University of Cambridge Oriental Publications No. 38

Ethiopian Biblical Interpretation

University of Cambridge Oriental Publications
published for the
Faculty of Oriental Studies

See page 489 for the complete list

Ethiopian Biblical Interpretation

A Study in Exegetical Tradition and Hermeneutics

ROGER W. COWLEY

CAMBRIDGE UNIVERSITY PRESS
Cambridge
New York   New Rochelle
Melbourne   Sydney

Published by the Press Syndicate of the University of Cambridge
The Pitt Building, Trumpington Street, Cambridge CB2 1RP
32 East 57th Street, New York, NY 10022, USA
10 Stamford Road, Oakleigh, Melbourne 3166, Australia

First published 1988

Printed in Great Britain by
Cambridge University Press

British Library cataloguing in publication data

Cowley, Roger W.
Ethiopian biblical interpretation: a study
in exegetical tradition and hermeneutics.
– (University of Cambridge oriental
publications; no. 38).
1. Bible – Criticism, interpretations, etc.
– Ethiopia
I. Title   II. Series
220.6′0963   BS500

Library of Congress cataloguing in publication data

Cowley, Roger W.
Ethiopian biblical interpretation: a study in exegetical
tradition and hermeneutics/Roger W. Cowley.
      p.   cm. – (University of Cambridge oriental publications:
no. 38)
Originally presented as the author's thesis (D.D.) – Cambridge
University, 1985.
Bibliography: p.
Includes indexes.
ISBN 0-521-35219-3
1. Bible – Criticism, interpretation, etc. – History. 2. YaI'tyoṗyā
o'rtodoks tawāḥedo b'eta kerestiyān – Doctrines – History. 3. Oriental
Orthodox churches – Ethiopia – Doctrines – History. I. Title.
II. Series.
BS500.C68   1988
220.6′0963 – dc19   87-34790

ISBN 0 521 35219 3

CONTENTS

P R E F A C E

This study seeks to answer the question, 'With which
exegetical tradition(s) does the traditional biblical (and
patristic) Amharic commentary material of the Ethiopian Orthodox
Church stand in essential continuity, and what are the processes
that have made this tradition what it is?' This formulation of
the question is largely the result of a private letter sent to
me in May, 1980 by Professor E. Ullendorff, in which he said,
'The time has surely come now to assess in some detail both the
provenance and the nature of the Ethiopian hermeneutical material'.

The plan of this study is as follows: an introductory
chapter leads on to some sample studies of very small areas of
commentary, with the aim of illustrating the use of non-Ethiopian
traditions, and the selection of material; this is followed
(ch. 3) by an investigation of the relationship of Ethiopian and
Jewish commentaries, a problem much more complex than that of
the relationships with Greek, Syriac, and Arabic commentary
materials. The main body of the study consists of the texts and
translations of the andǝmta commentary (AC) on Genesis 1.1-2.4
and Hebrews 1, preceded by surveys of the materials which have
contributed to Ethiopian understandings of creation and of
Christology respectively, and followed by comparative studies of
selected exegetical motifs. A final chapter (ch. 6) attempts
briefly to draw together some of the factors that have generated
the commentary.

The two central themes of 'creation' and 'Christology'
were chosen because they are basic to the Ethiopian Orthodox
presentation of the gospel, and are pervasive in the commentaries,
and in addition are so fully treated in other literatures that
they are very suitable for comparative study. Exegesis of the
prophetic literature and of the gospels should similarly have
been given fuller treatment, but some of the outline studies in
chapter 2 are intended partially to redress this imbalance.

If a geographical analogy may be used, this study attempts to draw a map of the continent of which Ethiopian Bible commentaries form a part. Parts of the continent are already well explored, and have only needed to be named in passing; other parts had been barely explored, and have required further examination in this study. Most of all, the 'trade routes' which link Ethiopian commentaries to other parts of the continent receive fairly detailed mapping, although at every corner there are further subsidiary routes and by-ways that could have been followed.

When I commenced the study of Ethiopian commentaries, they appeared to me to be a curious and isolated world of their own. Now, twenty years later, I see them as inheritors of much non-Ethiopian exegetical activity of the second to thirteenth centuries A.D., and (while distinctively Ethiopian in their present form) as parallel to medieval exegesis in other countries.

'Ethiopian' is used in this study of 'traditions found in Ethiopia', and not only of that which is uniquely Ethiopian. The reason for this is simply that it is generally impossible (except in instances of specific references to Ethiopian geography and history) to prove that a particular commentary pericope is uninfluenced by traditions of non-Ethiopian origin.

The books and manuscripts principally used for this study are listed in section 7. The works which have most greatly influenced me on the conceptual level are R. Murray, Symbols of Church and Kingdom; A Study in Early Syriac Tradition, I.R. Netton, Muslim Neoplatonists: An Introduction to the Thought of the Brethren of Purity, and A.C. Thiselton, The Two Horizons: New Testament Hermeneutics and Philosophical Description with special reference to Heidegger, Bultmann, Gadamer and Wittgenstein.

I am indebted to so many Ethiopian and non-Ethiopian scholars and friends that it is impossible to list them all; a number of them are listed in my The Traditional Interpretation of the Apocalypse of St. John in the Ethiopian Orthodox Church,

pp. x-xi. I am especially grateful to Dr. Getatchew Haile
(who in particular suggested many improvements to the
translations in sections 4.2 and 5.2), to Dr. S. Brock,
and to Professors E. Ullendorff and the late S. Strelcyn,
for much encouragement and assistance, to Oak Hill College,
which allowed me to complete the study during sabbatical
leave, to my wife and family for much support and fore-
bearance, and to Mrs. J. Milton for her typing.

    This study was submitted, together with some journal
articles on the same subject, in 1985 in application for
the degree of D.D. at Cambridge University. I acknowledge
with gratitude the award of the degree, and the kindness of
the Degree Committee of the Faculty of Divinity in allowing
me to incorporate in the published work some corrections
and additions, of the Publications Committee of the Faculty
of Oriental Studies in accepting the work for publication,
and of Cambridge University Press in the production of it.

ABBREVIATIONS

(Numbers in brackets refer to the sections of this study, or
the pages of <u>TIA</u>, where fuller explanations will be found.
For books and articles, fuller details will be found in 7.1 below).

<u>A</u>   Andəm (<u>TIA</u> p.3)

A.A.   Addis Ababa

<u>AAM</u>   Amməstu aʿəmadä məstir (5.1.5); unspecified page
                   numbers refer to the edition A.A. (Täsfa P.P.), 1952
                   E.C.

<u>ABKM</u>   <u>Abhandlungen für die Kunde des Morgenlandes</u>

AC   <u>Andəmta</u> commentary (<u>TIA</u> p.3); 'AC Gen.1.1' means 'the
                   <u>andəmta</u> (Amharic) commentary on the (Geez) text of
                   Genesis chapter 1 verse 1'

Acts   Acts of the Apostles

<u>AF</u>   <u>Äthiopistische Forschungen</u>

<u>AJSL</u>   <u>The American Journal of Semitic Languages and Literatures</u>

<u>AKAW</u>   <u>Abhandlungen der philosophisch – philologischen Classe
                   der Königlichen bayerischen Akademie der Wissenschaften</u>

Altaner   B. Altaner and A. Stuiber, <u>Patrologie</u>

<u>AM</u>   <u>Arägawi mänfäsawi</u> (TIA p.12)

BAC   R. Cowley, 'The Beginnings of the <u>andəm</u> Commentary
                   Tradition'

Bar.   Baruch (books of)

Baumstark   A. Baumstark, <u>Geschichte der syrischen Literatur</u>

BCEOC   R. Cowley, 'The Biblical canon of the Ethiopian
                   Orthodox Church today'

BFBS   British and Foreign Bible Society

<u>BJRL</u>   <u>Bulletin of the John Rylands Library</u>

B.L.   British Library (London)

<u>BIHRT</u>   <u>Bulletin d'information</u> of Institut de Recherche et
                   d'Histoire des Textes

<u>BK</u>   <u>Bəluy kidan</u>, Asmara, 1955 E.C.

<u>BMHE</u>   <u>The Book of the Mysteries of Heaven and Earth</u> (4.1.5)

B.N.   Bibliothèque Nationale (Paris)

Bowker   J. Bowker, <u>The Targums and Rabbinic Literature</u>

BSOAS   <u>Bulletin of the School of Oriental and African Studies</u>

BZ	Byzantinische Zeitschrift
BZNW	Beihefte zur Zeitschrift für die neutestamentliche Wissenschaft.
CBQ	Catholic Biblical Quarterly
CCSG	Corpus Christianorum Series Graeca
ch.	chapter
Chr.	Chronicles
CO	Chronicon orientale (4.1.7)
Col.	Colossians
Cor.	Corinthians
C.S.C.O.	Corpus Scriptorum Christianorum Orientalium
Cyr.	Writings of Cyril of Alexandria (TIA p.12)
Cyr E	Cyril, Ǝstəgubuʾ
Cyr P	Cyril, Päladyos
Cyr T	Cyril, Täräfä qerəllos
Dan.	Daniel
DAN	Doklady Akademiya Nauk, SSSR
DB	F. da Bassano, edition of Bible in Geez
Deut.	Deuteronomy
Did.	(Ethiopic) Didascalia
DTW	Dästa Täklä wäld, Addis yamarənna mäzgäbä qalat
E.C.	Ethiopian Calendar
Ecc.	Ecclesiastes
Ecclus.	Ecclesiasticus
EMML	Ethiopian Manuscript Microfilm Library (see 7.2 under W. Macomber and Getatchew Haile)
En.	Enoch
EOCCL	R. Cowley, 'The Identification of the Ethiopian Octateuch of Clement'
Eph.	Ephesians
Ep. Jer.	Epistle of Jeremiah
Est.	Esther
ET	Expository Times
Eth.	Ethiopian/Ethiopic
Ex.	Exodus
Ezra K	Ezra Kaləʾ, 1 Esdras
Ezra S	Ezra Sutuʾel, Ezra Apocalypse
Ez.	Ezekiel
Gal.	Galatians

GCS	Die griechischen christlichen Schriftsteller
Gen.	Genesis
GH	Gǝbrä hǝmamat (Holy Week lectionary)
Gibson	M.D. Gibson, The Commentaries of Isho'dad on the Epistles of St. Paul (Horae Semiticae XI part II)
Ginzberg	L. Ginzberg, Legends of the Jews
GOF	Göttinger Orientforschungen
GOTR	Greek Orthodox Theological Review
Graf	G. Graf, Geschichte der christlichen arabischen Literatur
Guidi	I. Guidi, Storia della letteratura etiopica
H	Hatäta, an explanation in a commentary
HA	Haymanotä abäw (5.1.4)
Hab.	Habakkuk
Hag.	Haggai
Heb.	Epistle to the Hebrews
HO	Hatäta orit, 'Questions on the Torah' (4.1.3.)
Hos.	Hosea
HTR	Harvard Theological Review
HUCA	Hebrew Union College Annual
IAT	(Abu'l-Faraj 'Abdallāh) ibn aṭ-Ṭaiyib
IATQ	'Questions' (HO) of IAT, EMML 1839 (4.1.3)
IBN	Išo' bar Nun; for his 'Questions', see 7.1 under E.G. Clarke
IM	Išo' dad of Merv
int (rod).	introduction (i.e. prologue, hypothesis etc.)
IRAN	Izvestiya Rossiy skoy Akademiya Nauk
JA	Journal asiatique
Jansma	T. Jansma, 'Investigations into the Early Syrian Fathers on Genesis'
Jas.	James
JBL	Journal of Biblical Literature
Jdg.	Judges
JE	Jerusalem Ethiopic (MSS preserved in Jerusalem)
Jer.	Jeremiah
JES	Journal of Ethiopian Studies
JJS	Journal of Jewish Studies
Jn.	(Gospel of) John
JNES	Journal of Near Eastern Studies

Jon.	Jonah
Josh.	Joshua
JQR	Jewish Quarterly Review
JRAS	Journal of the Royal Asiatic Society
JSOR	Journal of the Society of Oriental Research
JSS	Journal of Semitic Studies
JTS	Journal of Theological Studies
Jub.	Jubilees
Jud.	Judith
KBAW	Königlichen bayerischen Akademie der Wissenschaften
Kgs.	Kings
KWK	Kəflä giyorgis and Kidanä wäld Kəfle, Mäshafä säwasəw wägəss
Lam.	Lamentations
Lev.	Leviticus
LFP	R. Cowley, 'Ludolf's Fragmentum Piquesii'
Lk.	(Gospel of) Luke
LXX	Septuagint
Macc.	Maccabees
Mal.	Malachi
MEHI	R. Cowley, 'Mämhər Esdros and his Interpretations'
MGWJ	Monatsschrift für die Geschichte und Wissenschaft des Judenthums
MH	Kidanä wäld Kəfle, Mäshafä həzqə'el
MhG	Midraš haggadol on Genesis (page numbers refer to Margulies' edition)
MhH	Midraš hahefes on Genesis (page numbers refer to Habasselet's edition)
Mic..	Micah
Mk.	Mark
MK	Mäshafä kidan (TIA pp.11–12)
MO	Mämhərä orit (4.1.2 (iii))
MS(S)	manuscript(s)
MS R	MS Cowley 20 (7.5)
MS W	MS Cowley 1 (7.5)
MS Y	MS Cowley 31 (7.5)
MRAL	Memorie della Accademia Nazionale dei Lincei. Classe di Scienze morali, storiche e filologiche
MT	Massoretic text

MW	M̈aqdəm̈a ẅangel (TIA p.10)
Nah.	Nahum
Nat. Lib.	National Library
n.d.	not dated
NEB	New English Bible
Neh.	Nehemiah
NT	New Testament
NTIAC	R. Cowley, 'New Testament Introduction in the Andemta Commentary Tradition'
Num.	Numbers
Ob.	Obadiah
OC	Oriens Christianus
OCA	Orientalia Christiana Analecta
OCP	Orientalia Christiana Periodica
OKLS	Ostkirchliche Studien
OLP	Orientalia Lovanensia Periodica
Or.	orient(al)
OT	Old Testament
OTIAC	R. Cowley, 'Old Testament Introduction in the Andemta Commentary Tradition'
Pet.	Peter
PG	Patrologia Graeca (Migne)
Phil.	Philippians
Phm.	Philemon
PIAC	R. Cowley, 'Patristic Introduction in the Ethiopian Andəmta Commentary tradition'
PL	Patrologia Latina (Migne)
PN	R. Cowley, 'Preliminary notes on the balẅandəm commentaries'
P.P.	Printing Press
PO	Patrologia Orientalis
Prov.	Proverbs
pr.ed.	printed edition
Ps(s).	Psalms
PsJon.	(Targum) 'Pseudo-Jonathan'
Q̈al.	(Ethiopic) Q̈aleməntos (4.1.8); references to books and chapters are to the translation of S. Grébaut.
Qəd(dase)	Ethiopic Liturgy (see TIA p.13, and 7.1 under M̈ashaf̈a qəddase, M. Daoud, and G̈arima)

R	rabba, in parts of Midraš rabba (see 7.1 under H. Freedman)
RB	Revue Biblique
Rev.	Revelation
ROC	Revue de l'Orient Chrétien
Rom.	Romans
RRAL	Accademia Nazionale dei Lincei. Rendiconti della Classe di Scienze morali, storiche e filologiche
RSE	Rassegna di Studi Etiopici
RSO	Rivista degli Studi Orientali
RSV	Revised Standard Version (of the Bible)
Rt.	Ruth
Sam.	Samuel
SAQ	R. Cowley, 'Scholia of Aḥob of Qaṭar'
SBF	Studium Biblicum Franciscanum, Collectio minor
SBL	Society of Biblical Literature
SF	sənä fəträt (4.1.4)
SFA	Amharic SF; unspecified page numbers refer to the pr.ed. of Mogäs ʿ3qubä giyorgis
SFG	Geez SF; unspecified folio numbers refer to MS Cowley 40 (7.5)
SHAW	Sitzungsberichte der Heidelberger Akademie der Wissenschaften, philosophisch-historische Klasse
SKAW	Sitzungsberichte der philosophisch-historischen Klasse der Königlichen Akademie der Wissenschaften
SNTS	Society for New Testament Study
Song	Song of Solomon
Staab	K. Staab, Pauluskommentare aus der griechischen Kirche
Staal	H. Staal, Mt. Sinai Arabic Codex 151, I: Pauline Epistles (page numbers refer to the English translation, C.S.C.O. vol. 453)
T	Tarik, a historical pericope
TAV	Fischer, R.H. (ed.), A Tribute to Arthur Vööbus, Chicago, 1977.
TB	Babylonian Talmud
TFF	Tərgwame Felon Felgos (5.1.2 (iii))
TH	Təntä haymanot (4.1.4)

THBK	Theodore bar Koni, and his <u>Book of Scholia</u>; numbers refer to the section divisions of the edition of R. Hespel and R. Draguet , recension of Seert.
Thess.	Thessalonians
<u>TIA</u>	R. Cowley, <u>The Traditional Interpretation of the Apocalypse of St. John in the Ethiopian Orthodox Church</u>
Tim.	Timothy
Tit.	Titus
<u>TJ</u>	Talmud of Jerusalem
<u>TO</u>	Tərgwame orit, 'interpretation of the Torah' (4.1.2)
Tob.	Tobit
<u>TP</u>	Tərgwame pawlos, commentary on the Pauline corpus (5.1.2 (ii))
<u>TQ</u>	Tərgwame qälämsis, commentary on Rev. (<u>TIA</u> part II)
<u>TU</u>	<u>Texte und Untersuchungen zur Geschichte der altchrist-lichen Literatur</u>
T.V.	Textual variant
<u>TW</u>	Tərgwame wängel, commentary on the gospel(s) (<u>TIA</u> p.37)
v.	verse
<u>Vig.Chr.</u>	<u>Vigiliae Christianae</u>
<u>VOHD</u>	<u>Verzeichnis der orientalischen Handschriften in Deutschland</u> (ed. W. Voight and D. George)
<u>VV</u>	<u>Vizantiiskij Vremmenik</u>
Wisd.	Wisdom
<u>WM</u>	<u>Wəddase maryam</u>
<u>WZKM</u>	<u>Wiener Zeitschrift fur die Kunde des Morgenlandes</u>
YAWD	<u>Dərsan</u> of Yoḥannəs afä wärq (5.1.2 (i))
YAWT	<u>Tägsas</u> of Yoḥannəs afä wärq (5.1.2 (i))
<u>YML</u>	<u>Yalqut meʿam loʿez</u> (see 7.1 under Y. Culi); page numbers refer to vol. 1 of A. Kaplan's translation.
<u>ZA</u>	<u>Zeitschrift für Assyriologie</u>
<u>ZDMG</u>	<u>Zeitschrift der deutschen morgenländischen Gesellschaft</u>
Zech.	Zechariah
Zeph.	Zephaniah
<u>ZKM</u>	<u>Zeitschrift für die Kunde des Morgenlandes</u>
<u>ŽMNP</u>	<u>Žurnal Ministerstva Narodnago Prosveshcheniya</u>
<u>ZNW</u>	<u>Zeitschrift für die neutestamentliche Wissenschaft</u>
<u>ZVO</u>	<u>Imperatorskoye Russkoye Arkheologicheskoye obshchestvo. Zapiski Vostochnavo Otdeleniya</u>

1.   The study of the <u>andǝmta</u> commentary tradition

1.   THE STUDY OF THE ANDƎMTA COMMENTARY TRADITION.

        Traditional education in the Ethiopian Orthodox Church has much
in common with Jewish, Islamic, and other forms of traditional education. Its style and content have remained substantially unchanged
over a long period, it emphasizes oral instruction and memorisation,
and its aim is the thorough grasp of a defined corpus of learning.

        Study of the traditional Amharic commentary on certain Geez
texts, the andəmta commentary (AC), is the highest stage of this
Ethiopian church education. It has held this position since the
seventeenth century and probably earlier, and its scholars have been
influential, and respected by Ethiopians[1]. Publication of AC texts,
and of descriptions of AC study is, however, a relatively recent
development. The main indigenous accounts of aspects of AC study
are those by Liqä səltanat Habtä maryam Wärqnäh[2], Aläqa Ɉnbaqom Qalä
wäld[3], Aklilä bərhan Wäldä qirqos[4], Abba Kidanä maryam Getahun[5], and
Mämhər Mänkər Mäkwännən[6]. Some of the AC texts have been published

1. TIA pp.19–22, 54–56; MEHI.

2. Təntawi yä'ityopya sər'atä təmhərt, A.A.,1971 A.D. The main section
    on the AC is pp.212–222, and this appears in English translation in
    OTIAC pp.162–175.

3. Collection of Sources for the Study of Ethiopian Culture, Documents
    on Traditional Ethiopian Education, numbers 1 and 2, (in Amharic),
    duplicated by the Institute of Ethiopian Studies A.A., June and August
    1965 A.D.. The booklet in English, Imbaqom Kalewold, Traditional
    Ethiopian Church Education, New York, 1970 is an abridged version.

4. Märha ləbbuna, A.A., 1943 E.C.

5. Təntawiw yäqollo tämari, A.A., 1954 and 1955 E.C.

6. Mäshetä liqawənt, A.A.,1972 E.C., a brief biography of Dr. Ayyälä
    Alämu.

in Ethiopia, mainly at the instigation of the late Emperor Haylä səllase[7]. Although the prospects for further publication are currently poor, there are signs of modern interest in the AC as a resource for the expansion of Amharic[8], and the word 'andəmta' itself appears in some modern dictionaries with the meaning 'implication'[9].

Knowledge of the AC has been slow to reach other countries. Of nineteenth century travellers in Ethiopia, Samuel Gobat had extensive contact with the Ethiopian Orthodox Church, and mentions the celebrated AC teacher Mämhər Wäldä ab[10], and Antoine d'Abbadie formed friendships with teachers of the AC whom he names in his catalogue of his MSS (and probably his unpublished study notes, MSS B.N. d'Abbadie 228, 256–283, contain further material). However, as the AC is primarily an oral tradition, and MSS of its contents are usually in private possession and unimpressive in appearance, no substantial parts of it were included among the Ethiopian MSS which had reached European libraries during the late seventeenth to mid-nineteenth centuries. The situation improved slightly with d' Abbadie's MSS, and with the beginnings of the printing of the AC in the early twentieth century, but the works still attracted little non-Ethiopian attention, probably because of the scarcity of non-Ethiopians proficient both in Geez and Amharic, and because of the lack of any realisation that the works formed a substantial integral corpus of traditional commentary material.

7. <u>TIA</u> pp.6–14.

8. E.g. the article by Fəqrä dəngəl Bäyyänä, 'Yä'andəmta tərgwame lä'amarəñña ədgät', in <u>Zena ləssan</u> 2.2 (<u>Nähasse</u> 1974 E.C.), A.A.

9. E.g. <u>Täramaj mäzgäbä qalat</u>, A.A., 1968 E.C., prepared by the debating association of Ethiopian University teachers, p.294.

10. S. Gobat, <u>Journal of a Three Years' Residence in Abyssinia</u>.

At the time that I went to Ethiopia in 1963 A.D., most of the semi-popular books that an intending visitor was likely to read contained a description of the traditional church schools[11]. These accounts did not in general unambiguously identify the texts studied at the various stages of church education, and I found them difficult to relate to what I actually observed, especially in respect of the AC schools. I lived from 1963-4 near Dabat in Wägära, and from 1964-70 at Qobla (Jända) on the Dämbiya plain. In these rural areas, many churches have a teacher of reading and church chant (<u>zema</u>) attached to them, and some have a teacher of Geez poetry (<u>qəne</u>). The nearest schools for AC study were in Gondar, and they were physically inconspicuous – the school of Dr. Ayyälä Alämu near the church of Mädhane aläm, the school of <u>Mämhər</u> Käflä maryam Yəmär behind the church of Gəmja bet Maryam, and the school of <u>Mämhər</u> Ḥaddis Mädhane near Bata church, and latterly near Abiyä əgzi' – so it was some time before I actually saw a teacher or school of the AC. I remember, in these early days, looking at a copy of Mähari Tərfe's <u>Sostu mäsahəftä haddisat</u> (part of which I subsequently translated in <u>TIA</u>) in a book shop, and not being able to puzzle out what it was; and I declined to purchase a copy of the AC on the gospels on the grounds that I already possessed Geez and Amharic texts of the gospels, and was not specially interested in the further comment the volume contained. I had probably absorbed some prejudices about the state of biblical and patristic studies in the Ethiopian church, and for the most part I had not read, or even heard of, the non-Ethiopian sources which contributed to the AC tradition. Principally, however, I was unaware of the AC as a possible object of study, and conditions for study were unfavorable.

Certain other factors, however, did stimulate study – I sold a steady trickle of Ethiopian books to Mr. Thornton's bookshop in Oxford and so had the opportunity to read many books I could not afford to retain, I had a long correspondence with Fr. Dr. E.B. Eising about the Ethiopian canon of Scripture, arising from an article

11. E.g. S. Pankhurst, <u>Ethiopia, a cultural history</u>, Woodford Green, 1955, pp.232-283.

in <u>Sobornost</u>[12], I visited the school of Dr. Ayyälä and still vividly
remember his teaching of AC Hebrews 11, and, principally, I was
determined not to teach the Bible in Ethiopia without some understanding of the indigenous exegetical tradition. When a small Bible
school for church students was opened at Jända, I wished to obtain
a copy of AC Isaiah. Dr. Ayyälä agreed to lend his copy for copying,
but that was then needed for his students, and <u>Mämhər Kəflä</u> maryam
lent the copy he had inherited from <u>Mämhər Wäldä</u> sänbät. This was
the beginning of a long friendship, and enabled me to pay scribes to
copy MSS from the three Gondar schools. Some of the copies I sold
to the British and Bodleian Libraries, and some I retained (eventu-
ally bringing them to England in 1975-8). The only resistance to
this process was on the part of some AC teachers who did not want
'imperfect' copies of the AC to go abroad; they realized, however,
that the work of 'correcting and improving' the AC MSS was an unending one, and that a safe deposit of AC MSS in foreign libraries was
desirable.

In 1970, I moved to Makalle to work under the direction of
<u>Abuna</u> Yohannəs, and <u>Mäl'akä məhrät</u> Yared Gərmay allowed me to copy
or photocopy his AC MSS, advancing my collection to the point that
it became reasonable to think of acquiring a complete set of AC MSS.
I also purchased from the book-sellers in the Addis Ababa market
some of the printed AC volumes that were out-of-print, and made tape-
recordings of some of the AC MSS in the National Library, A.A.

In 1973 I moved to Gondar, and continued to have AC MSS copied,
assisted by a wide circle of Ethiopian friends, especially Deacon
Mänbäru Färrädä. In addition, I had begun to realize the importance
of commentaries in Geez as sources of the AC, and begun to collect
copies of MSS of these. I was much encouraged by <u>Abuna</u> Ĭndrəyas,
then archbishop of Gondar, whose teaching of the AC on the gospels
I attended. By 1977 I had read at least one copy of every part of
the AC, and the Geez commentary MSS that I had collected. During
1978 I translated the Geez and Amharic commentaries on Revelation

12. 'The Ethiopian Orthodox Church, some bibliographical notes',
<u>Sobornost</u>, Summer 1965, pp.45-51.

which appear in <u>TIA</u>, and then left Ethiopia, completing the work on <u>TIA</u> in Jerusalem during 1978-9.

Today the prospects for study of the AC materials are more favorable, as the EMML collection contains many microfilms of AC MSS, and further MSS are contained in the British and Bodleian Libraries and in my own collection (see 7.4 and 7.5 below), and editions and studies of some related Arabic and Syriac texts (notably Ibn aṭ-Ṭaiyib, Theodore bar Koni, Išoʿdad of Merv, and Mošе bar Kepha) have become available. Ironically, the situation of the actual teachers and students of the AC in Ethiopia is probably currently worsening, and it must be doubted whether it will continue much longer as a living tradition.

For the further study of the AC, the major <u>desideratum</u> is a critical edition, translation, and comparative source-critical study of the <u>exegetica</u> of Ibn aṭ-Ṭaiyib. Alongside this, the field is wide open for studies of the AC on selected books (Sister Kirsten Pedersen is currently undertaking study of AC Psalms), and of Geez commentaries and their Arabic antecedents.

2. Methodological soundings:

 2.1   The chronology of Noah's flood (Genesis 7–8)

 2.2   A tradition concerning the numbers of the written
       and unwritten languages of the descendants of Noah
       (Genesis 11.7–9)

 2.3   The ancestry of Melchizedek (Genesis 14)

 2.4   The <u>Diamerismos tēs gēs</u> (Joshua 6–7)

 2.5   'One who came from Edom' (Isaiah 63.1)

 2.6   Simeon (Luke 2.25)

 2.7   The magi (Matthew 2)

 2.8   The sinful woman who anointed Jesus (Matthew 26)

2.   Methodological Soundings.

> "Every methodological reflection is
> abstracted from the cognitive work
> in which one actually engages.
> Methodological awareness always
> follows the application of a method;
> it never precedes it"
> (P. Tillich, Systematic Theology, vol.I, ch.2.)

The miniature studies of this chapter are intended as a sondage, both historically, as an exploration of exegetical tradition, and methodologically, as an attempt to discern controlling hermeneutic. The restricted scope of their subjects allows consideration of more detail than is possible for the themes of creation and Christology (in chapters 4 and 5 below), and the choice of subjects is intended partially to redress the imbalance that would otherwise be caused by omission of material on the gospels and the prophetic literature. My article 'The "Blood of Zechariah" (Mt.23.35) in Ethiopian exegetical tradition' is a further study of the same type.

2.1   The chronology of Noah's flood (Genesis 7-8).

The Geez text of Genesis 7.11 cited in AC Gen.7.11 dates the commencement of the flood to the twelfth day of the second month of the six hundredth year of Noah's life; the Amharic comment identifies this second month as Ganbot, since Miyazya marks the change of year. This invites further study (i) to ascertain the origin of the reading 'twelfth day' (on which Geez MSS and printed texts appear unanimous[1]), and (ii) to compare with other sources the identification of the 'second month', especially in the light of Rabbinic dispute about this identification.

---

1. Texts and editions printed in A. Dillmann, Biblia Veteris Testamenti Aethiopica, Bd.1; O. Boyd, The Octateuch in Ethiopic, Part 1; F. da Bassano, Bəluy Kidan, vol.1; Bəluy Kidan, Asmara, 1955 E.C. I have further consulted a number of MSS not used in the editions listed above.

Some Hebrew sources represent the chronology as follows:

	Genesis MT[2]	R Eliezer[3]	R Joshua[3]	Jubilees[4]
Entry to ark		17th	17th	new moon of 2nd month
Beginning of flood, Gen.7.11	17th day 2nd month	Marhešvan	Iyyar	
Rain ceases		27th Kislev		new moon of 4th month
Ark rests on mountains, Gen.8.4.	17th day 7th month	17th Sivan, 7th month from Kislev		
Mountain tops visible, Gen.8.5.	1st day 10th month	Ab, 10th month from Marhešvan		
Waters dry, Gen.8.13.	1st day 1st month	1st of Tišri	1st of Nisan	17th day 2nd month
Exit from ark, Gen. 8.14.	27th day 2nd month			27th day 2nd month

The prevalent Jewish tradition identifies the 'second month' as
Marhešvan[5], and relates this to debate concerning the identity of the

2. Massoretic Hebrew text of Genesis.

3. Midraš haggadol on Gen.7.11, and Bərešit rabba 22.4 and 33.7; Rashi
    comm. in loc.; TB Roš haššana 11b–12a.

4. Jub. 5.22–32.

5. E.g. Bərešit rabba 33.7; Targum Pseudo-Jonathan in loc. (see J. Bowker,
    The Targums and Rabbinic Literature, pp.161–6) Pirke de Rabbi Eliezer
    (trans. G. Friedländer, p.167); Seder Olam ch.4 (ed. B. Ratner,
    Seder Olam Rabba); also Josephus, Antiquities, I.3.3. Further ref-
    erences in L. Ginzberg, Legends of the Jews, vol.I, pp.161–4, vol.V,
    p.184, and M.M. Kasher, Tora Šlema, vol.II (partial English trans. in
    M.M. Kasher, Encyclopedia of Biblical Interpretation).

month in which the world was created[6].

The most relevant Greek sources are the following:

	LXX[7]	Greek text reported by Išoʿdad[8]	Greek text reported by Bar Hebraeus[9]	Philo (Armenian text)[10]
Entry to ark		27th day 2nd month	20th of Iyar	
Beginning of flood	27th day 2nd month		27th day 2nd month	27th day of 7th month Nisan
Ark rests on mountains	27th day 7th month		27th day 7th month	27th day of Tišri
Mountain tops visible	1st day 11th month			1st day 10th month
Waters dry	1st day 1st month			} 27th day
Exit from ark	27th day 2nd month	1st day 3rd month	27th day 2nd month	} 7th month

6. E.g. Bərešit rabba 22.4.

7. Septuagint. See further J. Lewis, Study of the Interpretation of Noah and the Flood, especially Appendix I (though the references there to Ethiopian material are inaccurate in detail).

8. C. van den Eynde, Commentaire d'Išoʿdad de Merv sur l'ancien testament I.Genèse (translation) C.S.C.O. vol.156, pp.130-1.

9. M. Sprengling and W.C. Graham, Barhebraeus' Scholia on the Old Testament, part I, Genesis – II Samuel, on Gen.7.11; also E.A.W. Budge The Chronography of Bar Hebraeus, vol.I, p.6. The 'second month' is also identified as Iyar in Hippolytus' Arabic fragments to the Pentateuch, on Gen.8.1, in G.C.S. 1.2.90.

10. In Quaestions et Solutiones in Genesin, in F.H. Colson, G.H. Whitaker, and R. Marcus, Philo, questions 2,17,45,47.

In Syriac works, the identification of the 'second month' as Iyyar has become fairly general:

	Ephrem[11]	Isoʿdad of Merv[12]	Bar Hebraeus[13]	Cave of Treasures[14]	Book of the Bee[15]
Entry to ark	7 days before flood	10th day 2nd month Iyar	10th of Iyar	Friday, 27th of Iyar	
Beginning of flood	17th day 2nd month	17th day 2nd month	17th of Iyar		
Ark rests on mountains			17th day of first Tišri	17th day 7th month, first Tišri	
Mountain tops visible	10th month		second Kanūn	1st day 10th month Shebat	1st day 10th month
Sending of raven				10th of Adhar	10th month, Shebat
Waters dry	1st day 1st month			1st of Nisan	
Exit from ark	27th day 2nd month Yar	27th day 2nd month	27th of Iyar	Sunday in Iyar	

11. R.M. Tonneau, Sancti Ephraem Syri in Genesim et in Exodum Commentarii (C.S.C.O. Syr. 71 and 72), in loc.

12. C. van den Eynde, op.cit., in loc.

13. M. Sprengling and W.C. Graham, op.cit., in loc.

14. Syriac text in C. Bezold, Die Schatzhöhle; English translation in E.A.W. Budge, The Book of the Cave of Treasures.

15. English translation in E.A.W. Budge, Anecdota Oxoniensia (Semitic Series), vol. I, part II.

In some Arabic works, and Ethiopic versions of them, the chronology is as follows:

	Kitab al-majall[16]	Nazm al-jauhar[17]	Al-Makin Jirjis(Eth. text)[18]	Ibn at-Taiyib[19]	Gädlä Addam (Eth.text)[20]
Entry to ark	Friday, 17th of Adar		Friday 27th of Adar (=Mäggabit)	10th day 2nd month Ayar	27th of Gənbot
Beginning of flood				17th day 2nd month	
Ark rests on mountains		17th day 7th month Ilul(=Thut)	27th day 7th month Aylul (= Mäskäräm)		27th of Təqəmt
Mountain tops visible	diminution till 10th month Shebat	1st day 10th month	1st day 10th month		1st day 11th month
Sending of raven	10th of Adhar	(40 days later)	(40 days later)		
Waters dry			1st day 2nd month		2nd of Bärmuda (=Miyazya)
Exit from ark		17th day 2nd month Nisan(= Barmudah)		27th day 2nd month	27th of Gənbot

16. Arabic text and English translation in M.D. Gibson, Studia Sinaitica,VIII.

17. Eutychius' Annales, Arabic text ed. L.Cheikho, C.S.C.O. Arab.ser.III, t.VI. Latin trans. in Migne P.G. 111 cols.907-1156 (see col.916).

18. Cited from Ethiopic text of the Chronography of Giyorgis wäldä Amid, MS B.L. Orient 814 f.9b.

19. J.C.J. Sanders, Ibn at-Taiyib. Commentaire sur la Genèse, C.S.C.O. vols.274 and 5, translation pp.49-50. A similar identification is found in P. de Lagarde, Materialien zur Kritik und Geschichte des Pentateuchs, vol.II, p.74, line 32, on Gen.7.11.

20. Arabic text in A.Battista and B.Bagatti, Il Combattimento di Adamo. Ethiopic text in E. Trumpp, Der Kampf Adams.

Ethiopic Abušakər contains a variety of identifications. Near
the commencement of the work[21], the beginning of the flood, and the
date of the drying of the waters, are given as the 27th. of the second
month, and the date of the ark resting on the mountains as the 27th.
of the seventh month. The '27th. of the second month' is further
identified as the 10th. day of the first žāmadi (Arabic Jumādā), the
25th. day of bəsəns/bəsänša (Coptic Pachon), and the 20th. day of
ayär/ayar of Rome and Syria[22]. Further on in Abušakər[23], it is stated
that Noah entered the ark on the 27th. of Adar, and MS B.L. Orient
809 f.62b has a marginal note saying that this is a scribal error for
'25th.'. In the latter part of Abušakər[24], in the section which draws
on the Chronicon Orientale of ibn ar-Rahib and other sources, the
date of Noah's entry into the ark is given as Friday the 27th. of
Gənbot (B.L. Or. 809) or Mäggabit (B.L. Or. 810); these readings
may reflect a confusion, most probably in Ethiopic script, of Ayar
(Iyyar, equivalent to Gənbot) and Adar (equivalent to Mäggabit).

Further Ethiopic texts and versions show the chronology as
follows:

21. E.g. MSS B,L. Orient 809 f.21a and 810 f.27b.

22. Eutychius, PG 111 col.917 appears to be one source of this.

23. E.g. MSS B.L. Orient 809 f. 62b and 810 f. 95b.

24. E.g. B.L. Or. 809 f. 64a and 810 f. 98b.

	Ethiopic text of Gen.[25]	Maharka dangəl EMML 2101[26]	Mamhəra orit[27]			Ethiopic Qälemäntos[28]
			d'Abbadie 156 & 195	d'Abbadie 157	d'Abbadie 39	
Entry to ark		28th day of 2nd month Ayar	10th of Säne	10th of Säne	10th of Säne	
Beginning of flood	12th day 2nd month	17th of 2nd month	27th day 2nd month	23rd day 2nd month	27th day 2nd month	
Ark rests on mountains	12th day 7th month					
Mountain tops visible	1st day 11th month				Yäkkatit	17th (of Yäkkatit?)
Sending of raven	1st day 1st month				10th of Mäggabit	10th of Mäggabit
Waters dry		} 13th day	} 27th day	} 28th day		
Exit from ark		} 2nd month	} of ? month	} of 2nd month		6th of Miyazya

25. See fn. 1 above.

26. Ethiopian Manuscript Microfilm Library 2101(2), ff. 63a-148b, see catalogue by Getatchew Haile and W.F. Macomber, vol. VI, p.196.

27. Further see ch. 4.1 below.

28. Geez text in e.g. MS B.L. Orient 751. For a French translation of the section on the flood, see R.O.C. 1912, p.21 (incorrect in reading '7th. of Miyazya' where MSS have '6th.').

AC Genesis 7-8[29] identifies the months as follows:

Beginning of flood	12th day 2nd month, Gənbot
Ark rests on mountains	12th day 7th month, Ṭəqəmt
Mountain tops visible	11th month, Yäkkatit
Sending of raven	10th of Mäggabit
Waters dry	1st month, Miyazya
Exit from ark	12th day 2nd month, Gənbot

The following conclusions may be drawn from this survey:

(i)   The origin of the reading in Ethiopic texts of Gen.7.11 that the flood began on the 12th day of the month has not been established; it may represent a variant Arabic text, or an error in translation into Ethiopic.

(ii)   The identification of the 'second month' in the Syriac, Arabic, Ethiopic and Amharic materials surveyed is in general agreement with a Nisan new year (and in disagreement with a Tišri new year);   this raises, but does not answer, the question of contact between this tradition and the dispute between R. Eliezer and R. Joshua.

(iii) Some of the Syriac, Arabic and Ethiopic material surveyed follows the LXX chronology;   as commentaries in Ethiopic do not date the beginning of the flood on the 12th day of the second month, it is probable that they are dependent on sources nearer the MT and LXX, and (in this respect) independent of the prevalent Ethiopic text of Gen.7.11.

(iv)   The Syriac Cave of Treasures and the Arabic Kitab al-majall show some similarities, and the Book of the Bee, Gädlä addam and Qäleməntos bear lesser resemblances to them.

(v)   Ethiopic Abušakər and the chronography of Giyorgis wäldä Amid show similarities;   their precise relationship requires fuller investigation. Eutychius' Nazm al-jauhar is a source of both works, but the present survey does not very clearly illustrate this.

29. I have used the MS from which AC Gen.1 is reproduced in ch.4.2 below, MS W = Cowley 1.

(vi)   M̈amhər̈a orit appears to follow the tradition of identifying the 'second month' as Iyyar, but incorrectly identifies it as S̈ane; the recension of MO in MS B.N. d'Abbadie 39 appears to have used Q̈aleməntos as an additional source.

(vii)   The Ethiopic commentary of Məhərka dəngəl, although based on the Arabic text, or an Ethiopic version, of Ibn aṭ-Ṭaiyib's Firdaus an-nasrāniya, differs from it considerably in its chronology of the flood; in view of its internal inconsistency (in which Noah would have drowned), it probably used additional sources.

(viii) The idea of naming the months of the flood period is common to most of the materials surveyed; however, the equivalences Nisan = Miyazya, Iyyar = Gənbot etc. are so well established in Ethiopian materials that it cannot be concluded that in this specific example the AC is necessarily dependent on Syriac and Arabic commentary traditions.

2.2.   A tradition concerning the numbers of the written and unwritten
       languages of the descendants of Noah (Genesis 11.7-9)

S. Strelcyn[1] has compared the pericope on the numbers of written
and unwritten languages found in Midraš haggadol on Genesis 10.32[2] with
a pericope found in Geez materials[3]. The Geez pericope reads:

"The children of Noah were 3: Shem, Japheth, Ham. Of the
children of Shem, they spoke 25 languages, and they wrote 8 of the
writing systems, namely ʿaräbi, sorya, agawi, ʾəbrawi, farsawi, kälädawi,
həndi, sini. And of the children of Ham, they spoke 32 languages,
and they wrote 6 of the writing systems, namely qəbti, nobi, baša,
qilqi, fələstʿi, qwəbša. And of the children of Japheth, they spoke
15 languages, and they wrote 6 writing systems, namely yonanawi,
romawi, afrəngawi, gärgane, armanawi, ʾandələš. And all of them were
72 languages, 20 of which have a writing system, and 52 of which do
not have a writing system."

He shows that the Hebrew and Geez traditions resemble each other
in outline, in giving the same total number of languages, and in giving
names to the written languages; he concludes that, although the
details of the two traditions are very substantially different, they
must both be traced back to an ancient Jewish Yemenite source.

1.   'Une tradition éthiopienne d'origine juive yéménite concernant
     l'écriture', Rocznik orientalistyczny XXIII, 1 (1959), pp.67-72.

2.   E.g. M. Margulies, Midraš haggadol ..., Jerusalem, 1975, vol.1, p. קיצ;
     translation of relevant pericope in M.M. Kasher, Encyclopedia of
     biblical interpretation, vol. II, p.88.

3.   Strelcyn cites the pericope from Dillmann's Lexicon, col. 1378, but
     is mistaken in supposing Dillmann's source to have been MS. B.L.
     Dillmann XIX. Dillmann has quoted from an unspecified Vocabularium
     Aethiopicum, and the pericope is found, for example, in texts of
     Mämhərä orit (e.g. MS B.N. d'Abbadie 156 f.6a), and in B.N. Zotenberg 149
     f.46, B.L.Or.494 f.48b, Or.534 f.185b, EMML 2101 f.63b, 2088 f.140a,
     2849 f.82a, in texts of the Geez version of Giyorgis wäldä Amid (see
     below), and in a variant form in B.N. d'Abbadie 39 f.192a (which has 5
     as the number of written languages of the descendants of Japheth).

This conclusion may be correct, and may be further supported by the occurrence of the pericope in Midraš hahefes[4]; however, it should not be inferred from it that the Ethiopian material is directly dependent on Jewish Yemenite material which had, so to speak, crossed the Red Sea in a canoe, because a tradition similar in outline, approximating to the Geez (rather than the Hebrew) form, is found in various Syriac and Arabic works.

Of the Arabic works containing it, the earliest appears to be the Nazm al-ǧauhar of Saʿīd ibn Biṭrīq (877-940 A.D.)[5], from which it is cited in the anonymous commentary catena on Genesis and Exodus edited by de Lagarde[6], in commentary on Gen.11.9; later Arabic works in which it also appears are an anonymous commentary on the Psalms[7], and the al-Maǧmuʿ al-mubārak of Al-Makin Ğirǧis (the elder, 13th. cent.)[8] well-known in its Geez version as the chronography of Giyorgis wäldä Amid[9].

4. M. Ḥabaṣṣelet, Midraš hahefes, Jerusalem, 1981, p. קי״ט.

5. Latin translation in PG 111 col. 919; Arabic text in L. Cheikho et al., Eutychii Patriarchae Alexandrini Annales, C.S.C.O., Scr. arab. ser.III, t. VI-VII. Further see Graf II, pp.32-38, and M. Breydy in C.S.C.O. vol. 450.

6. P. de Lagarde, Materialien zur Geschichte und Kritik des Pentateuchs, vol. II, pp.92-3 (the section begins on p.92 line 14, and the paragraphs on Shem, Ham and Japheth on p.92 line 27, p.92 line 34,and p.93 line 7 respectively); on the work, see Graf II, pp.284-9, and the review by W.W. Müller of G. Bauer, Athanasius von Qūs. Qilādat at-tahrir fī ʿilm at-tafsir in Zeitschrift der Deutschen Morgenländischen Gesellschaft, Band 125 (1975), pp.168-71.

7. Graf II, pp.458-61.

8. Graf II, pp.348-51.

9. E.g. MS B.L. Orient 814.

Versions of the tradition in Syriac are contained in two brief chronicles published from MSS B.L. Add. 25,875 and Add. 14,541[10]; evidence for dating the origin of their contents is lacking.

Sources which list the numbers of languages and/or nations are very many, and the following is a small sample[11] which illustrates the variation among sources in Hebrew, Syriac, Arabic and Geez, and the correspondence of the Geez tradition cited above with that of Saʿīd ibn Biṭrīq:

Source:	Shem	Ham	Japheth	Actual total
Hebrew:				
Midraš təhillim[12]	26	30	14	72
Midraš haggadol	26	24	22	72
Midraš hahefes	24	24	22	70
Syriac:				
Chronica minora	22	13	37	72
Book of the Bee[13]	27	36	15	78
Arabic:				
Saʿīd ibn Biṭrīq	25	32	15	72
al Yaʿqubi[14]	19	16	37	72

10. E.W. Brooks, I. Guidi and I.-B. Chabot, Chronica minora fasc.3 (C.S.C.O, Syr.III. 4 = Syr. 5 and 6); the translations of the relevant passages are in Syr. 6,pp.278 and 281-3.

11. Further see e.g. Strelcyn, 'Une tradition ...'; J. Bowker, The Targums and Rabbinic Literature, pp.182-7; L. Ginzberg, The Legends of the Jews, I p.173, V pp.194-6.

12. Translation in W.G. Braude, The Midrash on Psalms, on Ps.9.7; Hebrew text in e.g. S. Buber, Midrasch Tehillim, Trier, 1892.

13. ch. XXII, E.A.W. Budge, The Book of the Bee.

14. Th. Houtsma (ed.), Ibn Wâdhih qui dicitur al-Jaʿqubî Historiae, Lugduni Batavorum, 1883, t.1, p.17, cited here from Strelcyn, 'Une tradition...'.

Source:	Shem	Ham	Japheth	Actual total
Geez:				
Book of the Mysteries of Heaven and Earth[15]	24	21/30	16	61/70
Geez pericope cited above	25	32	15	72

Some of these sources (though not the Geez pericope under examination) also allot numbers of 'islands'; whereas the Hebrew sources equally apportion 99 islands, the Arabic sources and the Geez version of Giyorgis wäldä Amid are quite different:

Source:	Shem	Ham	Japheth
Midraš haggadol and Midraš hahefes	33	33	33
Saʿid ibn Biṭriq, and Arabic and Geez texts of Giyorgis wäldä Amid[16]	no number given	26	12

The sources which contain a number and a list of names for the written languages may be tabulated as follows:

Source:	Shem	Ham	Japheth	Actual total
Midraš haggadol and Midraš hahefes	6	5	5	16
Syriac Chronica minora	5	4	6	15
Saʿid ibn Biṭriq, Giyorgis wäldä Amid, and Geez pericope cited above	8	6	6	20

Of the actual listed names of the written languages, the lists in the Geez pericope cited above are very similar to the lists of Saʿid ibn Biṭriq, rather less like the Syriac lists, and still less like the Hebrew lists - though even these show a measure of resemblance.

15. J. Perruchon and I. Guidi (completed by S. Grébaut), Le Livre des Mystères du Ciel et de la Terre, P.O. I. 1 and VI.3.

16. E.g. MS B.L. Orient 814, f.11b.

The material thus presents a good example of the problem of determining the relationship (or lack of it) between traditions similar in outline, but substantially different in detail. At first sight it seems that the earliest secure date for a tradition about the written languages is that of the <u>Annales</u> of Saʿīd ibn Biṭrīq. However, even if this is so, it does not explain how <u>Midraš hahefes</u>, the de Lagarde Arabic Catena, and the Geez <u>Mämhərä orit</u> have all come to use the tradition in commentary on Genesis 11.7–9; (<u>Midraš haggadol</u> uses it on Genesis 10.32). Either the three commentaries have made the same association independently, or they are dependent on one another directly or indirectly, or they have used some common literary source or oral tradition. <u>Mämhərä orit</u> may be related to the de Lagarde catena, but direct links of either with <u>Midraš hahefes</u> seem less likely, and I suggest therefore that a common source is involved, a source which contained numbers and names of written languages and used the material in commentary on Genesis 11.7–9.

Finally, it may be noted that this tradition does not appear in the Amharic AC corpus. It may be conjectured that it was found difficult to memorize, or felt to contribute little to the exegesis of Genesis 11; more probably, however, the reason may be that although <u>Mämhərä orit</u> contains much material in common with the AC tradition, it does not appear to have been directly used to a great extent by the AC compilers.

2.3.   <u>The ancestry of Melchizedek (Genesis 14)</u>

The AC corpus cites one account of the ancestry of Melchizedek, in which he is a Hamite, and refers to the existence of another account, in which he is a Shemite. The first of these is in AC Philoxenus p.39, which reads:

<u>'And this Mark was a Greek, an Egyptian</u>[1] <u>... and it was he who made a book concerning the reply to the ones who say that Melchizedek is the son of God.</u>
And it is he who wrote an answer book against the ones who said, "Melchizedek is the son of God"; citing <u>"who had no father and mother"</u>, they said, "He is the son of God". When people asked him (Mark) how the matter was, he spoke thus, "The descent and tribal division of the tribe of Ham is not written in the Torah, but he (Melchizedek) had a mother and father. Ḥasel begat Salem, Salem begat Melki, Melki begat a further Melki and Melchizedek. Their mother is called Sälima. Their father used to worship idols ..."'.

Similar material is contained in AC Ezekiel 16.3[2], and in Amharic annotations in MS B.L. Orient 809 f.63a (Ethiopic <u>Abušakər</u>), and the source is doubtless the tract on Melchizedek by pseudo-Athanasius[3], of which at least the greater part has been translated into Geez[4], probably from Arabic[5].

1. After the following comment, the text continues by saying that this Mark is to be distinguished from Mark the Syrian formerly called Malkos, and from Mark the less, disciple of Səlwanos.

2. <u>MH</u>, p.147, also partially in MS EMML 1278 f.761a.

3. <u>PG</u> 28, cols. 525-30. Material from this tract has also been used in the Ethiopic anaphora of Gregory (of Nyssa); see S. Euringer, 'Un frammento di Midrasch di Melchisedech nella Liturgia dell'Osanna Etiopica', <u>RSE</u> iii (1943), pp.50-60.

4. MS. B.N. d'Abbadie 156, f.131a-132a. The folios are in a different hand from the rest of the MS, and f.130b lacks continuation, so possibly the MS has been tampered with. The translation, which is not very close to the Greek text, runs as far as <u>ho potos autou drosos hon eleiche</u>.

The second account is in AC Hebrews 7.3, which reads:

'There is no book which says of Melchizedek, "So-and-so was his father, so-and-so was his mother". There is no book which says of him, "He was born on this day, he died on this day". If it is asked, "Is it not written in Sᵊnkᵊssar?", (it is said thus) because it was not written in the book of the Levites'.

This refers to Sᵊnkᵊssar, Pagume 3[6], which names Melchizedek's father as 'Qaynan son of Shem'. The source closest to this appears to be the 'Book of Adam and Eve'[7], which gives his father as Qaynam, son (or grandson) of Arphaxad. A number of other sources[8] represent him as a Shemite, and some of them, like Sᵊnkᵊssar, include the narrative of the burial of Adam's bones.

In addition to these names and identifications, a number of other accounts of Melchizedek's ancestry are found in Ethiopic, but have not entered the AC corpus proper:

(i)   His father is named as Faleq in many works, including Ethiopic

5. Graf I, pp.204-5, and references given there.

6. English translation in E.A.W. Budge, Book of the Saints, vol.IV, pp.1277-8.

7. Ethiopic text in E. Trumpp, Der Kampf Adams, p.126; English translation (unreliable in detail) in S.C. Malan, The Book of Adam and Eve, p.149 and notes on pp.237-8. See also Graf I, p.205, lines 4-10.

8. E.g. Book of the Bee (E.A.W. Budge, Anecdota Oxoniensia (Semitic Series) vol. I, part II, pp.33-4) ch.21 cites a 'Book of Chronography' as saying that Cainan son of Arphaxar son of Shem begat Shalaḥ and Malaḥ, and Malaḥ married Yozadak and begat Melchizedek; Book of the Rolls (M.D. Gibson, Studia Sinaitica, VIII; see also Graf I, pp.283-92) and Book of the Cave of Treasures (C. Bezold, Die Schatzhöhle; E.A.W. Budge, The Book of the Cave of Treasures) give similar names.

Qäleməntos[9], the chronography of Giyorgis wäldä Amid[10], a homily of
Rətuʿa haymanot on the twelve apostles[11], and miracle 24 of the 'Miracles
of the Father and the Son and the Holy Spirit' collected by Abunä
Bəṣuʿa amlak[12]. The source for this name is probably the Annales of
Eutychius (Saʿīd ibn Biṭrīq)[13]. The Ethiopic Mämhərä orit in MS B.N.
d'Abbadie 39 adds to Faleq a name for Melchizedek's mother, Sädäqa[14];
Ethiopic Abušakər (e.g. MSS B.L. Orient 809 f.63a and 810 f.96a) also
gives his mother's name as Sädäqa, but has Sala son of Arphaxad as his
father.

(ii)   The commentary on the Pentateuch in MS EMML 2101[15] names
Melchizedek's mother as Sultayəl and his father as Hərqälayəm son of
Känäʾan grandson of Ham. This is based on the opinion recorded by
Ibn aṭ-Ṭaiyib in his commentary on Genesis[16]; he has cited it from
Išoʿdad of Merv[17], who took it from Zacharias Scholasticus[18], who

9. See S. Grébaut's translation, ROC, 1912 p.23 and 136.

10. E.g. MS B.L. Orient 814 f.10b.

11. E.g. MS B.L. Orient 786 f.151b.

12. MS Berlin (Hammerschmidt and Six 113) or. quart. 993.

13. PG 111, cols. 917-8.

14. Fol. 79a.

15. Fol. 80b.

16. Geez translation in, e.g., MS B.N. d'Abbadie 28 f.24b; Arabic text
    and French translation in J.C.J. Sanders, C.S.C.O. vols. 274-5
    (Arab. 24-5), see vol. 275, p.60.

17. Syriac text and French translation in C. van den Eynde, C.S.C.O. vols.
    156-7 (Syr. 75-6), see vol. 156, p.159.

18. Syriac text and Latin translation in E.W. Brooks, C.S.C.O. vols. 83-4
    and 87-8 (Syr. 38-9, 41-2), see vol. 83, p.9.

attributes it to Epiphanius[19].

(iii)   Chapter 27 of the Chronicle of John of Nikiou says that Melchizedek 'was descended from the race of Sidus, son of (Egyptus) the king of Egypt and Nubia'[20].

(iv)   MS EMML 1839 f.30b identifies Melchizedek with Shem[21];   this is the commonest Jewish opinion[22], and also that of Ephrem[23].

(v)   The Mämhərä orit in MS B.N. d'Abbadie 156 says (f.6b) that Melchizedek's birth is 'from the seed of Känä'an'. This opinion is mentioned as a majority view in the Book of the Bee[24], and is perhaps to be traced back to Eustathius of Antioch[25].

(vi)   A marginal note in a Geez Abušakər, MS B.L. Orient 809 f.62b, identifies as Melchizedek the son of Shem who was called to help take up the body of Adam.

19. But it is not identical with Epiphanius' account in Panarion LV (PG 28).

20. English translation by R.H. Charles;   a slightly different text of this is cited in MH p.147, in comment on Ezek. 16.3.

21. EMML 1839 contains a Geez version of a compilation of 'questions' made by Ibn aṭ-Ṭaiyib. The first part corresponds fairly closely with Išoʿ bar Nun's questions, but (f.2b) omits Išoʿ bar Nun's question XIX on Melchizedek. On f. 12a, dependent on another source, Melchizedek is said to be a Canaanite, and on f.30b, probably dependent on Theodore bar Konis' Book of Scholia Mimrā II. 124, he is identified with Shem.

22. L. Ginzberg, Legends of the Jews, especially vol.V, pp.225-6.

23. Syriac text and Latin translation in R.M. Tonneau, C.S.C.O. vols. 152-3 (Syr.71-2).

24. Ch.21, see note 8 above.

25. B. Altaner, 'Die Schrift ΠΕΡΙ ΤΟΥ ΜΕΛΧΙΣΕΔΕΚ des Eustathios von Antiocheia', Byzantinische Zeitschrift, 1940, pp.30-47.

Of the known opinions[26] about Melchizedek's ancestry, almost all have reached Ethiopia. The only one lacking appears to be the account in some texts of 2 (Slavonic) Enoch that his mother was Sopanim/Sothonim, wife of Nir, the second son of Lamech[27], and possibly also the record of Epiphanius that his mother was Astarōth or Asterian[28] (but as he gives his father's name as Hēraklan, this may be Zacharias Scholasticus' source).

The compilers of the AC evidently had a wide choice of material. The concerns which prompted their selection appear to have been exegetical ones (rather than idle curiosity), as follows:

(i)   In AC Philoxenus p.39, the commentator is concerned with the refutation of the claim that Melchizedek is son of God, and therefore reports that he was a Hamite. Similarly, in the commentary on Ezekiel 16.3, the commentator uses the history of Jerusalem, of Melchizedek, and of the Canaanite occupation, to illustrate the text (that Jerusalem's ancestry was from the land of Canaan).

(ii)   In AC Heb.7.3, the commentator faces the apparent contradiction that whereas the author of Hebrews says that Melchizedek is 'without father or mother' and 'has no end of life', in Sənkəssar his father is named, and his death dated; it is to resolve this that the matter is raised.

26. The literature is vast; see especially V. Aptowitzer, 'Malkizedek, zu den Sagen der Agada', Monatsschrift für die Geschichte und Wissenschaft des Judentums, 70 (1926), pp.93–113; J. Bowker, The Targums and Rabbinic Literature, pp.196–9; R.Murray, Symbols of Church and Kingdom, p.180; P.J. Kobelski, Melchizedek and Melchirešaʿ; D.M. Hay, Glory at the Right Hand: Psalm 110 in Early Christianity.

27. J.H. Charlesworth (ed.), The Old Testament Pseudepigrapha, vol.I, pp.204 ff. (2 Enoch 71).

28. PG 41 cols. 973–4. K. Holl's text in G.C.S. reads Astarth.

The exegetical intent that has led to this selection of material in the AC may best be illustrated from AC Psalms 109 (110). 4:

'If it is asked, "In what does Melchizedek resemble the Lord?", it is because it says of Melchizedek, "who has no father or mother" – if it is asked, " Is it not written in Sənkəssar?", (the answer is that it is said) because it is not in the Levitical writing – and (similarly) the Lord has no mother for his former birth, nor father for his latter birth.

A.   It is because Melchizedek used to offer prayers with wheat and wine, and (similarly) the Lord has given to us in wheat his flesh, and in wine his blood.

A.   It is because it is not said of Melchizedek, "At this time he appeared, at this time he passed away", and (similarly) it is not said of the Lord, "At this time he appeared, at this time he passed away", as it says, "There is no origin to his time, nor end to his days".

A.   It is because it says of Melchizedek, "who is from the tribe of Ham"; he, having been born of Ham, appropriated priesthood without having been born from the house of Levi, and (similarly) the Lord, having been born of the house of Judah, appropriated priesthood without having been born from the house of Levi.'

This argument of this pericope is very similar to that found towards the close of the Ethiopic 'Second homily of Cyril of Alexandria on Melchizedek', where the four points made in AC Ps. 109.4 appear in the order 4,1,3,2[29]; although that homily does not specify Melchizedek's descent from Ham, this is insisted on in a further tract in the Ethiopic Qerəllos corpus[30].

29. The homily is in A. Dillmann, Chrestomathia Aethiopica, pp.93-98, where the relevant passage commences on p.97 line 8; also B.M. Weischer, 'Die äthiopischen Psalmen- und Qērlosfragmente in Erevan, Armenia', Oriens Christianus 53, pp.113-158, where the relevant passage is pp.130-7.

30. B. M. Weischer, op.cit., text pp.142-3, translation pp.152-3.

2.4.   The Diamerismos tēs gēs (Joshua 6-7).

The text of the Mämhärä orit contained in MS. B.N. d'Abbadie 156, fols.4a-19a, includes, on fols.16b-17b, a pericope on the lists of the nations descended from the children of Noah. This section is preceded by comment on the destruction and rebuilding of Jericho (Josh.6.26), and followed by the story of Achan (Josh.7); it appears somewhat intrusive into its context - though it may be considered to be related to the themes of Israelite resettlement in Canaan, and the fact and the morality of the dispossession of other peoples - and it is not contained in the other texts of MO described below in chapter 4.1.

This pericope is cited from the Geez version of the Ancoratus of Epiphanius, beginning from PG 43, col.220 (hoti kalos ho theos tou nomou = d'Abb. 156 fol.16b, col.2, fäkkare äsmä sännay ägzi'abäher zä'orit) and ending at PG 43, col.225 (ou gar muktērizetai ho theos hōs proeipon = d'Abb. 156 fol.17b, col.1, äsmä iyät'ebbäd ägzi'abäher bäkämä aqdämku nägirotä).

This Diamerismos tēs gēs in Epiphanius' Ancoratus has been studied by Piilonen[1], who includes in his summary of conclusions:

"1. The order of the Semite peoples in the MSS of Epiph. anc. 113,2 was confused by medieval copyists. The correct order is preserved in the numerous MSS of Anastasius Sinaita quaest. 28,7[2], which is an extract from Epiph. anc. 113 ....

2. The Διαμεριϲμος τῆϲ γῆϲ in Epiph. anc. 113 is not the inde - pendent work of Epiphanius. He took the main bulk, at least 156 (83%)

1. J. Piilonen, 'Hippolytus Romanus, Epiphanius Cypriensis and Anastasius Sinaita. A Study of the ΔΙΑΜΕΡΙϹΜΟϹ ΤΗϹ ΓΗϹ ', Annales Academiae Scientiarum Fennicae, series B 181, 1974.

2. PG 89, cols. 555-562; this is part of the work of the Pseudo-Anastasius, and not of the genuine questions, see M. Richard, 'Les Véritables "Questions et Réponses" d'Anastase le Sinaite', Bull. Inst. Rech. Hist. Textes 15 (1969), pp.39-56, reprinted in his Opera Minora III, Leuven, 1977.

of the 188 ethnic and geographical names from Hippolytus' chronicle[3]
of which a MS of type H_2 was available to him. Although Epiphanius'
dependence on Hippolytus admits of no doubt whatever, it must be
acknowledged that he treated the chronicle in an original fashion,
inserting into the lists 11 names totally foreign to Hippolytus ...."

The order of the Semite peoples in the list in d'Abb. 156 and
in the MSS of the Geez version of the Ancoratus which I have
examined (principally MS. B.L. Orient 740) is the same as that in
the Greek texts of (Ps.) – Anastasius Sinaita, and the same as
Piilonen's reconstruction of the true Greek text of the Ancoratus;
the Geez version of the Ancoratus therefore supports Piilonen's theory,
and appears to represent a Greek text superior (at least in respect
of this section) to any extant.

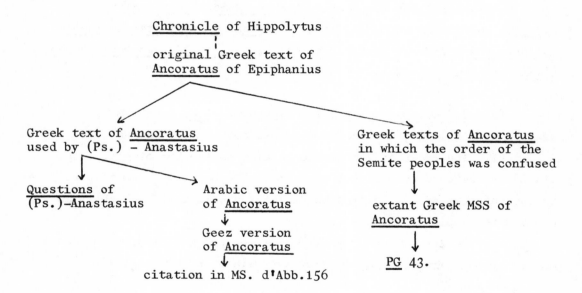

3. In GCS, Hippolytus, vol.4, pp.10–43.

The natural commentary context for this pericope on the lists of the nations seems to be Genesis 10, on which there are plentiful materials, amplifying and updating the Biblical lists, in Hebrew[4], Greek[5], and Syriac[6]. The Epiphanian material which has been translated into Geez, however, appears independent of these other materials (except for its dependence on Hippolytus); it has not been utilized in Geez or Amharic commentaries on Genesis 10, or, so far as I can discover, on other parts of the Bible (except for the use noted above in d'Abb. 156).

The following are possible reasons for the non-inclusion of this material in the AC:

(i)   The lists proved uncongenial to memorize.

(ii)   The lists did not, for the Ethiopians, aid understanding of Gen.10. AC Gen.10 contains a translation of the Geez Biblical text, and adds a few etymological and historical notes, but does not seem to feel the need for 'updating' the names – a process which would have been, from the Ethiopian view-point, a mere replacement of lists of names familiar from the Biblical texts by other names unfamiliar either from the Bible or from current Ethiopian geographical knowledge.

(iii)   The lists were available for consultation in MSS of the Geez version of the <u>Ancoratus,</u> and were therefore not repeated; in general, the AC does not idly repeat mere information from Geez historical and chronographic writings.

4. See P.S. Alexander, <u>The Toponomy of the Targumim</u>, Oxford D.Phil. thesis, 1974. This includes consideration of the Hebrew <u>Sefer Yosippon</u>; YwK, the Geez epitome of this, is, however, unrelated to the <u>Ancoratus</u>.

5. E.g. Josephus, Eusebius of Caesarea, Procopius; references in C. van den Eynde, <u>Commentaire d'Išodad de Merv I. Genèse</u>, <u>C.S.C.O.</u>, vol.156, p.142, note 1.

6. E.g. Išodad on Gen.10 in C. van den Eynde (<u>op.cit.</u>), and Theodore bar Koni in Mimrā II, 115-118, in R. Hespel and R. Draguet, <u>Theodore bar Koni Livre des Scolies</u> vol. I, <u>C.S.C.O.</u>, vol. 431, pp.128-9.

2.5.   'One who came from Edom'   (Isaiah 63.1)

AC Isaiah 63.1 has four interpretations of the text:

(i)   'The angel appears to him in the likeness of Hyrcanus when he destroyed Edom ...'

(ii)   'He sees the angel in the appearance of Cyrus when he destroyed Babylon ...'

(iii)   'Who is this who, having put on flesh, is born from the Virgin Mary?'

(iv)   'Who is this who, having put on a robe, goes out from the lithostratos towards Calvary?'

Comment on (iii) includes the note, '"Basor" means "flesh", as it says, "For 'Basor' is interpreted of 'flesh'", apparently mistakenly alluding to Hebrew basar, and demonstrating the existence of a Geez tradition[1] about the meaning of the place-name 'Bozrah'.

The interpretations of Isa. 63.1 concerning Hyrcanus and concerning Christ are also to be found in the Geez commentary on Isaiah in MS B.N. d'Abbadie 157. This is a composite of parts of two commentaries, or perhaps of one commentary and addenda[2], and contains

---

1.   Interpretation of Bosor as 'carnis/carnalis' is also found in e.g. Cyril of Alexandria, PG 70, col. 1381-2.

2.   This commentary is of Christian provenance, but scrapings and marginalia indicate that this MS has passed through Felasha hands. Ff.193a-222a contain comment covering Isa.1-66, with some gaps, and then ff.222a-227a contain comment on certain verses from Isa.38-66. Both parts contain some Amharic words, probably of the 18th. century. The former part contains a number of notes that 'the text is not correct' (zä'ikonä), and some of these show evidence of collation with the Hebrew text or a version very close to it; the former part also has atorawyan written for the commoner Geez asorawyan, possibly reflecting Syriac influence. That the two parts have a measure of independence (and are not a mere accident resulting from dislocation of page order) is demonstrated by a number of contradictions between them - e.g. on serenes (Isa.43.20 = LXX seirēnes), f.218b says 'the text is incorrect; it should read herodyanos' (Geez for 'stork'), while f.224a says 'which above its neck is a bird, and beneath it a man'.

two comments on Isa. 63.1 as follows:

(f.221b) '"Question from the prophet and answer from the angel. Who are you, a man self-reliant, and wonderful, and powerful, who came[3] from Edom[4]...". As for the explanation of this, the angel appeared to Isaiah in the form of Hyrcanus, a long time previously, so that he finish off the Edomites in conflict. There is (another interpretation): "And a self-reliant man came out[5] from Edom" - it is ...[6], because he was from Edom and from the region of Galilee ...'.

(f.226b) '"Who is the man who arrived[7] from Edom?" - the inheritance of Esau, his enemy, who quarrelled with Israel. As for "the one who made (him) come out" - (it is) Hyrcanus. And there is (another interpretation) which says "(It is) ...[8], who was born in Judah; it is near to Edom ...'.

The former part of this composite commentary contains several more Maccabean/Hasmonean references:

(a)   on Isa.7.24 (f.200a), the person 'who will again destroy the land' is Antiochus;

(b)   on Isa.22.20 (f.209a), Eliakim son of Hilkiah is understood to be, or to prefigure, Hyrcanus wäldä mäqabyan, who took both the priesthood and the kingdom;

3. z̤amäsa'äkä .

4. The lemma cites parts of the text of Isa.63.1-5, in some disorder. 'Question ... angel' appears as a part of the text of Isa.63.1 here, as it does also in AC Isa.63.1.

5. wäwäs'a.

6. krästos, 'Christ', was written here, but scraped out (as throughout this commentary except for f.223a, where it was overlooked).

7. z̤abäsha.

8. 'Christ', as in note 6 above.

(c)   on Isa.24.18 (f.210a), 'he who flees ... shall fall into the pit'
is understood to mean that those left over from Nebuchadnezzar's
invasion will be captured by Antiochus;   and

(d)   Isa.34.4-6 (f.215a-b) is referred, in an extensive passage, to
Hyrcanus' military successes, especially against Edom.

The Geez commentary on the minor prophets in e.g. MS B.N.
d'Abbadie 156 also makes reference to Hyrcanus, especially in the
commentary on Obadiah, which commences (f.116a), 'And he saw much
slaughter which will happen to the men of Edom, the descendants of
Esau, at the hand of Hyrcanus', and on Zechariah 11.14 (f.127a) which
refers   the 'breaking of the second staff' to the 'destruction of
the kingdom which happened at the hands of the Romans after the death
of Hyrcanus'.

There is further comment on Isaiah 63.1-64.4 in the t̲ə̲r̲g̲w̲a̲m̲e̲
n̲ä̲b̲i̲y̲a̲t̲ ('interpretation of the prophets') contained in G̲ə̲b̲r̲ä̲ ̲h̲ə̲m̲a̲m̲a̲t̲
and attributed to A̲b̲b̲a̲ S̈alama the m̲ä̲t̲ä̲r̲g̲w̲ə̲m̲[9];   the relevant section
is appointed for the third day hour on Friday:
'"Who is this"[10] as far as it says "they hope for your mercy"[11] _

9.   This t̲ə̲r̲g̲w̲a̲m̲e̲ n̲ä̲b̲i̲y̲a̲t̲ appears in the printed edition of G̲ə̲b̲r̲ä̲ ̲h̲ə̲m̲a̲m̲a̲t̲
       (A.A.,1942 E.C.) as comment on Job 23.2-24.25 (pp.103-5), 27.1-28.13
       (pp.207-10), 29.21b-30.10 (pp.293-5);   Prov. 3.5-15a (pp.151-2),
       9.1-11 (pp.121-2);   Wisd. 2.12-22 (pp.275-7);   Isa.1.2-9 (pp.269-71),
       5.1-9a (pp.59-61), 12.2-13.10 (pp.321-4), 61.1-7 (pp.204-6), 63.1-
       64.4 (pp.290-1);   Jer. 22.29-23.6a (pp.272-3), Prophecy against Pashhur
       (pp.273-5);   Dan.7.2-15 (pp.124-5);   Hos. 5.13b-6.3 (pp.152-4);   Zech.
       14.5b-11 (pp.355-8).   The note that A̲b̲b̲a̲ S̈alama 'prepared it from
       Arabic' is on p.358.

10. Isa.63.1.

11. Isa.64.4.

the interpreter said, "He says, 'Who is this who came out[12] from
Edom?'; the prophet said this concerning our Lord God Jesus Christ,
to whom be praise, for Edom is of the region of Galilee. But if the Jews
had said that he was from Galilee, they would have said among themselves, by reason of jealousy, 'Search in the books, that a prophet
does not arise from Galilee'[13]. (People) interpreted it further
concerning Edom, that it is 'Heaven', in accordance with the word of
David the prophet,'Who will take me to the walled place, and who will
lead me as far as Edom?'[14]; for the two words[15], in prophecy, indicate
our Lord Christ.

'He says, "And his clothes are red, which are from Basor" - God revealed
through the prophet what will happen at the time of his life-giving
sufferings, when the troops of Herod and Pilate clothed him in a red
robe, and they mocked him; and our Lord accepted this from them,
willingly, and so that he should fulfil the prophecy of the prophets...'

Of the interpretations in AC Isa.63.1, MS d'Abbadie 157, and
Gäbrä hämamat, the two interpretations in d'Abb. 157 are essentially
similar, and AC Isa. 63.1 shares with them the interpretations referring
to Hyrcanus and to Christ. The comment in d'Abb.157 f.221b shares with
Gäbrä hämamat the geographically inaccurate reference to Edom as
əm'adyamä gälila ('from/of the region of Galilee', 'one of the districts
of Galilee'). AC Isa.63.1 shares with Gäbrä hämamat the interpretation
referring to Christ's passion, and there are some shared interpretations
later in the section, such as the references to the 'pouring out of the
blood of the Jews' on Isa.63.6. The Hasmonean theme does not appear in

12. The printed text here, in common with e.g. B.L. MS Orient 2083 f.148b,
    reads zawäs'a, but many MSS read zäbäsha (e.g. B.L. Orient 597 f. 159b;
    598 f.123b; 599 f.105b; 600 f.101a; 601 f.70b); the text
    printed in Mäshafä tənbitä näbiyat, Asmara, 1977 E.C. also reads zawäs'a.

13. John 7.52.

14. Ps.60.9 (RSV).

15. i.e. 'walled place' and 'Edom'. AC Ps.59.9 does not comment on this;
    elsewhere these two terms are frequently referred to the Virgin Mary.

Gǝbrä hǝmamat at all, probably because, in a Holy Week lectionary, the
interest was narrowly Christological; however, the theme does not seem
to be found in Syriac or in Jewish comment on this chapter either, nor
does Hyrcanus' subjugation of Edom appear very prominently in Yosef
wäldä Koryon[16], and this raises the question of the source of this
interpretation. Some nineteenth century Protestant commentators[17]
refer to Hyrcanus in their comment on Isa.63, but I have not discovered
an ancient source for this.

It may be concluded that the materials on the interpretation of
Isa.63.1 surveyed above are related to one another as representatives
of a tradition, but are not derived from one another in a linear fashion;
that while all the materials interpret the verse Christologically, most
of them first understand it in a prior historical context; and that
the source of the references to Hyrcanus remains unidentified.

16. It is narrated in YwK 88, in a passage parallel to Josephus, Ant.
    13.9.1, and referred to again on YwK pp.167, 221 and 234.

17. E.g. E. Henderson, The Book of the Prophet Isaiah, London, 1840.

2.6.   Simeon (Luke 2.25).

The AC contains two traditions about Simeon:

(i)   that he was one of the LXX translators, as related in AC
Lk.2.26[1] (translated below), and

(ii)   that he was the author of 1 Esdras, as related in the AC
introduction to 1 Esdras[2].

In addition, he is well-known in Ethiopia as author of the Nunc
dimittis (Lk.2.29-32), and there are various references to him in
Geez literature.

The tarik pericope in AC Lk.2.26 reads as follows:

"There was a magnificent king called Bäṭlimos. By reason of
his magnificence, he ruled this world, melting it like wax and crushing
it like a shard. He knew the language of every country. He asked,
'What do I lack?', and people said to him, 'You lack the forty-six
books of the Old Testament, which contain much wisdom and many similes.
Because at that time he had authority over the Israelites, he sent
(a message), saying, 'Send me the scribes and the books'. They sent
him the forty-six books of the Old Testament and seventy-two scribes.
Two died on the way; to each of the seventy he allotted a young man
who would run errands for them, and to each pair he gave a tent.
This makes thirty-five. He allotted the smaller (books) to individuals,
and the greater (books) to pairs, telling them to write out the Hebrew
in the Greek language. The book of Isaiah fell to Simeon. While he
was writing, he reached the section which says, 'Behold, a virgin will
conceive and bear a son'. He wrote, 'A maiden will conceive', saying,
'Let alone a king of the Gentiles, would even a king of Israel accept
it from me if I wrote, "A virgin will conceive in virginity and give
birth in virginity"?' He became drowsy and slept; when he awoke, he
found 'maiden' scraped out, and 'virgin' written. He scraped out
'virgin', and wrote 'maiden'. A second time he became drowsy and slept;
when he awoke, he found 'maiden' scraped out, and 'virgin' written.

1.   Wängel qəddus, p.290 col.3-p.291 col.1.

2.   TIA p.16.

He scraped out '<u>virgin</u>', and wrote '<u>maiden</u>'. A third time he became drowsy and slept; when he awoke, he found '<u>maiden</u>' scraped out, and '<u>virgin</u>' written. When he intended to scrape it out, this was spoken to him – '<u>You will not die without seeing the anointed of God</u>'. If it is asked why it was like this, the secret was the wisdom of God. Because the books written in Hebrew were the ones that the wicked people would burn, he (God) saw to it that the ones written in Greek would be preserved when the ones written in Hebrew were lost. If it is said that his (Simeon's) age was five hundred, then he was two hundred and fifty when he wrote this, and after he had written this he lived for two hundred and fifty years. If it is said that it (his age) was three hundred, then he was one hundred and fifty when he wrote this, and after he had written this he lived for one hundred and fifty years. But Mämmər Esdras[3] said that he was a young man of fifteen years when he wrote this."

The major source of the above is clearly <u>Sənkəssar</u> for <u>Yäkkatit</u> 8[4], with the following details added from supplementary sources:

(i)   the reference to the O.T. books as 46 in number (probably Ethiopian in origin),

(ii)   the note that two translators died on the road (probably taken from the Ethiopic <u>Abušakər</u>[5], or the Ethiopic version of Giyorgis wäldä Amid[6]),

(iii) the opinion that Simeon lived to be 500 (probably from <u>Tərgwame wängel</u>, the Geez version of Ibn aṭ-Ṭaiyib's gospel commentary[7]), and

(iv)   the opinion that Simeon was 15 at the time of the LXX translation

3. I.e. Mämhər Esdros, on whom see MEHI.

4. E.A.W. Budge, <u>The Book of the Saints</u>, II, pp.602-4.

5. In section on reign of Ptolemy Philadelphus, e.g. B.L. MSS Orient 809 fol.85b, 810 fol.136a.

6. In section on Ptolemy's reign, e.g. B.L. MS Orient 814, fol.75a.

7. On Lk.2.25 ff., e.g. B.L. MSS Orient 731 fol.233a, 732 fol. 244a-b. His age is also given as 500 in AC <u>Qəddase Maryam</u> p.267.

(for which the AC notes M̈amhər Esdros as source; as noted elsewhere[8], I believe this to be Esdros' original thought, unless it represents a misreading of, or error in, a text of Giyorgis ẅäldä Amid's chronography, which gives Simeon's age as 95 when he went to Egypt).

Thus far the facts may be represented as follows:

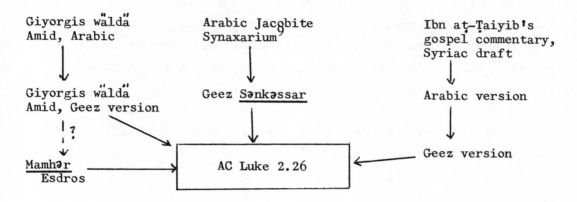

Giyorgis ẅäldä Amid, Arabic

Giyorgis ẅäldä Amid, Geez version

Mamhər Esdros

Arabic Jacobite Synaxarium[9]

Geez Sənkəssar

Ibn aṭ-Ṭaiyib's gospel commentary, Syriac draft

Arabic version

Geez version

AC Luke 2.26

In the Geez version of Giyorgis ẅäldä Amid, the section on Ptolemy Philadelphus, '94th. from Adam', falls into 3 parts:
(i)   a discussion of the length of his reign, naming the sources as 'ẅäldä Bäṭriq', 'ẅäldä Mänäkos', and 'Mänbägi' – namely, the Annales of Eutychius (Saʿid ibn Baṭriq)[10], the Chronicon Orientale of ibn

8. MEHI.

9. R. Basset, Le Synaxaire arabe jacobite; the section on Simeon is under Amchir 8th., P.O. XI, pp.803-805 ([769]-[771]).

10. PG 111, col.907- (section on Simeon on col.974); Arabic text ed. L.Cheikho, C.S.C.O. vol.50 (= Ar.6), see pp.ΛO ff. On Eutychius' sources, see M. Breydy, Études sur Saʿid ibn Baṭriq et ses sources (C.S.C.O. vol. 450 = Subs.69), Louvain, 1983.

ar-Rahib ("Abusǎkər")[11], and the <u>Kitab al-ʿUnwan</u> of Agapius (Mahbub)[12], (ii) the story of the LXX translation, including mention of Simeon 'who lived 300 years until Christ was born', and of Eleazar 'whom Antiochus killed', apparently based on the sources named in (i) above, (iii) a second account of the LXX translation, with no mention of Simeon; the source is named as Yosef wǎldǎ Koryon 'in the first section of his work'[13]. The reference and the actual wording identify the source as (the Arabic version of) the <u>Sefer Yosippon</u> (and not the actual works of Josephus), and Giyorgis wǎldǎ Amid seems to have been uncertain whether this second account was a doublet of the first or not.

Comparison of the details of the various accounts establishes the following relationships:

11. The relationship of (Geez) <u>Abusǎkər</u> to the (Arabic) <u>Chronicon Orientale</u> is described in chapter 4.1 below. Basically, <u>Abusǎkər</u> is a large calendrical chronographic work of which an expansion of the non-Muslim material of the <u>Chronicon Orientale</u> forms part. For the material on Simeon, see Arabic text and translation by L.Cheikho, <u>C.S.C.O.</u> vols.45 and 46 (= Ar.1 and 2), text p.ﵕﵕ, trans. p.38, and Geez version e.g. MSS B.L. Orient 809 fol. 85b, Orient 810 fol. 136a.

12. Arabic text and translation by A. Vasiliev in <u>P.O.</u> V.4, VII.4 and VIII.3. The section on Ptolemy is V.4 pp.641-5, and also p.658; the length of his reign (as 38 years) is also mentioned in the chronologies cited by Agapius from Julius Africanus (VII.4, p.557) and from 'Chrysostom' (VII.4 p.561).

13. In the Geez version of this work the story appears at the end of section 1 in the majority of the MSS used by Murad Kamil (<u>Des Josef ben Gorion (Josippon) Geschichte des Juden</u>, pp.49-51).

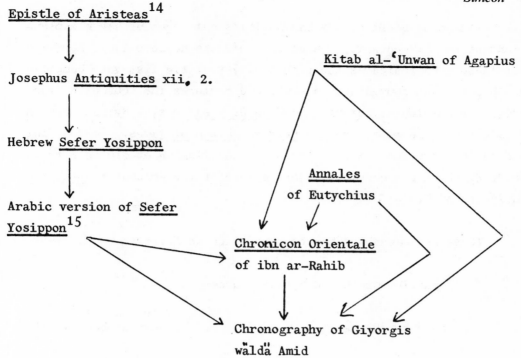

The commentary of Ibn aṭ-Ṭaiyib on Luke 2.25 ff.[16] contains 5 explanations of who Simeon was:

(i)   son of Joshua son of Jozadak ... who lived 500 years,

(ii)   son of Sirak ... who lived 250 years,

(iii)   high priest who read in the prophet, 'Behold a virgin ...',

(iv)   one of the 72 translators for Ptolemy,

(v)   one spared by the Holy Spirit to be a preacher concerning the birth of Christ.

J.F. Coakley has studied the sources of these traditions in his 'The Old Man Simeon (Luke 2.25) in Syriac Tradition'[17]. He begins

14. R.H. Charles (ed.), Apocrypha and Pseudepigrapha of the Old Testament, II, pp.83–122; further bibliography in J.H. Charlesworth, The Pseudepigrapha and modern research, pp.78–80, 274.

15. Graf. I, pp.221–3.

16. On the commentary, see Graf II, pp.166–9; for the relevant folios of MSS of the Geez version, see fn. 7 above.

17. Orientalia Christiana Periodica, XLVII.1 (1981), pp.189–212.

with a statement of Dionysius bar Ṣalibi's catalogue of seven explanations of who Simeon was; Ibn aṭ-Ṭaiyib's are numbers 1, 3, 4, 5 and
6 of these. He indicates the probability that the list goes back to
Mošе bar Kepha's commentary on Luke, and explores the sources of the
individual opinions - notably the <u>Cave of Treasures</u>, a Syriac version
of Eusebius' chronicle, and the <u>Protevangelium of James</u>. He does not
find an ancestry in Syriac exegesis for the linking of Simeon with
Isa.7.14, which has become a major feature of the account in <u>Sənkəssar</u>
and in the AC[18].

These relationships may be simplified as follows:

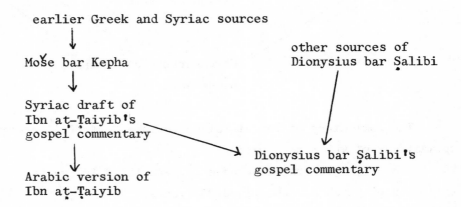

    earlier Greek and Syriac sources

    Mošе bar Kepha   other sources of
                                      Dionysius bar Ṣalibi
    Syriac draft of
    Ibn aṭ-Ṭaiyib's
    gospel commentary
                                      Dionysius bar Ṣalibi's
    Arabic version of   gospel commentary
    Ibn aṭ-Ṭaiyib

It seems possible that the tradition that Simeon wrote 1 Esdras is
derivative from Ibn aṭ-Ṭaiyib's first or second explanations (numbers
1 and 3 of Dionysius bar Ṣalibi), or perhaps from Dionysius' second
explanation (that Simeon was 'a righteous man who went down in the
captivity and despaired of restoration'), although that is lacking in
Ibn aṭ-Ṭaiyib.

There are further references in Geez to Simeon in <u>Gädlä Addam</u>[19]
(as a priest in the time of Nebuchadnezzar), in a poetic homily (on

18. Coakley, p.207; in this respect <u>Sənkəssar</u> represents a tradition
     quite different from that of the <u>Cave of Treasures</u>.

19. S.C. Malan, <u>The Book of Adam and Eve</u>, pp.196, 198 and 201.

'St. Simeon receiving our Lord') attributed to Cyril of Jerusalem[20] and translated into Geez[21] from Arabic[22], in the <u>Protevangelium of James</u>[23], in a homily attributed to Jacob of Serug[24] (which mentions Simeon's long life but gives no other specific details), in the Geez version of the 'Coptic–Arabic gospel catena' on St. Luke's gospel[25] (which does not add biographical details), and in a homily for Yäkkatit 8 attributed to Philoxenus of Mabbug[26].

It may be concluded that the sources on which this AC pericope on Simeon has drawn exhibit the historical interest of relating the origins of the Septuagint, and the hagiographical interest of identifying a gospel character about whom the gospels are reticent; the main concern of the AC itself, however, is the exegetical one of explaining the force of 'now' in Simeon's words, 'Now dismiss your servant ... because my eyes have seen your salvation'.

20. <u>PG</u> 33, 1187–1204.

21. E.g. B.L. MS Orient 773, ff. 164a –.

22. Graf I, p.335.

23. M. Chaîne, <u>C.S.C.O.</u> vols. 39 and 40 (= Aeth. 22 and 23), Geez text vol. 39, p.18, lines 27–9, corresponding to Greek <u>Protevangelium</u> 24.4.

24. E.g. MSS B.L. (Wright) Orient 774 ff. 43a–48b and Berlin (Hammerschmidt and Six 161) orient. fol. 3075, ff. 24a–29a.

25. MSS of the Geez version of the section on St. Matthew's gospel from this catena are not uncommon, but Tanasee (Hammerschmidt) 30 is the only MS of which I am aware containing the commentary on all 4 gospels. The section on Lk.2.25ff. is on Tanasee 30 ff. 100a–101a, approximately corresponding to de Lagarde, <u>Catenae in evangelia aegypticae quae supersunt</u>, pp.125–7.

26. EMML 1763 f.129a–132b.

2.7.   The magi (Matthew 2)

AC Matthew 2.3[1] contains the following account of the names and number of the magi; the intention of the comment is to explain why Herod and all Jerusalem were disturbed at their coming:

"... the city was disturbed together with him (Herod), like him, for (as the proverb says), 'The death of a king, the setting of the sun, is common to all'.

A. The three kings are called Mantusimar, Bädidasfa, Melku. Because they came each bringing ten thousand troops, he (Herod) was startled, was sad, when he heard this; and his people were startled, were sad, because exile had repeatedly come upon them.

If it is asked, 'Tä'ammärä iyyäsus[2] says "three (magi)", Tərgwame wängel[3] said "12"; is it not contradictory?', it is not contradictory; the matter is according to Tərgwame wängel. They set out as twelve. When they reached the river Euphrates, the emperor is called Fəršabur, and he took the nine away with him and they returned. If it is asked, 'For what reason?', it was because people told them that war had broken out against them to their rear. A. because their provisions were exhausted. A. because people told them that Jerusalem is cramped, and would not suffice for encampment. The real mystery, however, verifies that he (God) did not have them participate in the blessing of his (Jesus') birth.

If it is asked, 'How then does it say in the minor prophets,

1. Wängel qəddus, p.25 col.2.

2. I.e. The Miracles of Jesus; in the text edited and translated by Grébaut (P.O., XII.4, p.612), it is stated that the kings were three, but no names are given.

3. I.e. the Geez translation of Ibn aṭ-Ṭaiyib's gospel commentary, e.g. MS B.L. (Wright) Orient 731 f.21b-22a.

"Seven shepherds will arise, and eight troops"?,[4] it is because the seven had assumed the rank of emperor, but the five had not assumed the rank of emperor, and he spoke of them by saying 'their eighth one', counting them (the five) as one emperor; but the matter is according to Tərgwame wängel".

The names given here to the magi are found also (i) in Geez texts of the Protevangelium of James[5], and (ii) in the Geez recension of the Coptic-Arabic gospel catena[6]. However, as they do not occur in the Greek text or other oriental versions of the Protevangelium so far studied[7], nor in the Coptic text of the gospel catena as edited by de Lagarde[8], it seems that they have been interpolated into the Geez texts, which therefore cannot be uncritically accepted as sources for their appearance in the AC.

4. Mic.5.5. The AC on Mic.5.5 first interprets the 7 shepherds as the 7 archangels, and the 8th as the troops of the devil, and then interprets them of the kings/magi and their followers; it next discusses the apparent contradiction with Sənkəssar (rather than Tä'ammərä iyyäsus), but this may be an error, as Sənkəssar scarcely mentions the magi (Budge, Book of the Saints, p.789).

5. In M. Chaîne, Apocrypha de Beata Maria Virgine (C.S.C.O. vols. 39 and 40), text p.15, trans. p.13 gives the names as Tänisuram, Mälikä, and Sisəsba. MS B.L. Orient 743 f.86a gives them as Bä'əntä surawa, Mäläkän, and Bädeseba. See also A. d'Abbadie, Catalogue, p.114, on MS B.N. d'Abbadie 105.

6. E.g. B.L. Add. 16220 f.10b–11a, EMML 2088 f.9a–b.

7. For references see E. Hennecke, New Testament Apocrypha, vol.I, pp.370–1.

8. P. de Lagarde, Catenae in Evangelia; the pericope on the names of the magi would appear on p.5. See also Graf I, pp.481–3.

The AC has not recorded a considerable variety of other names for the magi[9] found in other works in Geez:

(i)   **Tərgwame wängel**, the Geez version of Ibn aṭ-Ṭaiyib's gospel commentary referred to in AC Mt.2.3, lists the following opinions[10]:

(a)   that the magi were 3, according to the number of their offerings, with 1000 followers,

(b)   that Jacob of Roha said they were 12, with more than 1200 followers,

(c)   that they were 8, in accordance with the prophecy of Micah 5.5,

(d)   that others say that they were 3 of royal descent and 9 important officials, the king who sent them was Fəršabur, and their names were

Hədwänäd	son of	Ɜrtabän,[11]
Šädäf	"	Kädfär,
Aršak	"	Mähadäs,
Zurwänäd	"	Wərwänd,
Arʾayahum	"	Käsri,
Artahašt	"	Hulit,
Ašnän buzən	"	Šäsrun,
Aduq	"	Hahum,
Ahsirəs	"	Säniban,
Šärduh	"	Bəldan,
Märduh	"	Nil.

9.   On the names in general see B.M. Metzger, 'Names for the nameless in the New Testament', Kyriakon, vol.I, pp.79–99;   U.Monneret de Villard, Le Leggende Orientali sui Magi Evangelici;   H. Kehrer, Die "Heiligen drei Könige" in der Legende und in der deutschen bildenden Kunst bis Albrecht Durer.

10. The text I have primarily used is B.L. Orient 731, fol.21b–22a.

11. Comparison with Mošе bar Kepha's list (see below) suggests that 'Hormizdad son of Sanatrus' has been omitted here;   the name is not contained in the relevant B.L. MSS – Or.731, fol.22a;   Or.732, fol.30a; Or.734, fol.12a;   Or.735, fol.36b;   Or.736, fol.15a–b. Alternatively, bar Bahlul's 'Ahduiyad' may have been omitted before Hədwänäd.

These opinions are variously found in a number of Syriac works, e.g. <u>The Book of the Bee</u> and bar Bahlul's <u>Lexicon</u>[12], but the actual selection of material is closest to that in Moše bar Kepha's 'Homilies on the gospels'[13], which, alongside Išoᶜdad of Merv's gospel commentary,[14] is a major source of Ibn aṭ-Ṭaiyib's gospel commentary.

(ii) The Geez adaptation of the Coptic-Arabic gospel catena gives the name of the magi's ancestor as Zärädäš, and continues with the information tabulated below[15]:

name in Coptic	name in Greek	age in years	gift
Bä'əntisuram	Gäspar	60	gold
Mälikun	Bälṭaser	40	incense
Bädisäsba	Malkəyos	20	myrrh

The 'names in Coptic' are the ones noted above as found in the AC and elsewhere. The 'names in Greek' are the familiar Gaspar, Balthasar, and Melchior, and they are also to be found, as Gäspar, Beltäzar, and Beləstor, in MS Rema 2[16], in comment on Mt.2.1-23 which begins, 'The interpretation of the magi and the journeying of the star, which Yohannəs the Syrian interpreted; you will find it in the <u>Tərgwame wängel</u> of Kämbat'.

(iii) <u>Gädlä addam</u> gives the magi's names as Hor, Bäsänaṭər and Qärsudan.[17]

12. References in Metzger, 'Names for the nameless', pp.83-4, and Kehrer, <u>Die "Heiligen drei Konige"</u>, pp.25-30.

13. Coakley, <u>The Homilies of Moše bar Kepha</u>, p.26ff.

14. Gibson, <u>Horae Semiticae</u>, V and VI.

15. The text I have primarily used is B.L. Add. 16220, fol.10b-11a; EMML 2088 fol.9a-b has only minor differences.

16. Hammerschmidt, <u>Äthiopische Handschriften vom Tänäsee</u>, vol.II, on MS 91 = Rema 2.

17. Metzger, 'Names', p.82; Geez text in Trumpp, <u>Der Kampf Adams</u>, p.168, translation and notes in Malan, <u>Book of Adam and Eve</u>, pp.205, 251-3. On the work, see Graf I, pp.201-3.

(iv)   A Marian homily for the festival of Lədäta[18] gives the names
and gifts as Awnəson (gold), Albatar (incense), Käsäd (myrrh);   this
is similar to the names given in Ludolf's <u>Lexicon</u>[19].

(v)   A 'Nägärä tənbitomu länäbiyat'[20] gives the names, tribes and
gifts as

Qäysor from the tribe of Shem who brought gold,

Maləq   "   Japheth   "   incense,

Sasnaniləs   "   Ham   "   myrrh.

MS EMML 2849 f.68b-69a gives these names as Qädäsər, Mäliho and Neləs,
and the names of the shepherds as Aser, Zablon, Yosṭos, Niqalimos, and
Bähəlm – a tradition probably distantly related to <u>The Book of the Bee</u>[21].
The linkage of Shem with gold, Japheth with incense, and Ham with
myrrh is also found in other sources, including the <u>Annales</u> of
Eutychius[22].

AC Matthew 2.1-11 considers the following questions about the
magi's origin, journeying, and gifts:

on v.1:

(i)   The meaning of <u>säb'a sägäl</u> ('magus').

(ii)   Prophecy concerning Bethlehem and Herod.

(iii)   The reason the magi came from the east.

(iv)   The prophecy that caused them to journey – the answer to this
mentions (a) their philosopher – ancestor Zärädäst, (b) their descent
from Balaam, (c) Ps. 72.10, (d) Baruch's journey to Athens, (e) Daniel's
prophecy[23].

18. E.g. MS B.L. Orient 692 f.19b.

19. Metzger, 'Names', p.82;   Ludolf, <u>Lexicon Aethiopico – Latinum</u>, 1661 ed.
    Appendix col. 539;   1699 ed. col. 329 (the column numbers are mis-
    printed in Metzger).

20. E.g. B.L. Orient 494 f.21b;   cf. EMML 7410 f.28b.

21. Metzger, 'Names', p.86.

22. <u>PG</u> 111, col. 915.

23. Cf. Išoʿdad's and Dionysius bar Ṣalibi's commentaries on Mt., <u>in loc.</u>

(v)   The reason God revealed the matter to them and not to others.

on v.2:

(vi)   Whether the star led them.

(vii)   Why they asked for the 'king of the Jews'.

(viii) The meaning of 'his star', and the question of whether it was really a star or an angel.

(ix)   Why it was by a star that they were led.

on v.3:

(x)   Why Herod and the people were startled at their coming – the comment is translated above.

on v.6:

(xi)   A story is told about how the prophet Micah saw a vision when passing through Bethlehem.

on v.11:

(xii)   The symbolism of the gifts:-

gold	kings	pure	martyrs	faith	angels
incense	idols	scented	hermits	hope	humans
myrrh	death	healing	believers	love	other
		and uniting			creations

(xiii) The question of the origin of the gifts – the answer relates how they were given to Adam by angels, reached Persia and Babylon, and were found by the magi; they gave them to Mary, and they were passed on to Peter and Clement.[24]

(xiv)   The question of their time of arrival – the answer gives the opinions that they arrived at the time of Jesus' birth, and that they arrived when he was two years old; it cites Epiphanius (incorrectly) to support the former of these.

(xv)   The question of the gifts and ages of the individual magi – the answer is as follows:

gift	age	tribe	symbolism of tribe
gold	20	Shem	kingship
incense	40	Japheth	priesthood
myrrh	60	Ham	the believers

24. This material is related to The Book of the Cave of Treasures, and is also mentioned briefly in Sənkəssar, Miyazya 6, and Ethiopic Qäleməntos (S. Grébaut, ROC, 1911, pp.169–70).

(xvi) The question of whether the magi received a spiritual reward.

The Geez materials most evidently used in the compilation of the Amharic comment outlined above are as follows:-

(i)   The translation of Ibn aṭ-Ṭaiyib's commentary on Matthew.

(ii)   The anonymous commentary covering Mt.1.18b-22.46 contained in B.L. MS Orient 731 fols. 142b-208b.[25]

(iii)   The Geez adaptation of the 'Coptic-Arabic gospel catena' on Matthew.

(iv)   Legendary material from works such as Gädlä addam and Qäleməntos, found also in Sənkəssar, and having general affinities with works such as The Book of the Cave of Treasures.

Detailed investigation of the relationship of the first two of these seems likely to be of interest for the study of later Syriac and Arabic Bible Commentaries. As far as the section on the magi is concerned, the facts are as follows:

(i)   the contents of Ibn aṭ-Ṭaiyib's comment (e.g. Or.731 fols.21b-28b) are almost verbally identical with that of Dionysius bar Ṣalibi's commentary on Matthew (C.S.C.O. vol.16, pp.67-87[26]),

(ii)   the Anonymous Commentary (i.e. Or.731 fols. 145b-147a) contains 12 numbered explanations, closely resembling Moše bar Kepha's and others' 'explanations of the coming of the magi':

Anonymous Commentary		Moše bar Kepha
1	=	explanation 1
2	=	" 2-3
3	=	" 6
4	=	" 7
5	=	" 8
6	=	" 9
7	=	" 10
8	=	" 11 (considerably short-ened)
9	=	" 12

25. Not mentioned in Wright's Catalogue;   see SAQ p.330-1.

26. I. Sedláček and I.-B. Chabot, C.S.C.O. Syr. II 98, V, I, fascicle 1.

Anonymous Commentary   Mošе bar Kepha

  10

  11   somewhat similar to George of Beʿeltanʼs explanation 7[27]

  12

(iii) Ibn aṭ-Ṭaiyibʼs comment and the Anonymous Commentary overlap; they both contain Mošе bar Kephaʼs explanations 1, 2 and 3, and some material from 11 also. However, while the Anonymous Commentary agrees with Mošе bar Kephaʼs third explanation in attributing Micah 5.5 to Isaiah, Ibn aṭ-Ṭaiyib correctly reads ʼMicahʼ.

  As far as the section on the magi is concerned, the relationships of the sources appear to be as follows[28]:

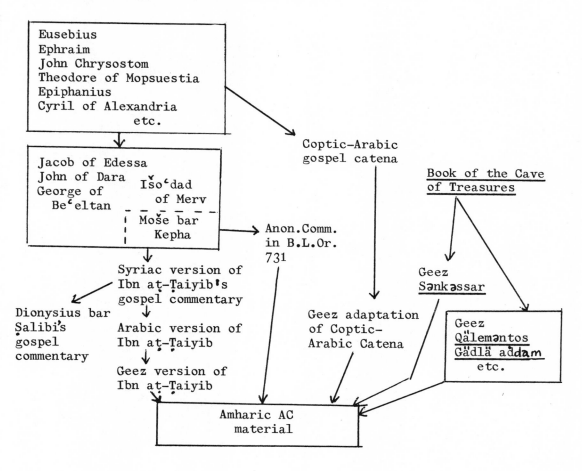

27. J.F. Coakley, <u>Homilies</u>.

28. Cf. the stemma in Beyer, <u>OC</u>, third series, I (1927) p.94; also Rendel Harris in introduction to Gibson, <u>Horae Semiticae</u>, vol.V.

It may be concluded that the AC has drawn on classical commentaries and on traditions of a more legendary nature; it mentions many of the classical 'questions' about the magi, using these to explain the text of Matthew 2, but it has exercised considerable selectivity from among the diverse materials available, especially those giving names to the magi.

2.8.   The sinful woman who anointed Jesus (Matthew 26)

AC Matthew 26.12[1] contains the following account of the sinful woman:

"This woman was one of beautiful appearance, from whom nothing was lacking from the hair of her head to her toe-nails. She had a mirror which showed her whole body. Having laid down her clothes and looked at her appearance, she said, 'What is the profit in being so beautiful when destruction and corruption are sure to come? They say that Jesus Christ, who forgives each person's sin, has come. I will go, having purchased perfume with which I will anoint him.' She had three hundred pieces of gold which she had gathered by fornication, and she went, carrying (them).

The devil, saying, 'She is escaping me; let me lead her astray at once', awaited her at the way-side <u>in the likeness of a young man of beautiful appearance</u>, resembling one whom she knew formerly. He said to her, 'Where are you going?' She was silent. He said to her, 'If you do not tell me, shall I not then tell you? A strange man has come to you, and you are going to buy perfume to anoint him'. 'Yes', she said to him. 'No, it's not that', he said to her, 'a man whose passion is not exhausted has come to you, and you are going to buy perfume to anoint him'. 'Yes', she said to him. 'No, it's not that', he said to her, 'a trader who will exchange much wealth for a little wealth has come to you, and you are going to buy perfume to anoint him'. 'Yes', she said to him. 'To each one you say, "Yes, yes"; which one is it?', he said to her.

She replied, 'As for your saying to me, "A strange man has come to you", the Lord, who is alien to this world, has come. As for your saying to me, "A man whose passion is not exhausted has come to you", he (the Lord) has come to die, the love of humankind having constrained him – as it says, "<u>Love drew the powerful son from his</u>

---

1. Amharic text in Ẅangel qǝddus, A.A., 1916 E.C., pp.179-80, and LFP p.44.

throne, and brought him as far as death"[2]. As for your saying to me,
"A trader who will exchange much wealth for a little wealth has come
to you", yes, (indeed,) because Jesus Christ, who will give much glory
for a little virtuous work, has come, I am going to purchase perfume,
with which I will anoint him'; when she invoked against him the name
(of Jesus), he disappeared for her, scattered like dust and diffused
like smoke.

There was a wealthy trader called Hadnok, and after this she
went and gave to him three hundred (pieces) of gold, saying, 'Bring
perfume which befits kings'. Because in their country there is no
falsehood, he said to her, 'But I have none that would fetch such a
price!' There was (some perfume) left over, David and Solomon having
been anointed with it, of which he (the trader) did not know, (but)
which his mother knew. She said to him, 'It is in such-and-such a
place; sell to her', and after he had sold it to her (the woman), she
brought (it) and anointed him (Jesus). Nor was it this alone - while
Salome and 'the brigand of the right hand' were carrying the Lord
when he went down to Egypt, he perspired on his clothing. When they
washed it, it (perfume) came to the surface. They placed this in a
container, and this was added to it (the royal anointing oil)".

The principal further Ethiopian materials relevant to the
interpretation of the story of the sinful woman may be grouped as
follows, according to their degree of verbal resemblance:
(i)   Materials containing the 'three questions': a Geez homily
attributed to John Chrysostom found e.g. in MS B.L. Orient 774
f.32a-43a[3], commencing dərsan zäqəddus wäbəsuʿ yohannəs afä wärq
bä'əntä bə'əsit hat'ət əntä qäb'atto lä'əgzi'ənä əfrätä. yəbe qəddus

---

2. Cited from qəddase, Qəddase maryam sect. 127 and Qəddase yohannəs afä
wärq sect. 53 in Mäshafä qəddase, A.A., 1951 E.C. (Geez and Amharic)
and M.Daoud, The Liturgy of the Ethiopian Church, A.A., 1954 A.D.
(English translation).

3. Also, e.g., in MS B.L. Orient 775 and Berlin (Hammerschmidt and Six 161)
Ms. orient. fol. 3075 f.15a-24a.

rətuⁿ lä̈nä̈ nəsmaⁿ wä̈nəlä̈bbu kwəllo gəbra .... I have not been able to
identify it with other (pseudo) - Chrysostomica[4]. It is a lenten
homily which commences with an exordium on the importance of turning
to good works. It continues with the story of the sinful woman who
wept over her sin, purchased unguent from a seller who asked her
the 'three questions', was tempted by Satan while on her way to Jesus,
and anointed Jesus in the house of Simon the Pharisee; Jesus told
Simon the story of the two debtors, and forgave the woman's sin. The
homily closes with an exordium on repentance and fasting. It is no
doubt ultimately dependent on Ephrem's homily <u>On the Sinful Woman</u>[5],
with which it has marked similarities, alongside some striking
differences.

The homily <u>Zena bə'əsit zä̈'əfrä̈t</u> contained in the burial service

4. On which see, in general, M. Geerard, <u>Clavis Patrum Graecorum</u>, II,
    Turnhout, 1974; J. de Aldama, <u>Repertorium pseudochrysostomicum</u>;
    Graf I, pp.342-352; and specifically, <u>PG</u> 59 cols.531-6, 61 cols.709-
    12, 727-34, 745-52; J.-M. Sauget, 'Une homélie syriaque sur la
    pécheresse attribuée a un évêque Jean', <u>Parole de l'Orient</u> 6/7 (1975/6),
    159-94; Y. ⁶Abd al Masīḥ, 'A Discourse by St. John Chrysostom on the
    Sinful Woman in the Saⁿīdic Dialect', <u>Bulletin de la Société d'Arch-
    éologie Copte</u> 15 (1958-60), 11-39; S. Grébaut, 'La Légende du parfum
    de Marie-Madeleine', <u>ROC</u> 21 (1918-19), 100-3; F. Graffin, 'Deux
    homélies anonymes sur la pécheresse', <u>L'Orient Syrien</u> 7 (1962),
    175-222; I. Guidi, 'La Traduzione Copta di un 'Omelia di S. Efrem',
    <u>Bessarione</u> 7, fasc. 70 (Jan.-Feb. 1903).

5. Syriac text and German translation in E. Beck, <u>Des heiligen Ephraem
    des Syrers Sermones</u> II, <u>C.S.C.O.</u> 311 (= Syr. 134), 78-91; 312 (= Syr.
    135), 99-113. English translation in P. Schaff and H. Wace (edd.),
    <u>Select Library of Nicene and Post Nicene Fathers</u>, second series,
    vol.XIII, pt. II, 336-41. On the later literature related to this
    homily, see A.C. Mahr, <u>Relation of Passion Plays to St. Ephrem the
    Syrian</u>, Columbus, 1942.

Mäshafä gənzät[6] corresponds closely with the section of this pseudo-Chrysostom homily which deals with the woman's fine clothing, her going to the perfumer, the perfumer's questions, the woman's answers, and her taking of the perfume. An old Amharic tract, the 'Fragmentum Piquesii',[7] contains the material of this Mäshafä gənzät homily with some expansions.

Literary comparison of these three works does not establish beyond doubt the nature of their interdependence, but the probability is that the Mäshafä gənzät homily is excerpted from the pseudo-Chrysostom homily, and that the Fragmentum Piquesii is a periphrastic translation and imaginative expansion of the Mäshafä gənzät homily, possibly written by someone who also knew the pseudo-Chrysostom material. The pseudo-Chrysostom homily contains conversations both between the trader and the woman, and between the devil and the woman; the Fragmentum Piquesii has taken up the first of these, and AC Mt.26.12 the second.

(ii)   Material on the source of the unguent: two appendices to the pseudo-Chrysostom homily[8], attributed to 'one of the holy fathers'. The first states that the unguent was left over from unguent with which the Virgin Mary had anointed the infant Jesus. The second states that the unguent was found on the clothing of the infant Jesus during the flight to Egypt; this is probably the source of the reference at the end of AC Mt.26.12 above, and a similar account is found in the Acts of Pilate, Greek recension B[9], and in AC Qəddase maryam[10].

6. Printed in Mäshafä gənzät, A.A., 1944 E.C., pp.164-166, and contained in most MSS of the work.

7. Text and translation in LFP.

8. E.g. MS B.L. Orient 774 f.41b-42a and 42a-43a.

9. M.R. James, The Apocryphal New Testament, pp.115-7.

10. Mäshafä qəddase, A.A., 1918 E.C., p.269, col.2.

(iii) An outline account of the story of the woman, contained in
Sǝnkǝssar for Yäkkatit 6^{11}, and an almost identical account (attributed
to Cyril) in the Geez version of the Coptic-Arabic gospel catena on
Mt.26.12^{12} (which additionally contains comment explaining the meaning
of albasṭiros). This material shows verbal correspondences with the
part of the pseudo-Chrysostom homily contained in Mäshafä gǝnzät, but
does not contain the 'three questions'.

(iv) Miracle 33 of the 'Miracles of Jesus', Tä'ammǝrä iyyäsus^{13}.
The following is a summary of it:

On Thursday (of Holy Week), Jesus was in the house of Simon.
In Jerusalem there was a prostitute called Mary, of the tribe of Judah;
she took 300 dinars of gold, and went to the chief trader, of the tribe
of Reuben, named Hadnok. He had the golden horn which had been in the
wilderness tabernacle, and which God had given to Moses for anointing
prophets and priests; Hadnok did not know the function of the oil in
the horn, though his mother knew. Mary bought the oil, went to the
house, and was refused admission. Jesus had her admitted, and she
anointed him, washed his feet, and asked for her sins to be forgiven.
Jesus told Simon the parables of the lost sheep and of the two debtors.
Judas Iscariot was angry.

This account, despite the similarities of outline, has no
verbal correspondence with the materials listed in (i)-(iii) above.
It contains elements from the various gospel accounts, and is doubtless
the source of the reference to Hadnok in AC Mt.26.12. The AC tradition
does not appear to have taken up the placing of the anointing of Jesus
on Thursday of Holy Week; Tä'ammǝrä iyyäsus does, however, share this
peculiarity with an apocryphal passion gospel, The Homily and Teaching

11. E.A.W. Budge, The Book of the Saints of the Ethiopian Church, vol.II,
 pp.597-8.

12. E.g. MS B.L. Add.16220 f.41b.

13. E.g. MS B.L. Orient 8824 f.122b-126a. It is not included in
 S. Grébaut's edition in PO vols. 12, 14, 17.

of our Fathers the holy Apostles, which is excerpted in the Holy Week lectionary Gəbrä həmamat[14].

(v)   Comment in the Geez version of Ibn aṭ-Ṭaiyib's gospel commentary, on Mt.26.12[15] and in appendices[16], dealing with the problems of reconciling the gospel narratives of the anointing. The affinities of this material are with Išoʿdad of Merv[17] and Mošе bar Kepha, not with the pseudo-Chrysostom homily.

AC Jn.12.11[18] contains two opinions about the problem of harmonisation. The first of these takes the Johannine account as correct, and explains the apparent divergence of the Matthaean one. The second says that there were two anointings – one by Mary the sister of 'the brigand of the right hand', who anointed Jesus' head on Wednesday, and one by Mary the sister of Lazarus, who anointed Jesus' feet on Saturday.

The probable relationships between these materials are as follows:

14. See R. Cowley, 'The so-called 'Ethiopic Book of the Cock' – part of an apocryphal passion gospel, The Homily and Teaching of our Fathers the holy Apostles'.

15. E.g. MS B.L. Orient 731 f.121a-122a.

16. E.g. MS B.L. Orient 731 f.1a-2a and 11a-b.

17. E.g. M.D. Gibson, The Commentaries of Ishoʿdad on the Gospels, Horae Semiticae V, pp.101-2.

18. Wängel qəddus, A.A., 1916 E.C., p.472.

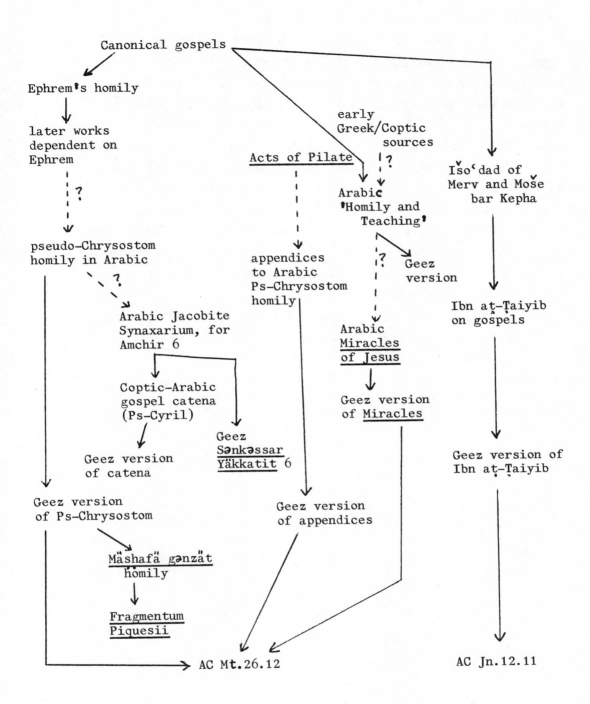

The following general points may be made about Ethiopian exegesis of the story of the sinful woman:

(i)   It is ultimately dependent on Ephrem's homily, <u>On the Sinful Woman</u>; however, while Ephrem's homily is most directly related to Luke 7, the Ethiopian commentary is attached to Matthew 26, and so, for example, suppresses the material on Simon and the parable of the debtors.

(ii)   Among the very widespread materials about the sinful woman, the traditions to which the Ethiopian commentary is related are the Syriac and Arabic ones, rather than the Graeco-Latin versions and adaptations of Ephrem's homily.

(iii)   The main interests of the Ethiopian comment are as follows:

(a)   aetiology, e.g. concerning the origin of the unguent,

(b)   biography, in giving background to a character of whom otherwise nothing is known,

(c)   narrative, in its liking for a well-shaped folk tale, and

(d)   reconciliation or harmonisation of the various gospel accounts.

3.   The question of the direct use of Jewish sources in

Ethiopian commentaries:

3.1   General considerations

3.2   Interpolations 'from Hebrew' in Geez texts of

Song of Solomon

3.3   References to 'Hebrew' and 'Arabic' in the section

on Genesis of the <u>Mämhərä orit</u> in MS d'Abbadie 156

3. THE QUESTION OF THE DIRECT USE OF JEWISH SOURCES IN
    ETHIOPIAN COMMENTARIES

3.1 GENERAL CONSIDERATIONS

   3.1.1. The following three questions are relevant to this
enquiry concerning direct use of Jewish sources in Ethiopian commentaries, and the third is the principal subject of this section:

(i)   whether direct use has been made of Hebrew biblical texts in
       the translation of biblical texts into Geez[1], and/or in the
       revision of the translation of biblical texts in Geez versions[2];

(ii)   whether the methodology of Ethiopian commentaries, and in
       particular of the AC, resembles that of rabbinic and other
       Jewish materials (see 3.1.3 below); and

(iii) whether there are parallels in the content of Ethiopian and
       Jewish commentaries, and if there are, how the existence of
       these parallels is to be interpreted (see 3.1.4 below).

   3.1.2. The argument of this section 3.1 is as follows:

1. See H.A.W. Pilkington, A critical edition of the Book of Proverbs in
    Ethiopic, and E. Ullendorff, 'Hebrew, Aramaic and Greek'. Writing of
    Geez MSS of Proverbs, Pilkington finds that while "the earliest
    group of MSS available to us is significantly more Septuagintal in
    character than the later MSS", yet "even the earliest group of MSS is
    not free from details which can only be assigned to the influence of
    a Hebrew Vorlage" (p.42), and "the pervasiveness of Hebrew influences
    in all groups of Ethiopic MSS suggests its use as a Vorlage at the
    beginning of the history of the Ethiopic text, and not merely as the
    source of a later recension" (pp.84-5). It is to be hoped that
    Pilkington's important study will be published; possible criticisms
    of it are that it may have narrowed too much the periods of history
    when translational activity was possible, and overlooked the contri-
    bution to translation and revision that may have been made by visitors
    to Ethiopia.

2. See footnote 1 above, and sections 3.2 and 3.3 below.

(i)   There are general similarities in methodology between the AC and rabbinic commentaries. These, like similarities of world-view, background, culture, and religious attitudes, demonstrate that the creative thinkers of the traditions had much in common, but they do not prove direct contact.

(ii)   There are parallels in the content of the AC and various Jewish sources. It should not, however, be asserted of any specific example that material was borrowed directly from Jewish sources into the AC, unless there are credible claims, in documented historical circumstances, that this was so.

The problem referred to in (ii) may be diagrammatically represented as follows:

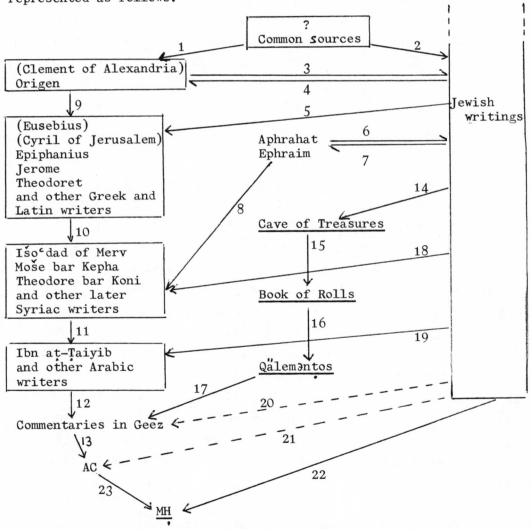

Many scholars[3] have performed the spade-work of listing material found in common in Jewish and Christian patristic works. Some of these have concluded, or implied, that this material must have moved along pathways 4, 5 and 7 of the diagram, without adequately considering the possibility of prior common sources (pathways 1 and 2), or of movement in the opposite direction (pathways 3 and 6), or of independent origins[4].

For pathway 4, de Lange writes: 'One conclusion which emerges is that, even granted a good deal of scepticism, there is enough evidence to prove that Origen does preserve aggadic material not found in earlier Greek sources ... . A second conclusion is that, nevertheless, a certain amount of scepticism is justified. Previous writers on the subject have sometimes been too willing to seize on a reference to 'the Hebrews' or on a rabbinic parallel and insist immediately that Origen is quoting a rabbinic aggadah.'[5]

Pathways 4, 5 and 7 have been surveyed, for example, by S. Krauss (on Justin Martyr, Clement of Alexandria, Origen, Eusebius, Ephraim and Jerome); he writes that he will "speak of such Agadas as were expressly and explicitly borrowed from the Jews", but also notes that for several of his examples there is no actual extant Jewish parallel[6].

3. References in the bibliography of de Lange, Origen and the Jews, under G. Bardy, L. Ginzberg, H. Graetz, S. Krauss, A. Levene, A. Marmorstein, B. Murmelstein, M. Rahmer; also É. Lamirande in Vigiliae Christianae 21; R. Loewe in Studia Patristica 1; C.J. Elliott, 'Hebrew learning among the Fathers' in Dictionary of Christian Biography, II, pp.850-72.

4. The writings of A. Levene, among others, are open to this criticism; see the critique by T. Jansma, Oudtestamentische Studien 12 (1958).

5. Origen and the Jews, p.123.

6. S. Krauss, 'The Jews in the works of the Church Fathers', JQR 5, pp.122-157; 6, pp.82-99, 225-261.

Pathway 7 has been extensively investigated[7]; Kronholm, for example, writing of Ephraim's hymns (not his biblical commentaries), has found "that the influence of Jewish Haggadah on the exegesis of Ephrem's hymns in no case can be called a literary one", but he notes "a particular affinity between the Ephremic Haggadah and that embedded in PRE," and also that "the closest connexion between the exegesis in the genuine hymns of Ephrem and that of the various Targumim is discernible in T^PsJon".[8]

Pathway 8 can be studied through the introductions and notes to the volumes of van den Eynde's translation of Išoʿdad's commentaries, and in general works on Syriac literature, and needs no further comment here. For pathway 18, on the other hand, it would be necessary to establish that material of apparently Jewish affinities found in the 8th.-9th. century Syriac commentators had been borrowed directly from Jewish sources, and had not travelled along pathways 7-8, or 5 and 10, or 4, 9 and 10 – a matter I believe to be incapable of proof. S. Brock concludes: "The vast majority of the Jewish traditions attested in Syriac literature reached Syriac writers before the end of the fourth century; these travelled by three different paths: incorporated into the Peshitta, by way of the apocrypha and pseudepigrapha, and independently of these two (whether orally or in written form is impossible to say; it is very possible that they travelled by both ways, and in the latter case the lost Adam literature is very likely to have been an important vehicle)'.[9]

7. T. Kronholm, Motifs from Genesis 1-11, and works noted in his bibliography under D. Gerson, S. Krauss, N. Treppner, T.-J. Lamy, S. Hidal; Also S. Brock, 'Jewish Traditions in Syriac Sources', JJS 30 no.2 (1979); R. Murray, Symbols of Church and Kingdom (especially pp. 281-288); J. Neusner, Aphrahat and Judaism; J.G. Snaith, 'Aphrahat and the Jews' (and works of S. Funk and F. Gavin noted there).

8. Motifs from Genesis 1-11, pp.222, 224.

9. Op.cit., footnote 7 above.

Pathways 8–13 are illustrated, for example, by sections 2.6, 2.7 and 2.8 above; alongside this line of transmission of material of the commentary type, there are lines of transmission of chronographic and legendary material, pathways 15–17 (to which Saᶜīd ibn Bitrīq, Giyorgis wälda Amid and Ethiopic Abušakər can be added), illustrated, for example, by sections 2.1, 2.3 and 2.7 above. Pathway 14 requires further study.[10]

Investigation of pathway 19 presents a problem similar to that of pathway 18. There exists in the writings of Ibn aṭ-Ṭaiyib and Al Makīn Jirjis, for example, material parallelled in Jewish writings, and lists of parallels can be drawn up; the lists can be used to demonstrate that some such material reached them via pathway 11, and from e.g. Saᶜīd ibn Bitrīq, but they do not elucidate the origins and transmission of the residuum.

Pathways 22–23 are a special case, that of the commentary on Ezekiel written by Kidana wald Kəfle with instruction from Kəflä giyorgis, which draws on material traditional in Ethiopia and also on rabbinic commentaries.[11]

As for transmission via pathways 20 and 21, it will be evident from the remarks above that I believe its existence to be unprovable, as with pathways 18 and 19, unless further evidence of the type available for pathways 22 and 23 should be found, relating to an earlier period.[12] The quest for such evidence is not a

10. See notes in J.H. Charlesworth, The Pseudepigrapha and modern research with a supplement, pp.91–2; 4.1 below on the Testament of Adam; and A. Götze, Die Schatzhöhle, Überlieferung und Quellen.

11. See my 'A Geez Prologue concerning the work of Mämhər Kəflä giyorgis on the text and interpretation of the book of Ezekiel', especially pp.110–2, and Berhanou Abebbé, Haymanotä abäw qäddämt.

12. On the question of rabbinic sources in another work of Ethiopic literature, the Kəbrä nägäst, see D.A. Hubbard, The literary sources of the Kebra Nagast; it is to be hoped that this work will be published.

hopeless one[13]; for example, MS EMML 932 f.121a[14] records that an
Abba Bäḥaylä maryam said, 'I indeed know the Arabic and Hebrew
languages, all the explanation of the books of law, for Isayəyyas
the Egyptian, the great teacher, taught me the book of interpretation
by the command of our king Naᶜod[15] that he teach me in the Arabic,
Hebrew and Greek languages, who is together with[16] Ɔnbaqom[17], whom
they call 'the great pride[18] of our country,' the brother of the great
teacher whose name is Ɔndrəyas, the well-known, teacher[19] of Däbrä
Libanos, whose great faith is known as far as the city of Alexandria,
among the archbishops, to the people of Ethiopia'. Such teachers may
have used Jewish sources at first hand; Abba Giyorgis of Gasəčča, for
example, uses Jewish traditions in his Arganonä wəddase (e.g. the
tradition that from the rock in the wilderness twelve streams of
water flowed, pr.ed. Addis Ababa, 1959 E.C. p.296). The historical
evidence currently available, however, is fragmentary, sometimes
unclear in detail, and uncertain of interpretation.

Two trivial examples will serve to illustrate the ambiguities
of literary comparison uncontrolled by historical and wider contextual
evidence:

13. See my 'A Geez Prologue ...' p.99, for notes of Ethiopian scholars
    who are alleged to have learned non-Ethiopian languages, MS B.L.
    Orient 737 f.12b for notes comparing Geez and Arabic texts of
    Ezekiel, and section 3.3 below.

14. I am indebted to Dr. Getatchew Haile for communicating this text to me.

15. Reigned 1494-1508 A.D.

16. zäməslä; it probably means that Isayəyyas and Ɔnbaqom were both
    teachers, but might mean that Ɔnbaqom and Bäḥaylä maryam were both
    pupils of Isayəyyas.

17. On whom see E.J. van Donzel, ᶜĒnbāqom.

18. Geez teməh; the translation assumes derivation from the Arabic root
    tmh.

19. Geez mämhər, probably to be understood here as 'abbot'.

(a)   ˈTorahˈ/ˈŌryātāˈ/ˈŌritˈ is said in Šemot R.   34.2, by Išoˁdad
at the beginning of his commentary on Genesis, and in AC Genesis
introduction (OTIAC p.136), to mean ˈlightˈ. In Šemot R. this is
justified by citing Prov. 6.23 (ˈand <u>torah</u> is lightˈ (ˀor)): In
Išoˁdad (and THBK <u>Mimrā</u> III.55), no explanation is given, but it
seems that (etymological) derivation from Hebrew ˀ<u>or</u> is assumed, and
Ōrešlem (Jerusalem), ˈlight and peaceˈ is offered as a corroborative
example. AC Gen., on the other hand, offers the name Erəmyas (Jeremiah)
as corroboration; AC Jer. introduction says, ˈErəmyas means "light",
as Eraˀel (? i.e. Uraˀel) means "light". A. It means "word" as they
interpret "<u>A holy er came down</u>" (Dan.4.10) to mean "a holy word",
"a holy angel".ˈ The intention of the Jewish source is homiletic,
and of the Syriac and Ethiopian sources apparently etymological (I
have not found such a reference in Arabic sources); the differences
between them preclude a conclusion that there has been literary
borrowing, but the possibility remains that the basic idea travelled
around.

(b)   Concerning the word ˈSadduceeˈ, it is commonly assumed that it
derives from the name Zadok (Ṣadoq), high priest in the time of
Solomon. In <u>Abot de Rabbi Nathan</u> (version B, ed. Saldarini, ch.10,
pp.85-6) it is associated with Saddok, disciple of Antigonus of Soko.
Syriac materials (surveyed by S. Brock, ˈSome Syriac Accounts of the
Jewish Sectsˈ) make the association with Zadok, identified variously
as ˈpriest in the time of Davidˈ, and ˈthe originator of their teachingˈ.
Giyorgis wälda Amid (e.g. B.L. Orient 814 f.76b) says ˈSadducees are
the people of one man from among the scholars of the Jews whose name
was Sadoq, whom the gospel calls "Saduqawyan".ˈ In the Geez version
of Ibn aṭ-Ṭaiyibˈs <u>Questions</u> (MS EMML 1839 f.47b) the material of
THBK <u>Mimrā</u> V.24 is reproduced almost <u>verbatim</u>, and further, probably
related, accounts of the Jewish sects are found in Ibn aṭ-Ṭaiyib on
Matthew (e.g. B.L. Orient 731 f.36a and 113a) and in the ˈCoptic-
Arabic gospel catenaˈ (e.g. B.L. Add. 16220 f.36a). The AC frequently
states that the Sadducees were named after Zadok (e.g. OTIAC, p.141;
<u>TIA</u>, p.175), but does not specify which one.

     The relationship of these Syriac, Arabic and Geez materials to
each other, and probably to the <u>Anakephalaiosis</u> of Epiphaniusˈ
<u>Panarion</u>, is clear, but although it is probable that the source for
the AC, in this specific example, is Ibn aṭ-Ṭaiyib, it remains

possible that the AC statement is an independent surmise, and also
that sources (such as Giyorgis wäldä Amid) that identify Zadok as a
scholar or leader, rather than as a high priest, are related to
Jewish sources such as Abot de Rabbi Nathan.

3.1.3.   The following are notes of methodological and formulaic
similarities between the AC and Jewish commentary materials. The
method by which the list was compiled was simply a reading of the
Ethiopian and the Jewish materials, with the aim of noting (for this
purpose) similarities other than similarities of content (on which
see 3.1.4. below). I have refrained from taking to one tradition
some preconceived and systematized list of the 'methods' or 'rules'
of the other tradition, in order to look for examples; such an
approach would be methodologically unsound, since it would undermine
the integrity of the traditions, and might give undue emphasis to
features which were common in one, but rare in the other.

Further details of the formulae of Talmudic discussion will be
found in L. Jacobs, The Talmudic Argument, ch.1, and of methods and
formulae in the AC in TIA, pp.46–53 and 164–6, and PN, pp.17–19.

(i)   The listing of complementary or contrasting opinions, very
frequent in the AC, and common in the midrashim, e.g. Bəresit R. 66.3,
Semot R. 29.7, Vayyiqra R. 4.1, 7.6, 18.2, 28.4, 30.10, Qohelet R.
7.1.3. In the AC these opinions are introduced by andəm, bo, yämmilu
allu etc. (TIA p.3), and in the midrash by davar aher, vəyeš 'omrin
(e.g. MhG p.124), etc.

(ii)   Notes of textual variants and emendations which should or may
be read, introduced in Hebrew by kətib and qəre, or by 'for x read y',
and introduced in Amharic by yəlal or sil näw. See Bəresit R. 19.8,
Qohelet R. 5.6 §1, TIA pp.4, 164, 185. In general, however, the AC
examples of this appear to be suggestions that the text could or
should be emended, whereas the Hebrew midrashic 'al tiqre (e.g. TB
Roš haššana 24a) is a homiletic device to obtain further interpretations
of the text.

(iii) A propensity for numbered lists and groups – very frequent in
the AC (e.g. TIA pp.49, 59, 219–21, 274), and in Jewish sources (e.g.
the list of famines in Targum rut 1.1 and elsewhere).

(iv)   Use of brief quotations to justify a specific interpretation. In Jewish literature this is the principle referred to as   gəzera šava, 'the inference from a similarity of phrases', and in the AC the corroborative quotation is followed by the formula əndil 'as it says'. See e.g. Bərešit R. 19.5, in which ləhaskil of Gen.3.6 is illustrated by maskil of Ps.89.1, and TIA p.207 where Zech.5.7 is cited to justify the interpretation of 'women' as 'sin' in Rev.3.4.

(v)   Reference to foreign languages to explain the meanings of words. In the midrashim these references are commonly to Arabic or Greek, see Bərešit R. 87.1, Šemot R. 3.1, 42.4, Vayyiqra R. 1.3, Ester R. 3.12; in the AC they are commonly to Arabic or Tigrinya, TIA pp.58, 246.

(vi)   Reasons why 'x is called y', and questions of the type 'Why is x called y?', where y is read in the text, and x is an inter-pretation which takes y as a symbol of x. See TIA pp.265–7, and Qohelet R. on Eccles.4.13, 'Why is (the good inclination) called "child"?'.

(vii) Interpretation of a text by referring it to successive historical periods. In the midrashim this is commonly applied either to 'the land' and 'the Messianic future', or to the series Babylonia, Media, Greece, Rome/Edom. See Bərešit R. 44.15, 48.10, 65.13, Bəmidbar R. 11.7, notes on Gen.15.9 in 3.1.4 below, and TIA pp.48–49, 169–171.

(viii) The investigation of how two apparently contradictory verses can be reconciled, in the AC commonly headed 'ərq' or introduced with ayəttallam. See TIA pp.51, 278, and Ekhah R. 2. 19 § 22 (concerning the reconciliation of Ps.119 vs.62 and 148) and Bəmidbar R. 11.7.

(ix)   The quest for reasons – e.g. 'Why was Lot's wife turned into salt?' See TIA pp.50–1, and notes on Gen.19.26 in 3.1.4 below .

(x)   The recording and answering of real or potential objections. In the AC the objection is commonly recorded as direct speech and followed by bəlo. See Bəmidbar R. 14.10, 'If you object that there

are actually fifty-eight (descendants of Esau), the answer is that ...',
cf. <u>TIA</u> pp.5, 327.

(xi)   The note that a particular line of interpretation involves,
or is free from, a specified difficulty. In the midrashim the lack
of difficulty is often expressed by <u>niha</u>, and in the AC by <u>ahun</u>
<u>yätämäčča</u>;   see e.g. <u>Bərešit R.</u> 5.9, and <u>TIA</u> pp.282-3, 332.

(xii)   Association of a group of <u>n</u> items with other Biblical groups
of <u>n</u> items - e.g. <u>Bəmidbar R.</u> 14.18, on the twelve dishes etc. of the
tabernacle, <u>Bəmidbar R.</u> 14.12 on many other numbers, and <u>TIA</u> p.53, on
twelve (apostles, gems etc.), and p.308 on ten (faculties, commandments
etc.).

(xiii) Comparison of two things by statements of the type '<u>x</u> has <u>z</u>,
and <u>y</u> (also) has <u>z</u>'. See <u>TIA</u> p.265, 'A locust has wings; (the
believers) have wings of grace', and <u>Ester R.</u> 10.12, 'A king wears
purple, and Mordecai wore purple'.

(xiv)   Notes on the distinctions between words of similar meaning -
e.g. in the midrashim, notes on the '3 types of torpor' (<u>Bərešit R.</u>
17.5, 44.17; <u>MhG</u> p.86; <u>MhH</u> p.80), and on the difference between
'violence' and 'robbery' (<u>Bərešit R.</u> 31.5), and in the AC, notes on
the 'types of fright' (<u>TIA</u>, p.48, also AC Ps.47 (48).5, Jer.1.17 and
Lk.1.12). This is to be distinguished from the talmudic and midrashic
<u>tarte mašma</u>ʿ (e.g. <u>TB Məgilla</u> 14b), in which one word is given an
alternative, or two-fold, meaning.

(xv)   Notes on the beneficial or harmful results of riches, sorrow,
etc. - e.g. in the midrashim, notes on 'riches that harm their
possessors, and other riches that stand them in good stead' (<u>Šemot</u>
<u>R.</u> 31.3), and in the AC, 'sickness which brings a reward', and 'sick-
ness which comes as a punishment' (<u>TIA</u> p.48).

(xvi)   Catenas of texts demonstrating a point from various different
parts of the scriptures (and, additionally, in the AC, from patristic
writings), e.g. <u>Bərešit R.</u> 48.11, 68.3, 74.14, <u>Šemot R.</u> 25.12,
<u>Rut R.</u> 4.5 and <u>TIA</u>, p.51, NTIAC, p.182.

(xvii) Reference to other parts of the corpus as to be understood as

included at a specific point, or as to be related in oral instruction;
see e.g. Šemot R. 10.1, 'The entire Midrash thereof is given in
Leviticus Rabbah ...', and NTIAC pp.168-9, 'Relate as for Matthew',

(xviii) Deduction from the use of the Hebrew definite article, or
from the use of the Geez third person singular suffix to a noun,
that the referent is unique - e.g. Bərešit R. 24.4, which understands
'the ship' of Jonah 1.4 to be Jonah's ship alone; AC Isa.1.3 feels
the need to explain betä əgzi'u, 'the house of his master', and offers
two opinions, firstly that it is a 'suffix with no owner', and secondly
that the house is the house of the owner of the animals (followed by
a long story about its history, see PN p.19 and also AC Mt.2.11).

(xix) General statements contrasting Israel and others, e.g.
Bərešit R. 52.5 on prophets of Israel and of the nations, and OTIAC
p.145, 'The Gentiles give their children attractive names'.

(xx) Imaginative expansion of the Biblical narrative, see Ester R.
7.13, Rut R. 3.6, 4.6, and TIA p.52.

(xxi) Pure conjecture - e.g. Bərešit R. 97 (in MSV, Soncino ed.
p.933) 'Who told him? Some say, Manasseh; others say, The physicians';
TIA, p.197, 'If it is asked what his work was, it is not known. A. it
is known; it was almsgiving'.

Summary and conclusions.

(a)   Parallels in method and phraseology between the AC and Jewish
materials are of common occurrence and of many various kinds. Within
the AC corpus, they are common to all its parts, and are not restricted
to the OT commentaries.

(b)   Although parallels to many of the shared features can be found
in other bible commentaries, it is my subjective opinion that the
parallels listed above are more impressive than similar lists for
other pairs of traditions would be.

(c)   The list demonstrates that the creative thinkers of each
tradition, and the tradents, were people of similar background and

outlook; it does not prove literary contact, and further consideration of it must also recognize the many real differences between the two traditions.

3.1.4.   The following is a list of some parallels in the content of Ethiopian commentaries and Jewish sources. The process of compilation was that, having read the whole AC corpus, I read the whole or parts of the Talmud and various midrashim and medieval Jewish commentators, and noted parallels; I did not search one corpus for certain predetermined motifs drawn from the other, or from elsewhere[20]. From the results, a sample was selected with the aim of representing the variety and range of parallels, rather than of selecting striking specimens.

A list of parallels could more easily have been compiled simply by using Ginzberg, Legends, Kasher, Tora šlema, Bowker, The Targums, and Dov Noy, Motif-index; however, I preferred to use primary sources, and, moreover, among the midrashim which in form, style, and content most resemble the AC, Midraš hahefes and Yalqut me'am lo'ez were not used by Ginzberg, and Midraš haggadol was only rather slightly used by him.

(i)   Gen.1.1–2.4. Many rabbinic parallels are noted in 4.4 below.

(ii)   Gen.2.1, and Revelation. Parallels to the successive millennia of world history.

In YML on Gen.2.1, the 'six days' of creation are interpreted as parallelling, or alluding to, the successive millennia of Adam, the flood, the exodus, the kings, the destruction of the temple, and the Messiah; the seventh day parallels the world to come. In AC Rev., the series of seven seals, instruments, and cups are similarly referred to successive millennia, though the details of the millennia are different (see TIA p.170).

20. On the dangers of parallelomania, see P.S. Alexander, 'Rabbinic Judaism and the New Testament'.

(iii)   Gen.2.4. The question whether heaven was created first, or earth.

This question is variously reported in Jewish sources as one of 'Alexander's questions' (YML 36; TB Tamid 32a), or as a dispute between the houses of Hillel and Shammai (MhG p.72 on Gen.2.4; MhH 68-9[21]). It is not asked so directly in the AC, but is referred to in AC Heb. 1.10 (see 5.2 and 5.5 below), and is implied in AC consideration of texts of Gen.1.2 which read 'but the earth' (and might be taken to imply that heaven was created later, but the earth had existed from eternity - see 4.2 and 4.3 below).

(iv)   Gen.2.21-22. The reason why it was from Adam's side that Eve was created.

AC Gen.2.21-22 says, 'This is because women were originally proud, and if he (God) had created her (Eve) from his (Adam's) forehead, they would have been wholly proud. Women have low esteem, and if he had created her from his foot, they would have been wholly despised. He created her from his middle, from his side, meaning, "Let her be over the family, and beneath her husband".'

A Jewish account similar in outline is found e.g. in Bərešit R. 18.2[22]. However, the emphasis of the Jewish story is on the prevention of certain faults supposedly characteristic of women ('not from the mouth, lest she be a tattler' etc.), while the Ethiopian version emphasizes the status of woman, a feature it shares with some western commentators (e.g. 'not made out of his head to rule over him, nor out of his feet to be trampled upon by him ...', Matthew Henry, in loc.), and for which its actual source is probably Ibn aṭ-Ṭaiyib's commentary on Genesis.

---

21. Also Bərešit R. 1.15; Vayyiqra R. 36.1; Bowker, The Targums, pp.102-3.

22. Further references in Ginzberg, Legends, I, 66 and V, 89 (where the reference to Bərešit R. 18.2 appears to be misprinted).

(v)   Gen.3.1. The serpent's appearance as a camel.

AC Gen.3.1 has a short <u>tarik</u> pericope reading, '(A source) says
"<u>in the likeness of the young of a camel</u>" – when the earth was originally created, this animal was created like a racing camel'. <u>MhG</u> p.92
line 22, on the same verse, similarly says 'and the form of the
serpent was according to the type of the camel'. Išoʿdad (<u>in.loc.</u>)
dismisses the idea, and so do IAṬ (<u>in.loc.</u>) and Məhərka dəngəl (<u>EMML</u>
2101 f.70b).

(vi)   Gen.3.8. The great stature of Adam, and his shortening.

References to Adam's great height at the time of creation, and
its reduction at the time of his trespass, are frequent in rabbinic
literature[23]. The idea appears to be absent from the AC corpus, but
the author of <u>Tərgwame qälämsis</u> (<u>TIA</u> p.148) recognises it as an opinion
in need of refutation.

(vii) Gen.4.23. Lamech's killing of Cain.

AC Gen.4.23 says, '... for in my blindness I struck Cain and
my guide and killed (them). <u>T.</u> ... While Lamech was being led along,
he said to him (his guide), "What is it that murmurs in the scrub?
Give me a stone". He picked one up, and gave it to him. When he
threw it, he struck him (Cain). He said to him, "Go and see it, for
my hand is hot". When he went, he found him fallen and threshing
around. Returning, he said to him, "You have killed Cain, the father
of the whole world". He (Lamech) wailed, and as he started to make
lamentation, he beat his breast and killed his guide.'

The commonest Jewish legend (Ginzberg,<u>Legends</u> I, 116-7;   V,
146-7; <u>MḥH</u> 92-3) relates that Lamech killed Cain with an arrow, and
inadvertently killed his (Lamech's) son, named as Tubal Cain in <u>YML</u>
301.

---

23. Ginzberg, <u>Legends</u>, I, 59,76; V, 79,99; Bowker, <u>The Targums</u>,
pp.118-9; <u>MhG</u> 70,98,109; <u>MḥH</u> 83; <u>YML</u> 228,275; <u>TB Erubin</u> 100b.

Despite the general similarities, the proximate source of the AC account appears to be Q̈aleməntos (ROC 1911, 227-8) and the Kitab al-majall (f.104a), and not the legend in its Jewish form, or the commentaries of e.g. Ephraim, Išoʿdad and Ibn aṭ-Ṭaiyib in loc.[24] It is probable, however, that there has been interaction (a) between Jewish sources and Ephraim, and (b) between Jewish sources and the sources of the Kitab al-majall.

This tradition has presented a problem for AC Jubilees 4.31, which faces the apparent contradiction as follows: 'If it is asked, "The Torah said his descendant killed him, but here it says his house collapsed on him – is it not contradictory?", then when he fell, struck by a stone, his sons took him up and put him in the house, and the house collapsed on him and he died.'

(viii) Gen.7-8. See section 2.1 above.

(ix)   Gen.10.9-10. Expansion of the story of Nimrod.

AC Gen.10.9-10 says that Nimrod was a powerful warrior who had a crown made in secret, claimed that it had descended from heaven for him, and reigned over Babylon. M̈amhərä orit (d'Abb.156 f.6a) says that Nimrod son of Kwərš built the cities of Roha, Nisibis, Nineveh and Kolona; from his kingdom arose the kingdoms of Persia and Babylon, and Cyrus was from his seed.

Jewish sources share an interest in Nimrod, but generally identify him with Amraphel, and see him as Abraham's great enemy[25],

24. Further see THBK Mimrā II.88, EMML 2101 f.74a col.3 - f.74b col.1 (which has Ibn aṭ-Ṭaiyib's material plus a version of the legend in which Cain is found at the door of Lamech's dwelling and stoned by him), M̈ashafä Hawi (which cites Theodoret as saying that Lamech killed Cain, e.g. B.L. Orient 776 f.221a); Ramban in loc. (which has Cain dying in the flood); Bowker, The Targums, pp.136-41, and Jerome Epist. xxxvi. 2-6 (PL 22 cols. 453-6).

25. Ginzberg, Legends, I, section on Abraham, passim, especially pp.189-217, and notes in vol.V; Ginzberg, Die Haggada, pp.88-9; YML on Gen. 11.31; Tora šlema on Gen.15.7.

themes which are absent from the AC (the AC sources here are probably
the chronographic works such as the <u>Chronicle</u> of John of Nikiou).

(x)   Gen.10.32 and 11.7-9. See section 2.2 above.

(xi)   Gen.15.9. Symbolism of the heifer, the she-goat, and the ram.

Some Syriac commentators interpret the 'heifer, ram and goat'
of three generations, the generations of Levi, Kohath and Amram,
namely the generation which first entered Egypt, the second generation,
and the third generation, which experienced bondage (Išoʿdad <u>in loc</u>.,
SAQ p.339). This interpretation is also found in IAṬ (<u>in loc</u>.), in
the <u>MO</u> (e.g. d'Abb.156 f.6b), and in AC Gen.15.9.

Levene (<u>Early Syrian Fathers</u> pp.239-40) in his comments on MS
Mingana 553 notes that this interpretation is without parallel in
rabbinic sources. However, the idea of interpreting the animals of
successive historical entities is shared with rabbinic sources, in
which (alongside their interpretation of actual sacrifices subsequently
to be commanded) they are interpreted of successive kingdoms – the
heifer of Babylonia, the she-goat of Media, and the ram of Greece[26].

(xiii) Gen.19.26. Lot's wife's incitement of her neighbours.

AC Gen.19.26, commenting on, 'And she became a pillar of salt',
says, 'It means she was a worthless woman. If one piles salt up, it
collapses; if one rests ones head on it, the head becomes bald; if
one throws it on a garden, it dries up the plants; if one throws it
into water, it becomes bitter. If salt is bitter, it is worthless –
it means she was worthless, because sin is called "salt". A. He made
her salt for a reason – because when she went to borrow salt, she said,
"The people who have come today are like jewels; do what you like
with them". (A). The Lord made her an example to hermits. Just as

---

26.   Bərešit R. 44.14-15, <u>MhG</u> pp.254-5; Media and Greece are reversed in
<u>MhH</u> p.135, and <u>YML</u> <u>in loc</u>.; for an interpretation relating 'dread',
'darkness' etc. to the successive kingdoms, see Šemot R. 51.7 and <u>PRE</u>
ch.28 .

she, when she returned to her country, became a stone of salt, so you, after you have become hermits, if you return to the world, you will be worthless ...'. AC Wisd.10.7 (= 7.8 in AC pr.ed.) has a similar account.

The story about her borrowing salt is found in MhH 157: 'She said to her neighbours, "Give me a little salt, for visitors have come to us", and the word passed from woman to woman until all the men of Sodom knew and came to Lot to demand them', and in some texts of Bərešit R. 51.5[27]. The story is also found in the commentaries of Išoᶜdad and Ibn aṭ-Ṭaiyib in loc., and no doubt IAṬ is the actual source for AC Gen.19.26.

(xiii) Gen.22.9. Isaac's request to be bound.

AC Gen.22, and the similar material in AC Qəddase maryam pp.233-4, are extremely rich repositories of traditional exegesis that repay study phrase by phrase. Comparison of them with Syriac materials (see S. Brock, 'Genesis 22 in Syriac Tradition', and 'Genesis 22: Where was Sarah?') show that almost all the exegesis is of East Syrian provenance. The apparent exception is in AC Gen.22.9, 'And he tied .... At this time, Isaac knew that he was a sacrifice. He said to him (Abraham), "It seems to me that you will sacrifice me. My father, bind me lest I thresh around and make you cut your hand". He bound, fastened, and tied him hand and foot, and threw him down.'

This may be compared with Bərešit R. 56.8, '"Father, I am a young man and am afraid that my body may tremble through fear of the knife and I will grieve thee, whereby the slaughter may be rendered unfit and this will not count as a real sacrifice; therefore bind me very firmly",' though the reason given for Isaac's request is a different one.

(xiv) Gen.22.13. The origin of the ram.

AC Gen.22.13 records three opinions: (i)that the sheep descended

---

27. For other reasons for the choice of salt, see Ginzberg, Legends, I, 255; V, 241-2; YML in loc.; PRE ch.25.

from heaven, (ii)that it came from Abraham's flock, and (iii)that it was 'found from the sealed tree of sabeq'.

MO records the opinion that the sheep was 'born suddenly from the tree by the wisdom of God', and some texts of MO (e.g. d'Abb.157 f.7b) record only this view. Others add a second opinion, that it was brought from the flock of Abraham by an angel (e.g. d'Abb.195 f.10a), and d'Abb.39 f.81b–82a attributes this view to Farāz (presumably IAṬ). D'Abb. 156 f.7a records the second opinion as, 'Some say (it was) from the flock of Abraham; and it was not created at once, as people say' (and the same words are found in IAṬ's Questions, EMML 1839 f.31b).

Jewish sources are also interested in the origin of the ram, and the main views represented are: (i)that it was one of the ten things created on the eve of Sabbath in the twilight (Pirqe abot 5.9; MhH p.167; YML in loc.), (ii)that it came from Abraham's flocks (MhH p.167; MhG p.356), and (iii)that it came from the mountains (Yalqut Šim'oni I.101).

Comparison with the materials surveyed in S.Brock's 'Genesis 22 in Syriac Tradition' shows that the Ethiopian commentaries contain little, if anything, that cannot be traced back to Syriac exegesis. It is possible that the AC opinion of a heavenly origin for the ram might reflect the Jewish story of its early creation[28].

(xv)   Ex.2.5. Pharaoh's daughter's bathing as a cure for a skin disease.

AC Ex.2.5 asks why Pharaoh's daughter went to the river, and gives five reasons, of which one is that she bathed as a cure for a skin disease called kobəs (TIA 50–1). Some Jewish sources say that she was smitten with leprosy, and went to bathe in cool water (Ginzberg Legends II, 266–7; V, 398; Šemot R. 1.23), and other reasons are

28. Further see Ginzberg, Legends, V, p.252; Bəmidbar R. 17.2; PRE ch.31; TJ Ta'anit 2.4; Iso'bar Nun question 29 (in Ethiopic translation as part of the version of IAṬ's Questions, MS EMML 1839 f.3b); S.G. Hall, Melito of Sardis, pp.76–7.

also offered (e.g. <u>YML in loc</u>.). This material does not appear in
the commentaries of IM or IAṬ. The name of Pharaoh's daughter given
in the AC is Ta̋rmut (as in Jub.47), and not Bitya (as in Jewish sources).

(xvi) Ex.7.1 and Rev.17.10. People who rejected God and claimed
      divinity.

      AC Rev.17.10 (see <u>TIA</u> p.331) lists Pharaoh, Ṣiruṣayda(*n*),
Nebuchadnezzar, Sennacherib, and Diocletian as rejectors of God.
Šemot R. 8.2 lists Hiram, Nebuchadnezzar, Pharaoh, and Joash as people
who claimed to be God, and <u>Bəmidbar R</u>. 14.1 and 21.23 contain similar
lists including Pharaoh, Sennacherib and Nebuchadnezzar.[29]

(xvii) Ex.15.8. The number of parts into which the sea was divided.

      The account of Isoʿdad (<u>in loc</u>.) that the Hebrews and Athanasius
say the sea was divided into twelve parts[30], and that John of Beth
Rabban says that it remained in one place, has entered Ethiopic via
Ibn aṭ-Ṭaiyib (MSS d'Abb.28 f.44b, EMML 2101 f.105b). The AC itself,
however, more commonly speaks of its being divided into two or three
parts (e.g. AC Ps. 135.13).

(xviii) Lev.10.1-2. Drunkenness as a reason for Nadab and Abihu's
      offence and punishment.

      AC Lev.10.1-2 says, 'Being drunk with wine, they (Nadab and
Abihu) made fire at another place which God had not commanded, and
brought (it).' The comment continues by saying that the reason for
their death is not here revealed, but that it will be explained in
Lev.10.16; the comment on that verse, however, (in the MSS I have
consulted) explains Moses' anger with Eleazar and Ithamar, but not
the reason for the death of Nadab and Abihu. Nevertheless, the implication of the whole passage in the AC is that their sin was (a)

29. Further lesser parallels in <u>Bərešit R</u>. 96.5 and <u>Bəmidbar R</u>. 9.24.

30. For references see van den Eynde, <u>C.S.C.O.</u> vol.179, p.39.

drunkenness, and (b) ignition of fire in an unauthorised place.

The AC has here made little use of Ethiopic materials. IAṬ's commentary (in Geez translation in MS d'Abb. 28 f.57a) is closely based on Išoʿdad (in loc., including the material from Michael, John of Beth Rabban, and Aphrahat that Išoʿdad quotes), and Məhərka dəngəl has rewritten IAṬ's comment (in EMML 2101, f.122a). IAṬ's Questions contain two sections on Nadab and Abihu (in Geez translation in EMML 1839 f.16b and 36a), of which the second is taken almost verbatim from THBK, Mimrā III.39.

Jewish sources do not in general see drunkenness as the main offence of Nadab and Abihu, but a number list it as one reason among others, e.g. Rashi in loc., where the opinion is attributed to Rabbi Ishmael.[31]

(xix) Num.2. The emblems of the tribes.

AC Num.2, MH on Ezekiel 1.28, and some Jewish sources specify the emblems on the flags of the tribes. Bəmidbar R. 2.7 and YML in loc. contain the developed Jewish form of this tradition, with emblems and colours for all the flags of the tribes. The following table shows the Ethiopian accounts and the Jewish ones most directly comparable,[32] though in making the comparison, the further similarity with the symbols of the four evangelists (Matthew a man, Mark a lion, Luke an ox, and John an eagle) should not be overlooked.

31. YML in loc. and Vayyiqra R. 20.9 also mention drunkenness, Bəmidbar R. 2.23 does not; further references in Ginzberg, Legends, III, 187–192; V, 75.

32. Further references in Ginzberg, Legends, III, 230–238, and VI, 81–83; his note 447 appears to contain errors of detail, especially in respect of Ephraim's emblem.

tribe	AC Num. 2		MH Ezek.˙1.28	Targum Yərušalmi Num. 2.	Midraš Leqah Tob Num.˙2˙
	account 1	account 2			
Judah	lion Gen.49.9	lion Gen.49.9	lion Gen.49.9	bar aryəwan 'son of a lion'	ʾry lion Gen.49.9
Reuben	man Gen.49.3	animal- he did animal- like deeds	man Gen.49.3	bar ayyala 'son of a hart'	dwdʾym dmwt ʾdm mandrakes in human form Gen.30.14
Ephraim	animal- Jeroboam descended from him	man – Joshua descended from him	cow/bull Deut.33.17	riba maiden	šwr bull Deut.33.17
Dan	eagle- he will worship Caesar's eagle	serpent – the false Messiah will come from him	eagle/ winged serpent Gen.49.17 Isa.30.6	hewe harman šerpent	nšr eagle Deut.32.11

This is a striking parallel, especially as (a) the principal difference between the two opinions in the AC, regarding the emblem of Dan,
is paralleled by a divergence in the targumic and midrashic traditions,
and (b) the material is not found, so far as I can discover, in
Syriac and Arabic commentaries. The authors of MH are known to have
used Jewish commentaries at first hand, but I have not in this
instance been able to identify the exact source they used although
the general affinities of the material are clear.

(xx)   Num.2 and Rev.21. The gems of the tribes.

AC Rev.21.26 (see TIA pp.365-370) associates the twelve sons
of Jacob individually with twelve gems, and also describes the gems
and associates them individually with the twelve apostles. In overall
plan, the section is reminiscent of Jewish sources (YML on Num.2;
Bəmidbar R. 2.7; Šemot R. 38.8-9) and also of some other Ethiopic
sources (Book of the Mysteries of Heaven and Earth, PO 6, pp.447-9;
further references in TIA p.366) and Greek sources such as Epiphanius'
De gemmis. Despite the number and variety of gem catalogues, I have
not been able to discover the actual source of either the AC list, or

of the two lists in the Book of the Mysteries of Heaven and Earth.[33]

(xxi) Deut.33.6. Moses' prayer for Reuben.

Moses' prayer for Reuben, and Reuben's posthumous rehabilitation, are referred to in a number of Jewish sources (see Dəvarim R. 7.5 and Ginzberg, Legends, V p.367 note 384, VI pp.154-5 note 920). This idea is developed in AC Deut.33.6, which relates that after Reuben's death, his bones were found to have blackened; when Moses blessed him, the bones whitened (see BSOAS 67 pp.358-9, and TIA p.366).

(xxii) Judges 12.6. The meaning of the word which the Ephraimites
          were told to say.

Dillmann's Geez text of Jdg.12.6 gives the word which the Ephraimites distinctively pronounced as mahsän, with the variant mämhəsan, both representing the LXX A text sunthēma, 'agreement, covenant' (and not the LXX B text stachus, 'ear of corn'). AC Jdg. 12.5-6 says that mämhəsan means 'May God be a refuge for me', and notes that members of the Agäw tribe are unable to pronounce Ethiopic/ Amharic /s/.

Kəflä giyorgis and Kidanä wäld Kəfle, in their Geez-Amharic lexicon, on mämhəsan (p.458) note, 'Instead of reading səbolet, it reads mämhəsan; it is in error';   and on səbolet (p.846), having given the definition 'head of grain', they add, 'But the teachers of the O.T. say that the word is səholet, and that its meaning is "May he throw me in the sea, or over a precipice".

The Mämhərä orit in MS B.N. d'Abbadie 156 (f.18b col.2) says, 'And they said to them, "Say mahsän" - (the text) is not (correct), but (it should read) sekol';   the MO in d'Abbadie 39 (f.150a) adds to this, 'And sekol is "a torrent of water".'

33. Further see W.W. Reader, JBL 100;   U. Jart, ST 24;   R.P. Blake and H. de Vis, Epiphanius de Gemmis;   Anastasius Sinaita, PG 89 col.311; EMML 7410 f.1a.

It may be concluded that alongside knowledge of Geez texts of Jdg.12.6 that follow LXX A, there was some (direct or indirect) Ethiopian knowledge of the MT of this verse (and possibly of LXX B also), and in addition there was concurrence in a rabbinic interpretation (e.g. Rashi's and Radak's commentaries <u>in loc.</u>) of šibbolet as 'stream of water' and not 'ear of corn'.[34]

(xxiii) 2 Chron.24.20-2 and Matt.23.35. The 'blood of Zechariah'.

Material on this is contained in my 'The 'blood of Zechariah' (Mt.23.35) in Ethiopian exegetical tradition' (<u>Studia Patristica</u>).

(xxiv) Ps.43 (44). 1 (2). The martyrdom of a woman and her sons.

Stories of the martyrdom of a woman and her sons at the command of an impious ruler are found in Ethiopian and in Jewish sources, with widely varying details. AC Ps.43(44).1 relates   how Eleazar's seven sons, and then his wife Mäkbəyu (or Mäbkəyu), were killed before him at the command of Antiochus. Some texts of <u>Gädlä sämaᶜ ətat</u> (e.g. EMML 2514 (42)) include the martyrdom of Mäkbəyu and her seven sons on <u>Nähasse</u> 8, and <u>TQ</u> on Rev.6.9 (see <u>TIA</u> p.104) knows of Mäkbəyu and her three or seven children.

A story similar in outline, but not containing the name Mäkbəyu, is found in <u>Sənkəssar</u> for <u>Nähasse</u> 8 (Eleazar, Salome, and seven children), LXX 2 Macc.6-7 (Eleazar, and a mother and her seven sons), LXX 4 Macc. 5-17, <u>Ekha R.</u> 1.16 § 50 (Miriam, daughter of Tanḥum/Naḥtum and her seven sons), and <u>TB Gittin</u> 57b.

The story is not found in Josephus, but it is contained in the Hebrew <u>Sefer Yosippon</u> (conveniently summarized in Charles, <u>Pseudepigrapha</u>, pp.657-8), and also in the Ethiopic epitome of <u>Sefer Yosippon</u>,

34. Further see Ginzberg, <u>Legends</u>, II, 138; V, 366; P.Swiggers, 'The word Šibbōleṭ in Jud.XII.6', <u>JSS</u> 26 (1981) 205-7; Theodoret's Questions on Judges (<u>PG</u> 80 col.505); Bar Hebraeus comm. <u>in loc.</u>; E.Y. Kutscher, <u>A History of the Hebrew Language</u>, pp.14-5; AC Ps. 77.11.

Zena ayhud (which in Murad Kamil's edition has the story of Eleazar on pp.53-6, and of the seven brothers, but without their mother being named Hannah, on pp.56-63). A more distant parallel is in Ethiopic I Maccabees, which relates the martyrdom of five sons of (the father) Maqabyos of Benjamin, at the order of Ṣiruṣaydan (see OTIAC pp.141-3).

Syriac commentaries are not unaware of the history of Antiochus and the Maccabees (e.g. Iso'dad on Daniel), but do not appear to use this martyrdom story. Iso'dad follows Theodore of Mopsuestia in interpreting Ps.44 of the Maccabees, as the AC tradition also does.

(xxv) Ps.67(68).27(28). The citing of 'There is Benjamin ...' in support of the claim that his tribe was first to enter the Red Sea.

Jewish sources relate that the first to enter the Red Sea at the exodus from Egypt was (a)Nahshon, prince of the tribe of Judah, or (b)the prince of the tribe of Benjamin. The former is the majority view; both views are found in TB Sotah 37a, and the latter one is there supported from Ps.68.28, 'There is little Benjamin their ruler'.

AC Ps.67.27 and AC Rev.21.26 (see TIA pp.368-9) also relate that the tribe of Benjamin was first to enter the sea, and AC Ps.67.27 gives Elo as the name of the prince of Benjamin. The placing of this story in commentary on Ps.67(68) is common to the Ethiopian and Jewish traditions (see Rashi and Məsudat david in loc.[35]); it appears not to be so used in other commentary traditions.

(xxvi) Ps.126.4. The quotation of Joshua 15.19 in comment on Ps.126.4.

AC Ps.125(126).4 reads, 'Like a river in Azeb' - as water flows from highland to lowland, as it returns to its place of origin, the ocean; as Achsah daughter of Caleb said, "And since you sent me to the land of Azeb, give us something in exchange".' This verse, Josh.15. (18)19, is also quoted in the commentary of Radak, and in Məsudat ṣiyyon, on Ps.126.4, though the point made is different, namely that

35. Further see Ginzberg, Legends III 21, 195, 221; VI 6, 75-6, 238; Semot R. 24.1; Bəmidbar R. 12.21, 13.7; PRE ch.42.

'<u>negeb</u>' means 'dry land'.[36]

(xxvii) Eccles.9.14. Historical and moral interpretation.

AC Eccles.9.14. and <u>Qohelet R.</u> <u>in loc.</u> both contain historical
and moral interpretations, as follows (two of the eight interpretations
of <u>Qoh.R.</u> are given as samples):

	AC Eccles. 9.14		<u>Qohelet R.</u>	
little city	Judah	humanity of the righteous	Egypt	body
few men	Judaeans	the righteous	Israel	limbs
great king	Sennacherib	the devil	Pharaoh	evil inclination
poor man	Hezekiah	the righteous hermit	Moses	good inclination

(xxviii) Eccles.11.5 and Rev.10.4. Seven concealed things.

In comment on Eccles.11.5, 'Thou knowest not what is the way
of the wind', <u>Qohelet R.</u> lists seven things concealed from man: 'the
day of death, the day of consolation, the profundity of divine judgement, the source from which one will profit, what is in the heart of
his fellow, what is in a woman's conception, and when the kingdom of
Edom will fall' (see also <u>Bərešit R.</u> 65.12 and <u>TB</u> <u>Pəsahim</u> 54b).

AC Eccles.11.5 is slightly similar: 'because there is no one
who knows what the way of death is, just as it is not known whether
the embryo in the womb of a woman who has conceived is male or female';

36. Text and translation of Radak in J. Baker and E.W.Nicholson, <u>The
Commentary of Rabbi David Kimhi on Psalms CXX-CL</u>. For <u>Məsudat siyyon</u>
see <u>Miqra'ot gədolot</u>. The use of <u>azeb</u>, corresponding to MT <u>negeb</u>, in
some Geez texts of both Josh.15.19 and Ps.126.4 is striking in view
of the fact that the LXX translates differently in each verse (<u>eis
gēn Nageb</u> and <u>en tō notō</u> respectively).

the list in AC Rev.10.4 of 'what the thunders said' (see <u>TIA</u> p.274)
is a closer parallel: faith, love, the day of death, sexual union,
the parousia, conception, mercy.

(xxix) Song 6.8–9. Interpretations referring to (a) the patriarchs,
      (b) books and (c) types of people.

    Both AC Song 6.8–9 and Šir R. 6.9 have in common three main
lines of interpretation, shown in the following table (from which the
further interpretations of Šir R. 6.9 § 4–5 are omitted for simplicity):

Song 6.8-9	interpretation of patriarchs		interpretation of books		interpretation of types of people	
	AC	Šir R.6.9§1 and Berešit R. 90.1	AC	Šir R. 6.9§2	AC	Šir R. 6.9§2-3
60 queens	offspring of Abraham and Keturah	–	NT books	tractates of Mishnah	apostles	companies of the righteous
80 concubines	children of Lot	–	OT books	sections in Leviticus	disciples	companies of the fairly good
maidens without number	other peoples	–	other books (awlad)	additional halakhot	spiritual offspring	disciples
my dove is only one	Isaac	Abraham	gospel	one principle of interpretation	Virgin Mary	one principle
the darling of her mother	Isaac, only child of Sara	Isaac	gospel	–	Virgin Mary	–
flawless to her that bore her	Isaac	Jacob	gospel	–	Virgin Mary	–
the maidens saw her	other peoples praised her	tribal ancestors	other books praised the gospel	–	spiritual offspring praise her	–

(xxx)   Rev.21.26.   Satan's assuming the appearance of Solomon.

The legend found in some texts of AC Rev.21.26 (see TIA p.372) is also found, substantially different in detail, in TB Gittin 68a–b;   see Ginzberg, Legends, IV pp.169–172;   VI pp.299–300.

Summary and conclusions:

(a)   It is possible to draw up an extensive list of parallels between Ethiopian and Jewish commentaries and related materials.

(b)   The Jewish sources which most resemble the AC in general format and style are Midras̆ haggadol and Midras̆ hahefes.

(c)   The Jewish sources which have most parallels with the AC in content are Targum Pseudo-Jonathan, MhG, MhH, PRE, Midras̆ rabba, and the non-halakhic portions of the Talmuds and Yalqut meʿam loʿez.   (The AC, like the Talmud, does contain rules for life of a halakhic type, but in detail the two are completely different).

(d)   While, for example, Abot de Rabbi Nathan shares with the AC a liking for numbered lists, and the Zohar has some motifs in common such as the great height of Adam[37], a reading of these sources, and others not mentioned in (c) above, shows that the material they contain is more remote from the traditions which have reached the AC.

(e)   For some of the parallels adduced, it is clear that the traditions have been transmitted to Ethiopia via Syriac and Arabic Christian commentaries, or via Christian chronographic works, or via compilations of legendary material such as the Kitab al-majall.   Of the examples given, iv, v and xii were probably transmitted by pathways 11 and 12, and vii by pathways 16 and 17.

(f)   Some parallels involve legends or stories of wide diffusion, the source of which may lie neither in Jewish nor in Ethiopian tradition;   xxiv, xxx, and the Alexander legends are possible examples.

37. See D.C. Matt, Zohar, pp.51, 210–11.

(g)   Some parallels are so slight that they may well be the result of independent thought, or of mere chance; ii, ix, xvi, and xxi are probable examples.

(h)   There remains a residue of parallels for which other paths of transmission cannot be proved, and for which transmission by pathways 20 and 21 is a possibility; however, the nature of the parallels is such that direct transmission should not be postulated in the absence of historical (rather than literary) evidence of its occurrence. Of the examples given, the strongest candidates for inclusion in this category are xix and xxv; weaker candidates are xii, xiv, xxii, xxvi and xxix, and xx requires further study (especially on the sources of the Book of the Mysteries of Heaven and Earth).

(i)   In no instance, except Kidanä wäld Kəfle's work on MH, can literary contact between the Ethiopian and Jewish traditions be seriously entertained on the basis of the evidence currently available. For some midrashim, such as YML, such literary contact is overwhelmingly improbable on historical and linguistic grounds (but that does not preclude the possibility of the common preservation of traditional, and perhaps oral, material). For other midrashim, the historical circumstances do not preclude cross-influence, or even literary con- tact, and it is of interest here that the two midrashim which most resemble the AC, MhG and MhH, contain material of Yemenite provenance.

(j)   Further investigation of this area will need to develop a more discriminating methodology, distinguishing the various historical and literary strata of the Ethiopian and Jewish sources. For example, the sources of the Cave of Treasures and the Kitab al-majall need inves- tigation, and the question of whether the AC parallels with PRE and Targum Pseudo-Jonathan have been mediated via Ephraim and Isoʿdad, or by other routes.

3.2.   Interpolations 'from Hebrew' in Geez texts of Song of Solomon.

Ethiopian tradition alleges a dual textual tradition for the Geez version of Song of Solomon, one from Hebrew (as chanted in church), and one from Greek (as taught in the commentary schools):

"In the Ethiopian Church there are two types of Old Testament: firstly, the Torah which was brought by Azaryas the chief priest in the time of Menelik the first is the Torah of the Levites, which Moses wrote;   secondly, the Torah which the person called Abba Sälama käsate bərhan brought in 328 E.C. is the one which the seventy elders of his country interpreted – and today every book of the Old Testament which the scholars of Ethiopia interpret is the interpretation of the seventy elders which Abba Sälama caused to be translated from Greek into Geez.   But the Old Testament which Azaryas the chief priest brought is used for prayer – but only the Song of Solomon, in chant, only in the church".[1]

Examination of texts of the Geez version of Song reveals a variable amount of material absent from the Hebrew text and from other versions;   AC Song 2.16[2] has a note, 'The Hebrew began (here)', meaning that this verse has the first of the interpolations, and that the interpolations are of Hebrew origin.   Ethiopian printed texts of Song (including editions of the Psalter) contain the interpolations variously, and the printed text of AC Song contains the maximum; they are not contained in the extracts from Song in the chant books.

There is an interesting reference in AC Kidan[3] to the interpolation in Song 5.1.   The subject is the origin of the wood on which Christ was crucified.   This is said to have been brought by an eagle from Paradise to King Saul, and subsequently to have been planted by

---

1.   Aklilä bərhan Wäldä qirqos, Mäshetä amin, p.18.   A briefer account, similar in outline, is given in the same author's Märha ləbbuna, p.13.

2.   Mäsahəftä sälomon wäsirak,   A.A., 1917 E.C., p.213.

3.   Mäshafä kidan, A.A., 1963 E.C., pp.9–10.

the Jordan. Then it was cut for Solomon's temple, but not used, and it cured the foot of the Queen of Sheba when she visited Solomon and accidentally kicked it. Solomon and Sheba, and the successive 28 kings attached money to it. Then the money went to Judas Iscariot, and the wood went to crucify our Lord. Here the commentary quotes, "The creeper of the vine which was cut from Hasison and planted at Golgotha; the creeper of the vine became my salvation, which is from God". (Whatever Hasison may originally have meant, it is currently used by Ethiopian monks in Jerusalem to refer to the Valley of the Cross.)

The dictionary of Kəflä giyorgis and Kidanä wäld Kəfle[4] is dismissive of the interpolations:

"In the Song (of Solomon) there is extra text which has no basis in the original, which the teachers interpret but the choristers do not chant, which came in after (the time of) Yared[5] like an admixture and like a gloss; people distinguish it from the Greek version and call it 'Hebrew'. However, they ought to call it 'Geez', and not 'Hebrew', because it is found only in Geez, and not, like other words of foreign origin, in Hebrew. It is absolutely unknown who called it Hebrew and inserted it in the middle (of the text) ...."

The existence and extent of the interpolations have been partially concealed by their omission from Gleave's edition[6], although they are to be found in at least some of the biblical MSS (e.g. in MS B.L. Add. 24990) which the introduction[7] claims were collated for

---

4. Mäshafä säwasəw wägəss, A.A., 1948 E.C., pp.17-18. A similar, briefer, comment occurs on p.219 under aksitos.

5. Sixth century A.D., traditionally the founder of Ethiopian church chant.

6. H.C. Gleave, The Ethiopic Version of the Song of Songs, London, 1951.

7. Gleave, pp.xvii-xviii, xxviii-xxix.

the edition. S. Euringer[8] noted a few of the interpolations, but it appears that the MS he used, Berlin Ms. or. fol. 397, only contains those in Song 3.11, 5.1, 6.10 and 7.3, and lacks the rest of the material.

It is possible that the interpolations were translated from a non-Ethiopian version of Song, and the presence in them of many non-Ethiopian words gives general probability to such a suggestion; however, a search of versions of Song in Aramaic, Greek, Latin, Syriac, Arabic, Coptic and Armenian has failed to reveal a non-Ethiopian source for the interpolations.

It may be tentatively suggested that the interpolated material may have originated as epexegetic glosses from the great Ethiopian scholar Abba Giyorgis of Gasəčča[9], on the grounds that the closest parallels to the interpolations are to be found in his Arganonä wəddase, both generally in style and in width of vocabulary, and in specific parallels, of which the most striking is እትጋነይ ፡ ለኪ ፡ እኢየፈሳለኝም ፡ ... ወግልፋት ፡ በዕንቄ ፡ ሰምር ፡ ወበ ፡ እጿሮግዮን ፡
(Arganon p.365[10], cf. interpolation in Song 3.10 given below).

The following table shows the parts of the Geez text of Song which appear in the printed version of AC Song[11], but not in Gleave's

8. *Die Auffassung des Hohenliedes bei den Abessiniern*, Leipzig, 1900, pp.31-3.

9. Died 1425 A.D.; see Taddesse Tamrat, *Church and State in Ethiopia 1270-1527*, pp.222-5; catalogue notes on MS EMML 1838; Getatchew Haile, 'On the Writings of Abba Giyorgis Säglawi from Two Unedited Miracles of Mary', *Orientalia Christiana Periodica*, 48 (1982), pp.65-91.

10. The page reference is to *Mäshafä arganon zä'abba Giyorgis*, A.A., 1959 E.C. The work has also been edited by P. Leander, Göteborg, 1922.

11. *Mäsahaftä sälomon wäsirak* (ed. *Mälʾakä gännät Kəfle), A.A., 1917 E.C., pp.205-235.

text or apparatus. The chapters and verses are those of Gleave's edition, and the line divisions of the interpolations are those of M̈azmurat ză̈dawit, Asmara (Franciscan Press) 1960 E.C., pp.279–298. The interpolations present many problems of translation, and the translations offered follow the interpretation of the AC. Further textual study of the interpolations should await a new critical edition of the Geez text of Song.

ch.	v.	words of text preceding interpolation	interpolation and 'translation'
2	16	ወእሳ፡ ኮተ፡	መኑ፡ ይትዓዳዋ፡ ለወልዱ፡ እኁየ፡ እስመ፡ ፃዑል፡ መዝራዕት፡ የማኑ፡
			Who trangresses against my young brother, for his right upper arm is above all?
2	17	ለወይጠል፡	ወይርእያክን፡ እዋልደ፡ ኢየሩሳሌም፡ ወንበር፡ ዲበ፡ ሰራፌል፡ ወዲበ፡ ፬ቱ፡ ኪሩቤል፡
			Let the daughters of Jerusalem see you (m.sing.), and sit above the seraphim and above the 4 cherubim
2	17[12]	ፉጥንጎ፡	ቅንዱ፡ እንተ፡ ወልዱ፡ እኁየ፡ ክመ፡ ወይጠል፡
			Spring, you, my young brother, like an antelope
3	6	እምገዳም፡	ከመ፡ ፌመና፡ ዘመፈሬ፡ ሰማይ፡ [13]
			like a cloud of the firmament of Heaven
3	6	ዕጣናት፡	ክልኤ፡ እንግባትኪ፡ ይወሐዛ፡ ሐሊብ፡
			your two breasts pour out milk
3	10	ዘብሩር፡	ሰርዲዮስ፡ ዘምስለ፡ ተርሴስ፡ ኢዮፖሎግዮስ፡ ዘምስለ፡ ሶፍር፡
			onyx with beryl, iyopologyos with sapphire
3	10	ዘወርቅ፡	እቀላሌሁ፡ ወእቀፈሊሁ፡ ኢያሴሜር፡
			its hole and its bindings are (the jewel) iyasemer
3	10	ዘሜላት፡	ሕንብርቱ፡ ዘቢሩሌ፡ ዘምስለ፡ ኢያስጴዱ፡ በገሕርይ፡ ክዱን፡
			its centre is of beryl with jasper, covered with pearl

12. Ch.3 v.1 in AC Song.

13. AC records the variant ዘመፈሬ፡ ውስተ፡ ሰማይ፡

| 3 | 11 | እለ ፡ | እሰ ፡ ዕለተ ፡ ሕማሙ ፡ ወእሰ ፡ ዕለተ ፡ ስቅለቱ ፡ ወእሰ ፡ ዕለተ ፡ ሞቱ ፡ |

on the day of his suffering and on the day
of his crucifixion
and on the day of his death

| 4 | 2 | ይሰነትዎ ፡ | ፸ወ፯ት ፡ እለ ፡ ይሰፍዱ ፡ |

which bear 77

| 4 | 4 | ውስቱቱ ፡ | ኅበ ፡ ኢይሬእዮ ፡ ሰብእ ፡ ወኢይበጽሑ ፡ ፀሐይ ፡ |

where man does not see it, nor the sun reach it

| 4 | 4 | ኃይላን ፡ | ወደረጓን ፡ እለ ፡ የዓቅቦዋ ፡ ፫ቱ ፡ እጓው ፡ |

the 3 men who guard it are powerful

| 4 | 6 | ስሒን ፡ ምዑዝ ፡ | ወእትቀባዕ ፡ እመዓዛሁ ፡ እቍልን ፡ ገዳም ፡ ወይበልዕዋ ፡ አዕዋፈ ፡ ቆላት ፡ ወኢይመውታ ፡ እስመ ፡ ይሐዱሱ ፡ ውርዘቶን ፡ |

and the olive trees of the open places will
be anointed from its scent,
and the birds of the lowlands will eat it and
will not die,
for they will renew their youthfulness

| 4 | 8 | ሃረጋዮት ፡ | ወታስተርእዪ ፡ ውስተ ፡ አድባሬ ፡ ጽባሕ ፡ |

and you (f. sing.) will appear on the hills
of the east

| 4 | 8 | ወጴርዎን ፡ | ትስቀዪ ፡ ጠለ ፡[14] |

(while) you (f.sing.) drink dew

| 4 | 10[15] | ወርዓት ፡ | ወሐሊቦን ፡ ይጥዕም ፡ እመዓር ፡ ወሃክር ፡ ወእምተምር ፡ ዘውስተ ፡ ገነት ፡ |

their milk is sweeter than honey and sugar,
and than the date which is in a garden

| 4 | 12[16] | ፈናወ ፡ ዚእኪ ፡ | ኅበ ፡ ኢይበጽሑ ፡ ወኢይኳርዮ ፡ ኄንያ ፡ |

where no-one reaches it nor craftsman digs it

| 4 | 13 | እቀጣዝ ፡ | ሰንፉሮስ ፡ ምስለ ፡ ጵርስቅላ ፡ |

juniper gum together with (the perfume)
pr∂sq∂la

14. AC suggests   እንዘ ፡ ትስቀዪ ፡ ጠለ ፡   should be understood.

15. Ch.4 v.9 in AC Song.

16. Ch.4 v.13 in AC Song.

5	1	እንጋውየ፡ወሰኔራ፡	እስመ፡እንሁዛን፡እሙንቱ፡ ወትእሳሃሙ፡ቅንአት፡ክመ፡ሰልባልያኖስ ፤ ሐረግ፡ወይን፡ሃዩ፡መዉኑኢትየ፡ ዘእምነዛሒሃን፡ይትሃዝም፡ወበጎልጎታ፡ይተከል፡

for they are stupid,

and jealousy seizes them like Sälbəlyanos.

The creeper of the vine has become my salvation,

which is cut from Hasison and is planted at Golgotha

5	2	ፉጽምት፡	ከመ፡ፋቄ፡ቅጡን፡ወክመ፡መሰንቆ፡ሐዋዝ፡ይታተፌሰሐኒ፡ልብየ፡ በሰሚዖተ፡

like shrill whistling and like a tuneful lyre

it made my heart rejoice in hearing it

5	3	እንገምየን፡	እስመ፡ተሐፀብኩ፡እነ፡በስሒን፡ወበእቅራሃዮን፡

for I have washed myself in white incense and

in (the perfume) aqrahyon

5	4	ስቀሬት፡	እስመ፡በሊህ፡ልቡ፡እምነኑ፡ናት፡

for his heart is sharper than a spear

5	9	እምሐልኳኑ፡	በፀሐይኑ፡ወበየርኅኑ፡ወበከዋክብትኑ፡

by sun, and by moon and by stars?

5	10	ወቀይሕ፡	ወዕፃወፉዋ፡እልፍ፡ወትእልፊት፡እዕላፋት፡

and tens of thousands and millions of millions

surround him

5	13	እሬዋት፡	እዕይንቲሁ፡ክመ፡ኮከበ፡ፅባሕ፡እለ፡ይዴዱሉ ፡[17]

like the morning star are his eyes, which

shine brightly

5	13	ፉጹም፡	ወልዱ፡እኁየ፡ይፄኑ፡ዝርቤን፡ያዑዝ፡ እልባሲሁ፡ዘዕብን፡ክመ፡ሰብአ፡ተርሴስ፡

my young brother smells of sweet z̈ärben,

his clothes of stone are like (the clothes of)

the men of Tarshish

5	14	ሰንቴር፡	እዕዛን፡ክብር፡ወዉዕዖ፡ዘኢየዉዕዖ፡እዴ፡ክበዴ፡

ear-rings of glory and a nose-ring that a

craftsman's hand did not fashion

6	1	preceding first እዴቴ፡	ወትቤ፡መርዓት፡

and the bride says

6	1	preceding second እዴቴ፡	ወትቤ፡እንኪሞስ፡

and the company (aksitos) says

6	9	ፉጽምትየ፡	ክነፋዋ፡ክንፊ፡ብሩር፡ ወገበዋቲሃኒ፡በሐመልማለ፡ወርቅ፡

her wings are wings of silver

and her sides are in strands of gold

---

17. AC records the variant ፀዓኮሁ፡ፀዓኬ፡ይዴዱሉ፡

6 10 ጸሐይ :   ሑረታቲሃ : በምሥጢር :
her paths are in mystery

6 11 እኁየ :   ወትቤ : እቅሌስያ :
and the company (aqlesya) says

6 11 ሙኃዝ :   ኃበ : ፈሪየ : እኽይሞስ :
where the akyamos gives fruit

7 4 ዘወይጠል :   እለ : ይፈለፉለ : ሐሊበ : ወንፈስ :
which pour out milk of the spirit

7 5 ብዘኃ : እያዉ :   ንግሥታት : ይፈቅዱ : ስነኪ : ወእሕዘብኒ :
                      የሐዉሩ : በፀዳልኪ :
queens desire your (f.sing.) beauty and
also the peoples walk in your brightness

7 6 ዌለት : ፉሑስ :   ማኅፈደ : ወርቅ : ለሰሎሞን :
                      ወመሠረቱ : ዘዕንቀ : እፍማርስጲስ : [18]
Solomon has a tower of gold
and its foundation is of the jewel admarəspis.

7 9 ወልዕልቱ :   ቱኃ : ሐንኮሉ : ለእርያም :
its great height (reaches) to Heaven

7 10 ወለልብንየ :   እዘብ : ወሊኅን : ወጸናታም : የዋውሑ : ጸፈሪ : ቤትኪ : [19]
                      ክሙ : ጸጎ : ሪሑ : ወካዕዉ : ሮማን : ወጸጎንቶስ :
                      ይምዐዝኒ : እፉሉ :
hyssop, fennel and rue surround the courtyard
of your (f.sing.) house.
His mouth smells to me like a rose and like
a pomegranate, and säbanyos

7 13 ሮማን :   ልብነ : ወወግሐጠ : ይምዐዝኒ : እፉሉ :
his mouth smells to me of storax and jasmine

7 13 ለክ :   ወይቲፈተዉ : እምነኩልነ : መፋቅሩ : [20]
they are more desired than other desirable things

18. AC records the variant   ዘዕንቁ : እፍማርስጲስ :

19. AC records the variant   ቤትክ :

20. AC suggests   እመፍቅዱ : ንፈነ :   as an alternative understanding.

| 8 | 5 | እንዛእኑኃ ፦ | ኮልኔ ፦ ዘበዕብራይስኬ ፦ እለ ፦ ቀሉዓን ፦ እዳዊሁ ፦ በዳሞ ፦ ሕርጌ ፦ ዘገለዓፍ ፦ |

kol (means) in Hebrew

'the one whose hands were dipped in the
blood of a heifer of Gilead'

| 8 | 5 | ወላዲተኃ ፦ | ፋቂቀ ፦ ይሳኮር ፦ ይሣለቁ ፦ ላዕሌክ ፦ |

the children of Issachar pour scorn upon
you (m.sing.)

| 8 | 6 | ፅንዕት ፦ | ዕንቄ ፦ ዮሣር ፦ [21] ኢይሰነሙን ፦ ሤጣ ፦ |

the jewel of <u>yosar</u> will not be her price

| 8 | 6 | ሲኦል ፦ | ቀንዓት ፦ ትበልዖሙ ፦ [22] ለልበ ፦ ብዙኃን ፦ በመዓት ፦ |

jealousy eats up the heart of many in wrath

| 8 | 6 | ላህባ ፦ | እስመ ፦ በቀንዓትሰ ፦ ኢይትረከብ ፦ ጸጋ ፦ እግዚእብሔር ፡ |

for the grace of God is not obtained by
jealousy

| 8 | 9 | ዘቄፍሮስ ፦ | ማኅፈድ ፦ ቀይሕ ፦ ዘያክንት ፦ ለሰሎሞን ፦ በኬብሮን ፡ |

Solomon has a red tower of jacinth in Hebron

| 8 | 11 | የዓቀሉ ፦ ፍሬሁ ፦ | እእላፍ ፦ ፍሬሁ ፦ በበዘቤሁ ፦ ፲ተ ፦ ፲ተ ፦ ለጽዮን ፦ ይሁብ ፡ |

tens of thousands are its fruit in its seasons.
He gives thousands to Zion

| 8 | 12–13 | ርእይዎ ፦ | ጉቡዓን ፦ ወስንዑዓን ፦ እንዘ ፦ ይነብሩ ፦ በሰላም ፦ ወእንዘ ፦ ይትረእዩ ፦ ማዕከላ ፦ እንዘ ፦ የሐውሩ ፦ ውስተ ፦ ገነተ ፦ ካልዓን ፡ |

assembled and in agreement while they live in
peace,
and while they are seen in her midst,
while they walk in the garden of others

21. AC records the variants ወርቀ ፦ ዮሣር ፡ and ወርቅ ፦ ወዮሣር ፦
ኢይሰነሙኑ ፦ ሤጣ ፦

22. AC suggests ትበልዕ ያ ፦ as more grammatical.

3.3   References to 'Hebrew' and 'Arabic' in the section on Genesis
of the Mämhərä orit in MS d'Abbadie 156.

Of the texts of Mämhərä orit examined (see 4.1 below), all contain
some references to 'Hebrew' and 'Arabic', but the copy in MS d'Abbadie
156, f.4a-19a has the most, and those in the section on Genesis are
listed below as a sample of the whole. The other texts of MO variously
either lack the individual references, or have a text substantially
agreeing with d'Abb.156, and so do not contribute to an elucidation of
its obscurities.

(i)   MS d'Abbadie 156 f.4a col.2, on Genesis 1.22: ወበዕብራይስጡ ፡
ይቤ ፡ ወለአናምርትስ ፡ ኢባረኮሙ ፡ ከመ ፡ ኢይብዝኁ ፡

"And in Hebrew it says, 'But the leopards he did not bless, lest they
multiply'".
There appears to be no textual or midrashic parallel for this; if,
however, anabərt were read for anamərt, it might be understood as a
reference to Behemoth and Leviathan (cf. e.g. Bəreŝit R. VII.4).

(ii)   f.4b col.1, on Gen.2.10: ወበዕብራይስጥ ፡ ይቤ ፡ ወያሐውሩ ፡
ውስተ ፡ ፬ እርእስተ ፡ ምድር ፡ ዘውእቶሙ ፡ ፋርስ ፡ ወሮምያ ፡
ሕንዱ ፡ ወኢትዮጵያ ፡ "And in Hebrew it says, 'And they go to 4 heads of
the land, namely Persia and Rome, India and Ethiopia'".
The lemma reads ወይትፈለሙ ፡ ለ፬ ወንዓዝዝ ፡   , doubtless reflecting
LXX ἀφορίζεται εἰς τέσσαρας ἀρχάς   ; the alleged
Hebrew, provided 'namely ... Ethiopia' is understood as comment, is
closer to MT היה לארבעה ראשים

(iii)   f.4b col.2 - f.5a col.1, on Gen.3.24 : ወኣዘዘሙ ፡ ለሱራፌል ፡
ከመ ፡ ይዕቀቡ ፡ ፍኖተ ፡ ገነት ፡ እንተ ፡ ትትወየጥ ፡ ዘ ፡ ኢኮነ ፡፡
ወበእብራይስጥ ፡ ይቤ ፡ ወኣዘዘሙ ፡ ለሱራፌል ፡ ወለኣንተ ፡ ትነፍፍ ፡
ወንጋሕት ፡ ወትትወየጥ ፡ --- ወበዓረቢስ ፡ ይቤ ፡ ወሠርዖ ፡
ለኪሩብ ፡ ዘውስተ ፡ እዴሁ ፡ ኵናተ ፡ እሳት ፡ እንተ ፡ ትትገረዥ ፡
ከመ ፡ ይዕቀብ ፡ ፍኖተ ፡ ገነት ፡፡

"'And he ordered the seraphim that they guard the way of the garden
which turns around' - (the text) is not (correct). And in Hebrew it
says 'And he ordered the seraphim and the knife which burns and turns
around' ... . But in Arabic it says, 'And he appointed the cherub in
whose hand is a sword of fire which glitters, that he guard the way of
the garden'".

The lemma here is at variance with Geez biblical texts (which
generally read '... seraphim and cherubim ... guard the way of the
tree of life'), and was probably translated as a part of the nucleus
of <u>MO</u>, and not quoted from a Geez version of Gen. In the alleged
Hebrew, ወለኧንተ ፡ --- ወቶተሐዐየኝ ፡   looks like an attempt to
translate MT ‏חׇיׅים הׇעׅץ דׇרׇך אׇת לׅשׁמׁר‎ .
The alleged Arabic appears to represent a version based on the LXX
(see the discussion of this verse in the commentaries of Išoᶜdad and
Ibn aṭ-Ṭaiyib on Gen.; <u>MO</u> has not taken the discussion directly from
their commentaries, where the wording is very different, cf. MS d'Abbadie
28 f.14b col.2 and EMML 2101 f.72b).

(iv)   f.5a col.2, on Gen.6.14 ፡ ርስዐተ ፡ ዘ ፡ ምዐዝንተ ፡፡ ወበዕብራይስን ፡
ይ ፡ ኧፈልሪሮተ ፡ ስሞ ፡ ዕፀ ፡ ውኧቱ ፡፡   "'Four-fold'
means 'cornered'. And in Hebrew it says 'anelrebot'; it is the name
of a tree."
The first comment is clearly related to LXX ἐκ ξύλων τετραγώνων,
but I have not found a convincing explanation for the 'Hebrew', unless
it represents <u>ʾln rbᶜt</u> , 'four-cornered tree'.

(v)   f.5b col.1, on Gen.6.16 ፡ ወበዕብራይስንስ ፡ ይቤ ፡ ፍድም ፡
ገበሪሃ ፡፡ ወዓርጋተ ፡ ተፁሪፉ ፡ ወተስካስ ፡ ፫ ፉሉምሳ ፡ ባዓሃበር ፡፡
ወበዕብራይስንስ ፡ (!) ይቤ ፡ ወግበር ፡ ለከ ፡ ሞወርጋተ ፡ ኧሓቲ ፡
ወኧልኤቲ ፡ ወሣልስ ፡፡ ወበዐሪቢስ ፡ ይቤ ፡ ግበር ፡ ለከ ፡ ወዓርጋተ ፡
ታሕታየ ፡ ወማኧከላየ ፡ ወላዕላየ ፡፡   "But in Hebrew it says,
'Complete ...? (<u>gäbäriha</u>). Decks, the second and third – (they are) 3,
separated individually. But in Hebrew it says, 'And make for yourself
decks, one and two, and a third'. But in Arabic it says, 'Make for
yourself lower, middle and upper decks'."
The LXX and MT of this verse are rather different, there are substantial
variants in Geez versions of it, and the account of the texts given
here in <u>MO</u> is not wholly clear; for <u>gäbäriha</u>, possibly <u>gəbräta</u> or
<u>tägbara</u>, 'her manufacture/work' should be read. The alleged Arabic is
close to the Arabic text printed in Walton's <u>Polyglott</u>.

(vi)   f.6a col.1, on Gen.10.2 ፡ ወፉቄቀ ፡ ያፌት ፡ ፯ ወኤልሳዕስ ፡
ኢሀሎ ፡ በኧብራይስን ፡ ወበነገልኧን ፡ ልሳናት ፡ ኧክ ፡ ዘሠልስ ፡
ተወልፉ ፡ ውኧቱ ፡፡   "And the children of Japheth were 7, but
Elsaᶜ is not (written) in Hebrew or in other languages, but he is of
the third generation."

This is a reference to the fact that some Geez texts of this verse place an Elsaᶜ after Yəhya(n) (=Javan), and thus have 8 sons of Japheth; these texts have a further Els(aᶜ) in Gen.10.4 as a son of Javan. The particularity seems to be distinctively Geez; this suggests that the author of this comment is using a Geez text as a base for reference, rather than translating ready-made textual scholia from another language. Saadia's Arabic version of this verse is notably different from the LXX and MT, and from this Geez version.

(vii) f.6b col.1, on Gen.12.8 : ወግዕዘ ፡ በህየ ፡ ውስተ ፡ ቤቴል ፡ ዘ ፡ ኢኮነ ። ወበዕብራይስጥሰ ፡ ይ ፡ ወግዕዘ ፡ እምህየ ፡ ወኀደረ ፡ ቅድመ ፡ ፅባሕ ፡ ቤቴል ።   "'And he travelled there to Bethel' – (the text) is not (correct). But in Hebrew it says, 'And he travelled thence and passed the night in front of the east of Bethel'." əmhəyyä corresponds well with MT mišsam, and two translations for miqqedem are conflated; if the commentator had the MT for reference, however, it is not clear why Hebrew hahara was mistranslated wahadärä .

(viii) f.6b col.1, on Gen.12.13 : ትሕየው ፡ ነፍስየ ፡ በዕብሬትኪ ፡ ዘ ፡ በዘመንኪ ። ወቦ ፡ እ ፡ ይ ፡ በሊቃፉኪ ። ዝሰ ፡ ነገር ፡ ኢይሰነኣዋ ፡ ዝቃል ። ወበዕብራይስጥ ፡ ይቤ ፡ በአርኪ ፡ በእርኪ ፡ ብ ፡ በእንቲእኪ ። "'May my soul live by your turn' – ('by your turn') means 'by your time'. And there are those who say, ('It means) 'by your wish''. But as for this matter, this word does not agree with it (i.e. with the context). And in Hebrew it says bä²aborki; bä²aborki means 'because of you'." The commentator rightly feels əbret to be unsuited to the context, and has apparently looked at the Hebrew of Gen.12.13 and found בעבורך (although the Hebrew word in the corresponding place in the verse is actually בגללך).

(ix) f.6b col.1, on Gen.13.3 : ወበዕብራይስጥ ፡ ይቤ ፡ ወተከለ ፡ ዳስተሎ ፡ ወቤተ ፡ በህየ ፡   "And in Hebrew it says, 'And he pitched a tent and dwelt there'."

(x) f.6b col.1, on Gen.13.10 : ርውይ ፡ ዘ ፡ ጥሉል ። ወበዓረቢስ ፡ ይቤ ፡ ዘቦቱ ፡ ምሥቃየ ፡ ማይ ፡ ዘውእቱ ፡ ወስኖ ። "'Watered' means 'wet'. But in Arabic it says, 'In which is a channel of water, namely a canal'."

The 'məsqay' could be related to Arabic سقًى (in the text in
de Lagarde, <u>Materialien</u>), or to MT mašqe.

(xi)   f.6b col.1-2, on Gen.14.4: ፲ወ፪ዓመት ፡ ለኮዶርጎሞር ፡ H ፡
ኢየሩ ፡ ወበዕብራይስጥ ፡ ይቤ ፡ ወተቀኑይ ፡ ለኮዶርጎሞር ፡ H ፡
፲ወ፪ዓመት ፡ ወኣይምዝ ፡ አጽረፉ ፡ ወበዐረቢስ ፡ ይቤ ፡ እከሰ ፡
ኮዶርጎሞር ፡ ቀነዮሙ ፡ ፲ወ፪ዓመት ፡ ወበ፲ወ፫ ፡ አጽረፉ ፡

"'The twelfth year of Chedorlaomer' - (the text) is not (correct). And
in Hebrew it says, 'And they were subject to Chedorlaomer, that is,
twelve years. And then they rebelled'. But in Arabic it says that
Chedorlaomer subjected them for twelve years. And in thirteen they
rebelled."
The point at issue here appears to be the question of whether the
rebellion lasted for one year (i.e. the thirteenth), or for thirteen
years, as discussed e.g. in Rashi's commentary and in <u>Midraš meᶜam loᶜ ez</u>
on this verse.

(xii)   f.6b col.2, on Gen.15.10-11: ወነሣእ ፡ Hንተ ፡ ኵሎ ፡ ወነፈኮ ፡
ኣማእከሉ ፡ ወአንበረ ፡ Hነፈሰ ፡ እንጸረ ፡ ካልኡ ፡ ወኢነፈሰ ፡ አዕዋፈ ፡፲
ወእብራይስጡ ፡ ይቤ ፡ ወወረዱ ፡ አዕዋፍ ፡ ኀበ ፡ እለ ፡ ተመትሩ ፡
Hወእፈ፡ውም ፡ ወውእጎ፡ያ ፡ አዕዋፍ ፡፡

"And he took up all this and divided it in its middle, and he placed
what he divided opposite its fellow, and he did not divide the birds.
In Hebrew it says, 'And the birds descended to the ones which were cut
up' - namely, birds of prey'."
The lemma is Gen.15.10 in a version so different in detail from other
Geez texts that it must be an independent translation, and not a
citation from a Geez biblical text. The 'Hebrew' continues with
Gen.15.11, but <u>əllä tämätru</u> resembles LXX τὰ διχοτομήματα
αὐτῶν   rather than MT <u>happəgarim</u>.

(xiii) f.7a col.1, on Gen.16.7: ገዳም ፡ ቡር ፡ H ፡ ኵሬ ፡፡ ወበ ፡ እ ፡
ይ ፡ ፀድ ፡፡ ወበእረቢ ፡ ቢር ፡፡   "'Wilderness
(of) <u>bur</u>' - it means 'pool'. And there are some who say 'olive tree'.
And in Arabic (it says) '<u>bir</u>'."
Geez versions of this verse generally read, 'And an angel of God found
her by a well of water in the wilderness of Bur on the path'; they
are thus rather shorter than the LXX, and have '<u>Bur</u>' for LXX/MT <u>Sour/Šur</u>.
Arabic <u>bi'r</u>, 'well', appears to have been read in the commentator's
Arabic text; Saadia has البِّير.

(xiv) f.7a col.1, on Gen. 18.6 : ወግበሪ ፡ ኃፍ3ተ ፡ ዘ ፡ ኃቦ ፲
በዓረቢሰ ፡ ይብል ፡ እብስሊ ፡ በእቶን ።   "'And make a bun' –
it means 'bread'; but in Arabic it says, 'Cook in the oven'."

(xv)   f.7a col.1, on Gen.18.8: ዐቄ3 ፡ ዘ ፡ ወገባዔት ። ወቦ ፡ ኽ ፡ ይ ፡
ሐይብ ። ወበዕብራይስጻ ፡ ይ ፡ ወእቅረበ ፡ ኦሙ ፡ ሐሊብ ፡
ወቅብኃ ፡ ወበልዑ ።   "'Curds' means 'whey'. And there
are some who say 'cheese'. And in Hebrew it says, 'And he brought to
them milk and butter and they ate'."
Geez texts of Gen. 18.8 commonly read <u>ᵓəqwanä wämäᶜarä</u>, 'curds and
honey'. The alleged Hebrew, represented in Geez as <u>haliba wäqəbᶜa</u>,
is closer to MT <u>hemᵓa wəhalab</u>, especially if <u>hemᵓa</u> is understood in
its post-biblical sense as 'butter' rather than 'curds'.

(xvi) f.7a col.1, on Gen.18.10 : ኸመ ፡ ካመ ፡ ዮም ፡ ትሬኸብ ፡ ሰራ ፡ (!)
ወፍሩ ፡ ዘ ፡ ኢይኣነ ። በዓረቢሰ ፡ ይቤ ፡ በዓመት ፡ ዘይመፅእ ።
          "'At the time like today Sarah will obtain a son' –
(the text) is not (correct). But in Arabic it says, 'In the year
which is coming'."

(xvii) f.7a col.1-2, on Gen.21.7 : መኑ ፡ ኽዮዘነሣዋ ፡ ለኽብርሃም ፡ ካመ ፡
ተሐፅን ፡ ለኽ ፡ ሰራ ፡ (!) ሕፃነ ፡ ዘ ፡ ሶበ ፡ ተፈሥሐት ። በእረቢሰ ፡
ይቤ ፡ መኑ ፡ ዜነዋ ፡ ለኽብርሃም ፡ ወይቤኮ ፡ ተሐፅን ፡ ለኽ ፡
ሰራ ፡ ሕፃነ ።   "'Who would have related to Abraham
that "Sara will suckle an infant for you"?' – it means (that it was
said) while she rejoiced. But in Arabic it says, 'Who related to
Abraham and said to him, "Sara will suckle an infant for you".'"

(xviii)f.7a col.2, on Gen.22.9 : ኸዐቀፀ ፡ ዘ ፡ እጐደቆ ። በዓረቢሰ ፡
ይቤ ፡ እሰሮ ፡ ፉ ሩረት ።   "'He entrapped him' – it means
'he threw him down'. But in Arabic it says, 'He bound him from behind'."

(xix) f.7b col.1, on Gen.25.30 : ኤዱም ፡ ብ ፡ ተብሲል ፡ ለ ነገት (!) ።
ወለስመ ፡ ዔሰው ፡ ኢየኃብር ፡ ሬፉከመሙ ፡ ወ ነ ግ ረ ፡ ዖ መ ፡ ለ ኤ ዱ ም ፡
ገነት ፡ በእብራይስጻ ። ሬፉ ፡ ዓይን ፲ ወለስመ ፡ ኤሳው ፡ እ ኈ ፍ ፡
ለ ኤ ዱ ም ፡ ገ ነ ት ፡ ፉ ግ ሬ ሩ ፡ ተ ፉ ሳ ። ወ ለ ስ መ ፡ ኤ ሳ ው ፡
ተ ብ ሲ ል ። ወ ቦ ፡ ኽ ሰ ፡ ይ ፡ ቀ ይ ሕ ፡ ብ ፡
"'Edom' means 'cooked food for a garden' (<u>gännät</u>). And the letters
and the interpretation of the garden Edom are not the same as the name
of Esau in Hebrew. Its letter is <u>ᶜayən</u>; and for the name of Esau it

is ʾaləf. The meaning of the garden Edom is ʿrejoicing', and of the
name of Esau ᵗcooked foodᵗ. And there are some who say it means ᵗredᵗ."
The commentator is distinguishing (the garden of) ʿeden (Geez ʾedom)
from ʾə dom (Geez ʾedom), the name given to Esau, and pointing out the
further association with Heb. ʾadom.

(xx)   f.8a, col.1, on Gen.36.33 : ባሶር ፡ ዘ ፡ እስመ ፡ ሀገር ፲ ወሀገረሰ ፡
ዘጌሳሙ ፨ እሳይያስኒ ፡ ዘ ፡ ይለብስ ፡ ወሢየ ፡ እልባሰ ፡ በባሶር ፡ ስሙ ፡
ሙኡቱ ፡ ሀገር ፨ ወጋሕቲ ፡ በልሳነ ፡ ግዕዝ ፲ ወበእብራይስጣ ፡
ይቤ ፡ ወይለብስ ፡ እልባሰ ፡ ዘሊረዩ ፡ በዳም ፨

"Basor (Bozrah) is the name of a place; and as for
the place, it is Esauᵗs. Isaiah also says, ᵗHe wears fine clothes in
Basorᵗ - it is the name of that (same) place. But only in the Geez
language; and in Hebrew it says, ᵗAnd he wears clothes dipped in
bloodᵗ."
The text of Isa.63.1ab in MS dᵗAbbadie 156 f.44b reads : ተስእሎ ፡
እምነሩይ ፡ ወተሰጥዋ ፡ እመልእን ፡ እንዘ ፡ ይሰብ ፡ ሙኑ ፡ ዝንቱ ፡ ዘወፅእ ፡
እምኤዱም ፡ ወይለብስ ፡ ቀደሐ ፡ እልባሰ ፡ ዘገሶር ፡ እንተ ፡ ብእኒ፡ወጎነህ ፡
ኃይል ፡ ወግራም ፡ እልባሲክነ ፡ ዘሊረዩ ፡ በዳም ፡   (and it carries a
marginal note Hərqa(nos) krəs(tos) gălila yəhud(a) qərubä edom, see
section 2.5 above). The commentator on Gen.36.33, however, appears to
have understood zäsiruy bädäm, ᵗdipped in bloodᵗ, as the Geez translation
of the part of the Hebrew text of Isa.63.1 for which his lemma has
ᵗin Bozrahᵗ.

(xxi) f.8a col.1, on Gen.37.2 : ወእምፅኡ ፡ ሶበ ፡ ዮሴፍ ፡ ሙፋት ፡
እኃዊሁ ፡ ኃበ ፡ እሉሉ ፡ ኢስራኤል ፡ ዘ ፡ ኢኮነ ፨ ወበዓረቢስ ፡ ይቤ ፡
ወእምፅኡ ፡ ዮሴፍ ፡ ሙፋት ፡ ሶበ ፡ እኃዊሁ ፡ ኃበ ፡ እሉሉ ፡

"ᵗAnd his brothers brought an evil
report against Joseph to his father Israelᵗ - (the text) is not (correct).
But in Arabic it says, ᵗAnd Joseph brought an evil report against his
brothers to his fatherᵗ."
The lemma here is the common text of Geez MSS. The two readings appear
to go back to the LXX katēnegken/-kan, and are discussed, e.g. in van
den Eyndeᵗs notes to his translation of Išoʿdadᵗs commentary on this
verse.

(xxii) f.8a col.1, on Gen.37.18 ; ወእሕሰሙ ፡ ለቀተሎቱ ፡ ዘ ፡ ቢስ ፡
እፉረጉ ፨ ወበእረቢስ ፡ ይቤ ፡ ወሀለዩ ፡ ለቀተሎቱ ፨

"'And they did evil to kill him' - it means 'they did wrong'. But in Arabic it says, 'And they thought to kill him'."

(xxiii)f.8b col.1, on Gen.47.31 : ከተማ፡ በትሩ፡ ዘ፡ ጽንፈ፡ በትሩ። ወበዕብራይስጥ፡ ይቤ፡ ውስተ፡ ከተማ፡ አራቱ።
"'The end of his staff' means 'the extremity of his staff'. But in Hebrew it says 'at the end of his bed'."
These readings correspond with LXX epi to akron tēs rhabdou autou and Hebrew ʿal roš hammitta respectively, but if the annotator had the MT before him, it is difficult to see why he did not write laʿəlä rəʾəsä ʿaratu (which is the reading of some Geez MSS).

(xxiv) f.8b col.1, on Gen.49.11: ወበዕፀ፡ ዘይት፡ አድጊሁ፡ ዘ፡ ኢኮነ፡ አላ፡ ወበሴሬቅ፡ አድጊሁ። ወበዓረቢሰ፡ ይቤ፡ በአዕጹቂሁ፡ አድጊሁ። ሴሬቅሰ፡ ይሰሐብ፡ ወይን። ወኵሉ፡ ነገረ፡ በረከተ፡ ለያዕቆብ፡ ዘጽሑፍ፡ ውስተ፡ ኦሪት፡ ኢየኃብር፡ ምስለ፡ ኦሪት፡ ዘዕብራይስጥ፡ ወዐረቢ።
"'And with an olive tree (he will bind) his donkey' - (the text) is not (correct), but (it should read), 'And with his choice vine (sereq) his donkey'. But in Arabic it says, 'With his branches his donkey'. 'Sereq' is a vine (which) is productive (?). And all the word of the blessing of Jacob which is written in the Torah does not agree with the Hebrew and Arabic Torah."
'Sereq' could represent Hebrew or Arabic in this verse, and is attested elsewhere in Geez. I have not found an Arabic text which reads 'with his branches'. For 'the Torah', MS B.N. d'Abbadie 195 f.12a reads 'our Torah'.

(xxv) f.8b col.2 on Gen.50.2 : ወአዘዞሙ፡ ዮሴፍ፡ ለእለ፡ ይገንዙ። ወበዕብራይስጥ፡ ይቤ፡ ለእለ፡ የሐንጥሙ። ለእለ፡ የሐንጥሙ፡ ዘ፡ ለእለ፡ ይገብሩ፡ ከመ፡ ኢይማስን፡ በድን። ለእለ፡ ያምዐዝዋ፡ ይትበሀል። "'And Joseph ordered the ones who were shrouding (the body of Jacob)'. And in Hebrew it says 'the ones who were embalming' (ḥnṭ); 'the ones who were embalming' means 'the ones who worked so that the corpse would not decay'. Alternatively, 'the ones who scented' is said.
Geez versions of Gen.50.2 present several variants; Dillmann reads : ወአዘዞሙ፡ ዮሴፍ፡ ለአግብርቲሁ፡ እለ፡ ይቀብሩ፡ ኀቤሁ፡ ለእለ፡ ይቀብሩ፡ ይቅብርዎ፡ (var. ያምዕዝዎ)፡ ለአቡሁ፡
which looks like a conflated text. Use of ḥnṭ may reflect the MT of

this verse, but the root is not unattested in Geez, and is also used in Saadia's Arabic version of this verse.

Conclusions.

These scholia are a perplexing collection. The presence of a transliterated Hebrew word, on Gen.12.13, shows that at some stage a Hebrew text was consulted, but a number of the comments show little, if any, contact with the MT. The current state of text-critical study of the Arabic Pentateuch precludes definite judgement on the 'Arabic'; although the notes on Gen.6.16 and possibly Gen.16.7 suggest Arabic influence, I have failed to identify any one text that would account for the majority of the references.

I conclude that although in the prehistory of these scholia some genuine textual criticism must have taken place, the author who inserted them into MO was more remote from the non-Ethiopian languages, and may have used Geez biblical texts with marginalia referring to variant readings, or Geez biblical texts which were believed to have been corrected on the basis of Hebrew or Arabic (but which in reality contained a Mischtext).

4.   Creation:

4.1   Survey of Ethiopian material related to the
      creation theme

    4.1.1   Biblical, apocryphal, and pseudepigraphical
              texts

    4.1.2   Commentaries on Genesis

    4.1.3   'Question and answer books'

    4.1.4   Hexaemeric literature

    4.1.5   The Book of the Mysteries of Heaven and Earth

    4.1.6   Homilies and miracles

    4.1.7   Chronographic works

    4.1.8   Ethiopic Qälemǝntos and Gädlä addam wähewan

    4.1.9   Miscellanea

4.2   Annotated translation of AC Genesis 1.1-2.4

4.3   Geez texts of Genesis 1.1-2.4

4.4   Comparative study of selected exegetical motifs

4.   C R E A T I O N

4.1   SURVEY OF ETHIOPIAN MATERIAL RELATED TO THE
       CREATION THEME.

This is a survey of materials known in Ethiopia, and of their
antecedents in other literatures. The subject of creation has attracted very extensive comment, spread across a wide range of literary
genres; this survey therefore attempts only outline coverage, with
fuller detail in some areas which have received less attention and
study elsewhere.

4.1.1. Biblical, apocryphal, and pseudepigraphical texts
        relevant to Ethiopian interpretation of creation.

The most relevant texts, in addition to Genesis, are Psalms
(especially 18(19), 103(104), and 135(136)), parts of Job, parts of
Wisdom, Ecclesiasticus 42.15-44.33, 4 Ezra 6-7 (4-6 in Ethiopian
capitation), Jubilees (especially 2-3), Enoch, Eth.1 Maccabees 27
(a retelling of the six days of creation, containing quotations from
Gen.1), Eth. 3 Maccabees 2-5 (concerning Adam and his fall), and parts
of Ethiopic Qäleməntos (see 4.1.8 below).

4.1.2. Commentaries on Genesis.

Genesis is the subject of a greater range of Jewish and Christian commentaries than any other Biblical book. The concern of this
study is with commentaries proper in Geez and Amharic, and their background in Hebrew[1], Greek[2], Syriac[3], and Arabic[4] commentaries, and also

---

1. Bowker, The Targums, gives a convenient survey.

2. See Devreesse, 'Anciens commentateurs grecs de l'Octateuque', Revue
    biblique 44-5.

3. Principally Ephraim, Narsai, Isoʻdad, Moše bar Kepha, Dionysius bar
    Ṣalibi, bar Hebraeus, and the Mingana catena (A. Levene, The
    Early Syrian Fathers on Genesis); for further details see Baumstark.

4. Principally Ibn aṭ-Ṭaiyib (Graf II, 162), an anonymous catena (Graf II,

with hexaemeric literature (surveyed in 4.1.4 below).

(i)   'Tərgwame orit zäsähafä Yohannəs afä wärq',
Geez translation of Ibn aṭ-Ṭaiyib's commentary on Gen.-Dt.,
and part of Joshua, contained in MS B.N. d'Abbadie 28, f.2a-86b
(incipits and further details are given in 7.3 below). The translation is close to the original, contains many Arabic words, and in
places is somewhat rough and obscure. The divisions of the text in
Genesis correspond with those in Sanders' edition of IAṬ's commentary,
and the text itself generally agrees with Naples cod. arab. 60 rather
than Vatican cod. arab. 37; it commences at C.S.C.O. vol. 275,p.3
line 27. A fragment of the beginning of the commentary is found in
MS A.A. Nat. Lib. 438/111 (=EMML 7410) f.128b-129a (two successive folios are numbered 128).

(ii)   'Tərgwame orit', a Geez commentary on the Pentateuch,
contained in MS EMML 2101 f.63a-148b (see EMML Catalogue, vol.VI
pp.195-6). The translation of the colophon is problematic, but the
cataloguer is probably correct in understanding it to mean that the
work was composed by Məhərka dəngəl, disciple of the celebrated
Ɉnbaqom, about 1610 A.D. The basis of the work is the commentary of
IAṬ. The degree of verbal correspondence between EMML 2101 and d'Abb.
28 suggests that Məhərka dəngəl worked both from a Geez text of the
type of d'Abb.28 and from an Arabic text of IAṬ; further to this, he
added material from other sources. The editorial process may be
illustrated by a translation of the opening of the work, with the
passages from IAṬ underlined:

(EMML 2101 f.63a) 'In the name of God the merciful and forgiving, who is three in persons and one in godhead, to him be praise for
ever and ever, Amen. We write the interpretation of the Torah which

4.   284), ? Markus ibn al-Qanbar (Graf II, 329 and Biblica 23) on Genesis,
ʿAbdallāh ibn al-Faḍl's commentary on the Hexaemeron based on Basil
and Gregory of Nyssa (Graf II, 56), and translations into Arabic from
Hippolytus (I, 307), Basil (I, 321), Gregory of Nyssa (I, 332),
Severianus (I, 355), Cyril of Alexandria (I, 360), Jacob of Serug
(I, 446), Jacob of Edessa (I, 455), John Chrysostom (II, 53), and
Dionysius bar Ṣalibi (II, 264).

came down from God into the hand of Moses, the greatest of the
prophets, son of Amram, son of Kohath, son of Levi, son of Jacob,
son of Isaac, son of Abraham, May peace be upon him, and upon them.
The interpretation of the name of 'Torah' is law and judgement and
statute and commandment; if people explain it in each way, its interpretation will be found. This book was lost in the exile of Nebuchadnezzar, together with other books. But the book of Daniel and
Ezekiel and Jeremiah and Habakkuk and Nahum and Zechariah and Haggai
and Tobit and Esther and Judith and Sirach were not lost, because
they were after the exile, as time passed on. And the one who
restored them was Ezra the priest, who was 14th. from Aaron the priest
(in the line of priests) who were before the exile, by divine power.
This Torah has 112 sections; and some say 127. And the number of its
stichoi is 16325. Then these books came from the Hebrew language into
the Greek language in the 260th. year after Ezra the priest in the
days of Ptolemy the second, who is called Philadelphus, the interpretation of whose name is 'lover of brethren', who was third from
Alexander. Ptolemy was great in speech and wisdom. He caused them
to be translated by the hand of 70 elders of the Jews, discerning and
knowledgable. This movement into (another) language was by divine
work; it had a secret mystery which will happen (again) as time passes.
Then, further, after a short time, it came from the Greek language
into the Syriac language. The ordinances of the book of the Torah
are divided into prophecy and narrative and keeping of laws and prayers
and wisdom and teaching and praise of God and discipline and reproach.'

This corresponds to Sanders' edition of IAṬ, C.S.C.O. vol.275,
p.3 line 27–p.4 line 9, with the omission of a passage giving further
details about translations into Syriac, which is also omitted in the
Geez version of IAṬ in d'Abb.28.

Although the material which Məhərka dəngəl has added to IAṬ is
mostly of non-Ethiopian origin, the precise use he has made of it is
an original and identifiable Ethiopian contribution to exegesis, and
therefore the translation of his commentary should advance the study
of Ethiopian biblical interpretation[5].

5. I am hoping to prepare a translation of EMML 2101 f.63a–95b.

(iii)   Works entitled M̈amhǝr(ä orit) or M̈amhǝr(ä) täs'iləyä.
Works bearing this title (here abbreviated <u>MO</u>) form a commentary
corpus which extends through the Octateuch, and it is probable that
further commentaries on Samuel, Kings etc. which follow in some MSS
of the works, and are written in a similar style, should also be considered a part of the corpus.

The works are contained in the following MSS:
MS B.N. d'Abbadie 39 f.66a-154b (Gen. f.66a-89b; Ex. f.90a-93b, 102a-
109b; Lev. 110a-117b; Num. f.118a-128b; Dt. f.128b-134a; Josh.
f.134a-139b; Jdg. f.139b-154a; Rt. 154a-b complete except for a
colophon; this is followed by commentaries on Sam., Kgs., Song,
Solomon, Ecclus., Didascalia, Chron., Jub., Job, Isa., Ez., Ezra, Dan.,
Jer., Macc., Tob., Jud., Esther, and 'prophets').
MS B.N. d'Abbadie 156 f.4a-19a (Gen. f.4a-9a; Ex. f.9a-12b; Lev.
f.12b-13b; Num. f.13b-15a; Dt. f.15a-16a; Josh. f.16a-18a; Jdg.
f.18a-19a; Rt. f.19a).
MS B.N. d'Abbadie 157 f.1a-50b (Gen. f.1a-12b; Ex. f.13b-24a, 36a-b;
Lev. f.36b-39b; Num. f.39b-43a; Dt. f.43a-45b; Josh. f.45b-47a;
Jdg. f.47a-50b; Rt. f.50b; this is followed by commentaries on Sam.,
Kgs., Chron., Dan., the minor prophets, and Isa.).
MS B.N. d'Abbadie 195 f.5a-15b (Gen. f.5a-13a; Ex. incomplete f.13a-
15b).
MS B.N. d'Abbadie 247 f.20a-22b (fragment on Gen. only).
MS B.N. Zotenberg 150 f.1-13 (Gen. and Ex. only).
Incipits are given in section 7.3 below.

Of the MSS listed above, only d'Abb. 39 gives the name of a
compiler; the incipit reads, 'In the name of God, the forgiving and
merciful, I commence the writing of the book which is called "Teacher
of the Torah" (M̈amhǝrä orit), which I, Isaac the monk (Yǝsḥaq m̈anäkos),
compiled, having enquired from the scholars of the books; as for the
profit of this, it teaches and it interprets words of the Torah ...'.
This Isaac does not appear to be the Felasha scholar-monk mentioned by
d'Abbadie[6], as the contents of the work are not of distinctively

6. A.Z. Aešcoly, 'Notices sur les Falacha', <u>Cahiers d'etudes africaines</u>,
vol. 2, 1961, pp.84-147; see pp.100-1.

Felasha provenance, and include a few Christological interpretations[7]; this does not preclude Felasha interest in the MO, and MS d'Abb. 157 has certainly passed through Felasha hands.

The text of MO, as represented by the MSS listed, is extremely variable, and consists of a common core to which various teachers have added citations from other works and miscellaneous textual notes. None of the extant texts is self-evidently the base on which other texts have been reworked.

The contents of MO consist of passages of commentary and 'questions and answers' in Geez, and 'explanations of difficult words' in Geez and Amharic. Many of the interpretations go back to Syriac and Arabic[8] commentaries, though some of the notes are so brief that a judgement cannot be made on the extent of their implications; on Gen. 1.2, for example, '"Spirit" means "wind"' may be intended simpliciter, or it may be siding with Ephraim against Basil. It is probable that the framework of MO is an adaptation from Arabic, but the Amharic explanations are doubtless indigenous Ethiopian work (as they contain old Amharic forms, and these vary between the MSS, the MO is a potentially valuable source for the study of local variation in early Amharic). All the texts of MO contain textual notes on comparisons between Geez, 'Arabic', and 'Hebrew' texts; these are most numerous in d'Abb. 156[9]. An edition of the MO would be a valuable tool in the study both of commentary traditions and of early Amharic. As it appears that the only known MSS of it are all in the Bibliothèque

7. The dating of the MS does not help to solve this problem, as the note in d'Abb. 39 f.155a on which Chaîne bases his dating of it in 1788 E.C. is a historical memorandum (which may have been recopied), and not a record of the date of copying.

8. There are points of contact with the catena on Genesis in P. de Lagarde, Materialien zur Kritik und Geschichte des Pentateuchs, vol.II, Leipzig, 1867.

9. See section 3.3 above.

Nationale, Paris, it may be that d'Abbadie and his Ethiopian acquaintances had a special interest in the work.

(iv) AC Genesis. Text and translation of AC Gen. 1.1-2.4 are given in section 4.2 below.

(v) Miscellanea and fragments:

(a) MS B.L. Orient 503 f.1a-4b contains comment on Gen.1-11, principally on creation; it is entitled targwame sǝnä̈ fǝträ̈tat, and its affinities are with the Ethiopic hexaemeric literature, and, to a lesser extent, with <u>MO</u>. MS JE 754 E f.1a-6a, headed targwame orit, contains excerpts from a text of the type of B.L. Or.503 f.1a-4b.

(b) MS B.L. Orient 484 f.188b contains a Geez memorandum resembling the AC introduction to Gen.

(c) A work entitled <u>orit zä̈fǝträ̈t zä̈tä̈rgwä̈ma yohannas afä̈ wä̈rq</u> is contained in EMML 7122 f.108a-109a and Bodleian MS Ind. Inst. Misc. 3 (not 4, as printed in Ullendorff's <u>Catalogue</u>, where the MS is no.85) f.51b-53a; this is a homily on the incarnation based on the story of Abraham, and not as the title suggests, a commentary on Genesis by John Chrysostom.

(d) Fragments contained in <u>Mä̈shafä̈ hawi</u> from 'John Chrysostom on the hexaemeron' (e.g. B.L. Or. 776 f.192a, 253a) and 'Theodoret on the Torah' (e.g. B.L. Or.776 f.115b, 167a, 260a).

4.1.3 <u>'Question and answer books'</u>.

Books of 'Questions and Answers' are a familiar genre of Greek[10], Syriac[11], and Arabic[12] Christian literature; their method has pre-

10. See G.Bardy in <u>RB</u> vols. 41 and 42.

11. See E.G. Clarke, <u>The Selected Questions of Isho bar Nun</u>, pp.7-13.

12. See S.H. Griffith in <u>OCP</u> 47, especially pp.170-1.

Christian antecedents, and possible links with Muslim apologetics (the
ʿilm al-kalām). MS EMML 1839 f.1a-48b contains an Ethiopic version
of a part of an important work of this type, the compilation of Ibn
aṭ-Ṭaiyib as contained e.g. in MS Vat. arab. 36. The opening of the
text reads, 'First section, of Yoḥannəs afä wärq, which the honoured
priest <u>Abba</u> Fəssəḥa Gäbrä əgzi'abəher wäld sännay collected .... And
this book recalls many profound questions, words and explanations,
from the book of the Torah, and prophets and kings, and from Job the
righteous, and from the book of Solomon the wise, and the explanation
of the psalms of David, and the gospel, and from the epistles of Paul,
and from the apostle, and from the book of the Acts of the apostles,
and concerning alms-giving, which is more than fasting and prayer ...'.[13]

The colophon on EMML 1839 f.48b reads 'The holy book is completed, which is called "Questions of the Torah" (<u>hatäta orit</u>), which
Yoḥannəs afä wärq, archbishop of Constantinople interpreted .... May
his blessing ... be with his beloved Ləbsä krəstos, enemy of the faith
of Urubanon and Afonsu, offspring of Leo, devouring wolves...'. The
colophon to the whole work, on f.382a, identifies Ləbsä krəstos as a
Jacobite. If the 'wolves' are Urban VIII and Alphonse Mendez, Ləbsä
krəstos lived at the time of Emperor Susənyos (1607-1632 A.D.).

The work consists of continuous questions and answers, and the
following divisions can be distinguished:

1. f.1a-6a: material commencing, 'For what reason did God create
darkness before light?', and ending 'How is it said that Phinehas son
of Eleazar son of Aaron ministered before God in those days (Judges 20.
28) when the time between him and Aaron was long?' The source of this
section is clearly Išoʿ bar Nun's <u>Book of Questions</u>, as in MS Cambridge
Add. 2017 f.1a-29a, but with questions 7, 10-11, 19, 30-1 and 34-5
omitted; IAṬ has edited some of the answers, but not, apparently,

---

13. Text given in EMML <u>Catalogue</u>, vol.V, pp.342-3. 'Yoḥannəs' is John
Chrysostom, and '<u>Abba</u> Fəssəḥa' is Abu'l faraj Abd'allāh ibn aṭ-Ṭaiyib.
Cf. Sanders, <u>C.S.C.O.</u> vol.275, pp.2-3.

with the intention of harmonising them with answers on similar topics
which recur later in the work.

2. f.6a–8b: material commencing, 'What is the reason that God
created the world while he is rich ...?', and ending 'Why was Eve
not startled by the serpent?'

3. f.8b–19a: material commencing, 'Why did Moses recall the creation
of heaven and earth?', and ending, 'What is the interpretation of the
word of the most high God which says, "No man sees me and lives"?'

4. f.19a–22b: material commencing with comment on the 'spirit' of
Gen.1.2, and ending, 'Why does the law of Moses command circumcision
on the eighth day?'

5. f.22b–39b: material beginning with creation and continuing with
questions on Gen.-Lev., Num., Josh., Jdg., Sam. and Ruth. The order
of the material, and most of its content, corresponds closely with
Theodore bar Koni's <u>Book of Scholia</u>, <u>Mimrā</u> I–III.[14] If it is supposed
that IAṬ had a copy of THBK, then the editorial processes were as
follows: (a) some sections were omitted, and some shortened, with a
tendency not to omit material which is also found in Išoʿdad, (b) some
questions were omitted, but their answers retained, (c) much philosophical and chronological material was omitted, and also many
'explanations of difficult words'.

14. The approximate correspondence is as follows, using the numbering of
Hespel and Draguet's edition of THBK: (f.22b) I.25, 46; (f.23a–b)
I.52–3, 55–6, 60,66,69,70,75–9; (f.24) I.80–6,93,95,97,99,100,103–4;
(f.25) I.107–9, II.1, 27, 37–43; (f.26) II.44, 50–2, 55, 57–8, 69,
71–3, 75–9; (f.27) II.80–90; (f.28) II.91–2 plus a section on Saturday and Sunday, 93–100; (f.29) II.102–109, 111 (fragment only), 112;
(f.30) II.113, 114, 119, 121, 124–6, 131; (f.31) 133–4, 137–9, III.
1–4; (f.32) III.5–11; (f.33) III.12–17; (f.34) III.19–20, 22–30;
(f.35) III.31–9; (f.36) III.40–5, 49–53; (f.37) III.54, 55 (items
105 and 136 and conclusion only), 56–63, 65; (f.38) III.66–71, 73–4,
72, 75–7; (f.39) III.78–9, 80 (beginning and ending only), 81 (items
3, 4, 7, 14 only), 82, V.20, III.92, III.55 (items 1–2, 5–17, 19–24,
26–32, 48–9, 57–8, 61–7, 99–100, 102, 105, 104 only).

6. f.39b–42a: material beginning, 'What is the word of David the prophet, which says concerning the prophets, to Saul, "Let not the heart of man fall upon him"?', and ending, 'By which path, and which direction, did Jonah come to the city of Nineveh?' The source is again Išoˁ bar Nun's Questions, as in MS Camb. Add. 2017 f.30a–39b.

7. f.42a–43b: material beginning, 'What is the reason that God brought reproach upon Eli by the tongue of Samuel?', and ending with the reason that God gives to each person a guardian angel.

8. f.43b–48b: material beginning with the reason why the Philistines took the ark, and ending with the story of Judith and a fragment on Pss. It shows substantial correspondence with THBK Mimrā III and V,[15] and editorial processes as in 5 above, though with even more shortening of some answers.

Further investigation properly belongs to Christian Arabic studies. However, it appears that (a) sections 2–4 and 7 may preserve material from lost Syriac question and answer books, (b) sections 5 and 8 may shed light on the question of recensions of THBK's Book of Scholia,[16] and on the question of the relationship between Išoˁdad, Išo bar Nun, THBK, MS (olim) Diyarbekr 22 (van Rompay), and MS Mingana 553 (Levene), and (c) sections 1 and 6 may reveal IAT's editorial Tendenz with respect to Išoˁ bar Nun. For example, on the 'spirit' of Gen.1.2, Išoˁ bar Nun's question 7 has been omitted from section 1 (it would occur on EMML 1839 f.1b–2a). In section 4 (f.19a) we find, 'The "spirit which was hovering over the water" he does not say concerning the Holy Spirit, but concerning the wind, according to the word of David the prophet which says, "The winds blow and the waters flow"' (Ps.147.8, cited by Išoˁ dad on Gen.1.2, and in Mingana 553). In section 5 (f.23b) it says, 'As for the spirit of which he

15. (f.43b) III.83,85; (f.44) III.87, 90–6; (f.45) III.98–103, 112, 104–6; (f.46) III.107–9, 111, 113–4, 116; (f.47) V.1–3, 23–25; (f.48) V.26–7 plus comment on Pss, V.22 plus fragment on Pss.

16. See L. Brade, Untersuchungen zum Scholienbuch des Theodoros bar Konai, pp.26–28, and R. Hespel and R. Draguet, C.S.C.O. vol.431, pp.14–18.

reminded them that it was hovering over the water, Basil says, 'It is the Holy Spirit', but Ta'odros says, 'It is the wind'. But the wind was not known. But the intention of the prophet is to speak concerning the creations, and not concerning the persons' (which is an unhelpfully abbreviated version of THBK Mimrā I.70).[17]

4.1.4 Hexaemeric literature.

F.E. Robbins defines 'Hexaemeron' as 'the title of certain treatises and series of sermons written by the Fathers of the Christian church commenting on the story of the creation of the world as told in Genesis, sometimes a simple exegesis and sometimes an allegorical version of the scriptural story'[18]. He demonstrates the influence of Greek philosophy (Plato, especially the Timaeus, and Aristotle, e.g. the De generatione et corruptione), and of Philo and other Jewish writings on the Greek and Latin hexaemera, and surveys the development of the form from Basil to his imitators, through works of a "less scientific nature" (Theodore of Mopsuestia, Diodore of Tarsus), or "more edifying and allegorical" (John Chrysostom, Anastasius Sinaita), to the "mere compilations" of the Byzantine chroniclers (Syncellus).

The hexameron did, however, take on a new life as, having been developed in Greek[19], it was taken up by Syriac writers[20], then by

17. Cf. van den Eynde, C.S.C.O. vol.156, p.19 lines 7,11-12, 22-3, p.20 lines 1-2; Sanders, C.S.C.O. vol.275, p.6 line 29-p.7 line 7; Clarke, Selected Questions, pp.23,75-83; Levene, Early Syrian Fathers, pp.72, 130; van Rompay, OLP 8.

18. The Hexaemeral Literature, p.1.

19. Principally (Ps).-Eustathius (PG 18, cols.707-94), Basil (PG 29, cols. 3-208; 30, cols.869-968), Gregory of Nyssa (PG 44, cols.61-256), Severianus of Gabala (PG 56, cols.429-500), Anastasius Sinaita (PG 89, cols.851-1078).

20. Notably Jacob of Edessa (ed. I.-B. Chabot), Mošе bar Kepha (ed. L. Schlimme), Emmanuel bar Šaḥḥare (Baumstark pp.238-9), and the 'second base' of Bar Hebraeus' Lamp of the Sanctuary (ed.J.Bakoš), which draws

Arabic writers[21], who in turn were adapted into Ethiopic[22] and
Amharic[23]. Despite the adaptations which have taken place in these
successive stages, comparison of Basil's In Hexaemeron with AC Gen.1
(translated in 4.2 below), as representatives of the ends of the range
of material, shows many shared features: 'By naming (heaven and earth)
he suggests the substance of the whole world' (Hex.I.7 and II.3; cf.
AC Gen.1.1); 'fire leaps out from stones' (Hex.I.7; cf. AC Gen.1.12);
the creation of darkness (Hex.II.5; cf. AC Gen.1.4); the spirit of
God (Hex.II.6; cf. AC Gen.1.2); provision of food for man (Hex.V.1
and 5; cf. AC Gen.1.12); non-seed-bearing plants (Hex.V.2; cf. AC
Gen.1.29); the illustrative use of the phases of the moon (Hex.VI.10;
cf. AC Gen.1.18); the nature of plant and animal life, and their production from elements which lack this life (Hex.VII.1 and VIII.1; cf. AC Gen.1.
20 and 22). More significant than selected parallels is the fact that
the topics with which Basil is concerned overlap about 70% with the
concerns and interests of AC Gen.1. By contrast, the parallels between AC Gen.1 and Gregory of Nyssa's De opificio hominis are rather
slight: 'Why man appeared last' (op.hom. II; cf. AC Gen.1.27);   the

20. on Moše bar Kepha; also translations of Basil (Baumstark p.78) and
    Gregory of Nyssa (Baumstark p.79).

21. Principally ʿAbdallāh ibn al-Faḍl (Graf.II, p.56), freely based on
    Basil and Gregory of Nyssa , and the Arabic Hexaemeron of Pseudo-
    Epiphanius of which the Ethiopic version has been edited by Trumpp
    (Graf I, pp.201-3); also fragments of Jacob of Edessa in the catena
    on Genesis edited by de Lagarde (Graf I, p.455), and, if it exists,
    the Arabic original of the Təntä haymanot mentioned below.

22. Principally the various Geez works called sənä fəträt, surveyed
    below; also the Geez version (edited by Trumpp) of the Arabic
    Hexaemeron of Ps.-Epiphanius, and the Geez Təntä haymanot, described
    below, probably a translation from Arabic.

23. The various Amharic works called sənä fəträt, surveyed below.

attack on the Anomoeans (op.hom.VI.3; cf.AC Gen.1.26-7); the upright
stance and sovereignty of man (op.hom.VII-VIII; cf.AC Gen.1.27-8); the
'vegetative soul', 'management according to sense', and 'rational
nature' (op.hom. VIII.4-5; cf. AC Gen.1.12, 26-7).

The Ethiopic work actually entitled Aksimaros is the text
published by E. Trumpp[24] from MS B.L. Orient 751 f.90a-105a, and
attributed to Epiphanius. This occasionally echoes Basil – e.g. the
darfilat and färäsä bahr of the 5th. day (Trumpp p.203) are reminiscent of Basil's delphines and hoi potamioi hippoi (Hex.VII.1 – the
dolphins are also found as far afield as Midras haggadol on Gen.,
p.52 and Book VII of Milton's Paradise Lost[25]). In general, however,
in vocabulary (e.g. in using anasər for the 'elements', instead of
täbayät), and in content (e.g. a nine-fold ouranology), this 'Aksimaros'
appears to stand outside the main line of tradition that has been
formative of the sənä fəträt and of AC Gen.1, and this is confirmed
by the fact that the quotations attributed to 'Aksimaros' in the
various works entitled sənä fəträt are not from Trumpp's text, but
are mostly, if not all, from another work, probably also translated
from Arabic, entitled Təntä haymanot.

The Təntä haymanot (TH) has been partially investigated by
A. Haffner[30], who notes some of the MSS and divides them according to
their textual resemblance into two groups, (i) B.L. Or. 818, B.N. Zot.
146, B.N. d'Abb. 67, and (ii) B.L. Or. 753, B.N. d'Abb.125. The work
is also found in Berlin (Dillmann 31) Ms.or.oct. 237 f.67-108a,
Tanasee (Hammerschmidt) 35 and Jerusalem Ethiopic 699 E; it is well
described in Zotenberg's B.N. Catalogue pp.246-7. Guidi's reference
to the '"Aksimaros" in 116 sections'[31] is doubtless to MS B.L.Or.753

24. Das Hexaemeron des Pseudo-Epiphanius. See also Graf I pp.201-3; A.
Haffner in Oriens Christianus N.S. 10/11; S.Grébaut 'Les manuscrits
éthiopiens de M.É. Delorme', ROC vols.19-21.

25. See also Ginzberg, Legends, V, pp.53-4.

30. Vienna Oriental Journal, 1912.

31. Storia della letteratura etiopica, p.69.

f.68a–83a, but this MS in fact has sections numbered 1–59 followed
by sections numbered 30–116, and some other MSS of the work lack the
section numbers, which are probably secondary. The work is a detailed
hexaemeron, concluding with brief material on Cain and Abel, and the
patriarchal genealogy as far as Isaac; it is a major source of the
Geʿez and Amharic works entitled sǝnä̈ fǝträt.

   To avoid confusion, it should be noted that the passages on
the fall of Satan found in (a) B.L. Or. 751 f.98a–101b (and printed
in Trumpp, Das Hexaëmeron, pp.194–203), (b) TH, in the narrative of
the fourth day of creation, and (c) in Wien Cod. aeth. (Muller) 19
f.56a–57b (and printed in Haffner, 'Eine äthiopische Handschrift')
are all verbally different; it is the material of (c) that has been
taken up e.g. in AC Rev.12.17 and AC Mäqdǝmä̈ wängel pp.15–16, probably via the sǝnä̈ fǝträt as an intermediate source.

   The Geʿez and Amharic works entitled sǝnä̈ fǝträt, and the
other Geʿez and Amharic works resembling them but not so entitled,
are very varied in length and in detail. It should not be assumed
that the Amharic works are necessarily a later development from the
Geʿez ones. MSS of Amharic sǝnä̈ fǝträt texts (SFA) are far more
numerous than of the Geʿez texts (SFG); the SFG appears generally to
correspond with one type of SFA, rather than with the other types;
and MSS of the SFA of moderate antiquity are not lacking (and are of
value for the study of old Amharic, e.g. Cambridge Or. 1798, B.L.
Add. 16222, Add. 24183). This suggests that the SFA was well established as a genre of old Amharic tract, and that the SFG developed
either partially in parallel with it, or even by derivation or imit-
ation from it.

   The principal areas of variability which may be used to describe the sǝnä̈ fǝträt are:

(a) Title. Sǝnä̈ fǝträt (e.g. EMML 23), tǝrgwame sǝnä̈ fǝträtat (e.g.
Berlin (Dillmann) 37, tǝrgwame zäyǝqäddǝm ǝmäshafä̈ orit (e.g. EMML
7122 f.3a) and other similar titles are found.

(b) Language. The works are in Geʿez, or in Amharic (and the library
at Däbrä gännät, Jerusalem, has one in Tigrinya, formerly the property
of an Abba Sinoda), with quotations in Geʿez; many of the texts con-

tain isolated Arabic words.

(c) The named sources. The fuller texts commonly name a profusion of sources, generally similar to those listed below from the printed SFA, and those listed in TIA p.293 from the SFG in MS Cowley 40; MSS Tel Aviv Faitlovitch 31 and 32 are especially rich in named sources; MS Cambridge Or. 1884 is unusual in citing a source täräfä wängel (which I have not identified).

(d) The nature of the work as primarily a hexaemeron, or primarily a commentary on the early chapters of Genesis. The inclusion of the latter as 'hexaemera' is less inconsistent than it appears, since the works form a spectrum, of which only the extremities are clearly distinguishable; MS B.L. Or. (Strelcyn) 8818 f.26a–38a, for example, is more strictly a hexaemeron, while Bodleian Ind. Inst. Misc. 3 f. 76a–122b is like a commentary, and more closely resembles AC Gen.1.

(e) The balance of exegetical and homiletic material. The shorter texts are generally principally exegetical; some fuller ones include extensive homiletic and allegorical material (e.g. Tel Aviv Faitlovitch 31).

Of these, it is principally (d), and to a lesser extent (e), rather than (a)–(c), which seem to point to the real, rather than the superficial, sub-divisions within the genre.

A fairly full text of the SFA has been published by Liqä mäzämmäran Mogäs ᵓquä giyorgis,[32] shorter versions are contained in various catechetical works,[33] and further MSS are listed in 7.4 below. The named sources of Mogäs' text are: the Bible (including apocrypha), 4 Ezra, Jubilees, Enoch, Eth. 3 Maccabees, Eth. Qälemäntos, Sinodos, Mäshafä kidan, Aksimaros, Mäqdämä wängel, John Chrysostom, Liturgy (Qäddase of 300, of John, of Mary, and təmhärtä həbuᶜat), the 'books

32. Mäshafä sənä fəträt məslä 5-tu aᵊmadä məstir, Asmara, 1955 E.C. pp.9–95.

33. E.g. Mäsärätä təmhərt, Täsfa P.P., A.A., 1949 E.C. pp.12–18.

of the monks' (Mar Yəshaq, Filkəsəyus, Arägawi mänfäsawi), Rətu'a
haymanot, Dərsanä mika'el, Dəggwa, and Anqäsä bərhan; the 'Aksimaros'
quotations are, as noted above, from the Təntä haymanot.

Further classification of the sənä fətrat is hindered by
the fact that MS cataloguers have rarely given incipits, apparently
assuming either that the works were all the same or that their variability precluded classification. For the SFA, the incipits that I
have found most frequent and characteristic are the following:

(a) SFA 1: እግዚአብሔር ፡ እምቀዳሞ ፡ ዓለም ፡ ነገፍነት ፡
በሶስትነት ፡ ነበረ ፡ እንፈነተን ፡ ኦስትነቱ ፡ ሳይዘከፍለው ፡
ሶስትነትንም ፡ እንፈነቱ ፡ ሳይመቀሉለው ፡ ከዚህም ፡
በኋላ ፡ ዓለምን ፡ ፈጠረ ፡

(or ዓለምን ፡ ፍፈጠር ፡ ሳኸው ፡ እሰበ ፡ እስዮም ፡ እልቀረ ፡   ),
found variably in B.L. Add. 24183, B.L. Or. (Strelcyn) 8818, Vat.
eth. 120, 123, 157, JE 698 E, JE 707E, Tel Aviv Faitlovitch 32 f.
77b–111b, and in Mogäs' printed text.

(b) SFA 2: (introduction in Geez followed by) ከዚያ ፡ በኋላ ፡
ዓለም ፡ ፍፈጠር ፡ ሳኸው ፡ ሪያስብ ፡ በወጋጌት ፡ በፃያ ፡
Hመኝ ፡ ቀን ፡ አያንት ፡ ፍንረት ፡ ፈጠረ ፡   ,
variably in B.L. Add. (Dillmann) 16222, Cambridge Or. 1798 f.78a–,
EMML 2169, and JE 708 E.

(c) SFA 3: እራት ፡ Hልፈት ፡ ማለት ፡ ዜና ፡ Hፍንረት ፡ --
መኑ ፡ ይወልፉ ፡ ስህዝንባበ ፡ ነኅበ ፡ መል ፡ እንዳስ ፡ እዮብ ፡ ,
variably in Cambridge Or. 1884 and Bodleian Ind. Inst. Misc. 3,
f.76a–122b.

Of these, SFA 3 is most like AC Gen. 1, and SFA 1 is most
like the SFG as represented by MS Cowley 40 (further MSS are listed
in 7.3 below, but it should not be assumed that they are all substantially the same). The incipit of this SFG is በስሞ ፡
እብ ፡ __ ንጽሐፍ ፡ __ መጽሐፈ ፡ ሥነ ፡ ፍንረት ፡ ፡ ህኋ ፡
እግዚአብሔር ፡ እምቀዳሞ ፡ ዓለም ፡ በትሥልስት ፡ ወተዋህፉት ፡
እንH ፡ ኢይከፍሎ ፡ ትስልስቱ ፡ ለተዋህፉት ፡ ወእንH ፡
ኢያስተጋብእ ፡ ተዋህፉት ፡ ለትሥልስት ፡ --- ወሁለP ፡
ፈነፈ ፡ ፈጦሮተ ፡ ዓለም ፡

While the dependence of the sənà fəträt on the Bible, Eth. Qàleməntos, and TH is clear, the transmission of its Aristotelian and neo-Platonic component is less clear. For example, in the SFG Porphyry is cited as holding that a blending of two or more of the four elements is necessary for the making of substances (f.15a), and täbiban ('wise ones', i.e. philosophers) are quoted as attributing the origin of cloud to the combination of wet vapour from the water and dry vapour from the earth (f.40a- an opinion reminiscent of that cited by Isoʿdad on Gen.1.13 from Aristotle). Such material may have passed via Isoʿdad and other Syriac commentators to Ibn aṭ-Ṭaiyib, but, additionally or alternatively, it may have been transmitted (a) via philosophical rather than exegetical writings - for example, from Yaḥya ibn ʿAdi to Ibn al-Ḥammār to Ibn aṭ-Ṭaiyib, who wrote a commentary on Porphyry's Isagoge,[34] or (b) via compilations of legendary material, and thence to TH.

In conclusion, it should be noted that the following works are not hexaemera:

(a) three tracts in Bodleian MS Aeth. g. 9 (Ullendorff 84), which are about prayer and Christian discipline,

(b) Cambridge Or. 1876, which approximates to the computus genre, and

(c) B.L. Or. 814 f.2-4, of which f.4 and 2, and f.3 are two discontinuous extracts from Eth. Qàleməntos book 1, ch.2.

4.1.5   The Book of the Mysteries of Heaven and Earth.

This Geez work (Mäshafä məstirä sämay wämədr, here abbreviated BMHE) includes substantial comment on the work of creation. The text which has been edited[35] is that of MS B.N. Zotenberg 117,

34. S.M. Stern, 'Ibn al-Ṭaiyib's Commentary on the Isagoge'; also Graf II pp.156-7, 233-249, and bibliography under Endress, and Platti.

35. Ed. and trans. by J. Perruchon and I. Guidi, completed by S. Grébaut; trans. by E.A. Wallis Budge.

but MS EMML 2161 contains another text of it, of which Getatchew
Haile (EMML Catalogue vol.VI pp.266-70) notes that it has more than
the edited texts and contains evidence that indicates that its
author may not have been Abbā Baḥāyla Mikāʾēl, as is usually assumed,
but his disciple (lit. "son") Yesḥaq.ᵗ Some of the excess of EMML
2161 over Zot. 117 is also to be found in EMML 2229 f.167a-174b,
which forms a brief hexaemeron.

Some apparently related material is contained in the Zena
nägäromu läsəllase contained in MS Conti Rossini (Strelcyn) 62 f.71a-
82b, and EMML 1882 f.3a-12a, of which Getatchew (EMML Catalogue,
vol.V p.392) notes, ᵗThe composition is influenced more by the
Mestira Samāy wa-Medr of Abbā Baḥayla Mikāʾēl than by the Sena fet-
rat.ᵗ

In general, while many of the topics covered in BMHE – the
names of the heavens, the names and disposition of the tribes of
angels, the names of the languages of the world – are also mentioned
in Ethiopian commentaries, the details are different, though in
some cases overlapping. The author of BMHE has incorporated con-
flicting sources,[36] and usually simply conflates them. Some material has been taken from BMHE into the AC – e.g. a list of the
rulers of the churches in Rev.2-3 (see TIA p.196), but in most
instances the relationship, if it exists at all, is complex and
indirect, as the following example of the names given for the prophet
Zephaniahᵗs parents shows:

Source	Zephaniahᵗs father	Zephaniahᵗs mother
AC Zeph.introd. MS Cowley 18 p.175	Kus, son of Godolya	Nəhəba
BMHE (P.O. vol. VI p.399)	Sedeq or Gotonyal	Meroba or Nəhəb
Ethiopic Lives of the Prophets, MS EMML 7410 f.23a	Kwəs	Merob
Ethiopic Sənkəssar, Hamle 4	Kus	–
Greek Lives of the Prophets, Epiphanius recensio altera (Schermann p.58)	Chousē	–
MS B.L. Add.24990, marginal notes	Ayaqidäqi	Nəhəba

36. E.g. the association of jewels with the tribes of Israel in P.O.
I p.66 and VI pp.447-9.

It seems that <u>BMHE</u> is the creation of an individual of independent mind who has utilized many sources, including some which are unique to him[37] (and which I have not been able to identify); the work will repay further study, but such study is likely only to be peripherally relevant to the mainstream of Ethiopian commentary tradition.

4.1.6. <u>Homilies and miracles</u>.

Ethiopic literature includes both indigenous homilies and translations; not infrequently there is doubt about the genuineness of their attributed authorship. The interests of the homilies, including those on creation, are generally those of adding detail to, and systematising, the Biblical narratives, and of making moral and doctrinal applications. In several works arranged for reading on monthly festivals, homilies and miracles are both included in the lections; in such works the material relating to creation is commonly found appointed for the months <u>Tarr</u>, <u>Yakkatit</u>, <u>Maggabit</u> and <u>Miyazya</u>, possibly reflecting the Ethiopian reckoning that the world was created in <u>Maggabit</u>, or the practice in some branches of the Christian church of expounding the hexaemeron during Lent.

(i)   Severianus of Gabala's homily <u>Peri pisteōs</u> (<u>De fide</u>, <u>PG</u> 60 cols.767-72), in Geez translation,[38] forms a part of the Ethiopic <u>Qerallos</u> corpus. It has contributed to the reservoir of proof-texts of the AC, and is cited e.g. in AC Gen.1.26 and AC Heb. 1.8. Part of the homily concerns creation.

(ii)   The <u>Kitab al-Idah</u> of Severus ibn al-Muqaffaʿ has been translated into Geez, under the titles <u>Mashafa sawiros</u>, <u>Mashafa hadar</u>, and <u>Kabra haymanot</u>. The second of its homilies contains material on creation.[39]

---

37. See e.g. S.Strelcyn, 'Une tradition éthiopienne d'origine juive yéménite', pp.69-70. Further on the author see catalogue notes on MS EMML 3012.

38. Printed in A.Dillmann, <u>Chrestomathia Aethiopica</u>, pp.77-88, and B. Weischer, <u>Qerellos IV.3</u>.

39. See Graf II, pp.309-11, and catalogue notes on EMML 2145; for the text of the second homily, I used MS B.L. Or. 773 f.15b-43b.

(iii) The Zena nägäromu läsəllase, mentioned in 4.1.5 above,
appointed for reading in Mäggabit in EMML 2846 f.16b-25b.

(iv) Part of Dərsanä ura'el, e.g. EMML 1942 f.34b-37a, appointed
for Mäggabit, which is about the creation of the angels; the cataloguer notes that it is similar to sənä fəträt texts.

(v) Dərsanä mika'el[40] contains (a) a passage about the angels
in the section for the month Tərr, and (b) a passage on creation
in the section for Miyazya.

(vi) Dərsanä gäbrə'el[41] contains (a) in the section for the month
Tahsas a short passage about Adam, (b) in the section for Tərr a
passage from 'alätəqarfu' (i.e. the 'Miracles of Jesus'[42]) concerning the fall of Satan, and (c) in the section for Yäkkatit a section
from 'Aksimaros' (excerpted from the account of the creations of
the sixth day in Təntä haymanot).

(vii) The work Tä'ammərihomu lä'ab wäwäld wämänfäs qəddus, 'The
miracles of the Father and the Son and the Holy Spirit', collected
by Abunä Bəṣu'a amlak, found, apparently uniquely, in MS Berlin
(Hammerschmidt and Six 113) orient. quart. 993, and well described
in the catalogue description, contains a retelling of some of the
narratives in the Pentateuch; a substantial part of the work concerns Gen.1-4.

40. The work is described in the catalogue notes on EMML 1133 and 2865,
and Berlin (Hammerschmidt and Six) 86, and was published in Geez
and Amharic edited by Aläqa Ayyalew Tamməru, A.A., 1969 E.C.

41. The work is described in the catalogue notes on EMML 1311, and was
published in Geez and Amharic by Nəburä əd Mäkwəriya Abəyye hoy,
A.A., 1969 E.C.

42. This work, Tä'ammərä iyyäsus, is described in the catalogue notes
on EMML 2050 and Berlin (Hammerschmidt and Six) 155, and the greater
part of it was published by S. Grébaut.

4.1.7 Chronographic works.

After the beginnings of chronography as an independent discipline in Alexandria in the third century B.C.,[43] chronographic works were produced by later writers in Hebrew[44], Greek[45], Syriac[46] and Arabic[47]; many of these comment on the date and manner of creation, and some of them – notably Agapius, Eutychius, the Chronicon orientale, and Al-Makīn Jirjis – lie within the band of tradition that has continued into Ethiopian commentaries. The main chronographic works known in Ethiopic are (a) the Chronicle of John of Nikiu, probably originally written in Greek, and known in Ethiopia as Yohannəs mädäbbär,[48] (b) the work known in Ethiopia as Abušakər,

43. See B.Z. Wacholder, 'Biblical Chronology in the Hellenistic World Chronicles'.

44. E.g. the Seder ʿolam (ed. B. Ratner).

45. Notably Hippolytus (Altaner p.166), Julius Africanus (Altaner 209-10), Eusebius (Altaner p.218), further authors mentioned in Altaner pp.229-235 (including John of Nikiu), and later Byzantine chroniclers such as Syncellus.

46. Notably Semʿōn Barqayā (based on Eusebius, Baumstark pp.135-6), Jacob of Edessa (Baumstark p.254), Eliyā bar Sīnayā (Baumstark pp. 287-8), Michael the Great (Baumstark pp.299-300), Bar Hebraeus (trans. E.A. Wallis Budge; Baumstark pp.318-9).

47. Notably Eutychius/Saʿīd ibn Biṭrīq (PG 111 cols. 907-1156, and M. Breydy) and Yahyā ibn Saʿīd (Graf II pp.32-5, 49-51), Agapius/Mahbub (II pp.39-41 and A. Vasiliev), Chronicle of Seʿert (II pp.195-6), Severus ibn Muqaffaʿ (II pp.300-6), Al-Makīn Jirjis the elder (II pp.348-51), Chronicon orientale and Abuʾl-Faḫr al Mutanaṣṣir (II pp.434-6), Abu-l Barakāt (II pp.439-41); also translations of Elias of Nisibis (i.e. Eliyā b. Sīnayā, II pp.188-9), Michael the Great (II p.267), and Bar Hebraeus (II pp.274-5).

48. See Graf I pp.470-2; edition of H. Zotenberg; translation of R.H. Charles; TIA p.44.

and (c) the Ethiopic version, known as Giyorgis wäldä Amid, of the Arabic chronography of Al-Makin Jirgis the elder. In addition to these, there are varied chronological[49] and calendrical[50] works which will not be further considered here.

The Ethiopic work commonly referred to as Abušakər[51], and contained e.g. in MSS B.L. Add. 16252, Or. 809-813, is a compilation of two major parts. MSS commence with a numbered list of about 59 section titles. This list is followed by:

(a) the text of chs. 1-46, and 48 (numbered 47),

(b) a series of short numbered sections, running from '1. Adam' (though the first few sections frequently lack numbers) to '166. Heraclius'; this series commences after ወሰመይ ፡ ወሬኅን ፡ ፄፋቅ ፡ ኢ.የፋ ሰ ኅዖም ፡ of ch. 48, and its incipit is ኦወዩኦ ሔ ፡ ቀኅምንምኦ ፡ ሬፄኦ ፡ ፄፇርኦ ፡ ሐዋርዴ ፡ ዴ.ቤ ፡ ወሶበ ፡ ሐዴወ ፡ ኦዉም ፡ ፳፯ ወ ፲ ፋወተ ፡ ኢኦኦ ፡ ፻ወፏ ፋወተ ፡ ኦም ሐዴወተ ፡ ወሰኦ ኦ ፬ ፡ ,

49. E.g. the ləda̋ta̋ addam in EMML 7410 f.43a-46b.

50. On which see O.Neugebauer, Ethiopic Astronomy and Computus, and 'Abū-shāker and the Ethiopic Hasāb'.

51. It should be distinguished from (a) Amharic or Geez treatises on computus (bahrä hassab) ascribed to Abušakər (e.g. EMML 1104), (b) a book printed under the title Abušakər, A.A. 1962 E.C.,which contains the beginning of the complete work in Geez with Amharic translation (pp.1-32 = MS B.L. Or. 810 f.4a-6a; pp.32-75 = Or. 810 f.7a-10a), a work of computus in Amharic (pp.75-146) and calendrical tables and miscellanea (pp.146-210), (c) the "Buch des Beweises" (Graf II pp.431-2) which Getatchew Haile has suggested (EMML Cata-logue vol. VI, on MS EMML 2369) may be related to Mashafä tälmid, (d) the 'History of Alexander, taken from Abušakər', found in e.g. MS B.N. Zotenberg 146 f.189b-192b (see Zotenberg's Catalogue, and Graf II pp.432-3), and (e) the Arabic Chronicon orientale of ibn ar-Rahib, formerly ascribed to Abū Sakir ibn Butrus.

(c) the text of the chapters appearing as numbers 52 and 54-57 in the table of contents (and somewhat variably numbered in the body of the book),

(d) the text of ch.50, and

(e) a history of the patriarchs of Alexandria, running from 'Mark, the first patriarch' at least as far as '95. Gabriel VII'.

Some MSS (e.g. B.L. Or. 809) follow the order (a)-(e), and others (e.g. B.L. Or. 810, Or. 5085, and Add. 16252) have the order (a), (b), (d), (e), (c). Sections (a), (c) and (d) belong together, and approximately correspond with the table of contents of the work; these will be referred to as 'Abušakǝr part I'. Sections (b) and (e), which will be referred to as 'Abušakǝr part II', also belong together, and appear to be an expansion of the Arabic <u>Chronicon orientale</u> (<u>CO</u>) which has been intruded into the framework of 'the 59 chapters' (with a few omitted[52]). This arrangement, and outline correspondence with the <u>CO</u>, may be illustrated as follows:

52. Some MS catalogues note chapters 47, 49, 51, 53, 58-9 as 'wanting'. This means that there is no section of text in the body of the work corresponding to these numbered titles in the table of contents; it does not mean that the section in question has been uniquely omitted from the MS described. Dillmann's procedure in cataloguing B.L. Add. 16252 is the clearest - namely to translate the table of contents, and to note for certain chapters, 'Hoc caput in textu deest'.

Subject	Pages in Cheikho's Latin Translation of CO	folios in MS B.L.Or. 809.	folios in MS B.L.Or. 810	folios in MS B.L. Add. 16252
Abušakər table of contents	–	7a–8b	4a–6a	3a–10a
Abušakər part I, chs.1–46, 48	–	8b–63b	7a–97a	10a–322a
(Abušakər part II) Adam	1	63b	97a	322a
21. Abraham	8	65a	100a	333b
27. Moses	9	66a	101b	338b
50. Eli	15	71b	110b	371a
51. Samuel	15	72b	112b	377a
53. David	16	75a	117a	393a
55. Rehoboam	18	77a	120b	405b
68. Manasseh	27	81a	128a	428a
76. Evilmerodach	31	83a	131b	438a
85. Artaxerxes the Great	35	85a	135a	447a
birth of Christ	41	88a	140a	461a
116. Titus	47	89b	142b	467b
166. Heraclius	55	'94b–95a	150b	488b–489b
(part I) chs.52,54–7	–	95a–104b	178a–192a	565a–604b
(part I) ch.50	–	104b–105b	150b–152b	489b–493b
Islamic history	56–109	–	–	–
(part II) history of Alexandrian patriarchs – preface	–	106a	152b	493b
Mark, first patriarch	110	106a	153a	495a
Athanasius, son of Kalil, 76th patriarch	152	122a–b	176a	558b–559b
subsequent patriarchs	153–4	122b–123b	176b–178a	559b–564b
end of MS		123b	192a	604b

The editorial processes which would lead to the production of Abušakər part II from the CO are:

(a) from the CO, omission of the material on the Caliphs,

(b) to the remaining chronological tables of the CO (on Jewish history, the Roman emperors, and the Alexandrian patriarchs) which already contained the chronologies of wäldä mänäkos (i.e. ibn ar-Rahib) and əlfakər krəstun (i.e. Abu'l-Faḥr al Mutanaṣṣir), addition of columns giving the chronologies of Sāᶜid wäldä Bäṭriq (i.e. Eutychius),

Maḥbub mänbuzawi (i.e. Agapius), Yoḥannəs afä wärq (probably 'John Chrysostom' as cited in Agapius), (Wäldä) Epifanyos, and Səᶜidawyan, and

(c) addition into the framework of the CO of a variable amount of material from other sources, including the OT, Eth. Qäleməntos and other chronographic works.

Abušakər part I has also clearly undergone expansion, as, for example, B.L. Or. 809 contains, passim, passages of Geez text which are absent from B.L. Or. 810. The named sources of the work are very many[53], and include Basil of Caesarea's Hexaemeron (e.g. B.L. Or. 810 f.22a).

Abušakər and the chronography of Giyorgis wäldä Amid contain some material in common; the question of the relationship between them is evidently complex, and can only be resolved after the preparation of critical editions of at least parts of the relevant texts[54].

4.1.8. Ethiopic Qäleməntos and Gädlä addam wähewan.

The contents of these works include material of a legendary nature concerning creation. Ethiopic Qäleməntos is a substantial, seven part work, found e.g. in MSS B.L. Or. 751 f.2a-89b, B.N. d'Abbadie 78 and EMML 1141; the greater part of it has been published in French translation by S. Grébaut[55]. Gädlä addam wähewan, the 'Acts of Adam and Eve', is an Ethiopic adaptation of an Arabic

53. See list in Dillmann's catalogue notes on MS B.L. Add. 16,252.

54. See 'Le Chronicon orientale de Butros ibn ar-Rahib et l'Histoire de Girgis el-Makim', ROC 28 (1931-2), pp.390-405.

55. 'Littérature Éthiopienne Pseudo-Clementine', ROC 1911 pp.72-78 (outline of contents), ROC 1911,1912,1913,1914,1915-17,1918-19, 1920-21,1927-28, and Aethiops year 3 no.2, pp.21-23 (translation); see also EOCCL and Graf I pp.283-292.

work, of which the Ethiopic text has been published by E. Trumpp[56] from MS B.L. Or. 751 f.105a-171b; it is also found e.g. in MS EMML 722, and has been translated into English by S. Malan[57].

The identity of these works and of the other works, such as the Syriac <u>Cave of Treasures</u> and Arabic 'Apocalypse of Peter', to which they are related, has become somewhat confused in the second-ary literature. Because Eth. Q̈al. contains the material of the Syriac <u>Testament of Adam</u> (dyʼtyqy dʼbwn ʼdm), and material similar to the Arabic <u>Book of the Rolls</u> (Kitāb al-majāll) and the Syriac <u>Cave of Treasures</u> (Meᶜarat gazzē), the secondary literature contains references to the 'Ethiopic Book of the Rolls',[58] the 'Ethiopic text of <u>The Cave of Treasures</u>'[59], and the 'Arabic-Ethiopic Testament of Adam'[60], as though these were additional independent works. The

56. <u>Der Kampf Adams</u>. Graf I pp.201-3 describes the Arabic text of this as the second part of a work of which the first part is the Arabic text of the pseudo-Epiphanian hexaemeron (of which the Ethiopic version was also published by Trumpp). These two works are associ-ated in the MSS used by Trumpp — München cod. arab. 243, and B.L. (Ethiopic) Or. 751 f.90a-105a, 105a-171b - but <u>G̈adl̈a addam ẅahewan</u> is found separately in some other Ethiopic MSS.

57. <u>The Book of Adam and Eve</u>. Malan's translation claims (preface, p.vi) to be made from Trumpp's text, but I have used the Arabic notes in Trumpp's apparatus; this raises the question of which text has actually been translated - an ambiguity revealed by the first foot-note on p.1. The work is unreliable in detail, containing errors (e.g. <u>s̈amen</u> is translated 'south', and <u>d̈abub</u> 'north'), and apparent misprints (e.g. 'Tkarnt' for <u>Təqəmt</u> on p.156).

58. Graf I p.292, S.E. Robinson, <u>The Testament of Adam</u>, p.142 (Robinson has given warnings about this problem on p.18).

59. M. Stone, <u>Armenian Apocrypha</u>, p.42. On the <u>Test. Adam</u>, this work valuably complements Robinson's.

60. C. Bezold, 'Das arabisch-ẅathiopische Testamentum Adami'. The Ethiopic text printed in this article is excerpted from MSS of Eth. Q̈al. (B.L. Or. 751, 752, 753).

matter is especially confused by Battista and Bagatti's study, which, under the title <u>La Caverna dei Tesori</u>, has re-printed M.D. Gibson's Arabic text of the <u>Kitāb al-majāll</u>, and which refers to Eth. Qäl. as the 'Libro delle Rivelazioni'.

The facts are that C. Bezold published a Syriac text of Me'arat gazzē opposite a similar untitled Arabic text[61]. M.D. Gibson published an Arabic text similar to Bezold's Arabic text, and entitled <u>Kitāb al-majāll</u>[62]. P. de Lagarde criticized Bezold for not pointing out (a) that his Arabic text (from Paris arab. 76) was only one of four similar MSS in the B.N. (the others being 77-79), and (b) that in all these MSS his text forms part of a larger work, an 'Apocalypse of Peter'[63]. This 'Apocalypse of Peter' to which de Lagarde refers is not the Greek Apoc. Pet. (as conjecturally re-constructed[64]), but an extensive Arabic work which de Slane[65] notes is the same, at least in outline, as MS Bodleian 294, more fully described by A. Nicoll in his Bodleian catalogue[66]; it is similar in parts to Eth. Qäl., but should not be equated with it.

61. C. Bezold, <u>Die Schatzhöhle</u>.

62. M.D. Gibson, <u>Apocrypha Arabica</u> (I. <u>Kitāb al-Magäll</u>) in <u>Studia Sinaitica</u> no. VIII.

63. P. de Lagarde, <u>Mittheilungen</u> III, pp.74-6, and further references in Graf I, pp.198-200.

64. E. Hennecke <u>N.T. Apocrypha</u>, vol. II, pp.663-683; R. Cowley, 'The Ethiopic work which is believed to contain the material of the ancient Greek Apocalypse of Peter'.

65. Baron de Slane, <u>Catalogue des manuscrits arabes de la Bibliothèque nationale</u>, on MS 76.

66. A. Nicoll, <u>Bibliothecae Bodleianae cod. mss. orientalium catalogi</u>, pt. II, vol. I, pp.49-54, on no. XLVIII = Bodl.294.

Bezold[67] suggested the following affinities:

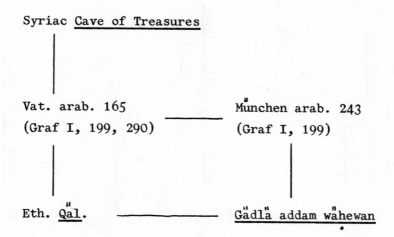

Syriac <u>Cave of Treasures</u>

Vat. arab. 165 ——— München arab. 243
(Graf I, 199, 290)   (Graf I, 199)

Eth. <u>Qäl</u>. ——————— <u>Gädlä addam wähewan</u>

Full investigation will require critical texts of the Arabic
'Apocalypse of Peter' and of Eth. <u>Qäl</u>., but in the meantime the
following further relationships may be suggested:

67 <u>Die Schatzhöhle</u>, vol. I, p.ix.

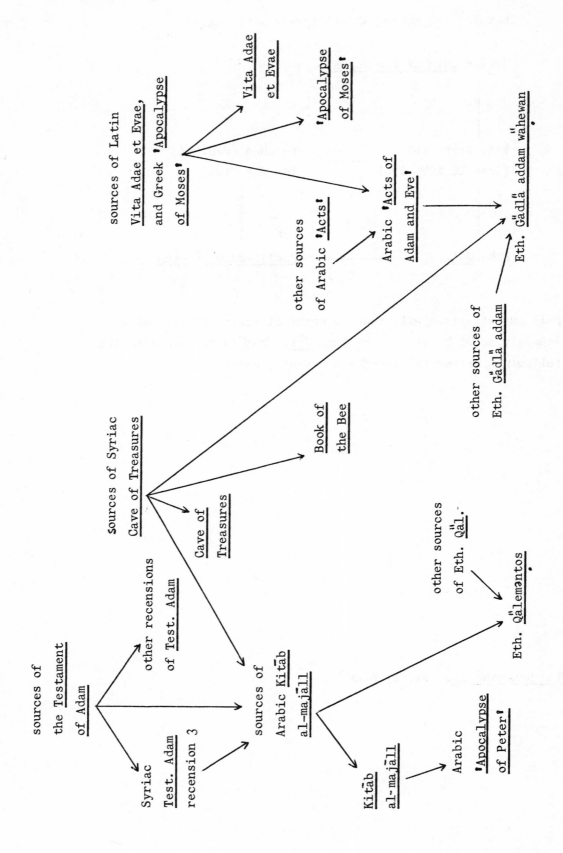

4.1.9. Miscellanea.

(i) D̮əhrä wängel. The Holy Week lectionary *Gəbrä ḥəmamat* contains passages of Bible commentary for reading after the gospel lections; most are headed *d̮əhrä wängel*.[68] I have not been able to ascertain their origin. The reading for dawn on Monday, following Mark 11. 12-26, is a brief commentary on the seven days of creation, commencing, 'At the first God made heaven and earth, and adorned them like this by the spirit of his mouth, and he covered the darkness, and he brought the light, and he distinguished them by new names ..[69]'.

(ii) Hymns. The opening stanzas of the hymn *Ṭäbibä ṭäbiban* (Dillmann, *Chrestomathia*, p.108) describe God's activity in creation. The hymn in MS Dublin (Cerulli) 950 contains, 'I bow down to your (m. sing.) godhead, you who created darkness before you made light'.

(iii) Felasha texts. The *Tə'əzazä sänbät* and *Abba elyas*[70] commence with outline accounts of the seven days of creation. W. Leslau has noted that the sources of *Tə'əzazä sänbät* are "mostly Jewish", with a few Christian elements, but that "some legends amplifying various accounts of the Bible, such as the creation of Adam, the story of

68. The passages are found in the printed edition of *GḤ* (A.A., 1942 E.C.) on pp.40,44,47,52,53,57,64,75,79,84,92,93,99,100,109,114,118,128,135, 136,139,142,148,149,157,162,166,173,179,180,183,186,188,189,192,197, 203,212,232,243,251,256,264,267,287,309,341,366-7,372-3,381,395,408. They each end ክርስቶስ፡ መድኀኒነ፡ መጽአ፡ ወሐመ፡ ወበሕማማቲሁ፡ አድኀነነ። or ንሰብሖ፡ ወንወድሶ፡ ወናልዕሎ፡ ስሞ፡ ኄሰመ፡ ውእቱ፡ ገብረ፡ ለነ፡ ምሕረተ፡ በከመ፡ ዕበየ፡ ሣህሉ።

69. *GḤ*, pr.ed.p.64.

70. Texts and French translation by J. Halévy, *Té'ĕzāza Sanbat*; English translation by W. Leslau, *Falasha Anthology*.

Abraham and his relation to Nimrod, and others, are of Arabic rather than Jewish origin".[71] It is unlikely that distinctively Felasha texts have greatly influenced Ethiopian Christian Bible commentaries;[72] however, the possibility must not be overlooked that legendary elements in the Christian commentaries also may have Islamic traditions as their proximate source – Leslau presumably means that some Jewish stories of Adam and Abraham have reached the Felasha texts in a form resembling that of some Arabic sources, rather than that these stories are ultimately not of Jewish origin.

(iv)   Magical texts. Some texts of <u>Ləfafä sədq</u> contain an introduction[73] (not included in Budge's edition[74]) which says that the text was written by God the Father prior to the creation of heaven and earth, and outlines the work of creation.

71. <u>Falasha Anthology</u>, pp.8–10.

72. For a possible exception to this, see A.Z. Aešcoly, 'Notices sur les Falacha', pp.100–1.

73. <u>Salot bäʾəntä ləfafä sədq wämängädä sämay wäzena həmamatihu läkrəstos,</u> A.A.,1962 E.C.,pp.7–14.

74. <u>The Bandlet of Righteousness</u>, London, 1929.

፩ ምዕራፉ።

፩ በቀዳሚ፡ገብሬ፡እግዚእ፡ብሔር።
ሰማየ፡ወምድረ፡በቀዳሚ፡ሥሳ
ጡኑ፡በቀዳማዊ፡ቃሉ፡እሁድ፡ብሶ
ርጎ፡ሰማይና፡ምድርን፡ፈጠረ።
ፖ፡በቀዳማዊ፡ልጁ፡በመጀመሪያ።
መፍጠሬ፡ፖ፡በመጀመሪያ፡ዕለት፡በ
መጀመሪያ፡ሰዓት፡ኃደሜ፡ጣታ፡እሁ
ዱ፡በወርኀ፡ሰማዩን፡ምድርን፡ፈ
ጠረ፡የፈጠረበት፡ወንጌሳዊ፡ቶሐን
ሩ፡ወርኁ፡ወጋቢት፡ቀኖሩ፡፳፱፡ዕ
ከቱ፡ዐስተ፡እሑዱ፡ሰዓቱ፡ሠርኀ፡፩
ዉ፡ሉተታ፡ሰላሴቅ ድ መ፡ዓሰም።
እንድነታቸዉ፡፫ነታቸዉን፡ሳይጠ
ቀልለዉ፡፫ነታቸዉ፡፮ነታቸዉን፡ሳይ
ከፍሎዉ፡ቪሰከሉ፡ቪቀዴሱ፡ይኖሩ፡
ነበር፡ማን፡ይመሰግናቸዉል፡ቢሉ፡
እርሱ፡ገወቀ፡ፖ፡ጮ ስጋና፡የገሀር
ያቸዉ፡ስለሆነ፡ምስጉን፡ገሕርያ
ቸዉ፡እብራቸዉ፡ስሕሞሬ፡ነዉ፡እ
ምቅድመ፡ይፍጥር፡መላእክቱ፡እት

4.2   ANNOTATED TRANSLATION OF AC GENESIS 1.1 - 2.4a[1]

Chapter 1

(1) At the first, God made heaven and earth

By his first authority, by his first word, on Sunday, at dusk,

he created heaven and earth;

A. by his first son, in his first creating;

A. on the first day, at the first hour, Saturday evening,

Sunday at dusk[2], he created heaven and earth.

At the time when he created, the evangelist was John[3], the

month Mäggabit, the number (of the day) 29, the day the day of

Sunday, the hour dusk.

H. Prior to the world, the (members of the) Trinity were in

existence, being glorified and praised, without their unity

absorbing their trinity, nor their trinity dividing their unity.

If it is asked, 'Who praised them?', only he (God) knows[4];

A. it is because praise is of their nature, because their nature

which is praised remained with them, as it says, 'Before he

created the angels for praise' (p.3),

1. Translated from the text reproduced opposite, MS W, Cowley 1,
    pp.2-17, copied by Deacon (now Dr.) Mänbäru Färrädä from a MS of
    Mämhər Wäldä sänbät formerly kept by Mämhər Kəflä maryam Yəmär at
    the school of Gəmja bet Maryam, Gondar. Notes are added of some
    of the variants of MS Y, Cowley 31, copied by Kal'ay Kiros from
    a MS of Mäl'akä məhrät Yared Gərmay of Makalle (now Abunä Märha
    Krəstos of Asmara). For abbreviations and conventions of the
    translation, see table of abbreviations and TIA pp.164-6; for
    other MSS of AC Gen., see 7.4 below.
2. I.e., 7 p.m. on Saturday.
3. I.e., on the 4-year cycle of the Ethiopian calendar in which
    successive years are named after the evangelists, this was a
    year of John.
4. For 'only he knows', MS Y has '(they praised) each other'.

ፍሮ፡ 0_ስብሕተ_ እብ ፡ ወወልዱ፡
ወመንፈ_ስቅዱስ፡ እላ፡ ምሉ_ዑ_ው
ስተ፡ ኖኅኜ፡ እንዲ_ል_፡ ክዚህም_
በጄሳ፡ ክብራቸው፡ አብ ጃቸው_ እ
ጎደቀረ፡ እ ው_ቀው፡ ሰጣ ኹንን፡ የሚቀ
ድስ፡ ሰጣ ኹንን_ የሚ ወር ሱ፡ እንፍ
ጠር፡ ብኮው፡ እ ሰ ኩ_ እ ስ በ ው_ ም
እልቀሬ፡ ሪ ው_ ና፡ መሳ ንክ ትን_ ደ ህ ን
ደ ል ም ፡ ፊ ጠ ሩ ፡ ፡ ደ ህ ነ ን ም ፡ ሱ እ ◯_
ነ ገ ር ፡ ፌ ጥ ር ታ ል ፡ ክ ሐ ሊ ነ ቱ ን ፡ ባ ዕ
ል ነ ቱ ን ፡ ር ኩ ብ ፡ ዘ እ. ይ ት ረ ክ ብ ነ
ቱ ን ፡ ራ ት ዕ ነ ቱ ን ፡ ስ ◯ ግ ለ ጿ ፡ ፡ ክ ሐ
ኢ ነ ቱ ፡ ደ ህ ን ፡ ባ ለ ም ፡ እ ም ፃ በ ፡ እ ል
በ ፡ ◌ ነ በ ያ ፡ እ ም ጥ ደ ፡ መ ፍ ጠ ሪ ፡
ባ ዕ ል ነ ቱ ፡ ዝ ሬ ፡ ባ ለ ያ ን ፡ ብ ዙ ፡ ሐ ው_
ጠ ር ቱ ፡ ሊ ያ በ ኮ ፡ ሊ ያ ጠ ግ ፡ ጠ ◌ ፡ ላ
ለ ው ፡ ጠ ◌ ፡ ሠ ጋ ፡ ላ ለ ው ፡ ሠ ግ ፡ የ ሰ
ጠ ፡ እ ን ደ ሆ ነ ፡ ባ ስ ◌ ግ ነ ቱ ፡ ደ ታ ወ ቃ ል
ጎ ታ ም ፡ ባ ዙ ፈ ን ፡ ፍ ጥ ሪ ታ ች ን ፡ እ ን ስ
ሳ ቱ ፡ እ ሬ ዊ ት ን ፡ ሰ ው ን ፡ ፌ ጥ ሮ ፡ እ
ዝ ር እ ት ን ፡ እ ት ክ ል ት ን ፡ መ መ ገ በ
ሪ ቀ ን ፡ ፍ ጥ ሪ ታ ች ን ፡ መ ሳ ኡ ን ግ ቱ ን ፡
ፌ ጥ ሮ ፡ መ ን ፈ ሳ ዊ ፡ ም ል ክ ብ ፡ ቅ ዳ ሴ
ን ፡ ወ መ ነ ጉ ቱ ባ ዕ ል ነ ቱ ን ፡ ያ ገ ል ጻ ል ፡ ፡
ር ኩ ብ ነ ቱ ፡ በ ሰ ህ ነ ፡ ፍ ጥ ሪ ት ፡ በ እ እ
ም ር ፡ ጠ ጋ ዩ ◌ ፡ ተ መ ር ም ው ፡ ደ ታ ወ
ቃ ል ፡ ዘ እ. ይ ስ ተ ር እ ፡ እ ግ ዚ አ ብ ሔ ር ፡
እ ም ፍ ጥ ሪ ት ኇ ያ ለ ም ፡ ይ ተ በ ወ ቅ ፡ በ
ፍ ጥ ሪ ቱ ፡ ኤ ፍ ጃ ሪ ቱ ፡ እ ን ዲ ል ፡ ዘ እ ደ

the glory of the Father and the Son and the Holy Spirit <u>was</u>

<u>not diminished, but was complete in everything</u>'.[1]

   After this, knowing that their glory was confined to

themselves alone, they thought, 'Let us create that which will

praise our name, (and) which will inherit our name'. They did

not fail to act on their thought; they created human kind,

and angels, and this world.

   He created this for 4 reasons - to reveal his omnipotence,

his wealthiness, his transcendent immanence, and his equity.

His omnipotence - his creating this world, bringing it from

non-existence to existence.

His wealthiness - today, if a rich man who has invited people

and brought them food and drink gives <u>täjj</u>[2] to the one who asks

for <u>täjj</u>, and meat to the one who asks for meat, his wealthiness

will become known; the Lord, too - the fact that he created

material creations, the tame and wild animals and humans, and

feeds (them) with grains and plants, and the fact that he

created immaterial creations, the angels, and feeds (them) with

spiritual food, (namely) praise, reveals his wealthiness.

His immanence is known by the wonder of his creation (and) by

being examined by the character of the mind, as it says, '<u>God,</u>

<u>who has not been seen from the creation of the world, is made</u>

<u>known through his creation, to his creation</u>'[3].

---

1. <u>Qəd</u>. of 300, sect. 31, also cited in SFA p.9, SFG fol. 1v, and
   KWK p.777.
2. A fermented honey drink.
3. Rom. 1.20.

ቅሪክብንቱ፡ባሕርዩ፡እደመረመሩ
ምና፡ሩቲፅነቱም፡ዱይብኮስ፡ቢ
ክዩ፡በንስሔ፡እንዓይመለስ፡እውፅ
በታው፡ከእደም፡ሰጥቆበታል፡እ
ደም፡ቢበድል፡በንስሔ፡እንዲመ
ለሱ፡እውፅ፡መአእክቱን፡እስጠ
ብቅኤታል፡ወእዘዞሙ፡እኪ ሩቤል
ወሉራፌል፡ዘውስተ፡እደዊሆ
ሙ፡ሰዶሬ፡እሳት፡እንተ፡ትትመ
ይየጥ፡ካመ፡ዱፅቀቡ፡ፍኖተ፡እ
ዩ፡ሕይወት፡ከመ፡ኢደግን፡እደ
ም፡ተሳቢሉ፡እንዲ ል፡ዩህሩ
ትፅነቱን፡ይገልጻል፡በዚህ፡ቀን
ኚ፡ፍጥረት፡ሩጥራል፡ምኅና፡
ምን፡ናቸው፡ቢሉ፡ነፍስ፡እሳ
ት፡ማይ፡መሬት፡ጽልመት፡መሳኔ
ክት፡ብራሕ፡ሰማይ፡ናቸው፡የሰማ
ዩና፡የምድርን፡ተፈጥሮ፡ተናግ
ሩ፡የቁቀረት፡ስለምን፡ሳዶና
ገሩቸው፡ቀሩ፡ቢሉ፡በሕመዩ፡በ
ምድ፡ር፡ምሉዓን፡ኣሆኑ፡ብኩ
እንድ፡ም፡ሰሩም፡ነፍስ፡ባይ
ሉ፡እሳቱ፡ባይክ፡እው፡ማይ፡ባይ
ዱሳል፡ቸሉ፡እነዚህ፡ኃይእን፡ፈ
ጥሪታት፡ናቸው፡እንስቶቸው፡
ቢሆን፡መናፍቃን፡እነዚህ፡እደ
ገዙት፡ፈጠሪ፡ባ ሉ፡ነበርኛ፡ነመ
ናፍቃን፡ምኅንኘት፡ስመጥፈቺ

His transcendence - because his nature cannot be examined.

His equity - knowing that when the devil apostasized he would

not repent, he gave his place to Adam; knowing that when

Adam offended he would repent (col. 2), he caused angels to

guard him, as it says, 'And he commanded the Cherubim and

Seraphim, in whose hands was a sword of fire which flickered

back and forth, that they guard the way of the tree of life,

lest Adam enter audaciously'.[1] This reveals his equity.

On this day he created 7 created things. If it is asked

what they are, they are wind, fire, water, earth, darkness,

angels, and the bright heaven.

If it is asked why, having spoken of the creation of

heaven and earth, he did not speak of the remaining ones, it

was because he considered they pervaded heaven and earth.[2]

A. It was to remove a reason from the heretics, because

Solomon says 'powerful wind', 'powerful fire', 'or powerful

water'[3]; these are powerful created things, and if he had

mentioned them, the heretics would have said that he created

while these assisted him[4].

1. Gen. 3.24, with an addition.
2. MS Y reads, 'Heaven and earth are like a house, since (the
   remaining ones) are stored in them'.
3. Wisd. 7.20, 16.19, 13.2 (LXX capitation; the AC capitation
   is different).
4. MS Y places here the note on the date of creation, and adds a
   note on the creation of angels from wind and fire, citing Eth. 3
   Macc. 4.8 (Amharic capitation).

አንድ ም፡ እሩን፡ በተራ፡ ያመጣ
ቹዋል፡ የጮእ ሻን፡ ተፈጥሮ፡ ወ
ቅልመኑ፡ መልዕልተ፡ ቀላዪ፡ ብ ኮ፡
የነፉስ፡ ተፈጥሮ፡ ወጮን ፉተኈ
ግሢእ ብሐር ደ ዴ ል፡ መልዕ ሁተ
ጣይ፡ ብ ኮ፡ የመእ ን ከተ ን ፡ ተፈጥ
ሮ፡ ወእ ዘዘ መ፡ ለ ኪ ፈ ጌል ፡ ወ
 እሁ ራተ ፡ ል ፡ ብ ኮ፡ የመጣ ዋል ፡ ም
ድ ሩ ፡ ህ ለ ወ ት ፡ ሰ ራ ቀ ፡ ም ጅ ር
ኔ ፡ ሲ ል ፡ ነ መ ፡ ም ድ ር ም ፡ ከ እ ዘ
ር እ ት ፡ ከ እ ተ ክ ል ኑ ፡ ከ ሰ መ ፡ ባ ይ
ፀ ን ፡ ነ በ ሬ ቹ ፡፡ ዮ ፡ ሰ ሟ ይ ን ፡ ከ ግ ሁ
ፈ ጠ ረ መ ፡ ብ ኮ ፡ ነ ክ ር ና ፡ ግ ሁ ፡ መ
ለእ ክ ተ ፡ ና ቹ መ ፡ ም ድ ር ፡ ግ ን ፡ ከ እ
ዘ ር እ ት ፡ ከ እ ተ ክ ል ት ፡ ለ ፊ ተ ን ፡ ነ
በ ሬ ቹ ፡ እ ም ተ ካ ተ ፡ ይ ሳ ል ፡ ከ ጥ ን
ት ፡ ፅ ም ሮ ፡ ዮ ፡ ከ ን ቱ ታ ፡ ብ ድ ወ ተ
ይ ሳ ል ፡ ከ እ ዘ ር ዕ ት ፡ ከ ን ቱ ፡ ሁ ና ፡
ም ድ ረ በ ዴ ፡ ሁ ና ፡ ነ በ ሬ ቹ ፡ ዮ ፡ ህ ለ
ወ ት ፡ ወ ኢ ህ ለ ወ ት ፡ ይ ሳ ል ፡ ህ ለ መ
ት ፡ ፃ ል በ ፡ እ ግ ዚ እ ብ ሐ ር ፡ ወ እ ሁ
ለ መ ት ፡ በ ተ ፈ ጥ ሮ ፡ በ መ ታ የ ት ፡
እ ል ነ በ ሬ ቹ ም ፡ ዮ ፡ ህ ሎ መ ት ፡ ወ ኢ
ታ ከ ተ ር ኊ ፡ ይ ሳ ል ፡ ህ ለ መ ት ፡ በ ተ
ፈ ጥ ሮ ፡ በ መ ሀ ፡ ተ ሸ ፉ ና ፡ እ ት ታ

A. (It is because) he will now introduce them in order - he
introduces the creation of darkness, saying <u>'and darkness was
over the deep</u>',[1] the creation of wind, saying <u>'the wind of God
hovered over the water</u>,'[1] and the creation of angels, saying
'<u>and he commanded the Cherubim and the Seraphim</u>'.[2]

(2) <u>but the earth was bare</u>

Reading <u>'and the earth'</u> - and the earth was bare of grains,
plants, and humankind (p.4).

A. (Reading <u>'but the earth'</u>) - he had said, 'He created heaven
with its belongings, and its belongings are the angels'; but
the earth was bare of grains and plants.

(A T.V.) reads <u>'from ancient times'</u> - beginning from ancient
times.

A. (A T.V.) reads <u>'emptiness</u>', <u>desertedness'</u> - it was empty
of grains, it was desert.

A. (A T.V.) reads <u>'it was and it was not'</u> - <u>it was</u> - in the
heart of God[3]; <u>and it was not</u> - it was not in visible created
state.

A. (A T.V.) reads <u>'it was and it was not visible'</u> - <u>it was</u> -
in the created state; (<u>and it was not visible</u>) - it was not
visible because it was covered by water.

1. Gen. 1.2.
2. Gen. 3.24.
3. Cf. Jub. 2.2.

ፎይምያነበር፡ወኢኮነት፡ድሉት፡
በእዝርኤት፡በእትናልት፡እስ
ተዘጋጅቸም፡ነበር፡ወድልመት፡
ምልፅልተ፡ቃሳይ፡የሷእጣን፡ፊ
ጥር፡እወጣ፡ሷእጣው፡ስውሃ
ው፡ላይ፡ስፉር፡ነበር፡ወመንፈ
ሠእግዚእብሔር፡ይዲልል፡መ
ልዕልተ፡ማይ፡የነፋሕን፡ተፈጥር
እወጣ፡እግዚእብሔር፡የፊጠሪ
ው፡ነፋት፡በሷሃው፡ካይ፡ሰፍጮ
ጄ፡ነበር፡መንፈሰ፡እግዚእብ
ሔር፡ያለውንም፡መሻፍቃን፡የ
ሚግል፡ፊቅ፡ለማይት፡ሕይወት፡
የሚሆ፡ኑቹው፡ማይኅን፡የሚይ
ዓሪቹው፡ነፋስ፡ነው፡ሰለዚ
ብሎ፡ተርኈጮታል፡ትርጊሜ፡
ኑፊትም፡በዋ፡ምቀፉ፡የሚ ሆዋ፡
የሴብ፡መንፈሷቅ ዱስ፡ግዞና
ሎ፡ነው፡ብኪል፡ሣዋሮሱ፡ክእ
መቤታቸን፡ይመ፡ድንግልጮን፡የ
ካፊኦ፡የመንፈስቅ ዱሱ፡ምሳሴ

<u>and it was not prepared,</u>

It had not been prepared with grains and plants.

<u>and darkness was over the deep,</u>

He introduced the creation of darkness, (saying), 'The darkness
abode over the water'.

<u>and the wind of God hovered over the water,</u>

He introduced the creation of the wind, (saying), 'The wind
which God created abode over the water'. As for that which he
calls '<u>wind of God</u>', a scholar called Măsafqan[1] interpreted
(it), saying, 'It is the wind, which is life for the waters,
(and) which purifies the waters'.[2] And <u>Tərgwame orit</u> says, 'It
is a likeness of the gift of the Holy Spirit, which is given in
baptism'.[3] Severus says, 'It is a likeness of the Holy Spirit
who separated from our Lady the blood of virginity'[4] (col. 2).

1. <u>mpassqana</u>, Theodore of Mopsuestia.
2. The view of Theodore (and Ephraim), as cited e.g. in the com-
    mentaries of IM and IAṬ on Gen.1.2., and THBK <u>Mimrā</u> I.70. MS Y
    here adds, 'As it says - '<u>Because the winds are the moving</u>
    <u>principle of the waters</u>'.'
3. This form of words is not found in the exemplars of <u>TO</u>
    examined in this study.
4. I have not located this quotation in the writings of Severus
    of Antioch or Severus of Esmunain. MS Y attributes it to Basil,
    and the following one to Severus.

ነወ፡ ብፌል፡፡ በሶልዩ፡ሱ፡በማሕፀኒ፡
እንዲነኮርምያ ስ፡ኤንዴነዉሐንሱ፡የ
ሚ፡ ሳኖ፡የመዒፈ፡ትቅጰዴ ሽ፡ ምሳሌ፡
ነወ፡ ብፌል፡ ወዩቤ፡ እግዚአብሔር
ከዩ ጐ፡ ብርሃን፡ ወ ኾነ፡ ብርሃን፡ እ ግ ዚ
አብሔር፡ ብርሃን፡ ዩ ፈጠረ፡ ዩፈጠረ፡
ብ ከ ወ፡ እ ዘ ዚ ፡ ብርሃ ን ያ ወ፡ ተ ፈ ጠ ሬ ፡፡
ወር እ ዮ ፡ እ ግ ዚ አ ጠ ሔ ር ፡ ለ ብ ር ሃ ን ፡
ከ ወ ፡ ሠ ና ዩ ፡ እ ግ ዚ አ ብ ሔ ር ፤ ፡ ብ ር ሃ
ን ን ፡ የ በ ቃ ፡ ፉ ጥ ሬ ት ፡ እ ን ዴ ሆ ነ ፡ አ ወ ዩ ፡
ፈ ጠ ሬ ፡፡ ከ መ ፡ ሠ ና ዩ ፡ ባ ለ ወ ፡ ከ መ ፡ ጦ
ብ ፡ ዩ ካ ል ፡ ከ መ ፡ ሠ ና ዩ ፡ ማ ለ ት ፡ ነ ወ ፡
ጠ ቢ ት ፡ ማ ለ ት ፡ ሠ ና ዩ ፡ ማ ለ ት ፡ እ ን ዴ
ሆ ነ ፡ ወ ፊ ለ ጠ ፡ እ ግ ዚ አ ብ ሔ ር ፡ ሰ
ሰ ከ ለ ፡ ብ ር ሃ ን ፡ ወ ማ ፅ ከ ለ ፡ ፁ ል ወ
ት ፡ እ ግ ዚ አ ብ ሔ ር ፡ በ ጨ ለ ማ ሪ ፡ በ ፀ
ር ሃ ን ፡ ወ ኪ ፎ ል ፡ ዼ ን በ ር ፡ ስ የ ፡ ታ ሪ ኪ ፡
ከ ዩ ኩ ን ፡ ብ ር ሃ ን ፡ ያ ለ በ ት ፡ ም ኽ ን ያ
ት ፡ ም ን ዿ ነ ወ ፡ ቢ ኮ ፡ ጌ ታ ፡ መ ሳ እ ከ

Basil says, 'It is a likeness of the Holy Spirit, who is given

in the womb to such as Jeremiah and John'.[1]

(3) <u>and God said, 'Let there be light', and there was light,</u>

And God commanded, saying, 'Let light be created, let it be

created'[2], and light was created.

(4) <u>and God saw the light, that it was beautiful,</u>

God created the light, knowing that it was a worthy creation.

(A.T.V.) reads '<u>that it was tob</u>' for 'that it was beautiful';

it means '<u>that it was beautiful</u>', just as 'Tobit' means '<u>beautiful</u>'.[3]

<u>and God divided between the light and the darkness.</u>

God made a boundary between darkness and light.

T.[4] If it is asked why he said, '<u>Let there be light</u>', (it is

1. See Basil <u>Hexameron</u> II.6; the opinion, but not this form of
   words, is attributed to Basil by IM and IAṬ on Gen.1.2 (but
   cf. IBN question VII).
2. Possibly dittography.
3. MS Y here adds a further supposed cognate by quoting Ps.44.1
   (LXX), 'like the pen of a scribe <u>zätäbätäbä</u>', where the AC (on
   Ps.44.1) interprets <u>zätäbätäbä</u> as 'which (writes) beautifully';
   this appears to be innocent of the fact that <u>tob</u> is a Hebrew word.
4. MS Y relates this story more fully, much as it appears in AC
   Rev.12.17 (see translation in <u>TIA</u> pp.293-6); similar material is
   found in AC<u>MW</u>, SF, and <u>Aksimaros</u> for Wednesday.

ኅን፡ ሕያዋን፡ ለባዉይን፡ ነባብይን፡ እ
ዕራት፡ ፈጣሬቸዉ፡ ነበር ና፡ ምንት፡
ኃያና፡ እምባዕይ ቴ፡ መዓእን፡ ወመፄ
ፈጠሪና፡ ወሜወ፡ በበርእሰነት፡ ተፈ
ጠርና፡ ተባጋሉ፡ ዴያብሎሽን፡ ኩሉ
ኩ፡ ሰላይ፡ አጼርን፡ ፈጥሮት፡ ነበር
ና፡ ከወዴሳይ፡ እኔ፡ ፈጠር ኩ፡ የሜ
ጽምዑ፡ አጣ፡ ካወዴታፉ፡ እንዴ
ኪኩ፡ ሰማ፡ እኔ፡ ፈ ጠርኩ፡ ለበል
ብሎ፡ እሰበ፡ እሶበ ም፡ እልቀሪ፡ እኔ
ፈጣሪወመ፡ ለፍጡራን፡ አለ፡ ይንጊ
ዘ፡ የሱ፡ ወገዮፉ፡ ከ፫፡ ተክፍለዋል
የተጠራጠራ፡ እኩ፡ አወን፡ ፈጠር
ከን፡ ያኩ፡ እኩ፡ ምን፡ እንተ፡ ቱ ፈጣ
ሪባ፡ እኛ፡ ፈጠርንህ፡ እን ፬፡ ያረመ
እኩ፡ የተ ጠራጠራት፡ በእየር፡ ቀርተ
ዋል፡ አወን፡ ፈጠርክን፡ ያሉት፡ ወዴ
ዚህ፡ ዓለም፡ ወርዲዋል። ምን፡ እን
ትቻፈጣሬን፡ እኞ፡ ፈ ጠርገህ፡እ
ኑ፬፡ ያሉት፡ እጠረዉ፡ ወርዲዋል
ያንጊዜ፡ በመላእኸት፡ ሸብር፡ ፀናባ
ቸዉ፡ ወእንጉዱ 9መ፡ ወልእክ፡ ሶላ
ም፡ ስቃሉ፡ እንዴራል፡ ቀዱ ሳ፡ ገባ
ር እል፡ ንቁም፡ በበ፡ ሕካዊና፡ ኑስ

because) the angels said to each other - for the Lord had created them living, understanding, and speaking - 'What are we? From where did we come, and who created us? And were we created each by ourselves?' Because he (God) had created the devil in the highest place of all, he (the devil) lacked a voice from above saying, 'I created', and he heard them (the angels) below talking like this. He thought he would say, 'I created', and did not fail to act on his thought. He said, 'I am the creator of the created beings'. At that time his tribes were divided into 3. Some doubted; some said, 'Yes, you created us'; some said, 'What do you mean that you created us - rather we created you!' (p.5). The doubters remained in the air; the ones who said, 'Yes, you created us', descended to this world; the ones who said, 'What do you mean that you created us - rather we created you!', descended together with him (the devil). Then the angels were very troubled, and as it says, 'An angel of peace quietened them with his word', St. Gabriel reassured them, saying, 'Let us stand firm in our respective states until we find our God',

ካንሪ፡ካቦ፡ አእምላካን፡ ብከ፡
እጹን ቴ ቻዋል። ዛሬ፡ ድል፡ የተነሳ
ን፡ ጦር፡ በጋ፡ እሪበኝ፡ ጋስህ፡ ድ
ና፡ ብኰ፡ እንዲ ያጸናው፡ ለብሰ
ይዓቅሉት፡ ይበቃው፡ ይህ፡ ነው፡ ወ
በእንተዝ፡ ይስዋ፡ ይጹር፡ ዜናህ
ለማርያም፡ እንዲ.ል፡ ከዚህ፡ በኂላ፡
ጨርሰው፡ ሳደክዱ፡ ሎይ ክዱ፡ ሰይ
ኩን፡ ብኰ፡ ብር ሃኑን፡ ፈጠራከቸው፡
ደህ፡ ዓሙቀት፡ ሁይቸው፡ ቀዳሉ፡ ቅ
ዱሉ፡ ቅዳሉ፡ ብለው፡ እመሳግዳ
ል፡ ሐተታ፡ ሶለይዐን፡ ጌቸን፡ በእርም
ሞ፡ ብርሃንን፡ በነቢብ፡ ፈጠረ፡ ቢ
ኩ፡ በእርሞው፡ በነቢግም፡ ወፍጠ
ር፡ ይቻለኛል፡ ሲል፡ መጻፋቃን፡ በእር
ሞሞ፡ እንጅ፡ በነቢብ፡ ሜቢብ፡ እን
ጅ፡ በእርማሞ፡ መፍጠር፡ አይቻለው
ም፡ ግኰ፡ ነበርና፡ ጌን፡ በእርሞሞ
ፈጠሪ፡ እሩን፡ ዓን፡ ሰማዐይን፡ ወለ
እክቱ፡ አሉና፡ ብርሃንን፡ በነቢብ፡ ፈ
ጠሪ፡ በ፡ ደህግሲያን፡ የልቡና፡ ነቢብ
ነው፡ ወዘይንብብ፡ ጽድቀ፡ በልቡ
እንዲ.ል፡ የውስ፡ ቢሆን፡ ቢፈት፡ ጨለ
ማን፡ ፈጥሮ፡ ሢላ፡ ብርሃንን፡ ሶለም
ን፡ ፈጠሪ፡ ቢኰ፡ በፈት፡ ጥበሃን፡ ፈ

just as today a good warrior reassures a defeated army,
saying, 'Stand firm where you are'. It was this that made
him worthy for the Annunciation, as it says, '<u>And because of</u>
<u>this it befitted him to bear news to Mary</u>'. After this,
before they (the angels) completely apostasize,[1] he (God)
created light for them,[2] saying, '<u>Let there be</u>'. This became
knowledge for them, and they praised him saying, '<u>Holy, holy,</u>
<u>holy</u>'.[3]

H.[4] If it is asked, 'Why did he create the 7 in silence, but
light with speech?', (it was) to show that he could create
(both) in silence and with speech, because heretics would have
said, 'He cannot create with speech, but only by silence, or
not by silence, but only with speech'. He created the 7 in
silence; but now, because there are listening angels, he
created light with speech.

A. If it is asked, 'If this is so, it is speech of the intel-
lect, as it says, "<u>And who speaks righteousness in his heart</u>"[5];
if that is so, why, having created darkness first, did he
create light afterwards?' (col. 2),

1. <u>lay̆əkədu</u> is probably a scribal error and has been left
   untranslated.
2. This is the point of the narrative, to state the reason why
   God said 'Let there be light'.
3. MS Y here adds a note on the Trinity.
4. MS Y has the following material in a different order.
5. Ps. 14(15).2.

ጥሮ፡ኂኅ፡ጨለማን፡ቢፈጥር፡ወ
የዩ፡እምላክ፡ ብርሃንን፡ ቢፈጥር፡
እኩዱ፡እምላክ፡ ጫየጨለማኂ
ፈጠረ፡ግሉ፡ ነበርኖ፡ ካመናፍቃን
ምኅንየቱን፡ልማጥፋት፡ ዪ ኧሜ
ቢፈት፡ ብርሃንን፡ ፈጥሮ፡ ኂኅ፡ ጨ
ለማን፡ ቢፈጥር፡ ዕኩዱ፡ እምላክ፡
ጨለማን፡ ቢፈጥር፡ ወናዩ፡ እምላ
ክ ፡ ብርሃንን ፡ ፈጠረ ፡ ቢኩ ፡ ይሆ ዒ
የኦምʼ፡ ቢ ኩ ፡ የጫ ዖልፈ ወን ፡ በ ሜ
ት ፡ የማ ዖልፈ ወ ን ፡ በ ኂኅ ፡ መ ፍ ጠ ር
ክፉ ወ ን ፡ በ ሜ ት ፡ በ ጐ ወ ን ፡ በ ኂ ኅ
ማ ጾ ጣ ት ፡ ሌ ጋ ታ ፡ ል ማ ደ ፡ ኅ ወ ፡ በ
ሜ ት ፡ የ ጫ ዖ ልፈ ወ ን ፡ ደ ሆ ነ ን ፡ ዓ ለ
ም ፡ ዒ ወ ር ሶ ፡ በ ኂ ኅ ፡ የ መ ዖ ል ፈ ወ
ን ፡ መ ን ግ ሥ ተ ፡ ሰ ማ ዖ ት ን ፡ እ ን ዴ ዖ
ወ ር ሱ ን ፡ በ ሜ ት ፡ የ መ ታ ል ፉ ፡ ኧ ሌ ት
ን ፡ ወ ር ቱ ፡ በ ኂ ኅ ፡ የ ጫ ታ ል ፈ ወ ኁ
ወ ን ጌ ል ን ፡ ኧ ን ዴ ወ ሰ ል ል ን ፡ በ ሜ ቱ ፡ መ
ክ ሌ ወ ኁ ን ፡ እ ም ጥ ዱ ፡ ኂኅ ፡ ፃ ጋ ወ
ኁ ፡ ክ ብ ሌ ኁ ፡ ኧ ን ዴ ሰ ጠ ን ፡ ኧ ን ዴ ዚ
ሃ ዖ ም ፡ በ ሜ ት ፡ ጨ ለ ማ ን ፡ ፈ ጥ ሮ ፡ በ
ኂኅ ፡ ብ ር ሃ ን ን ፡ ፈ ጠ ሌ ፡ ል ደ ኁ ን ፡
ብ ር ሃ ን ፡ ዖ ል ወ ን ፡ ደ ዘ ወ ፡ በ ዚ
ህ ፡ ቀ ን ፡ ፰ ፡ ፉ ጥ ሬ ቱ ፡ ፈ ጠ ሬ ፡ ደ ኻ ኁ ፡
ን ገ ር ግ ን ፡ በ ኹ ሉ ሌ ፡ ወ ጋ ብ ሌ ፡ ኧ ግ
ዚ ኧ ብ ሔ ር ፡ ሰ ብ ዓ ተ ፡ ዘ ወ ዲ ፡ ደ ላ
ል ና ፡ በ ዚ ህ ፡ ደ ሬ ታ ኹ ፡ ደ ህ ም ፡ ብ ር

a reason

it was to remove⸝from the heretics, because if, having

created light first, he had created darkness afterwards,

they would say, 'While a good god created the light, an evil

god created the darkness.'

If it is objected that if, having created light first, he

had created darkness afterwards, they could still say,

'While an evil god created the darkness, a good god created

the light', it is the Lord's custom to create what is transient

first, and what is not transient afterwards, to bring evil

first, and good afterwards; just as, having first caused (us)

to inherit this transient world, he will afterwards cause us

to inherit the kingdom of heaven which is not transient; just

as, having first made the Torah which is transient, afterwards

he made for us the gospel which is not transient; just as,

having first brought tribulation, afterwards he gave us grace

and glory. Similarly, having first created darkness, he

created light afterwards.

Citing, 'Let there be light', they say, 'On this day he

created 8 created things'[1]. But because in Kufale it says,

'And God made seven species'[2], they are refuted by this. For

1. I.e., they say that light is an eighth, additional to the
seven already listed.

2. Jub. 2.3 (Charles), 2.8 (Geez text).

ሃፉ። ከሰባቱ። ልዩ። እዶደለም።። የ
ተዳፈን ጊ እሳት። በጭድ። በገለባ።
እንዲገልጡት። በእሳት። ግሕርደት
ወጭድ። ፳በረውን። መግለጹ ፥
ው።። ደጎዱሰ። ዓለም። በምን። ፷ኝ
ቁ። ፈጥ ወታል። ቢሉ። በሶርደ ፡ ቋ
ቁ። ፈጥ ወታል።። በሶርደ ። ቋንቁ
እግዚአብሔር። ማከት። ፰ዌን ።ሠ
ኑ።ፍንሪት። የፈጠረ ፥ ማኮት ፡ ነው
ኢ ንድም። በዕብራይስጥ። ቁንቁ።
ፈጥ ወታል።። ይህም ኢ ታ ወቅ። አብ
ርሃም ፥ ወተና ገ ሮ። እግዚአብሔ
ር። በልሳነ። ፍጥሪት። ደሰዋል። ወ
ደመዮ። እግዚአብሔር። ለ ብር
ሃን። ወፅልተ ። እግዚአብሔር ፡ ብ
ርሃንን። መዓልት። እለው። ሠፈ
ህ። ማሊት። ነው። ሰው። ሲጽርብ
ት። ሲግርበት። የሚ ውል። ስለ ዮ
ነ ። ወ ኑነ። ሌሊ ተ። ወጸጥሐ። ጪ
ለማ። ሁም። እድ ሮ። ነጋ።። ወኮ፞ኑ።
መዓልተ። ብር ሃ ንም። የነ፥ ያ ፪ ዙ፞ ኡ።
ሮ። እዶ ደለም። በዛሬው። ስለታ ወ
ቀ።እን፮ያ ፞ም። ነቢ ደ። ውሬ። ገ ወቀ።
ተ የ ግ ወ ታ ል።። ወ ኡነ። ፭ ዪ። ዕ ለ ተ ፥ ፲

this light is not separate from the seven; it is the revealing

of what was concealed in the element of fire, just as people

reveal a smothered fire with stubble or straw.

If it is asked, 'But in what language did he create this

world?', he created it in the language of Syria (p.6), (for)

in the language of Syria, '**əgziꞌabəher**'[1] means 'God who created

the 22 wonders of creation'.

A. He created it in the Hebrew language; this is known as it

says of Abraham, '<u>And God spoke to him in the language of</u>

<u>creation</u>'[2].

5. <u>And God named the light 'day-time'</u>,

God called the light 'day-time'; it means '<u>work</u>', because

humankind spends the day toiling and labouring[3].

<u>and there was night, and it became dawn</u>,

It became dawn, the night having passed in darkness. [4]<u>And</u>

<u>there was day-time</u> - and there was light[4]; ('day') was not

previously established - (rather, it is so called) because

it is known by what happens today.

A. Moses the prophet spoke it according to that with which

he was familiar.

1. əgziꞌabəher is the Geez name for God.
2. Jub. 12.26 (Charles) = 13.15 (Eth.).
3. Here MS Y adds '<u>and (he called) the darkness 'night-time'</u> -
   he called it 'rest', because humankind spends the night resting,
   having spent the day toiling and labouring'.
4-4. It is not clear if any part of this is intended to be text;
   MS Y omits it.

ፊቶ፡መዓልት፡ፎዱ፡ዕለት፡ሆነ፡
ዕለት፡ብሂል፡ዘይሰተዛወትዎሙ፡
ለመዓልት፡ወሰሌሊት፡እንዲል፡
(እሌ፡ወርቅ፡ተዓዝዕ፡እዩ፡)

፭ ወደቡ፡እግዚእብሔር፡ለዩኩ
ን፡ጠፈር፡ማዕከለ፡ፅማይ፡ዘመ
ልዕልተ፡ጠፈር፡እሁድ፡ማታ፡ለሰ
ቁ፡እጣቢይ፡እግዚእ፡ብሔር፡በው
ሃቄ፡መካነል፡ጠፈር፡ይፈጠ
ር፡እኩ፡ከመ፡ይፋልጥ፡ማዕከ
ለ፡ማይ፡ወማዕከ፡ለ፡ወመይ፡
በውቅያኖስ፡በሐዮስ፡መካነል፡
ደንበር፡ይሆን፡ዘንዱ፡ወኮነ፡ከመ
ሁ፡እንደዘዘው፡ሆነ፡ማእት፡ተ
ፈጠሬ፡ጠፈር፡ማለትያ ይሊ፡ዱ
ኀዕ፡ማለት፡ራው፡ለሐሞስ ኃደ
ጅንፈ፡ነውና፡ሸድም፡ቤቱ፡መለ
ት፡ነው፡በውስጡ፡ሰው፡እራዊት፡
ኜ፡እንሹሳ፡ይምር፡በታልነ፡ወገብሬ፡

and there was 1 day.

Night-time and day-time were 1 day, as it says, 'A "day"

means that which comprises day-time and night-time';   see

Afä wärq Tägsas[1].

6.   And God said, 'Let there be a täfär between the water[2] which

is above the täfär[2].

On Sunday evening, at dawn of Monday, God said, 'Let a täfär

be created in the midst of the water,

so that it divide between water and water;

so that it be a boundary between wəqyanos and hanos[3].

and it was so.

It happened as he commanded,   meaning, 'It was created'.

Täfär means 'power', 'strength' (col. 2), because it is

power, strength to the hanos.

A.   (Täfär) means 'house', because in it live humankind, and

wild and tame animals.

1.   Probably alluding to YAWT p.110, but this is not the source
     of the quotation, which is cited in SFA (p.26), SFG (fol. 14r),
     and referred to the 'awaləd' in KWK p.415.

2-2. This piece of text appears to have been brought forward from
     v.7. täfär translates Greek stereoma.

3.   The lower and upper waters respectively.

ኤግዚኡእብሔር፡ ጠፈሪ፡ ማዕነሎ፡
ማይ፡ ዘታሕተ፡ ጠፈር፡ ወማዕነስ፡
ማይ፡ ዘመልዕልተ፡ጠፈር፡
ወኮነ፡ ክማሁ፡ ይእውን፡ ወገብረ፡
እግዚእብሔር፡ ጠፈሪ፡ ብኩ፡ እመ
ጠወ፡ በሕሞ ሱዒ፡ በውቀይኖስ፡መ
ክነል፡ ደንበር፡ ሰ ዮ፡እብነት፡ በ ክ
ምዓሎ፡ቀቀብ፡ ይላል፡ በዚህ፡ ኤሊ
ት፡ ውቀይኖሽና፡ ሕሞስ፡ ኤንደሐ
ጅት፡ጠፈ፟ር፡ ኤንደሰይፉ፡ ሁነው
እድረዋል፡፡

I ወስመዮ፡ኤግዚእብሔር፡ ለውን
ተ፡ ጠፈር፡ ሰማይ፡

እግዚእብሔር፡ ጠፈርን፡ ሰዕስ፡ማ
ይ፡ ጣ ከ ኣ፡ ነ ው'፡ ደ ፈ ጣ፡ ፲ ቱ ን፡ ሰ ማ
ይ ት፡ ሰ ማ ይ፡ ይ ላ ቸ ዋ ል፡ ሰ ዕ ስ፡ ማ
ይ፡ ማ ለ ት፡ ነ ው ን፡ ብ ኩ ወ ፡ ል ዑ ል ፡ ማ ለ
ት፡ ነ ው፡፡

ወ ር ኣ ይ ፡ እ ግ ዚ እ ብ ሔ ር ፡ ከ መ ፡ ሠ ና
ይ ~ የ በ ቃ ~ ፉ ጥ ረ ት ፡ እ ን ዴ ሆ ነ ፡ እ ወ
ቆ ፡ ፈ ጠ ረ ው ፡ ፡

ወ ኮ ነ ~ ሌ ሊ ተ ፡ ወ ጸ ብ ሐ ~
ጨ ለ ማ ~ ሁ ኖ ፡ እ ድ ሮ ፡ ነ ጋ ፡ ፡

ወ ኮ ነ ~ ፪ ተ ፡ ዕ ስ ተ ~
ሁ ሉ ት ~ ዕ ለ ት ~ ሆ ነ ፡ ሐ ተ ታ ~ ሁ ለ ኟ ዕ

7. And God made a täfär between the water which is beneath the
    täfär and the water which is above the täfär.

    Saying, 'And God made a täfär', he (Moses) introduced that of
    which he said, 'And it was so'. He (God) delineated a
    boundary between ḥanos and wəqyanos.

    Another text reads 'in the likeness of a scabbard'; that
    night, wəqyanos and ḥanos passed the night like a scabbard,
    and the täfär like a sword.

8. and God named that täfär 'sämay',[1]

    God (called) the täfär ('sämay'), which means səʿälä may
    ('picture of the water'). If it is objected. 'It[2] says
    "sämay" of the 7 heavens[2] – does that mean "picture of the
    water"?', then it means 'most high'.

    and God saw that it was beautiful.

    He created it, knowing that it was a worthy creation.

    And there was night, and it became dawn;

    It became dawn, the night having passed in darkness.

    and it was 2 days.

    It was 2 days.

1. Sämay represents Greek ouranos; the suggestion that it means
    səʿälä may is a play on words.
2-2. In place of this, MS Y reads 'It says, 'At the first, God
    created heaven'.'

ሶት፡ ሁለት፡ ፍጥረቶ፡ ፰፡ ሁኖ፡ ኢብነ
ት፡ በአምሳለ፡ አዝርቅ፡ ይላል፡ ጠ
ፈርን፡ በሰማያዊ፡ ቀለም፡ አምሳል፡
ፈጥሮታል፡፡ እጅግም፡ ሊበሩ፡ ዓ
ይን፡ ይበዘብዝ፡ ነበርና፡ እጅግ
ም፡ ቢጨልም፡ ለዓይን፡ ይከብዱ፡
ነበርና፡ ይኸንንም፡ የዓይን፡ ማረፊያ፡
ሊሆን፡ ፈጥሮታል፡፡ ጠፈር፡ ባይኖር፡
ማረፊያ፡ አጥቶ፡ የእንስሳ፡ የዓራዊ
ት፡ ዓይን፡ ወልቆ፡ ወልቆ፡ በወደቀ፡
ነበርና፡

፱ ወይቤ፡ እግዚአብሔር፡ ለይትጋባ
እ፡ ማይ፡ ዘመትሕተ፡ ሰማይ፡ ውስ
ተ፡ ፩ዱ፡ መካን፡

ሰኞ፡ ማታ፡ ለማክሰኞ፡ አጥቢያ፡ ከ
ጠፈር፡ ለታች፡ በዚህ፡ ዓለም፡ ያለ
ውን፡ ውሃ፡ ባንድ፡ ቦታ፡ ተወስኖ፡
የብሱ፡ ይገለጽ፡ አለ፡፡

ወኮነ፡ ከማሁ፡

እንዳዘዘው፡ ሆነ፡ አንድም፡ የብሱ፡
ይላል፡ ይህ፡ ዓለም፡ የብሱ፡ ሁኖ፡ ይ
ገለጽ፡ አለ፡ ተገለጸ፡፡

H.   Day 2, created things 8[1].

Another text reads 'in the likeness of Nile blue'.   He created

the tåfär in the likeness of the colour blue, because if it

were very bright, it would dazzle the eye, and if it were very

dark, it would have overshadowed the eye (p.7);   he created

this to be a resting place for the eye, because if there had

been no tåfär, the eyes of tame and wild animals would have

dropped out and fallen, lacking a resting place.

9.   And God said, 'Let the water which is beneath såmay be

gathered into 1 place';

On Monday evening, at dawn of Tuesday, he said, 'Let the dry

land be revealed, the water which is in this world, beneath

the tåfär, having been confined in one place.

and it was so.

It happened as he commanded.

A.[2] (A.T.V.) reads 'dry land'[2].   He said, 'Let this world

be revealed as dry land';   it was revealed.

1.   8 is the total of 7 on day 1, and 1 on day 2;   MS Y adds Jub.
2.4b (Charles), 'And he made one species' (on the second day).

2-2.   In place of this should probably be read, with MS Y, 'and let
yåbs (dry land) appear - he said, 'Let dry land appear'.
(A.T.V.) reads yåbså ('on dry land')'.

ወእስተጋብእ፡ማይ፡ውስተ፡ም
ዕላዲሁ፡ወእስተርእዩ፡የብስ፡
ውሃው፡በሟ፡ወሐንበት፡ዮቻ፡ቲወስ
ነ፡የብሱ፡ተገለዬ፡ልተታ፡ከዚህ፡እስ
ከብራሕ፡ሰሟዬ፡ዴርስ፡የነበረዉ
ን፡ውሃ፡ክ፪፡ክፍሎ፡ሲቶዉን፡እር
ግቶ፡ጠፈር፡እድርገታል፡ከዚህ፡ክ
ላይ፡ያለዉ፡ብጽብፅ፡ውሃ፡ነዉ፡
ስዉን፡ሐሞስ፡ብኮታል፡ሲሶዉን፡
ዴህን፡ዓለም፡እኔፉ፡ክፍሎ፡ጌኛ
ዉን፡እዓ፡እጉድጉዬ፡በዚዩ፡ወስ
ዮቻል፡ስዉን፡ዉቅይዎስ፡ካኮታል፡

፩ ወሰመዮ፡እግዚእብሔር፡ከየብሱ
ምድሪ፡እግዚእብሔር፡የብሔን፡ም
ድር፡እለዉ፡ማሕዴር፡ማለት፡ነዉ፡
ባለም፡ዕላዲ፡ሁ፡ሰሟዬ፡ሰሟይ፡ሰጣ
ዮ፡ገሐሪ፡ዉ፡

ውሃዉ፡የተወሰነበትን፡ቦታ፡ባሕር፡

፪

እለዉ፡፡ጉድጊዱ፡ማለፉ፡ነዉ፡
ወርእዩ፡እግዚእጠሔር፡ካመ
ሠናይ፡እግዚእብሔር፡የበቃ፡
እንዴሆነ፡እዉቆ፡እዘጋዠ፡

And the water gathered into its gathering place, and dry

land appeared;

The water was confined in the place where it was confined;   the

dry land was revealed.

H.   Having divided into 3 the water which reached from here

as far as the bright heaven[1], he solidified a third part and

made it t̤äf̈är.   That which is above this is fluid water;   he

called its name ḥanos.   Having divided this world into 7, and

dug out the 7th. portion, he confined the (remaining) third in

this world;   he called its name wəqyanos.

10.   and God named the dry land 'mədr',

God called the dry land 'mədr' ('earth');   it means maḥdär[2]

('dwelling place').

and the gathering place of the water he named 'baḥr'.

He called the place in which the water was confined 'baḥr'

('sea') (col. 2);   it means 'pit'.

And God saw that it was beautiful.

God made preparation, knowing that it was worthy.

1.   bəruh s̈amay, probably intended to mean 'the sky', cf. TQ on
     Rev.4.6 (translation in TIA pp.93-6).

2.   Possibly a play on words, cf. 1.8 above, and section 4.4.19
     below.

፸፭ ወይቤ፡እግዚእብሐር፡ለታ
ብቁል፡ምድር፡ሐመልመለሳ፡
ዑር፡ዘደዘራዕ፡በዘርኡ፡ወስ
ለዘመዱ፡ወለኵእርእርእየሁ
ከዚሀም፡ምድርን፡ለምለምኣ
ቱበት፡መስካ፡ቢያየት፡ አድም
፱፡ወር፡በጋ፡ገበሬ፡ሲያንቀረቅ
ባት፡የባጀች፡እርቻ፡ሁዶ፡ቢያየ
ት፡ሰኞ፡መታ፡ማክሰኞ፡እጥቢያ
ጌታ፡በየመልኩ፡በየወገኑ፡በየ
ዘሩ፡የሚዘራውን፡ዘር፡ፉክ
ል፡ምድር፡ታስገኝ፡እለ፡

ወደገብር፡ፍሬሁ፡ዘእመወስ
ጤቱ፡ዘርዕ፡ዘደወድእ፡
ዘእምፍሬሁ፡ሲል፡ነው፡ዘራ፡ነገር
ሁ፡የሚገኛውን፡ፍሬ፡የሚያፈ
ላውን፡ዘፍ፡ተክል፡ታስገኝ፡እ
ለ፡ጤፍ፡ዘርቾ፡ጤፍ፡አንዴ፡ዘ
ርቾ፡አንዴ፡መለት፡ነው፡ዘእ
ምወስቱ፡ቢል፡ከውሱጡ
ዘራ፡የሚገኝ፡እንዲ፡ዱቄባ፡እን
ዲ፡ቆል፡ያለውን፡ዘእምታሕቱ፡
ቢል፡እንዲ፡ሸንኩርት፡እንዲድ
ኒች፡ዘኤምገቦሁ፡ቢል፡እንዲ
ገብስ፡እንዲ፡ማ ጫላ፡ያለውንታ
ስገኝ፡

11. <u>And God said, 'Let the earth produce greenery of grass which is</u>

<u>sown[1] each according to its seed, its species, and its similitude,</u>

And then, when he saw the earth looking like fresh liver,

A. when he saw it like arable land over which a ploughman had

laboured for the 9 summer months[2], on Monday evening, at dawn

of Tuesday[3], the Lord said, 'Let the earth bring forth plants,

seed, each according to its form, its type and its seed.

<u>and[4] which makes its fruit, from within which is seed which</u>

<u>comes out,</u>

He said, 'Let it produce plants, seed, which will give fruit

- reading <u>'which is from it'</u> - the seed of which will be

obtained from it'.   It means (obtaining) <u>teff</u>[5], having sown

<u>teff</u>, and wheat, having sown wheat.

If <u>'which is from within it'</u> is read, (it means) 'the seed of

which is found within it', like the pumpkin and the gourd.

If <u>'which is beneath it'</u> is read, (it means 'the seed of which

is found beneath it'), like the onion and the potato.

If <u>'which is on its side'</u> is read, (it means 'the seed of

which is found on its side'), like barley and maize[6].

1. Although the LXX <u>speiron</u> is active, the Geez is passive (cf.
   variant reading <u>'which seeds'</u> recorded by Dillmann from Bible
   Society MS I).
2. I.e. it was completely bare.
3. MS Y reads (surely incorrectly), 'on Tuesday evening, at
   dawn of Wednesday'.
4. The lemma here omits <u>'tree which fruits'</u>.
5. The grain <u>Eragrostis tef</u>.
6. MS Y adds, 'If <u>'which is on its head'</u> is read, (it means 'the
   seed of which is found on its head'), like <u>teff</u>, wheat,
   Ethiopian maize, and millet'.

ወዘዴአ ሙን ፡ በበዘመዱ ፡ ዲቦ ፡
ምድር ፡

በምድር ፡ ላይ ፡ በየወገኑ ፡ የሚሆ
ነውን ፡ ዘር ፡ ተክል ፡ ታሰንኝ ፡ እሷ ፡

ወኮነ ፡ ከማሁ ፡
እንዲለው ፡ ሆነ ፡ ወለት ፡ እሰገነች ፡፡
ወእውጽእት ፡ ምድር ፡ ሐመል
ዋለ ፡ ሣዕር ፡ ዘይዘራዕ ፡ በበዘ
ርዑ ፡ ወበበዘመዱ ፡ ወለቡ ፡ እር
አየሁ ፡

ወኮነ ፡ ከማሁ ፡ ያለውን ፡ እጩዱ
እት ፡ ምድር ፡ ብሌ ፡ እመጣው ፡ ም
ድርም ፡ በየመልኩ ፡ በየወገኑ ፡ በዮ
ዘሩ ፡ የሚዘራውን ፡ ዘር ፡ ተክል ፡ እሷ
ገነች ፡፡

ወእየ ፡ ዘደፈ ራፈ ፡ ወዘደገብ
ር ፡ ፍሬ ከሁ ፡ ዘእምውስቱቱ ፡ ዘ
ርዑ ፡ ዘይወጽእ ፡ በበዘመዱ ፡ መ
ልዕልተ ፡ ምድር ፡
እውጽእት ፡ ምድር ፡ መል ዕልተ ፡
ምድር ፡ ብለህ ፡ ጣጠም ፡ ምድር ፡
ዘሩ ፡ ከቱ ፡ የሚነኝውን ፡ ፍሬ የ
ሚያፈራውን ፡ ተክል ፡ ዘር ፡ በ
የወገኑ ፡ በዚህ ፡ ዓለም ፡ እሰገኙ ።

<u>and which will be each according to its species, upon the
earth'</u>.

He said, 'Let it produce plants, seed, which will be according to its type, upon the earth' (p.8).

<u>And it was so.</u>

It happened as he said, meaning, 'It produced'.

(12.) <u>And the earth brought out greenery of grass which is sown,</u>
<u>each according to its seed, and its species, and its</u>
<u>similitude,</u>

Saying, '<u>The earth brought out</u>', he introduced that of which
he said, '<u>And it was so</u>'. And the earth produced plants,
seed, sown each according to its form, its type, and its
seed.

<u>and tree which fruits, and which makes its fruit, from</u>
<u>within which is seed which comes out according to its species,</u>
<u>upon the earth.</u>

Place in parallel '<u>the earth brought out</u>', '<u>upon the earth</u>'.
The earth produced, in this world, each according to its type,
plants, seed, which fruits fruit from which its seed is
obtained.

ወር እየ፡ እግዚአብሔር፡ ካሜ
ሠናዩ፡

እግዚአብሔርም፡ የባቆ፡ፍኖሪ
ቱ፡ እንዲሆን፡ አውቆ፡ ፊጠሪ፡ሐተ
ቱ፡ ሰዚህም፡ ቀን፡ ፩፡ ፍጥረታትን፡
ፊጠሪ፡ ወገብሪ፡ እግዚአብሔር
፱ተ፡ ዘመዷ፡ እንዲ_ል፡ በጥፍር
የሚቀልዬ፡ እነወዱን፡ እነትርጕ
እነዚህን፡ የመሰለውን፡ ሁሉ፡ ፪፡
ወገን፡ በመጭዱ፡ የሚታወዪ፡
እንዲገብሱ፡ እንዲአንዬ፡ ይሉፉን፡
እነዚህን፡ የመሰሉ፡ ሁሉ፡ ፫፡ ወገ
ን፡ በመጥሪቢ፡ የሚቆሪጡ፡
እንዲቀንዝ፡ እንዲዘግባ፡ ይለው
ን፡ እነዚህን፡ የመ ሰሳ፡ ሁሉ፡ ፬፡ ወ
ገን፡፡ ፬ኛ፡ ሪይወ፡ ገነትን፡ ምነወ፡
ሪይወ፡ ገነቱ፡ ካዚህ፡ ዓለም፡ ፬ይው፡
ልዩ፡ የቸወን፡ ቢሉ፡ አወን. ልዩ፡ ናቸ
ው፡ ብርሃን፡ አይለየቸውም፡ኛ፡ ፍ
ሬው፡ ቆርጠው፡ ወጸ እፍ፡ ወሶደ
ውት፡ መለሶ፡ ቢሉ፡ተኳተው፡ ደገ
ኛሉኖ፡ እነዚህንም፡ ለመሰብሰብ.
እንዲ መቹ፡ እጅሮን፡ እስገኛኰ፡ ቸዋ
ል፡፡ እኼ ሌታው፡ ቡቃይ፡ እኼ ሌታ
ው፡ ዘርዝር፡ እኼሌታው፡ እሾኢ
እኼሌታው፡ ዷሪቆ፡ ሁነው፡ተገኝተ
ዋል፡ ፬ድ፡ ሒዜ፡ የዷሪሉ፡ እንዲሆን.
ሰው፡ ይ‌ጎሪፊልኖ፡ መገኛተ ቸውም፡

And God saw that it was beautiful.

And God created, knowing that it was a worthy creation.

H. On this day, he created 4 created things, as it says, 'And God made 4 species'[1]. One group - the ones that are nipped off with the finger nails, like the vine, the citron, and all which resemble them. One group - the ones that are reaped with a sickle, like barley, wheat, and all which resemble them. One group - the ones that are chopped with an axe, like wanza and zägba[2] (col. 2), and all which resemble them. Fourthly, the trees of Gännät[3].

If it is asked whether the trees of Gännät are different from the trees of this world, yes, they are different, because light is not separated from them, and because if one picks the fruit, puts it to the mouth, and turns back (to the trees), they are found to have replaced it.

He (God) produced these (the plants) in a manner convenient for gathering (their fruit) - some were produced as shoots, some as unripe fruit, some as ripe fruit, and some dry, because if they were all ready at the same time, human kind would be in difficulties.

1. Jub. 2.8 (Charles).
2. Highland trees, Cordia africana and Podocarpus gracilior.
3. I.e., Eden or Paradise.

ከመሬት፡ሲለሀነ፡ተፈጥራቸው፡ክ
ቷቱ፡ባሕርይት፡ነው፡፡ የውሃ፡ባሕር
ይ፡እንዲላቸው፡ለመጠየቅ፡ቢልቁ
ል፡ቅንጫብ፡የወጉት፡እንደሆነ፡ደ
ም፡ይወጣዋል፡፡ ይህ፡የወሀ፡ባሕር
ይ፡እንዲላቸው፡ይወዱቃል፡፡ ቆርጠ
የጣኩት፡እንደሆነ፡ይበሰጥሳል፡ይ
ህ፡የመሬት፡ባሕርይ፡እንዲላቸው፡
ይወዱቃል፡አስታና፡አስታ፡ይዋጡ
ት፡እንደሆነ፡እሳት፡ይወጣዋል፡ይህ
የእሳት፡ባሕርይ፡እንዲ ላቸው፡ይሰ
ሪዳል፡፡ የነፋስ፡ባሕርይ፡እንዲላቸው
ለመጣየቅ፡በነፋስ፡ይድንጋሩ፡፡ በነፋ
ስ፡ይጣባኩ፡ይፈላኩ፡ይደርቃሉ፡፡

ወንደሲ፡በቀ ላትፉ፡በሑ ነት፡
ነፋስ፡ይነዉባ፡ወይማስን፡እስመ፡
ነፋስ፡ይገዝጽጮ፡ለፉ ሪ፡እንዲል፡
ለነዚህም፡ሁለት፡ሩ ለት፡ባጣር፡
አካቸው፡፡ ነፋስ፡ቆሪ ር፡ነው፡፡
ደ ቡ ስ፡ነው፡፡ መሬት፡ርጡብ፡ነው፡፡
ዱ ቡ ስ፡ነው፡፡ እሳት፡ዉ ዉደ፡ነው፡ ደ
ቡ ስ፡ነው፡ ዉሃ፡ቀሊር፡ነው፡ ርጡብ፡
ዉ፡፡ መሬትና፡ነፋስ፡ጠበ ጮች፡ናቸዉ
ዉ ሃ፡በመን ካቸዉ፡ሁ ሯ፡ይሰታር

Because they (the plants) were produced from the earth, their created nature is from the 4 elements. To verify that they have the element of water - if qwəlqwal[1] or qənčəb[2] is pierced, juice comes out; this verifies that they have the element of water. If it is cut and thrown down, it rots; this verifies that they have the element of earth. If asta is struck against asta[3], fire comes out; this proves that they have the element of fire. To verify that they have the element of wind - they grow by the wind, by the wind they flower, they produce fruit, they dry up, as it says, 'But as for the faculty of plants, in the motion of the wind they lengthen and they perish'[4], because the wind fattens the fruit'[5].

Each of these (elements) has two properties: wind is cold, (and) it is dry[6]. Earth is wet, (and) (p.9) it is dry, fire is burning, (and) it is dry. Water is cold, (and) it is wet. Earth and wind are opponents, and water, being between them, makes reconciliation, being, in its

1. Cacti, species of Euphorbia and Opuntia.
2. Another succulent plant.
3. Erica arborea; MS Y adds 'dog', Ferula communis.
4. Cited from MW, see NTIAC p.149.
5. MS Y omits this quotation, which is also quoted in SFA p.41; its source is unidentified.
6. For 'dry', MS Y, apparently correctly, has 'burning'.

ቃል። በቀዳርነቱ። ክነፋሱ። በር ጡብ
ነቱ። ክመሬት። ጋር። ሁም። እሳትዮ። ወሃ
ጠበኞች። ናቸዉ። ነፋሱ። በመንክላቸ
ዉ። ሁም። ያስታር ቃል። በደሩስነቱ።
ክእሳት። በቀዉሪነቱ። ክዉሃ። ጋር። ሁ
ም። ክዚህ። በታች። ያሉ። ዓለማት። መ
ሏራቃቸዉ። ክዚህ። እንዲጠፈር። ና
ቸዉ። እንዲ ህስ። ባዶሆን። ነፋሱ። እ
ላቱን። እነሳስዶ። እሳት። ዉሃዉን። እ
ነፍሮት። ዉሃ። መሬቱን። እግሬዮት።
በዚህ። ቫሎም። ያሉት። እዝርእት።
እትክልት። ጊፌሬ። በተንተኘቱ ጉ። ነበ
ሬ። እንድ ም። ክሐሊነቱ። እኝንቱቸዋ
ል። እንጅ። የተያይዙ። ናቸዉ። እነዚህ
ም። ሁለቱ። ክቡዲን። ናቸዉ። ነፋሱ
እሳት። ሁከት። ቀሊካን። ናቸዉ። ያየ
ኤን። ናቸዉ። ወጣተዉ። ቫለመኝ። እ
ንዲያጠኳት። ሁከቱ። ክቡዲን። ማየ
መሬቱ። ተጭነዉ። ይዘዋቹዋል። ክቡ
ዱ። ወደታች። እንዲወርዱ። ቀሊኩ
ተሸክመዉ። ይዘዋቹዋል። እነዚህም።
፪። ባሕርዩቱ። ፬ን። ክፍክሰዘመን ተ
ክፍሎዉ። ይመግጉታል። ክመጋቢቱ።

coldness, at one with wind, and in its wetness, at one with earth.   Fire and water are opponents, and wind, being between them, makes reconciliation, being, in its dryness, at one with fire, and in its coldness, at one with water.

The[1] distance between the worlds which are beneath this is[1] like (the distance) from here to the t̤äfär.   If it were not so, the wind would have fanned the fire, the fire would have boiled the water, the water would have heated the earth, and the grains and plants which are in this world would have been charred, would have sizzled.

A.   They (the worlds) are contiguous, but his (God's) omnipotence sustains them.

These two (water and earth) are heavy[2];   the (other) two, wind and fire, are light, they are powerful.   Lest they (wind and fire) issue forth and destroy the world, the two heavy ones, water and earth, press on them and hold them down.   Lest the heavy ones descend to the bottom, the light ones bear them and hold them up.

These 4 elements share the custodianship of the 4 seasons[3].

1-1.   In place of this, MS Y has, 'Just as these exist in this world, so they exist in the foundation of the earth.   The foundation is wind, then fire, then water, then earth.   The distance (of one from the other) is .....'.   SFA p.38 adds further details.

2.   This paragraph continues the theme of the tiered cosmology, made explicit in MS Y, note 1 above.

3.   MS Y says that these seasons are periods of 91 days each.

ቌቿ ቀን፡ ዪምሮ፡ እስከ ሰ፡ ቌቿ፡የ
መሬት፡ ባሕርይ፡ ይመገባል፡ ወርኈ
ፀዱይ፡ ይለዋል፡ ወርኈ፡ መሬት፡ ማለ
ት፡ ነው፡ ይህ፡ ይታወቄ፡ ዘንድ፡ ድን
ጋይ፡ ቢፈረቅሌ፡ ጋን፡ ቢያነሩ፡ ቡቃ
ይ፡ ይገኛል፡ ክስኔ፡ ከቌቿ፡ ዪምሮ፡
እስክ መሩከሪ ም፡ ቌቿ፡ የዉሃ፡ ባሕ
ቌ

ርይ፡ ይመገባል፡፡ ወርኋ፡ ክረምት፡
ይለዋል፡ ወርኋ፡ ማይ፡ ማለት፡ ነው፡፡
ይህ፡ ይታወቅ፡ ዘንድ፡ እፍላጉ፡ ይመ
ሳኩ፡ ኤንቅዕት፡ ይመነጫኩ፡፡ ከመስ
ከሪም፡ ቌቿ፡ እስክታሕሳስ፡ ቌቿ፡ ፋ
ሱ፡ ይመገባል፡ ወርኋ፡ መፀዉ፡ ይለ
ዋል፡ ወርኋ፡ ነፋስ፡ ማኅረ፡ ነው፡፡ ይ
ህ፡ ይታወቅ፡ ዘንድ፡ እዝር እት፡ እሕ
ክልት፡ ይያጠባሉ፡ ይፈራኩ፡ ከታ
ህሰስ፡ ከቌቿ ዪምሮ፡ እስከ ወጋ
ቢት፡ ቌቿ፡ ቀን፡ እጻት፡ ይመገባ
ወርኋ፡ ሐጋይ፡ ቋይለዋል፡ ወርኋ
እጻት፡ ማለኈ ነው፡ ይህ፡ ይታወ
ቅ፡ ዘንግ፡ መሬቱ፡ ሁሉ፡ እንደ
ባት፡ ይቃጠላል፡ እዝር እት፡ እትክ
ልት፡ ይይርቃኩ፡ ይህስ፡ ይሁን፡ የ
ከረምት፡ ዉሃ፡ መሞቂ፡ የበጋ፡ ዉ
ሃ፡ መቀዝቀዙ፡ ሲለ ምነዉ፡ ቢሉ፡ በ

From M̈aggabit 25 until S̈ane 25[1], the element earth is custodian.
It (the source) calls it 'the period of s̈ad̈ay'; it means 'the
period of earth'. To make this known, one finds a shoot
(underneath) if one dislodges a stone or lifts up a pot (during
this period).

From S̈ane 25 until M̈ask̈ar̈am 25[2], the element water (col.2)
is custodian. If (the source) calls it 'the period of kər̈amt';
it means 'the period of water'. To make this known, the rivers
are full and the springs bubble up.

From M̈ask̈ar̈am 25 until Taḥsas 25[3], wind is custodian.
It (the source) calls it 'the period of m̈as̈aw'; it means 'the
period of wind'. To make this known, the grains and the plants
flower and give fruit.

From Taḥsas 25 until M̈aggabit 25[4], fire is custodian.
It (the source) calls it 'the period of hagay'; it means 'the
period of fire'. To make this known, all the earth burns like
fire, and the grains and the plants dry up.

If it is asked, 'Let this be granted, but why is it that
the water of the rainy season is hot, and the water of the
summer is cold?', in the rainy season the burning heat is

1. About April 3 - July 2.
2. About July 2 - October 5.
3. About October 5 - January 3.
4. About January 3 - April 3.

ክረ ምጹ፡ ዊሪዴ፡ ተሸድ ዴ፡ ወደ ሙሬ
ት፡ ውሩጥ፡ ይገባል፡ ሙቀቱ፡ እውሃ
ው፡ ይሰማየል፡፡ በዚህ፡ ዓለም፡ ያሉ
እዘርኗት፡ እትክልት፡ ያብግኑ፡ ይሬ
ሬ ኩ፡፡ የክረምት፡ ውሃ፡ መሞቁ፡
ስለዚህ፡ ነው፡፡ በስጋ፡ ቀር፡ ተሸ ዴ፡
ወደ ሙ ሬት፡ ውስጥ፡ ይገባል፡ ቁ
ሊቱ፡ ወደ ሙሬት፡ ውስጥ፡ ይገግ
ቱ፡ ለውሃ፡ ይሰማል፡ የስጋ፡ ውሃ፡
ሙቀ'ዝቀዙ፡ ስለዚህ፡ ነው፡፡ ይኅዝ

ወደ ቬ፡ እግዚእብሔር፡ ሐይኩኑ፡
ብርሃ ኖት፡ ውስተ፡ ጠፈሪ፡ ሰሙዪ፡
ጠፈርየ፡ ሰማይ፡ ጀድ፡ ወገኑ፡ ማክሰ
ጮ፡ ማቱ፡ ለሪሑሪ፡ እጥ ሪይ፡ ጌተ፡ በሰ
ማይ፡ ፀሐይ፡ ጨ ሪቃ፡ ከዋክብት፡ ይሬ
ሬ ጠሩ፡ እለ፡ ለኑ ድ ጀ ሙ፡ ሰማይ፡ በ ማ

ግል፡ ጠፈር፡ ፀሐይ፡ ጨ ሪቃ፡ ክዋ
ክብት፡ ይሬ ጠሩ፡ እ ኩ፡፡

ክ ወ፡ ያብርሑ፡ ዴ በ፡ ምዴ ር፡፡
ዘዚህ፡ ዓለም፡ ያ በ ሩ፡ ዘንድ፡፡

ወ ይ ፍ ል ጡ፡ ሙ ዕ ክ ለ ፡ ሙ ዓ ል ት ፡ ወ
ሙ ዕ ክ ለ ፡ ሌ ሊ ት፡

በ ሙ ዓ ል ቱ ኝ፡ በ ኬ ሊ ት፡ ሙ ክ ነ ል፡ ይ ኝ
በ ር፡ ሁ ነ ው፡ ይ ለ ይ ፡ ዘ ን ድ፡፡

banished and enters the earth, its heat is felt by the water

(in the earth), and the grains and plants in this world flower

and fruit. This is why the water of the rainy season is hot.

In summer, coldness is banished and enters the earth; its

coldness is felt by the water. This is why the water of the

summer is cold.[1]

(End of) period (of instruction)[2].

(14.) And God said, 'Let there be lights in the tȁfȁr of sämay,

(Grouping) tȁfȁr and sämay together (as the same) - on Tuesday

evening, at dawn of Wednesday, the Lord said, 'Let sun, moon,

and stars be created in sämay'.

A. He said, 'In the tȁfȁr (p.10) which is called sämay,[3] let

the sun, moon, and stars be created'.

so that they shine upon earth,

so that they shine in this world,

and so that they separate between day-time and night-time,

so that they separate between day-time and night-time, being

a boundary,

1. MS W has here omitted v.13; MS Y has, 'And it was three days' -
    Day three, created things twelve' (cf.1.8).

2. guba'e; MS Y has mᴣqwam.

3. MS Y has 'in the sämay which is called tȁfȁr'. The Geez
    expression wᴣstȁ tȁfȁrȁ sämay (representing Greek en tō stereōmati
    tou ouranou) is felt to need explanation.

ወይኵኑ፡ ለትቅያማርታት፡
ለመዓልትና፡ ለሌሊቱ፡ መለይ፡ ምልል
ክት፡ ይሆኑ፡ ዘንድ፡፡ ፀሐይ፡ ኩጕመ
ጢ፡ ጨረቃ፡ እትገባ፡ ተነሱ ቸ፡ ከዚ
ህ፡ ደረስሁ፡ ደላልያ፡ ዮ፡ እንድም
ምሳሴ፡ ይሆኑ፡ ዘንድ፡ ሐተታ፡ ፀሐ
ደ፡ መውጣቱ፡ የመወለዳ ጁን፡ በጠ
ፈር፡ ማብራቱ፡ በዚህ፡ ዓለም፡ የመ
ዋሪቻን፡ መግጋቱ፡ መዋታ ጓን፡
ተመልሶ፡ መውጣቱ፡ የመነሳታ ቻን፡
ምሳሌ፡ ነው ን፡፡ ወ ስእዝመናት፡
ፀ፡ ክፉ ኡ፡ ዘመን፡ ብሎ፡ ለመ ቂ
ጠር፡ ወለመዋሪላት፡ ፲፡ ቀን፡ ብ
ሎ፡ ለመ ቂ ጠር፡፡ እንድም፡ ፴ ፡ ቀ
ን፡ ብሎ፡ ለመ ቂ ጠር፡፡ ወለዓመ
ታት፡ ፫፻፷፭፡ ቀን፡ ዓመት፡ ብሎ
ለመ ቂ ጠር፡ ማልክት፡ ሊሆኑ፡ ፀሐ
ይንና፡ ጨረቃን፡ ከዋክብትን፡ ፈጠሪ

<u>and so that they be for signs,</u>

so that they be a distinguishing mark for day-time and for

night-time, as one would say, 'I set out at sun-rise, or at

the setting of the moon, and reached here'.

A. (it is) so that they be a simile[1].

H. For the rising of the sun is a likeness of our birth,

and its shining in the ẗaf̈ar a likeness of our living in

this world; its setting is a likeness of our death, and its

rising again, of our resurrection.

<u>and for times,</u>

He created the sun, moon, and stars to be a sign, to reckon

saying, '4 seasons',

<u>and for days,</u>

to reckon saying, '7 days',

A. to reckon saying, '30 days',

<u>and for years,</u>

to reckon saying, '365 days a year'.

1. <u>məssale</u>, 'proverb, likeness, allegory, simile, similitude;

this is an alternative understanding of <u>tə'əmərt</u>, 'sign'.

ወይኩት፡ ለእብርሃ፡ በወፈሪ፡ሰ
ማይ፡ ከመ፡ ያብርኁ፡ ለዱበ፡ም
ድር፡ ሰማይ፡ በሚባል፡ ጠፈር፡
ነው፡ በዚህ፡ ዓልም፡ ያበራ፡ዘንድ፡
ዕሐይ፡ ጨረቃ፡ ከዋክብት፡ ይፈጠ
ሩ፡ እለ።

ወኑነ፡ አማሁ፡ እንዲስዉ፡ ሆነ፡
ማፈ፡ ተፈጠሩ።

ወገብረ፡ እግዚእብሔር፡ ፪ተ፡ ብርሃ
ናተ፡ ዐበይተ።

ወኩሎ፡ ከማሁ፡ ያለዉን፡ ንብረ፡ብሶዉ
እጠጣዉ፡ ጌታ፡ ከከዋክብቱ፡ የወበ
ልጡ፡ ዐሐይ፡ ጨረቃን፡ አቈቍብት፡ ፈጠረ

እንድም፡ ዳጋጎቹ፡ ፍጥረት፡ ዐሐይ
ጨረቃን፡ ፈጠረ።

ዘየዐቢ፡ ብርሃን፡ ከመ፡ ይምስል
ክ፡ መዓልተ።

ከጨረቃ፡ የሚበልጥ፡ አድም፡
ደገኛ፡ ፍጥረት፡ የሚሆን፡ ዐሐይ፡
በመዓልቱ፡ ይመግብ፡ዘንድ።

ወዘየንዕስ፡ ብርሃን፡ ከወ፡ይም
ልክ፡ ሌሊተ፡ ምስለ፡ ከዋክብቱ፡
ከዐሐይ፡ ሰክፍሉ፡ ብርሃን፡ የሚያን
ጀ ሪ፡ ጨረቃ፡ ከከዋክብት፡ ጋር፡ ይመ
ግብ፡ዘንድ።

(15.) <u>and so that they be for shining in the täfär of sämay,</u>

<u>so that they shine upon earth;</u>

He said, 'Let sun, moon, and stars be created, so that, being

in the <u>täfär</u> which is called <u>sämay,</u> they shine in this world'.

<u>and it was so.</u>

It happened as he said, meaning, 'They were created' (col.2).

(16.) <u>And God made 2 great lights,</u>

Saying, '<u>He made</u>', he (Moses) introduced that of which he

said, '<u>And it was so</u>'. The Lord created the sun and moon,

which are greater than the stars.

A. He created important created things, the sun and moon[1].

<u>the light which is greater, so that it rule the day-time,</u>

(He created) the sun, which is greater than the moon - A.

which is an important created thing[2] - so that it be custodian

in the day-time.

<u>and the light which is less, so that it rule the night-time,</u>

<u>together with the stars,</u>

(He created) the moon, which is less than the sun in its portion

of light, so that, together with the stars, it be custodian (in

the night-time).

1.   'Greater than the stars' and 'important' are alternative
     interpretations of <u>ᶜabbäyt,</u> 'great'.
2.   Cf. note 1 above - these are two interpretations of
     <u>zäyäᶜabbi,</u> 'which is great'.

ወቤሞሙ፡ኧ እግዚእብሔር፡
ዉስተ፡ጠፈረ፡ሰማይ፡ከመ፡ያበ
ርኁ፡ዲበ፡ምድ ረ።
እንባቆሙ፡ሲል፡ነዉ፡በዚህ፡ዓለም.
ይክሉ፡ዘንድ፡ፈጥሮ፡ጠፈር፡ደሙ.
በዕ፡ሰማይ፡እግ ራ ቸዉ፡
ወይኹንዓሙ፡ለመዓልት፡ወለሌ
ሊት።
በመዓልትም፡ለሌሊትም፡ይመባ
ቡ፡ዘንድ።
ወዩፍልጡ፡ማዕክለ፡መዓልት፡ወ
ማዕክለ፡ሌሊት።
በመዓልቹም፡በሌሊትም ፡ረ መዓ ሩ.
ዘንድ ን ድንበ ር፡ሁነዉ ፡ይሎዩ፡ዘ
ንድ ።
ወርእየ፡ኧግዚአብ ሔ ር፡ክመ፡ክ
መ፡ሠናይ፡የበቁ ፡ዲ ኃ ግ፡ኧ ን ዩ ሁ
ሩ፡እወቆ።ፈጠረ፡ሕ ሩ ታ ።ጫ ረ
ቃ ፡በ ዀ ቸ ዉ፡ኔ ካ ሮ ሱ ፡ተፈጥ ራ ፡ኽ
ታበ ረ ፡ ቆ ዩ ታ ፡ገ ብ ታ ለ ቸ ፡ ፀ ሐ ይ ።በ
ምዕ ራ ብ ፡መ ሽ ከ ት ፡ ተ ፈ ጥ ሮ ፡ወ ዩ
ይ ዉ ፡ ታ ዩ ቹ ፡ ገ ብ ቷ ል ፡ ፀ ሐ ይ ፡ ኧ ኽ ራ
ቢ ሁ ፡ ኧ ን ዲ ል ፡ ኧ ን ድ ም , ፀ ሐ ይ ፡ በ

(17)   and God appointed them in the täfär of sämay, so that they shine

upon earth.

Having created (them) so that they shine in this world -

reading anbäromu ('he placed them' for semomu 'he appointed them')

- he placed them in the sämay called täfär,

(18)   and so that they judge the day-time and the night-time,

so that they be custodians in both day-time and night-time,

and so that they divide between day-time and night-time;

and so that, being a boundary, they make separation, in day-time

and night-time.

and God saw that it was good.

He created, knowing that they were worthy, important, created

things.[1] (p.11).

H.   The moon, having been created in the 4th. kekros[2], remained

shining and set;   the sun, having been created in the window of

the west, appeared and immediately set, as it says,

'Also the sun knew its entrance'.[3]

1.   MS Y has abbreviated the material thus far on v.16, but adds
     quotation of Jub.2.11 (Charles), 'And he made three species'
     (on the fourth day).

2.   kekros, 'one sixtieth part of 24 hours', i.e. 24 minutes;   Dillmann,
     Lexicon col.859, KWK p.531.

3.   Ps.103 (104). 19, apparently poorly copied in the MS;   'entrance'
     represents Geez maʿərab, which may also mean 'west, place of
     setting', but is understood as 'entrance' in AC Ps.103.19.

፪ኛ ፡ ኪክሮስ ፡ ተፈጥሮ ፡ ሲያገሪ
እያመሽቶ ፡ ገብታል ፡ ጨረቃ ፡ በመሉ
ብርሃን ፡ ተፈጥራ ፡ ስታስረ ፡ እድሪ
ገብታለች ፡ ወገበርከ ፡ ወሪ ፡ በእድ
ሚሁ ፡ እንዲል ፡ እንደ ፡ ም ፡ ጨረ
ቃ ፡ ዘመልበት ፡ ተፈጥራ ፡ ስታበራ
እድሪ ፡ ገብታሶች ፡ ፀሐይ ፡ በነጠህ
ተፈጥሮ ፡ ሺያ ሰራ ፡ እድሮ ፡ ጨ
ረቃ ፡ ለገባቸበት ፡ ሞኝት ፡ ገብጬል ፡
ወገበርከ ፡ ወርኃ ፡ በእድሚሁ ፡ ፀ
ሐይኒ ፡ እእመረ ፡ ምዕለቢሁ ፡ እንዲ
ል ፡ ተፈጥሬቸ ዉ ንም ፡ ከዚህ ፡ ደ
ንገራ ታል ፡ ፀፀ ሐይ ፡ ተፈጥሮ ፡ ከነፈ
ሱ ፡ ክእሳት ፡ ነዉ ፡ ፀጨረቃ ፡ ተፈጥ
ሮ ፡ ከውሃ ፡ ክነፈሱ ፡ ነዉ ፡ ደኑ ም ፡
ዴታ ወቅ ፡ ዘንዴ ፡ ፀሐይ ፡ ትመቃለኝ ፡
ተደም ቃሴ ች ፡ ጨረቃ ፡ ትደመቃስኝ
እት ሞቅም ፡ እንዴም ፡ የሁሉም ፡
ተፈጥሬቸዉ ፡ ከነፈሱ ፡ ክነእሳት ፡ ነ
ዉ ፡ ፀሐይን ፡ መወቂ ፡ ድመቂ ፡ ቢስ
ት ፡ ትመቃለኝ ፡ ትደምቃለች ፡ ጨረ
ቃን ፡ ድመቂ ፡ እትመወቂ ፡ ቢለት ፡ ትደ
መቃለኝ ፡ እትሞቅም ፡ የነዚህ ፡ ነገሬ

A.   The sun, having been created in the 4th. <u>kekros</u>, remained
shining until evening, and set;   the moon, having been created
with full light, spent the night shining, and set, as it says,
'And you made the moon in its maturity'[1].

A.   The moon, having been created in fullness, spent the night
shining and set;   the sun, having been created at dawn,
[2]spent the night shining[2], and set in the portal in which the
moon had set, as it says, '<u>And you made the moon in its maturity,
and the sun also knew its entrance</u>'.[3]

(Teachers) speak here of their creation.   The creation of
the sun is from wind and fire;   the creation of the moon is
from water and wind.   To make this known, the sun is hot and
bright;   the moon is bright and is not hot.

A.   The creation of both (sun and moon) is from wind and fire.
As he (God) said to the sun, 'Be hot, be bright', it is hot and
bright;   as he said to the moon, 'Be bright, do not be hot', it
is bright and not hot.

1.   Ps. 103 (104).19;   'maturity' represents Geez ᶜɘdme, 'age',
which is understood to mean 'fullness' in AC Ps. 103.19.

2-2.   Possibly 'spent the night making its circuit', or 'spent the day
shining' is intended.

3.   Ps. 103 (104).19.

ለ፥ብርሃናቱ፡ ዉ፡ እንደምነ፡ዉ፡ቢ
ኩ፡ ለየኩን፡ ብርሃን፡ ክስዉ፡ እር
ፉ፡ ባወቀ፡ ፲፪፡ ክፍለ፡ ብርሃን፡ እ
ምጥዱ፡ ፳፫ን፡ ሰዐሐዩ፡ ፱ን፡ ለዉ
ሬቃ፡ ፬ን፡ ለ ንቀክ ብኢ፡ ፮ን፡ ለ

፲፮

ደዉ ፩፡ ሱ ፵ዱ ታል፡ ወመሠልቱ
ታ፡ ለዐሐዩ፡ ያዉ እዉ ዉ፡ ከእድግ
ር ፡ እንደ ል፡ እ ንደ ምጸ፡ በሬም
ኸ፡ ወቱ ነሠ ኸ፡ ማሪ ብዬ ተ፡ እም
ዘ ወር ኝ፡ ይሳል፡ ብሎ፡ ሱ ለ ን መ
ለዐሐዩ፡ ሰ ኞ ዱ ታል፡ ፉ ራ ነ
ክ ብ ኸ ፡ በ ኞ ቂ ቱ፡ ፤ ታ፡ ብርሃ እ
ን ፡ ፉ ኞ ሮ፡ ከ መ ስ ክ ት፡ እ ሳ ይ ዱ ዉ
ወ ሰ ኝ ኽ ቱ፡ እ መ ሰ ን ኒ፡ ደ ይ ብ ሱ
ኽ ፡ ቀ ድ ሱ፡ ቢ ሉ ቱ፡ እ ን ሰ ፡ እ ዉ
ዉ ፡ እ ማ ዝ ን ፉ፡ ሐ ሬ ር፡ እ ፈ ሱ፡
፳ ኝ ፡ እ ዱ ር ጋ ኹ ሁ፡ ብ ታ መ ተ ዖ
ኑ ኝ ፡ ኤ ወ ዱ ለ ሁ፡ እ ለ ፡ ዱ ሀ፡ ቀ ሐ
ት ፡ ፉ ኞ ሬ ቱ፡ እ ስ ክ መ ቿ፡ ዱ ረ ሱ
ዱ ታ በ ያ ል፡ ብ ሎ፡ በ ኢ ዮ ር፡ ክ ሱ
እ ጋ ን ት ፡ ደ ር ሮ ታ ል ፡፡ ረ ዉ ሱ፡ ዖ ሐ
ዱ ፡ ጨ ረ ቃ፡ ከ ዋ ነ ብ ቱ ን ፡ ፉ ኞ ሮ፡
ኙ ሳ ይ ቿ ዉ፡ መ ሰ እ ኽ ቱ፡ እ መ ሰ ን ኒ፡
ወ እ መ ፡ ተ ፉ ኞ ለ ፡ ክ ዋ ነ ብ ቱ ደ ሱ
ብ ሐ ኒ ፡ መ ሰ ነ ክ ቱ የ ፡ እ ን ደ ል ፡ እ ር

If it is asked what their apportionment of light is, after he said, 'Let there be light', he brought 7 portions of light, by what (only) he knows, and gave 3 to the sun, 2 to the moon, 1 to the stars, and 1 to (col. 2) the clouds, as it says, 'And the third part of the sun will burn up the hills'[1].

A. If it is objected that in Enoch it says, 'And it receives seven-fold more than that of the moon',[2] (then) he gave it all to the sun.

T. - a part of a fuller account[3]. The Lord created light, and showed it to the angels. The angels gave praise. When they told the devil to give praise, he said, 'But I have stepped away from this inclination; but I would like it if you praised me, making me a 4th. (member of the Trinity)'. He (God), saying, 'For how long will this erring creature remain proud?', added him to the demons in iyyor[4]. On the fourth (day), having created the sun, moon, and stars, he showed them (to the angels); the angels gave praise, as it says, 'And when my stars were created, my angels praised me'.

1. Ecclus. 43.4. Similar material is found in AC Ecclus. 43.4, and comparable material different in detail in SFA pp.48-9.
2. Possibly En. 72.37 (Charles). MS Y, in place of this, cites En. 73.6, and SFA p.49 cites En. 22.4 = En. 73.3 (Charles).
3. Similar, or complementary, material is found, e.g. in AC Rev. 12.17 (see TIA), Aksimaros for Wednesday (especially the 'Vision of Gorgoryos' which it includes), SFG, SFA pp.70-4, and AC MW pp.15-16.
4. One of the 7 heavens, the 5th. from the highest.

ሩ፡ሳይ፡መስዓኝ፡ቀረ። በጨልሰማ፡
እጐነድጵዮ፡በመካ፡ካይ፡እዉ
ርዩታል።ዘሬ፡ንጐሰዉ፡የተጣላ
ዉኝ፡ሰዉ፡በርጥካብ፡ቆልርበ
ት፡ጣቅሰወ፡ገዴል፡እንዴይኈኝ
ከዉ። ይህዎም፡ምሳጌ፡ነዉ።ፀ
ሐይ፡የኝ፡ጥእን፡ምሳጌ። ፀሐይ፡
በዋስዮ፡ ደንቾ፡እንዴ፡ዮሪ፡ኃጥ
እንዎም፡ በኝ፡ጢእት፡ ፀንተዉ።
ይዮራሉ፡ኝ፡ ሜነቀ፡የበድ፡ቃን፡ም
ቴሌ፡ ሕፀ፡ እንድ፡ታ፡ደርግ፡ ዳድ
ቃንዖ፡ ያጠእት፡ ፩ድ። ጊጴ፡ ድል
ስትነሳ፡ቸዉ፡ ፪ድ። ጊዜ፡እ፡ህሉ፡
ድ፡ል፡ ሲነፋ፡ት። ይዮራሉ፡ኝ። ስጠ
ዩ፡ይ፡ፀደድቅ፡ ዳድ፡ቅ፡ ዉሉጣበ፡ይ፡ት
ነዣኤ፡እንዴ፡ል፡ እንድ፡ዎም። ፀሐዩ፡የዳ
ድቃኝ፡ በጠርኅኡ፡ፀንቾ፡እንዴ፡፩ም
ር፡በምግባር፡በትሩፋት። ፀንተ፡ዉ፡
ይዮራሉ፡ሜ፡ሬቃ፡የኝ፡ጥ፡እን፡ ሕፀፀ፡
እንዴ፡ይደርግ። ያጥእንዎም፡ ፀዉቀተ
ቸዉ፡ እያ፡ነስ፡ ይሔዲፀ፡ኝ። ሉ፡ሉ፡ ሰአ
ብዩ፡ የነዴፄ፡ ካመ። እንተ፡ ዉርኝ፡
እንዴ፡ለ፡እንድ፡ም። ፀሐ፡ይ፡የኝ፡ታ፡
ሜ፡ረቃ፡የ፡ሕፀርይ፡ት፡ ንዋ፡ንክሑ፡ት። ም
ፉል፡ይ፡አ፡ር፡ድ፡እ፡ት። ምሳጌ፡እንድ፡ም።

He (the devil) failed to give praise. He (God), enfolding
him in darkness, threw him down on Mecca,[1] just as today a
king will have a person with whom he is angry wrapped in a
fresh animal skin and thrown over a precipice.

This is a simile. The sun is a likeness of the sinners,
because just as the sun remains strong in its burning, so
also the sinners remain strong in sin. The moon is a likeness
of the righteous, because just as the moon wanes, so also the
righteous live sometimes sin defeating them, and at other
times they defeating it (p.12), as it says, 'The righteous
one falls seven times, and rises up seven times'[2].

A. The sun (is a likeness) of the righteous; just as (the
sun) remains strong in its light, so (the righteous) remain
strong in good deeds and virtue. The moon (is a likeness)
of the sinners, because just as (the moon) wanes, so also the
knowledge of the sinners becomes less and less, as it says,
'The heart of the mad wanes like that of the moon'[3].

A. The sun is a likeness of the Lord, the moon of the
apostles, and the stars of the disciples.

1. Cf. AC MW p.15 col.1.
2. Prov. 24.16, also cited in SFA p.52.
3. Ecclus. 27.11 (though the text differs from that in AC Ecclus.),
    also cited in SFA p.52.

በሕይ፡ የገለመዱ፡ ጨራቃ፡ የጋለ፡
፲፡ ክዎዝብቱ፡ የጋለ፲፡ ምሳሴ፡ ፕቀ
ፊ፡ግልዕ፡ካብሩን፡

፲፯ ወኮነ፡ ሌፊተ፡ ወይሕብሕ፡
 አለማ፡ ሆኑ፡ አድ፡ዎ፡ነገ፡
ን፡ ፩፡ተ፡ሰለተ፡

፩፡ቀን፡ሆነ፡ ሰላፉ፡ ፪፡ ፍጥሬቱ፡
፲፬፡

ወይቤ፡እግዚእብሔር፡ ላታ፡ ወጾእ፡
ማይ፡ ዘይትሕወስ፡ ዘሎ፡ መንፈሬ፡
ሕይወት፡

ሬቡሪ፡ ማታ፡ ከሕሰሙሪ፡ እኖሪይ፡
ደመ፡ፙሱ፡ የሌላተ፡ ግሕር፡ በደ
መ፡ነፉሪ፡ ሕፀዎን፡የሆሪ፡ ፍጥሬታ
ተን፡ታስገኝ፡ እሰ፡

ወእፀዋፈ፡ ዘይሠርፋ፡ ወልዕልተ፡
ይዐድር፡ ወመትሕተ፡ ሰማይ፡
ካጠፌር፡ ብታቱ፡ ክያዐድር፡ በአይ፡
የሚ፡በሪ፡እፀዋሬንያ፡ታስገኝ፡እሊ
ወኮነ፡ክማሁ፡

ይገኙ፡እንዲሪ፡ተገኙ፡

A. The sun is a likeness of the one that bore one hundred,
the moon of the one that bore 60, and the stars of the one
that bore 30[1]. Quote 'The glory is different ...'[2].

19. And it became night-time, and it dawned;
It became darkness; the night having passed, it dawned.

and it was day 4.
It became 4 days. The day was 4, the created things 15.

(20) And God said, 'Let the water bring out that which moves, in
which is the spirit of life,
On Wednesday evening, at dawn of Thursday, he said, 'Let the
sea, which contains no animal faculty[3], produce created things
which are living with animal faculties'.

and birds which fly above earth and below sämay';
He said, 'Let it produce birds which fly beneath the ẗafär
and above earth'.

and it was so.
As he said, 'Let them be produced', they were produced.

1. Referring to Mt.13.8 and parallels.
2. I.e. the teacher is instructed to quote 1 Cor. 15.41.
3. dämä näfs, see also NTIAC p.149 for the part of MW which
    deals with the (Aristotelian) 'vegetative, sensitive, and
    rational faculties'.

ወገሪ፡እግዚእብሔር፡ እኖብርተ፡
ፀበዩት፡፡

ጌታ፡ታላላቅ፡ፍጥረታት፡የሚሆኑ፡
ብሔሞትንና፡ሌዋታንን፡ፈጠረ፡፡
ወነጎኩ፡ነፍሰ፡ሕይወት፡ዘይትሐወስ
ዘአውፅኡ፡ማይ፡በበዘመዶ፡
በየወገኑ፡ባሕር፡ያስገኝቸው፡በል
በቸው፡የሚንቧቧትን፡በዳመ፡ነፍሰ
ሕይዋን፡የሚሆኑትን፡ፍጥረታት፡
ፈጠረ፡ብሔሞትና፡ሌዋታን፡ቲፈን
ፈቸው፡ከእንስሳ፡ወገን፡ነበረ፡ፀጸ
ዬት፡ስለሆኑ፡ለዬዱ፡እጧቸው፡፡
ወነጎኩ፡አዕዋፈ፡ዘዶወርፈ፡በበዘ
ጦዳሙ፡፡

በየጦዋገን፡በየወገናቸው፡የሚ፡በራ፡
እዕዋፍን፡ሁሉ፡ፈጠረ፡
ወርእየ፡እግዚእብሔር፡ከመ፡ሠናይ
ዬ፡የበቁ፡ፍጥረታት፡እንደሆኑ፡እጧ
ቅ፡ፈጠረ፡፡
ወባረኮሙ፡እግዚእብሔር፡ወይቤ፡
ብዝኑ፡ወተጋዝኡ፡ወምልዑዋ፡ኩጡ
ፅርየዉስተ፡ምጽር፡
እዕዋፍንም፡በዚህ፡ዓለም፡ይበዙ፡
ዘንድ፡እዘዣቸው፡ሐተተ፡በዚህ፡ቁን
፫፡ፍጥረታት፡ፈጥሬል፡በልባቸው፡

21. And God made great monsters (col. 2),

The Lord created Behemoth and Leviathan, which are great

created things.

and every soul of life which moves, which the water brought

out, each according to its species,

He created created things which are living with animal

faculties, which crawl on their belly, which the sea produced,

each according to its type. The created nature of Behemoth

and Leviathan was from the type of tame animals, (but)

because they were great, he mentioned them separately.

and all the birds which fly, each according to their species;

He created all the birds which fly, each according to their

various types.

and God saw that it was good.

He created, knowing that they were worthy creations.

(22) And God blessed them, and said, 'Be many and multiply[1]

in the earth',

And he ordered the birds, that they be many in this world.

H. On this day he created 3 created things - ones which

1. After this 'and fill the earth' has been deleted in MS W.

የሚሳቤ፡ በእግራቸው፡ የሚጇክሪ
ከሉ፡ በክንፋቸው፡ የሚበራትን፡
እንዲቆቅ፡ እንዲ ጅግራ፡ ይራትን፡፡ እን
ዚህን፡ የመስክ፡ ሁሉ፡ ጃጅ፡ ወገን፡ በ
ክንፋቸው፡ የሚ በራትን፡ እንዳ9ፉ፡
እንዳ ግሶር፡ ያራትን፡ እነዚህን፡ የመ
ስስ፡ ሁ ሉ፡ ጃ ወገን፡ መገኘቻቸው፡ ምን
ም፡ ከ ግሕር፡ ቢ ሆን፡ ተፈጥሮቻቸው፡ ክ
ፎ ዱ፡ ግሕርያት፡ ነው፡፡ ከነዚ ህግሁ፡ ከባ

ሕ ር፡ ተገኝ ተው፡ በዚ ያው፡ ያን ተው፡
የቀሉ፡ እኮ፡፡ ጃ ጅ፡ ጊ ዚ፡ ወዴ የብሶ፡
ጄ፡ ጊ ዚ፡ ወዴ ግሕር፡ የሚ ቡ፡ ኩኩ፡
ስ ሪ ው፡ ስ ሪ ው፡ ስ ሪ ው፡ የ ፌ ያ፡ እኩ፡
ዩ ጁ ው ም፡ ምሳ ሌ፡ ነው፡ በሕ ር፡ የ 9
ምቀ ት፡ በ ግሕ ሩ፡ ያን ተ ው፡ የ ቀ ሩ ቱ፡
ብ ክ ር ስ ፖ ቸ ው፡ ያን ተ ው፡ የ ሚ ው
ሩ፡ ስ ዋ ኝ፡ ም ሳ ሌ፡ ነው፡፡ ስ ሪ ው፡
ስ ሪ ው፡ የ ሉ ያ ሩ ት፡ ወ ዴ ክ ህ ዴ ቱ፡ የ ሉ
ዱ፡ ስ ዋ ኝ፡ ም ሳ ሌ፡ ነው፡፡ ጃ ጅ፡ ጊ
ዚ፡ ወ ዴ ባ ሕ ር፡ ፅ ጅ፡ ጊ ዚ፡ ወ ዴ የ
ብ ስ፡ የ ሚ መ ዜ ሉ፡ ክ ር ስ ቲ ያ ን፡ ክ
መ ኝ፡ እ ስ ላ ም፡ ወ ዴ መ ሆ ን፡ እ ስ ላ
ም፡ ክ መ ሆ ን፡ ክ ር ስ ቲ ያ ን፡ ወ ዴ መ

crawl on their belly[1], ones which run on their legs, and
ones which fly with their wings. The ones like partridge
and guinea fowl, and everything that resembles these, are
1 group[2]. The ones that fly with their wings, like small
birds and hawks[3], and everything that resembles these, are
1 group[4].

Even though they are produced from the sea, their
created nature is from the 4 elements[5] (p.13).

From among these, there are some which, having been
produced from the sea, have remained there. There are
some which go at one time to dry land, and at another to
the sea. There are many which fly away. This is a simile.
The sea is a likeness of baptism. The ones which remain
living in the sea are a likeness of the people who stand
firm in their Christian baptism. The ones which fly away
are a likeness of the people who have gone off to apostasy.
The ones which go to and fro, at one time to the sea, and
at another to the dry land, are a likeness of the people
who go to and fro, from being a Christian to

1. MS Y gives the spider and the lizard as examples.
2. I.e. the group which run.
3. ʿof and nəsr; nəsr may mean 'eagle', but here it seems to
    be a generic term for birds of prey, and ʿof for other birds.
4. I.e. the group which fly. MS Y says there are 4 groups, but
    only lists these 3.
5. (and not from water only).

ሆን፡ የሚመስሉ፡ ሰዎች፡ እምሳሌ፡
ነው፡፡ አንድም፡ ወባረኮሙ፡ ለ፪
ሆሙ፡ በአሐቲ፡ በረከት፡ ይላል፡ ብዙ
ሁሉም፡ የበገኑ፡ ነው፡ ብኩ፡ ባሕር፡
የዚህ፡ ዓለም፡ በባሕር፡ ዲንተው
የቀሩት፡ በሚስታቸው፡ ዲንተው፡
ቈርበው፡ ጺጽቀው፡ ከሠራቱ
ን፡ በኋላቱን፡ እውጥተው፡ የሚ
ኖሩ፡ የ፩ብእ፡ ዓለም፡ ምሳሌ፡ ነ
ው፡፡ በሌው፡ በሌው፡ የሌዩት፡ ሕ
ድግዎ፡ ወመንንዎ፡ ለዝ፡ ዓለም፡
ብለው፡ የሌዩ፡ የመናንያን፡ ምሳሌ፡
ነው፡፡ ፩ድ፡ ጊዜ፡ ወይየብስ፡ ፩ድጊ
ዜ፡ ወይባሕር፡ የሚሉ፡ ተድላ፡ ዓለ
ም፡ ሲያናባቸው፡ ወይፅበ፡ ገዳ
ም፡ ዕፀበ፡ ገዳም፡ ሲያዩቸው፡ ወ
ደተድላ፡ ዓለም፡ የሚሉ፡ ሰዎች፡
ምሳሌ፡ ነው፡፡ ይመ፡ ነፍስ፡ ከሌ
ላት፡ ባሕር፡ በይመ፡ ነፍስ፡ ሕያዋን፡
፲፯
የሚሆኑ፡ ፍጥረታት፡ እንዲተገኙ፡
ለምዕመናን፡ ምንጊንያቱ፡ ሕይወ
ት፡ የሚሆን፡ ጌታ፡ ከእመቤታች
ን፡ ለመገኘቱ፡ ምሳሌ፡፡
፳፫ ወኮነ፡ ሌሊተ፡ ወጸብሐ፡፡
ዕለተ፡ ሆኖ፡ አድሮ፡ ነጋ፡

being a Muslim, and from being a Muslim to being a Christian.

A.   If it is objected that it says, 'And he blessed the 2 of them with one blessing'[1], then it is all (a simile) of good - the sea is a likeness of this world. The ones that remained in the sea are a likeness of the people of the world[2] who remain with their wives, receive the eucharist (with them), are righteous, and give tithes and first fruits. The ones that fly away are a likeness of the hermits who went away, saying, 'Leave this world, and renounce it'[3]. The ones who go at one time to dry land and at another to the sea are a likeness of people who, when the pleasures of the world weigh upon them go to the privations of the monastery, and when the privations of the monastery weigh upon them, go back to the pleasures of the world.

The production of created things which are alive with the animal faculty from the sea which has no animal faculty[4] (col.2) is a simile of the production of the Lord, who is the principle of life for the faithful, from our Lady (Mary).

23.   and it became night-time and it dawned,

It became dark;   the night having passed, it dawned.

1.   Also cited in SFA p.58, but the source is unidentified; possibly it is an expansion of Gen.1.22.
2.   I.e. people who have not taken monastic vows.
3.   Source unidentified;   it may not be an actual quotation.
4.   See 4 Ezra (2 Esd.) 6.48 (NEB capitation).

ወኮነ፡ ፮ቱ፡ ዕለተ፡
፮፡ዕለት፡ ፲፰፡ ፍጥረት፡ሆነ።
ወይቤ፡እግዚአብሔር፡ለታው
ጽእ፡ባሕርይምድር፡ዘመዱ፡እንስሳ
ሐመሙስ፡ማታ፡ ለዓርብ፡አጥቢ
ያ፡የእንስሳ፡ወገን፡የሚሆን፡ፍ
ጥረት፡ሁሉ፡ይፈጠሩ፡አለ።
ወዘይትሐወስ፡በልባቸው፡የ
ሚሳቡ፡በእግራቸው፡የሚ
ሽከረከሩ፡ፍጥረታትን፡ሁ
ሉ፡ምድ፡ታስገኝ፡አለ።
ወአራዊተ፡ምድር፡ዘበበዘመ
ዱሙ።
በዚህ፡ዓለም፡የሚኖሩ፡ፍጥ
ረታትን፡ታስገኝ፡አለ፡ሎቱኤል፡
እዝራ፡ወእዕዋፊ፡ዘይሠርሩ፡
ጣበሎ፡ጨምሮበታል።
ወኮነ፡ከማሁ፡እንዳለው፡ሁነ፡
ማለት፡አስገኘ።
ወገብረ፡እግዚአብሔር፡እንስ
ሳ፡በበዘመዱ፡
ጌታ፡እንስሳትን፡በየወገናቸው፡ፈ
ጠረ።በክንፋቸው፡የሚበሩ፡
ፍጥረታትን፡ፈጠረ፡

and it was day 5.

It became day 5, 18 created things.

(24) And God said, 'Let the earth bring forth species of tame
animals,

On Thursday evening, at dawn of Friday, he said, 'Let every
created thing which is of the tame animal type be created'.

and that which moves,

He said, 'Let the earth produce all created things which
crawl on their belly and run on their feet'.[1]

and the wild animals of the earth, each according to their
species';

He said, 'Let it produce created things which live in this
world'. Sutu'el Ezra has added to it, saying, 'and birds
which fly'[2].

and it was so.

It happened as he said, meaning, 'It produced (them)'.

(25) And God made tame animals, each according to its species,

The Lord created tame animals, each according to their types;
he created created things which fly with their wings.

1. MS Y adds 'horse, mule, cow, bull' as examples of these.
2. 4 Ezra (= 2 Esd.), probably 6.47 (NEB capitation).

ወነሱሎ፡ ዘደኅሐ ወሪ፡ ውሪቱ፡
ምድር፡ ሰበ ዘመዱ፡፡

በልባጡው፡ የሚሳቡትን፡ በኅግ
ራቸው፡ የሚሽከረከሩትን፡ በየ
ወገናቸው፡ ፈጠረ፡ ወእራዊተ፡ ም
ድር፡ ሰበ ዘመዱ፡፡

የምድር፡ እራዊትንም፡ በየገናቸ
ው፡ ፈጠረ፡፡

ወርእየ፡ እግዚእብሔር፡ ከመ፡ ሠ
ናዬ፡ የበቁ፡ ፍጥረታት፡ እንደ ሆዱ፡
አዉቆ፡ ፈጠረ፡ በዚህም፡ ቀን፡ ፫፡
ፍጥረታት፡ ፈጥሮል፡፡ ወገብረ፡ እ
ግዚእብሔር፡ ሠ ከሰተ፡ ዘመዱ፡
እንዲ ል፡ በልባቸው፡ የሚሳቡ፡
ቱን ቀዳቃሾችን፡ እንደ ሿሪሪቱ፡እ
ንዲ እንሿላ ሪቱ፡ያ ሉቱን፡ ሁሉ፡ ፬፡
ወገን፡ በእዋራቸው፡ የሚ ሽነረ
ክ ሬ ቱ፡ እራዊት፡ እንስሳትን፡ ፯ድ
ወገን፡ በክን ፈ ቸው፡ የሚ በረ
እንስርት፡ እ ዕዋፍን፡ ፮ ድ ወገን
እ ድ ር ን፡ ፈ ጥ ሮ ል፡ እ ነ ዚ ህ ም፡ መ
ንኘታ ቸው፡ ከ የ ብስ ፡ ስ ለ ሆ የ ፡ ፖ ራ
ጥ ራ ቸው ፡ ከ ፎ ቱ ፡ በ ሕ ጭ ዩ ቱ ፡ ነ
ው ፡ ፡ ዕ ሰ ት ፡ ስ ድ ሰ ት ፡ ፍ ጥ ረ ት ፡ ፬ ፡

and everything that moves in the earth, each according to

its species,

He created ones which crawl on their belly (p.14),

and which run on their feet, each according to their type.

and wild animals of the earth, each according to its species;

He created the wild animals of the earth, each according to

their type.

and God saw that it was good.

He created, knowing that they were worthy creations.

On this day[1] he created 3 things, as it says,

'And God made three species'[2]. He created, making 1 group

the ones that move around crawling on their belly, like spiders

and lizards, another group the wild animals and the tame

animals that run on their legs, and another group the hawks

and small birds[3] that fly with their wings.

Because they were produced from dry land their created

nature is from the 4 elements.

Day six, created things 21[4].

1. I.e. day 5.
2. Jub. 2.13 (Charles), 2.17 (Geez).
3. See comment on 1.22 above.
4. 21 is the total so far, leaving only human kind as the 22nd.

ወይቤ፡ኡግዚእብሔር፡ንግበር፡
ሰብአ፡በእርአያነ፡ወለአምሳሊነ፡
ጌታ፡ዓርብ፡ብነግሕ፡በጆ፡አምሳል፡
በጆ፡እርአይ፡ሰዉን፡እንፍጠር፡ኡ
ሐቱ፡ንግበር፡ማለት፡ይጅነቱ፡
በእርአይነ፡ማለቱ፡የኰነት፡፡እንደ
ም፡ንግበር፡ይሉዉ፡ያንድነት፡የሰ
ስትነት፡ደሆናል፡ንግበር፡ብኰ፡ማብ
ዣቱ፡የኰነት፡ኤንደ፡፩፡ቃል፡ሁም፡ን
ግበር፡ማለት፡ያይነት፡እየሬቸዉ፡
ቃል፡ልብ፡እሱቱንፉሱ፡ቢሞራቸዉ፡
ኤኔ፡ካድርግ፡እንተ፡እድርግ፡አሉያ
ድርግ፡ገሉ፡ነበርያ፡፡ኢዴቤ፡እግበር፡
ኤነ፡ወእንተ፡ ጠበር፡ ወዴግበር፡ዝኰ፡
ኤካ፡ይቤ፡ኤግዚእብሔር፡ንግበር፡
እንዲልል ፡፡ በእርአይነ፡ያለዉ ምጀኝት ፡
የኰነት፡ደሆናል፡በኰቱ፡እርእይ፡ጀድ
ሰዉ፡ ጠገኙት፡ ያንድነት፡በእርእይነ፡ጠ
ኰ፡ ጠዘርዘሩ፡የኰነት፡ሠራሴን፡በ ጠ
ን፡እንመስላቑዋስን፡ቢሉ፡ሠካሴ፡
ሰባዉይን፡ነካብይን፡ሕደዉን፡ናቸዉ፡
እኞም፡በነፍስ፡ሰባዉይን፡ነገብይን፡
ሕደዉን፡ነገና፡እንድም፡ለሰዉ፡ልብ

(26) <u>And God said, 'Let us make man in our appearance and in</u>

<u>our likeness,</u>

On Friday, at dawn, the Lord said, 'Let us create man in

our likeness and in our appearance'.

H.   '<u>Let us make</u>' (shows) the unity of (God);   '<u>in our</u>

<u>appearance</u>' (shows) the trinity[1].

A.   His saying '<u>let us make</u>' may show (both) unity and

trinity - his saying '<u>let us make</u>' in the plural shows the

trinity, (and) his saying '<u>let us make</u>' while being as one

voice shows the unity, because if each of them individually

had a voice, a heart, and breath, they would have said,

'Let me make (it)', 'You make (it),' 'Let him (col. 2)

make (it)', as it says, '<u>It does not say "Let me make (it)"</u>,

<u>or "You make (it)" or "Let that one make (it)"</u>,

<u>but God said "Let us make"</u>[2].'

Also his saying '<u>in our appearance</u>' may show (both) unity

and trinity.   The production of 1 person in the appearance of

the 3 shows the unity;   his saying '<u>in our appearance</u>' with

the (plural) pronominal suffix shows the trinity.

If it is asked, 'To what shall we liken (the members of)

the Trinity?', (the members of) the Trinity are understanding,

speaking, and living, because we, in (our) soul, are under-

standing, speaking, and living.

1.   Material similar in intent, but different in detail, is
found e.g. in SFA p.66, and in <u>AAM</u> pp.17-8.
2.   Cyr. T., Severianus of Gabala (B.M. Weischer, <u>Qērellos IV 3</u>,
pp.44-5.).

ቃል፡ እስትንፋሱ፡ እንዲ ለው፡ ሠላ
ሴም፡ በልብ፡ ለቃል፡ ስ እስትንፋሱ ደ
ወሲራሉና፡ አንድም፡ ለሰው፡ ፍጹም፡
መልክ፡ እንዲለ ው፡ ለሠላሴያ፡ መልክ
አላቸ ው ን፡ ነእምን፡ ከመ ብ፡ ለ እ ዐዢ
ኒ ጥሐር፡ መልክ ገባት፡ ጽ ዱ ቃት፡ ዓይ ን
ወ እዝ ን፡ እ ዐ ደ ው፡ ወ እ ዕ ጋ ር፡ ወ ρ
እሉ፡ ተርፉ፡ እ ያ ቤ ሆ ን፡ አ ገ ላ ት፡ እ ን
ዲ ል፡፡ እ ን ድ ም፡ በ እር እ ይ ን፡ ወ በ እ ም
ቂ ሊ ን፡ ከ መ ደ ከ ሔ ን ን፡ ይ ላ ል፡፡ ሠላ ሴ
በ ገ ሕ ር ደ፡ የ ሚ ገ ዙ ች ን፡ እ ኛ፡ በ ዓ ጋ፡
እ ን ገ ዛ ስ ግ ና ፡፡ ቡ ፡ በ እር እ ይ ፉ ፡ ከ መ
ይ ኑ ዕ ን ን፡ ይ ላ ል ፡፡ ከ መ ደ ኑ ሔ ን ን ፡ ዓ
ሣ ተ ፡ ግ ሕ ር ፡ ወ እ ራ ዊ ተ ፡ ም ድ ር ፡ ወ
እ እ ዋ ፈ ፡ ሰ ማ ይ ፡ ፡

እ ራ ዊ ት ን ፡ እ ዕ ዋ ፍ ን ፡ ዓ ሣ ት ን ፡ ይ ገ ዝ ፡
ዘ ን ድ ፡ ኡ ዱ ም ን ፡ እ ን ፍ ጠ ር ፡ እ ሉ ፡፡

A. Because just as a person has a heart, a voice, and breath, so also (the members of) the Trinity are likened to heart, voice, and breath.

A. Because just as a person has a complete form, so also (the members of) the Trinity (each) have a form, as it says, 'We believe that God has real bodily parts - eye and ear, hands and feet, and he has organs which are in addition to these'[1].

A. (A T.V.) says '.... in our appearance and in our likeness, in order that he judge'[2] - because we govern by grace the ones that (the members of) the Trinity govern by nature.

A. (Another T.V.) says '.... in our appearance, in order that he judge'[3].

in order that he judge the fishes of the sea, and the wild animals of the earth, and the birds of heaven[4],

They said, 'Let us create Adam, so that he govern the wild animals, the birds, and the fishes,

1. Also quoted in some texts of AAM, in the Məstira̋ səllase, e.g. SFA p.97, where it is attributed to the '300' (Nicene fathers); the text does not appear in the qəddase of the 300, or in the part of HA attributed to them, but similar words occur elsewhere in HA, notably HA Athanasius of Alexandria, p.88.

2. The 'text' has been read as wa̋yəkwa̋nnən (as read by Dillmann); the variant noted here is ka̋ma̋ yəkwa̋nnən (as read by BK).

3. Translation and comment on this variant appear to have been omitted.

4. sa̋may, hitherto transliterated in this translation.

ወእንስሳሃ፡ ወኵሉኮ፡ ምድረ፡
እንስሳትን፡ ዓለሙን፡ ሁሉ፡ ደገዛዘ
ንድ፡፡

ወኮቶሎ፡ ዘይትሐወሱ፡ ዲበ፡ ምድር
ር፡ በምድር፡ የሚመላለሱን፡

ሁሉ፡ ደገዛ፡ ዘንድ፡፡ አዳምን፡እንፍጠ
ር፡ እሉ፡፡

፲፻ ወጊዞ፡ እግዚአ፡ ብሔር፡ ሎፚለእ
መሕየዉ፡ በእመሳለ፡ እግዚአብሔ
ር፡ ጌታ፡ እዳምን፡ በራሱ፡ እምሳ
ል፡ ፈጠረዉ፡ እብ፡ ቢሉ፡ ወወልዱ
በመንፈ፡ቅዱሱ፡ እምሳል፡ እዳምን፡
ፈጠረዉ፡ እንድ፡ያ፡ ወልዱ፡ ቢሉ
በእብ፡ በመንፈ፡ ስቅዱ፡ ሱ፡ እምሳል፡ ፈ
ጠረዉ፡ እንድ፡ያ፡ መንፈ፡ ስቅዱ፡ ስ
ቢሉ፡ በእብ፡ በወልድ፡ እምሻል፡ፈ
ጠረዉ፡፡ ሰለያዉን፡ እዳያዉን፡ብንግሕ፡
የቀሩ፡ችን፡ ባሠርኌ፡ ፈ ጠረ፡ ቢሉ፡የ
ሠርኌ፡ ቱኵ ታደ፡ ጭኌጭ ነዉ፡፡ እነ
ዚያን፡ እላዋቄች፡ ናቸዉ፡ ሲል፡ የነግ
ሕ፡ተኵ ታዩ፡ ብርሃን፡ ነዉ፡እርሱን
ም፡እላዋቄ፡ ነዉ፡ ሲል፡ ነዉ፡፡ ይኹ ሱ
ይሁን፡እዝዬን፡ በፌት፡ ፈጥሮ፡ እርሲ
ን፡ በኌ ላ፡ መፈጠሩ፡ ስላ ምነዉ፡ ቢ
ሉ፡ በሰዉ፡ ልመያ ዘራ፡ ባለ ፚ፡ በፈ

and also the tame animals and all the earth,

so that he govern the tame animals and all the world'.

and everything that moves upon the earth'.

They said, 'Let us create Adam, so that he govern everything
which goes to and fro on the earth' (p.15).

27. And God made the human in the likeness of God;

The Lord created Adam in his own likeness. If it is said
(that it was) the Father (who created him, then) he created
Adam in the likeness of the Son and of the Holy Spirit.

A. If it is said (that it was) the Son (who created him,
then) he created him in the likeness of the Father and of
the Holy Spirit.

A. If it is said (that it was) the Holy Spirit (who created
him, then) he created him in the likeness of the Father and
of the Son.

If it is asked why he created Adam at dawn, but the
others at dusk, dusk is followed by darkness, and by this
he said of those (other created things), 'They are ignorant';
dawn is followed by day-light, and by this he said of him
(Adam), 'He is knowledgeable'.[1]

If it is asked why, while this is so, he created those
first, and him (Adam) afterwards, it is according to human
custom; just as today a rich man, having first prepared

---

1. Reading (apparently with MS Y), <u>awaqi</u> for <u>alawaqi</u>.

ት፡ ምግቡን፡ አዘጋጅቶ፡ ጂላ፡ ሰውን፡
እንዲ፡ ጠላ፡ ጌታም፡ በፊት፡ ምግቡን፡
ፈጥሮ፡ በኔስ፡ እርሱን፡ ፈጠረ፡ ያወ
ስ፡ ቢሆን፡ እቅንዶ፡ እንዲ፡ ሊያ፡ እነሱ
ን፡ እጐንብሾው፡ እንዲ፡ ሐዱ፡ እድር
ጎ፡ ሰአያን፡ ፈጠላቸው፡ ቢሉ፡ የገ
ሾና፡ የተገኘ፡ ምልክት፡ ነው፡ እ
ንደም፡ እነዚያ፡ ተሰሩ፡ ትንሣኤ፡ የ
ካቱውም፡ ሰሩ፡ ግን፡ ተሰሩ፡ ትንሣ
ኤ፡ አሰው፡ ቢል፡

ተከዕተ፡ ወእንሠተ፡ ገብሮሙ፡
ሴትና፡ ወንድ፡ እድርጎ፡ ፈጠላቸ
ው፡ በዘራው፡ ክታወቀ፡ ብኮ፡ እንድ፡ 🔯

ም፡ በርሱ፡ ጋሕርይ፡ እለጀና፡ እን
ዲህ፡ አለ፡

🔯 ወግሪኮሙ፡ ወዴቤኮሙ፡ ብዝኁ፡
ወተባዝኁ፡ ወያምልዕዋ፡ ለምድ
ር፡ ወቅንይዋ፡

አዘዘሙ፡ ቢል፡ ነው፡ ብዙ፡ የብዙ፡
ብዙ፡ ሁኑ፡ ወምልዕዋ፡ ለምድር፡
ወቃኒዋ፡ ያንድርንም ፡ ያስችጋ
ሂት፡ ብኮ፡ እዘዛቸው፡

the food, subsequently invites people (to eat), so the Lord, having first created the food, subsequently created him (Adam).

If it is asked why, even if that is so, he created him (Adam) so that he walked upright, but those so that they walked stooping, it is the mark of the governor and the governed.

A. (By it) he means that those have no hope of resurrection, but he (Adam) has the hope of resurrection.

<u>male and female he made them.</u>

He created them, making them female and male[1] - he (Moses) spoke (thus), since they are known (by these names) today (col.2).

A.[2] (he spoke thus) because she is in his nature[2].

28. <u>And he blessed them and said to them, 'Be many, and multiply, and fill the earth, and rule it,</u>

Reading <u>azzäzomu</u> ('<u>he commanded them</u>', for <u>barakomu</u> 'he blessed them') - he commanded them, saying, 'Be many, very many, <u>and fill the earth and rule it</u> - and fill the earth, govern it'.

1. Or 'woman and man'.

2-2. MS Y here reads <u>ba'addamawinnätəmm alläccənna,</u> 'because she also exists within the state of being Adam'. The problem faced is that if Adam alone was created, and if he was in the image of God, in what sense could he be said to be 'male and female'? Cf. <u>Bəresit Rabba</u> VIII.1.

ወኔሌንን ዎጮ። አዳሣተ። ባሕር። ወ
ለእስራዊተ። ምድር።

ዓ ሠተን ። የምድርንዐ። እ ራዊ
ት ። ግዚቻ ዉ ። ብኬ ። እዘዛቻ ዉ ።
ለእሰዋፊ ። ሐ ማይሪ ። ወ ለ ፖ ሉ ። እ
ንስሲ ። ወ ለ ነ ፖ ሉ ። ዘ ደ ት ። ሐ ወ ስ ዚ
በ ። ምድ ር ። የ ሰ ማ ይ ። እ ን ዋ ፍ ን ፆ ።
እ ን ስ ሳ ት ን ። በ ዚ ህ ። ዓ ለ ም ። የ ሟ ጠ
ከ ለ ሰ ዉ ን ። ሁ ሉ ። ግ ዚ ቻ ዉ ። ብ ሔ ።
እ ዘ ዛ ቻ ዉ ።።

፴፱ ወ ደ ሪ ። እ ግ ዚ እ ብ ሔ ር ። የ ሁ ። ወ
ሀ ብ ኰ ነ ገ ወ ። ን ሶ ሰ ። ሐ መ ል ማ ለ ።
ሣ ዕ ር ። ዘ ደ ዘ ራ ዕ ። ወ ደ ባ ቄ ል ። በ
በ ዘ ር ዉ ። ወ ት ዘ ር ዕ ዖ መ ዉ ። ዲ ባ ።
ዖ ዐ ር ።።

በ የ ወ ገ ኇ ። በ የ ዘ ሩ ። የ ሟ ዘ ራ ዉ ን ።
የ ሟ በ ቅ ሰ ዉ ን ። ዘ ራ ተ ኅ ል ። ሁ ሉ ።
በ ዚ ህ ። ዓ ለ ም ። ት ዘ ራ ት ። ዘ ን ድ ።። እ ን
ሦ ። ሰ ጠ ኜ ቹ ሁ ። ፖ ። ሰ ኛ ቻ ኞ ሁ እ ከ
ሁ ነ ። ዘ ር ዕ ዎ ። ዘ ራ ቹ ።።

ወ ነ ኡ ኤ ። እ ፀ ። ዘ ሀ ለ ዉ ። ዉ ስ ቱ ቱ ።
ዘ ር ዉ ። ዘ ደ ዘ ራ ዕ ። በ በ ፍ ሬ ሁ ።
በ ዘ ሩ ። ባ ዉ ስ ጡ ። ይ ለ ዉ ን ። ፍ ሬ
ዉ ። የ ሟ ዘ ራ ዉ ን ። ተ ክ ል ። ሁ ሉ

<u>and judge the fishes of the sea and the wild animals of the</u>

<u>earth,</u>

He commanded them, saying, 'Govern the fishes and also the

wild animals of the earth'.

<u>and the birds of heaven, and all the tame animals, and all</u>

<u>that move upon earth'.</u>

He commanded them, saying, 'Govern the birds of heaven,

and the tame animals, and all that go to and fro in this world.'

29. <u>And God said, 'Behold, I gave you all greenery of grass which</u>

<u>is sown and sprouts, each according to its seed, and which</u>

<u>you will sow upon the earth,</u>

'Behold, I gave you, so that you sow it in this world, every

plant, seed, which is sown and which sprouts each according

to its type, according to its seed'.

A.   'because I have given it to you, <u>sow it</u> - sow it.'

<u>and every tree within which is its seed, which is sown each</u>

<u>according to its fruit,</u>

I gave you every plant within which is its seed,[1] of which its

fruit is sown (p.16) -

1. Reading <u>zäru</u> for bäzäru.

ሰጠኒቹሁ፡ብእንጬትነት፡የሜዘ
ራ፡ተክል፡እሰና፡
ፈክጮ፡ይኑን፡ከጮ፡መጥልዐ፡
አኖተ፡ምግብ፡ዴሆኖቹሁ፡ዝንድ፡
ሰጠኒቹሁ፡
ወለኮኩ፡ዓራዊተ፡ምድር፡ወለ
ኮሉ፡እዐዋፈ፡ስጫዴ፡
ከእራዊትያ፡ለእዐዋፍም፡ምግብ፡
ዴሆን፡ዝንድ፡ሰጠኒቹሁ፡፡
ወለኮኩ፡ዘይችሐወሰ፡ዴ፡በ፡ም
ድር፡ዘቦ፡መንፈሰ፡ሕይወት፡
በደመ፡ነፍስ፡ሕያው፡ሁኖ፡በም
ድር፡ለሜ፡ዋር፡ሁሉ፡ምግብ፡ኪ
ሆን፡ዘራን፡ተክሎን፡ሰጠኒቹኩ፡
ወለኮኩ፡ሐመልማለ፡ሣዕር፡ይ
ኩንክጮ፡መጥልዒ፡
ዘራ፡ተክሎ፡ምግብ፡ዴኦናቹሁ፡
እኔ፡ወኮነ፡ከጣሁ፡እንዲ፡ለጮ፡

for there are plants which are sown[1] as wood[2].

so that for you it may be food,

(He said), 'I gave (it) to you, so that it be food for you'.

(30) and for all the wild animals of the earth, and for all the
birds of heaven,

'I gave (it) to you, so that it be food for the wild animals
and the birds'.

and for everything which moves upon earth, in which is the
spirit of life,

'I gave you plants, seeds, so that it be food for everything
which lives on earth, which is alive with the animal faculty'.

and for[3] all greenery of grass, let it be food for you';

He said, 'Let the plants, the seeds, be food for you'.

and it was so.

It happened as he said.

1. MS Y, which has otherwise considerably abbreviated this whole
    section, adds here ÿammittäkkäl, 'which is planted'.
2. I.e. planted as cuttings, not sown as seed.
3. 'for' may be omitted if lä̈ - is taken as an object marker
    marking objects of 'I gave you' in v. 29; as BK and Dillmann
    both read wäkwəllu, the inclusion of -lä̈- in MS W may in any
    case be a scribal error.

ሆነ። ወርእየ፡ እግዚአብሔር፡ ኵ
ሎ፡ ዘገብረ፡ ከመ፡ ጥቀ፡ ሠናይ፡
እግዚአብሔር፡ የፈጠረው፡ ፍጥ
ረት፡ ሁሉ፡ ፍጹም፡ ያማረ እጅግ፡
ያማረ፡ ፍጹም፡ የበቃ፡ ፍጥረት፡ እ
ንደሆነ፡ አውቆ፡ ፈጠረ። እስካሁ
ን፡ ወርእየ፡ እግዚአብሔር፡ ከመ፡
ሠናይ፡ እያለ፡ መጥቶ፡ ከአዳም፡ ላ
ይ፡ ሲደርስ፡ ጥቀ፡ ሠናይ፡ አለ፡ የሰ
ው፡ ተፈጥሮ፡ ከሁሉ፡ እንዲበ
ልጥ፡ ለማጠየቅ። ሰሎሞን፡ የሠ
ነ፡ ፍጥረትን፡ ነገር፡ ሲናገር፡ መጥ
ቶ፡ ወፍሠሐየኒ፡ ጥቀ፡ በእጓለእ
መሕያው፡ እንዳለ።
ወኮነ፡ ሌሊተ፡ ወጸብሐ፡
ወኮነ፡ ሌሊተ፡ ወጸብሐ፡
ጨለማ፡ ሁኖ፡ አድሮ፡ ነጋ።
ወኮነ፡ ሰዱስተ፡ ዕለተ፡
ዕለት፡ ስድስት፡ ፍጥረት፡ ፳፪፡ ሆነ።

ምዕራፍ፡ ፪፡

፩ ወተፈጸመ፡ ሰማይ፡ ወምድር፡ ወኵ
ሉ፡ ዓለሞሙ፡
ፍጥረተ፡ ሰማይ፡ ወምድር፡ ወፍጥረተ፡
ኵሉ፡ ዓለማሙ፡ ሲል፡ ነው። የሰማይ
ና፡ የምድር፡ የሠራዊቶቻቸውም፡ ተ

(31)   <u>And God saw all that he made, that it was very beautiful;</u>

God created, knowing that every created thing which he created

was a very beautiful, perfect, worthy created thing.   Until

now, he (Moses) had been saying, '<u>And God saw that it was</u>

<u>beautiful</u>'; when he reached Adam, he said '<u>very beautiful</u>',

to prove that the creation of human kind was greater than all

(else), just as Solomon, after having been speaking of the

matter of the wonders of creation, said, '<u>And my joy was very</u>

<u>great in the human</u>'[1].

[2]<u>and it became night-time, and it dawned</u>[2] (col. 2),

The night having passed in darkness, it dawned.

<u>And it was day six.</u>

It was day six, 22 created things.

Chapter 2

1.   <u>And heaven was completed, and earth, and all their world,</u>

<u>Reading 'the creation of heaven and of earth, and the creation</u>

<u>of all their world'</u> - all the creation of heaven and of earth

and of their companies was completed.

1.   Prov. 8.31, the AC to which contains comment similar to the
     above.   For <u>tə́qqä</u>, MS Y reads <u>dä́qiqä</u>, which is closer to the
     AC text of Prov. 8.31.

2-2. This lemma appears twice, doubtless by dittography, at the
     foot of col. 1 and the top of col. 2.

ፌጥሮ፡ ኩሉ፡ ተፈጸመ፨ ሕቱቃ፡ የ
ሰማይ፡ ወላዋት፡ ፀሐይ፡ ጨረቁ፡ክ
ዋክብት፡ የምድር፡ ወላዋት፡ እፀዉ
ዐዕፅን፡እንስሳት፡ አራዊት፡ ናቹው፡
ወፈጸመ፡እግዚአብሔር፡ ግብሮ፡ዘ
ገብረ፡ እግዚኡባሔር፡ የፈመረው፡ን
ፁዋረት፡ ኩሉ፡ ፌጥሮ፡ ፈጸመ፡ማ
ከት፡ ሰማይን፡ እነግሡ፡ ምድርን፡ክ
ነልበሱ፡ ፌጥሮ፡ ፈጸመ፨ ሕቱቁ፡
እስ ነሁን፡ ባዕድ፡ ፍጥረት፡ ሰኔዖር
ሰንብቴ፡ ነበረ፡ እንግዴ ህ ወዲ ህ
ግን፡ ግብሮ፡ እምግብር፡ ቢሬሳ
እንጅ፡ ኬሳ፡ ሰዕድ፡ ፍጥረት፡ አዴፊ
ጠርቃ ሃ፡ እንዲ ህ፡ እስ፡ ወአእረፊ
ኬግዜእብሔር፡ በሰብዐ ት፡ ዕለት፡
እም ሽ ሉ፡ ግብሩ፨

እግዚኡብሔር፡ በ፯ኛ ው፡ ቀን፡ ሰ
ረ፡ ከመሥራት፡ አሬፊ፨ አሬፊ፡ ማለ
ቱ ም፡ በ ጌታ፡ ድ ኣ ም፡ ኮ ሮ በ ት፡ አዴ
ዴ ስ ም፨ ወፈጠረ ን፡ ተ ወ፡ ሰ ል ነ ው፡
ወገሊ ብ፡ እግዚእብሔር፡ እሰ ስ ት ፡ሰ
ብዕ ት፡ ወቀዴ ሰ ፨

እግዚእብሔር፡ ከ፯ ፀ ላ ታ ፡ ሳ ዬ ዱ፡

H.   The companies of heaven are sun, moon, stars; the companies

of earth are trees, stones, tame animals, wild animals.

(2)   and God finished his work which he did,

God completed (it), having created all the created things

which he had begun, meaning, 'He completed (it), having created

heaven with its belongings and earth with its garments'.

H.   He (Moses) spoke thus because until now he (God) had spent

the time creating alien[1] created things, but from now on it

will multiply rather by natural increase, and no other alien

created thing will be created.

and God rested on the seventh[2] day from all his work,

On the 7th day God rested from doing work. However, its

saying 'he rested' does not mean that the Lord experienced

tiredness; it means 'he ceased creating'.

(3)   and God blessed the seventh day, and sanctified it,

God honoured the 7th. day, separating (it) from the 6 days (p.17).

1.   I.e. of new species not previously created.
2.   Here the ordinal number is used, whereas hitherto the
cardinal numbers have been employed.

፺ኛዩቱን፡ ቀን፡ እክበሬ።
እስዎ፡ ባቲኡፉሬፄ፡ እምኮኡ፡ግብ
ሩ፡ዝእዳዝ፡ ዪግበር፦
ዪለሠሬ፡ ዘንድ፡ ከፄመረ ዉ፡ ሠራሁ
ሉ፡ እርጭ ጋታልፕ፡ ሐተታ፡ መናፉ
ቁን፡ ፍፕሬት፡ ነበረ ዉ፡ ፅለቱ፡ እስ
ቀበቱ፡ እንፄ፡ እንዴዩኡ፡ ፮ ቀን እ
ተሬፄ፡ ፅለትስ፡ ነበረ ዉ፡ ፍፕሬት፡
እኮቀበ ት፡ እንፄ፡ እንዴዩኡ፡ እም
ኑቶኡ፡ ዓብሬ፡ እስ።

፯ ዝንቴ፡ ፍፕረት፡ በማዬ፡ ወያምድ
ር፡ እመ፡ ኮነት፡ ፅለት፡ እንተ ግቲ
ገብሬ፡ እማዚእጠሐር፡ ሰማዩ ወም
ድር፡ ሰማይንና፡ ምድርን፡ የፈጠረ
ባት፡ ፅለት፡ እሑድ፡ በተገኘት ጊዜ
የፅመዩፕ፡ የምድር፡ ተፈፕ ፆ፡ ዪህ፡
ነዉ። ወኮኑ፡ ሐመልማለ፡ ሐፅ

<u>because on it he rested from all his work that he had commenced</u>

<u>doing.</u>

(He honoured it) because on it he rested from all the work

which he had begun to do.

H. He left an extra day, lest heretics say, 'He had (further)

created things, but the days were exhausted too soon for him';

he said '<u>from all his work</u>', lest they say, 'He had (further)

days, but the created things were exhausted too soon for him'.[1]

4. <u>This is the creation of heaven and earth, at the time when</u>

<u>was the day in which God made heaven and earth.</u>

This is the creation of heaven and earth, at the time the day,

Sunday, was obtained, on which he created heaven and earth .....

1. After this, MS Y reads <u>məqwam</u>, making 1.1 - 2.3 (rather than
    chapter 1) its first major division of text and commentary,
    one 'period of instruction'.

4.3.   Geez texts of Genesis 1.1–2.4.

The establishment of a critical Geez text of Genesis requires a methodological rigour that has not yet been exercised. The existing editions, useful though they are, are open to criticism on grounds of accuracy, and they have not drawn on sources of textual evidence other than actual biblical MSS. Moreover, the question of the existence of Geez versions independent of one another has not been answered.

A. Dillmann prepared the first critical edition of the Geez version of the Octateuch[1], using as his primary source MS Bible Society 169[2] (Dillmann's F), and noting the variants of 3 other MSS. O. Boyd prepared a further critical edition[3], using as his primary source MS B.N. Zotenberg 3[4] (Boyd's Y), and adding variants from another MS (Codex Haverfordensis, R), but taking the readings of Dillmann's MSS directly from Dillmann's printed edition.

This means that deficiencies in Dillmann's edition may have misled Boyd. In Dillmann's printed text of Gen. 1, some departures from the actual readings of F are those noted in the annotationes to the edition, p.5 (orthography), and pp.26–7 (preferred variants), but the printed text exhibits additional differences in punctuation and

1. A. Dillmann, Biblia Veteris Testamenti Aethiopica,Bd. I, Leipzig, 1853.

2. M.R. Falivene and A.F. Jesson, Historical Catalogue of the Manuscripts of Bible House Library, London, 1982, pp.70–2.

3. O. Boyd, The Octateuch in Ethiopic, in Bibliotheca Abessinica, parts I and II, Leiden and Princeton, 1909–11.

4. H. Zotenberg, Catalogue des mss. Éthiopiens de la Bibliothèque nationale, Paris, 1877, pp.4–6.

word division (though Dillmann exercised decreasing editorial licence
as he progressed through Gen.), and it fails to distinguish consistently
the work of a corrector, and it contains a few errors. Thus the
chapter markings at 1.1 (ክፍል ፡ ፩) and 2.1 (ክ ፡ ፪) are
Dillmann's, and the numbering of the verses in F is the work of a
second hand. The further work of the corrector(s) of F is as follows:

1.1   after ወምድር the words ወሀለወ ፡ ዕምቅናት ፡ have been
partially erased (and Dillmann omits them);

1.2   from ወመልዕልተ ፡ ቀላይ ፡ , ወ has been deleted;

1.2   ይጸልል ፡ has been corrected to ይዴልል ፡ ;

1.4, 1.6 and 1.18, መኸነለ has been corrected to ባኸነለ ፡ ;

1.16   ይመልክ ፡ ሌሊተ ፡ has been corrected to ይምልክ ፡ ሌሊተ ፡ ;

In 1.18 (ወይኩ፦ንንፀ ፡), 1.20 (ወመትሕተ ፡) and 1.30 (ይኩ፦ንክሙ ፡),
there are corrector's scrapings which obscure the reading;

1.31, at the end of the verse, the second double dots are a corrector's
addition.

In general, Dillmann has reproduced the correctors' readings. The
main differences between the printed text and the actual text of F are
as follows (the readings of F are cited second):

1.2   ‹ ኢታስተርኢ › ኢታስተሪኢ

1.8   ‹ ወኅኅ ፡ ሌሊተ › ኅኅ ፡ ሌሊተ

1.9   ‹ ወታስተርኢ › (see <u>lec. var.</u>)   ወታስሪኢ

1.9   ‹ ወተጋብኡ › ወተጋብኡ

1.9   ‹ ምኅካዲሁ ፡ ወእስተርኡየ › ምኅካዲሁ ወ ፡ እስተርኡየ

1.10   ‹ ባሕለ › ባሕር

1.14   ‹ ወለመዋዕል › ወመዋዕል

1.21   ‹ ያሬ › ያፈ

1.29   ‹ ዘርኡ › ዠርኡ

2.4   ‹ ወምድር › ወምድር

      Thus in 1.8, for example, Boyd has been misled into thinking
that F is in agreement with Y in reading ወኅኅ ፡ , and in 1.9 Boyd
has assumed, on the basis of Dillmann's <u>lectiones variantes</u>, that F
reads ወታስተርኢ ፡ . Boyd evidently suspected the existence of this
problem, as he writes[5] about F:

      "In his annotations Dillmann rarely gives any indication of the
secondary origin of its readings, although he refers in his description

---

5.   O. Boyd, <u>The Octateuch in Ethiopic</u>, p.xvii.

of the MS to the large part that comparison and emendation have played
in the creation of this text, especially in Genesis. It would
probably be a profitable task for some scholar to examine the MS afresh
with this edition of Y before him, to ascertain how far those emended
places coincide with the places where F differs from Y."

    Such examination of the major corrections of F in Genesis shows
that in general the original text of F was closer to Y (and that the
tendency of the corrections is to bring agreement with the readings
of H ('Codex Halensis', MS B.N. Zotenberg 1 and 2), though this
merely confirms that G.M. Vansleb, the copyist of H, copied the
corrections of F rather than the original text). For example, in
Gen.8.2, F read ወተኅሠተ ፡ (agreeing with Y), and a corrector has
added or substituted ወተኀፅወ ፡ . In Gen. 9.13, F read ቄምዓ፟ ፡
(agreeing with Y), and a corrector has altered it to ቄምዓ፟ት ፡ ,
which, on the basis of Dillmann's text, Boyd has taken as the original
reading of F. Of the major corrections in F, in Gen. 10.8, 12.8,
17.26, 24.61, 27.14, 27.40-1, 29.10-11, 34.11-12, 35.21, 39.12, 15,
it is only at 24.61 that the correction, rather than the original,
approximates to the reading of Y. For example, at 34.11-12, Boyd
reads (v.11)... ወለእኅፀ፟ይ ፡ (v.12) ሪስይ ፡ ኢት ፡ ..., and shows the
addition of ሪክበኙ ፡ ... after ወለእኅፀ፟ይ ፡ as the reading of F
and H; in fact, the addition ሪኽበኙ ፡... is the work of a corrector
of F.

    The other published Geez texts containing Gen.1 are:
(i)   Geez Octateuch and Jubilees (BK)[6];
(ii)   four volume Geez-Amharic diglot Bible[7];
(iii) F. da Bassano's edition of the Geez Bible (DB)[8], and
(iv) the printed text of Gəbrä həmamat (GH)[9], where Gen. 1 is

6. Bəluy Kidan, vol.I, (Maḥbärä ḥawaryat) Asmara, 1955 E.C.

7. Mäṣhaf qəddus bägəʿazənna bäʾamarəñña yätäsafä, London, not dated.

8. F. da Bassano, Bəluy Kidan, Asmara, 1922-6.

9. Wäldä mikaʾel Bərhanä mäsqäl (ed.), Gəbrä həmamat, A.A., 1942 E.C.,
    pp.57-8.

appointed for reading at dawn on Monday of Holy Week.
Of these, <u>BK</u> and the diglot are very similar, <u>BK</u> tends to agree with
Dillmann's text rather than with Boyd's, and <u>GH</u> appears to represent
a scholarly revision of a text of the type used in DB.

Further MS evidence (in addition to biblical MSS not utilized
by Dillmann, Boyd and da Bassano[10]) is to be found in Geez texts of
Gen. 1 which occur as lemmas in Geez commentary MSS (e.g. B.N. d'
Abbadie 28, EMML 2101), as lemmas in Geez and Amharic commentary MSS
of the <u>Mämhərä orit</u> type, as lections in service books (e.g. <u>Säʿatat,
Gəbrä həmamat</u>), and as citations in chronographical works (e.g.
<u>Abušakər</u>[11], <u>Giyorgis wäldä Amid</u>[12]);   certain textual readings may be
found attacked or defended in various homilies (e.g. of Rətuʿa
haymanot), and some variant Geez readings are noted in the Amharic AC.
Textual evidence of these types must be used critically, since many
of the relevant works are translations or adaptations from Arabic,
and their Geez versions may therefore be of value for the text
criticism of the Arabic originals rather than for the text criticism
of the Geez Bible;   others have polemic intent, and must be interpreted
accordingly.

The commentary in EMML 2101 contains a text of Genesis which
appears to be an independent translation, subjected at some stage to
scholarly revision and slight expansion, for example, in Gen. 1.2
it reads   ወለ ምዉርሰ ፡ እሞ ፡ ፈጠሮ ፡ ሀለወት ፡ b ሩቅ ፡ ,
and in 1.14   ወነው ፡ ይኩኑ ፡ ለተእምራት ፡ ወለሐሳበ ፡ እዝመናት ፡
ወለ ኁ [ን] ቄ ፡ ወዋዕል ፡ ወእውራሳ ፡ ወ ዓመታት ፡ .
From 1.8 onwards the numbered days of creation are given a number
greater by one than that of the Hebrew text.

10. For example, most notably EMML 2098, also EMML 1839, 1842 and 1929,
    and in addition EMML 510, 1163, 2388, 2436, 2532.

11. E.g. B.L. Orient 809 f.14b–15a, Orient 810 f.17a–b.

12. E.g. B.L. Orient 814 f.6b.

The fifteenth century horologium (M̈ashafä sä̈ʿatat) in MS Bible Society 173 (Cowley XXV) contains on f.136b–137a a text of Gen.1.1–11 which exhibits the following readings not contained in the printed texts and *apparati* mentioned above:

1.2   ወሰዓስዕልት ፡ ቀሳይ

1.2   ይጸልል

1.6   ይኩን ፡ ምፈፈ

1.6   ይፍልጥ ፡ ማኸስለ ፡ ማይ ፡ ወማኸስለ ፡ ምፈC

1.7   < ማኸስለ ፡ ማይ ፡ ዘታኅት ፡ ምፈC > *omitted*

1.10   < ለማይ > ለሰማይ

The first two of these readings agree with the original text of Dillmann's F.   Where the text of this horologium differs from __BK__, it tends to agree with Boyd's Y.

The homily of Rətuʿa haymanot on the Incarnation of the Word, for the 29th. of M̈aggabit[13], assumes a text of Gen. 1.1–2 which reads 'At the first God made the heaven; but the earth was from former times ...', and attacks the view "that God did not create earth with heaven in the beginning; it was already there since eternity"[14]. The prevalence of this reading can be seen from MSS of Gəbrä̈ həmamat, e.g. B.L. Orient 597 f.21a reads በቀዳሚ ፡ ገብረ ፡ እግዚእስለዮC ፡ ሰማየ ፡፡ ወያዖፈርስ ፡ ሀለወት ፡ እያትክት ፡   , and a corrector has added ወያዖፈፈ ፡ after ሰማይ ፡   ; B.L. Orient 600 f.15a agrees with the uncorrected text of Or.597, and so does Or.601 f.12a, except that it reads ሰማይ ፡ for ሰማይ ፡ .

The AC on Gen.1[15] preserves the following variant readings:

13. I have used B.L. Orient 786 f.79b; it is also found in e.g. Berlin (Hammerschmidt and Six 148) Ms. orient. quart. 1165 f.25a–35b.

14. Catalogue notes (__Catalogue__ vol.VI pp.454–5) on EMML 2375 (9).

15. As contained in MSS W and Y translated above.

Text (a question mark indicates   Variant
that it is not certain which
words the variant replaces)

1.2   ? (add after ሀሎወት፥)   እምትነት ፥

1.2   ?   ኮንቶታ ፥ ብፁወታ ፥

1.2   ?   ሀሎወት ፥ ወኢሀሎወት ፥

1.2   ?   ሀሎወት ፥ ወኢታስተርኢ ፥

1.4   ክሞ ፥ ሠናይ ፥   ክሞ ፥ ጠብ ፥

1.7   ?   በኢምሳለ ፥ ቀቀብ ፥

1.7–8 ?   በኢምሳለ ፥ አዝሩቅ ፥ / እዝርቅ ፥

1.9   የብስ ፥   የብስ ፥

1.26   በእርኢያነ ፥ ወበኢምሳሊነ ፥   በእርኢያ ፥ ወበኢምሳሊነ ፥
       ወይኰንን ፥   ክሞ ፥ ይኰንን ፥

  "   "   በእርኢያነ ፥ ክሞ ፥ ይኰንን ፥

Of these, the reading ወኢታስተርኢ ፥ in 1.2 looks like accommodation
to LXX <u>aoratos</u>, and the previous two readings resemble Aquila's
<u>kenōma kai outhen</u> and Theodotion's <u>(ou)then kai outhen</u>.   The variant
on 1.4 is the most striking case known to me where the AC has preserved
a common Hebrew word as variant to a common Geez word;   I have not
found the reading in MSS.

     The AC on Gen.1–2.4 contains the following suggested textual
improvements:

         Text   Emendation
1.2   ምፁርሰ ፥   ምፁርኒ ፥
1.11   ዘእምውስቴቱ ፥   ዘእምጼሉ ፥
  "   "   ዘእምታሕቱ ፥
  "   "   ዘእምገቦሉ ፥
  "   "   ዘእምርእሱ ፥
1.17   ሤሞሙ ፥   እንበሎሙ ፥
1.28   ባርኮሙ ፥   እዘዞሙ ፥
2.1   ሰማይ ፥ ወምፁር ፥ ወኵሉ ፥   ፍጹረተ ፥ ሰማይ ፥ ወምፁር ፥
         ዓለሞሙ ፥   ወፍጹረተ ፥ ኵሉ ፥ ዓለሞሙ ፥

     It may be concluded that the Geez version of Genesis requires
further study which will
(i)   represent the MS evidence unambiguously,

(ii)   use further biblical MSS not available to previous editors,

(iii)   use further textual evidence from Geez and Amharic commentaries, and from citations in other works, and

(iv)   assess whether extant texts derive from a single archetype
or not.

4.4   COMPARATIVE STUDY OF SELECTED EXEGETICAL MOTIFS

4.4.1   The reasons for God's creating.

AC Gen.1.1 gives four reasons for God's creating – to reveal
his omnipotence, his wealth, his transcendent immanence, and his
equity. A similar list of reasons is given in the sᵊnä fᵊträt and
its sources[1], and in SFA pp.15-16 they are homiletically linked to
the four elements (wealth, earth; mercy and generosity, water;
omnipotence, fire; judging, wind). The sources are also concerned
to point out that God did not create in order to fulfil some lack
or need in himself[2]. Jewish sources contain similar ideas – e.g.
Šemot R. 17.1, "Everything which God created during the six days of
creation was created for his glory and for the fulfilment of his
will."

4.4.2   'At the first' (Gen.1.1).

The Geez text of Gen.1.1 translates LXX en archē by baqädami.
Qädami is commonly used as an adjective, and so the AC suggests some
nouns to be understood – 'first authority/word/son/creating/day/hour';
qädami can, however, quite properly be used as a substantive (Dillmann,
Lexicon, col.464), and raises no problem of the type that arises
from Hebrew bᵊrešit (apparently a pregenitive lacking a following
noun[3]). Nor is there a link (a) with exegesis explaining why Syriac
qadmaya or Hebrew miqqedem is not used in this verse[4], (b) with
exegesis linking Hebrew bᵊrešit to Syriac rešita[5], (c) with Jewish

1.   SFA (Mogäs) pp.14-16;   TH (Ṭanasee 35 f.72b);   IATQ (EMML 1839
     f.6a col.2).

2.   SFG (Cowley 40) f.3b.

3.   Rashi on Gen.1.1.

4.   Jansma pp.95-6. Targum Onkelos reads bᵊqadmin. The Ethiopic text
     of Prov. 8.22 uses the root qdm – this is the verse referred to in
     the interpretation of the Fragmentary Targum, see Bowker pp.98,100.

5.   Jansma pp.91-3.

interpretations of reṧit as Torah/Moses/ḥalla/tithes/first-fruits,[5] or (d) with Greek questionings concerning the archē.[6]

4.4.3 Things created prior to the creation of heaven and earth.

There are various Jewish accounts of things created long before the heaven and the earth[7] (to be distinguished from things created on the eve of the Sabbath at twilight[8]), and the idea, though not the same detail, is found in some Christian commentators - John Philoponus, for example, has preserved Theodore of Mopsuestia's refutation of Basil of Caesarea who asserted that angels were created prior to the creation of heaven and earth[9].

TH has been influenced by ideas of an earlier creation, as, following the quotation of Gen.1.1-2, it reads (f.81a): 'For first he said, "At the first God made heaven", water having been created before the earth; until then the earth was not made. And as for this which says, "But the earth was from former times, and it did not appear, and it was not prepared", (it is) true, for its existence was from former times. It was first, together with those four elements; it did not precede them or follow them, for at one time, by one word, the four of them were created'.

The SFG in d'Abbadie 156, however, opposes the idea of the prior creation of the earth (f.3a): '"But the earth was from former times" - it is not that it was formerly created, but because it was not revealed from Sunday until the dawn of Tuesday, for water concealed it'. Similarly IAT on Gen.1.1, for example, says that heaven

---

6. On which see J.C.M. van Winden, 'In the beginning', Vig.Chr. 17 (1963), pp.105-121.

7. Ginzberg I pp.3-8, V pp.3-6 (Ginzberg's promised 'Excursus 1' appears never to have been published); TB Pasahim 54a; Tanna de be Eliyahu 31; Bareṧit R. 1.4; Ṧemot R. 15.22; Rashi on Gen.1.1; PRE ch.3.

8. Bowker, The Targums, pp.113-5.

9. Jansma, pp.98-9.

and earth were new creations, and God (alone) was pre-existent; this view is generally prevalent in the sources known in Ethiopia. AC Gen.1.2 does, however, reflect the debate about whether the reading 'but the earth' implied the pre-existence of the earth from eternity, a view opposed in a homily of Rətuʿa haymanot (see 4.3 above).

4.4.4 The date of creation.

AC Gen.1.1 dates the first day of creation as the 29th. day of Mäggabit (the seventh Ethiopian month, equivalent to Hebrew Adar, Coptic Phanemoth, Arabic Baramhāt, and approximating to March) in a year of the evangelist John, at dusk on Sunday (i.e. Saturday evening). This identification is found in other Ethiopian sources[10], and some have (the error or variant?) Mäggabit 22nd.[11]

Some Jewish sources also date creation, but are divided about whether it occurred in Nisan or Təsri. MhG on Gen.1.11, MhH on Gen. 1.14, and Vayyiqra R. 29.1, for example, give Elul 25 as the date of the creation of the world, making Təsri 1 the date of the creation of Adam. YML on Gen.1.14-19, on the other hand, cites from Abudraham the opinion that the first night of creation was the eve of Adar 23 (cf. YML on Gen.2.7).

Ethiopic Abusakər approximates to the latter of these Jewish opinions. MS B.L. Or. 809 f.17a records the views that the first Sunday of creation was (a) Baramhāt 29 = Adar 25, (b) Baramhāt 22 = Adar 18, (c) Bärmuda (Coptic Pharmuthi) 3 = Adar 29, and (d) Bärmuda 14 = Nisan 9[12]; on f.18a-b it records the creation of sun and moon on Adar 21/Mäggabit 25 (agreeing with (b) above), and the creation of Adam on Mäggabit 26/27, and says that Yoḥannəs wäldä səʿid wäldä

10. SFG f.2b gives the date as Mäggabit 29 'by solar computation', or 12th of 'diyʿəlhəz' (i.e. dū l-hijja, the last month of the Islamic calendar).

11. MS B.N. Zotenberg 149 f.48b.

12. MS B.L. Or. 810 contains opinion (a), but lacks (b)-(d). Opinion (b) is found in Agapius' Kitāb al-ʿUnwān.

b̈aträq[13] dates creation on Sunday the 22nd. day of the 7th. month,
M̈aggabit.

Syriac and Arabic commentaries on Gen. appear not to date
creation itself, but say that the sun first shone on Paradise on the
15th. or 4th. of <u>Nisan</u> (Išoʿdad and IAṬ on Gen. 2.9). Q̈aləməntos
book II ch.4 says that creation took place in <u>Nisan,</u> Ethiopian
<u>Miyazya,</u> and <u>BMHE</u> section 4 gives the date of the 'birth' of Adam
as <u>Miyazya</u> 7.

4.4.5   <u>The numbers of created things by day.</u>

The total numbers of the creations of the six days are given
by some Ethiopian and Jewish sources as 22, and the common source
for this is probably Jubilees 2. In the distribution of the creations
to the days, AC Gen. 1 follows Jub. 2 closely, as follows:

day	total	creations
1	7	wind, fire, water, earth, darkness, angels, bright heaven (AC Gen.1.1)
2	1	firmament (AC Gen.1.8)
3	4	plants plucked by hand, reaped with sickle, chopped with axe, trees of Paradise (AC Gen.1.12)
4	3	sun, moon, stars (AC Gen.1.14)
5	3	animals created from water which crawl on their belly, run on their legs, fly with their wings (AC Gen.1.22)
6	4	animals created from the earth which crawl on their belly, run on their legs, fly with their wings (AC Gen.1.25), and man (AC Gen.1.26-31).
	22	total

Some texts of the sən̈a fətr̈at[14] have a pattern differing

13. Presumably Yaḥyā ibn Saʿīd (Graf II, pp.49-51) is meant, but the
reference is not to his <u>History</u> (ed. Kratchkovsky and Vasiliev).

14. E.g. <u>Ÿahaymanotənna ÿas̈alot m̈ashaf</u>, A.A., 1955 E.C., and <u>M̈as̈ar̈aẗa
təmhərt</u>, A.A., 1949 E.C. (which have the same text); Ayyalew Tamməru,
<u>Ÿäʾityopya əmn̈at b̈asostu həggəgat</u>, p.134; also <u>MO</u> (e.g. MS B.N. dʾ
Abbadie 156 f.4a).

slightly from the above, as they list light as an eighth creation
of the first day, and omit 'trees of Paradise' from the third day.
The question whether the creations of the first day are to be counted
as seven or eight is familiar from Syriac commentary materials[15];
the discrepancy over the counting of the creations of the third day
as three or four is reconciled in SFG (f.17a), which says that they
are three in the methods for gathering them, and in their fructiferous
parts, but four in the places in which they are found.

Among Jewish sources, it is Midraš tadše which is closest to
AC Gen. 1, (and which appears to be based on a slightly different
understanding of Jub. 2):

day	total	creations
1	7	heaven, earth, water, darkness, breath, the deeps, light
2	1	firmament
3	4	gathered water into one place; drew sweet water from earth; herbs; trees
4	3	sun, moon, stars
5	3	reptiles, fowl, fish
6	4	beasts, cattle, reptiles, man

The majority of Jewish sources, however, have accounts which
lack Ethiopian parallels, notably (a) the scheme of three creations
on each of the six days (with an alternative in which six are created
on the sixth day)[16], and (b) the scheme of ten or eight creations on
the first day in which tohu and bohu are included as two creations.[17]

4.4.6   The creation of darkness.

AC Gen. 1.1 lists darkness among the seven creations of the
first day; in this it agrees with THBK's list of the seven kyānē

---

15. Clarke, Selected Questions, pp.58-62; THBK Mimrā I. 97 (also in IATQ,
    EMML 1839 f.24b col.2); Išoʻdad (and IAT) on Gen.1.1 and 1.22.

16. Bərešit R. 11.9.

17. Ginzberg, Legends, I p.8; YML on Gen. 1.3,5; Yalqut Səmʻoni in loc.;
    TB Hagiga 12a.

(Mimrā I.53), and with Theodore of Mopsuestia, Iso͑dad, and <u>Book of</u> <u>the Bee</u> 6, and is in disagreement with Basil, Ephraim, Diodore and Theodoret[18].

AC Gen. 1.4 discusses why darkness was created before light, a question also raised in the <u>sanā fətrāt</u>[19], in Syriac and Greek 'questions',[20] and in Jewish sources as one of 'Alexander's questions'[21].

The SFA (Mogās p.25) also raises the questions (a) why God worked throughout the twenty four hours, (b) why he created darkness, and (c) why he created darkness in silence.

4.4.7   The creation of the angels.

(a) When were they created?

AC Gen.1.1 lists the angels among the creations of the first day, and this is in agreement with Jubilees 2, most Ethiopian sources,[22] IAṬ and Iso͑dad on Gen.1.1, and a minority of Jewish sources[23].

18. Jansma pp.103–4; Bar Hebraeus on Gen.1.2; Jansma, 'Barhebraeus' Scholion on the words 'Let there be light'.' See also Iso͑dad and IAṬ on Gen.1.2–3, and <u>TIA</u> p.100.

19. SFG (Cowley 40) f.6a, 10a; also <u>MO</u> (e.g. B.N. d'Abbadie 156 f.4a).

20. IBN question 1 (discussion in Clarke, <u>Selected Questions</u>, pp.44–54); THBK <u>Mimrā</u> I.83; IAṬQ in EMML 1839 f.1a, 19a–b, 24a (but IAṬ has here edited his sources more than usual); Theodoret, <u>Quaestiones</u> 7.

21. E.g. <u>TB Tamid</u> 32a; <u>YML</u> on Gen.1.1. Ethiopian sources appear to have no parallel to the Jewish suggestion (e.g. Ramban <u>in loc.</u>) that by hośekh in Gen.1 is meant the element fire.

22. Sannā fətrāt; Mogās Ɉqubā giyorgis, <u>Mārha sədq bahlā haymanot</u>, pp. 34–5 (citing Severus of Esmunain and Eth. Qāl.)

23. E.g. <u>YML</u> on Gen.1.5. The majority Jewish opinion favours the second or fifth day (<u>MhH</u> p.41; <u>MhG</u> p.25; <u>Bərešit R.</u> 1.3 and 3.8; <u>YML</u> on Gen.1.8; Ramban <u>in loc.</u>; Bowker, pp.107–8).

Ethiopian sources are not quite unanimous. SFG (f.13a) records an opinion that the angels were created on Tuesday, and SFA (pp.29-30) records D∂rsana̋ mika'el as saying that they were created on Monday; both harmonize these by saying that they were created on Sunday, but received their places for service on Monday/Tuesday.

(b) From what were they created?

AC Gen.1.1 says (in some MSS) that the angels were created from fire and wind, and this is the common opinion of the AC[24] and of its sources,[25] claiming the support of Eth. 3 Macc. 3.22, and Ps. 103(104).4. The AC also recognises the opinion that they were created ex nihilo, and SFA (pp.19-20) notes that if it is said that until Tuesday all creations were ex nihilo, then the view of TH may be followed - 'If they (the angels) had been created from wind and flame, they would have died and decayed like us.'

(c) Why did Moses not mention their creation?

AC Gen.1.1 gives three reasons why Genesis lists only heaven and earth as creations of the first day - (i) the other creations were included with heaven and earth,(ii) heretics might suppose that the created elements assisted God in creation, and (iii) Moses would subsequently mention the other creations. The first of these is paralleled in Basil, Hexaemeron 1.7. Apart from that, the reasons given in the AC are different from those most commonly found in its sources - namely, that the angels were not mentioned (i) lest people worship them, and (ii) because God taught Moses about the material creation, but not the creation of spiritual beings.[26]

---

24. See 5.5.15 below and e.g. AC Q∂ddase, p.217. For comparison with Jewish opinions, see Ginzberg V, p.21.

25. E.g. s∂na̋ f∂trát.

26. E.g. IAṬ and Išo'dad on Gen.1.4; IBN question 2; IAṬQ (EMML 1839 f.1a-b, 6b); Theodoret, Quaestiones, 2-4. For the same question in a Jewish source, see Abarban'el's question 2 on Gen.1.

(d) Why did they not appear until the time of Hagar?

This question is not discussed in AC Gen.1, but is raised three times in IAṬ's Questions (in Geez translation in EMML 1839 f.1a-b, 11b, 30b); the third of these is taken from THBK M̲i̲m̲r̲ā̲ II. 125.

(e) What is the number of their divisions?

Ethiopian commentary materials generally hold that the angels were originally created as 100 tribes (nägäd) in 10 settlements (kätäma).[27] Of these some fell, and the remaining ones formed nine groups allocated to various heavens. The names of the 9 correspond with those given in IAṬ's and Iso'dad's commentaries on Gen.1.4, dependent on (Ps.)- Dionysius, D̲e̲ c̲o̲e̲l̲e̲s̲t̲i̲ H̲i̲e̲r̲a̲r̲c̲h̲i̲a̲, P̲G̲ 3, cols. 120-569.

4.4.8 The duration of the work of creation.

Some Jewish and Christian sources suggest that all, or some, of the creations were created on the first day, and that the hexae-meral scheme of Gen.1 merely represents the periods when the creations were revealed.[28] This is referred to in the SFA (Mogäs p.38), 'But if it is objected that there was no creative act outside Sunday, then "he created" means "he polished, smoothed out, set in order"'. The view is opposed in a SFG (MS B.N. d'Abbadie 156 f.3b): "Why did God not create 22 creations on one day, namely Sunday? Explanation – it was not because of weariness, but so that the angels should know that he is creator and maker." This reason is similar to one of the reasons given by IAṬ and Iso'dad on Gen.2.2-3 for the six day dura-tion of creation – to put the creations in an order, to instruct the spiritual beings, to show that the world is not of spontaneous origin or eternal duration, and to prefigure the six thousand years of the world's existence.

27. E.g. AC M̲W̲ p.15.

28. E.g. Bar Hebraeus on Gen.1.5 reports Jacob of Edessa as supporting simultaneous creation, and Gregory of Nazianzus and John Chrysostom (P̲G̲ 53 col.35) as taking the opposite view; Basil, H̲e̲x̲a̲e̲m̲e̲r̲o̲n̲ I.6; Bərešit R. 12.4; Ginzberg, L̲e̲g̲e̲n̲d̲s̲, I p.23, V p.34.

4.4.9   The 'wind of God' (Gen.1.2).

AC Gen.1.2 translates 'mänfäsä əgzi'abəher' by əgzi'abəher yäfättäräw näfas, 'the wind which God created', and assumes that this refers to the creation of wind (one of the four elements). It cites Theodore of Mopsuestia in support of this view, and cites an unspecified commentary on the Torah, Severus, and Basil as holding that the 'mänfäs' referred to is the Holy Spirit. This well-known difference of opinion is represented in most of the Ethiopian commentary materials and their sources, and in general they agree in supporting Theodore and Ephraim[29], the main exception being Severus of Əsmunain, probably the Severus referred to in AC Gen.1.2 (Mäshafä Sawiros, e.g. MS B.L. Or.773 f.31a, 116b).

4.4.10   'Hovering' (Gen.1.2).

The Geez text of Gen.1.2 has yəselləl 'hovers over, abides upon', and the Amharic translation in AC Gen.1.2 reads säfro 'abiding'; the meaning is clear, so the AC (in common with IAT on Gen.1.2) does not become involved in discussion of the type of the Syriac commentators' comparison of mrahhpā and metyabblā (see Išoʿdad on Gen.1.2 and Jansma p.106).

4.4.11   The use of speech in creation.

AC Gen.1.4 asks why God created the seven (wind, fire, water, earth, darkness, angels, the bright heaven) in silence, but used speech in the creation of light. It answers that (i) it was to prevent heretics saying that he could create only in silence, or only by speech, and (ii) it was for the sake of the listening angels. The further legendary material in AC Gen.1.4 and many sənä fəträt

29. Theodoret, Quaestiones 8; Išoʿdad, IAT, and Bar Hebraeus on Gen. 1.2; IATQ (see end of section 4.1.3 above); THBK Mimrā I.70; MO (e.g. MS B.N. d'Abb.156 f.4a); Moše bar Kepha, Hexaemeron (ed. Schlimme, book II, ch.4); further discussion in Jansma, pp.104-6; van Rompay, 'Išoʿ bar Nun and Išoʿdad of Merv', OLP 8; K. Smoronski, 'Et Spiritus Dei ferebatur super aquas', Biblica 6 (citing a wide range of Jewish, Latin, Greek and Syriac, but not Arabic or Ethiopian, interpretations); Bərešit R. 2.4 (identifying the 'spirit of God' as the 'spirit of the Messiah').

texts concerning the doubts of the angels about their origin is used as amplification of the second reason — God spoke to reassure them. These two reasons are essentially those of Theodore of Mopsuestia (as represented in Book VII of John Philoponus' *De opificio mundi*[30]), namely that God created first in silence because beings that could hear were not yet created, and because it should not be thought that God needed an instrument in creation. These ideas run right through Ethiopian commentary materials and their sources[31], and have a partial parallel in Jewish sources in Abarban'el's question 3 on Gen.1.

4.4.12 The direction from which God spoke saying, 'Let there be light'.

This is not specified in the account of the angels and the creation of light in AC Gen.1.4, but in some parallel accounts (e.g. AC Rev.12.17, <u>TIA</u> p.294) it is said that it was from the east that God poured out the sea of light. The reason given is that that was the direction where the devil was not present, and this view is echoed in the SFG in MS **B**.N. d'Abbadie 156 f.3a: '"He made a voice heard" — it happened from the east, lest the thought of the angels be sullied by devilish thoughts".

That the direction was from the east is found also in the commentaries of Išoʿdad and IAṬ on Gen.1.3-4, and in IBN's question IV. In his commentary IAṬ has used Išoʿdad, but in his questions

---

30. For this and other references see Jansma pp.99-100.

31. 4 Ezra 6.39; Išoʿdad and IAṬ on Gen.1.22; THBK <u>Mimrā</u> I.46,53,97 (all in Geez version of IAṬ's questions, EMML 1839 f.22b,23a,24b); IAṬQ (EMML 1839 f.6b); SFG, B.N.d'Abbadie 156 f.3a; Clarke, <u>Selected Questions</u>, pp.58-9; Moše bar Kepha, <u>Hexaemeron</u> (ed. Schlimme, book II, chs.5-7); Jansma, 'Barhebraeus' Scholion on the words, 'Let there be light'.'

(IATQ, EMML 1839 f.1a col.3) he has reproduced IBN's question and answer IV, which is partly derived from Ephraim and Basil of Caesarea.[32]

4.4.13 The language of creation.

AC Gen.1.4 says that God used the language of Syria, and adds the alternative opinion that he used Hebrew. There are many references to this in Ethiopian commentaries and their sources[33], and at least three distinct questions are found discussed: (a) in what language did God say, 'Let there be light'?, (b) in what language did he speak with Adam?, and (c) was Hebrew/Aramaic/Syriac one of the languages produced at Babel, or did it antedate the confusion of tongues? Išoʿdad and IAT discuss the matter in comment on Gen. 1.3-4 and 11.1. It is not surprising that Syriac commentators generally opt for Syriac as the language of creation; in this they have the support, e.g., of Theodoret's Questions on Genesis 60 (PG 80, col.165), and claim the support of Theodore of Mopsuestia. Jewish commentaries generally, and some Christian ones, opt for the holy tongue, Hebrew[34]. Eth. Qäleməntos (book I, ch.20) says that the language of Adam was Syriac, and that those who say it was Hebrew lie (B.L. Or. 751 f.15a).

4.4.14 The day on which the devil fell.

Extensive legendary material on the fall of the devil is found both in the AC corpus[35] and in its sources. Išoʿdad and IAT in their commentaries on Gen.3.1 record the opinions that he fell

---

32. E.g. Clarke, Selected Questions, pp.22, 66-9.

33. IAT (B.N. d'Abbadie 28) on Gen.1.4; Məhərka dəngəl (EMML 2101 f.64a); Mäshafä arganon p.262; THBK Mimrä II, 42,113; Jansma pp.154-5; IATQ (EMML 1839 f.10b col.3, 25b col.3, 30a col.1).

34. MhG on Gen.2.23; MhH on Gen.11.6; Ginzberg, Legends, V pp.205-6.

35. E.g. TIA pp.293-6; AC Qəddase pp.284-5; AC MW pp.15-16.

on Sunday, Wednesday, or Friday. THBK <u>Mimrā</u> II.71, in which his fall
is on Wednesday or Friday, has passed into Ethiopic as part of IATQ
(EMML 1839 f.26b col.1).   The AC, which has some of this material
on Gen.1.4 and 18, has become the legatee of a variety of traditions,[36]
and the SFA (Mogäs, pp.70-74) has conflated them by relating that
on Sunday the devil fell from Heavenly Jerusalem to Iyyor, on Wednesday he declined to live in this world, on Thursday he fell to
Antortos, and on Friday he despaired.

4.4.15 <u>The creations of each hour of the first day</u>.

Jewish sources contain various accounts of the creative
activity of each hour of the sixth day[37], but apparently not for the
first day[38]. Such accounts do, however, appear in the <u>sənä fəträt</u>,
and the most systematised one is in Mogäs' SFA. It is closely paralleled in the SFG, and the account of the creations of the day hours
are partly paralleled in <u>TH</u>, and to a lesser extent in Trumpp's
<u>Aksimaros</u>.

The SFA scheme is as follows:

Night hour 1: 4 elements and darkness

       2-8: the 7 heavens, beginning from the uppermost, <u>mänbärä</u>
<u>mängəst</u>, <u>sərha aryam</u>, <u>sämay wədud</u>, <u>iyyärusalem</u>
<u>sämayawit</u>, <u>iyyor</u>, <u>rama</u>, <u>erär</u>, at hourly intervals.

     9-12: the angels in <u>iyyärusalem sämayawit</u>, <u>iyyor</u>, <u>rama</u>, <u>erär</u>.

Day hour 1: descent of Satna'el from <u>iyyärusalem sämayawit</u> to
<u>iyyor</u>

36. E.g. see <u>TH</u> for Wednesday (Tanasee 35 f.85a-88b, which includes the
devil's descent on Mecca); SFG (Cowley 40) f.9a, 37b-38a (similar
to SFA); Trumpp's 'Aksimaros' for Wednesday; Eth. <u>Qäl</u>. book II
ch.4 (in which the devil falls on the first hour of Friday); Budge,
<u>Cave of Treasures</u>, p.55.

37. See below, 4.4.37.

38. The general plan is reminiscent of the Horarium of the <u>Testament
of Adam</u>, but the details are quite different.

Day hour 2:   angels praise the Trinity

     3:    the angels in <u>iyyärusalem sämayawit</u> are anointed

   4-6:   the cherubim, seraphim, and <u>haylat</u> in <u>iyyor</u> are

            anointed (at hourly intervals)

   7-9:   the <u>arbab</u>, <u>mänabərt</u>, and <u>səltanat</u> in <u>rama</u> are anointed

 10-12:   the <u>mäkwannənt</u>, <u>liqanat</u>, and <u>mäla'əkt</u> in <u>erär</u> are

            anointed.

<u>BMHE</u> book I has a different scheme, in which in hours 2-9 of the night (? or day), groups of angels are successively created, the <u>mäla'əkt</u>, <u>mänabərt</u>, <u>səltanat</u>, <u>aga'əzt</u>, <u>haylat</u>, <u>räbbäwat</u>, <u>mäkwannənt</u>, and <u>arbab</u>.

4.4.16 <u>Cosmology</u>.

(a) The separation of <u>hanos</u> and <u>wəqyanos</u>.

AC Gen.1.6 describes the separation of <u>hanos</u>, 'upper waters', and <u>wəqyanos</u>, 'lower waters', by the <u>täfär</u>, 'firmament', generally understood as the visible blue heaven/sky. This is depicted in a diagram in MS B.L. Or. 503 f.1b:

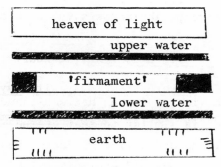

(b) The worlds beneath the earth.

AC Gen.1.12 refers to the 'worlds beneath', or the 'found-ations of the earth', and MS Y describes the earth as resting on water resting on fire resting on wind – a statement reminiscent of <u>TB Hagiga</u> 12b, which has the earth resting on pillars resting on water resting on mountains resting on wind resting on storm resting on the arm of the Holy One.

A more complex description of '20 worlds' is found in SFA (Mogäs p.38), SFG (Cowley 40 f.16a) and in the AC corpus (e.g. AC <u>Qəddase</u> p.261), and its source is probably the <u>TH</u> (e.g. Ṭanasee 35 f.83a–b). The '20 worlds' are:

9 of fire: (3 places of angels (? Erär, Rama, Iyyor), heavenly
Jerusalem, sämay səfhət, mänbärä mängəst, sərha mäqdäsu,
the fire beneath Jerusalem, and Gehenna),

4 of water: (2 heavens which came from water, wəqyanos, and the
male water which ascended in the heaven),

5 of earth: (Bärbaros, this earth, Paradise, the land of the
blessed, the land of the living),

2 of wind: (Babel which is above Bärbaros, and the wind beneath
the water of heaven).

(c) The heavens.

The AC and its sources are legatee to traditions of one, three,
seven and nine heavens, and considerable conflation has resulted[39].
SFA (pp.18–19) says there are seven heavens, and that they are like
the storeys of a castle building, so Moses was able to speak of them
as one; this is the commonest Ethiopian view, and is further explained in the sänä fəträt in MS Faitlovitch (Tel Aviv) 32:
'Jubilees says seven heavens, Aksimaros only one. Jubilees sees the
ladder of light and says seven; Aksimaros says one because the
foundation is one'.

(d) The 'spheres'.

While the Ethiopian view of 'seven heavens', and 'heaven
like a tent over the world' is similar to that of the Talmud and
the Apocryphal literature, the Greek view of 'seven heavenly spheres
encircling the earth' has also reached Ethiopia, albeit in a confused and misunderstood form[40].

39. The material of THBK Mimrä I.76–7 has reached Ethiopia in the Geez
version of IATQ (EMML 1839 f.23b); Eth.Qäl. book I ch.2, and book
II ch.2; Jansma pp.119–20; TH; Trumpp's Aksimaros; Basil Hexaemeron III.3; Theodoret Quaestiones 11. BMHE section 1 has a list
of names for six of the seven heavens which partially differs from
the list in the sänä fəträt. The Hebrew names are again different
(TB Hagiga 12b; Vayyiqra R. 29.11; Ginzberg I p.9, V p.9–10 etc).

40. TIA pp.94–6; G. Sarfatti, 'Talmudic Cosmography'.

4.4.17 <u>The matter from which the firmament was created.</u>

The views of 'Basil', that the firmament was created from nothing, and of Theodore of Mopsuestia, that it was created from water, are reported concisely in THBK <u>Mimrā</u> I.75, and thence have reached Ethiopia in the Geez version of IAṬ's questions (EMML 1839 f.23b); Išoᶜdad on Gen.1.6 points out that the <u>ex nihilo</u> view is not that of Basil, but of 'others'.[41] Another of IAṬ's questions (EMML 1839 f.8b) assumes that the firmament was made from water, and gives as a reason that on the further side of it there should be a world for immortal creations, while this world would be for mortal creations. SFA (p.28) may be referring to this in saying that humans, seeing the firmament, would understand that they have a heavenly inheritance. Some other accounts of the sᵊnä fᵊträt[42] refer to God's 'making the water firm like iron' in the creation of the firmament, and this is essentially the view of Ephraim, that it was 'congealed like ice from the waters'.

4.4.18 <u>The nature of the 'waters above the firmament'.</u>

The material of THBK <u>Mimrā</u> I.81, reporting and opposing the opinion of Origen that the 'waters above the firmament' are spiritual powers, is found in abbreviated form in IAṬQ (in Geez translation in EMML 1839 f.24a). IAṬ similarly mentions Origen in his commentary on Gen.1.7 (in Geez translation in d'Abbadie 28 f.4b); the parallel passage in Išoᶜdad on Gen.1.7 adds Basil as holding Origen's view[43], and Bar Hebraeus adds Athanasius (i.e. <u>PG</u> 27, col. 1333) and Gregory of Nyssa (i.e. <u>PG</u> 44, col.442; for Origen, see <u>PG</u> 12, col.1680). A partial parallel in Jewish sources is found

41. See Jansma pp.114–6.

42. E.g. Ḥaylä mäsqäl Gäbrä mädhᵊn, <u>Sᵊrwä haymanot</u>, p.14.

43. Išoᶜdad is mistaken about Basil, see <u>Hex.</u> III.9; the matter is further discussed in D.S. Wallace-Hadrill, <u>Christian Antioch</u>, pp.27–9.

in <u>YML</u> on Gen.1.7, 'The "water" above the firmament is not a physical liquid, but an ethereal fluid which we call "spiritual substance".'

4.4.19 The meaning given to 'sămay' (Gen.1.8).

AC Gen.1.8 says that <u>sămay</u>, 'heaven', means <u>sǝʿǝlă may</u>, 'picture of the water'.[44] This appears to be a play on words of the type of the midrashic association, e.g. in Bǝrešit R. 4.7, of Hebrew <u>šamayim</u> 'heaven', with <u>eš</u> and <u>mayim</u>, 'fire' and 'water', and with other words of similar sound.[45] This type of play on words is rare in the AC (but common in Jewish sources), and it is of interest that this Ethiopian example involves a word corresponding with a Hebrew word which is very richly so treated in the midrash.

It must be doubted whether the statement in AC Gen.1.10 that <u>mǝdr</u>, 'earth', means <u>mahdăr</u>, 'dwelling place',[46] is a further example of such a play on words, since it is coupled with the statement that <u>bahr</u>, 'sea', means <u>gwǝdgwad</u>, 'pit'.

4.4.20 The colour of the firmament.

AC Gen.1.8 cites what appears to be understood as a variant reading of the Geez text of Gen.1.8, <u>băʾamsală azrǝq</u>, 'in the likeness of Nile blue', and says that the firmament was this colour so that it would be restful for the eye. This idea is found in IAṬ's commentary on Gen.1.7-8, and Bar Hebraeus on Gen.1.7 attributes it to Gregory of Nyssa.[47]

44. Also found e.g. in SFG f.12a.

45. Further examples in Bǝrešit R. 4.7; <u>TB</u> <u>Hagiga</u> 12a; Ramban on Gen.1.8.

46. The source of this appears to be IAṬ's commentary on Gen.1.9-12; see also Išoʿdad on Gen.1.10, and Jansma pp.120-1.

47. See also SFG f.13a; Išoʿdad on Gen.1.6. AC Qǝddase p.282 gives (? the variant) kămă mayă azrăq and translates it into Amharic ǝndă arăngwade, 'like green' - but this different translation merely relates to a varying Ethiopian perception of colour.

4.4.21 The statement 'God saw that it was good' of the creations of the second day (Gen.1.8).

The Geez text of Gen.1.8 contains the words 'and God saw that it was beautiful', so the AC does not enter into attempts to wrest a meaning from their omission – as some Jewish[48] and Syriac[49] commentators do.

4.4.22 The divisions of land and sea.

These are described briefly in AC Gen.1.9, and receive mention elsewhere in the AC corpus (e.g. AC Qəddase, p.282). The SFG (f.15b) says that Ezra saw the land (mədr) divided into seven divisions, of which four are named as 'water' (may), 'Negeb' (nageb), 'earth' (maret), and 'desert' (mədra bädəw). SFA (pp.36-7) explains that 'nageb' is the wall of earth which bounds the earth that was moved to one side when God placed the ocean (wəqyanos) in its position; 'admas' is its other boundary. SFA continues by saying that God divided the land (mədr) into six, and placed wəqyanos in one division; it names four of the remaining five divisions as the place of distillation of hail (yäbäräd masriya), the home of Behemoth and Leviathan, the home for humans, and 'nageb'. The material is somewhat confused and conflated, and reflects a pre-scientific cosmology. It has links with IV Ezra 6.42 and 1 Enoch 60.9-10.[50]

4.4.23 The portals of the winds.

In the course of discussion of the ordering of the earth and

48. E.g. Bərešit R. 4.6; Rashi on Gen.1.8; Jansma pp.110-111.

49. E.g. Išoʿdad on Gen.1.7-8; IBN question V. IAṬ on Gen.1.7-8 notes that the words are lacking in the Syriac text, but present in Greek; the Geez version of this in MS B.N. d'Abbadie 28 f.4b, and in the commentary of Məhərka dəngəl, says that the words are present both in Greek and in Syriac.

50. See also IBN question 9 (in IAṬQ, EMML 1839 f.2a); Išoʿdad on Gen.1.6; Ginzberg, Legends, V p.13.

the waters on Tuesday, the SFG (f.17a–b) refers to an apparent disagreement between Enoch, who says that the winds come out of twelve
portals, and Epiphanius, who says there are twenty four. The reference to Enoch is doubtless to 1 Enoch 76, and 'Epiphanius' may
refer to the TH (f.82a), which supports 'twenty four windows'.
SFG and SFA (p.37) reconcile the apparent discrepancy by saying
that Enoch counts the exits for the winds, and Epiphanius adds their
entrances. AC Gen.1 does not refer to the matter, possibly because
it would be assumed to be familiar from the sᵊnä fᵊträt.

4.4.24 Homiletic treatment of the fruiting of plants.

AC Gen.1.11 records several variant readings of the Geez
text which relate to the parts of plants where fruit or seed is
formed. SFA (pp.44–6) gives a homiletic treatment, likening the
root of the plant to our Lord, the fruit formed from the root, or
from the top of the plant, to those who believe the Lord's teaching,
and the fruit formed from the side of the plant to those who
believe the apostles' teaching.

4.4.25 The properties of the four elements.

AC Gen.1.12 has a (slightly confused) account of the dual
properties of each of the four elements which is similar to that in
MhH on Gen.1.2, as follows:

	AC Gen.1.12	MhH on Gen.1.2
wind/air	cold and dry/burning	cold and damp
earth	wet and dry (!)	cold and dry
fire	dry and burning	hot and dry
water	cold and wet	cold and damp

The SFG (f.3b) has a slightly different account, and a
further account (shared with SFA p.13) in which each element is
allotted three properties:

	2 properties	3 properties
wind	burning, damp	burning, damp, dark
earth	dry, cold	dry, cold, dark
fire	burning, light	burning, light, dry
water	damp, cold	damp, cold, light.

AC Gen.1.12 and SFG (f.3b) also note that earth and wind
are opponents, and water reconciles them; and fire and water are
opponents, and wind reconciles them. This is similar to the account
in MhH on Gen.1.2, which has, like the AC, air and earth as opponents, with water in between them, but, unlike the AC, earth and
fire as opponents, with air in between them. SFA (p.14) adds to
the account in the SFG a more complicated scheme taking the elements in groups of three – e.g. when water, wind and earth are
opposed, fire reconciles them, sharing burning with the wind, light
with the water, and dryness with the earth.[51]

SFG (f.5a–b) applies this material homiletically, likening,
for example, the opposition of wind and earth to the human mis-
conception that God is an oppressor because he knowingly created
evil things.

4.4.26 The four seasons.

AC Gen.1.13 sets out the four seasons as follows:

			custodian
saday	Maggabit 25 to Säne 25	April – June	earth
kərämt	Säne 25 to Mäskäräm 25	July – Sept.	water
mäsaw	Mäskäräm 25 to Tahsas 25	Oct. – Dec.	wind
hagay	Tahsas 25 to Maggabit 25	Jan. – Mar.	fire

This correctly places the Ethiopian rainy season (kərämt) in
July – Sept., but fails to recognise that the Ethiopian year does
not have four climatically distinct seasons – non-Ethiopian sources
have been re-used here.

The account in IATQ (EMML 1839)f.24b col.3), which is very
loosely based on THBK Mimrā I. 103, has the following:

---

51. Further see Mose bar Kepha, Hexaemeron (ed. Schlimme, book IV,
    section A, ch.14).

kərämt ('winter') begins on <u>Tahsas</u> 24,

hagay ('summer') begins on <u>Säne</u> 24,

sädäy ('autumn') begins on <u>Mäskäräm</u> 24, and

mäsäw ('spring') begins on <u>Mäggabit</u> 24.

This corresponds with the seasons of the middle latitudes of the northern hemisphere, and (from the Ethiopian view-point) misplaces 'kərämt' in Jan. - Mar.

This material has an overall similarity to, but apparently no detailed correspondence with, Jewish comment on the four seasons (təqufot, *e.g.* <u>MhH</u> on Gen.8.22).

4.4.27 <u>The creations of each hour of the third day.</u>

The SFG (f.14b) gives the following account of the creations of each hour of the night of the third day of creation (and also points out, f.14a, that as with God one day is a thousand years, each of these 'hours' is 83 years and 4 months):

Night hour 1:   Bärbaros

          2:     fire placed over Bärbaros

          3:     wind placed over the fire

          4:     heaven placed over the wind

          5:     earth made from Bärbaros

          6:     land of the blessed created

          7:     land of the living

          8:     Paradise

          9:     plants created in Paradise

        10:     plants in land of the living

        11:     plants in land of the blessed

        12:     plants on earth.

4.4.28 <u>The relative positions of the sun and moon at the time of their creation.</u>

AC Gen.1.18 records the opinions (a) that the sun and moon were created at the same time in the 'hight of Wednesday' (i.e. Tuesday afternoon - evening), and that the sun quickly set, and (b) that the moon was created and shone through the night, and the sun was subsequently created at dawn on Wednesday and shone through

the day. The account seems a little confused, and is clearer in
Məhərka dəngəl's edition of IAṬ (EMML 2101), where he says that
either (a) the sun was created in the west four hours before the
end of the day, and the moon was created in the east, or (b) – and
here he merely follows IAṬ – the sun was created in the east and
the moon in the west, or (c) both were created in the east, and the
sun travelled during the day while the moon waited for the night.

The SFG is aware of this debate, which goes back at least to
Ephraim. It rejects (f.21b) the opinion of Mārha ʿəwwər that the
sun was created on Tuesday, and supports the view, attributed to
the Torah, ṬH, Qāl., and Abušakər, that the sun was created on
Wednesday; it also says (f.21a), in agreement with Ephraim, that
the sun was created in the east, and the moon in the west.[52] IAṬ,
in his comment on Gen.1.18, records the views of Theodore of Mopsuestia that the luminaries were created on Wednesday (i.e. Tuesday)
night, and of others who say they were created at dawn. The SFA
(p.48) agrees with Theodore.

Where does the sun spend the night? IAṬ on Gen.1.4 (in Geez
translation in d'Abbadie 28 f.4a) records the opinions of (a)
Theodore of Mopsuestia, that it hides behind mountains, (b) Narsai,
that it is hidden by an angel, (c) Ephraim, that it is immersed in
the ocean, and (d) 'others', that it goes around under the earth.
The fourth of these is reflected in SFA (p.48) which says the sun
spends the night 'circling by way of the south!'

4.4.29 The elements from which the heavenly bodies were created.

AC Gen.1.18 records two opinions: (a) that the sun was
created from wind and fire, but the moon from water and wind, and
(b) that the sun and moon were both alike created from wind and fire.
The SFA (pp.48–9) agrees with the former opinion, and supports the
statement about the sun by citing 1 Enoch 72.4. This interest is
common to the sources of Ethiopian commentaries, though in general

---

52. Jansma pp.122–5; Ephraim's opinion is cited in Moše bar Kepha's
Hexaemeron (ed. Schlimme, book II, ch.33).

they state, without differentiation, that the luminaries were created from wind, light, and fire.[53]

4.4.30 The apportionment of light to the luminaries.

AC Gen.1.18 says that of seven portions of light, three were given to the sun, two to the moon, one to the stars, and one to the clouds, and it notes the apparent discrepancy with Enoch (presumably 1 En.72-3, though the actual quotation in AC Gen.1.18 is nearer to Eth. Qäleməntos Book VI, e.g. B.L. Or. 751 f.80b, or to Isa.30.26). This view is shared with AC Ecclus.43.4 and TH f.84b. The SFA (p.49) has a mathematically more subtle scheme, in which, of the total light, the sun received 6/7ths., the moon 6/49ths., and the stars 1/49th., thereby preserving agreement with Enoch that the sun is seven times brighter than the moon. BMHE for day four, on the other hand, has a mathematically impossible scheme, in which of twelve parts of light for the sun, God took six, and allotted four of them to the moon, one to the stars, one to the waters, one to the clouds, and one to the lightning.[54] The Jewish legend of the diminution of the moon's light as a punishment[55] does not appear to have entered Ethiopian commentary sources.

4.4.31 The stars as custodians.

SFA (p.49) and SFG (f.23a-b) for Wednesday speak of the stars Narʾel, Bərkaʾel, Məlʾel, and Həlmälmelek as each custodians (mäggäbt) over 91 days of the year.[56] This is clearly dependent

---

53. Išoʿdad and IAṬ on Gen.1.14-18; IBN question 6, in Geez translation in IATQ (EMML 1839 f.1b col.3), discussed in Clarke, Selected Questions, pp.71-5.

54. Cf. Budge, Cave of Treasures, p.50.

55. E.g. Targum Pseudo-Jonathan on Gen.1.16; Bowker p.105; TB Hullin 60b, quoted in Ramban in loc.; Ginzberg I pp.23-6, V pp.34-41 .

56. Fully set out in Asräs Yänesäw, Yakam mättasäbiya, pp.37-40.

on 1 Enoch.82.13. The material does not appear in AC Gen.1, nor e.g. in IAṬ's commentary.

4.4.32 Homiletic treatment of the sun, moon and stars.

AC Gen.1.18 likens the luminaries as follows:

sun	sinners	righteous	the Lord	hundred-fold crop
moon	righteous	sinners	the apostles	sixty-fold
stars	–	–	the disciples	thirty-fold (Mt.13.8)

Similar material is found in the SFA (p.52), and other commentators variously apply it homiletically – IAṬ on Gen.1.14-19, for example, likens the rising and setting of the sun and the waxing and waning of the moon to human life and death, and material similar to this also is found in the SFA (p.54).

4.4.33 The 'monsters' of Gen.1.21.

AC Gen.1.21 understands the 'great anabᵊrt' to be Behemoth and Leviathan. This opinion is not found in the commentaries of, for example, IAṬ, Bar Hebraeus, and Iꞁoꞔdad, but a number of Jewish sources interpret the tanninim of Leviathan and its mate.[57]

4.4.34 Homiletic application of the three creations of the fifth day.

SFA (Mogas pp.59-60) gives four homiletical applications, of which the second is similar to material contained in AC Gen.1.22:

animals which	1	2	3	4
crawl on their belly	kingdom	ordinary people of the world	the three sons of Noah	the three persons of the trinity
run on feet	priesthood	monks		
fly with wings	baptism	martyrs		

57. E.g. Targum Pseudo-Jonathan on Gen.1.21; Bowker pp.97, 105-6.

4.4.35 <u>Homiletic treatment of the days of creation</u>.

SFA (Mogas) likens the days of creation to major Christian
doctrines, in a pattern approximating to the 'five pillars of
mystery' (<u>AAM</u>), as follows:

Sunday   - doctrine of the Trinity,

Tuesday   - doctrine of the Incarnation,

Wednesday - ordinance of the church,

Thursday   - doctrine of Baptism,

Friday   - doctrine of the resurrection of the dead.

A different account is found in the SFA in MS Faitlovitch (Tel
Aviv) 31:

'Let there be light' - the angels praising at the birth of Christ,

Monday   - our Lord at 12 years old,

Tuesday   - our Lord at 30 years old,

Wednesday - the time of our Lord's ministry,

Thursday   - the people who believed by the preaching of the apostles,

Friday   - the people who believed by the preaching of our Lord.

<u>BMHE</u> section 3 contains a further account:

Monday   - Ascension of our Lord,

Tuesday   - Pentecost,

Wednesday - Transfiguration,

Thursday   - Last Supper and Eucharist.

It is the first of these which has some contact both with
AC Gen.1 and apparently with   earlier Christian writings. Thursday, the day of creation of creatures from the waters, not unnatur-
ally attracted the idea of baptism, and both AC Gen.1.22 and SFA
pp.57-8 liken the water creatures to the baptized, the terrestrials
to the unbaptized, and the amphibians to the doubters. A similar
idea is found in Severian of Gabala, <u>De creatione</u> 4.2 (<u>PG</u> 56, col.
458-9).

4.4.36 <u>The interpretation of Gen.1.26</u>.

Comment on this verse has principally raised the questions
of (a) the revelation of the Trinity, and (b) the nature of the

imago Dei[58]. Ethiopian commentary materials generally assume a full Trinitarianism, in common with Antiochene traditions[59], and see the imago Dei in Adam's a'əmro, 'knowledge, understanding',[60] though these ideas are not extensively developed in AC Gen.1.

4.4.37 The creations of each hour of the sixth day, and the creation of Adam and Eve.

Ethiopian commentary materials contain no systematised account of the creations of each hour of the sixth day of the type that is found in Jewish sources[61]. They do, however, rather variously, specify the hour of the creation of Adam. AC Gen.1.26 states that Adam was created at dawn on Friday. SFA (pp.74-9) says that Adam was created at dawn on Friday, and Eve on the eighth day after him; Adam was taken on the fortieth day and placed in Paradise at the third hour on Friday, Eve was placed there on the eightieth day, and they then remained there seven years prior to their expulsion. SFG (f.32a) gives the time of Adam's creation as 'dawn, the third hour, on Friday'. AC Gen.2.7 alludes to the apparent discrepancy in

58. R. McL. Wilson, 'The Early History of the Exegesis of Gen.1.26'; N. Zeegers-Vander Vorst, 'La création de l'homme (Gn.1.26) chez Théophile d'Antioch'; L.van Rompay, 'Išo' bar Nun and Išoʿdad of Merv'; John Chrysostom, Homily X on Gen., PG. 53 cols.81-90; Theodoret, Quaestiones 19-20; Jansma pp.127-134; Moše bar Kepha, Hexaemeron (ed. Schlimme, book II, chs. 47-8); IBN question 12; THBK Mimrā II.1; Išoʿdad on Gen.1.26; Bar Hebraeus on Gen.1.27; IAT on Gen. 1.26; IATQ (EMML 1839 f.2a, 19b, 25a); SFA p.65; Bowker pp.106-8.

59. AC Gen.1.26 quotes from Severianus of Gabala, PG 56, cols.474-8.

60. E.g. TH (Tanasee 35) f.89a; MO (d'Abbadie 156 f.4a-b).

61. See e.g. Ginzberg, Legends, V pp.106-7 (note 97); A.J. Saldarini, The Fathers according to Rabbi Nathan, pp.303-5; PRE ch.11 and Chronicles of Jerahmeel (ed. M. Gaster); YML on Gen.2.7; Vayyiqra R. 29.1; MhH on Gen.1.26.

timing, and says, 'Here the Holy Spirit speaks as though God gave him sonship that very day. But <u>Aksimaros</u> says that the angels ... took Adam into the garden on the fortieth day'. IAṬ on Gen.2.2 states that Eve was created 'after the sixth day', but in Məhərka dəngəl's commentary (EMML 2101) this appears as, 'Eve was created at the sixth hour after the creation of Adam; some say "at the third hour".' Eth. Q̈aleməntos (book I ch.3) has Adam placed in Paradise at the third hour on Friday, but Adam and Eve only remaining there for three hours before their expulsion.

Of these, the SFA and other parallels in the AC corpus itself (e.g. AC <u>Qəddase</u> p.229) are dependent on Jubilees. IAṬ's commentary is based on Iso^cdad's, and Məhərka dəngəl's appears to be based on a conflation of Ethiopian opinion with a poor text of IAṬ.[62] THBK <u>Mimrā</u> II.77, rejecting the opinion that Adam was in Paradise 30 years, appears in IAṬQ (Geez version in EMML 1839 f.26b, reading '33 years'), but does not receive mention in the AC, doubtless due to the dominance of the Jubilees tradition. The account in Eth. Q̈al. has partial parallels in Eutychius (<u>PG</u> 111 col.911), and in some other Christian and Jewish sources (Ginzberg, <u>Legends</u>, V pp.106–7).

Concerning the creation of Eve, AC Gen.1.27 hints that she was 'contained within the nature of Adam', a motif common in Jewish and Christian sources.[63] AC Gen.2.21–2 says that Eve was created when Adam was 'between sleep and wakefulness';[64] it discusses why she was created from Adam's side (see 3.1.4 (iv) above), and whether the rib from which she was created was his right or left one.[65]

62. The translation in MS B.N. d'Abb. 28 of IAṬ on Gen.2.2 reads 'but if she was created after 6', and does not specify 'hours' or 'days'.

63. R. Murray, <u>Symbols of Church and Kingdom</u>, pp.301–3; Ginzberg, <u>Legends</u>, V pp.88–9.

64. Cf. Ginzberg, <u>Legends</u>, I pp.67–8;

65. AC Gen.2.21–2 gives reasons for both opinions. IAṬ <u>in loc</u>. opts for the right, and, like Iso^cdad, records the view of Henana that it was the left. The SFG in MS d'Abb. 156, f.3b, says it was the right rib, while the SFG in MS Cowley 40, f.40a, says the left.

4.4.38 The preparation of food for Adam prior to his creation.

AC Gen.1.27 says that Adam was created subsequent to other creations so that his food would be ready for him in advance. The source of this is probably the SFA (p.69) or IAṬ's commentary on Gen.1.26-7, which contain similar statements. A Jewish parallel is found e.g. in Bərešit R. 8.6.

4.4.39 Adam's upright stance.

AC Gen.1.27 says that Adam was created standing upright as (a) it is the mark of his governing the other creatures, and (b) it is the mark of his hope of resurrection. These are the two reasons given by THBK Mimrā II.57 (in the Geez version of IAṬQ in EMML 1839 f.26a). The second reason, but not the first, is similar to that given by Iso'dad and IAṬ on Gen.2.7. The proximate source for the AC account is probably the SFA (see Mogäs p.69).

4.4.40 The place of the creation of Adam.

AC Gen.1 does not specify the place where Adam was created, but elsewhere in the AC (e.g. AC Ps.73 (74).12) it is stated as 'bäma 'əkälä mədr bä'iyyärusalem,' 'in the middle of the earth, in Jerusalem'. This is also found in the SFG (f.35a, 'in the middle of the earth') and SFA (p.65, 'in the middle of the earth at Qäranyo (Calvary)'). The identification of the place of the creation of Adam, and/or of the resting place of his bones, with the site of the crucifixion of Jesus is an important theme in Ethiopian legend and art, and it has a Jewish parallel in the statements that he was created from the 'place of atonement', the Temple site (e.g. Bərešit R. 14.8).

4.4.41 The Sabbath.

AC Gen.2.2-3 points out that God did not experience tiredness from creating, but 'ceased from all his work' lest heretics say he lacked time, or that he lacked things to create. This is similar to THBK Mimrā II.86, which is found in Ethiopic in IAṬQ (EMML 1839 f.27b; other material on the Sabbath occurs on f.20a and f.28a). The theme of the first week as a type of the seven thousand year duration of the world (IAṬ and Bar Hebraeus on Gen. 2.2) is not developed in AC Gen.2, nor is the 'honouring' of the Sabbath emphasized (see Jansma pp.136–7).

4.4.42 Multiplication by natural increase.

AC Gen.2.2 says that after the six days of creation (when new things had been created ʻəmhabä albo' - ex nihilo, or from other materials unlike them), there would be no further alien (baʻəd) creation, but the species already created would multiply by natural increase (gəbr əmgəbr). Similar comments are found in Išoʻdad's and IAṬ's comments on Gen.2.2 (and see also Jansma pp.135–6).

4.4.43 Summary and conclusions.

(i)   AC Gen.1 and its proximate sources contain a variety of categories of material – the interpretation of words, theology, natural science, cosmology, calendrics, and homiletic application.

(ii)   Of proximate sources, the dependence of AC Gen.1 on the commentary of IAṬ on Genesis, the sənä fəträt, TH, and the books of Jubilees, Enoch and IV Ezra has been clearly demonstrated.

(iii)   Of anterior sources, links with Theodore of Mopsuestia, Ephraim and Basil are very pervasive, and there are specific links with other ancient writers, such as Ps.-Dionysius.

(iv)   As far as mediate sources are concerned, the questions and ideas common in Syriac writers like Išoʻdad and Theodore bar Koni have entered Ethiopian tradition, principally via IAṬ.

(v)   Eth. Qäleməntos has been utilized, especially in the sənä fəträt literature, but some of the material it contains has been explicitly or implicitly rejected.

(vi)   BMHE (and Trumpp's Aksimaros) stand to one side of the AC tradition; they share some common material with the AC, but are not representatives of the same exegetical tradition.

(vii)   AC Gen.1 has many parallels with Jewish commentaries; none of the parallels is such as would prove direct borrowing from one tradition into the other.

(viii) Some topics commonly raised in the sources of the AC are absent from AC Gen.1 itself; it seems likely that the student would be assumed to be familiar with them from other works, rather than that they were deliberately excluded on principle.

5. Christology:

    5.1   Survey of Ethiopian material related to Christology, and to the epistle to the Hebrews in particular

        5.1.1   Material associated with the text of the epistle to the Hebrews in biblical MSS

        5.1.2   Commentaries on Hebrews

        5.1.3   Creeds and other liturgical texts

        5.1.4   Patristic works other than commentaries

        5.1.5   Theological tracts

        5.1.6   Refutation of heresies

        5.1.7   Parts of the <u>andəmta</u> corpus

        5.1.8   Modern works

    5.2   Annotated translation of AC Hebrews 1

    5.3   Patristic quotations in AC Hebrews 1

    5.4   Geez texts of Hebrews 1

    5.5   Comparative study of selected exegetical motifs

5.   C H R I S T O L O G Y

5.1   SURVEY OF ETHIOPIAN MATERIAL RELATED TO CHRISTOLOGY,
       AND TO THE EPISTLE TO THE HEBREWS IN PARTICULAR.

This is a survey of materials known in Ethiopia, and of their
antecedents in other literatures. Christological issues have been of
such importance for the Ethiopian Orthodox Church that almost all
Geez literature, and some Amharic literature also, has relevance to
them; this survey therefore attempts only outline coverage, with
fuller detail in areas which (i) are closely related to Ethiopian
interpretation of Hebrews, and (ii) have received less attention and
study elsewhere.

5.1.1   Material associated with the text of the epistle to
         the Hebrews in biblical MSS.

(i)   Prologues.
Three types of prologue may be distinguished: (a) prologues
attached to the epistles in biblical MSS, (b) Euthalian hypotheses,
and (c) prologues in commentaries. Of these, (c) are considered in
5.1.2 below. Geez representatives of (a) and (b) are classified in
in my review of the EMML Catalogue vol.VII (in JSS), and the numbering
system proposed there is here followed. Of the prologues to Hebrews,
number 3.1.14 belongs to a series of prologues to the Pauline epistles
of which some others appear ultimately derivative from the Marcionite
prologues[1], and prologue number 3.4.14 is a translation of the
Euthalian hypothesis, PG 85, cols.773-6. All the five Geez prologues
to Heb. (and more may be discovered) show points of contact with each
other, with other prologues in biblical MSS (e.g. of the Vulgate),
with prologues in commentaries (e.g. Ephraim's and Iso͗cdad's), and
with AC Heb.; the following is a translation of them:

---

1.   Cf. L. Brade, 'Die Herkunft von Prologen in den Paulusbriefexegesen',
     OC 60.

Prologue 3.1.14[2]

The reason of the epistle of the Hebrews is for verification concerning the grace of Christ to all, not for the Jews by themselves. Many times God spoke by the mouth of his prophets, but especially by the mouth of Isaiah, concerning the promulgation of one new law, and Isaiah spoke in the place of God the Father, concerning Christ, and said, 'Is it a small thing to you that you are named my servant, and that you establish the people of Jacob, and the dispersion of Israel, and you bring them back? Behold, I made you a light to the nations and a saviour as far as the bounds of the earth.' And in this epistle the apostle shows that in the gospel law was the fulfilment of all grace, and that it is eternally existent and sufficient for the saving of the soul. And further he shows, concerning the weakness of the first law, that it has no sufficiency, and its passing away is for this reason. And further he shows the supremacy of Christ, one in nature and one in union[3]. The perseverance of the apostle was for this reason, that the Jews who entered into the law of truth were desirous of remaining attached to the law of the Torah, so that they might live by keeping two laws. When some of the people who are called Nazarenes heard (this), they persisted in this error.[4] And when the apostle heard, he brought an end to their teaching. He wrote[4] to them this epistle, in the Hebrew language, and subsequently Luke translated it from Hebrew into Greek.

And in this epistle, Paul opposes these (people). And further he shows in it that the grace of belief in Christ and the law of the gospel suffices by itself for the salvation of the soul. And he

2. Translated from MS Cambridge Or. 192 f.109b–110b, with corrections from MSS B.L. Or. 526 f.4b, Or. 528 f.110a–111a, and Or. 530 f.164a–165a.

3. B.L. Or. 530 has 'and (his) nature is one after the union'.

4-4. B.L. Or. 530 has 'And when he desired to bring an end to their teaching, he wrote'.

verifies the death of that law[5], which kills the ones who obey its laws[5]. And further he shows (a matter) to the ones who say that this epistle is not Paul's, but Luke's or Clement's, or if not, one of his disciples'. And they used to think this for 2 reasons. 1 of them is because Paul did not write his name at the head of this epistle according to his custom in all his (other) epistles; and the second reason is because of the abundance of the word of wisdom which is in it, and the directness of the matter for the one who disputes. [6]And in this there was a straightforward reply to all[6]. For the Jews used to hate Paul because of his disputation with them in the Holy Spirit, and because he desired[7] a little of their law, which had no sufficiency; and because of this he did not write his name for them, thinking that they would reject it, and would not accept the words in it. And the second reason[8] (is that) Paul wrote in the epistle of the Hebrews direct words and a matter which ends disputation – this matter is not a marvel when he himself is a Hebrew, and he used to speak to (his) fellows in their words, and turn them back to belief, in the Greek language; and his speaking in direct and correct words is not like Hebrew. But the church believes that this epistle is Paul's, and Diyonasyos Aryosfagos[9] in his homily brings many citations from this epistle, saying, 'My teacher Paul said'. All the 14 books of Paul are completed.

5-5. Following B.L. Or. 526 and 530. Or. 528 has 'which kills the ones who remain attached to its laws'. Camb. Or. 192 has 'we will kill the ones ...'.

6-6. It is not clear whether this should be attached to what follows, or to what precedes.

7. Possibly 'he did not desire' should be understood.

8. As this is the second 'second reason', the following material may be from another source.

9. I.e. 'Dionysius the Areopagite'.

Prologue 3.2.14[10]:

The reason of the apostle's writing to the Hebrews was because of many various matters. For the Hebrews who were living in the land of Judah and in all the lands of the Gentiles were opponents against Christ and against his disciples, because of their teaching. Nevertheless, after his ascension to heaven many from among them believed in the name of our Lord when they saw the miracles and wonders which were done at the hands of the apostles. But, while they believed, they kept the law of the Torah, and they honoured it more than the law of the gospel; they made the law of the gospel an addition to their law. Moreover, the apostles did not at that time urge them speedily to leave the law of the Torah, but they left them to observe (it) together with the law of the gospel, until the time when the teaching of the faith would be revealed in all the world. And because of this, the Jews who believed used to refrain from the foods of the Gentiles, and distance themselves from their company. Nor was it the Jews alone who were doing this, but the apostles also. There was a time when they were behaving like this because of the Jewish people who were believing, as this apostle said in his epistle, 'And when Cephas arrived at Antioch, I opposed him to his face, because before people came from James he had been eating with non-Jews, and when they came he withdrew from them because he feared the ones from among the Jews ; and the ones who had entered into this work were many, and Barnabas also was united with them, and was partial towards them, Gal.2.11-14[11]. But that Peter behaved like this (is because) previously Jewish believers who were in Jerusalem had criticized him, at the time when people returned from the house of Cornelius, the officer of Caesarea, and they had argued with him, saying, 'You went in to non-Jews, who were not circumcized, and ate together with them'.

10. Translated from Mǎhari Tǝrfe, Yǎqǝddus Pawlos mǎshaf, pp.595-603, and slightly corrected from MS B.L. Orient 529 f.54b-56b.

11. The reference is given in the printed text, but not in MSS.

Thus they were extremely jealous when they heard the report of Paul's and Barnabas' teaching and preaching among all the Gentiles, and (heard) that many miracles were done for them, and many Gentiles believed by their preaching, and that the apostles left the Gentile believers uncircumcized and unobservant of the law of the Torah. And they sorrowed with great sorrow when they recollected the passing of their Torah, and of the office of the Levites, and of the sacrifice of animals, and of all the ordinance of their fathers; and (when they recollected) the promise which was from the beginning for them alone, they were greatly disturbed. And they counselled together and sent to the country of Antioch resolute false brethren who would disturb the world, in order to deceive the believing Gentiles, so that they would be circumcized and observe the law of the Torah, as it is said in the Acts of the Apostles, 'And there were some who went down from the regions of Judah, and taught the Gentiles, saying to them, "If you are not circumcized according to the law of Moses, you cannot live".' And because of this, the Gentiles at Antioch were extremely disturbed, and argued with Paul and Barnabas. And they counselled that they send Paul and Barnabas, and their companions also, to the apostles and the priests[12] who were in Jerusalem, to verify for them the matter which would profit them. Having been sent from the church, they reached Jerusalem, and all the churches which were with the apostles and priests received them; and they reported to them what God had done for them among the Gentiles, and how the Holy Spirit descended upon them without their being circumcized, (and) the apostles and priests rejoiced greatly. And there were some people of the Pharisees who believed, who rose up and went to the apostles, saying to them, 'It is proper that we command them to observe the law of Moses and be circumcized'. But the apostles refused, and said to them, 'Do not be hard upon the Gentiles who have turned (to the gospel), and do not make them carry a heavy burden which neither our fathers nor we could (bear); but by the grace of God all of us will live. However, we will command them to distance themselves from that which people sacrifice to gods, and dead things, and blood, and sexual immorality, and (also) that what they hate for themselves they should not do to their fellow'.

12. <u>qäsisan</u> – 'priests' or 'elders'.

And from that time jealousy filled their heart, and they were sorrowful, and they were separated from the apostles, and they conferred with their leaders, and they sent brethren who were worse than at the first, to deceive the Gentiles, so that they be circumcized. And they compelled the Jews also, and made them remember the law of the Torah, that it is honoured, and was given from God at the hand of an angel and at the hand of Moses their prophet, and by it their fathers used to be governed, and because of this it is impossible for them to forsake it in any respect. And further they made them remember the ordinance of the office of the Levites, and the ordinance of sacrifice, and all the work of the tabernacle, together with the temple, and the sprinkling of blood which was in it, and the forgiveness of sins. And when they introduced all this stumbling block and doubt into the heart of the believing Jews, they wanted to turn back and retreat from the faith towards the ordinance[13] of their fathers.

And while they were in this state, the apostle Paul heard, and thought that he would strengthen them. And he verified for them that there was change in the first law, by reason of its weakness, for there was no sufficiency in it, nor did the Torah have any authority at all. And further he verified for them that that Torah was a shadow of the good that will come. And further the apostle desired (to explain that) its removal is in that which is proper for being removed, citing a testimony from the word of God, which he spoke by the mouth of Jeremiah, 'I will ordain for the house of Israel and for the house of Judah a new law, and it is not like that law which I ordained for their fathers when I took them out of the land of Egypt, because they did not remain within my ordinance, and I rejected them'. And concerning the priesthood of the Levites, he verified for them that it was not from the first, saying, 'But if that which they do for the people had been completed through the priesthood of the Levites, why then was it desired that another priest be appointed whose priesthood was like that of Melchizedek?', rather than saying 'like the appointment of Aaron', because their priesthood had to pass away, and since their priesthood passed away, their Torah will pass away. And further he showed, by a good testimony, the removal of their sacrifice, which

13. Reading sərʿata for səryata with Or. 529.

is meet for abolition. And he said concerning this, 'When he came
into the world, he said, "You did not desire sacrifice and offering,
but you clothed me with flesh; you did not take pleasure in sacrifice
for sin. At that time I said, 'Behold me, I came to do your will[14],
O my God'".' And he said, 'This word removes the former, so that it
establish the latter, in order that we be sanctified by the offering
of the flesh of the one who pleased him'.

And he wrote this epistle concentrating on spiritual wisdom;
and he omitted mention of his name at the beginning of his epistle,
for this apostle did not write his name, saying, 'From Paul an apostle',
like all his (other) epistles, because he knew that his relatives
would hate him intensely, and all the Jewish people would reject him,
because he was removing their law and reproaching them, and (because)
he loved the erring Gentiles who had believed. But if the apostle
had written his name[15] at the beginning of this epistle, who would
have read his epistle, and who would have given heed to it?[16] Rather,
they would have been dispersed quickly, breaking up the gathering
without hearing the word of wisdom which is in it. Similarly, this
(apostle) omitted mention of Moses' name at the beginning of his
epistle, and he wrote in place of it, 'In many matters and in many
portions God gave information to our fathers, in his prophets, from
former times'. And he said this verifying that the first ordinance
came by the hand of a servant. But as for the messianic ordinance,
he says, 'But in the latter days he spoke to us in his son, whom he
made inheritor of all'. And further he verified that he is the light
of the glory of the Father, and the likeness of his image, who holds
everything in the power of his word. And further he wrote to them
so that they should hear, after they had read a little, and should
know the deficiency of Moses and the honour of our Lord. For he says,
'Like Moses, so he also is righteous and faithful to the one who sent
him, over all his house; nevertheless, his honour is much greater
than Moses', just as the honour of the owner of a house is greater

14. Here m̈akärku, lacking in Or.529, has been left untranslated.

15. Reading səmä.

16. 'To it' supplied from Or.529.

than (the honour of) his house. For humans make every house, but
God is the maker of everything. And Moses was faithful in all his
house like its custodian, so that he be his witness in all the work
which he spoke. But Christ was like a son in his house.'

And further, this apostle wrote to the ones who were tested,
and suffered much suffering, who believed from among their unbelieving
relatives, because, by reason of observing the first law, people
would bring many perils upon them, and beat them, and imprison them,
and plunder their possessions, and they would bring them before kings
and officials, so that they change their faith; and he commanded
them to be strong in tribulation. And he warned them, saying, 'It
is very terrible to fall into the hand of God'. And he said to them,
'Remember the period when they baptized you, how you endured suffering
and were abused, how they tortured you and mocked you, and how you
were united with me in my imprisonment, and in the plundering of your
property, and in the joy which you received - and now, also, be
patient in the same way, and be strong in your faith'. And he spoke
to them of the power of the faith which God made operative for the
ones who were determined in their believing, so that they should
complete all that they intended - these are the former ones, whose
names he recalled, from Abel to Stephen the first martyr. And after
this he commanded the believers to live in love and charity with
their brethren. And he said to them, 'Do not forget to receive
strangers, for there are some whom he appointed to receive angel
strangers'. And further he commanded them to remember prisoners who
were tortured because of the faith. And as for adulterers who go to
the wife of another man, and those who desert the union with a woman
by reason of the yoke of asceticism and of purity, he gave them to
understand (the matter), saying, 'Marriage is honourable everywhere,
and their bed has no impurity. But God will judge the adulterers and
the ones who are unclean'. And he commanded that they greatly
honour the teachers, and he said, 'Remember your leaders who spoke
the word of God to you; seeing their good deeds, resemble (them) in
their faith. For Jesus Christ is the same, yesterday, and today, and
for ever'. And concerning them he further emphasized that they should
honour them and fear them, and he said, 'Obey your leaders and be
subject to them, for they persevere by reason of your souls, as ones

whom they will monitor on your account[17]; let them do this with joy, and not be wearied by it'. And further he entrusted the poor to them, saying, 'Do not forget mercy to the poor and participation with them, for a sacrifice like this pleases God'. And he sealed (the epistle) by saying, 'The grace of our Lord be with you all, Amen'.

It was written in Italy, and sent by the hand of Timothy.

Prologue 3.3.14[18]:

The reason for the epistle to the Hebrews is that they had been at the beginning perfect in faith, but as the time lengthened their faith waned, and they wished to call Christ a prophet like Moses, or an angel like Raphael, who remained in the house, and abode[19] as a servant. But concerning his divinity they doubted, saying, 'How can a god be incarnate?' Further, they recollected the ordinance of their laws and their altar; they said among themselves, 'How did we enter this law which has no chief priest and no altar?' It is by reason of humility that he desists from mentioning his name at the head of this epistle, for all (people) who send an epistle to the ones who are greater than they do not write their name; also he did this to make them great, because they preceded him in the faith. It was written in Rome and sent by the hand of Timothy.

Prologue 3.4.14[20]:

His epistle to the Hebrews. This was sent from Italy by the

17. Or.529 reads '...monitor before God on your account', and ends here.

18. Translated from MS Manchester Rylands (Strelcyn) 19 f.187a.

19. Reading wäbetä; alternatively, this may be a dittography, and 'and abode' should be omitted.

20. Translated from MS B.N. d'Abb. 130 f.114b–115a, with some corrections from Bodleian Bruce 81 (Dillmann XV) f.93b. Neither MS is free from scribal error and minor obscurity, and the translation is eclectic; d'Abb. 130 is nearer to the Greek of PG 85, cols. 773–6, from Tēs pros Hebraious to teleioi tēn Epistolēn.

hand of Timothy. And the reason of its sending was that the Jews, when they made firm the laws of the Torah and its study, for this reason made the apostle Paul a teacher for all the Gentiles, and he was sent among them to preach the gospel, and when he had written to all the Gentiles he later wrote the epistle to the Hebrews who had believed from among the people of the circumcision, (an epistle) which speaks clearly of the coming of Christ. And he says in it that the shadow of the Torah is inoperative and has passed away. Firstly, he showed them that the prophets were sent for this reason, that they relate the coming of Christ; and after them, he himself came and verified for them that the prophets are servants, and indicated his coming, and Christ is the son of God, and in him was all creation; and that the son of God must become man and abolish death by the sacrifice of his flesh, and raise it up by the power of his divinity, and ascend to Heaven, and in it he will come again for judgement at the time of the resurrection of the dead, and every eye will see him, and he will judge them in justice and in equity, because he is their creator. And further he verified that the salvation of human kind is not in the blood of goats and the blood of heifers, but in the blood of Christ. And he showed them further that the Torah has no authority at all, but is the shadow of the good which will come, which is written in it. And he said to them that the people[21] will not rest, but the day of rest is fitting for us all ...[22]. And further he verified and made clear that the true priesthood is not from the house of Levi. And he said that the fathers were justified by faith, and not by doing the laws of the Torah. And then he ordered those (people) that they preach, and he accepted their patience by praise which concerns Christ[23], and he taught them that they should honour priests, and he sealed his epistle.

21. I.e. the Jews alone.

22. Here d'Abb.130 reads nǎhallu, and Bruce 81 hallo; neither fits the syntax of the sentence.

23. The text is not wholly clear.

<u>Prologue 3.12.2.14</u>[24]:

  The fourteenth epistle. To the Hebrews. And the number of the headings of its lections is 11 lection headings; and the number of its <u>stichoi</u> (<u>qal</u>) is 703 sentences (nägär).

  He wrote this epistle from Italy, in Hebrew, and Luke the evangelist translated it into Greek; other people say Aqleməs[25] (translated it). And he sent it with Timothy his disciple. And the reason which prompted him to write it was that many of the Jews did not wish to believe that Christ is God, but they used to make him merely like Moses the prophet, doer of signs and wonders. And Paul sent them this epistle, indicating in it the honour of Christ, (which is) more than Moses and than angels and prophets, and (showing) that he is greater than they in the divinity in which he was united, and that he is equal to them in the humanity. And he elucidated for them that the Christly law is better than the former law, because it was a guide for us to the law of perfection and towards the end which is fitting, the Christly law. And he explained this to them with testimonies from the word of the Torah of Moses and from the books of the prophets. And he sealed this epistle (with) good counsels and godly commands and spiritual lessons. May the supreme God help (us) to know and perform it[26].

(ii) <u>Testimonia</u>.

  (a) Lists of numbers of <u>testimonia</u>:

  Lists of the numbers of <u>testimonia</u> in Hebrews, similar to that in <u>PG</u> 85 cols. 721-2, commencing, 'of Genesis 3, of Exodus 3, of Deuteronomy 6 ..., ' are found e.g. in MSS B.N. d'Abbadie 130 f.106a and Bodleian Bruce 81 (Dillmann XV) f.88b.

24. Translated from MS B.N. d'Abb. 130 f.93b.

25. I.e. Clement; the spelling reflects Arabic influence.

26. This is followed by a quotation from Heb.6, and a comment on hospitality.

(b) Lists of <u>testimonia</u>:

d'Abb. 130 f.106a–b and Bruce 81 f.88b–89a contain the 30 <u>testimonia</u> in Hebrews written out as in <u>PG</u> 85, cols. 739–44, commencing '1. Psalm 2, 15, You are my son ...'. MS d'Abb. 130, f.96a–b contains the same 30 <u>testimonia</u>, but instead of being consecutively numbered, they are divided into 10 sections (kəfl), apparently corresponding to a system of capitation.

(iii) Chapters.

(a) Notes of numbers of chapters:

The number of the larger divisions of the text of Hebrews is variously given as 7 (Bruce 81 f.87a), 10 (d'Abb.130 f.96a–b), 11 (d'Abb. 130 f.93b), 12 (d'Abb.119), 13 (AC), 23 (B.N. Zot. 45 and 47,[27] and B.L. Or. 13264[28]), and 28 (d'Abb.130 f.115a–b). The number of the smaller divisions of the text is given as 11 (Bruce 81 f.87a), 62 (d'Abb. 130 f.103b), and 65 (d'Abb.119). Further numbers may be found and clearly many sources are involved.

Of these numbers, the '7 larger chapters' belong to a capitation system running through the Pauline corpus, virtually the same as that in Iso'dad's commentary and in the <u>Tərgwame Pawlos</u>; the '28 larger chapters' are the Euthalian 22 (<u>PG</u> 85 cols. 717–8) differently numbered.

(b) Lists of <u>titloi</u>:

d'Abb. 130 f.115a–b contains a list of 28 chapter headings corresponding with the Euthalian list in <u>PG</u> 85, cols. 777–80.

(iv) Stichometry.

MSS give various numbers for the numbers of <u>stichoi</u> (qal) in Hebrews, and in some instances the lack of proportion with the numbers for the other epistles shows that differing sources have been conflated, or that scribal errors have been made, as the following examples show:

27. Probably B.N. Zot. 46 also.

28. The number is misprinted as '32' in Strelcyn's <u>Catalogue</u>.

MSS		Stichoi in Heb.	Stichoi in Phil. (for comparison)
(i)	B.N. Zot.45 and 47, BFBS 184 (Cowley XX), B.L. Or. 13264, MS Cowley 20 f.228b–229a	347	212
(ii)	B.N. d'Abb.130 f.130b, Bruce 81 f.87a	755 (or 655)	218
(iii)	d'Abb. 130 f.93b	703	208

The third of these (of which the full list is given in JSS, in my review of EMML Catalogue vol.VII) is similar to the numbers in the Euthalian list in PG 85 cols. 715–8, and to those given by Scrivener (A Plain Introduction, I, p.68).

5.1.2. Commentaries on Hebrews.

The Pauline corpus has attracted fewer commentators than have the gospels, but there is still a rich background in Greek[28],

28. Principally John Chrysostom (PG 63 cols. 9–236; 64 cols. 479–92), Theodoret (PG 82 cols. 673–786), fragments of Origen (PG 14 cols. 1307–10), Eusebius (PG 24 cols. 605–6), Theodore of Mopsuestia (Staab pp.200–12), Cyril of Alexandria (PG 74 cols. 953–1006), Severian of Gabala (Staab pp.345–51), Gennadius of Constantinople (Staab pp.420–22), Oecumenius of Trikka (Staab pp.462–469), Photius of Constantinople (Staab pp.637–652), various later writers (see bibliographies in commentaries on Hebrews by C. Spicq and P.E. Hughes), and comment in other exegetica and dogmatica by writers such as Athanasius.   See also F.M. Young, 'Christological Ideas in the Greek Commentaries on the Epistle to the Hebrews'.

Syriac[29] and Arabic[30] commentaries on Hebrews against which the Geez
and Amharic commentary material listed below may be studied.

(i)   John Chrysostom's <u>Homilies on Hebrews</u>. These homilies were
translated from Greek (<u>PG</u> 63 cols. 9-236;   64 cols. 479-92) into
Arabic by ʿAbdallāh ibn al-Faḍl (Graf II pp.52-6), and then into
Geez (MSS are listed in 7.3 below).   The Geez text with AC was published under the title <u>Dərsan</u> and <u>Tägsas zäqəddus yohannəs afä wärq</u>
(<u>TIA</u> p.13).   In this printed edition the 'admonitions' (<u>tägsasat</u>)
are separated from the 'homilies' (<u>dərsanat</u>), and appear as a group
subsequent to them.   This arrangement is found in some MSS, but in
others each 'admonition' appears as the conclusion of each 'homily',
as in the Greek text.   The printed edition also omits John Chrysostom's introduction, but the Geez version of this is found in some
MSS (e.g. B.L. Or. 740 f.1a-3a, Or. 739 f.3a-5b), sometimes accom-
panied by a Geez <u>bios</u> of John (e.g. B.L. Or. 741 f.7b-9b).

        Excerpts from the homilies are found in other works in Geez:
(a)   In <u>Gəbrä həmamat</u>, pr. ed. pp.244-5 cited from homily VIII;
p.297 cited from homily VII;   p.329 cited from homily XXVIII[31].   The

---

29. Principally Ephraim (Baumstark p.37-8;   published by Mechitharists),
    Paul of Edessa (Baumstark p.190), Ĭsoʿdad (Baumstark p.234;   pub-
    lished by M.D. Gibson), Laʿzar of Beth Qandasā (Baumstark p.271),
    Severus the monk (Baumstark p.279), Bar Hebraeus (Baumstark p.314;
    published by M. Loehr), and other writers whose works are not cur-
    rently known to be extant (such as Ḥenanā of Adiabene, and the
    author of the commentary translated into Arabic in Mt. Sinai Codex
    151 and published by H. Staal).

30. Principally Ibn aṭ-Ṭaiyib (Graf II p.163), an anonymous commentary
    of Coptic provenance (II pp.384-6), Ibn Kātib Qaiṣar (II p.463), and
    translations of John Chrysostom's <u>Homilies on Hebrews</u> (II p.55-6),
    and of a Syriac Nestorian commentary translated into Arabic by Bishr
    ibn al-Sirrī and published by H. Staal from Mt. Sinai Arabic Codex 151.

31. Other passages of 'tägsas' in <u>GH</u> (e.g. pr. ed. pp.173, 192, 213, 278,
    350) are not from YAWT.

text in the printed edition of GH is the same as that in the printed
edition of YAWD, pp.161-5, 149-50, and 418-9 respectively.

(b)   In Haymanotä abäw, pr. ed. pp.220-226 cited from homily V;
pp.226-230 and 230-234 from homily VI; p.243 cited from homily IV[32].
The version is not the same as that of the Geez MSS of the complete
homilies, and does not correspond very closely with the Greek text.

(c)   In Mäshafä hawi there are two extracts attributed to John
Chrysostom on Hebrews (e.g. B.L. Or. 776 f.102b and 118a); they
appear to be two different expansions of the same passage of Chrysostom's homily III.11 on charity towards 'heretics, heathen and
Jews'.

(d)   In some theological tracts of the ammǝstu aʿǝmadä mǝstir
type (see 5.1.5 below) there are brief extracts from the homilies;
e.g. the haymanot lämmiyyäkkäs in EMML 7122 contains two excerpts
from homily III.2 (YAWD pr. ed. pp.54-6) and one excerpt from homily
XV.4 (YAWD pr. ed. p.276) on f.67b.

      There is a reference to Chrysostom on Heb.1.3 in Mäshafä
tälmid (e.g. B.L. Or. 779 f.86b), but it appears not to be an actual
quotation.

(ii)   Tǝrgwame Pawlos. This is an important Geez commentary on the
Pauline corpus, found, together with TQ on Revelation, in MSS B.L.
Or. 13830 and Cowley 33-4 (see TIA p.65). The opening of its com-
mentary on Hebrews shows considerable agreement with that in MS
Vatican arabic 43, f.276b-300b[33], and it is probable that the TP

32. For further details see Graf in OCP 3 pp.345-402, and 7.3 below.

33. I am indebted to Msgr. J.M. Sauget for verifying this for me; a
    fuller comparison of Or. 13830 and Vat. arab. 43 is necessary to
    establish their precise relationship.

and <u>TQ</u> contained in B.L. Or. 13830 are translated from, or based on,
an Arabic text of the type of the anonymous commentary of Coptic
provenance contained in Vat. arab. 43 f.1b–300b and 307b–344b and
described in Graf II pp.384–6.

<u>TP</u> commences (on Romans): 'Interpretation of the first
letter which he wrote to Rome when he was in Corinth, and sent by
the hand of Phoebe. And the reason of the writing of it was to the
far-off people, after they had believed at the hand of Peter, because he wished to strengthen them concerning the assurance of the
faith, and further to assure them that he had not been separated
from the time when Peter taught them. And he wrote this letter not
seeking vain-glory for himself, and he sent (it) to them, lest the
wisdom of the Greeks and the teaching of the barbarians and that
which resembles them should suffice them. Chapter one ....' The
Geez incipits of <u>TP</u> are given in 7.3 below, and extracts from <u>TP</u>
on Heb.1 in 5.5.

(iii) <u>Tərgwame Felon Felgos</u>. This is a substantial Geez commentary on the Pauline corpus contained in MSS B.L. Or. 13964 and
Cowley 35. Its rubrics are <u>nägärä pawlos</u> ('word of Paul'), introducing the lemmas, and <u>felon/felgos tärgwämä wäyəbe</u>, introducing
comment by 'Felon' and by 'Felgos', two commentators I have not been
able to identify. The section on Galatians, for example, commences:
  'In the name of the Father ... . The word of Paul: "His
servant, who was not from humankind, but because of our Lord Jesus
Christ, and God who raised him from the dead". Felon commented and
said: "We believe; 'and I Paul was sent an apostle to the people
of Galatia'. And it was not because of humans but because of God,
the holder of all the world, who rose from the dead by the power of
his godhead." The word of Paul: "All our brothers who were with
me in the church of Galatia." Felgos commented and said: "All the
souls of the Christians, we who are joined together in Galatia, to
the ones who join in the glory of the faith together with me. Peace
to you, and the grace of God ...".' The commentary, as this sample
shows, has a somewhat flat and pedestrian character. The lemmas
represent an old Geez text-type (see 5.4 below), the Geez incipits
are given in 7.3 below, and extracts from the commentary on Heb.1
will be found in 5.5 below.

(iv)   Prologues in commentaries. The printed edition of the AC on
the Paulines includes one Geez <u>hypothesis</u> for each epistle (of which
the one for Hebrews is number 3.2.14, translated in 5.1.1 above),
and one Amharic prologue for each epistle, which has points of contact with the various Geez <u>hypotheses</u>, but is not the same as any
of them. Geez commentaries do not contain any substantial prologues
to the Paulines (except for John Chrysostom's introduction to his
<u>Homilies on Hebrews</u> found in some MSS); however, a number of pro-
logues to Hebrews in Greek, Syriac and Arabic commentaries have
points of contact with the Ethiopian commentaries - notably those
of Theodoret (<u>PG</u> 82 cols. 673-678), Išoʿdad (Gibson pp.101-2),
Sinai Arabic Codex 151 (Staal pp.221-3), and Bar Hebraeus (ed. M.
Loehr; the prologue says that the epistle was sent with Timothy
from Rome, and translated into Greek by Clement or Luke).

(v)   Miscellanea. Among collections of Amharic explanations of
Geez words may be found notes of commentary on Hebrews, e.g. in MS
Bodleian Bruce 81 f.95b, a collection commencing 'Of Hebrews. "Rod
of righteousness" means "power of righteousness".'

(vi)   AC Hebrews. Text and translation of AC Heb.1 are given in
section 5.2 below.

5.1.3   Creeds and other liturgical texts.

The liturgy of the Ethiopian Orthodox Church[34] contains
extensive doctrinal teaching, and the material on the Trinity and
on Christology is especially to be found in the anaphoras of St.
Mary, of the Three Hundred, of St. John Chrysostom, and of St. Cyril.

The creeds accepted by the Ethiopian Orthodox Church are

34. Geez text published in various Ethiopian editions; Geez-Amharic
diglot in <u>Mashafa qəddase</u>, A.A., 1951 E.C.; AC in <u>Mashafa qəddase</u>,
A.A., 1918 E.C.; English translation by M. Daoud, <u>The Liturgy of
the Ethiopian Church</u>, A.A., 1954 A.D.; study in E. Hammerschmidt,
<u>Studies in the Ethiopic Anaphoras</u>, Berlin, 1961.

those contained in the liturgy, namely the 'amaknǝyu zähawaryat'[35] (Creed of the Apostles') and the ṣ̈alotä haymanot'[36] (the Niceno-Constantino politan creed). In addition to these, the church knows of other statements of credal type contained in the work Haymanotä abäw, notably the 'twelve commands given to Constantine, son of Constantine' by Athanasius (HA, pr. ed. A.A., 1967 E.C., pp.83-90), the creed of Epiphanius from the Ancoratus (pp.192-3), Cyril's 'teaching of the faith' (pp.256-9), a credal statement of Severus of Antioch (pp.356-62), and various anathemas, especially those of Gregory of Nazianzus (pp.559-62), and the 'chapters' of Cyril[37] (pp.562-575).

In addition to the Niceno-Constantinopolitan creed itself, some 'credal expansions' are found included in 15th.-16th. century Ethiopic horologium MSS (Mashafä säⁿatat), e.g. Bible Society Cowley III, IV and XXV (BFBS 176, 177 and 173 respectively). Some of these expansions contain the text of the Niceno-Constantinopolitan creed together with brief historical statements about it (e.g. BFBS 176 f.123a-b, part of which is the same as HA pr. ed. pp.46-7), others contain related patristic citations or near citations, e.g. "The Father is the begetter and not the begotten. The Son is the begotten and not the begetter. And the Holy Spirit is the one who comes out from the Father, and takes up from the Son. Three names, one God, the Father and the Son and the Holy Spirit. Their kingdom is one and their authority is one, and from among angels and humans they bow down to them once, and we also, having believed, bow down to the Father and the Son and the Holy Spirit, for ever and ever, Amen" (BFBS 176 f.129b). This emphasis on 'one prostration' may

35. Daoud, Liturgy, pp.51-2; it is not the same as the Western 'Apostles Creed'.

36. Daoud, Liturgy, pp.122-3; it does not contain 'filioque'.

37. The 'chapters of Cyril' may instructively be compared with their Nestorian refutation appearing in L. Abramowski and A.E. Goodman, A Nestorian Collection of Christological Texts, pp.75-88.

have had polemical intent (see Getatchew Haile, 'Religious
Controversies', pp.125-7).

5.1.4. Patristic works other than commentaries.

The following are the principal works which fall in this
category, are known in Ethiopia, and contain material on Christology:

(i)   The Ethiopic Qerəllos corpus, consisting of the De recta fide,
book 1 of the Prosphoneticus ad Reginas, and the Quod Christus sit
unus of Cyril of Alexandria, together with some writings of other
church fathers, and some further writings attributed to Cyril, in
Geez translation;   a critical text and translation of the greater
part of the corpus has been published by B.M. Weischer (see 7.1
below).

(ii)   Haymanotä abäw, a Geez version of a large Arabic compilation
of writings of early church fathers and later patriarchs of Alexandria and Antioch[38];   the work treats (somewhat repetitively) of
the doctrines of the Trinity and Incarnation, and its main aim is
the defence of non-Chalcedonian Christology. A consecutive reading
of HA clearly demonstrates how it is that the Ethiopian Orthodox
Church maintains a non-Chalcedonian position. The Nicene and early
post-Nicene fathers are cited as teaching that the incarnate Christ
was (in) one həllawe ('being, state of existence', a translation
equivalent of hupostasis, phusis, and ousia). The post-Chalcedonian
writings then represent the pro-Chalcedonians as holding that the
incarnate Christ was (in) two həllawes (i.e. 'en duo phusesin') –

38. The Arabic work and its sources are excellently described by
    G. Graf, 'Zwei dogmatische Florilegien der Kopten' (see also Graf
    II, pp.321-3). The Ethiopic version is described in outline in the
    catalogue notes to MS B.N. Zotenberg 111, and has been published,
    with Amharic translation, A.A., 1967 E.C.

and this is seen as contradicting the Nicene homoousios.[39]

(iii) Mäshafä sawiros, the Geez version of the Kitab al-Idah of Severus of Esmunain.[40]

(iv) Tälmid, a Geez theological treatise described in the catalogue notes to MS EMML 2369.

(v) Mäshafä hawi, the Geez version of the Arabic translation of the Pandektēs of Nikon.[41]

(vi) Rətu'a haymanot, a collection of Geez homilies described in the catalogue notes to MS EMML 2375 (and see also Getatchew Haile, 'Religious Controversies').

5.1.5. Theological tracts.

(i) Təmhərtä həbu'at/Ɉlmästo'agya.
     Təmhərtä həbu'at is a part of the Geez version of the Syriac

39. Further see V.C. Samuel, 'One Incarnate Nature of God the Word'; Habte Mariam Worquineh, 'The Mystery of the Incarnation'; R. Cowley, 'The Ethiopian Church and the Council of Chalcedon'; and, in general (but from a Greek Orthodox viewpoint), M.G. Fouyas, The Person of Jesus Christ.

40. On the Arabic original, and bibliography of the Ethiopic version, see Graf II pp.309–11; for an outline of the Geez text, see catalogue notes on MS EMML 1195.

41. The Arabic version is described in Graf II pp.64–6, and a Geez MS is described in the catalogue notes to MS B.N. Zotenberg 110.

Testamentum Domini.[42] It is excerpted and attached to the Ethiopic
liturgy,[43] and is commonly included alongside the Psalter as a part
of Ethiopian elementary Christian instruction. At a higher level
of instruction the AC on it is taught, and its contents, which are
mainly Christological, are frequently used as a quarry of proof-
texts in other parts of the AC corpus.

Əlmasto'agya is a slightly differing recension of the
Təmhərta habuʿat found in the work Haymanota abäw,[44] and commented
on as a part of AC HA.

(ii)   Works based on the pattern of the 'five pillars of mystery'.
        The 'five pillars of mystery' (amməstu aʿəmada məstir, here
abbreviated AAM) are the doctrines of the Trinity, the Incarnation,
Baptism, the Eucharist, and the resurrection of the dead. This
pattern of presentation of basic Christian doctrine is latent in
the Niceno-Constantinopolitan creed itself, and more evident in the
'twelve commands given to Constantine, son of Constantine' by
Athanasius;[45] it is fundamental to Ethiopian Orthodox systematic

42. Syriac text in I.E. Rahmani, Testamentum Domini Nostri Jesu Christi;
    English translation of Syriac by J. Cooper and A.J. Maclean; French
    translation of Syriac by F. Nau and P. Ciprotti (where Təmhərta
    habuʿat corresponds to book I.XXVIII.2-12 of the Syriac Octateuch
    of Clement). Geez text and German translation in E. Hammerschmidt,
    Äthiopische liturgische Texte; Italian translation of Geez in O.
    Raineri, 'La «Dottrina degli Arcani».' The Ethiopic version of the
    Testamentum Domini, with French translation, has been published by
    R. Beylot (but the edition is methodologically unsatisfactory).

43. Mashafa qəddase, A.A., 1918 E.C., pp.1-23 (with AC).

44. Haymanota abäw, A.A., 1967 E.C., pp.21-7, and see my review of R.
    Beylot, Testamentum Domini Éthiopien. On the textual tradition of
    the Testamentum Domini, see R. Coquin, 'Le Testamentum Domini'.

45. See Graf I p.313; HA (printed diglot) pp.83-90; Cowley, 'An
    Ethiopian Orthodox Catechism'.

theology, and is found both in older Geez and Amharic texts, and in modern printed works based on traditional sources.[46] The following are the main features that may be used for description and classification of works following this pattern:

(a)   Title. While ammǝstu a‘ǝmadä mǝstir is the commonest title, works bearing other titles such as qalä haymanot,[47] haymanotä abäw hawaryat,[48] tǝmhǝrtä haymanot,[49] haymanot rǝtǝ‘ǝt,[50] nägärä haymanot and haymanot lämmiyyäkkäs yähaymanotǝn ammälaläs ǝndih näw[51] may have

46. For printed versions see e.g. Yähaymanotǝnna yäsälot mäshaf, A.A., 1955 E.C. pp.21–46 (in Amharic, translated in Cowley, 'An Ethiopian Orthodox Catechism'); Mogäs ‘Iqubä giyorgis, Mäshafä sännä fǝträt mǝslä 5-tu a‘ǝmadä mǝstir, Asmara, 1957 E.C. pp.96–126 (in Amharic with quotations in Geez); Ammǝstu a‘ǝmadä mǝstir, A.A. 1952 E.C., pp.99 (in Amharic with quotations in Geez, fuller than Mogäs' edition, and including a brief mäqdǝmä haymanot); Haylä mäsqäl Gäbrä mädhǝn, Sǝrwä haymanot, A.A., 1960 E.C., pp.37–137 (in Amharic, traditional in outline); Habtä maryam Wärqnäh, Ya’ityopya ortodoks täwahǝdo betä krǝstiyan ǝmnätǝnna tǝmhǝrt, A.A., 1963 E.C. (in Amharic; an Ethiopian Orthodox systematic theology in a more modern style); Ayyalew Tammǝru, Ya’ityopya ǝmnät bäsostu hǝggǝgat, A.A., 1953 E.C., pp.119–74.

47. See catalogue notes on Berlin Ms. orient. oct. 1290 (Hammerschmidt and Six 62.II) and orient. oct. 1295 (Hammerschmidt and Six 67.I).

48. E.g. EMML 1036.

49. E.g. Berlin Ms. orient. oct. 1008 (Hammerschmidt and Six 24.II), and Cowley, 'A text in Old Amharic'.

50. E.g. B.L. Add. 16199 (Dillmann XV).

51. E.g. Berlin Ms. orient. quart. 1017 (Hammerschmidt and Six 137.II), Bodleian MS Clarke Or. 39, EMML 7122 f.57a–107b, B.L. Add. 16222, B.N. d'Abbadie 122, and B.N. Mondon-Vidailhet (Chaîne) 35 (221). The structure of the text in EMML 7122 is unusual, and it may be that it should be regarded as a five-part 'haymanot rǝtǝ‘ǝt' (f.53a–57a, f.62b–82b, f.93b–f.98a, f.98a–104a, f.104a–107b) in Geez, into which haymanot lämmiyyäkkäs in Amharic (f.57a–62b) and nägärä täwahǝdo wäqǝb‘at in Geez (f.82b–93b) have been intruded.

contents following the <u>AAM</u> pattern.

(b)   Language. The works are in Geez, or in Amharic with quotations in Geez; as some exemplars commence in Geez and continue in Amharic, or <u>vice versa</u>, it does not seem that language indicates any fundamental distinction within the genre.

(c)   The named sources. Some of the works name many sources, others only a few. Some works (e.g. EMML 7122 f.57a-107b) name predominantly biblical and patristic sources, others (e.g. Mogäs' printed text) include quotations from Eth. Qälemäntos and similar works of a legendary nature, and from Ethiopian chant such as Dəggwa. EMML 7122 f.57a-107b names the following sources: (from the Bible) Job, Psalms, Prov., Macc., prophets, gospels, Paul, Peter, Mäshafä kidan; (from the liturgy) anaphoras of John, of Mary, and of the Nicene fathers; Arägawi mänfäsawi, Philoxenus of Mabbug; Mäqdämä wängel; Dionysius the Areopagite, Aforosyos, Herenewos (? = Hierotheus), Cyriacus ('Kirakos' and 'Kiryaqos'), Eraqlis (? = Proclus), <u>Abba</u> Sälama (of Ethiopia), the 'Blessed Interpreter' (mätärgwəm bəsu'awi), Ephraim, Theodotus of Ancyra, Gregory Thaumaturgus, Epiphanius, Eusebius, Gregory of Nazianzus, Gregory of Nyssa, Basil of Caesarea, John Chrysostom, Jacob Baradaeus; (bishops of Rome) Abulidəs (?= Hippolytus or Julius), Vitalis, Innocent; John of Jerusalem; (patriarchs of Alexandria) Macarius, Athanasius, Shenuti, John, Christodulus, Cyril, Gabriel, Zachariah, Cosmas, Alexander, Philotheus, Theodosius; <u>Abba</u> Mikael of Atrib and Malig and <u>Abba</u> Yohannəs of Burləs (compilers of <u>HA</u> and Sənkəssar); Severus of Esmunain; George disciple of Anthony (compiler of <u>Hawi</u>); St. Mäqabis; (patriarchs of Antioch) Ignatius, Basil, John, Severus, Dionysius; Rətu'a haymanot. This list is very similar to that given in the catalogue notes on MS **B.L.** Add. 16199 (Dillmann XV).

(d)   The formal structure of the work as a catechism proper[52], or as a 'question and answer book' after the style of Cyril's discourse with Palladius,[53] or as neither of these. It is probable that the

---

52. E.g. Cowley, 'An Ethiopian Orthodox Catechism' and Getatchew, 'Materials for the study of the Theology of Qəbat'.

53. E.g. EMML 7122 f.53a-107b.

catechetical form developed in response to doctrinal controversies, with the Roman Catholics, and internally (especially over the question of Christ's 'anointing' (qəbᶜat)).

(e) The presence or absence of a preface to the 'five pillars', a (variable) mäqdəmä haymanot.[54]

The AAM texts thus present many parallels with the sənä fəträt texts – a group of works, following a common plan, of variable title and text, drawing on many named sources, well established as an Old Amharic tract,[55] and found also in Geez texts which are probably a development parallel to the Amharic texts (rather than the source from which they were translated); moreover, sənä fəträt and AAM texts commonly occur together, in this order, in MSS.

(iii) Other tracts. There are many further theological tracts, the majority in Geez, with a large minority in Amharic; many of these cover the doctrines of the Trinity and the person of Christ, e.g. the Geez Mäzgäbä haymanot published with Amharic translation, A.A. 1959 E.C., pp.1–113.

5.1.6. Refutation of heresies.

Most works of Christian doctrine known in the Ethiopian Orthodox church include material in refutation of other doctrinal positions. The major Christological disputes referred to are those associated, in the early church period, with Sabellius, Arius, Apollinarius, Macedonius, Nestorius, and the Council of Chalcedon, and, in the later period, with the Roman Catholics, and the internal

54. Present e.g. in Amməstu aᶜəmadä məstir, A.A. 1952 E.C. pp.5-9, in Amharic; EMML 7122 f.108a-109a has a different 'preface', in Geez.

55. Getachew, 'Materials for the study of the Theology of Qəbat'; Cowley, 'A Text in old Amharic' (containing a text which Getatchew ('Religious controversies', p.134) suggests is of Ǝstifanosite provenance).

Ethiopian Christological controversies.[56] The major work devoted
entirely to the refutation of heresies is the Mashafa mastir of
Giyorgis of Gasəčča.[57] It will be found described in catalogue
notes on MSS EMML 1191, 1831, 2426, 2429 and B.N. Zotenberg 113.[58]

5.1.7. Parts of the andəmta corpus.

Christological material is found in the AC (a) to the OT,
especially on certain passages which are interpreted as messianic
prophecies (such as Gen.49, Isa.53, Lam.5, Pss.2, 8, 44, 109 (LXX
numbering), Ezek.44.2, parts of Daniel), which are given a typological Christological interpretation (such as Song of Solomon),
which contain apocalyptic (such as 4 Ezra), and which have been
prominent in Christological debate (such as Prov.7-8 and Isa.61.1),
(b) to the NT, in passages such as AC Jn.1.1 and Jn.17, Mt.3,
Rom.1.3-4, Heb.1 and Rev.6, and (c) to the patristic works, especially Qerəllos, Haymanotä abäw, Qəddase, and Yohannəs afä wärq.[59]

5.1.8. Modern works.

Modern Amharic works dealing with Christology are briefly
noted here as evidence of a continuing concern with the Christological debate, and not as works which may have directly incluenced
the AC tradition. The religious controversies of the fourteenth
and fifteenth centuries, which were "the main impetus for the growth

---

56. For a summary, and further bibliography, see D. Crummey, Priests
and Politicians, pp.14-27.

57. Dr. Yaqob Beyene is preparing a critical edition of the work. See
also Getatchew Haile, 'Religious Controversies'.

58. These catalogue notes identify as Manichaeus the heretic named as
'Mänkəyon/s'; I believe he is more probably to be identified as
Marcion (cf. notes on AC Heb.1.4 below).

59. For identifications, see TIA pp.12-13.

of Ethiopic literature during those two centuries", are reflected
in theological works which "constitute today part of the literary
tradition of the Ethiopian Orthodox Church"[60] the controversies
with Roman Catholics in the sixteenth century, and the subsequent
internal (mainly Christological) controversies, resulted in contem-
porary literary remains,[61] and continued in various forms, and in
the twentieth century Amharic books of the following types have
been produced:

(i)   restatements of classical Ethiopian Orthodox (tä̈waḥǝdo)
doctrine, based on classical sources such as those noted in 5.1.3-6
above,[62]

(ii)   refutations by Ethiopian Orthodox scholars of a book written
in Italian (and translated into Amharic) by an Ethiopian Roman
Catholic, <u>Abba</u> Ayyälä Täklä ḥaymanot,[63]

(iii) books written and published in Ethiopia as presentations of
Ethiopian Orthodox doctrine, but subsequently judged heretical and
banned.

Group (iii) is represented by two works:

1. <u>Ǝgziʾabǝher kaňňa gara</u>. yägetaččǝn sǝggawenna tä̈waḥǝdo mǝstir
('God with us. The mystery of the incarnation and the union of our

---

60. Getatchew Haile, 'Religious Controversies', quoted from pp.135 and 134.

61. See e.g. D. Crummey, <u>Priests and Politicians</u>, ch.2;   E. Cerulli,
<u>Scritti teologici etiopici dei secoli XVI-XVII</u>;   Getatchew Haile,
'Materials for the study of the Theology of Qǝbat'.

62. E.g. <u>Blatta</u> Pawlos, <u>Mǝstirä sǝllase</u>;   Habtä maryam Wärqnäh, <u>Yaʾityopya
ortodoks tä̈waḥǝdo beta krǝstiyan ǝmnätǝnna tǝmhǝrt</u>.

63. The Italian original is P. Mario da Abiy-Addì, <u>La Dottrina della
Chiesa Etiopica dissidente sull'unione ipostatica</u>, Rome, 1956.
Bibliographical details of the Amharic version, and of the Amharic
refutations of it, are given in Cowley, 'The Ethiopian Church and
the Council of Chalcedon'.

Lord'), by Abba Filəppos (formerly Ethiopian archbishop in Jerusalem), written in 1956 E.C., printed in 1957 E.C. at the Bərhanənna sälam Press, A.A., pp.1-68. The author says that in the person (akal) of Christ there are two natures (bahrəyat), the divine nature (bahrəy mäläkotawi) and the human nature (bahrəy säb'awi) (p.55), that it is not alien to Ethiopian Orthodox doctrine to say that the two natures 'exist united' (täwahədäw yənorallu) (p.61), and that the churches should unite on the basis of the Nicene faith (p.62). It is no doubt principally on the basis of the first of these statements that copies of the book were destroyed, and the author temporarily placed under house-arrest.

2. Ortodoks haymanot. andänna mäshaf ('The Orthodox Faith. First book'), by Abuna Gäbrə'el (formerly Ethiopian archbishop of Eritrea), published by the Ethiopian Studies Centre, P.O. Box 868, Asmara, in 1983 (A.D.), pp.1-111.

The book is written in question and answer form, as a catechism covering the major Christian doctrines. The author rejects 'one single nature' (and nätäla bahrəy) of the incarnate Christ as Eutychian, and rejects 'two natures' (hulätt bahrəyat) as Nestorian; he says that the Ethiopian Church accepts 'one nature in the union' (and bahrəy bätäwahədo) and 'one united nature' (and wəhud bahrəy) (pp.26-7). He continues by saying that after the two natures became one person, they experienced no separation, but continued in the union; the two exist, being one, in the union, each retaining its own character (hulättumm bäyyätäbayaccäw säntäw bätäwahədo and honäw yənorallu) (p.33). It seems that the statement that 'both natures were united in one person' was seen by the Synod of the Ethiopian Orthodox Church as Chalcedonian and heretical; the book was banned, and on 22nd May 1984 the author was deposed, and on 25th July 1984 excommunicated. The Ethiopian Government rejected accusations against the author of attempting to foment religious strife in Ethiopian society.

ምዕራፍ ፡ ፮ ።

ክፍል ፡ ፩ ።

፩ ፡ በብዙን ፡ ነገር ፡ ወበብዙን ፡ መክፈልት ፡ አይድዐ ፡ እግዚአብሔር ፡ ለአበዊነ ፡ በነቢያቲሁ ፡ እምትክት ። ዘጐል ፡ ፲፪ ፡ ፲ ፡ ፰ ፡ ሮሜ ፡ ፫ ፡ ፪ ፡ ፪ ጢም ፡ ፫ ፡ ፲፮ ።

አምስት ፡ ሺህ ፡ ክምስት ፡ መቶ ፡ ዘመን ፡ እስኪፈጻም ፡ እግዚአብ
ሔር ፡ በነቢያት ፡ አድሮ ፡ ለአባቶቻችን ፡ ተናገረ (በብዙን ፡ ነገር ፡) በአሠ
ርቱ ፡ ቃላት ፡ (ወበብዙን ፡ መክፈልት ፡) ወነበበ ፡ ወነበቦ ፡ ባለው ፡ (በብዙን ፡

5.2   <u>ANNOTATED TRANSLATION OF AC HEBREWS CHAPTER 1</u>[1]

Chapter 1

Section 1[2]

1.   <u>In many matters and in many portions God gave information to</u>

     <u>our fathers, in his prophets, from former times</u>, Num.12.7,8;

     Rom.3.2;   2 Tim.3.16.

     Until the five thousand five hundred years was completed, God,

     abiding in prophets, spoke to our fathers, <u>in many matters</u> -

     in the ten commandments, <u>and in many portions</u> - in that which

     he said, '<u>And he said to him, and he said to him</u>'[3] (p.607).

1.   Translated from the text reproduced opposite, from <u>Liqä̈ liqawnt</u>
     Mähari Tərfe, <u>Yä̈qəddus pawlos mä̈s̲h̲af</u>, A.A., 1948 E.C., pp.606-
     615.   On Mä̈hari's life and editorial activity, see <u>TIA</u>, pp.159-
     60.   Notes are added of some of the variants of MS R, Cowley
     20 (see 7.5 below).   The Biblical references contained in the
     printed text are not generally found in MSS;   the references
     attached to the portions of Geez text are very similar to those
     in <u>Addis Kidan</u>, manufactured in the United States of America
     by National Bible Press, Philadelphia, 1938 E.C., and the
     references placed in the Amharic comment are probably Mä̈hari's
     own.

2.   In this edition, the division into chapters is the commonly
     accepted one; the 'sections' are as follows: (1) Heb.1.1;
     (2) 3.1:   (3) 4.14;   (4) 5.10;   (5) 6.13;   (6) 9.1;   (7) 9.11;
     (8) unmarked;   (9) 10.19;   (10 and 11) unmarked;   (12) 12.1;
     (13) 13.1.

3.   I.e. the (570) commands which God spoke to Moses;   OTIAC p.136.

ነገር ፡) በምሳሌ ፡ (ወበብዙኅ ፡ መክፈልት ፡) እንበለ ፡ ምሳሌ ። በምሳሌ ፡ በመ
ሰበ ፡ ወርቅ ፡ በተቅዋመ ፡ ወርቅ ፡ በማዕጠንተ ፡ ወርቅ ፡ በበትረ ፡ አሮን ፡
እንበለ ፡ ምሳሌ ፡ በዘፈቀደ ። (እንድም ፡ በብዙኅ ፡ ነገር ፡) በብዙኅ ፡ ኀብረ ፡
ትንቢት ፡ (ወበብዙኅ ፡ መክፈልት ፡) በብዙኅ ፡ ኀብረ ፡ አምሳል ፡ ተናገረ ።
ኀብረ ፡ ትንቢት ፡ ወነገርነኒ ፡ ከመ ፡ ሕፃን ፡ ወከመ ፡ ሥርው ፡ ዘውስተ ፡ ምድር ፡
ጽምዕት ። ምድርኒ ፡ ትሁብ ፡ ፍሬሃ ፡ ጽጌ ፡ አስተርአየ ፡ በውስተ ፡ ምድርን ።
ወናሁ ፡ ድንግል ፡ ትፀንስ ፡ ወትወልድ ፡ ወልደ ፡ ኢሳ ፡ ፯ ፡ ፲፬ ፡ ያለው ፡
ነው ። ኀብረ ፡ አምሳል ፡ በአምሳለ ፡ ነበልባል ፡ ወሐመልማል ፡ ዘፀአ ፡ ፫ ፡ ፪ ፡
፫ ። በአምሳለ ፡ ፀምር ፡ ወጠል ፡ ዘመሳ ፡ ፮ ፡ ፴፯ ፡ ፴፱ ። በአምሳለ ፡ ዕብን ፡
ዳን ፡ ፪ ፡ ፴፬ ። በአምሳለ ፡ ብእሲ ፡ መከሀ ፡ ኢሳ ፡ ፷፪ ፡ ፭ ። በአምሳለ ፡
አንበሳ ፡ መፍርህ ፡ ዕዝ ፡ ፪ ፡ ፴፪ ። ይህን ፡ የመስለ ፡ ነው ፡

(A.) He spoke <u>in many matters</u> - in similes[1]; <u>and in many</u>
<u>portions</u> - without similes. 'In similes' - in the golden
omer, in the golden lampstand, in the golden censer, in the
rod of Aaron[2]; 'without similes' - in whatever he chose.

A. He spoke <u>in many matters</u> - <u>in many various forms of</u>
<u>prophecy</u>; <u>and in many portions</u> - <u>in many various forms of</u>
<u>likeness</u>. 'Various forms of prophecy' is that which he said,
'<u>But our word is like a child, and like a root which is in</u>
<u>a thirsty land</u>'[3], '<u>And the land will give its fruit</u>'[4], '<u>A</u>
<u>flower appeared in the midst of our land</u>'[5], '<u>And behold, a</u>
<u>virgin will conceive, and she will bear a son</u>'[6], Isa. 7.14;
'various forms of likeness' is that which resembles this -
<u>in the likeness of flame and verdure</u>, Ex.3.2,5: <u>in the likeness</u>
<u>of fleece and dew</u>, Jdg. 6.37,40: <u>in the likeness of a stone</u>,
Dan.2.34: <u>in the likeness of a proud man</u>, Isa.63.1: <u>in the</u>
<u>likeness of a terrible lion</u>, Ezra 2.36[7].

1. <u>məssale</u> - 'parable, similitude, allegory, sign, symbol,
    likeness', cf. AC Gen. 1.14 and notes.
2. These are interpreted symbolically of the Virgin Mary, cf.
    <u>WM</u> for Sunday.
3. Isa. 53.2.
4. ? Lev. 25.19.
5. Song 2.12.
6. MS R additionally quotes, '<u>For from you will come forth a</u>
    <u>king</u>' (Mic.5.2). These quotations are understood as
    prophecies of the birth of Jesus from Mary, and are also
    found in various Marian hymns.
7. Probably Ezra Apocalypse (NEB 2 Esdras 11.37). These quota-
    tions are understood as similes of the Virgin Mary or Christ.

አንድም ፡ ዋዌውን ፡ ትቶ (በብዙን ፡ ነገር ፡ በብዙን ፡ መክፈልት ፡) ይላል ፡
በብዙ ፡ ክፍለ ፡ ዘመን ፡ በብዙ ፡ አነጋገር ፡ እግዚአብሔር ፡ በነቢያት ፡
አድሮ ፡ ለአባቶቻችን ፡ ተናገረ ።

በዘመን ፡ አበው ፡ በዘርዕክ ፡ ይትባረኩ ፡ ኵሎሙ ፡ አሕዛበ ፡ ምድር ፡
ብሎ ፡ ዘፍጥ ፡ ፳፪ ፡ ፲፰ ።

በዘመን ፡ መሳፍንት ፡ ነቢየ ፡ ያነሥእ ፡ ለክሙ ፡ እምአኃዊከሙ ፡ ዘከ
ማየ ፡ ወሰሉ ፡ ስምዕዎ ፡ ብሎ ፡ ዘዳግ ፡ ፲፰ ፡ ፲፭ ።

በዘመን ፡ ነገሥት ፡ እስመ ፡ እምፍሬ ፡ ክርሥክ ፡ አነብር ፡ ዲበ ፡ መን
በርከ ፡ ብሎ ፡ መዝ ፡ ፻፴፩ ፡ ፲፩ ።

በዘመን ፡ ካህናት ፡ መቅዲስ ፡ ትትሐነጽ ፡ እስከ ፡ ክርስቶስ ፡ ንጉሥ ፡
ብሎ ፡ ዳን ፡ ፱ ፡ ፳፭ ።

፯ ፡ ወበዲኃሪስ ፡ መዋዕል ፡ ነገረነ ፡ በወልዱ ።

አምስት ፡ ሺህ ፡ ካምስት ፡ መቶ ፡ ዘመን ፡ ከተፈጸመ ፡ በኋላ ፡ ግን ፡
በልጁ ፡ ሀላው ፡ ኹኖ ፡ ነገረን ፡ (ሐተታ ፡) በወልዱ ፡ ያለውና ፡ በነቢያቲሁ ፡
ያለው ፡ ንባብ ፡ ቢያሳብረው ፡ ምሥጢር ፡ አያሳብረውም ፡ በነቢያቲሁ ፡
ያለው ፡ አድሮ ፡ ሲል ፡ ነው ።

ዘለሊከ ፡ ነብብክ ፡ በአፈ ፡ ዳዊት ፡ ጉብርክ ፡ በመንፈስ ፡ ቅዱስ ፡ እንዲል ፡ ግብ
ሐዋ ፡ ፬ ፡ ፳፭ ።

በወልዱ ፡ ያለው ፡ ሀልው ፡ ኹኖ ፡ ሲል ፡ ነው ። በዚህም ፡ በወልዱ ፡
ባለው ፡ የአሪትን ፡ ሕፀፀ ፡ የወንጌልን ፡ መብለጥ ፡ ነገረን ። አሁን ፡ ሰው ፡ ሰውየ

A.   Omitting the (conjunction) 'and', it will read 'in many
matters in many portions - God, abiding in prophets, spoke
to our fathers, in many periods of time in many fashions of
speech, saying, in the time of the patriarchs, 'In your seed
all the peoples of the earth will be blessed', Gen.22.18,
and saying, in the time of the judges, 'He will raise up for
you a prophet from among your brethren, who is like me; hear
him', Deut.18.15, and saying, in the time of the kings, 'For
from the fruit of your belly I will seat upon your throne',
Ps.132.11[1], and saying, in the time of the priests, 'The
temple is built until the time of Christ the king', Dan.9.25.[2]

2.   but in the latter days he spoke to us in his son,
But after the five thousand five hundred years was completed,
he spoke to us, being existent in his son.
H.   Even though the text equates 'in his son' and 'in his
prophets', the meaning does not equate them - 'in his prophets'
means 'abiding (upon them)', as it says, 'Of whom you yourself
spoke in the mouth of David your servant in the Holy Spirit',
Acts 9.25; 'in his son' means 'being existent (in his son)'.
In this, in saying 'in his son', he spoke to us of the in-
adequacy of the Torah, and the superiority of the gospel.

1.   According to the Hebrew, not LXX, enumeration.
2.   MS R omits these 4 quotations.

ውም ፡ ተራ ፡ ነገሩም ፡ ተርታ ፡ የኽነ ፡ እንደኽነ ፡ ብላቲናውን ፡ ሰዶ ፡ ነገሩን ፡ ይቆርጣል ። ሰውየውም ፡ ደግ ፡ ነገሩም ፡ ደግ ፡ የኽነ ፡ እንደኽነ ፡ ግን ፡ እሱም ፡ ሔዶ ፡ ቢሉ ፡ ልጁንም ፡ ሰዶ ፡ ቢሉ ፡ ነገሩን ፡ ይቆርጣል ። እንደዚህም ፡ ኹሉ ፡ አሪት ፡ ሕጊቱም ፡ ተርታ ፡ ሰዎችም ፡ ተርታ ፡ ነበሩና ፡ በነቢያት ፡ አድሮ ፡ ነገረን ፡ አለ ።

፰፻፵፯   መልእክት ፡ ኅበ ፡ ዕብራውያን ።

ወንጌል ፡ ግን ፡ ሕጊቱም ፡ ደግ ፡ ሰዎችም ፡ ደጋግ ፡ ናቸውና ፡ በልጁ ፡ ሀልዉ ፡ ኾኖ ፡ ነገረን ፡ አለ ።

በነቢያቱሁ ፡ እንዳለ ፡ ብዩ ፡ ነገረክሙ ፡ ያላለ ፡ በወልዱ ፡ ያለ ፡ ስለምን ፡ ነው ፡ ቢሉ ፡ ብዩ ፡ ብሎ ፡ ቢኽን ፡ ለራሱ ፡ ሲቆርስ ፡ አያሳንስ ፡ ባሉት ፡ ነበ ርና ፡ ትላንት ፡ ከኛ ፡ ጋራ ፡ የነበረ ፡ ብላቲና ፡ ምን ፡ ጊዜ ፡ ከዚህ ፡ ደርሶ ፡ እን ዲህ ፡ ይለናል ፡ ባሉት ፡ ነበርና ። እንድም ፡ እሱ ፡ እንደመምህር ፡ እነሱ ፡ እንደ ፡ ደቀ ፡ መዝሙር ፡ በኾኑ ፡ ነበርና ፡ ደጋግ ፡ ናቸሁ ፡ ለማለት ። ትክት ፡ የሚ

Nowadays, if the other person is ordinary and his business commonplace, a man will send a servant and complete the business. But if the other person is important and his business important, the man either goes personally or sends his son, and completes the business. Just like all this, he said of the Torah, because both the law is commonplace and the people commonplace, 'He spoke to us, abiding in the prophets' (p.608).

But as for the gospel, because both (its) law is important and (its) people important, he said, 'He spoke to us, being existent in his son.'

   If it is asked, 'Why is it that, just as he said 'in his prophets', he said 'in his son', but not 'he spoke to you in me'[1]', it is because if he had said 'in me', they would have said to him, 'When one breaks (bread) for oneself, one does not make (it) small'[2]; (it is) because they would have said to him, 'Since when did the young man who yesterday was with us attain to this, that he speaks thus to us?'
A. (It is) because (otherwise) he would have been like a teacher, and they like disciples - he means, 'You are important'.[3]

1. I.e. 'Why did Paul not include himself among those through whom God spoke?'
2. A proverbial reproach to the greedy.
3. MS R adds, 'He said 'he spoke to us', including himself with them.'

ለው ፡ ልጅነት ፡ አጥተተንበት ፡ በፍዳ ፡ ተይዘዘንበት ፡ የነበረው ፡ ዘመን ፡ ነው ።
ደኃሪ ፡ የሚለው ፡ ልጅነት ፡ ያገኘንበት ፡ ከፍዳ ፡ የዳንበት ፡ ዘመን ፡ ነው ።
ዘረሰዮ ፡ ወራሴ ፡ ለኩሉ ፡ መዝ ፡ ፪ ፡ ፰ ። ዮሐ ፡ ፭ ፡ ፎ።ቴላ ፡ ፭ ፡ ፲፮ ።

ኵሉን ፡ ገንዘብ ፡ ባደረገለት ፡ በልጁ ፡ ሀልዉ ፡ ኹኖ ፡ ነገረን ። ሰአል ፡
እምኔየ ፡ እሁብከ ፡ አሕዛብ ፡ ለርስትከ ፡ ክለው ፡ ጋራ ፡ አንድ ፡ ነው ፡ መዝ ፡ ፪ ፡ ፰ ፡
ረሰዮና ፡ እሁብከ ። (ስዓልም ፡ ብትል ፡) ወራሴና ፡ ለርስትከ ፡ ለኩሉና ፡ አሕዛብ ፡
ያለው ፡ አንድ ፡ ነው ።

ይህን ፡ ለምን ፡ ይሻዋል ፡ ቢሉ ፡ መንግሥታተ ፡ ሰማይ ፡ የለም ፡ ላሉት ፡ መን
ግሥተ ፡ ሰማይ ፡ ይሏቸዄል ፡ ሔላን ፡ (አለ ፡) የባሕርይ ፡ ልጁ ፡ ሥጋ ፡ ኾኒልና ፡
መንግሥተ ፡ ሰማይን ፡ ያወርሳቸዄል ፡ ለማለት ።

ወቦቱ ፡ ፈጠሮ ፡ ለኩሉ ።

ኵሉን ፡ በፈጠረበት ፡ በልጁ ፡ ሀልዉ ፡ ኹኖ ፡ ነገረን ።
ወኩሉ ፡ ቦቱ ፡ ኮነ ፡ ክለው ፡ ጋራ ፡ አንድ ፡ ነው ።

'Former times' is the period when we lacked sonship, and were
in bondage to punishment.

'Latter (days)' is the period when we obtained sonship and
were saved from punishment.

whom he made inheritor of all, Ps.2.8; Jn.1.3; Col.1.16.
He spoke to us, being existent in his son, to whom he caused
everything to be appropriated. This is the same as that which
says, 'Ask from me, I will give you peoples for your inheritance', Ps.2.8. 'He made him' and 'I will give you' (or
'ask'), 'inheritor' and 'for your inheritance', 'of all' and
'peoples' are the same.

    If it is asked why he wants this, it is to say to the
ones who say, 'There is no kingdom of heaven', 'Is there any
other which they call for you the kingdom of heaven?[1] Because
the son of his nature has become flesh, he will cause you to
inherit the kingdom of heaven'.

and in whom he created everything,
He spoke to us, being existent in his son, in whom he created
everything. This is the same as, 'And everything was in him'[2].

1. On the syntax of this sentence, see LFP.
2. MS R identifies the source of this quotation as 'the gospel'
    - i.e. Jn.1.3.

፭ ፡ ዘውእቱ ፡ ብርሃነ ፡ ስብሐቲሁ ።

የኔትነቱ ፡ መታወቂያ ፡ በሚኸን ፡ በልጁ ፡ ሀልዉ ፡ ኾኖ ፡ ነገረን ።
ብርሃነ ፡ ፀሐይ ፡ ከኃይን ፡ ጋራ ፡ ተዋህዶ ፡ ክበቡን ፡ እንዲያስታውቅ ፡ እሱም ፡
ሥጋን ፡ ተዋህዶ ፡ ዘርእየ ፡ ኪያየ ፡ ርአየ ፡ ለአቡየ ። እነ ፡ ወአብ ፡ ፩ ፡ ንሕነ ። እነ ፡
በአብ ፡ ወአብ ፡ ብየ ፡ እያለ ፡ አባቱን ፡ አስታውቋልና ።

ወአምሳለ ፡ አርአያሁ ፡ ፩ ፡ ቆሮ ፡ ፱ ፡ ፱።ቄላ ፡ ፮ ፡ ፲፯።

በመልክ ፡ የሚመስለው ፡ በባሕርይ ፡ የሚተካከለው ።

ዘይእናዝ ፡ ኵሎ ፡ በኀይለ ፡ ቃሉ ።

በኀያል ፡ ቃልነቱ ፡ ኵሉን ፡ ፈጥሮ ፡ የሚገዛ ። ዘይእናዝ ፡ ኵሎ ፡ ያለውና ፡
ወበቱ ፡ ኵሉ ፡ ኮነ ፡ ያለው ፡ አንድ ፡ ነው ። እግዚአ ፡ አኀዜ ፡ ኵሉ ፡ እንዲል ።
ቀዳሚሁ ፡ ቃል ፡ ያለውና ፡ በኀይለ ፡ ቃሉ ፡ ያለውም ፡ አንድ ፡ ነው ።

3. <u>who is the light of his glory,</u>

He spoke to us, being existent in his son, by whom his lordship is made known. Just as the light of the sun, being
united with the eye, makes known its circular shape, so also
he, being united with flesh, has made known his father,
saying, '<u>The one who saw me saw my father</u>'[1], '<u>I and the father
are one,</u>'[2] '<u>I am in the father and the father is in me</u>'.[3]

<u>and the likeness of his image,</u> 2 Cor.4.4; Col.1.15.
who is like him in form, who is equal to him in nature.

<u>who holds everything in the power of his word;</u>
who, in his property of being the powerful word, created
everything and rules (it). '<u>Who holds everything</u>' and '<u>And in
him was everything</u>'[4] are the same, as it says, '<u>O Lord, holder
of all</u>'[5]; similarly, '<u>Its beginning is the word</u>'[6] and '<u>In
the power of his word</u>' are the same.

1. Jn.14.9.
2. Jn.10.30.
3. Jn.14.10. Here MS R adds (cf. printed edition on verse 4
    below), 'In (the writing of) the scholar it says '<u>the shining
    of his glory</u>' (sǎdalǎ səbhatihu); this is the same as '<u>I am
    the light of the world</u>'' (Jn.8.12).
4. Jn.1.3.
5. Prayer of Manasseh v.1.
6. Jn.1.1.

ወውእቱ ፡ በህላዌሁ ፡ ገብረ ፡ በዘያነጽሕ ፡ ኃጢአተነ ፡ ም ፡ ፪ ፡ ፲፰ ፡ ፳፯ ።

በአካለ ፡ ህላዌሁ ፡ ብሎ ፡ ሊቁ ፡ ወስዶታል ፡ በተለየ ፡ አካሉ ፡ ከኃጢአታ
ችን ፡ ያነጻን ፡ ዘንድ ፡ በሚያነጻን ፡ ገንዘብ ፡ የሚያነጻበትን ፡ ሥራ ፡ ሡራ ፡
(ሐተታ) ከብሉዩ ፡ ሊቀ ፡ ካህናት ፡ ሲለይ ፡ የብሉዩ ፡ ሊቀ ፡ ካህናት ፡ የሚያነ
ጻቸው ፡ እሱ ፡ የሚነጹት ፡ ሕዝቡ ፡ የሚያነጻበት ፡ ደሙ ፡ ልዩ ፡ ልዩ ፡ ነው ።
ደሙ ፡ ደመ ፡ ላሕም ፡ ደመ ፡ ጠሊ ፡ ነውና ።

ምዕራፍ ፡ ፮ ።	፻፲፱

ከአጣቢም ፡ ሲለይ ፡ አጣቢ ፡ የሚያጥበው ፡ እሱ ፡ የሚታጠበው ፡ ልብሱ ፡
የሚያጥብበት ፡ እንዶዱ ፡ ሳሙናው ፡ ልዩ ፡ ልዩ ፡ ነው ። እሱ ፡ ግን ፡ የሚያነ
ጻን ፡ እሱ ፡ ራሳችን ፡ የምንነጻ ፡ እኛ ፡ ሕዋሳቱ ፡ የሚያነጻበት ፡ ደሙ ፡ ነውና ፡
አንጡነቱ ፡ ከባቱ ፡ ያገናኘዋል ፡ ከእናቱ ፡ አያገናኘውም ፡ መንጪነቱ ፡ ከባቱም ፡
ከናቱም ፡ አያገናኘውም ፡ ከአባቱ ፡ እንዳያገናኘው ፡ ለዕሩቅ ፡ ቃል ፡ ደም ፡ የለ

and he, in his essence, did (the work) by which he cleanses our sin, ch. 9.14, 26.

The scholar[1] has cited it, saying, 'In the person of his essence'. In his separate person, in order that he cleanse us from our sin, in the measure that he cleanses us, he did the work by which he cleanses us.

H. He is distinguished from the chief of the priests of the old (covenant): (as for) the chief of the priests of the old (covenant), it is he who cleanses them, those who are cleansed are the people, and that with which he cleanses is the blood; they are all different from each other, for the blood is the blood of an ox or the blood of a goat (p. 609). He is distinguished from a washer (of a garment) - the person is the washer who washes it, that which is washed is the garment, and that with which he washes is the əndod[2] or soap; they are all different from each other.

But he - it is he who is ourself who cleanses us, the ones who are cleansed are we, his members, and it is his blood by which he cleanses (us). His property of being a cleanser links him with his father; it does not link him with his mother. His property of being the one by whom cleansing is made links him neither with his father nor his mother. It does not link him with his father,

---

1. I.e. a patristic writer; these quotations are assembled and identified in the notes following this translation, 5.3.
2. A plant Phytolacca dodecandra, used as a detergent.

ው·ምና ። ከእናቱም ፡ እንዳያገናኛ*ነው* ፡ የዕሩ·ቅ ፡ ብእሲ ፡ ደም ፡ አያነጻምና ።
ይህን ፡ ለምን ፡ ይሻዋል ፡ ቢ.ሉ ፡ መከራ ፡ አይ*ን*ካን ፡ ላሉ·ት ፡ እሱ·ስ ፡
እንኳ ፡ እጸድቅ ፡ አይል ፡ ጻድቅ ፡ እከብር ፡ አይል ፡ ክቡ·ር ፡ ለናንት ፡ ብሎ ፡
መከራ ፡ የተቀበለ ፡ እናንትማ ፡ ልትከብሩ·በት ፡ መከራ ፡ ብ·ትቀበሉ ፡ በዛን ፡ ለ*ማ*
ለት ። አንድ·ም ፡ መልአክ ፡ እንብለው ፡ ላሉ·ት ፡ መላእክትማ ፡ ምን ፡ ሥ*ጋ* ፡
አላቸው·ና ፡ መ*ሥ*ዋዕት ፡ ኸ*ነ*ው· ፡ ይመግቢ*ች*ኋል ፡ የባሕርይ ፡ ል*ጁ* ፡ ግን ፡ ሥ*ጋ* ፡
ኸኒ·ልና ፡ መ*ሥ*ዋዕት ፡ ኸኖ ፡ ይመግባ*ች*ኋል ፡ ለ*ማ*ለት ። አንድ·ም ፡ *ነ*ቢ·ይ ፡ እን
በለው· ፡ ላሉ·ት ፡ የዕሩ·ቅ ፡ ብእሲ ፡ ሥ*ጋ* ፡ ቢ.በሉ·ት ፡ ይመራ·ል ፡ ይተኩ·ሳል ፡
እንጂ ፡ ሕይወትን ፡ ይ·ኸናል ፡ ከፍዳ ፡ ያ*ነ*ጻል ? የባሕርይ ፡ ል*ጁ* ፡ ግን ፡ ሥ*ጋ* ፡
ኸኒ·ልና ፡ በሱ· ፡ ደም ፡ ትነጻላ*ች*ሁ· ፡ ለ*ማ*ለት ።

ወ*ነ*በረ ፡ በየ*ማ*ን ፡ ዕበዩ ፡ በሰማያት ፡ *ማ*ቴ ፡ ፳፯ ፡ ፷፪ ።
በልዕልና ፡ ክብ·ር ፡ ባለው· ፡ ዕሪ*ና* ፡ ተቀምጦ ፡ *ነ*በረ ። (ሐተታ ፡) በሰማያት ፡

since the Word alone has no blood; it does not link him with his mother, since the blood of a mere man does not cleanse.

[1]If it is asked why he wants this, (it is to refute) the ones who said, 'Let not tribulation overtake us', to say (to them), 'But when even he, a righteous person who did not seek righteousness, an honoured person who did not seek (his own) honour, accepted tribulation on your behalf, is it too much (for you) if you also receive tribulation, so that you be glorified through it?'

A. (It is to refute) the ones who said, 'Let us call him 'an angel'', to say (to them), 'As for angels, what flesh have they that, having become a sacrifice, they would feed you? But because the son of his nature has become flesh, he, having become a sacrifice, will feed you'.

A. (It is to refute) the ones who said, 'Let us call him 'a prophet'', to say (to them), 'If one eats the flesh of a mere man, it is bitter, it burns - but will it be life? Will it cleanse from condemnation? But because the son of his nature has become flesh, by his blood you are cleansed'[1].

<u>and he sat at the right hand of his splendour in the heavens,</u> Mt. 27.64[2].

He had sat in supremacy, in equality of glory.

1-1. MSR abbreviates this section, reading, 'If it is asked why he wants this, (it is) for the former one and the latter one; <u>tarik</u> as before'.

2. The reference is taken from Mahari's source (see note 1 on AC Heb.1.1 above), but appears to be incorrect.

ማለቱ ፡ ቦታ ፡ ወስኖበት ፡ አይደለም ፡ በክብር ፡ ሲል ፡ ነው ፡ እስመ ፡ ነቢር ፡
በዐሪና ፡ ያኤምር ፡ ጎብ ፡ ተዋህዱ፦ቶሙ ፡ በክብር ፡ እንዲል ፡ (አራ ፡ ወ) ።

፵ ፡ ወተለዓለ ፡ እመላእክት ።

መዓርገ ፡ መላእክትን ፡ እንደጫማ ፡ ረግጦ ፡ (በልዕልና ፤ ክብር ፡ ባለው ፡
ዐሪና ፡ ተቀመጠ ።

ዘመጠነዝ ፡ ጎየሰ ፡ ወወረሰ ፡ ስመ ፡ ዘየዓቢ ፡ እምእስማቲሆሙ ፡ ወይከብር ፡ ፈል ፡ ፱ ፡ ፱ ።

ይህን ፡ ያህል ፡ መሻልን ፡ የተሻለ ፤ ይህን ፡ ያህል ፡ መብለጥን ፡ የበለጠ ፡
ከስማቸው ፡ የበለጠ ፡ ስምን ፡ ገንዘብ ፡ ያደረገ ፡ ቾኛ ፡ መዓርገ ፡ መላእክትን ፡
እንደጫማ ፡ ረግጦ ፡ ነብረ ። ለመኑ ፡ ማንሽ ።

አንድም ፡ ይህንን ፡ ያህል ፡ መሻልን ፡ የተሻለ ፡ ይህን ፡ ያህል ፡ መብለ

H. 'In the heavens' does not mean that he confined him
spatially[1]; it means 'in glory', as it says, 'For sitting
in equality indicates their union in glory'[2], (Chrysostom).

4. and he was higher than the angels,

Having set foot as with a shoe upon the ladder[3] of the angels,
he sat in supremacy, in equality of glory.

who in this measure was better, and inherited a name which
is greater than their names, and is (more) glorious,
Phil.2.9.

He who is indeed this much better, he who is indeed this much
greater, having appropriated a name which is greater than
their name, had set foot as with a shoe upon the ladder[3] of
the angels. 'To whom' (starts) a new sentence[4].

A. He who is indeed this much better, he who is indeed this

1. MS R adds 'as a king would confine a person with whom he has
    quarrelled, saying, 'Don't put on long trousers (sānafil),
    don't take your stick, don't leave such-and-such a place'.
2. MS R reads the quotation, 'For saying 'right' points to their
    union in glory'.
3. Or 'high rank'.
4. I.e. 'to whom', the first words of Heb.1.5, may be taken as the
    beginning of a new sentence, as in this interpretation, or as
    linked to the end of v.4, as in the next interpretation.

ጥን ፡ የበለጠ ፡ ከስማቸው ፡ የበለጠ ፡ ስምን ፡ ገንዘብ ፡ ያደረገ ፡ ኸኖ ፡ ለሙኑ ፡ እመላእክቲሁ ። አንድም ፡ (በዘመጠነዝ ፡) በዚህን ፡ ያህል ፡ መሻል ፡ የተሻለ ፡ በዚ ህን ፡ ያህል ፡ መብለጥ ፡ የበለጠ ፡ ከስማቸው ፡ የበለጠ ፡ ስምን ፡ ገንዘብ ፡ ያደ ረገ ፡ ኸኖ ፡ ነበረ ፡ ለመኑ ፡ ማንሽ ፡ ነው ።

አንድም ፡ በዚህን ፡ ያህል ፡ መሻል ፡ የተሻለ ፡ በዚህን ፡ ያህል ፡ መብለ ጥን ፡ የበለጠ ፡ ከስማቸው ፡ የበለጠ ፡ ስምን ፡ ገንዘብ ፡ ያደረገ ፡ ኸኖ ፡ ለመኑ ፡ እመላእክቲሁ ፡ ይቤሎ ፡ (ሐተታ ፡) ከዚህም ፡ ብላቴናውን ፡ ወደላይ ፡ እያወጣ ፡ እያወረደ ፡ በሚያስለምድ ፡ ሰው ፡ አምሳል ፡ ተናገረ ። እንደማውጣት ፡ ነገረን ፡ በወልዱ ፡ ይላል ፤ ቢፈራ ፡ በዚህ ፡ ምክንያት ፡ ደዌ ፡ ይደርበትን ፡ ብሎ ፡ መልሶ ፡

39

፫፻፲ መልእክት ፡ ኀበ ፡ ዕብራውያን ።

እንደማውረድ ፡ ዘረሰዮ ፡ ወራሴ ፡ ለኵሉ ፡ ይላል ፤ ይልመደው ፡ እንጂ ፡ እንደ ፈራን ፡ ይቅር ፡ ብሎ ፡ መልሶ ፡ እንደማውጣት ፡ ወቦቱ ፡ ፈጠሮ ፡ ለኵሉ ፡ ዘውእቱ ፡ ብርሃነ ፡ ስብሐቲሁ ፡ ወአምሳለ ፡ አርአያሁ ፡ ዘይእኅዝ ፡ ኵሉ ፡ በኃ ይለ ፡ ቃሉ ፡ ይላል ።

much greater, having appropriated a name which is greater than
their name, <u>to whom from among his angels (does he say ....)</u>?[1]

A.   (Reading) <u>bäzämätänäzə</u>[2] - he who is indeed better by this
much, he who is indeed greater by this much, appropriated a
name which is greater than their name.

<u>'To whom'</u> starts a new sentence.

A.   He who is indeed better by this much, he who is indeed
greater by this much, having appropriated a name which is greater
than their name, <u>to whom from among his angels does he say ...</u>?[3]

H.   Here he speaks according to the simile of a person who is
training his child, making him ascend and descend. Like making
(him) ascend, he says, <u>'He spoke to us in his son'</u>. Like
making (him) descend again, when (the child) is afraid, being
worried that for this reason he will fall ill (p.610), he says,
<u>'whom he made inheritor of all'</u>. Like making (him) ascend again,
saying, 'Will he remain fearful? Rather, let him get used to
it.', he says, <u>'and in whom he created everything, who is the</u>
<u>light of his glory, and the likeness of his image, who holds</u>
<u>everything in the power of his word.</u>'

1.   This links v.5 to v.4, and does not take <u>lämännu</u> ('to whom')
     as a <u>manša</u> (fresh start).

2.   This is a variant reading for <u>zämätänäzə</u>, and is noted by MS R
     as an <u>'abənnat'</u> (textual variant); in fact, <u>bäzämätänäzə</u> is
     read in the texts of the B.F.B.S., the Asmara N.T. (1953 E.C.),
     and the Franciscan edition (Asmara, 1952 E.C.), see 5.4 below.

3.   This interpretation firstly reads <u>bäzämätänäzə</u>, and secondly
     does not take <u>lämännu</u> as a <u>manša</u>, see note 1 above.

እንደማውረድ ፡ ወውእቱ ፡ በህላዌሁ ፡ ገብረ ፡ በዘያነጽሕ ፡ ኃጢአተነ ፡ ወነበረ ፡ በየማነ ፡ ዐበዩ ፡ በሰማያት ፡ ወተለዓለ ፡ እመላእክት ፡ በዘመጠነዝ ፡ ኅየሰ ፡ ወወረሰ ፡ ስመ ፡ ዘየዓቢ ፡ እምአስማቲሆሙ ፡ ወይከብር ፡ ይላል ።

እንድም ፡ ማውረድ ፡ ይቀድማል ፡ ብሎ ፡ ነገረነ ፡ በወልዱ ፡ ዘረሰዮ ፡ ወራሴ ፡ ለኵሉ ፡ ይላል ።

እንደማውጣት ፡ ወቦቱ ፡ ፈጠሮ ፡ ለኵሉ ፡ ዘውእቱ ፡ ብርሃነ ፡ ስብሐቲሁ ፡ ወአምሳለ ፡ አርአያሁ ፡ ዘይእኅዝ ፡ ኵሎ ፡ በኃይለ ፡ ቃሉ ፡ ይላል ።

እንደማውረድ ፡ ወውእቱ ፡ በህላዌሁ ፡ ገብረ ፡ በዘያነጽሕ ፡ ኃጢአተነ ፡ ይላል ።

እንደማውጣት ፡ ወነበረ ፡ በየማነ ፡ ዐበዩ ፡ በሰማያት ፡ ወተለዓለ ፡ እመላ እክት ፡ በዘመጠነዝ ፡ ኅየሰ ፡ ወወረሰ ፡ ስመ ፡ ዘየዓቢ ፡ እምአስማቲሆሙ ፡ ወይ ከብር ፡ ይላል ።

እንድም ፡ እመዓርግ ፡ ውስተ ፡ መዓርግ ፡ ብሎ ፡ ሊቁ ፡ ወስዶታል ፡ (ዮሐ ፡ አፈ ፡) ወደሰገነት ፡ እያወጣ ፡ በሚያስለምድ ፡ ሰው ፡ አምሳለ ፡ ተናገረ ፡ እንደ ማስጻህ ፡ አይድዐ ፡ እግዚአብሔር ፡ ለአበዊነ ፡ በነቢያቲሁ ፡ እምትክት ፡ ይላል ፡ አይድዐ ፡ ያለውንም ፡ ይዞ ፡ ሰባልዮስ ፡ አንድ ፡ ገጽ ፡ ብሎ ፡ ተነሥቷል ። መጀመሪያ ፡ እርከን ፡ እንደማስያዝ ፡ ነገረነ ፡ በወልዱ ፡ ይላል ። በዚህ ፡ ይረ ታል ፤ ጨርሶ ፡ አይረታም ፤ ስም ፡ ይሰጣል ፡ በዘመነ ፡ አበው ፡ አብ ፡ በዘመነ ፡

Like making (him) descend (again), he says, 'And he, in his essence, did (the work) by which he cleanses our sin, and he sat at the right hand of his splendour in the heavens, and he was higher than the angels, who in this measure was better, and inherited a name which is greater than their names, and is (more) glorious'.

A. If it is objected that making (him) descend comes first, (then, like making him descend) he says, 'He spoke to us in his son, whom he made inheritor of all'. Like making (him) ascend, he says, 'and in whom he created everything, who is the light of his glory, and the likeness of his image, who holds everything in the power of his word.' Like making (him) descend (again), he says, 'and he, in his essence, did (the work) by which he cleanses our sin'. Like making (him) ascend (again), he says, 'and he sat at the right hand of his splendour in the heavens, and he was higher than the angels, who in this measure was better, and inherited a name which is greater than their names, and is (more) glorious.'

A. The scholar has cited it, saying, 'From rank to rank' (John Chrysostom). He spoke in the likeness of a trainer who makes someone climb up to a roof[1]. Like making (him) crawl, he says 'God gave information to our fathers, in his prophets, from former times'. Sabellius arose, seizing on 'he gave information', and saying 'one face'[2].

Like causing (him) to step on the first step, he says, 'He spoke to us in his son'. By this, he (Sabellius) is refuted, (but) he is not completely

1. Or 'balcony'.
2. Representing Greek <u>prosopon</u>.

ሥጋዌ ፡ ወልድ ፡ በዘመነ ፡ ሐዋርያት ፡ መንፈስ ፡ ቅዱስ ፡ ተባለ ፡ ብሂል ።
በወልዱ ፡ ያለውንም ፡ ይዘው ፡ ጎድረት ፡ የሚል ፡ ሳምሳጢ ፡ ጸውሎስ ፡
ፍጡር ፡ የሚል ፡ እርዮስ ፡ ተነሥተዋል ፡ እስመ ፡ ሶበ ፡ ሰመዮ ፡ ወልደ ፡ በጊ
ዜሃ ፡ ተንሥአ ፡ ሳምሳጢ ፡ ጸውሎስ ፡ ወአስተማሰሎ ፡ በግእዝ ፡ ብዙኃን ፡ እን
ዲል ፡ (አፈ ፡ ወር ፡) እስራኤል ፡ ወልድየ ፡ ዘበኩርየ ፡ ተብለዋል ። ጸድቃን ፡
ውሉደ ፡ እግዚአብሔር ፡ ይባላሉ ፤ በጀጋ ፡ የሚወለዱ ፡ የእነዚያ ፡ ልደት ፡ ይብ
ቃዋ ፡ ብሂል ። ኹለተኛ ፡ እርከን ፡ እንደማስያዝ ፡ ዘረሰዮ ፡ ወራሴ ፡ ለኵሉ ፡
ይላል ፡ ሰባልዮስ ፡ በዚህ ፡ ይረታል ። ሳምሳጢ ፡ ጸውሎስ ፡ ግን ፡ ወረሰዮ ፡
ከመ ፡ ድኩም ፡ ይላል ፡ (አፈ ፡ ወር ፡) ይኸውም ፡ እንጂ ፡ ድካም ፡ ቢኖርበት ፡
ነው ፡ መዋርስቲሁኬ ፡ ለክርስቶስ ፡ ንሕነ ፡ ያላቸው ፡ የእነዚያ ፡ ይብቃዋ ፡ ብሂል ።
ሐዋርያ ፡ ግን ፡ በንድ ፡ በረሰዮ ፡ ፍጹም ፡ አምላክነቱን ፡ ፍጹም ፡ ሰውነቱን ፡
ተናገረ ። ሐዋርያስ ፡ ተናገረ ፡ ባቲ ፡ በቃለ ፡ ፍጻሜ ፡ እንዲል ።(አፈ ፡ ወር ፡) በንድ ፡
በእርአያ ፡ የሰውነትንም ፡ የአምላክነትንም ፡ ነገር ፡ እንደተናገረ ፤ ያለውን ፡ ረሰዮ ፡

refuted, because he (Sabellius) allocates a name, and says, 'In the time of the fathers, he (God) was called '<u>father</u>', in the time of the incarnation he was called '<u>son</u>', and in the time of the apostles he was called '<u>holy spirit</u>'.

Seizing on '<u>in his son</u>', Paul of Samosata, who said '<u>resting</u>'[1], and Arius, who said '<u>created being</u>' arose, as it says, '<u>For when he named him 'son', in that time arose Paul of Samosata, and he likened him to the character of many (people)</u>', (Chrysostom). He (Paul of Samosata) said, 'The Israelites are called '<u>my son, my first born</u>', (and) the righteous are called '<u>sons of God</u>' - so let the birth of these who are begotten by grace suffice him (Jesus).''

Like causing (him) to step on the second step, he says, '<u>Whom he made inheritor of all</u>'. By this, Sabellius is refuted. But Paul of Samosata said, 'It says, "<u>And he made him like a feeble one</u>" (Chrysostom). This is indeed (said) because he is feeble[2] - so let the matter of these of whom he said, '<u>But we are the legatees of Christ</u>[3]' suffice him'. But the apostle, in one (word), in '<u>he made him</u>', declared his perfect godhead and perfect manhood, as it says, '<u>But the apostle spoke in it, in a word of perfection</u>'[4] because, just as he declared the matter of both his manhood and his godhead in one (word), in '<u>he showed</u>', (so) he does not say '<u>whom he made</u>' of him who has (an origin in time),[5] nor '<u>inheritor</u>' of him who has no (origin in time).

1. hədrät, 'dwelling'- i.e. the Word rested upon/the human Jesus.
2. This sentence is clearer in the parallel passage in AC YAWD 34, yəkʰäwəmm ənji dəkamun yasräddal.
3. Rom. 8.17.
4. The text in AC YAWD 33 is slightly different. 'Perfection' represents Geez fəssame 'finality, completion, completeness'.
5. This is explicit in MS R, which reads tənt yalläwn ... tənt yälelläwnəmm.

የሌለውንም ፡ ወራሴ ፡ አይለውምና ። ሦስተኛ ፡ እርከን ፡ እንደማስያዝ ፡ ወቦቱ ፡
ፈጠሮ ፡ ለኵሉ ፡ ይላል ፤ ሳምሳጢ ፡ ጸውሎሱ ፡ በዚህ ፡ ይረታል ፡ ወበዛቲ ፡

ምዕራፍ ፡ ፳ ። ፫፻፲፩

ቃል ፡ ነሣተ ፡ ምክሮ ፡ ለሳምሳጢ ፡ ጸውሎስ ፡ ኄሡር ፡ እንዲል ፡ (አፈ ፡ ወር ፡)
እርዮስ ፡ ግን ፡ አለሁ ፡ አለሁ ፡ ተንክር ፡ ተንክር ፡ ይላል ፡ ወእርዮስሰ ፡ ዓዲሁ ፡
ይትገዓዝ ፡ ወእለ ፡ እርዮስሰ ፡ ኢኄደጉ ፡ ተጋዕዘቾሙ ፡ እንዲል ፡ (አፈ ፡ ወር ፡)
እኔስ ፡ ምን ፡ እላለኋ ፤ አንጠረኛ ፡ ዘሬት ፡ መዶሻውን ፡ ሥርቶ ፡ የቀረውን ፡
ኋላ ፡ እንዲሠራ ፡ ሽክላ ፡ ሠሪ ፡) ማኖሪያውን ፡ ሥርታ ፡ የቀረውን ፡ ኋላ ፡ እን
ድትሠራ ፡ ፈጥሮ ፡ ፈጠረበት ፡ እላለሁ ፡ እንጂ ፡ ሌላ ፡ ምን ፡ እላለሁ ፡ ብሏል ።

አራተኛ ፡ እርከን ፡ እንደማስያዝ ፡ ዘውእቱ ፡ ብርሃነ ፡ ስብሐቲሁ ፡ ይላል ፡
በዚህ ፡ ይረታል ።

ከዚህ ፡ በኋላ ፡ በተሣለ ፡ ባሊሆ ፡ መሃል ፡ ልቡን ፡ የተወጋ ፡ ጠላት ፡
መነሣት ፡ እንዳይቻለው ፡ መነሣት ፡ አልተቻለውም ።

ብርሃነ ፡ ስብሐቲሁ ፡ ያለውንም ፡ ፀዳለ ፡ ስብሐቲሁ ፡ ብሎ ፡ ሊቁ ፡ ወስዶ
ታል ። ብርሃነ ፡ ስብሐቲሁ ፡ ያለውንም ፡ ይዞ ፡ መርቅያን ፡ ዝርው ፡ ነው ፡ የፀ

Like causing (him) to step on the third step, he says, 'and in whom he created everything'. By this, Paul of Samosata is refuted (p.611), as it says (Chrysostom), 'And in this word he destroyed the counsel of the wretched Paul of Samosata'. But Arius still makes his presence felt, as it says (Chrysostom), 'But Arius still contends and the Arians have not forsaken their contention'. He (Arius) has said, 'What other, then, should I say than that (God), having created (Jesus), created (other things) in him, just as a metal worker, having first made his hammer, subsequently makes everything else (using the hammer as a tool), and just as a woman who makes pottery, having first made its mould, subsequently makes everything else (using it)?'

Like causing (him) to step on the fourth step, he says, 'who is the light of his glory'; by this he (Arius) is refuted. After this, it is not possible for him to arise, just as it is not possible for an enemy who has been stabbed right in the heart with a sharpened knife to arise.

The scholar has taken 'light of his glory', and cited it as 'shining of his glory'.[1] Also Märqəyan[2] arose seizing on 'light of his glory', and

1. This phrase, 'shining of his glory' appears in the text of Hebrews as quoted in YAWD 23; it is thus an alternative translation of the text of Hebrews, rather than a distinctive interpretation of John Chrysostom's.
2. In John Chrysostom's Homilies on Hebrews, II.2 (PG LXIII col.22), on which this passage is based, the Greek text mentions Sabellios, Markellos, Foteinos, and Markiōn; the Geez translation (of the Arabic version of the Greek) printed in YAWD p.34 col.2 represents these names as Säbalyos, Märkəlos, Qorontyos (probably by confusion of Arabic f and q), and Märqəyan. However, in YAWD 28 (=PG LXIII col.20, Hom.II.1), Geez Märqəyan represents Greek Markellos; in YAWD 55 (=PG col.29, Hom.III.1), Greek Markiōn is represented by Geez Mänkəyon, and Greek Markellos is represented first by Geez Märkəlan, and subsequently by Märkənon.

ሐይ ፡ ይብቃው ፡ ብሎ ፡ ተነሥኋቷል ። አምስተኛ ፡ እርከን ፡ እንደማስያዝ ፡ አም
ሳለ ፡ እርአያሁ ፡ ይላል ፡ በዚህ ፡ ይረታል ።

እምሳለ ፡ እርአያሁ ፡ ያለውንም ፡ ይዘው ፡ ንግበር ፡ ሰብእ ፡ በአርአያን ፡
ወበአምሳሊ.ነ ፡ ያላቸው ፡ የነዚ.ያ ፡ ይብቃዋል ፡ ብለዋል ። እርአያሁ ፡ ያለውንም ፡
ሊቁ ፡ ዘባሕርይሁ ፡ ብሎ ፡ ወስዶታል ፡ በዚህ ፡ ይረታሉ ፤ ይህስ ፡ የሊቅ ፡ ቃል ፡
ነው ፡ አያስረታም ፡ ብሎ ፡ ስድስተኛ ፡ እርከን ፡ እንደማስያዝ ፡ ዘይእኅዝ ፡
ኵሎ ፡ በኃይለ ፡ ቃሉ ፡ ይላል ፡ በዚህ ፡ ይረታሉ ። ዘይእኅዝ ፡ ኵሎ ፡ ያለው
ንም ፡ ይዘው ፡ ቢያስይዙት ፡ አይገዝ ፡ ቢያስገዙት ፡ አይገዝ ፡ አለን ፡ ብለዋል ፡
በኃይለ ፡ ቃሉ ፡ በለው ፡ ይረታሉ ። ከዚህ ፡ በኋላ ፡ መነሣት ፡ የተቻለው ፡
የለም ። እንደማውረድ ፡ ወውእቱ ፡ በህላዌሁ ፡ ገብረ ፡ በዘያነጽሕ ፡ ኃጢአተን ፡
ይላል ። እንደማውጣት ፡ ወነበረ ፡ በየማን ፡ ዕበዩ ፡ በሰማያት ፡ ወተለዓለ ፡ እመ
ላእክት ፡ በዘመጠነዝ ፡ ኃየሰ ፡ ወወረሰ ፡ ስመ ፡ ዘየዓቢ. እምአስማቲሆሙ ፡ ወይ
ከብር ፡ ይላል ።

saying, 'He is diffuse - let (the light) of the sun suffice him.'[1]

Like causing (him) to step on the fifth step, he says, 'the likeness of his image'; by this he (Mārqəyan) is refuted.

People have seized on 'likeness of his image', and said, 'Let the matter of those of whom he said, 'Let us make man in our image and in our likeness' suffice him.'[2] but the scholar has taken 'his image' and cited it as 'of his nature', and by this they are refuted.

If it is objected that this is the word of a scholar (and not of the Bible)[3], and cannot be used in refutation, then, like causing (him) to step on the sixth step, he says, 'who holds everything in the power of his word'; by this they are refuted. Also, having seized on 'who holds everything', (some) have said, 'Is there anyone who fails to hold when they put (something) in his hand, who fails to rule when they give (him) ruling authority?';[4] they are refuted by 'in the power of his word'. After this, there is no-one who can arise.

Like making (him) descend, he says, 'And he, in his essence did (the work) by which he cleanses our sin'; like making (him) ascend, he says, 'And he sat at the right hand of his splendour in the heavens, and he was higher than the angels, he was better by this much, and he inherited a name which is greater than their names, and is (more) glorious'.

1. I.e. 'the Son is a diffuse emanation of the Godhead, like the corona of the sun'.
2. I.e. 'he is merely human, like Adam and Eve'.
3. MS R makes this explicit, reading, 'Heretics are refuted from the Old Testament and New Testament, and not from (the word of) a scholar'.
4. This Amharic sentence contains asyndetic relative clauses.

፭ ፡ ለመኑ ፡ እመላእክቲሁ ፡ ይቤሎ ፡ እምእመ ፡ ኮነ ፡ ወልድየ ፡ አንተ ፡ ወአነ ፡ ዮም ፡ ወለድኩከ ፡ መዝ ፡ ፪ ፡ ፯ ፡ ።

ክኹን ፡ ጀምሮ ፡ ክሡላእክት ፡ ወገን ፡ አንተ ፡ ልጅ ፡ ነህ ፡ እኔም ፡ አባ ትህ ፡ ነኝ ፡ ማንን ፡ አለው ፡ ።

ወካዕበ ፡ ይቤ ፡ አነ ፡ እከውኖ ፡ አብሁ ፡ ወውእቱ ፡ ይከውነኒ ፡ ወልድየ ፡ ፪ ሳሙ ፡ ፯ ፡ ፲፬ ።

ዳግመኛ ፡ እኔ ፡ አባት ፡ እኾነዋለሁ ፡ እሱም ፡ ልጅ ፡ ይሆነኛል ፡ ማነን ፡ አለ ፡ (ሐተታ ፡) ወልድየ ፡ አንተ ፡ ወአነ ፡ ዮም ፡ ወለድኩክ ፡ ባለ ፡ ጊዜ ፡ ዳዊ ትን ፡ አነ ፡ እከውኖ ፡ አቡሁ ፡ ወውእቱ ፡ ይከውነኒ ፡ ወልድየ ፡ ባለ ፡ ጊዜ ፡ ናታንን ፡ አላነሣም ፡ ስለምን ፡ ቢሉ ፡ በኢየሩሳሌም ፡ የነበሩ ፡ አይሁድ ፡ ምሁ ራን ፡ መጻሕፍተ ፡ ነቢያት ፡ ነብሩና ፡ አዋቆች ፡ ናቸሁ ፡ ለማለት ፡ ለአዋቂ ፡ አይ ነግሩ ፡ ለአንበሳ ፡ አይመትሩ ፡ እንዲሉ ፡ ።

5. <u>to whom from among his angels did he say, from the time when he was,</u>[1]

<u>'You are my son, and I today begat you'</u>? Ps. 2.7.

Beginning from the time when he was, to whom, from the class of

angels, did he say, 'You are my son, and I am your father'?

<u>and further (to whom) did he say, 'I will be to him his father, and</u>

<u>he will be to me my son'</u>? 2 Sam. 7.14.

Further, to whom did he say, 'I will be father to him, and he will

be son to me'?

H. If it is asked why it is that when he said, <u>'You are my son, and</u>

<u>I today begat you'</u>, he did not mention David, and when he said, <u>'I</u>

<u>will be to him his father, and he will be to me my son'</u>, he did not

mention Nathan, it is with the intention of saying, 'You are knowledge-

able people' - because the Jews who lived in Jerusalem were learned

in the books of the prophets, as people say (in the proverb), 'One

does not tell a knowledgeable person (what he knows already), one

does not cut up (meat) for a lion' (p. 612).

1. <u>'from the time when he was'</u> - if the text is considered in isolation,
it is not clear whether the Geez əm'amä konä, and its Amharic translation, are part of the quotation or not, nor whether it should be
understood to mean 'since the time when Christ existed', or (like
the Greek original <u>pote</u>) 'at any time'.

፮፻፲፬ **መልእክት ፡ ናብ ፡ ዕብራውያን ፡ ።**

ወአሙ ፡ ካዕበ ፡ ፈነዎ ፡ ለበኵሩ ፡ ውስተ ፡ ዓለም ፡ ይቤ ፡ ይስግዱ ፡ ሎቱ ፡ ኵሎሙ ፡ መላእክት ፡ እግዚአብሔር ፡ ሮሜ ፡ ፰ ፡ ፳፱ ፡ መዝ ፡ ፺፮ ፡ ፯ ።

ምዕግድ ፡ ሳያደላድሉ ፡ ዓምድ ፡ ማቆም ፡ እንዳይቻል ፡ አኰነኖ ፡ ሳልል ፡ ይሰግዱ ፡ ብዩ ፡ ብል ፡ አይቀበሉኝም ፡ ብሎ ፡ አኰነኖ ፡ አለ ፡ ብሎ ፡ ሊቁ ፡ ወስዶታል ። ሥጋን ፡ ከባሕርይ ፡ ልጁ ፡ ጋራ ፡ አዋህዶ ፡ ይህን ፡ ዓለም ፡ ባስገ ዛለት ፡ ጊዜ ፡ መላእክት ፡ ይሰግዱለታል ፡ አለ ። ወአሙ ፡ ቦዐ ፡ በኵርም ፡ ይላል ፡ ነበረ ፡ ላለው ፡ ዋዜ ።

፯ ፡ ወበእንተ ፡ መላእክቲሁሰ ፡ ይቤ ፡ ዘይሬስዮሙ ፡ ለመላእክቲሁ ፡ መንፈስ ፡ ወለእለ ፡ ይትለአክዎ ፡ ነደ ፡ እሳት ፡ መዝ ፡ ፻፫ ፡ ፬ ።

ስለመላእክትስ ፡ ሊቃነ ፡ መላእክትን ፡ ሠራዊተ ፡ መላእክትን ፡ ከእሳት ፡ ከነፋስ ፡ የፈጠራቸው ፡ እሱ ፡ ነው ፡ አለ ። (ሐተታ ፡) የመላእክት ፡ ተፈ ጥሮ ፡ ከእሳት ፡ ከነፋስ ፡ ነው ፡ ቢሉ ፡ የተመቸ ፡ ወሰብ ፡ ኢያእኩትክ ፡ ለፈጠረክ ፡ እምነበልባለ ፡ እሳት ፡ ወእምነፋስ ፡ ፈጠረ ፡ ህየንቴከ ፡ ሰብአ ፡ ዘማሬ ፡ እማይ ፡ ወእመሬት ፡ እንዲል ፡ (መቃ ፡) እምነብ ፡ አልቦ ፡ ነው ።

(6). and when, further, he sent his first born into the world he said,
'All the angels of God will bow down to him,' Rom. 8.29, Ps.96.7.
The scholar has cited it, saying, 'He said "he put him in
authority", saying, 'They will not accept (it) from me if I say
"they will bow down" before I say "he put him in authority"',
just as it is impossible to erect a pillar without preparing
the base. He said, 'The angels bow down to him at the time when,
having caused the union of flesh with the son of his nature, he
subjugated this world to him'.
(A T.V.) reads 'and when the first born came' - the conjunction
'and' refers back to 'he sat'.

7. but concerning his angels, he said, 'Who makes his angels spirit,
and the ones who serve him a flame of fire', Ps. 104.4.
But concerning angels, he said, 'It is he who created the chief
angels and the troops of the angels, from fire and from wind'.
H. If fits (the interpretation better) if it is said that the
creation of angels is from fire and wind, as it says, 'And when
you did not praise him who created you from a flame of fire and
from wind, he created in your place a human who would sing praise,
from water and from earth' (Macc.[1])

1. Eth. 3 Macc.4.8 (Amh. capitation).

ቢሉ ፡ በግብር ፡ ስለመሰሏቸው ፡ እሳት ፡ ነፋስ ፡ ኃያላን ፡ ናቸው ፡ መላእ
ክትም ፡ ኃያላን ፡ ናቸውና ፤ እሳት ፡ ነፋስ ፡ ረቂቃን ፡ ናቸው ፡ መላእክ
ትም ፡ ረቂቃን ፡ ናቸውና ፤ እሳት ፡ ነፋስ ፡ ፈጣኖች ፡ ናቸው ። መላእክትም ፡
ፈጣኖች ፡ ናቸውና ፤ እሳት ፡ ነፋስ ፡ ፈጻምያን ፡ ፈቃድ ፡ ናቸው ። መላእክትም ፡
ፈጻምያነ ፡ ፈቃድ ፡ ናቸውና ።

፱ ፡ ወበእንተ ፡ ወልዱሰ ፡ ይቤ ፡ መንበርከ ፡ እግዚኦ ፡ ለዓለመ ፡ ዓለም ።
ስለ ፡ ልጁ ፡ ግን ፡ አቤቱ ፡ ጌትነትህ ፡ ቀዳማዊ ፡ ነው ፡ አለ ።

በትረ ፡ ጽድቅ ፡ ወበትረ ፡ መንግሥትከ ።
     (ወበትረ ፡ መንግሥትከ ፡ በትረ ፡ ጽድቅ ፡) የጌትነትህም ፡ ሥልጣን ፡
የባሕርይህ ፡ ነው ፡ አለ ። አንድም ፡ (መንበርክ ፡ በትረ ፡ ጽድቅ ፡) ጌትነትህ ፡
የባሕርይ ፡ ሥልጣን ፡ ያለው ፡ ነው ፡ (ወበትረ ፡ መንግሥትከ ፡ ለዓለም ፡)
የጌትነትህም ፡ ሥልጣን ፡ ቀዳማዊ ፡ ነው ፡ አለ ።

If (on the other hand) it is said (that the creation of angels) is
ex nihilo, it is because they (the angels) resemble them (fire and
wind) in nature. Fire and wind are powerful, and angels are
powerful; fire and wind are insubstantial, and angels are insubstantial; fire and wind are swift, and angels are swift; fire
and wind are performers of (his) will, and angels are performers
of (his) will.[1]

8. but concerning his son he said, 'Your throne, O Lord, is for ever
and ever,

But concerning his son, he said, 'O Lord, your lordship has
precedence'.

the rod of righteousness, and the rod of your kingdom,

(Reading) 'and the rod of your kingdom is a rod of righteousness'
- he said, 'And the authority of your lordship is of your nature'.
A. Reading 'your throne is a rod of righteousness' - 'Your
lordship is (lordship) which has authority by nature'.
Reading 'and the rod of your kingdom is for ever' - 'And the
authority of your lordship has precedence.

1. An annotator of MS R here adds examples of occasions on which God
used wind - 'He destroyed the tower of Shinar with it, he suspen-
ded the adulteress upon it, he destroyed the troops of Paragmon with
it'- and examples of the use of fire, e.g. the destruction of
Sodom and Gomorrah.

አንድም ፡ (መንበርከ ፡ ወበትረ ፡ ፡ መንግሥትከ ፡ በትረ ፡ ጽድቅ ፡ ለዓለም ፡)
ጌትነትህ ፡ የባሕርይ ፡ የሚኸን ፡ የጌትነትህም ፡ ሥልጣን ፡ ቀዳማውያን ፡
ናቸው ፡ አለ ። ፫ያ ፡ ቀዳማዊ ፡ ዘአምቀዳማዊ ፡ ያሉትን ፡ ቴዎፍሎስ ፡
ዘለዓለም ፡ እምዘለዓለም ፡ ፁሎ ፡ ወስዶታል ፡ ጌትነቱን ፡ ሥልጣኑን ፡ በመን
በር ፡ በበትር ፡ መስሎ ፡ ተናገረ ፡ ንጉሥ ፡ ከዳርቻ ፡ ከጋብቻ ፡ ለመጣ ፡
ሰው ፡ እርድ ፡ አንቀጥቅጥ ፡ የሚባል ፡ ልብስ ፡ መንግሥት ፡ ለብሶ ፡ ግራ ፡
ቀኝ ፡ መከዳ ፡ ሰይፉን ፡ ተንተርሶ ፡ ጠርሙዝ ፡ በሎታውን ፡ ከራስጌው ፡
አሰቅሎ ፡ ኃያላኑን ፡ በቀኝ ፡ በግራ ፡ በሬት ፡ በኋላ ፡ አሰልፎ ፡ ግባ ፡
ይለዋል ፡ ለኔ ፡ ብትገዛ ፡ ጠላትህን ፡ በዚህ ፡ ፡ እጠፋልይለሁ ፡ ለኔ ፡ በትገዛ ፡
ግን ፡ አንተን ፡ በዚህ ፡ እጠፋሃለሁ ፡ ሲለው ፡ ነው ። እሱም ፡ ሕጉን ፡

A. Reading 'your throne and the rod of your kingdom are a rod
of righteousness for ever' - 'Your lordship, and also the
authority of your lordship, which is of (your) nature, have
precedence'.

That which the 300 said, 'The first, who is from the first'[1],
Theophilus cited, saying, 'The eternal, from the eternal'[2].
He spoke[3] likening his lordship and his authority to a throne
and to a rod, as when a king puts on the royal robes called
arəd angätqət[4] for a man who has come from the border country,
or from the frontier[5], rests himself on cushion and sword to
left and right, hangs up his mace[6] at his head, lines up his
warriors to right and left, in front and behind, and says to him,
'Come in', meaning, 'If you submit to me, I will destroy your
enemy for you with this; but if you do not submit to me, I
will destroy you with this' (p.613).

1. Nicene fathers in HA (diglot edn. p.50).
2. Theophilus of Alexandria in HA (diglot edn. p.253). A similar
    passage is found in AC Ps. 44.6, which contains a further
    sentence also found in MS R, 'Just as he said 'You are of the
    first, and you are of the present' of that which Thomas said,
    'My lord and my god'' (cf. AC Jn.20.28 and AC Song 5.6).
3. MS R shortens this paragraph.
4. See TIA p.192, notes on AC Rev.1.13.
5. gabəcca commonly means 'marriage', but appears to be used here
    in contrast to darəcca.
6. tärmuz bälota is an ancient Ethiopian symbol of authority, a
    cudgel with four iron spikes, DTW p.591 and AC Ps.2.9.

ብትጠብቁ ፡ በንደዚህ ፡ ያለ ፡ ሥልጣን ፡ ይጠብቃችኋል ፡ ባትጠብቁ ፡ ግን ፡ በንደዚህ ፡ ያለ ፡ ሥልጣን ፡ ያጠፋችኋል ፡ ለማለት ፡ ነው ።

መንበረሰ ፡ ሰበ ፡ ሰማዕስ ፡ ለብዎ ፡ ለመንበር ፡ ድልወተ ፡ መለኮት ፡ ዘው እቱ ፡ እግዚእና ፡ ወሥልጣን ፡ እንዲል ፡ (ሳዊር ።)

ሷ ፡ አፍቀርከ ፡ ጽድቀ ፡ ወጸላእከ ፡ ዓመፃ ።

ጽድቅ ፡ ወደድህ ፡ ሓሰትን ፡ ጠላህ ፡ ማለት ፡ ሰው ፡ መኸንን ፡ ወደ ድህ ፡ ሰው ፡ አለሙኸንን ፡ ጠላህ ። አንድም ፡ ዘመንን ፤ ቀጠሮን ፡ አሥሩ ፡ ቃላትን ፡ ሕግጋተ ፡ መስቀልን ፤ ትንቢተ ፡ ነቢያትን ፤ መፈጸምን ፤ ወደድህ ፡ አለመፈጸምን ፡ ጠላህ ።

ወበእንተዝ ፡ ቀብዐከ ፡ እግዚአብሔር ፡ አምላክከ ፡ ቅብዐ ፡ ትፍሥሕት ፡ ዘይ ዔይስ ፡ እምእለ ፡ ከማከ ። መዝ ፡ ፵፬ ፤ ፯ ፡ ኢሳ ፡ ፷፩ ፡ ፩ ግብ ፡ ሐዋ ፡ ፲ ፡ ፴፰ ።

ስለዚህ ፡ እግዚአብሔር ፡ መንፈስ ፡ ቅዱስን ፡ በርግብ ፡ አምሳል ፡ በራ ስህ ፡ ላይ ፡ አኑሮ ፡ ወልድየ ፡ ፍቁርየ ፡ ዘጎረይኩ ፡ ወቦቱ ፡ ሠመርኩ ፡ ብሉ ፡ እንዳንት ፡ ካሉ ፡ ሰዎች ፡ መረጠህ ፡ ለዞ ። ዘይዔይስ ፡ በነቢዱ ፡ የለም ፡

He, too, means, 'If you keep his law, he will guard you with
authority like this, but if you do not keep it, he will
destroy you with authority like this,' as it says, 'But
when you hear 'throne', understand the throne proper to the
godhead, namely lordship and authority' (Sawiro[1]).

9. you loved righteousness, and you hated lawlessness,
'You loved righteousness; you hated falsehood' means,
'You loved becoming human; you hated not becoming human'.
A. (It means) 'You loved fulfilling the time, the appointment[2],
the ten commandments, the sufferings of the cross, the prophecy
of the prophets; you hated not fulfilling (them)'.

and because of this, the Lord your God anointed you with the
ointment of joy, which is better than the ones who are like
you', Ps.45.7, Isa.64.1, Acts 10.38.
Because of this, God chose you, he separated you from people
like you, placing the Holy Spirit in the likeness of a dove
on your head, and saying, 'My son, my beloved, whom I chose,
and in whom I am pleased'[3].

1. This quotation, also quoted e.g. in AC Rev.4.5, is from Cyr.T.,
    Severianus of Gabala (cf. AC Gen. 1.26), see 5.3.5 below.
2. I.e. the time and the appointment for the incarnation.
3. Mt.3.17 and parallels, but the text cited here is different
    from the accepted AC Geez text.

ሐዋርያ ፡ ተናግሮታል ። ሐዋርያ ፡ ዘይኔይስ ፡ ያለውንም ፡ ቄርሎስ ፡ ቅብኻ ፡
ነክራ ፡ ዮሐንስ ፡ አፈወርቅ ፡ ዘአልቦ ፡ መስፈርት ፡ ብለው ፡ ወስደውታል ።
እምእለ ፡ ከማከ ፡ ያለውንም ፡ ዮሐንስ ፡ አፈ ፡ ወርቅ ፡ መኑ ፡ እሙንቱ ፡
እለ ፡ ከማሁ ፡ አከኑ ፡ ውሉደ ፡ ሰብእ ፤ ቄርሎስም ፡ ዘውእቶሙ ፡ ንሕነ ፡
ብለው ፡ ወስደውታል ።

፲ ፡ ወካዕበ ፡ ይቤ ፡ አንተ ፡ እግዚአ ፡ አቅደምከ ፡ ሣርዖታ ፡ ለምድር ።
አቤቱ ፡ ዳግመኛም ፡ ምድርን ፡ አስቀድመህ ፡ የፈጠርካት ፡ አንተ ፡ ነህ ፡
አለ ፡ ⟨ሐተታ ፡⟩ አቅደምከ ፡ ከማን ፡ ቢሉ ፡ ከሰማይ ፤ ምነው ፡ የሰማይና ፡ የም
ድርማ ፡ ተፈጥሮ ፡ በቀዳሚ ፡ ገብረ ፡ እግዚአብሔር ፡ ሰማየ ፡ ወምድረ ፡

(The word) 'which is better' is not in (the word of) the prophet; the apostle spoke it.[1] And that which the apostle said 'which is better', Cyril cited, saying, 'a wonderful ointment', and John Chrysostom cited, saying, 'which is without measure'. That which (the apostle) said 'than the ones who are like you', John Chrysostom cited, saying, 'Who are the ones who are like him - are they not human kind?', and Cyril cited, saying, 'namely us'.[2]

10. and further,[3] he said, 'You, O Lord, caused the founding of the earth to take precedence,

He said, 'O Lord.' Further, you are the one who previously created the earth'.

H. If it is asked, 'You caused to take precedence - from whom?', (it is) from heaven. If it is asked, 'But as for the creation of heaven and éarth, was it not at the same time, as it says "At the first, God made heaven and earth"

---

1. Cf. AC Ps.44 (45).7.
2. These patristic quotations are identified in 5.3 below. An annotator of MS R has here added an interpretation 'of Mä(mhər) Kə(fle)' - 'God, the father of your nature, caused you to be united with a union of nature which is different from that with which the apostles, the believers, who are like you, have been united'.
3. In the Geez text, 'and further' is most naturally understood as an introductory formula; the AC Amharic translation, however, has probably taken it as part of the quotation.

እንዲል ፡ ዘፍጥ ፡ ፩ ፡ ፳ ፡ አንድ ፡ ጊዜ ፡ አይደለምን ፡ ቢሉ ፡ የሰማይ ፡ ተፈጥሮ ፡
ግብር ፡ እምግብር ፡ ነው ፡ ቢሉ ፡ አቅደምክ ፡ የተመቸ ፡ እምነበ ፡ አልቦ ፡ ነው ፡
ቢሉ ፡ አቅደምክ ፡ በመታየት ፡ ከዚህ ፡ እስከ ፡ ብሩህ ፡ ሰማይ ፡ ውሀ ፡
መልቦት ፡ ነበር ፡ ለይትጋባእ ፡ ማይ ፡ ውስተ ፡ ምዕላዲሁ ፡ ብሎ ፡ በወሰ
ነው ፡ ጊዜ ፡ አስቀድማ ፡ ምድር ፡ ታይታለች ፡ ዘሬውኑ ፡ ቅሉ ፡ ምድር ፡
ትታያለች ፡ ሰማይ ፡ አይታይም ፡ ።

መግብረ ፡ እዴዊክ ፡ እማንቱ ፡ ሰማያት ፡ ።

ሰማያት ፡ የጅህ ፡ ፍጥረቶች ፡ ናቸው ፡ ።

፲፮ ፡ እማንቱሰ ፡ ያትጎጉላ ፡ ።

እነሱ ፡ ያልፋሉ ፡ ።

ወአንተሰ ፡ ትኄሉ ፡ ።   አንተ ፡ ግን ፡ አትልፍም ፡ ።

አንድም ፡ አንተ ፡ እግዚአ ፡ አቅደምክ ፡ ሣርሮታ ፡ ለምድር ፡ ።

     ሥጋን ፡ አስቀደመህ ፡ የፈጠርካት ፡ አንተ ፡ ነህ ፡ አለ ፡ (ሐተታ ፡)

(Gen. 1.1) ?', <u>you caused to take precedence</u> fits (the interpretation) best if (it is replied that) the creation of
heaven is a fashioning from something else. If, (on the
other hand), it is said that it (the creation of heaven) is
<u>ex nihilo</u>, then <u>you caused to take precedence</u> refers to its
appearance, because from here up to the bright heaven had
been full of water, and the earth appeared previously (to
the appearance of heaven) when he delimited it, saying,
'<u>Let the water be gathered together in its gathering place</u>'[1];
even today, earth is seen and heaven is not seen[2].

<u>and the heavens are the work of your hands,</u>
The heavens are the creations of your hand.

11. <u>but they will perish,</u>
They will pass away.
<u>but you will exist.</u>
But you will not pass away.

A.[3] <u>You, O Lord, caused the founding of the earth to take</u>
<u>precedence,</u>
He said, 'You are the one who previously created the flesh'.

1. Gen. 1. 9.

2. An annotator of MS R has here added some material also found
   in AC Gen. 1.

3. This is a further interpretation of v. 10f. In some AC texts
   such a repetition would be introduced by <u>bəläh mälləs</u>, see PN 10.

አቅደምከ ፡ ከማን ፡ ቢሎ ፡ ከነፍስ ፤ ምነው ፡ የነፍስና ፡ የሥጋማ ፡ ተፈጥሮ ፡

<u>ጀፀ፲፪</u>   መልእክት ፡ ጎበ ፡ ዕብራውያን ፡ ፡

ንግበር ፡ ሰብእ በአርአያነ በአርኣያነ ፡ ወበአምሳሊነ ፡ ሲል ፡ አንድ ፡ ጊዜ ፡ አይደለምን ፡
ቢሎ ፡ የነፍስ ፡ ተፈጥሮዋ ፡ እምጎበ ፡ አልቦ ፡ ነው ፡ ቢሎ ፡ አቅደምከ ፡
የተመቸ ፤ አራቱ ፡ በሕርያት ፡ የተፈጠሩ ፡ እሁድ ፡ ነው ፤ ነፍስ ፡ የተፈጠ
ረች ፡ ዓርብ ፡ ነውና ፡ ፡

ግብር ፡ እምግብር ፡ ነው ፡ ቢሎ ፡ አቅደምከ ፡ በመታየት ፡ ዘሬውን ፡
ቅሉ ፡ ሥጋ ፡ ትታያለች ፡ ነፍስ ፡ አትታይምና ፡ ፡

ወግብረ ፡ እደዊክ ፡ እማንቱ ፡ ሰማያት ፡ ፡

ነፍሳት ፡ የጅህ ፡ ፍጥረቶች ፡ ናቸው ፡ ፡

እማንቱሰ ፡ ይትጎጉላ ፡ ፡

እንዲህ ፡ ሲል ፡ ያውካል ፡ ፡ አንድም ፡ አባ ፡ ለትፁን ፡ አሳሽተው ፡

H. If it is asked, 'You caused to take precedence - from whom?', (it is) from the soul. If it is asked, 'But as for the creation of the soul and the flesh (p.614), was it not at the same time, as it says, 'Let us make man in our appearance and in our likeness'[1]?', you caused to take precedence fits (the interpretation) better if it is said that the creation of the soul is ex nihilo, because it was on Sunday that the four elements were created, and it was Friday that the soul was created. If, (on the other hand), it is said that (the creation of the soul) is a fashioning from something else, then you caused to take precedence refers to its (the flesh's) appearance, for even today the flesh is seen and the soul is not seen.

and the heavens are the work of your hands,
Souls are the creations of your hand.

but they will perish,
[2]When it says so, it becomes difficult (to interpret)[2].
A. (It is) like the soul whose destruction Abba Lá́tṣun caused, by having caused it to be rubbed

1. Gen. 1.26.

2-2. MS R omits these words.

እንዳስጠፋዋት ፡ ነፍስ ፤ ይህጣ ፡ ከክብርም ፡ ከኃሣርም ፡ አልኽነችም ፡ ሲል ፡
ነው ፡ እንጀ ፡ በነፍስ ፡ ምን ፡ ጥፋት ፡ አለ ፡ ቢሉ ፤ ይህስ ፡ መጽሐፍ ፡
ኢ.ዘከረ ፡ ፫ት ፡ ዓለጣተ ፡ አላ ፡ ፪ተ ፡ ይላል ፡ ከክብር ፡ ከወጡ ፡ ኃሣር ፡
ከኃሣር ፡ ከወጡ ፡ ክብር ፡ ነው ፡ ከዚህ ፡ የወጣ ፡ የለም ፡ ብሎ ፡ በኃጢ.
አት ፡ የምትለወጥ ፡ ስለኽነ ፤ መለያየት ፡ የጋራ ፡ ስለኽነ ።
እንተሰ ፡ አንተ ፡ ክመ ።
    አንተ ፡ ግን ፡ መቸም ፡ መች ፡ ትኖራለህ ፡ (ኳለ ፡) አታልፍም ።
ወኵሉ ፡ ከመ ፡ ልብስ ፡ ይበሊ. ።
    ኵሉ ፡ እንደልብስ ፡ ያልፋል ፡
ወከመ ፡ ሞጣሕት ፡ ትጠውሞሙ ፡ ወይጠወጡ ፡ መዝ ፡ ፻፩ ፤ ፳፮ ፤ ፳፯ ፤ ኢሳ ፡ ፶፩ ፤ ፮ ፤ ሩኡ.
                                            ዮሐ ፡ ፩ ፡ ፲፱ ፡ ም ፡ ፳፫ ፡ ፴ ።
    እንደሽግሌ ፡ መ.ጋረጃ ፡ ትጠቀልላቸዋለህ ፡ ይጠቀለላሉ ፡ ያን ፡ አን

(to powder)[1]. If it is asked, 'But what destruction does the soul have - as for this (story), it (only) means that it (the soul) was neither in glory nor in perdition?', indeed, it says, 'The book did not mention 3 worlds, but 2'[2]. If it is objected that if one goes out of glory (there is) perdition, and if one goes out of perdition (there is) glory, and there is no other outside this , (then it is said) because it (the soul) is changed by sin, (and) because the separation affects both (the soul and the flesh)'.

<u>but you, you are the same,</u>

He said, 'But you abide for ever; you do not pass away'.

<u>and everything grows old like a garment,</u>

Everything passes away like a garment.

<u>and like a cloak, you will roll them up, and they will be rolled up,</u> Ps.102.27,28, Isa.34.4, Rev.6.14, 13.8.

You will roll them up like a curtain of săgle[3]; they will be rolled up. Just as people fold one into two, and

1. MS R omits asassǝtăw. The reference is to the story of <u>Abba Lătsun</u> in e.g. Sǝnkǝssar, Săne 17, and the point is the narration of the destruction of a soul. See also Graf I p.535, AC Ecc.3.16, AC Cyr.Ǯ, and catalogue notes on MS EMML 1939.

2. In MS R the text of this quotation appears as wă'izăk(k)ără măshaf amlakawi 3-tă măkanată alla 2-tă.

3. <u>săgle</u> is a type of cloth, but the dictionaries do not describe it in detail.

ዱን ፡ ከኹለት ፡ ኹለቱን ፡ ከአራት ፡ አራቱን ፡ ከስምንት ፡ አጥፎ ፡ በሳ
ጥን ፡ እንዲከቱት ፡ ሰዓቱን ፡ በዕለት ፡ ዕለቱን ፡ በወርኀ ፡ ወርኁን ፡ በዓመት ፡
ዓመቱን ፡ በሽህ ፡ ሽሁን ፡ በኹለት ፡ ሽህ ፡ ኹለቱን ፡ ሽህ ፡ በአራት ፡
ሽህ ፡ አራቱን ፡ ሽህ ፡ በስምንት ፡ ሽህ ፡ አጥፈህ ፡ በኀልፈት ፡ ሣጥን ፡
ትከተዋለህ ።

ትቈልጠሙ ፡ ወይትቈለጡ ፡ ይላል ፡ እንደሌታቀን ፡ ግምጃ ፡ ትለዋው
ጣቸዋለህ ፡ ይለዋወጣሉ ።

ወአንተሰ ፡ አንተ ፡ ክመ ።

አንተስ ፡ መቸም ፡ መች ፡ አንተ ፡ ነህ ።

ወዓመቲከኒ ፡ ዘኢየኀልቅ ።

ዘመንህም ፡ የማይፈጸም ፡ ነው ።

፲፫ ፡ ለመኑ ፡ እመላእክቲሁ ፡ ይቤሎ ፡ እምአመ ፡ ኮነ ፡ ንበር ፡ በየማንየ ፡ እስከ ፡
አገብኦሙ ፡ ለጸላእትከ ፡ ታሕተ ፡ መከየደ ፡ እገሪከ ፡ መዝ ፡ ፻፲ ፡ ፩ ።

ከኾነ ፡ ጀምሮ ፡ ከመላእክት ፡ ወገን ፡ ጠላቶችህን ፡ በእግርህ ፡ እርግጥ ፡

two into four, and four into eight, and put it away in a
chest, so you, having folded the hour into a day, the day
into a month, the month into a year, the year into a
thousand, the thousand into two thousand, the two thousand
into four thousand, and the four thousand into eight
thousand, will put it (the world) away in the chest of the
passing away.

(A T.V.) reads 'you will change them, and they will be
changed'[1] - like letaqän[2] cloth, you will change them
around, and they will be changed around.

but you, you are the same,

But you, you are always yourself,

and your year, moreover, is unending,

and your period of time does not come to an end.

13. To whom from among his angels did he say, from the time when
he was[3], 'Sit at my right hand until I put your enemies
under the stool of your feet', Ps.110.1.
Beginning from the time when he was, to whom, from the class
of angels, did he say - who is it to whom he said -

1. MS R marks the reading 'you will roll them up ....' as a
    variant (abännät), and so has probably understood 'you will
    change them ...' as the text.
2. letaqän is an iridescent fabric, KBT 48.
3. See notes on AC Heb.1.5.

በእጅህ ፡ ጭብጥ ፡ አድርጌ ፡ እስካስገዛልህ ፡ ድረስ ፡ በዕሪናዬ ፡ ኑር ፡ (ያለው፣

ምዕራፍ ፡ ፩ ።   ፯፻፱፻፳፭

ማንnው ፡) ማንን ፡ አለው ። ጸሳዕት ፡ አይሁድ ፤ መናፍቃን ፤ አጋንንት ። እገር ፡
ሥልጣነ ፡ መለከት ፤ ረድኤት ፤ ሐዋርያት ፤ መስቀል ።

፻፬ ፡ አከነ ፡ ኩሎሙ ፡ መላእክት ፡ መንፈስ ፡ እሙንቱ ፡ ወይትፌኔዉ ፡ ለመልእክት ፡
በእንተ ፡ እለ ፡ ሀለዎሙ ፡ ይረሱ ፡ ሕይወተ ፡ ዘለዓለም ፡ ዘፍጥ ፡ ፳፩ ፡ ፯ ፡ መዝ ፡ ፻፵፩ ፡ ፰፡ ፻፳፡ ፲፫
መላእክትማ ፡ የዘለዓለም ፡ ደጎነትን ፡ ይወርሱ ፡ ዘንድ ፡ ስለአሳቸው ፡ የሚ
ወጡ ፡ የሚወርዱ ፡ ፍጡራን ፡ አይደሉምን ፡ (ሐተታ ፡) በመላእክትማ ፡ ምን ፡
ተልእከ ፡ አለባቸውና ፡ እንዲህ ፡ አለ ፡ ቢሉ ፡ ዘሬ ፡ በዚህ ፡ ዓለም ፡ ሰው ፡
የጸለየውን ፡ ጸሎት ፡ ያቀረበውን ፡ መሥዋዕት ፡ ለማሳረግ ፡ ይወጣሉ ፡ ይወር
ዳሉ ፡ ኂላ ፡ ግን ፡ ዋጋቸውን ፡ ተቀበለው ፡ አርፈው ፡ የሚኖሩ ፡ ስለኸነ ። እን
ድም ፡ የዘለዓለም ፡ ደጎነትን ፡ ይወርሱ ፡ ዘንድ ፡ ስለሳቸው ፡ ሰዎች ፡ የሚወጡ ፡
የሚወርዱ ፡ ፍጡራን ፡ አይደሉምን ፡ መንፈስ ፡ እሙንቱ ፡ ማለቱ ፡ ግን ፡ መል
አክ ፡ እንበለው ፡ ላሉት ፡ መላእክትማ ፡ ምን ፡ ሥጋ ፡ አለቸውና ፡ መሥዋዕት ፡
ኸነው ፡ ይመግቢቸኋል ። የባሕርይ ፡ ልጁ ፡ ግን ፡ ሥጋ ፡ ኸኒልና ፡ መሥዋዕት ፡
ኸነ ፡ ይመግበቸኋል ፡ ለማለት ።

'Abide in equality with me, until I subjugate your enemies
to you, making (them) trodden by your feet and grasped in
your hand'? (p. 615).

'Enemies' (are) Jews, heretics, demons; 'feet' (are) the
authority of the godhead, (divine) assistance, apostles,
the cross.

14. Are not all the angels spirit, and are they not sent for
service, because of the ones who must inherit eternal life?
Gen. 24.7, Ps. 34.8, 91.11.
As for the angels, are they not created beings who ascend
and descend for the sake of those who must inherit eternal
salvation?
H. If it is asked, 'What service is laid upon angels, that
he spoke thus?', it is because they ascend and descend to
take up the prayer which in this world a person has prayed,
or the sacrifice he has offered, but afterwards they will
abide resting, having received their reward.
A. Are they not created beings who ascend and descend
because of the people who must inherit eternal salvation?
But his saying 'They are spirit' is (to refute) the ones who
said of him (Jesus), 'Let us call him an angel'. He means,
'As for the angels, what flesh have they, that they should
become a sacrifice and feed you? But the son of his nature
has become flesh, that, being a sacrifice, he should feed you'.

5.3. Patristic quotations in AC Hebrews 1.

5.3.1 Quotations attributed to John Chrysostom (all from his Homilies on the Epistle to the Hebrews):

(i)   in AC Heb.1.3   አሰመ፡ ነቢር፡ በዕሩይ፡ ይኤምር፡ ኅቡ፡ ተዋሕዶሙ፡ በክብር፡   'For sitting in equality indicates their union in glory';

YAWD p.45 col.2.

PG 63 col.24 ἡ γὰρ συνεδρία οὐδὲν ἕτερον δείκνυσιν, ἢ τὸ ὁμότιμον   ; Gardiner[1] p.373 col.1, 'For the "sitting together" implies nothing else than equal dignity'.

(ii)   in AC Heb.1.4   እመዓርግ፡ ውስተ፡ መዓርግ፡   'from rank to rank';

YAWD p.13 col.2.

PG 63 col.15 Εἶτα ἀναβαθμοῖς χρώμενος   ; Gardiner p.367 col.1, 'using degrees of ascent'.

(iii)   in AC Heb.1.4   አሰመ፡ ሶበ፡ ሰሞዖ፡ ወልደ፡ በዝኩ፡ ተንሥአ፡ ሰጎሳሙ፡ ጳውሎስ፡ ወአስተዋግሰሙ፡ በግዙኅ፡ ብዙኃ፡   'For when he named him 'son', in that time arose Paul of Samosata, and he likened him to the character of many (people)';

YAWD p.33 col.2.

PG 63 col.21 Εἶπεν Υἱὸν, καὶ εὐθέως ἐφέστηκε Παῦλος ὁ Σαμοσατεὺς, λέγων αὐτὸν εἶναι Υἱὸν ὡς τοὺς πολλούς   ; Gardiner p.371 col.2, 'He names Him "Son", and immediately Paul of Samosata comes on him, saying that he is a son, as the many are'.

(iv)   in AC Heb.1.4   ወልሰዖ፡ ክመ፡ ፉጹ፡ም   'and he made him like a feeble one';

YAWD p.34 col.1.

PG 63 col.21 ἐκεῖνος μεν ἀσθενείας λέγων εἶναι   ; Gardiner p.371 col.2, 'it comes of weakness'.

(v)   in AC Heb.1.4   አ፡ፕፈ፡ተ፡ነገረ፡ ባቲ፡ በቃለ፡ ፍጹም፡   'But the apostle spoke in it, in a word of perfection';

YAWD p.33 col.2.

1.   Translation of Chrysostom's Homilies on Hebrews by F. Gardiner, in P. Schaff (ed.), A Select Library of the Nicene and Post-Nicene Fathers, series 1, vol.XIV, pp.335-522.

PG 63 col.21 Ἀλλ' ἔδωκεν αὐτῷ καιρίαν πληγην ;
Gardiner p. 371 col.2, 'But he gives him a fatal wound'.

(vi)   in AC Heb. 1.4 ወበዝኬ : ፈሰ : ፃወተ : ግዝዐ : ለሕሱም : ዳውሎስ : ዛውC :   (for ፃውC)   'And in this word he destroyed the counsel of the wretched Paul of Samosata';

YAWD p.34 col.1.

PG 63 col.22 ἔβαλεν ὕπτιον ἀναισχυντοῦντα τὸν Σαμοσατέα; Gardiner p.371 col.2, 'For by saying ..., he strikes backwards the impudent Samosatene'.

(vii)   in AC Heb. 1.4 ወአርዮስ : ዓዲሁ : ይትዓዛዝ : ወኢሊ : አርዮስ : ኢኀደጉ : ተጋብኦቶሙ :   'but Arius still contends, and the Arians have not forsaken their contention';

YAWD p.34 col.1 (ወአርዮስ : ዓዲሁ : ይትቀወም :   )

PG 63 col.22 ὁ δὲ Ἄρειος ἔτι ἰσχυρὸς εἶναι δοκεῖ ; Gardiner p.371 col.2, 'while Arius still seems to be strong'.

(viii) in AC Heb.1.9 ዘአልቦ : መስፈርት :   'which is without measure';
YAWD p.56 col.2 (እን : በመስፈርት :   )

PG 63 col.29 οὐκ ἐκ μέτρου   ; Gardiner p.376 col.1, 'not ... by measure' (of Christ's reception of the Spirit).

(ix)   in AC Heb. 1.9 መኑ : አሙንቱ : እለ : ይመስሉ : እንዘ : ወኢአ : ሰብአ :   'Who are the ones who are like him – are they not human kind?';

YAWD p.56 col.1.

PG 63 col.29 Τίνες δέ εἰσιν οἱ μέτοχοι, ἀλλ᾽ ἢ οἱ ἄνθρωποι   ; Gardiner p.376 col.1, 'But who are these His "fellows" other than men?'.

5.3.2   Quotations attributed to 'a scholar' (liq)(all from John Chrysostom's Homilies on Hebrews):

(i)   in AC Heb.1.3 በአካለ : ህላዊሁ :   'in the person of his essence';
this appears to refer to the phrase (ወ)አርአየ : አካሉ : ዘባሕርያቱ : 'the manifestation of the person of his nature', YAWD p.13 col.2, p.19 col.1, p.28 col.2, p.34 col.2 and p.37 col.1, corresponding to Greek χαρακτὴρ τῆς ὑποστάσεως αὐτοῦ   (e.g. PG 63 col.15), and translated by Gardiner 'express image of his person' (e.g. p.367 col.1).

(ii)   in AC Heb. 1.4 ፀዳለ : ስብሐቲሁ :   'shining of his glory';
the text of Heb.1.4 read as the lemma in the printed version of YAWD,

p.13 col.2, has Ө&ሕ᎓ ሕባሕቲሁ᎓ where the lemma in the printed version of AC Heb. reads ብርሃ᎓ ሕባሕቲሁ᎓ 'light of his glory'; this corresponds to Greek ἀπαύγασμα τῆς δόξης, PG 63 col.15, 'the brightness of his glory', Gardiner p.367 col.1.

(iii) in AC Heb. 1.4 ዘግሕ ፁ ሑ᎓ 'of his nature'; this appears to refer to the references noted in 5.3.2 (i) above, especially YAWD p.13 col.2 in the lemma (Heb.1.3-4).

(iv) in AC Heb. 1.6 ኣኖᎌ ዎ᎓ 'he put him in authority'; YAWD p.50 col.2.

PG 63 col.27 ἐγχειρίση αὐτῷ ; Gardiner p.375 col.2, 'when he putteth (the world) into his hand'.

5.3.3   Quotation attributed to 'the 300' (i.e. the Nicene fathers):
in AC Heb. 1.8   ቀዳማዊ᎓ ዘእምቀዳማዊ᎓   'the first who is from the first';
Haymanotä abäw[2], p.50.
Mansi II p.1063[3], _aeternus ab aeterno_ (in Latin translation of Arabic documents about the Council of Nicaea).

5.3.4   Quotation attributed to Theophilus (of Alexandria):
in AC Heb. 1.8 ዘሳዕሳዊ᎓ እምዘሳዕሳዊ᎓   'the eternal, from the eternal';
Haymanotä abäw, p.253;   Geez and Arabic text in B. M. Weischer,

2.   In section attributed to the Nicene fathers;   the page number is that of the Geez-Amharic diglot printed edition, A.A., 1967 E.C.

3.   J.D. Mansi, Sacrorum conciliorum nova et amplissima collectio, Florentiae, 1757 -   .   Mansi vol. II, p.1063 col.1 line 48 - col.2 line 30 corresponds with Haymanotä abäw pp.50-51, ch.19 vs.1-10.   On the identification of the contents of Haymanotä abäw, see G. Graf, 'Zwei dogmatische Florilegium der Kopten', Orientalia Christiana Periodica 3 (1973) pp.49-77, 345-402;   on Arabic texts relating to the Council of Nicaea, see Graf, Geschichte, I pp.586-593.

Q̄erellos IV.3[4], pp.132–3.
PG 46 col.912 ἀίδιος ἀιδίου   ; from Gregory of Nyssa's De vita
S. Gregorii Thaumaturgi.

5.3.5   Quotation attributed to 'Sawiro' (Severianus of Gabala[5]):
in AC Heb.1.8 ወእንበለ፡ ስበ፡ ሰምዕከን፡ ኣበ፡ ለመንበር፡ ፄፄውት፡
መለኮት፡ ዘውእቱ፡ እግዚእን፡ ወሥልጣን፡   'But when you
hear "throne", understand the throne proper to the godhead, namely
lordship and authority';
cited from the Ethiopic Q̄erḁllos corpus, B.M. Weischer, Q̄erellos IV 3,
pp.62–3.
PG 60 col.772 Ἀλλὰ θρόνον ὅταν ἀκούσῃς Θεοῦ, θεοπρεπῶς
νομτέον θρόνον, τουτέστιν, ἐξουσίαν, βασιλείαν,
κυριότητα   ; from a homily of Severianus, among the
spuria of John Chrysostom.

5.3.6   Quotations attributed to Cyril (of Alexandria):
(i)   in AC Heb.1.9 ቅብዕ፡ ዕፁብ፡ 'a wonderful ointment ';
cited from the Ethiopic Q̄erḁllos corpus, B.M. Weischer, Q̄erellos III[6],
pp.78–9 (reading በቅብዕት፡ ዕፁብ፡   ).
PG 75 col.1277 ἐξαιρέτῳ τινὶ χρίσει   ; from Cyril's
Quod unus sit Christus.
(ii)   in AC Heb. 1.9 ዘውእቱሙ፡ ንሕነ፡   'namely us'; cited from
the same sentence as 5.3.6 (i) above, τουτέστιν ἡμᾶς.

5.3.7   Unattributed quotation (from Isaac of Nineveh):
in AC Heb. 1.12 መፅሐፍ፡ ዪዘኔሬ፡ ፲ት፡ ዓሕዐት፡ እስ፡ ፮ት፡   (MS R reads
ወዪዘኔሬ፡ መፅሐፍ፡ እግሙህነዮ፡ ፲ት፡ መዐየት፡ እስ፡ ፮ት፡),

4   Traktate des Severianos von Gabala, Gregorios Thaumaturgos und Kyrillos
von Alexandrien, Äthiopistische Forschungen 7.

5.   'Sawiro(s)' more commonly represents the name Severus.

6.   Der Dialog, Dass Christus einer ist᾽ des Kyrillos von Alexandrien,
Äthiopistische Forschungen 2. The reference in Dillmann's Lexicon
col.668 to MS B.L. Add.16200 f.73 does not correspond to the present
numbering of the folios of this MS, in which the phrase occurs on
f.76a.

'The book did not mention 3 worlds, but 2';

printed version of Mar Yəshaq[7], p.62 col.2, which reads እስሞ ፡ ወዩሐራ ፡
እምላነዌ ፡ ኢመሐሬነ ፡ ፫ተ ፡ መዓናተ ፡ እስ ፡ ዘንተ ፡ ባሕቲቶ ፡ _ _ ናሁ ፡ ተጓሙቀ ፡
በዘንተ ፡ ቃል ፡ ክሞ ፡ ጸዋትው ፡ እክ ፡ ፫ተ ፡ እስ ፡ ፪ተ ።

Syriac text edited by P. Bedjan[8], p.88, l' gyr 'lpwn ktb' tlt'
'trwt' ... 'pl' tlt gwd' 'mr hrk' 'l' trtyn;

English translation by A.J. Wensinck[9], pp.59–60, 'For the Scriptures
do not teach three places ... Here the Scriptures do not mention
three classes, but two ...'.

5.3.8   Identification of the quotations in AC Heb.1 has
shown that:

(i)   they are all of non-Ethiopian (i.e. Greek/Syriac/Arabic) origin;

(ii)   the works cited are all parts of the literature commented on in
the AC corpus;

(iii)   the major source of citations in this section is John
Chrysostom's Homilies on Hebrews; (comparison with the rest of the AC
shows that this work is an important quarry for citations throughout
the corpus, but that, as is to be expected, proportionately greater
use is made of it here);

(iv)   some of the citations deal with matters of definition – they
are dicta of recognised authority, a basis for further exegetical
activity;

(v)   'the scholar has taken it' (liqu wasdotal) is usually associated
with phrases representing a specific understanding – i.e. a narrowing –
of the text being commented on, and thereby a development of doctrine.

7. Mar Yəshaq, A.A., 1920 E.C. (Geez text with AC, edited by Aläqa Dästa
Esäte).

8. Mar Isaacus Ninivita De Perfectione Religiosa.

9. Mystic treatises by Isaac of Nineveh ....

5.4   GEEZ TEXTS OF HEBREWS 1.

No critical edition of Geez texts of Hebrews has yet been prepared. Biblical MSS containing the epistle, lemmas in commentaries, and citations in other works, are available for study, although MSS are less plentiful than for the gospels (Metzger, The early versions of the New Testament, pp.223-32, 236). Of Geez MSS containing Hebrews, the oldest known appears to be B.N. Zotenberg 45 (1378 A.D.). Milan, Biblioteca Ambrosiana MS.B.20 inf., EMML 2198, and possibly Addis Ababa Nat. Lib. 27, are 15th. cent. MSS; B.N. Zotenberg 46 and Vatican Eth. MS 5 are of the 16th. cent. or earlier, and 17th. cent. MSS are more plentiful - e.g. EMML 656, 1944, 2160 and 2927, and the B.L. MSS noted below.

The use of lemmas for text-critical purposes is complicated by the possibility that the lemma, together with the comment, may have been translated into Geez from a language other than Greek (cf.4.3 above). This possibility is almost certainly realized in the Geez version of John Chrysostom's Homilies on Heb., where the lemma at ch.1 begins (cited from the printed text, AC YAWD p.1[1]):

ብብዙኃ ፡ ነገር ፤ ወበብዙኅ ፡ ዐሳክፌልት ፡ አይፋሮ ፡ እግዚእብሔር ፡ ቀዲሙ ፡ ለአበዊነ ፡ በነቢያቲሁ ፡፡ ወበጊዜሰ ፡ በዛቲ ፡ መዋዕል ፡ ተናገረነ ፡ ለነ ፡ በወልዱ ፡ ዘረስዮ ፡ ወራሴ ፡ ለኵሉ ፡ ወቦቱ ፡ ፈጠሮ ፡ ለዓለም ፡፡

and in the Geez Tərgwame Pawlos (a Geez version or adaptation of an anonymous Arabic commentary on the Corpus Paulinum, see 5.1 above, and Graf II, pp.384-6) where the lemma begins (MS Cowley 34, p.55):

ብብዙኃ ፡ ጾታ ፡ ወበብዙኃ ፡ እግኋኅል ፡ ነገር ፡ እግዚእብሔር ፡ ለአበዊነ ፡ ኰዕለ ፡ ፍሳነ ፡ ነቢያት ፡ በዘመን ፡ ቀዲዐዋ ፡፡ ወበዝንቱስ ፡ ዘመን ፡ ፊ,ፃራዊ ፡ ነገረነ ፡ በወልዱ ፡ -- (the lemma is then abbreviated); the text cited in the comment in TP, however, is: በኵሉ ፡ ፅፍል ፡ ወበኵሉ ፡ ነገር ፡ አይፋእ ፡ እግዚእብሔር ፡ ለአበዊነ ፡ ውስተ ፡ ጐ ፡ ነቢያት ፡ --

---

1.   As far as MS evidence for this text is concerned, MSS B.L. Orient 740 f.6a and 741 f.10a have the same text as the extract given; Or. 739 f.5b reads ... la'abäwinä q̈adimu wäbädäharissä ..., Or.738 f.3a reads ... la'abäwinä wädäharissä ..., and Or.737 f.13a reads ... bä'afä näbiyat ... .

However, without further study the possibility cannot be excluded that such lemmas represent different recensions of Geez versions of the Greek text of Heb. This possibility is strikingly realized in T̲a̲r̲g̲w̲a̲m̲e̲ ̲F̲e̲l̲o̲n̲ ̲F̲e̲l̲g̲o̲s̲ (MSS B.L. Orient 13964 and Cowley 35), where Heb.1.1-4 is read as follows:

በብዙኅ፡ ነገር፡ ወበብዙኅ፡ ወዕንገፈልፈት፡ እደፊእ፡ እግዚእብሔር፡ ለአበዊነ፡ በነቢያቲሁ፡ በዚህሌ፡ ወወፅዐነ፡ ነገሬነ፡ በኅንተ፡ ወልዱ፡ ዘረሰዮ፡ ወራሴ፡ ለኵሉ፡ በኅንቲአሁ፡ ፈጠሮ፡ ለዓለም፡ በብርሃነ፡ ስብሐቲሁ፡ ዝውእት፡ እርእይ፡ ዘእሩ፡ ክሞ፡ ይገኒይ፡ ኵሉ፡ ለቃለ፡ ኃይሉ፡ ወገብረ፡ በኅንቲአሁ፡ በዘያፈድኅ፡ ጋሜት፡ ወነበረ፡ በየማነ፡ እቡሁ፡ በሰማያት፡ ወኅዘ፡ ወመነገዘ፡ ሐየስ፡ እሰላእንተ፡ ወወርዮ፡ ወስሙ፡ ለወራሴ፡ ክቡር፡ ውኅቱ ፨

Comparison with the extract given in Zotenberg's <u>Catalogue</u> (p.45) from the 14th. cent. MS B.N. Zotenberg 45 shows that the two texts are almost identical; and comparison with the post-sixteenth century '<u>textus receptus</u>' given below shows that the two versions are so different that they should not be contained within a single critical apparatus.

In addition to such sources, there are citations from Hebrews, and from the Pss. quotations in Heb.1, in other Geez works, though these are, for text-critical purposes, even more remote from Geez versions of the Greek N.T., and for Heb.1 the position is complicated by the fact that Pss. quotations will have been known to copyists in an established text. For example, Ps.44 (45) is cited in the first homily of Severus of Esmunain, in a passage in which Severus probably had Heb.1 in mind; the text in MS B.L. Orient 773 f.9a reads <u>bä̈trä̈</u> <u>sᵊdq bä̈trä̈ mä̈ngᵊstkä̈</u> (against the lemma in AC Ps.44.6, but agreeing with a textual variant noted in AC Ps.44.6 and with some of the MSS noted below).

The following text of Heb.1 is reproduced from <u>Wä̈ngel qᵊddus</u> ..., Asmara, 1953 E.C., p.324, and the apparatus below records the variants of the following sample of MSS and printed texts. The purpose of the apparatus is to illustrate the degree and type of variation within the more modern '<u>textus receptus</u>', and the background to the variant readings which the AC itself has recorded; it is not intended as a full sample text-critical study.

A.   Lemmas of AC printed text (as in 5.2 above)

B.   Textual variants recorded in AC (as in 5.2 above)

C.   BFBS edition (Ẅangel qəddus ..., Bible Society of Ethiopia, 1979)

D.   Da Baṣṣano Franciscan edition (Haddis kidan, Asmara, 1952)

E.   Vol. 4 of the Amharic and Geez diglot Bible (M̈ashaf qəddus ..., 4 vols., London, undated)

F.   MS B.L. Orient 526, f.45b-46a (17th. cent.)

G.   MS B.L. Orient 527, f.62b (18th. cent.)

H.   MS B.L. Orient 528, f.111a-b (18th. cent.)

I.   MS B.L. Orient 529, f.56b (17th. cent.)

J.   MS B.L. Orient 530, f.165a-166a (17th. cent.)

K.   MS B.L. Orient 531, f.186b-187a (17th. cent.)

L.   MS B.L. Orient (Strelcyn) 13264, f.56a-b (17th.-18th. cent.)

M.   MS Manchester Rylands (Strelcyn) 19, f.83a-b (19th. cent.).

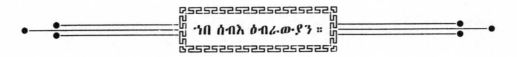

መልእክት ኅበ ሰብእ ዕብራውያን ።

ምዕራፍ ፩ ፥ ክፍል ፩ ።

፩   በብዙኅን ነገር ወበብዙኅን መክፈልት አይድዐ እግዚአብሔር ለአበዊነ በነቢ
፪   ያቲሁ እምትካት ። ወበደኃሪስ መዋዕል ነገረነ በወልዱ ዘረሰዮ ወራሴ ለኵሉ
፫   ወቦቱ ፈጠር ለኵሉ ። ዘውእቱ ብርሃነ ስብሐቲሁ ወአምሳለ አርአያሁ ዘይኦ
    ኅዝ ኵሎ በኃይለ ቃሉ ። ወውእቱ በህላዌሁ ገብረ በዘያነጽሕ ኃጢአተነ ወነ
፬   በረ በየማነ ዕበዩ በሰማያት ። ወተለዐለ እመላእክት በዘመጠነዝ ኅየሰ ወወረሰ
፭   ስመ ዘየኀቢ. እምእስማቲሆሙ ። ወይከብር ። ለመኑ እመላእክቲሁ ይቤሎ እም
    አም ኮነ ወልድየ አንተ ወአነ ዮም ወለድኩከ ፡ ወካዕበ ይቤ አነ አከውኖ
፮   አባሁ ወውእቱኒ ይከውነኒ ወልድየ ። ወአመ ቦአ በኵር ውስተ ዓለም ይቤ
፯   ይሰግዱ ሎቱ ኵሎሙ መላእክት እግዚአብሔር ። ወበእንተ መላእክቲሁስ ይቤ
፰   ዘይሬስዮሙ ለመላእክቲሁ መንፈስ ወለእለ ይትለአክዎ ነደ እሳት ። ወበእንተ
    ወልዱስ ይቤ መንበርከ እግዚአ ለዓለም ዓለም በትረ ጽድቅ ወበትረ መንግሥ
፱   ትከ ። አፍቀርከ ጽድቀ ወዐመዋ ጸላእከ ወበእንተዝ ቀብአከ እግዚአብሔር
፲   አምላክከ ቅብአ ትፍሥሕት ዘይኔይስ እምእለ ከማከ ። ወካዕበ ይቤ አንተ እግ
፲፩ ዚአ አቀደምከ ሣርርታ ለምድር ወግብረ እደዊከ እማንቱ ሰማያት ። እማንቱሰ
    ይትሐጎላ ወአንተሰ ትሄሉ ወኵሉ ከም ልብስ ይበሊ. ወከመ ሞጣሕት ትጠ
፲፪ ውሞሙ ። ወይትዌለጡ ። ወአንተሰ አንተ ከመ ወዐመቲከኒ ዘኢየኀልቅ
፲፫ ለመኑ እመላእክቲሁ ይቤሎ እምአም ኮነ ንበር በየማንየ እስከ አገብአሙ ። ለጸ
፲፬ ላእትክ ታሕተ መከየደ እገሪከ ። አኮኑ ኵሎሙ መላእክት መንፈስ እሙንቱ
    ወይትፌነዉ. ለመልእክት በእንተ እለ ሀለዎሙ ይረሱ ሐይወተ ዘለዓለም ።

v. 1. < ወብዙኃ > በብዙኃ B . < መካፈልት > ወካፈልት J .

v. 2. < ወበፋኅሪስ > ወበፋኅሪ CDIJKL ; በፋኅሪ FM . < ወሬሴ > ወሬሲ E . < ወሂቶ > ዘሒቶ CDGHIJKL ; ወሐሎቶ M .

v. 3. ኵሎ + ግብሪ I . < በዘደናጹሕ > ዘደናጹሕ G . < ኃሚእተነ > ኃሚእተ J . < በሰዓያት > ዘበሰዓያት M .

v. 4. < በዘመመጠዝ > B ዘመጠናዝ A ; ዘመመናዝ:ኵሎ EFGHIL ; ዘበመመጠዝ:ኵሎ JK ; በዘመጠናዝ:ኵሎ M . < እግዝእሰማቲሆሙ : ወይሰብር > ወይሰብር:እግዝእሰማቲሆሙ F ; omit ወይሰብር CD .

v. 5. ይቤሎ + እግዚእብሔር FGHIJKLM . < እግዚአው:ኮነ > omit E . < እነ > omit F . < እገሩ > እጉሁ IJL . < ወውእተኒ > ወውእተ AEFL .

v. 6. < ወእመ:ቦእ:በኵር > B ወእመ:ናቦበ:ፈናያ:ለበኵሬ A ; ወእመ ናቦበ : ፈናያ : ለበኵር CD . < ይቤ > omit J .

v. 7. < ወበእንተ > በእንተ G . < መላእንቲሆስ > መላእንቲሆ CDEJKL . < ዘደሬስዮሙ > ሬስዮሙ FGHIJLM .

v. 8. < ወንበርክ __ ወንግሥትክ > ? ወንበርክ:በቱሬ:ጽፉቅ:ወበቱሪ : ወንግሥትክ:ለዓለም B ; ? ወንበርክ:ወበቱሪ:ወንግሥትክ:በቱሬ : ጽፉቅ:ለዓለም B . < ለዓለው > ለዓለም H . < በቱሬ __ ወንግሥትክ > በቱሬ:ጽፉቅ:በቱሪ:ወንግሥትክ CDGJKL ; ? ወበቱሪ:ወንግሥትክ: በቱሬ : ጽፉቅ B .

v. 9. < ወዐሰዓ:ጸላእክ > ወጸላእክ:ዓሰዓ ACD . < ወበእንተዝ > በእንተዝ EGJ ; በእንተ I . < እማሳእክክ > እማሳኪክ I . < ዘደኄደስ > ዘደኄ ስ J ; omit CDG (corr.) .

v. 10. < እማንተ > እማጡ GH ; እማቲ L .

v. 11. < እማንተስ > ወእማንተስ I . < ተጠውጥሙ > ተቴልጠሙ B ; ወይጠውጡ G ; ተጠውጡ H . < ወደተጀሩ > ወይጠወሙ AH ; ወይመውሙ: ወእሙንተ:ይተጀሩ E ; ወይመውሙ:ወእሙንተስ:ይተጀሩ FIKM ; ወይመውሙ : እሙንተስ : ይተጀሩ JL .

v. 12. < ወእንተስ > እንተስ E . < ዘኢየኅልቅ > እኢየኅልቅ L .

v. 13. ይቤሎ + እግዚእብሔር FGHIJKLM . ኮነ + ወዕፋዎ E . < እገብኡሙ > እገብዖ F . < ለጸላእትክ > ለዐርክ E .

v. 14. < እኮኑ > ወኮኑ E . < መላእንት > መላእክተ E . < ወደተፈናዉ > ወደተፈናዎ F ; ወደተፈናዉ I . < ለመዕልእክት > ለመላእክት EF . < ዘለዓለም > omit CDGHIJKLM .

Summary and conclusions:

(i)   Of the textual variants recorded in AC Heb.1, those in verses
4 and 6, and one of the variants in v.8, are found in other texts or
MSS.   The variants in vs. 1 and 11 are not found in the other textual
witnesses examined;   and the status of two of the 'variant texts' of
v.8 is unclear.

(ii)   The texts of C and D are identical in this chapter. G, H and
I form a group with similarities, and so do J and L.   E contains the
most scribal errors, and J and I also contain a number. M shows a
tendency to conflate.

(iii)   The main textual crux in the chapter is in v.6, in the reading
'and when further he sent (his) first-born' against 'and when the
first-born came'. The former is the reading of at least some older
MSS, and is read in the lemma of <u>TFF</u>;   the latter, which may have been
influenced by John Chrysostom's Homily III (<u>ho de Paulos eisodon autēn</u>
<u>onomazei</u>) or by other doctrinal <u>Tendenz</u>, is general in the MSS
examined from the 17th. cent. onwards, and also appears to be the text
assumed by <u>TP</u>.

(iv)   On the sample of evidence presented, in every verse of the
chapter except 1, 3, 9-10 and 12, there are readings on which the
witnesses are sufficiently divided as to preclude judgements about a
'correct' reading.

(v)   For some of the variants, the weight of evidence is sufficiently
against the Asmara edition used as the base text that it cannot be
assumed that it adequately represents even the more recent MS tradition.

(vi)   The degree of variation here recorded demonstrates the methodological problems of including "Ethiopic evidence" in critical appara-
tuses to the Greek N.T., and of forming conclusions about the textual
families to which the Geez is related.

5.5   COMPARATIVE STUDY OF SELECTED EXEGETICAL MOTIFS.

5.5.1   The many 'matters' and 'portions' (Heb.1.1).

John Chrysostom (Hom.I) does not draw a distinction between
the 'times and manners', and says that the phrase means 'in different
ways'; he continues by quoting Hos.12.10, as Iso'dad and Theodoret
also do. Iso'dad has a longer comment on the 'portions and forms',
defining them (Gibson, p.102) as 'the varieties of the knowledge of
God, which he taught bit by bit according to the weakness of the early
ages and times'; and later (p.103) he speaks of the threefold
revelation in former times, from God, from the angels, and from
similitudes, and the threefold revelation in latter times, from God
the Father, from the Word who dwelt in a body, and from the Body who
speaks with the world. This latter comment is found also in the
Tərgwame Pawlos (TP, see 5.1 above; page references are to MS Cowley
34), 'Just as at the first God was likened and revealed himself by
three likenesses, namely by God — behold, he is powerful and honoured —
and by angels, and their likenesses, so our Lord Christ was likened
for us in three likenesses and their reasons — by God the Father, and
by his Word which dwelt in flesh, and by his appearance in flesh' (p.56).

On the 'divisions and words/likenesses', TP (pp.55-6) says,
'"In every division and in every word" ...; "in every division" —
this (means) the ordinances of God, powerful and honoured. And it
happened at the time of the creation of Adam and Eve, and the oblation
of Abel and the sinning of Cain, and the transmigration of Enoch, and
the completion of the faithfulness of the former people, at the time
of the flood and the saving of Noah from it, at the time of the choosing
of Abraham, and the report of Joseph through that which he obtained
from his brothers, and their subjection to him after this, and their
departure from Egypt, in all that happened of the work and history of
Israel, and the commandment that was handed over on Mount Sinai, and
more beside all this. "In every likeness" — (this means) that God,
supreme and honoured, revealed himself to his prophets, and (also)
his being sent to human kind, and his being likened to many forms and
likenesses; formerly, he appeared to his prophets, and he spoke to
them in human fashion, and he appeared to Adam walking in the garden,
and there are other people to whom he appeared in sleep, and to others

awake, to some in fire or in cloud, to some in the likeness of angels, and to some in the likeness of a noble, or in the likeness of a spirit'.

This comment is almost identical with that in Mt. Sinai Arabic Codex 151, an Arabic translation from Syriac, edited by H. Staal (page numbers refer to Staal's translation; for this comment, see p.224, notes 1-2). It has some similarities with the commentaries of Theodoret, Severian, Ephraim and Išoʿdad. Theodoret (PG 82, cols. 677-8) distinguishes 'dispensations' and 'visions', and refers to Abraham, Moses, Elijah, Micah, Isaiah, Daniel and Ezekiel as having seen visions or semblances of God. Severian distinguishes the 'dispensations' of Adam, Cain, Noah, and Abraham from the giving of laws to Adam, Noah, Abraham and Moses (Staab, p.346). Ephraim mentions Noah, Abraham, Moses, and the Israelites in the wilderness. Išoʿdad distinguishes oral communications of God's law to such as Adam, Noah, and Abraham (Gibson, p.102) from visions granted to Abraham, Moses, and Isaiah (Gibson, p.103).

There is a further close parallel in a passage attributed to John Chrysostom in Gǝbrä hǝmamat (pr.ed. pp.350-2): ' ... and he appeared to Adam like a man who walks in a garden, so that he heard the sound of his heel on the ground. And he appeared to our father Abraham like a man who passes on the road. And he appeared to Jacob like a man who sits on a ladder which reaches from earth to heaven. And he appeared to Moses in the tree of patos, and in a small cloud. And he appeared to Joshua in the likeness of an angel, and to Isaiah in the likeness of a man ... . And Paul the apostle said, "In many portions and in many likenesses ...".'

The Tǝrgwame Felon Felgos (TFF) has understood the text to mean, 'In many words ... God ... spoke to us concerning his Son', and the comment therefore emphasizes Messianic prophecy, rather than the contrast between the former and latter times; the comment says, '"In many words" - the prophets prophesied that Christ would come for the salvation of the sons of men; "and in many divisions" - how in their flesh the prophets saw concerning his crucifixion, and death, and resurrection ...'.

The AC, translated in 5.2 above, suggests three distinctions between the 'matters and portions', and interprets them as (i) the ten

commandments and the other commandments, or (ii) similes and plain
speech – the similitudes being such as the furniture of the tabernacle
and temple, and Aaron's rod, or (iii) various forms of prophecy and
'likenesses' such as the stone of Daniel. Išoᶜdad (Gibson p.103)
similarly mentions the rod, the plate, the serpent, and the ark (of
the covenant).

5.5.2 The reasons why Paul did not say 'he spoke to you in me'.

John Chrysostom (Hom.I.1) gives three reasons why Paul did not
oppose 'himself' to 'the prophets' – (i) to avoid speaking great things
concerning himself, (ii) because his hearers were not yet perfect, and
(iii) because he wished to exalt his hearers. AC YAWD (p.4) explains
reason (ii) by saying that the hearers were not yet perfect in their
love for him, a statement doubtless to be linked with suggestions in
introductions to Hebrews (e.g. Išoᶜdad, Gibson p.101; Geez introductions in 5.1 above; also mentioned in Staal p.221) that if Paul's
name had appeared at the head of the epistle, the intended recipients
would not have read it. AC Heb.1.2 says that Paul was avoiding (i)
the appearance of self-aggrandisement, (ii) rejection from the hearers
because of their familiarity with him, and (iii) making the hearers
seem unimportant; these reasons approximate to those of John Chrysostom,
and (the Geez version of) his first homily is no doubt the source for
both the idea of the pericope, and for the reasons stated in it.

5.5.3 Comparison of the former and latter days (Heb.1.1-2).

Commentators variously emphasize either the superiority of
gospel to law, or the place of both in God's plan. John Chrysostom
(Hom.I.2) says that the Old and New Covenants are both of God, and
Išoᶜdad emphasizes that in the former times God was really teaching
'according to the weakness of the ages' (Gibson, pp.102,103). AC Heb.
1.2 contrasts the dispensations more sharply – the former times are
characterised as the period when human kind lacked sonship and was in
bondage to punishment, and the latter times as the period when human
kind obtained sonship and was saved from punishment.

5.5.4 The Son as inheritor of all (Heb.1.2).

AC Heb. 1.2 quotes Ps.2.8 in illustration of this idea, and has
probably taken the quotation from John Chrysostom's homily I.2; TP
(p.56-7) is also closely dependent on John Chrysostom: 'He points to
the flesh which he took up from us, because he is inheritor of all by
way of union in God the Word, the divine nature, because it is not
possible for a mere man to be inheritor over all. And Chrysostom says,
"As for his saying,'(He is) inheritor, who is over all', (it is)
according to the flesh, after the word of David in the second psalm,
'Ask of me, and I will give you the nations for your inheritance'.
Also Peter says in Abräksis that God made him Lord and Messiah ." '

Iso'dad (Gibson p.104) has a briefer, similar comment, but
Gibson's annotations suggest that his quotation 'Thou shalt inherit all
nations' is Ps.82.8, not Ps.2.8; reference to Iso'dad's commentary on
these Psalms does not conclusively demonstrate which one he intended.

Theodoret similarly refers to Christ's humanity (ouch hōs Theos,
all'hōs anthropos, PG 82, cols. 679-80), but quotes Rom.8.17, and not
Pss.

The commentary edited by Staal (p.224 note 4) does not cite the
psalm, but emphasizes the theme of inheritance according to the flesh -
' ... the person who was taken, who by his union with God the Word
took authority in heaven and earth'.

5.5.5 The refutation of misguided opinions.

In AC Heb.1 vs.2, 3 and 14, certain views are mentioned as held
by some of the recipients of the epistle, and as refuted by it,
especially the views of those who say (i) 'there is no kingdom of
heaven', (ii) 'let not tribulation overtake us' (i.e. 'we will not
reach spiritual perfection through suffering), (iii) 'let us call
Jesus an angel', and (iv) 'let us call Jesus a prophet'. This material
does not appear in this form in John Chrysostom or Iso'dad, but is
prominent in the AC Amharic introduction to Heb. (Yáqəddus pawlos
mashaf, pp.604-6); this Amharic introduction contains, in an
expanded form, material of the type of the Geez introduction
in MS Rylands 19 (introduction no. 3.3.14, see section 5.1 above).

5.5.6 Christological terminology in Hebrews 1.3.

The Christological terminology found in Heb.1.3 raises textual, translational, and theological questions. The terms used here have reached the AC by at least two routes, and the two may have interacted. The stages are that (i) the NT text formed the lemma in John Chrysostom's homilies, (ii) John Chrysostom's homilies were translated into Arabic, (iii) the Arabic version of John Chrysostom's homilies was translated into Geez, and the NT text was translated into Geez and revised in various ways, and (iv) both the Geez version of the homilies and a Geez version of the NT text were commented on in Amharic in the AC; clearly, the probability exists that at stage (iii) there was cross-influence between the versions of the texts, and that at stage (iv) there was cross-influence between the commentaries. The two routes may be diagrammatically represented as follows:

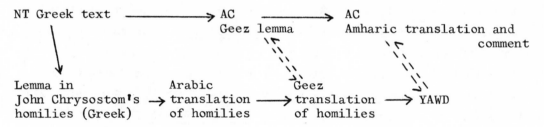

The Greek <u>charaktēr tēs hupostaseōs autou</u> appears in the Geez lemma of AC Heb.1.3 as <u>amsalä ar'ayahu</u>, 'the likeness of his image/ appearance', and the AC interprets this (see 5.2 above) as 'who is like him in form (<u>mälk</u>), who is equal to him in nature (<u>bahrəy</u>); in the printed text of AC YAWD, on the other hand, the Greek is repre-sented in the lemma (p.23, at the head of Homily II) by <u>aräya akalu zäbahrəyhu</u>, 'the image of the person/substance (<u>akal</u>) of his nature (<u>bahrəy</u>)', while the Amharic comment (especially p.37) refrains from translating the phrase.

Subsequently in Heb.1.3, John Chrysostom has read <u>di'heautou</u> (<u>katharismon</u>) (cf. Theodoret, <u>PG</u> 82, cols.683-4) and this is probably the Greek text underlying both the reading <u>bähəllawehu</u> common in Geez texts of Heb.1.3, and the reading <u>bä'ənti'ahu</u> of e.g. B.N. Zotenberg 45 and the lemma in <u>TFF</u>. In the printed text of AC YAWD, <u>di'heautou</u> is represented in the lemma (p.23, at the head of Homily II) by <u>bä'akalä zi'ahu</u>. AC Heb.1.3 translates <u>bähəllawehu</u>, 'in his

essence' by b̈äẗäl̈äyyä̈ akalu, 'in his person (akal) which is separate/
distinct'; AC YAWD does not comment on b̈äʔakalä̈ ziʔahu (and the
translation of the relevant passage of homily II is in slight disorder).

Iso⁽dad has also read, 'And He in His own Person made the
cleansing ...' (Gibson, p.105), and comments on it referring 'person'
to 'the manhood that was taken'. TP (p.58) comments, '"In his essence
(hǝllawe) he did (the work) by which he cleanses us from our sins ..." —
(this means) that this flesh which he took up from us, after his
passion, cleansed us from our sins and from our every error; for he
became one in essence (hǝllawe) with the divinity (m̈äläkot)'.

Clearly the opportunity has not been missed for making
Christological bricks with very little straw. The terms akal, bahrǝy,
and to a lesser extent hǝllawe, have become theologically charged from
centuries of debate (see further section 5.1 above), and in particular
the process that led to the use of akal z̈äbahrǝy to represent hupostasis,
and akal or hǝllawe to represent heautou, is a considerable step in
the development of doctrine, already partially taken in comments on
Heb.1.3 by Severianus of Gabala (ek tēs ousias, Staab, p.346, line 27)
and Theodore of Mopsuestia (ton charaktēra tēs phuseōs, Staab, p.201,
line 33).

5.5.7 The 'light of his glory', not the 'light of God' (Heb.1.3).

Theodore of Mopsuestia, commenting on apaugasma tēs doxēs
(Heb.1.3), says, 'Rightly he did not say "of God", but "of glory"'
(kalōs ouk eipen tou theou alla tēs doxēs, Staab, p.201, line 28).
This is strikingly paralleled in TP (p.58), '"Light of his glory" —
he does not say "light of God"; (this is) exaltation of his name,
and reproach for the one who presumes to make an impossible investigation'.

Both Theodoret (PG 82, cols.681–2) and AC Heb.1.3 quote Jn.14.9
in illustration of 'the light of his glory'.

5.5.8 The 'light of his glory' (Heb.1.3) illustrated by the sun.

AC Heb.1.3 says, 'Just as the light of the sun, being united

with the eye, makes known its circular shape, so also he, being united
with flesh, has made known his father'. The two principal points made
here are (i) the unity of Christ's divinity and humanity, and (ii) the
Son as the revelation of his Father. Iso῾dad (Gibson, p.104) makes
a similar comment, '... there are not times and no space for his
causation; just as the sphere of the sun to its radiance, and the
light that is with us to its splendour'; the point here, however, is
the temporal and spatial co-existence and equality of Father and Son.
TP (p.58) makes the same point, '... then there is no separation
between them, neither time nor duration; and he is like the sun, in
which there is no separation between its light and its heat, and,
further, like fire which is not separated from heat, nor the heat from
rays of light', and so does the commentary edited by Staal (pp.224-5,
note 8).

This illustration of the sun is not used by John Chrysostom
in his second homily, possibly because such language could be used to
teach subordinationism - a possibility to which the interpretation of
TFF seems particularly open, 'He is the light of his glory and the
manifestation of the face of God (ar'aya gásu lá'əgzi'abəher)'. The
illustration is specifically opposed by Photius of Constantinople,
ouk apo tou hēliou, ouk apo tou puros ... (Staab, p.638, lines 20-21).

5.5.9 The nature of 'holding everything' (Heb.1.3).

The commentaries principally consider the following questions:
(i) whether God the Father or God the Son was creator, (ii) whether
God the Son 'holds everything' by his own authority, or by the
Father's command, and (iii) whether the work of 'holding' is to be
understood as 'upholding' or as 'governing'; that is, the phrase is
related either to the status or to the continuing activity of God
the Son.

Iso῾dad (Gibson, p.105) brings together status and activity,
by saying, '... he not only calls him the Maker, but shews that He
made everything by unspeakable power, if from His word all things
depend', and the commentary edited by Staal does so more clearly: 'He
meant that he is the creator of all, and that he by his almighty

power established everything in the condition in which it is. That
is, he is the creator of all and keeper of all according to his
creation' (Staal, p.224, note 7, which appears to be related to
'controls' rather than to 'glory').

TP (p.58) says, 'Concerning the one who says, "The nature
(bahrəy) of his godhead is not strong (sɘnuʿ), and he has no omnipotence (kɘhilot) over work", he indicated further and recollected
his first birth, saying, "He is the holder of all by the word of his
power and his omnipotence." Athanasius says that he said this concerning his work; and Ḥanan says, "In saying 'the power of his word'
he means 'his authority and lordship', for his power is a witness to
him and to his nature, that he is omnipotent over all work.'

John Chrysostom, in discussing this in Homily II, refers the
phrase to 'upholding', as against 'governing' (eipe pherōn. ouk eipe
kubernōn). In Geez translation these appear as ahazi and sāraʿi
respectively, presenting a problem to one stream of opinion among the
AC commentators (AC YAWD pp.41-2), which sees no essential distinction
between the two words; another opinion sees a distinction, and comments,
'Because the Honofe (Ḥanafi) say of him that he did the work having
been commanded'. The form of words in AC Heb.1.3, 'who rules, having
created everything, in his property of being the powerful word',
appears to be intended to combine the ideas of ruling and creating,
and to remove any idea that 'his word', 'his power', or indeed 'the
Son', might be a mere agent.

In considering whether 'the Father commanded and the Son obeyed',
John Chrysostom (Hom.II.2), Theodoret (PG 82, cols.681-2), and
Theodore of Mopsuestia (Staab, p.202, lines 5-6) all cite Gen.1.3
(the reference Gen.1.3, 6 is misprinted in Staab, apparently on the
basis of PG 66,col.954).

5.5.10 'He sat ... in the heavens' (Heb.1.3) does not imply spatial
confinement.

AC Heb.1.3 understands 'in the heavens' to mean 'in glory', and
not to imply spatial confinement. TP (p.58) similarly explains
'sitting' and 'the right hand'. John Chrysostom (Hom.II) also dismisses

the idea of enclosing God spatially, in the passage leading up to the
sentence actually quoted in AC Heb.1.3.

5.5.11 The illustration of training a child to climb.

In John Chrysostom's Homily I.3, and in AC Heb.1.4, the successive statements about the Son are likened to the gentle leading of a
child up to some high place. The first account in AC Heb.1.4 sets out
two upward and two downward stages, as follows: (i) up – 'He spoke
to us in his son', (ii) down – 'whom he made inheritor of all', (iii)
up – 'in whom he created everything ... who holds everything in the
power of his word', (iv) down – 'he ... cleanses our sin ... and
inherited a name which ... is more glorious'. A further opinion in
AC Heb.1.4 partially reverses the direction of the stages, but the
purpose of the illustration, and its source in John Chrysostom's
Homily I.3 are clear. The other commentaries surveyed do not contain
this illustration.

5.5.12 Successive steps in the refutation of named heretics.

In John Chrysostom's Homily II, and in AC Heb.1.4, the successive statements about the Son are likened to stages or steps in the
refutation of the main early Christological heresies. In AC Heb.1.4
they appear as follows:–
1st. step, 'He spoke to us in his son', partially refuting Sabellius;
2nd. step, 'whom he made inheritor of all', completely refuting
Sabellius;
3rd. step, 'in whom he created everything', refuting Paul of Samosata;
4th. step, 'who is the light of his glory', refuting Arius;
5th. step, 'the likeness of his image', refuting Märqəyan;
6th. step, 'who holds everything in the power of his word', refuting
all heretics.

The confusion over the identity of Märqəyan is noted in 5.2
above, in the annotations to AC Heb.1.4; on the basis of the actual
part of John Chrysostom's Homily II on which the AC comment is based,
it seems that Marcion, rather than Marcellus, is here intended, but it
is also possible that the inconsistencies introduced in the process of
translating the homilies into Geez prevented Ethiopian scholars from
correctly differentiating the two characters and their teachings.

TP (p.57) mentions the reproaching of Paul of Samosata (by
'in whom he created the world') and of Arius, Cyril of Alexandria
(PG 74, cols. 953-1006 on Heb.1.4) mentions the Arians, Valentinians,
and Carpocratians, and Theodoret (PG 82, cols. 681-2) mentions the
Sabellians, Photinians, Marcellus, Paul (of Samosata) and Arius, but
the material is not ordered in the same way as in John Chrysostom's
Homily II, which is clearly the source for AC Heb.1.4.

5.5.13 Quotations from the Old Testament.

The quotations are as follows:

in Heb. 1.5:	Ps. 2.7 and 2 Sam. 7.14;
in Heb. 1.6:	Ps. 96 (97). 7;
in Heb. 1.7:	Ps. 103 (104). 4;
in Heb. 1.8-9:	Ps. 44 (45). 6-7;
in Heb. 1.10-11:	Ps. 101 (102). 25-27;
in Heb. 1.13:	Ps. 109 (110). 1.

Išoʿdad (Gibson, p.105) and the commentary edited by Staal
(p.225, note 13) additionally recognize the quotation in Heb.1.6 as
a text of Deut.32.43; Išoʿdad on Deut.32.43 attributes the exact
words to the version of Symmachus. The commentary edited by Staal
identifies the sources of most of the quotations, apparently using the
Hebrew, rather than the LXX, enumeration of the psalms.

In AC Pss., there are comments on Ps.2.7, Ps.103 (104). 4,
Ps.44 (45). 6-7, Ps.101 (102). 25-27, and Ps.109 (110). 1 which are
similar to, and in fact mostly verbally identical with, those found
in AC Heb.1 as translated in 5.2 above. One difference, however,
between AC Heb. and AC Pss. lies in the treatment of the word
zäyəheyyəs, 'which is better', in Heb.1.9. AC Heb.1.9 says of this,
'(It) is not in (the word of) the prophet (i.e. David); the apostle
spoke it'. AC Ps.44 (45). 7, which does not have zäyəheyyəs in the
lemma, comments, 'That which St. Paul said, "which is better", John
Chrysostom cited saying, "with oil of joy".' The AC is correct in
recognizing zäyəheyyəs as an addition to the verse, but is incorrect
in supposing the addition to be Pauline and to have been 'cited' by
John Chrysostom; the word is not even found in all Geez texts of
Heb.1.9 (see 5.4 above; nor is it found in the text in TFF). The

AC comments do, however, illustrate the general attitude of the AC commentators to OT quotations in the NT: (i) that the OT passages have an abiding significance and validity, and (ii) that they can be used creatively, and 'developed', by the NT writers, and later by patristic authors.

5.5.14 <u>The entry of the first-born into the world (Heb.1.6)</u>.

The Geez version of this verse contains a major textual crux, as to whether 'he sent the first-born' or 'the first-born came' should be read (see 5.4 above); both readings use the Geez perfect, whereas the Greek <u>hotan</u> with aorist subjunctive <u>eisagagē</u> would be better represented by the Geez imperfect, and this has predisposed Ethiopian commentators to see a reference to a past event (though they do, of course, share this with e.g. John Chrysostom's Homily III, and Theodoret, <u>PG</u> 82, cols.685-6). AC Heb.1.6 says, 'The angels bow down to him at the time when, having caused the union of flesh with the son of his nature, he subjugated this world to him', and locates the 'coming' as the incarnation. <u>TFF</u> makes this even more explicit with a passage about the worship of the angels and magi at Bethlehem.

Some of the commentaries, however, are aware of opinions which refer the 'coming' to a later event. In the commentary edited by Staal (p.225, note 13), the possibility is noted that 'when he has entered' 'can be interpreted concerning the second coming of Christ, according to the saying of Gregorius the brother of Basilius'; a similar opinion is attributed in <u>TP</u> (p.59) to Athanasius: 'When the first-born came into the world, he says, "All the angels of God will bow down to him". Paul's mention of "bowing down" gives us to understand that we should bow down to him, and this also is David's saying, "All the angels will bow down to him". As for the first-born who came into the world, it is the humanity of our Lord Jesus Christ, who is first-born from Mary the virgin and from the resurrection, as is said in another place, "He will be the first-born of many brothers". By "his coming" he means the first appearance of our Lord. And our Lord's saying in the gospel, "A sower went out in order to sow" is his appearance in flesh. He intends by this to give (us) to understand that our Lord went out among us, and appeared in public,in order to turn us from error to obedience to God; for when a king has spoken against the people and distanced them from his sight, the one who would be a reconciler, and would improve their deeds, goes out to them and turns them back to the service of the king by his message. And Paul's saying in this place, "He came into the world" means that he (Christ) is the likeness of a king who comes among his people and turns them from error by the method of a reconciler. And Athanasius says that the apostle's saying here, "When the first-born came into the world" (refers to the time) prior to his second coming.'

This section of TP reads as a combination of the beginning of John Chrysostom's Homily III, and Staal p.225, note 13, with perhaps a sideways glance at Theodore bar Koni's Book of Scholia, Mimrā IX. 20 (1) (and no material from Iso͗ͨdad); it is not being suggested, however, that this was its actual literary history.

5.5.15 Questions related to creation.

The following matters related to creation are mentioned in AC Heb.1: (i) on 1.7, the question of whether angels were created from fire and wind, or ex nihilo, (ii) on 1.10, the questions of whether heaven and earth were created at the same time, and of whether heaven was fashioned from something else or created ex nihilo, (iii) on 1.10 (but following the beginning of 1.11) the questions of whether souls can be destroyed, and of whether they are created ex nihilo, and (iv) on 1.11, the eight thousand year duration of the world.

John Chrysostom, Theodoret and Iso͗ͨdad do not have material of this type in their commentaries on Hebrews, though many commentators consider them in commentaries on Genesis (see section 4.4 above).

AC Ps.103 (104). 4 contains a comment on the creation of the angels similar in outline, but different in detail, to that in AC Heb.1.7: 'For the creation of angels is from fire and wind. If it is objected that it says, "But if they were created from wind and fire, they would die and decay like us", then their creation is ex nihilo, as it says, "But the creation of angels is from divine light".'

TFF gives a fuller account: 'But truly angels are ones created by a flame of fire; they are spiritual (beings) which are created by a flame of fire and from wind, and from heat, and from rays of light, and from wärawəre' (wärawəre is the translation equivalent of 'topaz'

and of 'marble', but its precise significance was probably not understood by the Geez writer).

AC Heb.1.7 continues with a more symbolic interpretation of
the 'fire and wind', and this is found also in the commentary edited
by Staal (p.225-6, note 14), and in TP (p.60), '... because they
hasten and give service for our salvation and for bringing us to the
good things which are prepared for us, and which come for our sakes.
And Cyriacus says he calls the angels 'spirits' with reference to the
speed of their service, and the wisdom of their race (i.e. 'their
running', rusätomu; perhaps räd'etomu 'their help' should be read).
And he names them 'fire' by reason of the strength of their power.'

5.5.16 The symbolism of 'throne' and 'rod' (Heb.1.8).

AC Heb.1.8 understands 'throne' as 'lordship', and 'rod' as
'authority', and similar ideas of divinity and royalty are found in
John Chrysostom (Hom.III.2), Cyril of Alexandria (PG 74, cols.961-2),
Theodore of Mopsuestia (Staab, p.202), and Iso'dad (Gibson, p.105-6),
and in the quotation in AC Heb.1.8 from Severianus of Gabala. TFF
emphasizes the eternal nature of the Son's throne: '... not like a
noble of this transient world ..., but the throne of the Son of God
is eternal, unto all generations ..., and there is no end to his
kingdom'.

A second interpretation of the symbolism of the rod is found
in Iso'dad (Gibson, p.105-6), Staal p.226, note 16, and, as follows,
in TP (pp.59-60), 'But concerning the Son he says, "Your throne, O
Lord, is for eternity, and your rod is spread out over all creation"....
In saying "a rod spread out", this is the rod of rule, because a rod
is that which springs up from a root, and is high up; it is from the
nature of the root. He intends to verify by this that the nature of
the Son is from the nature of the Father.'

5.5.17 The anointing of the Son (Heb.1.9).

AC Heb.1.9 makes two main points in interpreting this idea:
(i) Christ's solidarity with human kind, and (ii) the descent of the
Holy Spirit upon him at his baptism; the AC comment is innocent of
the polemics of the qǝb'at controversy in the Ethiopian church.

TP passes over this topic, and Išoᶜdad has little to say on
it; the other commentators surveyed point out that this is said
'concerning his humanity', and that 'the manhood is anointed' (TFF;
Staal, p.226, note 17; John Chrysostom Hom. III.2; Theodoret, PG 82,
cols. 687-8; Cyril of Alexandria, PG 74, cols.961-2).

5.5.18 The identity of 'your enemies' (Heb.1.13).

AC Heb.1.13 and AC Ps.109 (110). 1 both identify the 'enemies'
as 'Jews, heretics, demons'; most commentators do not feel the need
for an identification, but TFF develops it as a major topic: 'Who
are "your enemies" - are they not Satan and his demons, and the
wicked Jews, the crucifiers of Jesus Christ, whom Satan caused to err
against the creator of the whole world; and further, not they alone,
but all who hate the name of Christ? They must enter into the depths
of Sheol, and this is the footstool of God, for the prophet says,
"Heaven is my throne, and earth is my footstool," because beneath
the earth it is completely the depth of Sheol, and it is beneath the
feet of Christ, and all who erred entered beneath the earth into the
depths of Sheol. And at that time Christ will reign for the martyrs
and the righteous and the heavenly angels, and Christ will reign over
them, because he received from his father the kingdom and the authority
for ever and ever, for the authority of his father was given to him.'

5.5.19 Summary and conclusions.

(i)   The most evident linkages established are (a) dependence of
AC Heb.1 on John Chrysostom's homilies I-III; (b) dependence of
TP on John Chrysostom, and on material of the type of the commentary
edited by Staal.

(ii)   The relationship of AC Heb.1 and TP on Heb.1 appears to be
indirect - that is, they have made independent selections from
commentary material of the types of John Chrysostom, Theodoret,
Theodore of Mopsuestia, Išoᶜdad, and Staal's commentary.

(iii) Although Išoᶜdad's use of Theodore of Mopsuestia is well-
documented, this material on Heb.1 does not clearly illustrate it.

(iv)   <u>TFF</u>, while not contradicting the other Ethiopian and related materials, is not a representative of the exegetical tradition to which the materials listed in (ii) above belong.

6.   Hermeneutical implications of this study

6.   HERMENEUTICAL IMPLICATIONS OF THIS STUDY.

"Not the intention of the author, which is supposed to be
hidden behind the text; not the historical situation common to the
author and his original readers; not the expectations or feelings
of these original readers; not even their understanding of themselves as historical and cultural phenomena. What has to be appropriated is the meaning of the text itself, conceived in a dynamic
way as the direction of thought opened up by the text."

(P. Ricoeur, Interpretation Theory, p.92[1]).

Hermeneutics is generally understood to be 'the study of
the principles and rules of interpretation and understanding'[2].
However, the concept of 'rule of interpretation' is (I believe) too
elusive to be useful, and, moreover, the AC does not contain explicit interpretative rules. Therefore this chapter addresses the
hermeneutical question in the form, 'What are the processes that
have generated the AC and made it as it is? This is considered
under the headings (i) 'middot', (ii) commentary tradition, (iii)
doctrine, (iv) availability of material, (v) shaping of material,
(vi) 'haggada', (vii) 'midraš' and 'targum', (viii) 'horizon', and
(ix) conclusions.

6.1   'Middot'.

Has Ethiopian commentary been generated by the application
of 'rules of hermeneutics'?

Jewish sources list the seven middot of Hillel[3], the thirteen
middot of Ishmael[4], and thirty three middot 'by which the aggada

---

1. Quoted from P. Ricoeur, Essays on Biblical Interpretation, p.16
    (essay by L.S. Mudge).

2. H.W. Frei, The Eclipse of Biblical Narrative, p.9.

3. Bowker, The Targums, pp.315-8.

4. MhH pp.8-11; The Authorised Daily Prayer
    Book, 1962, pp.14-15.

(or 'the tora') is expounded'[5], and refer to a midraš of forty-
nine middot[6]. The AC does not contain such numbered lists of 'rules'[7],
but it does exhibit methodological and formulaic parallels with the
Jewish material, as shown in 3.1.3 above.

'Middot' (in this context) is usually translated 'exegetical
principles', or 'rules of interpretation'. The actual middot, however, are principles of logic rather than of hermeneutics, and some
are a matter of common sense. The extent to which Jewish Bible
commentary has in reality been generated by the use of middot can
only be judged subjectively, since in many instances it appears
that the middot have been used to support a conclusion already
reached by other means. In Ethiopian commentary, the formulaic
parallels with the Jewish middot (notably the 'inference from a
similarity of phrases') only appear generative of the comment in
the case of commonly adduced parallels, commonly cited proof texts,
and maxims of the type that the biblical literature 'does not necessarily observe chronological order', and 'is not careful to observe
the grammatical categories of number and gender'.

It seems, in any case, that Jewish and Ethiopian 'rules'
are generalisations arising from actual engagement in exegetical
debate, rather than expressions of a philosophical interpretative
system which has been separately constructed and then applied to
the text. I am unconvinced that it is possible to construct a system, the application of which reveals 'the meaning of the text';

5. MhH pp.12–19.

6. H.G.Enelow (ed.), The Mishnah of Rabbi Eliezer, p.19.   Additionally
    see W.S. Towner, The Rabbinic "Enumeration of Scriptural Examples",
    especially pp.251-5, and S.B. Sofer, Sefer kəritot.

7. The list of 'yatərgwame səltu' (types of interpretation) given by
    Maḥari Tərfe and translated in PN pp.17-18 is (a) not necessarily
    traditional material, and (b) not really 'principles of exegesis'
    (see TIA pp.46–53). Aklilā bərhan Wälda qirqos in Marha ləbbuna,
    p.12 states, 'In the period when Ɉcage Qalā awadi was əcage, because
    he was very learned, the limit (dəmbär) of the interpretation of books,
    of the content and ordinance of zema, and of the style of qəne, was
    defined'; it is not clear that 'rules' of interpretation are meant,
    nor have I been able to find 'rules' attributed to him.

attempts to do so appear only to raise the spectre of an infinite
hierarchy of criteria of criteria by which the meaning of the
meaning which has been educed may be further elucidated and evaluated.

6.2 Commentary tradition.

The most evident conclusion of this study is that the AC
stands in fundamental continuity with earlier commentaries, especially those of the 'Antiochene' tradition.

This statement, however, requires clarification, firstly
because the term 'Antiochene' has become a source of some confusion.
It is a geographical term, and can therefore legitimately be used
of the tradition of Biblical interpretation historically associated
with (Syrian) Antioch, provided that the historical period and
principal tradents are specified. Some writers have used 'Antiochene'
of an abstract concept of the 'essentials' of a school of interpretation, and then applied this concept to exegetes like John
Chrysostom who were leading Antiochenes, to demonstrate that he was
only 'for the most part consistent with Antiochene exegesis'.[8] So
treated, 'Antiochene' becomes a modern idealisation divorced from
historical reality; here, it is understood to mean the Biblical
interpretation which characterised the church of Antioch and is
associated principally with the names of Lucian, Paulinus, Diodore,
Eustathius, John Chrysostom, and Theodore of Mopsuestia.

Secondly, while it is clear that there is literary continuity and communality of thought between these Antiochenes and the
AC, and that there is no comparable link with Origen, Clement of
Alexandria and other Alexandrines, it is also evident that Antio-
chene (and Alexandrine) discussions of <u>allēgoria</u>, <u>theōria</u> and <u>tupos</u>
(to say nothing of <u>paradeigma</u>, <u>ainigma</u>, <u>skopos</u> etc.) have not

---

8. E.g. <u>ET</u> June 1982, p.265.

reached Ethiopia in intelligible form[9]; the exegetical fruit has been transmitted, but the root of its theoretical basis has been detached and lost, so it cannot be claimed that Antiochene exeget- ical theory is generative of Ethiopian Bible commentary – it is rather that Antiochene theory has generated Antiochene exegesis, and that this has been transmitted to Ethiopia.

The presence in the AC of material of allegorical type may be felt to weaken the exclusiveness of its Antiochene connections. For example in AC Qəddase maryam pp.233-4 the story of the ʿaqeda is followed by: 'Isaac is a likeness (məssale) of this world, the sheep is a likeness of the Lord .... Isaac is a likeness of the godhead, the sheep a likeness of the manhood, the knife a likeness of the authority of God, and the blade a likeness of suffering and death .... The thought of Abraham is a likeness of the grave, Isaac is a likeness of the Lord .... The fire is a likeness of the Holy Spirit, the wood a likeness of the cross, and the two servants are likenesses of the two brigands ...'[10]. However, there is no suggestion in the AC that the original events did not happen, or were unimportant, there is no (explicit or implicit) 'theory of allegory', and the reader will probably feel that these are exam- ples of homiletic application, and not allegory proper. The AC does emphasize that events which happened 'at the time' may also have a fulfilment, or fuller significance, and that the former things

9. See further A. Kerrigan, St. Cyril of Alexandria; F.M. Young, 'Christological Ideas in the Greek commentaries on the Epistle to the Hebrews'; J. Guillet, 'Les exégèses d'Alexandrie et d'Antioche'; H.N. Bate, 'Some Technical Terms of Greek Exegesis'; H.S. Nash, 'The Exegesis of the School of Antioch'. Terms such as theōria and tupos are used, for example, in IBN questions 1 and 4 (see Clarke, Selected Questions, p.53), but in the process of translation into Arabic, editing, and translation into Geez, their original signifi- cance has been completely obscured.

10. Similar material is found in AC Gen.22.

happened 'for our instruction'[11], but does not minimize the importance of the original event, or use allegorisation to evade moral
problems arising from the text.[12]

When such homiletic application veered towards typology, it
potentially raised doctrinal, especially Christological, problems.
For example, S. Brock (in 'Genesis 22 in Syriac Tradition', p.17)
writes, 'It was probably typological reasoning that gave rise to
the opinion ... that only the ram had a miraculous birth. Yet
further reflection on the unsuitable implications of such typology,
as far as Antiochene theology was concerned, led late East Syrian
writers to reject the entire tradition, and to assert instead that
an angel took an ordinary ram from Abraham's flocks ...'. Debate
of this type has left its mark on AC Gen.22: 'If it is said that
the sheep descended from Heaven, it is a likeness of the Lord's
descent from Heaven. If it is said that the sheep came from Abraham's
flock, (then) it is a likeness of (the Lord's) birth from Abraham's
people. If it is said that (the sheep) was obtained from the sealed
tree of sabeq, (then) it is a likeness of the Lord's birth from
our Lady in sealed virginity.'

Finally, it may be asked whether there was perhaps an
earlier non-Antiochene Ethiopian commentary, with a relationship to
the AC similar to the relationship of Jubilees to Midraš rabba;
this question requires further investigation.

6.3   Doctrine.

Non-Chalcedonian formulae are common-place in the AC, but
substantive doctrinal discussion is not at all prominent. This is
surprising in view of the long history of doctrinal dispute inside
Ethiopia, and in view of the contrast between the Nestorianism of
Theodore of Mopsuestia, Išoᶜdad, and Ibn aṭ-Ṭaiyib on one hand, and
the condemnation of Nestorius in the Ethiopic liturgy, in AAM, in

---

11. See TIA pp.49-50 (where I have been incautious in using the term
    'allegory').

12. Cf. R.P.C. Hanson, Allegory and Event.

<u>HA</u>, and in other works. It seems that the Ethiopian church was
able to reject the formula in which the teaching of Nestorius was
encapsulated ('two <u>akal</u> ('persons'), and two <u>bahrəy</u> ('natures')),
while accepting much of the exegetical work of writers who were
Nestorians. This suggests that the study of doctrine has not been
one of the main factors generative of Ethiopian biblical exegesis.

There is evidence of objection to the interpretations of IAṬ
on the grounds of his Nestorianism, and apparently especially because he did not interpret characters like Zerubbabel simply as
types of Christ; possibly his works were translated after the AC
had partially crystallised, or they gained currency among the
Felashas, and for these or other reasons lacked full acceptance
among AC teachers.[13] However, in the current state of study, the
evidence concerning rejection of IAṬ's <u>exegetica</u> is rather slight,
and should be seen as the exception which proves the rule that his
influence has been very pervasive, and that narrow doctrinal concerns have scarcely affected Ethiopian exegesis.

6.4   <u>Availability of material</u>.

It is unlikely that any one Ethiopian commentary scholar had
access to all the Ethiopian materials surveyed in sections 2, 4.1
and 5.1 above, but it seems very probable that the AC tradition as
a whole has been able to draw on them all. These Ethiopian materials
are mostly translations or adaptations from Arabic, and thus there
has been a process of selection, partly accidental and partly inten-
tional, from the available Arabic materials; these in turn will
have been available for a variety of ecclesiastical, geographical,
and accidental reasons. Some material is likely to have become
effectively unavailable through suppression – for example, in the
traditions surveyed in this study, Origen is so consistently referred
to as a heretic as to make it unlikely that any of his works would
later gain acceptance.

13. See R. Cowley, 'A Geˤez document reporting controversy concerning
    the Bible commentaries of Ibn aṭ-Ṭaiyib'. On Christological concerns
    of Christian commentators, see J. Baskin, <u>Pharaoh's Counsellors</u>,
    especially pp.119–120.

A number of factors probably influencing the choice of material included in the AC are noted in chapter 2; the following seem to be the principal ones:

(a) the date of translation into Geez – traditions accepted early were not dislodged, though they might be supplemented, by those arriving later;

(b) congruity with already accepted tradition;

(c) effective availability of MSS;

(d) association with celebrated teachers;

(e) memorability;

(f) church use of the non-Biblical texts drawn on as sources of commentary;

(g) discontinuities caused by historical disturbances.

6.5   Shaping of material.

The reader of the AC soon becomes aware that the comment has its own characteristic shape and style, and that it is easy to supply lacunae and correct copying errors in AC MSS, because of the patterned structure of the material.[14]

The typical ordering of the AC is: (i) Geez text, (ii) periphrastic Amharic translation, preceded or immediately followed by grammatical elucidation, (iii) illustration of the text – illustrative stories, explanation of details or obscurities, (iv) application and homiletic development. The sentence structure also shows characteristic patterns.

The exegetical content of the AC is largely dependent on sources external to the corpus, but the shaping and ordering of the material is not, and must be attributed to the Ethiopian scholars who are recorded as having formed and developed the AC tradition.

14. This does not mean that some elements may not undergo relocation – as may be seen, e.g. by comparing MSS of the AC on the gospels with the pr.ed., or by comparing AC Gen. 22 with the parallel material in AC Qəddase maryam.

It is they who digested the sources, and formed a body of material
which was then further shaped by the processes of transmission by
tradents.[15]

6.6   'Haggada'.

'Haggada', 'non-halakhic interpretation', is a Jewish category which seems a natural description of the parts of the AC
which expand Biblical narrative after the manner of a story-teller.
Haggadic elements appear in the AC both as expansions of the actual
text under consideration, and as illustrations imported into the
context of the commentary on other texts, though there seems to
be no essential difference between the materials found in these two
situations.[16]

Two points should especially be noted:
(i) After a particular haggada has developed and then stagnated in
a non-Ethiopian tradition, it may later develop further in the AC.
The transition to another culture presumably provided a stimulus to
redevelopment (and it would be very interesting to know the dynamics
of the process). This is illustrated, for example, by 2.6 above.

(ii) Elements in the AC which might be considered to be 'legendary'
are frequently, if not always, derived from scriptural exegesis;

15. On the Ethiopian teachers, see TIA pp.31-2 and MEHI; for Jewish
    parallels, see J. Neusner, From Mishnah to Scripture: The Problem
    of the Unattributed Saying, and In Search of Talmudic Biography:
    The Problem of the Attributed Saying.

16. For situations outside commentary there may be distinctions to be
    made, as Vermes concludes (of Jewish materials): 'Haggadic extracts
    figuring as examples in homiletic works, or as premises for ethical
    or legal conclusions in scholastic discussions, are not to be con-
    fused with authentic exegetical tradition. These are severed from
    their scriptural context, and although in most cases they echo the
    old Haggadah, they are definitely extraneous to it, and secondary
    to what may be called, in the broadest sense, targumic exegesis'
    (Scripture and Tradition in Judaism, p.229).

the stimulus to narration is the Biblical text itself and the obscurities, ambiguities, and potentialities it is perceived to contain.[17]

6.7   'Midraš' and 'targum'

The terms midraš and targum have occasionally been used in description of the AC. If such categorisation is proper, it might be suggested that there are parallels between the situations and processes in which the Jewish and Ethiopian materials were produced.

Unfortunately, discussion of 'the literary genre midrash' has been confused by (a) lack of agreement over the meaning of 'genre', a term not precisely defined in the study of stylistics, and (b) the attempt to name a category already intuitively recognised (thus provoking debate about its precise limits).[18] The use of targum to refer to versions, especially the Aramaic versions of the Hebrew Bible, presents a similar problem of definition.[19]

Certainly the AC shares features with the midrašim and targumim (concern for literalism,[20] expansionist and anti-anthropomorphic tendencies, for example), but as midraš and targum are essentially Jewish categories, and even within Jewish studies they are described rather than defined, it must be concluded that these terms should not be used in analysis of the AC, and it should not be assumed that the Jewish and Ethiopian materials have been produced as a result of similar processes.

17. For a Jewish parallel, see T. Kronholm's study of Rut R. in G. Larsson (ed.), Annual of the Swedish Theological Institute, vol. XII (1983).

18. See, e.g. R. le Déaut, 'Apropos a Definition of Midrash', and its extensive references; further bibliography in J. Neusner, Midrash in Context.

19. See Bowker, The Targums, p. 3.

20. For example, the AC, in commenting on 'He married his wife', points out that the woman was not his wife until he had married her.

6.8   'Horizon'.

The studies of K.E. Bailey (see bibliography) have shown how cultural similarities between the N.T. situation and the world of later Syriac and Arabic exegetes may give their works a special value for insights into the gospels; the same may be true, to a lesser extent, of the AC.

However, as the traditional Ethiopian world-view has been moulded by the Bible, and Ethiopian material culture is not unlike that of Biblical times, the question of 'horizon' does not present itself to the Ethiopian commentator. Because the cultural and situational gap is seen to be slight, or is not perceived at all, the theoretical problem, that the horizon of the exegete is not the horizon of the text, remains unfelt, and is therefore not one of the factors generative of commentary.

6.9   Conclusions.

The Ethiopian AC commentary tradition is an exegetical tradition which is in essential continuity with Antiochene exegesis, and which has been moulded into its present form by Ethiopian scholars. Although its sources have been variously influenced by hermeneutic theories and doctrinal concerns, these theories and concerns have not influenced the Ethiopian development of the tradition. The intention of the AC is to elucidate the text, in the belief that what is written is written for our instruction.

7.1   <u>GENERAL BIBLIOGRAPHY</u>

This bibliography lists the works referred to (often by short titles) in this study, and a selection of the further works which have been used but are not specifically mentioned. Ethiopian manuscript catalogues are omitted here, and listed in 7.2. General works on biblical studies and on Ethiopian studies, lexicons, encyclopedias, concordances, editions of versions of the Bible, and patristic texts in the <u>PG</u> and <u>PL</u>, are mostly omitted.

Aarne, A.A. (translated and enlarged by S. Thompson), <u>The Types of the Folktale. A classification and bibliography</u>, (FF Communications</u> 184), Helsinki, 1961.

Abarban'el, <u>Peruš Abarban'el ʿal hattora</u>, printed in Israel, n.d. (ed. princ. is Samuel de'Archivolti, Venice, 1579).

ʿAbd al Masīḥ, Y., 'A Discourse by St. John Chrysostom on the Sinful Woman in the Saʿīdic Dialect', <u>Bulletin de la Société d'Archéologie Copte</u> 15 (1958–60), pp.11–39.

Abramowski, L. and Goodman, A.E., <u>A Nestorian Collection of Christological Texts: Cambridge University Library MS. Oriental 1319</u>, Cambridge, 1972.

Aescoly, A.Z., 'Notices sur les Falacha ou Juifs d'Abyssinie d'après le «Journal de Voyage» d'Antoine d'Abbadie', <u>Cahiers d'études africaines</u> 2 (1961), pp.84–147.

Agapius, see Vasiliev, A.

<u>Aggadat bəresit</u>, see Buber, S.

Aklila bərhan Wälda qirqos, <u>Marha ləbbuna</u>, A.A., 1943 E.C. <u>Mašheta amin</u>, A.A., 1946 E.C. 'Zena masahəfta bəranna', <u>Proceedings of the Third International Conference of Ethiopian Studies, Addis Ababa, 1966</u>, A.A. 1970, vol.II, pp.133–9.

Albeck, H., <u>Midraš bəresit rabbati</u>, Jerusalem, 1940.

de Aldama, J., <u>Repertorium pseudochrysostomicum</u>, (Documents, études et répertoires publiés par l'Institut de Recherche et d'Histoire des Textes</u> X), Paris, 1965.

Alexander, P.S., The Toponymy of the Targumim with special reference
  to the Table of the Nations and the Boundaries of the land
  of Israel, Oxford D. Phil. thesis (unpublished), 1974.
  'Rabbinic Judaism and the New Testament', ZNW 74 (1983),
  pp.237-246.

Allenbach, J. et.al. (edd.), Biblia patristica: Index des citations
  et allusions bibliques dans la littérature patristique,
  Paris, 1975-77.

Altaner, B., 'Die Schrift ΠΕΡΙ ΤΟΥ ΜΕΛΧΙΣΕΔΕΚ des Eustathios von
  Antiocheia', BZ 40 (1940), pp.30-47.
  and Stuiber A., Patrologie: Leben, Schriften und Lehre der
  Kirchenväter, Freiburg, 1978.

Alula Hidaru and Dessalegn Rahmato (edd.), A Short Guide to the
  Study of Ethiopia. A General Bibliography, Westport and
  London, 1976.

Amməstu aʿəmadä məstir, A.A. (Tästa P.P.), 1952 E.C.

Andəmta, see Gäbrä ab et al., Gäbrä krəstos, Gäbrä krəstos, Gärima,
  Kəfle et al., Kidanä maryam, Mähari, Tewoflos, Wäldä rufaʾel
  et al.

Aphrahat, see Lafontaine, G., Neusner, J., Owens, R.J., Snaith, J.G.

Aptowitzer, V., 'Malkizedek, zu den Sagen der Agada', MGWJ 70
  (1926), pp.93-113.

Armstrong, G.T., Die Genesis in der Alten Kirche, Justin, Irenäus,
  Tertullian. (Beiträge zur Geschichte der biblischen Herm-
  eneutik 4) Tübingen, 1962.

Asräs Yänesäw, Yäkam mättasäbiya, Asmara, 1951 E.C.

Ayyalew Tamməru, Yäʾityopya əmnät bäsostu həggəgat, A.A., 1953 E.C.
  (ed.), Dərsanä mikaʾel, A.A. (Tənsaʾe P.P.), 1969 E.C.

Bacha, P., 'S. Jean Chrysostome dans la littérature arabe', in
  Χρυσοστομικα : Studi e ricerche intorno a S. Giovanni
  Crisostomo, Roma, 1908, pp.173-187.

Bachmann, J., Der Prophet Jesaia nach der aethiopischen Bibel-
  uebersetzung, Berlin, 1893.

Bailey, K.E., Poet and Peasant: A Literary Cultural Approach to the Parables in Luke, Grand Rapids, 1976.
'Hibat Allah ibn al-ʿAssāl and his Arabic thirteenth century critical edition of the gospels (with special attention to Luke 16:16 and 17:10)', Theological Review (The Near East School of Theology Beirut, Lebanon), vol.1 no.1 (1978), pp.11-26.
Through Peasant Eyes: More Lucan Parables, Their Culture and Style, Grand Rapids, 1980.

Baker, J. and Nicholson, E.W., The Commentary of Rabbi David Kimhi on Psalms CXX-CL, (Cambridge University Oriental Publications 22), Cambridge,1973.

Bakoš, J., Le candélabre des sanctuaires de Grégoire Aboulfaradj dit Barhebraeus, PO 22.4 and 24.3, Paris, 1930-3.

Bar Hebraeus, see Bakoš, J., Jansma, T., Khoury, J., Loehr, M., Sprengling, M. and Graham, W.C.

Barr, J., 'St. Jerome's Appreciation of Hebrew', BJRL 49 (1966-7), pp.281-302.

Basil of Caesarea, see Giet, S., Wace, H. and Schaff, P.

Baskin, J., Pharaoh's Counsellors: Job, Jethro, and Balaam in Rabbinic and Patristic Tradition (Brown Judaic Studies Series 47), 1983.

da Bassano, F., Bəluy Kidan, Asmara, vol.I, Octateuch, 1915 E.C.; vol.II, Kgs., Chron., Ezra, 1916 E.C.; vol.III, Tobit to Wisd., 1917 E.C.; vol.IV, prophets and (LXX) Macc., 1918 E.C.

Basset, R., Le Synaxaire arabe jacobite, PO 1.3 (Tout, Babeh), 3.3 (Hatour, Kihak), 11.5 (Toubeh, Amchir), 16.2 (Barmahat, Barmoudah, Bachons), 17.3 (Baounah, Abib, Mésoré), 20.5 (Tables).

Bate, H.N., 'Some Technical Terms of Greek Exegesis', JTS 24 (1922-3), pp.59-66.

Battista, A., and Baggati, B., La Caverna dei Tesori, (SBF 26), Jerusalem, 1979.
Il Combattimento di Adamo (SBF 29), Jerusalem, 1982.

Baumstark, A., Geschichte der syrischen Literatur, Bonn, 1922 (repr. 1968).

Beck, E., <u>Des heiligen Ephraem des Syrers Sermones, II</u>, <u>C.S.C.O.</u>
311 (= Syr. 134), 312 (= Syr. 135).

Bedjan, P., <u>Mar Isaacus Ninivita De Perfectione Religiosa</u>, Paris,
1909.

Belaynesh Michael, Chojnacki, S. and Pankhurst, R. (edd.), <u>The</u>
<u>Dictionary of Ethiopian Biography</u>, vol.I, <u>From Early Times</u>
<u>to the End of the Zagwé Dynasty c.1270 A.D.</u>, A.A., 1975.

<u>Bəluy Kidan</u>, vol.I, Asmara (Mahbärä hawaryat), 1955 E.C. (Geez
Octateuch and Jubilees).

Berhanou Abebbé, <u>Haymanotä abäw qäddämt: La foi des pères</u>
<u>anciens</u> (Studien zur Kulturkunde 79), Stuttgart, 1986.

Beyer, G., 'Die evangelischen Fragen und Lösungen des Eusebius in
jakobitischer Überlieferung und deren nestorianische Paral-
lelen', <u>OC</u>, neue Serie, zwölfter bis vierzehnter Band, for
years 1922-4, publ. 1925, pp.30-70, and dritte Serie, Band
1 (1927), pp.80-97, 284-292.

Beylot, R., <u>Commentaire éthiopien sur les bénédictions de Moïse et</u>
<u>de Jacob, C.S.C.O.</u> vols. 410, 411 (= Aeth. 73, 74), Louvain,
1979.
<u>Testamentum Domini Éthiopien</u>, Louvain, 1984.

Bezold, C., <u>Die Schatzhöhle</u>, Leipzig, 1883 and 1888.
<u>"Kebra Nagast". Die Herrlichkeit der Könige</u>, <u>KBAW</u> 23.1,
München, 1905.
'Das arabisch-äthiopische Testamentum Adami', <u>Orientalische</u>
<u>Studien Theodor Nöldeke zum siebzigsten Geburtstag</u>, Gieszen,
1906, pp.893-912.

Bickerman, E.J., <u>Chronology of the Ancient World</u>, London, 1968.

Bigg, C., <u>The Christian Platonists of Alexandria</u>, Oxford, second ed.
1913.

Black, G.F., <u>Ethiopica and Amharica; A List of Works in the New</u>
<u>York Public Library</u>, New York, 1928 (reproduced from the
<u>Bulletin of the New York Public Library</u>).

Blake, R.P. and de Vis, H., <u>Epiphanius de Gemmis</u>, (Studies and Documents II), London, 1934.

Bloemendaal, W., <u>The Headings of the Psalms in the East Syrian Church</u>, Leiden, 1960.

<u>Book of the Bee</u>, see Budge, E.A.W.

Bowker, J., <u>The Targums and Rabbinic Literature</u>, Cambridge, 1969.

Boyd, O., <u>The Octateuch in Ethiopic</u>, Leiden and Princeton, part I (Gen.), 1909; part II (Ex. and Lev.), 1911.

Brade, L., <u>Untersuchungen zum Scholienbuch des Theodoros bar Konai. Die Übernahme des Erbes von Theodoros von Mopsuestia in der nestorianischen Kirche</u>, <u>GOF</u> I.8, Wiesbaden, 1975.
'Die Herkunft von Prologen in den Paulusbriefexegesen des Theodoros bar Konai und Ishodad von Merv', <u>OC</u> 60 (1976), pp.162-71.
'Nestorianische Kommentare zu den Paulusbriefen an der Wende vom 8. zum 9. Jahrhundert', <u>ZDMG</u> Suppl. 4 (1980), pp.145-7.

Braude, W.G., <u>The Midrash on Psalms</u>, (Yale Judaica Series, vol.13), New Haven, 1959.
<u>Pesikta rabbati</u>, (Yale Judaica Series, vol.18), New Haven and London, 1968.
and Kapstein I.J., <u>Pĕsikta dĕ-Rab Kahăna</u>, London, 1975.
<u>Tanna dĕbe Eliyyahu: The lore of the School of Elijah</u>, Philadelphia, 1981.

Breydy, M., <u>Études sur Saʿīd ibn Batriq et ses Sources</u>, <u>C.S.C.O.</u> vol. 450 (= Subs. 69). (See also <u>C.S.C.O.</u> vols. 471-2).

Brock, S.P., 'Syriac Studies 1960-1970: A classified bibliography', <u>Parole de l'Orient</u> 4 (1973), pp.393-465.
'Some Syriac accounts of the Jewish sects', <u>TAV</u> pp.265-76.
'Jewish traditions in Syriac sources', <u>JJS</u> 30 (1979), pp.212-32.
'Genesis 22 in Syriac Tradition' in Casetti, P., Keel O., Schenker, A. (edd.) <u>Mélanges Dominique Barthélemy: études bibliques offertes a l'occasion de son 60e anniversaire</u>, (<u>Orbis biblicus et orientalis</u> 38), Fribourg/Göttingen, 1981, pp.1-30.

'Syriac Studies 1971–1980: A classified bibliography',
Parole de l'Orient 10 (1981–2), pp.291–412.

'Genesis 22: Where was Sarah?', ET 96 (1984) no.1, pp.14–17.

Syriac Perspectives on Late Antiquity, London, 1984.

Brooks, E.W. and Chabot, I.-B., Chronica minora, fasc. 2, C.S.C.O.
vols. 3, 4 (= Syr. III, 4), Louvain, 1904.

Brooks, E.W., Guidi, I. and Chabot, I.-B., Chronica minora, fasc. 3,
C.S.C.O. vols. 5, 6 (= Syr. III, 4), Louvain, 1905, 1907.

Buber, S., Midraš Leqah Tob (on Gen. and Ex.), Wilna, 1880.
Midrasch Aggadah, Vienna, 1894.
Midrasch Tehillim, Trier, 1892.
Aggadath Bereshith, Cracow, 1903.

Buchanan, G.W., To the Hebrews, (Anchor Bible), New York, 1972.

Budge, E.A. Wallis, 'The Book of the Bee', Anecdota Oxoniensia
(Semitic Series), vol. I, part II, Oxford, 1886.
The life and exploits of Alexander the Great, London, 1896.
Contendings of the Apostles, London, (text and translation)
vol. I, 1899; vol. II, 1901; (translation only) 1935.
One Hundred and Ten Miracles of Our Lady Mary, London, 1923.
The Book of the Cave of Treasures, London, 1927.
The Book of the Saints of the Ethiopian Church, Cambridge,
1928 (translation of Sǝnkǝssar).
The Bandlet of Righteousness, London, 1929.
The Chronography of Bar Hebraeus, Oxford, 1932.

Bundy, D., 'The "Questions and Answers" on Isaiah by Išoʿ bar Nūn',
OLP 16 (1985), pp.167–178.

Cave of Treasures, see Bezold, C., Budge, E.A.W.

Cerulli, E., Il libro etiopico dei Miracoli di Maria e le sue fonti
nelle letterature del Medio Evo latino, Roma, 1943.
Scritti teologici etiopici dei secoli XVI-XVII (Studi e
Testi) Città del Vaticano, 1958, 1960.
La Letteratura Etiopica, Milan, 1968.

Chabot, I.-B., <u>Iacobi Edesseni Hexaemeron seu in opus creationis</u>
<u>libri septem</u>, <u>C.S.C.O.</u> vol. 92 (= Syr. II, 56 = Syr. 44;
text only, for translation see Vaschalde, A.).
and Tonneau, R.M., <u>S. Cyrilli Alexandrini commentarii in</u>
<u>Lucam</u>, <u>C.S.C.O.</u> vols. 70, 140 (= Syr. IV, 1 = Syr. 27, 70).

Chaîne, M., <u>Apocrypha de Beati Maria Virgine</u>, <u>C.S.C.O.</u> vols. 39, 40
(= Aeth. I, 7 = Aeth. 22, 23).
'Répertoire des salâm et de malke'e contenus dans les manuscrits éthiopiens des bibliothèques d'Europe', <u>ROC</u> 1913,
pp.183-203, 337-47.
'Le Chronicon Orientale de Butros ibn ar-Rahib et l'histoire
de Girgis el-Makim', <u>ROC</u> 28 (1931-2), pp.390-405.

Charles, R.H. (ed.), <u>The Apocrypha and Pseudepigrapha of the Old</u>
<u>Testament</u>, Oxford, 1913.

<u>The Chronicle of John, Bishop of Nikiu, translated from</u>
<u>Zotenberg's Ethiopic Text</u>, London, 1916.

Charlesworth, J.H., <u>The Pseudepigrapha and modern research with a</u>
<u>supplement</u>, Ann Arbor, 1981.
(ed.), <u>The Old Testament Pseudepigrapha</u>, vol. I, New York,
1983.

Chase, F.H., <u>Chrysostom: A Study in the History of Biblical</u>
<u>Interpretation</u>, Cambridge, 1887.

Chavel, C.B., <u>Ramban (Nachmanides): Commentary on the Torah</u>,
New York, 1971-6.

Cheikho, L., <u>Petrus ibn Rahib. Chronicon orientale</u>, <u>C.S.C.O.</u>,
vols. 45, 46 (= Ar.III, 1 = Ar. 1 and 2).
<u>Eutychii patriarchae Alexandrini annales</u>, <u>I</u>, <u>C.S.C.O.</u> vol.
50 (= Ar.III, 6 = Ar.6).
Carra de Vaux, B. and Zayyat, H., <u>Eutychii patriarchae</u>
<u>Alexandrini annales, II</u>, <u>C.S.C.O.</u>, vol.51 (= Ar.III, 7 =
Ar.7).

Chesnut, R.C., Three Monophysite Christologies: Severus of Antioch,
        Philoxenus of Mabbug, and Jacob of Serug, Oxford, 1976.

Chojnacki, S., Major Themes in Ethiopian Painting, (AF 10),
        Wiesbaden, 1983.

Chronicles of Jerahmeel, see Gaster, M.

Chronicon orientale, see Cheikho, L.

Chrysostom, see John Chrysostom.

Clarke, E.G., The selected Questions of Ishō bar Nun on the
        Pentateuch, with a study of the relationship of Ishōᶜdādh
        of Merv, Theodore bar Kōni and Ishō bar Nun on Genesis,
        Leyde, 1962.

Coakley, J.F., The Homilies of Mošе bar Kepha on the early chapters
        of the gospels, (unpublished Cambridge PhD thesis, PhD 10353,
        Sept. 1977).
        'The Old Man Simeon (Luke 2.25) in Syriac Tradition', OCP
        47.1 (1981), pp. 189-212.

Colson, F.H., Whitaker, G.H. and Marcus, R., Philo, Harvard,
        1929-53.

Cooper, J. and Maclean, A.J., The Testament of Our Lord,
        Edinburgh, 1902.

Coquin, R., 'Le Testamentum Domini: problèmes de tradition
        textuelle', Parole de l'Orient 5.1 (1974), pp.165-88.

Cowley, R.W., 'The Ethiopian Orthodox Church, some bibliographical
        notes', Sobornost, Summer 1965, pp.45-51.
        'The Ethiopian Church and the Council of Chalcedon',
        Sobornost 6/1 (1970), pp.33-38.
        'Preliminary notes on the balåandəm Commentaries', JES 9.1
        (1971), pp.9-20.
        'The Beginnings of the andəm Commentary Tradition', JES
        10.2 (1972), pp.1-16.

'Old Testament Introduction in the Andemta Commentary Tradition', <u>JES</u> 12.1 (1974), pp.133-75.

'The Biblical Canon of the Ethiopian Orthodox Church Today', <u>OKLS</u> 23.4 (1974), pp.318-23.

'A text in Old Amharic', <u>BSOAS</u> 37/3 (1974), pp.597-607.

'An Ethiopian Orthodox Catechism on the 'Five Pillars of Mystery', <u>Sobornost</u> 7.4 (1977), pp.298-306.

'New Testament Introduction in the Andemta Commentary Tradition', <u>OKLS</u> 26. 2/3 (1977), pp.144-92.

'The Identification of the Ethiopian Octateuch of Clement', <u>OKLS</u> 27.1 (1978), pp.37-45.

'Patristic Introduction in the Ethiopian Andəmta Commentary Tradition', <u>OKLS</u> 29.1 (1980), pp.39-49.

'Scholia of Aḥob of Qaṭar on St. John's Gospel and the Pauline Epistles', <u>Le Muséon</u> 93. 3-4 (1980), pp.329-43.

'Ludolf's <u>Fragmentum Piquesii</u>: an old Amharic tract about Mary who anointed Jesus' feet', <u>JSS</u> 28/1 (1983), pp.1-47.

'A Geez Prologue concerning the work of Mämhər Kəflä giyorgis on the text and interpretation of the Book of Ezekiel' in Segert, S. and Bodrogligeti, A.J.E. (edd.), <u>Ethiopian Studies, Dedicated to Wolf Leslau</u>, Wiesbaden, 1983, pp.99-114.

The Traditional Interpretation of the Apocalypse of
St. John in the Ethiopian Orthodox Church, (Cambridge
Oriental Publications 33), Cambridge, 1983.
Review of EMML Catalogue vol.VII, in JSS, 29/2 (1984),pp.325-338.
'The Ethiopic work which is believed to contain the material
of the ancient Greek Apocalypse of Peter', JTS n.s. 36.1
(April 1985), pp.151-3.
'The so-called "Ethiopic Book of the Cock" - part of an
apocryphal passion gospel, The Homily and Teaching of our
Fathers the holy Apostles', JRAS 1985, pp.16-22.
'The 'blood of Zechariah' (Mt. 23:35) in Ethiopian exeget-
ical tradition', Studia Patristica XVIII, vol.I, pp. 293-302.
'Mamhar Esdros and his Interpretations', Ethiopian Studies:
Proceedings of the sixth international conference, Tel Aviv,
14-17 April 1980, (ed.) Goldenberg, G., Rotterdam/Boston,
1986, pp.41-69.
Review of R. Beylot, Testamentum Domini Éthiopien, JSS,
(forthcoming).
'A Geʿez document reporting controversy concerning the
Bible commentaries of Ibn aṭ-Ṭaiyib', RSE XXX (1984-1986),
pp.5-13.

Crossan, J.D., The dark interval: towards a theology of story,
        Niles, Illinois, 1975.

Culi, Y. (Rabbi), translated by Kaplan, A., The Torah Anthology
        MeAm Lo'ez, New York, 1977 - .

Cyril of Alexandria, see Chabot, I.-B. and Tonneau, R.M.,
        Kerrigan, A., Weischer, B.M.

Danby, H., The Mishnah, Oxford, repr. 1954.

Daoud, M., The Liturgy of the Ethiopian Church, A.A., 1954 A.D.

Dästa, Mämhər (= Abunä Abrəham) (ed.), Arägawi mänfäsawi, A.A., 1922 E.C.

Dästa Ɜsäte, Aläqa (ed.), Mar Yəshaq, A.A., 1920 E.C., (AC on Mar Yəshaq).

Dästa Täklä wäld, Addis yamarəñña mäzgäbä qalat, A.A., 1962 E.C.

Daube, D., 'Rabbinic Methods of Interpretation and Hellenistic Rhetoric', HUCA 22 (1949), pp.239–264.

le Déaut, R., 'Apropos a Definition of Midrash', Interpretation 25 (1971), pp.259–282.

Derenbourg, J., Oeuvres complètes de R. Saadia ben Iosef al-Fayyoumī, 5 vols. Paris, 1893–9, repr. in 2 vols., Hildesheim and New York, 1979.

Dərsanä gäbrə'el, see Mäkwəriya.

Dərsanä mika'el, see Ayyalew.

Devreesse, R., 'Anciens commentateurs grecs de l'Octateuque', RB 44 (1935), pp.166–191; 45 (1936), pp.201–220, 364–384.
'La méthode exégétique de Théodore de Mopsueste', RB 1946, pp.207–241.
Essai sur Théodore de Mopsueste (Studi e Testi 141), Vatican City, 1948.

Didymus the Blind, see Nautin, P. and Doutreleau, L.

Díez Macho, A., Neophyti 1. Targum Palestinense MS de la Biblioteca Vaticana, Madrid–Barcelona, 1968–79.

Dillmann, A., Biblia Veteris Testamenti Aethiopica, Leipzig, 1853–94.
Lexicon Linguae Aethiopicae, Lipsiae, 1865 (repr. New York, 1955).
Chrestomathia Aethiopica, Lipsiae, 1866.

Dionysius bar Ṣalibi, see Sanders, J.C.J., Sedláček, I., Sedláček, I. and Chabot, I.-B., Vaschalde, A.

van Donzel, E.J., ʿEnbāqom, Anqasa Amin (La Porte de la Foi), Leiden, 1969.

Doutreleau, L., Origène: Homélies sur la Genèse, (Sources Chrétiennes 7 bis), Paris, 1976.

Drijvers, H.J.W., <u>East of Antioch.   Studies in early Syriac Christianity</u>, London, 1984.

Egan, G.A., <u>Saint Ephrem, an exposition of the Gospel</u>, C.S.C.O. vols. 291-2 (= Arm.5-6).

Emmanuel bar Shaḥḥare, see Ten Napel, E.

Ǝnbaqom Qalä wäld, <u>Collection of Sources for the Study of Ethiopian Culture, Documents on Traditional Ethiopian Education</u>, nos. 1-2 (in Amharic), duplicated by Institute of Ethiopian Studies, A.A., June and August 1965 A.D. (see also Imbaqom).

Endress, G., <u>The works of Yaḥyā ibn ʿAdī.   An analytical inventory</u>, Wiesbaden, 1977.

Enelow, H.G., <u>The Mishnah of R. Eliezer, or The Midrash of the thirty-two Hermeneutical Rules</u>, New York, 1933.

Ephraim, <u>S. Ephrem Syri Commentarii in Epistolas D. Pauli nunc primum ex Armenio in Latinum sermonem a patribus Mekith-aristis translati</u>, Venetiis, 1893.
    see also Beck, E., Egan, G.A., Hidal, S., Jansma, T., Kronholm, T., Leloir, L., Mahr, A.C., Tonneau, R.M.

Epiphanius, see Blake, R.P. and de Vis, H., Haffner, A., Trumpp, E.

Epstein, I. (ed.), <u>The Babylonian Talmud</u>, London, 1948-62.

Euringer, S., <u>Die Auffasung des Hohenliedes bei den Abessiniern. Ein historisch - exegetischer Versuch</u>, Leipzig, 1900.
    '« Schöpferische Exegese » im äthiopischen Hohenliede', <u>Biblica</u> 17 (1936), pp.327-344, 479-500.
    'Ein äthiopische Scholienkommentar zum Hohenlied', <u>Biblica</u> 18 (1937), pp.257-76, 369-82.
    '« Schöpferische Exegese » im äthiopischen Hohenliede. Nachträge', <u>Biblica</u> 20 (1939), pp.27-37.
    'Un frammento di Midrasch di Melchisedech nella Liturgia dell'Osanna Etiopica', <u>RSE</u> 3 (1943), pp.50-60.

Eusebius of Caesarea, see Beyer, G.

Eustathius of Antioch, see Altaner, B., Spanneut, M.

Eutychius of Alexandria, see Breydy, M., Cheikho, L.

Fǝqrä dǝngǝl Bäyyänä, 'Yäʾandǝmta tǝrgwame läʾamarǝnna ǝdgät', <u>Zena lǝssan</u> 2.2, A.A., Näḥasse 1974 E.C.

Filəppos, Abba, Əgziʾabəher kanna gara, A.A., 1957 E.C.

Fouyas, M.G., The Person of Jesus Christ in the Decisions of the
  Ecumenical Councils, A.A., 1976.

Freedman, H. and Simon, M., The Midrash Rabba, London, 1939 and
  reprints.

Frei, H.W., The Eclipse of Biblical Narrative, New Haven and
  London, 1974.

Friedländer, G., Pirke deRabbi Eliezer, London, 1916.

Gäbrä ab, Aläqa, Tabqe, Aläqa and Wäldäyäss, Gra geta (edd.) Fətha
  nägäst, A.A., 1958 E.C. (AC on Fətha nägäst).

Gäbrä krəstos, Abba (ed.), Filkəsyus, A.A., 1920 E.C. (AC on
  Filkəsyus).

Gäbrä krəstos, Liqe (ed.), Yohannəs afa wärq, Tagsas, A.A., 1915
  and 1924 E.C.
  Yohannəs afa wärq, Dərsan, A.A., 1923 E.C. (AC on John
  Chrysostom's Homilies on Hebrews).

Gäbrəʾel, Abuna, Ortodoks haymanot, Asmara, 1983 A.D.

Gärima, Mämhər (= Abuna Mikaʾel) (ed.), Mashafa qəddase, A.A., 1918
  and 1926 E.C. (AC on the Ethiopic liturgy).

Gaster, M., The Chronicles of Jerahmeel, (repr.) New York, 1971.

Gəbrä həmamat, see Wäldä mikaʾel.

Geerard, M., Clavis Patrum Graecorum, Turnhout, 1974-.

Gertner, M., 'Midrashim in the New Testament', JSS 7 (1962), pp.
  267-92.

Getatchew Haile, 'Materials for the study of the Theology of Qəbat',
  Proceedings of the Sixth International Conference of
  Ethiopian Studies, Tel Aviv , pp.205-250.
  'Religious Controversies and the Growth of Ethiopic Liter-
  ature in the Fourteenth and Fifteenth Centuries', OC 65
  (1981), pp.102-136.
  'On the Writings of Abba Giyorgis Säglawi from Two Unedited
  Miracles of Mary', OCP 48 (1982), pp.65-91.
  'The Homily of Zärʾa Yaʿəqob in Honour of St. John the Evan-
  gelist, EMML 1480, ff.48r-52v', OC 67 (1983), pp.144-66.

Gibson, M.D., <u>Apocrypha Arabica. Kitab al-Magall or The Book of</u>
<u>the Rolls</u>, (<u>Studia Sinaitica</u> VIII), London, 1901.

    <u>The Commentaries of Isho⁶dad on the Gospels, Horae Semiticae</u>
<u>V</u> (translation), VI (Syriac text, Mt. and Mk.), VII (Syriac
text, Lk. and Jn.), Cambridge, 1911-.
    <u>The Commentaries of Isho⁶dad on the Epistles of St. Paul,</u>
<u>Horae Semiticae</u> XI, pt. 1 Syriac, pt.II English, Cambridge,
1916.
    <u>The Commentaries of Isho⁶dad on the Acts and Catholic</u>
<u>Epistles, Horae Semiticae</u> X.

Giet, S., <u>Basile de Césarée. Homélies sur l'Hexaeméron</u>, (<u>Sources</u>
<u>chrétiennes</u> 26 bis), Paris, 1968.

Gignoux, Ph., <u>Homélies de Narsaï sur la création</u>, <u>PO</u> 34.3-4,
Turnhout, 1968.

Ginzberg, L., <u>Die Haggada bei den Kirchenvätern und in der apokry-</u>
<u>phischen Literatur</u>, Berlin, 1900.
    <u>Legends of the Jews</u>, Philadelphia, 1911-38.

Giyorgis of Gasəčča, see Getatchew, Leander, P., <u>Mäshafä arganon</u>.

Gleave, H.C., <u>The Ethiopic Version of the Song of Songs</u>, London, 1951.

Gobat, S., <u>Journal of a Three Years' Residence in Abyssinia</u>,
London, 1834 and 1847.

Götze, A., <u>Die Schatzhöhle, Überlieferung und Quellen</u>, <u>SHAW</u>, Abh.4,
Heidelberg, 1922.

Graf, G., <u>Geschichte der christlichen arabischen Literatur</u>, (<u>Studi</u>
<u>e testi</u> vols. 118, 133, 146, 147, 172), Vatican City, 1944-53.
    'Zwei dogmatische Florilegium der Kopten', <u>OCP</u> 3 (1937), pp.
49-77, 345-402.
    'Ein arabischer Pentateuchkommentar des 12. Jahrhunderts',
<u>Biblica</u> 23 (1942), pp.113-138.

Graffin, F., 'Deux homélies anonymes sur la pécheresse', <u>L'Orient</u>
<u>Syrien</u> 7 (1962), pp.175-222.

Grébaut, S., 'Littérature Éthiopienne Pseudo-Clémentine', <u>ROC</u> 1907,
pp.139-51, 285-97, 380-92; 1908, pp.166-80, 314-20; 1910,
pp.198-214, 307-23, 425-39; 1911, pp.72-84, 167-175, 225-
233; 1912, pp.16-31, 133-144, 244-252, 337-346; 1913, pp.

69–78; 1914, pp.324–330; 1915–17, pp.33–7, 424–430;
1918–19, pp.246–252; 1920–1, pp.22–28, 113–7; 1927–8,
pp.22–31.

'La Légende du parfum de Marie-Madeleine', ROC 1918–19,
pp.100–3.

Les miracles de Jésus, PO 12.4, 14.5, 17.4.

and Roman, A., 'Un passage eschatologique de Qalēmentos',
Aethiops year 3 no.2, pp.21–3.

Greer, R.A., Theodore of Mopsuestia, Exegete and Theologian,
London, 1961.

Griffith, S.H., 'Chapter ten of the Scholion: Theodore Bar Kōnī's
Apology for Christianity', OCP 47.1 (1981), pp.158–88.
'Theodore bar Kōnī's Scholion: A Nestorian Summa contra
Gentiles from the first Abbasid century', in Garsoïan, N.,
Mathews, T. and Thompson, R., East of Byzantium: Syria and
Armenia in the Formative Period, Washington, 1982, pp.53–72.

Grossfeld, B., A Bibliography of Targum Literature, New York, 1972
(vol. I), 1977 (vol. II).

Guerrier, L. and Grébaut, S., Le Testament en Galilée de Notre-
Seigneur Jésus-Christ, PO 9.3.

Guidi, I., 'La Traduzione Copta di un'Omelia di S. Efrem',
Bessarione 7, fasc. 70 (Jan.–Feb. 1903).
Chronica minora, fasc.1, C.S.C.O. vols. 1, 2 (= Syr. III,4),
Louvain, 1903 (see also Brooks, E.W.).
Storia della letteratura etiopica, Roma, 1932.

Guillaumont, A., 'Un midrash d'Exode 4, 24–26 chez Aphraate et
Ephrem de Nisibe', TAV pp.89–95.

Guillet, J., 'Les exégèses d'Alexandrie et d'Antioche, conflit ou
malentendu?', Recherches de Science Religieuse 34 (1947),
pp.257–302.

Habasselet, M., Midraš hahefes, Jerusalem, 1981.

Habtä maryam Wärqnäh (Liqä saltanat), Yä'ityopya ortodoks täwahədo
betä krəstiyan əmnätənna təmhərt, A.A. (Bərhanənna sälam P.P.),
1963 E.C.
Təntawi yä'ityopya sərʿatä təmhərt, A.A. (Bərhanənna sälam
P.P.), 1963 E.C.

Habte Mariam Worquineh (= Habtä maryam Wärqnäh), 'The Mystery of
    the Incarnation', GOTR 10/2 (1964-5), pp.154-60.

Haddis Kidan: wängel qəddus zä'əgzi'ənä wämädhaninä iyyäsus
    krəstos wämäsahəftihomu lähawaryat qəddusan (Geez N.T.),
    Asmara (Franciscan Press), repr. 1952.

Haffner, A., 'Eine äthiopische Handschrift der k.k. Hofbibliothek
    in Wien zu den pseudo-epiphanischen Werke', Vienna Oriental
    Journal (= Wiener Zeitschrift für die Kunde des Morgenlandes)
    26 (1912), pp.363-87;
    'Das Hexaëmeron des Pseudo-Epiphanius', OC n.s. 10 (1923,
    for years 1920-21), pp.91-145.

Haile-Gabriel Dagne, 'The Scriptorium at the Imperial Palace and
    the Manuscripts of Addis Ababa Churches', Proceedings of the
    Eighth International Conference of Ethiopian Studies, Addis
    Ababa, November 26-30, 1984 (forthcoming).

Halévy, J., Te'ézäza Sanbat. Commandements du Sabbath, Paris, 1902.

Hall, S.H., Melito of Sardis. On Pascha and fragments, Oxford, 1979.

Hammerschmidt, E., Äthiopische liturgische Texte der Bodleian
    Library in Oxford, (Deutsche Akademie der Wissenschaften zu
    Berlin, Institut für Orientforschung no.38), Berlin, 1960.
    Studies in the Ethiopic Anaphoras, Berlin, 1961.

Hanson, A.T., The Living Utterances of God, London, 1983.

Hanson, R.P.C., Allegory and Event, London, 1959.

Hay, D.M., Glory at the Right Hand: Psalm 110 in Early Christianity
    (SBL Monograph series 18), Abingdon, 1973.

Hayek, M., 'Ammār al-Basrī. Apologie et Controverses, (Recherches
    publiées sous la direction de l'Institut de Lettres Orien-
    tales de Beyrouth, Nouvelle série B. Orient Chrétien tome V),
    Beyrouth, 1977.

Haylä mäsqäl Gäbrä mädhən (Liqä liqawnt) et al., Sərwä haymanot,
    A.A. (Artistic Press), 1960 E.C.

Haymanotä abäw, A.A. (Tənsa'e zäguba'e P.P.), 1967 E.C.

Henderson, E., The Book of the Prophet Isaiah, London, 1840.

Hennecke, E. (ed. Schneemelcher, W., trans. Wilson, R.M.), <u>New Testament Apocrypha</u>, London, 1963–5.

Henry, Matthew, <u>An exposition of all the books of the Old and New Testament</u>, London, 1725.

Hespel, R. and Draguet, R., <u>Théodore bar Koni: Livre des Scolies (recension de Séert)</u>, I, <u>Mimrè</u> I–V; II, <u>Mimrè</u> VI–XI, <u>C.S.C.O.</u> vols. 431–2 (= Syr. 187–8), Louvain, 1981, 1982. (For the recension of Urmiah, see <u>C.S.C.O.</u> vols. 447–8, 464–5).

Hibat Állah, see Bailey, K.E.

Hidal, S., <u>Interpretatio Syriaca. Die Kommentare des hl. Ephram des Syrers zu Genesis und Exodus</u>, Lund, 1974.

Hirschberg, J.W., <u>Jüdische und christliche Lehren im vor- und frühislamischen Arabien</u>, Cracow, 1939.

Hoenerbach, W. and Spies, O., <u>Ibn aṭ-Taiyib. Fiqh an-nasraniya «Das Recht der Christenheit»</u>, <u>C.S.C.O.</u> vols. 161–2 (= Ar. 16, 17), vols. 167–8 (= Ar. 18, 19), Louvain, 1956, 1957.

Hoffmann, G., <u>Opuscula nestoriana</u>, Kiel, 1880.

Hofmann, J., <u>Die äthiopische Übersetzung der Johannes-Apokalypse</u>, C.S.C.O. vols. 281–2 (= Aeth. 55–6), Louvain, 1967.
<u>Die äthiopische Johannes-Apokalypse kritisch untersucht</u>, <u>C.S.C.O.</u>, vol. 297 (= Subs. 33), Louvain, 1969.

Horner, G.W. (ed.), <u>The Coptic Version of the New Testament in the Northern Dialect</u>, Oxford, 1898–1905.
<u>The Coptic Version of the New Testament in the Southern Dialect</u>, Oxford, 1911–24.

Hubbard, D.A., <u>The literary sources of the Kebra Nagast</u>, unpublished PhD thesis, St. Andrews University, 1956.

Hughes, G., <u>Hebrews and Hermeneutics. The epistle to the Hebrews as a New Testament example of Biblical Interpretation</u>, (SNTS monograph 36), Cambridge, 1979.

Hughes, P.E., <u>A Commentary on the Epistle to the Hebrews</u>, Grand Rapids, 1977.

Ibn aṭ-Taiyib, see Cowley, R., Hoenerbach, W. and Spies, O., Sanders, J.C.J., Stern, S.M.

Imbaqom Kalewold, Alaka, <u>Traditional Ethiopian Church Education</u>, New York, 1970 (see also Ɜnbaqom).

Isaac of Nineveh, see Bedjan, P., Dästa Ɜšäte, Wensinck, A.J.

Isaverdentz, H., <u>The uncanonical writings of the Old Testament</u>, Venice, 1901.

Išoʿ bar Nun, see Clarke, E.G., van Rompay, L., Bundy, D.

Išoʿdad of Merv, see Gibson, M.D., Levene, A., van den Eynde, C., van Rompay, L., Vosté, I.M. and van den Eynde, C.

Jacob of Edessa, see Chabot, I.-B., Martin, P., Phillips, G., Vaschalde, A.

Jacob of Serug, see Jansma, T.

Jacobs, L., <u>The Talmudic Argument</u>, Cambridge, 1984.

James, M.R., <u>The Biblical Antiquities of Philo</u>, London, 1917.
<u>The Apocryphal New Testament</u>, Oxford, 1924.

Jansma, T., 'Investigations into the Early Syrian Fathers on Genesis', <u>Oudtestamentische Studien</u> 12 (1958), pp.69–181.
'L'Hexaméron de Jacques de Sarûg', <u>L'Orient Syrien</u> 4 (1959), pp.3–42, 129–62, 253–84.
'Une homelie anonyme sur la chute d'Adam', <u>L'Orient Syrien</u> 5 (1960), pp.159–82, 253–92.
'Théodore de Mopsueste. Interpretation du Livre de la Genèse: Fragments de la version syriaque (BM Add. 17189 f.17–21)', <u>Le Muséon</u> 75 (1962), pp.63–92.
'Narsai and Ephraem. Some observations on Narsai's Homilies on Creation and Ephraem's Hymns on Faith', <u>Parole de l'Orient</u> 1 (1970), pp.49–68.
'Barhebraeus' Scholion on the words 'Let there be light' (Gen.1:3) as presented in his 'Storehouse of Mysteries',' <u>Abr Nahrain</u> 13 (1972/3), pp.100–14.

Jart, U., 'The Precious Stones in the Revelation of St. John xxi. 18–21', <u>Studia Theologica</u> 24 (1970), pp.150–81.

Jastrow, M., <u>A Dictionary of the Targumim, the Talmud Babli and Yerushalmi, and the Midrashic Literature</u>, repr. New York, 1950.

Jellicoe, S., <u>The Septuagint and Modern Study</u>, New York – London, 1968.

John Chrysostom, see ⁽Abd al Masīḥ, Bacha, P., Chase, F.H.,
  Liqe Gäbrä krǝstos, Schaff, P.

John of Nikiu, see Charles, R.H.

John Philoponus, see Reichardt, W.

Kaplan, S.B., The Monastic Holy Man and the Christianization of
  Early Solomonic Ethiopia, (Studien zur Kulturkunde 73),
  Wiesbaden, 1984.

Kasher, M.M., Tora Šlema (in Hebrew), Jerusalem, 1895–; partial
  English translation in Encyclopedia of Biblical Interpretation, New York, 1953–.

Kǝflä giyorgis and Kidanä wäld Kǝfle, Mashafä säwasǝw wägǝss
  wämäzgäbä qalat haddis, A.A., 1948 E.C.

Kǝfle, Mäl'akä gännät, Haylä sǝllase, Aläqa and Märsǝ'e hazän
  Wäldä qirqos, Blatta (ed.), Mäsahǝftä sälomon wäsirak, A.A.,
  1917 E.C. (AC on books of Solomon and Ecclus.).

Kehrer, H., Die "Heiligen drei Könige" in der Legende und in der
  deutschen bildenden Kunst bis Albrecht Dürer, (Studien zur
  deutschen Kunstgeschichte, Hft. 53, 1894 etc.).

Kelly, J.N.D., Early Christian Doctrines, London, 1958.

Kerrigan, A., St. Cyril of Alexandria, Interpreter of the Old
  Testament, (Analecta biblica no.2), Roma, 1952.

Khoury, J., Le candélabre du sanctuaire de Grégoire Abou'lfaradj
  dit Barhebraeus. Quatrième base: de l'incarnation, PO
  31.1, Paris, 1965.

Kidanä maryam, Abba (ed.), Tǝmhǝrtä habu⁽atǝnna sälotä kidan,
  A.A., repr. 1963 E.C.

Kidänä maryam Getahun, Tǝntawiw yäqollo tämari, A.A., 1954 E.C.

Kidänä wäld Kǝfle, Mashafä hǝzqǝ'el, Dire Dawa, 1916 E.C.

Kilgour, R. (ed), The New Testament in Syriac, London, 1950.

Kimhi, D., see Baker,J. and Nicholson, E.W., Talmage, F.E.

Kinefe-rigb Zelleke, 'Bibliography of the Ethiopic Hagiographical
  Traditions', JES 13.2 (1975), pp.57-102.

Kisch, G., <u>Pseudo-Philo's Liber Antiquitatum Biblicarum</u>, Notre
    Dame, Indiana, 1949.

<u>Kitab al-Majall</u>, see Gibson, M.D.

Knibb, M.A., 'The Ethiopic version of the lives of the prophets:
    Ezekiel and Daniel', <u>BSOAS</u> 43 (1980), pp.197-206.
    'The Ethiopic version of the Lives of the Prophets, II:
    Isaiah, Jeremiah, Haggai, Zechariah, Malachi, Elijah,
    Elisha, Nathan, Ahijah, and Joel', <u>BSOAS</u> 48.1 (1985),
    pp.16-41.
    and Ullendorff, E., <u>The Ethiopic Book of Enoch</u>, Oxford, 1978.

Kobelski, P.J., Melchizedek and Melchireša', (<u>CBQ</u> monograph series
    10), Washington, 1981.

Kratchkovsky, I. and Vasiliev, A., <u>Histoire de Yahya-ibn-Saʿid
    d'Antioche</u>, <u>PO</u> 18.5, 23.3.

Krauss, S., 'The Jews in the works of the Church Fathers', <u>JQR</u>
    5, pp.122-157; 6, pp.82-99, 225-261.

Kronholm, T., <u>Motifs from Genesis 1-11 in the genuine hymns of
    Ephrem the Syrian</u>, Lund, 1978.
    'The Portrayal of Characters in Midrash Ruth Rabbah.
    Observations on the formation of the Jewish hermeneutical
    legend known as 'biblical haggadah',' in Larsson, G. (ed.),
    <u>Annual of the Swedish Theological Institute</u>, vol.12,
    Leiden, 1983, pp.13-54.

Kropp, M., 'Ein äthiopischer Text zu Peter Heyling: Ein bisher
    unbeachtetes Fragment einer Chronik des Fāsiladas', in
    Rubenson, S. (ed.), <u>Proceedings of the Seventh International
    Conference of Ethiopian Studies, University of Lund, 26-29
    April 1982</u>, A.A., Uppsala, and East Lansing, 1984, pp.243-
    256.

Kutscher, E.Y., <u>A History of the Hebrew Language</u>, Leiden, 1982.

Lafontaine, G., <u>La version arménienne des oeuvres d'Aphraate le
    Syrien</u>, <u>C.S.C.O.</u> vols. 382-3 (= Arm. 7, 8), 405-6 (= Arm.
    9, 10), 1977, 1979.

de Lagarde, P., <u>Der Pentateuch koptisch</u>, Leipzig, 1867.
    <u>Materialien zur Kritik und Geschichte des Pentateuchs</u>,

Leipzig, 1867.

Catenae in Evangelia aegypticae quae supersunt, Goettingae, 1886.

Mittheilungen, 4 vols. Göttingen, 1884-91.

Laistner, M.L.W., 'Antiochene Exegesis in Western Europe during the Middle Ages', HTR 40 (1947), pp.19-31.

Lamirande, É., 'Étude bibliographique sur les Pères de l'Eglise et l'Aggada', Vig.Chr. 21 (1967), pp.1-11.

Lampe, G.W.H. and Woolcombe, K.G., Essays in Typology (Studies in Biblical Theology 22), London, 1957.

de Lange, N.R.M., Origen and the Jews, (Cambridge Oriental Publications 25), Cambridge, 1976.

Leander, P., Arganona Weddase, nach Handschriften in Uppsala, Berlin, Tübingen und Frankfurt a.M., Göteborg, 1922.

Leloir, L., S. Éphrem. Commentaire de l'Évangile concordant, version arménienne, C.S.C.O, vols. 137, 145 (= Arm. 1, 2), Louvain, 1953, 1954.

Leslau, W., Falasha Anthology (Yale Judaica Series 6), New Haven, 1951.

An annotated bibliography of the Semitic languages of Ethiopia, The Hague, 1965.

Levene, A., The early Syrian Fathers on Genesis, London, 1951.

'Remarque sur deux commentaires syriaques de la Genèse', L'Orient Syrien 5 (1960), pp.55-62.

'Some observations on the commentaries of Isho'dad Bishop of Hadatta and of the Manuscript Mingana 553 on Genesis', TU 79 (1961) (= Studia Patristica 4), pp.136-42.

'The Blessings of Jacob in Syriac and Rabbinic exegesis', TU 92 (1966) (= Studia Patristica 7), pp.524-30.

Lewis, J., A Study of the Interpretation of Noah and the Flood in Jewish and Christian Literature, Leiden, 1968, repr. 1978.

Lockot, H.W., Bibliographia Aethiopica: Die Äthiopienkundliche Literatur des Deutschsprachigen Raums, (AF 9), Wiesbaden, 1982.

Loehr, M., <u>Gregorii Abulfaragii bar Ebhraya in Epistulas Paulinas adnotationes</u>, Göttingae, 1889.

Loewe, R., 'The Jewish Midrashim and Patristic and Scholastic Exegesis of the Bible', <u>Studia Patristica</u> 1, pp.492–514.

Lowy, S., <u>The Principles of Samaritan Bible Exegesis</u>, (Studia Post-Biblica 28), Leiden, 1977.

Ludolf, H., <u>Lexicon Aethiopico-Latinum</u>, Frankfort, 1661 and 1699.

Mahari Tərfe, <u>Liqä liqawnt</u> (= <u>Abunä</u> Petros) (ed.), <u>Yäqəddus Pawlos mäshaf</u>, A.A., 1948 E.C. (AC on Pauline corpus). <u>Mäsahəftä haddisat sostu</u>, A.A., 1951 E.C. (AC on Acts, Catholic epp. and Rev.).

Mahr, A.C., <u>Relation of Passion Plays to St. Ephrem the Syrian</u>, Columbus, 1942.

Mäkwəriya Abəyye hoy (ed.), <u>Dərsanä gäbrə'el</u>, A.A. (Tənsa'e zäguba'e P.P.), 1969 E.C.

Malan, S.C., <u>The Book of Adam and Eve, also called the Conflict of Adam and Eve with Satan</u>, London, 1882.

Mänkər Mäkwännən (Mämhər), <u>Mäshetä liqawnt</u>, A.A., 1972 E.C.

Mansi, J.D., <u>Sacrorum conciliorum nova et amplissima collectio</u>, Florentiae, 1757–.

Margulies (= Margolioth), M., <u>Midraš haggadol</u>, Jerusalem, repr. 1975.

Mario da Abiy-Addi, P., <u>La Dottrina della Chiesa Etiopica dissidente sull 'Unione Ipostatica</u>, (<u>OCA</u> 147), Rome, 1956.

Marshall, I.H. (ed.), <u>New Testament Interpretation: Essays on Principles and Methods</u>, Grand Rapids, 1977.

Martin, P., 'L'Hexaméron de Jacques d'Édesse', <u>JA</u> sér.8, tom.11 (1888), pp.155–219, 401–40.

<u>Mäsärätä təmhərt</u>, A.A. (Täsfa P.P.), 1949 E.C.

<u>Mäshaf qəddus bägə'əzənna bä'amaranna yätäsafä</u>, 4 vol. Geez and Amharic Bible reproduced by photolithography in London, n.d.

<u>Mäshaf qəddus yäbəluyənna yähaddis kidan mäsahəft</u>, A.A., 1953 E.C. (large Amharic Bible).

Mäshafä arganon zäʾabba giyorgis, A.A. (published by Aläqa Wäldä
        hanna Täklä haymanot), 1959 E.C.

Mäshafä ganzät, A.A. (Tansaʾe zägubaʾe P.P.), 1944 E.C.

Mäshafä qaddase, A.A. (Täsfa P.P.), 1951 E.C. (Geez and Amharic
        diglot; for AC Qaddase see Gärima).

Mäshafä tanbitä näbiyat, Asmara (Mahbärä hawaryat), 1977 E.C.

Matt, D.C., Zohar. The Book of Enlightenment, London, 1983.

McKnight, E.V., Meaning in Texts: The Historical Shaping of a
        Narrative Hermeneutics, Philadelphia, 1978.

Meeks, W.A. and Wilken, R.L., Jews and Christians in Antioch in
        the first four centuries of the common era (SBL Sources
        for Biblical Study 13), Missoula, 1978.

Mastirä sallase, see Pawlos.

Metzger, B.M., The Text of the New Testament: Its Transmission,
        Corruption and Restoration, 2nd. ed., Oxford, 1968.
        'Names for the nameless in the New Testament', in Kyriakon
        (Festschrift for J. Quasten, Münster, 1970), vol.I, pp.79-99.
        The Early Versions of the New Testament: Their Origin,
        Transmission, and Limitations, New York/London, 1977.

Midraš aggada, see Buber, S.

Midraš barešit rabbati, see Albeck, H.

Midraš haggadol, see Margulies, M.

Midraš hahefes, see Habasselet, M.

Midraš leqah tob, see Buber, S., Padwa, A.M.

Midraš meʿam loʿez = Yalqut meʿam loʿez.

Midraš rabba, see Freedman, H. and Simon, M.

Midrash Tadshe with Pirke Eliyyahu and Nisteroth Rashbʾi, followed
        by Likkute Kelale ha-GeRa", Johannesburg, 1858 (Midraš tadše
        also edited by Jellinek, A., Bet haMidrasch vol.III,
        Leipzig, 1853-77, and by Epstein, A., Vienna, 1887).

Midraš tahillim, see Braude, W.G., Buber, S.

Milton, J., Paradise Lost and Paradise Regained, (with notes by
        D. Masson), Clinton, Mass., 1968.

Miqraʾot gadolot, many edd.

Mogäs ǝqubä giyorgis, <u>Liqä mäzämmǝran, Mäshafä sǝnä fǝträt mǝslä 5-tu aʿǝmadä mǝstir</u>, Asmara (Mahbärä hawaryat Press), 1955 E.C.

<u>Märha sǝdq bahlä haymanot</u>, Asmara (Mahbärä hawaryat Press), 1969 E.C.

Monneret de Villard, U., <u>Le Leggende Orientali sui Magi Evangelici</u>, (<u>Studi e testi</u> 163), Vatican City, 1952.

Mose bar Kepha, see Coakley, J.F., Schlimme, L.

Moss, C., <u>Catalogue of Syriac Printed Books and Related Literature in the British Museum</u>, London, 1962.

Müller, W.W., review of Bauer, G., <u>Athanasius von Qūs</u>, <u>ZDMG</u> 125 (1975), pp.168–71.

Murad Kamil, <u>Des Josef ben Gorion (Josippon) Geschichte des Juden, Zena Ayhud</u>, New York and Berlin, 1937.

Murray, R., <u>Symbols of Church and kingdom: a study in early Syriac tradition</u>, Cambridge, 1975.

Narsai, see Gignoux, Ph., Jansma, T.

Nash, H.S., 'The Exegesis of the School of Antioch. A Criticism of the Hypothesis that Aristotelianism was a Main Cause in its Genesis', <u>JBL</u> 11 (1892), pp.22–37.

Nau, F. (trans.) and Ciprotti, P. (ed.), <u>La Version Syriaque de l'Octateuque de Clément</u>, Paris, 1967.

Nautin, P. and Doutreleau, L., <u>Didyme l'Aveugle: sur la Genèse, Sources chrétiennes</u> 233 (1976), 244 (1978).

Netton, I.R., <u>Muslim Neoplatonists. An Introduction to the Thought of the Brethren of Purity</u>, London, 1982.

Neugebauer, O., <u>Ethiopic Astronomy and computus</u>, (Österreichische Akademie der Wissenschaften philosophisch-historische Klasse. Sitzungsberichte, Bd. 347. Veröffentlichungen der Kommission für Geschichte der Mathematik, Naturwissenschaften und Medizin, Hft. 22), Vienna, 1979.

'Abū-Shāker and the Ethiopic Hasāb', <u>JNES</u> 1983, pp.55–8.

Neusner, J., <u>Aphrahat and Judaism. The Christian–Jewish Argument in Fourth-Century Iran</u>, (Studia Post-Biblica 19), Leiden, 1971.

Midrash in Context: Exegesis in Formative Judaism,
Fortress Press, Philadelphia, 1983.
_From Mishnah to Scripture: The Problem of the Unattributed
Saying_, 1983.
_In Search of Talmudic Biography: The Problem of the
Attributed Saying_, 1984.

Nicoll, A., _Bibliothecae Bodleianae codicum manuscriptorum orientalium catalogi, partis secundae volumen primum Arabicos
complectens_, Oxford, 1821.

Noy, Dov (= Neumann, D.), _Motif-Index of Talmudic-Midrashic
Literature_, Bloomington, 1954.

Origen, see Doutreleau, L., de Lange, N.R.M.

Oulton, J.E.L. and Chadwick, H., _Alexandrian Christianity_,
(Library of Christian Classics vol.2), London, 1954.

Owens, R.J., _The Genesis and Exodus citations of Aphrahat the
Persian Sage_, Leiden, 1983.

Padwa, A.M., _Midraš Leqah Tob_ (on Lev., Num., Deut.), Wilna, 1884.

Pankhurst, S., _Ethiopia, a cultural history_, Woodford Green, 1955.

Pawlos, _Blatta, Mastirä sallase_, A.A., 1903, E.C., repr. 1960 E.C.

Pearson, J.D., _Oriental MSS Collections in the Libraries of Great
Britain and Ireland_, London, 1954.

Perruchon, J. and Guidi, I. (completed by Grébaut, S.), _Le Livre
des Mystères du Ciel et de la Terre_, _PO_ 1.1, 6.3.

Pesikta dé-Rab Kahäna, see Braude, W.G. and Kapstein, I.J.

Pesikta rabbati, see Braude, W.G.

Petit, F., 'L'édition des chaînes exégétiques grecques sur la
Genèse et l'Exode', _Le Muséon_ 91 (1978), pp.189-94.
_Les Oeuvres de Philon d'Alexandrie, Quaestiones in Genesim
et in Exodum_, Paris, 1978.
(ed.), _Catenae Graecae in Genesim et in Exodum_, _CCSG_,
Leuven, 1977.

Phillips, G., _Scholia on passages of the Old Testament by Mar
Jacob, Bishop of Edessa_, London, 1864.

Philo, see Colson, F.H. et al., Petit, F.

Piilonen, J., 'Hippolytus Romanus, Epiphanius Cypriensis and Anastasius Sinaita. A Study of the ΔΙΑΜΕΡΙΣΜΟΣ ΤΗΣ ΓΗΣ', Annales Academiae Scientiarum Fennicae, series B 181, 1974.

Pilkington, H.A.W., A critical edition of the Book of Proverbs in Ethiopic, (unpublished) Oxford D. Phil. thesis, 1978.

Pirke de Rabbi Eliezer, see Friedländer, G.

Platti, E., La Grande Polémique antinestorienne de Yahyā b. ʿAdī, C.S.C.O. vols. 427–8, 437–8 (= Ar. 36–39).

Polzin, R.M., Biblical Structuralism. Method and Subjectivity in the Study of Ancient Texts, (Semeia Supplement), Fortress Press, Pennsylvania, 1977.

Propp, V. (trans. Scott, L.), Morphology of the Folktale, 2nd. ed., American Folklore Society and Indiana University, 1968.

Qälemantos, see Grébaut, S.

Qəddase, see Daoud, M., Gärima, Hammerschmidt, E., Mäshafä qəddase.

Qerəllos, see Weischer, B.M.

Quasten, J., Patrology, Utrecht/Brussels, 1950, 1953, 1960.

Rahmani, I.E., Testamentum Domini Nostri Jesu Christi, Mainz, 1899.

Raineri, O., 'La « Dottrina degli Arcani » (temherta hebuʿat) del Messale Etiopico Vaticano', Ephemerides Liturgicae year 95 (1981) no.6, pp.550–5.

Ramban, see Chavel, C.B.

Rashi, see Silbermann, A.M.

Ratner, B., Seder Olam Rabba, Wilna, 1894–7.

Reader, W.W., 'The twelve jewels of Revelation 21: 19–20: Tradition history and modern interpretations', JBL 100/3 (1981), pp.433–57.

Reichardt, W., Joannis Philoponi de opificio mundi Libri VII, (Scriptores Sacri et Profani fasc. 1), Leipzig, 1897.

Reinink, G.R., Studien zur Quellen- und Traditionsgeschichte des Evangelienkommentars der Gannat Bussame, C.S.C.O. vol.414 (= Subs.57), Louvain, 1979.

Richard, M., 'Le Véritables "Questions et Réponses" d'Anastase le
Sinaite', <u>BIRHT</u> 15 (1969), pp.39-56.

Ricoeur, P., 'Sur l'exégèse de Genèse 1, 1-2, 4a', in <u>Exégèse et
herméneutique</u>, Paris, 1971, pp.67-84 (the volume is the
Proceedings of a conference organised by the Association
catholique française pour l'étude de la Bible, Chantilly,
3-7 September, 1969).
<u>Interpretation Theory: Discourse and the Surplus of Mean-
ing</u>, Fort Worth, 1976.
(ed. by Mudge, L.S.), <u>Essays on Biblical Interpretation</u>,
London, 1981.

Robbins, F.E., <u>The Hexaemeral Literature: A Study of the Greek
and Latin Commentaries on Genesis</u>, Chicago, Illinois, 1912.

Robinson, S.E., <u>The Testament of Adam</u>, (SBL Dissertation Series
52), Chico, 1982.

Rondeau, M.J., <u>Les Commentaires Patristiques du Psautier, IIIe-Ve
siècles, vol.I: Les travaux des Pères grecs et latins sur
le Psautier</u> (<u>OCA</u> 219), 1982.

Roupp, N., 'Die älteste äthiopische Handschrift der vier Bücher
der Könige', <u>ZA</u> 16 (1902), pp.296-343.

Saadia, see Derenbourg, J.

Sachau, E., <u>Theodori Mopsuesteni Fragmenta Syriaca</u>, Leipzig, 1869.

Saldarini, A.J., <u>The Fathers according to Rabbi Nathan</u>, Leiden,
1975.
<u>Scholastic rabbinism: a literary study of the Fathers
according to Rabbi Nathan</u> (Brown Judaic studies 14),
Chico, 1982.

<u>Sälot bä'əntä ləfafä sədq wämängädä sämay wäzena həmamatihu
läkrəstos</u>, A.A., 1962 E.C.

Samir Khalil, 'La Tradition Arabe Chrétienne et la Chrétiente de
Terre-Sainte', in Jaeger, D.-M.A. (ed.), <u>Tantur Papers on
Christianity in the Holy Land</u> (<u>Studia Oecumenica Hieros-
olymitana</u> vol.1), Jerusalem, 1981, pp.343-432.

Samuel, V.C., 'One Incarnate Nature of God the Word', <u>GOTR</u> 10/2
(1964-5), pp.37-53.

Sanders, J.C.J., Inleiding op het Genesiskommentar van de
    Nestoriaan Ibn at-Taiyib, Leiden, 1963.
    Ibn at-Taiyib. Commentaire sur la Genèse, C.S.C.O. vols.
    274-5 (= Ar. 24-5), Louvain, 1967.
    'Le commentaire de Denis bar Salibi sur la Genèse', in
    Pestman, P.W. (ed.), Acta Orientalia Neerlandica, Leiden,
    1971, pp.46-50.

Sarfatti, G.B., 'Talmudic Cosmography', Tarbiz 35 (1965), pp.137-
    48 (in Hebrew, with English summary).

Sauget, J.-M., 'Une homélie syriaque sur la pécheresse attribuée
    a un évêque Jean', Parole de l'Orient 6/7 (1975/6), pp.
    159-94.

Schaff, P. (ed.), A Select Library of the Nicene and Post-Nicene
    Fathers of the Christian Church, New York, 1892-90 (vol.14
    includes John Chrysostom's Homilies on Hebrews).

Schermann, T., Prophetarum Vitae Fabulosae (in Bibliotheca
    scriptorum graecorum et romanorum Teubneriana), Leipzig,
    1907.

Schlimme, L., Der Hexaemeronkommentar des Moses bar Kepha, (GOF
    14), Wiesbaden, 1977.
    'Die Bibelkommentare des Moses bar Kepha', TAV pp.63-71.
    Der Johanneskommentar des Moses bar Kepha, (GOF 18),
    Wiesbaden, 1978.

Schneemelcher, W. (ed.), Bibliographia patristica: Internationale
    patristische Bibliographie, Berlin/New York, 1959-.

Schneider, R., 'Les titres des psaumes en éthiopien', in Cohen,
    D. (ed.), Mélanges Marcel Cohen, The Hague and Paris, 1970,
    pp.424-8.

Schwab, M., Le Talmud de Jérusalem, Paris, 1871-90.

Scrivener, F.H.A., A Plain Introduction to the Criticism of the
    New Testament, 4th. ed., 1894.

Seder Olam Rabba, see Ratner, B.

Sedláček, I., Dionysius bar Salibi. In Apocalypsim, Actus et
    Epistulas catholicas, C.S.C.O. vols. 53, 60 (= Syr.II,101
    = Syr. 18, 20), Louvain, 1909, 1910.

and Chabot, I.-B., <u>Dionysii bar Salibi commentarii in</u>
<u>evangelia</u>, <u>C.S.C.O.</u> vols. 15, 16 (= Syr. II, 98), vols. 77,
85 (= Syr. II, 98 = Syr. 33, 40), vols. 95, 98 (= Syr. II,
99 = Syr. 47, 49).

Sefer kəritot, see Sofer.

Sənkəssar, see Budge, E.A.W.

Sənnä fəträt, see Mogäs.

Sergew Hable Selassie, 'Two leading Ethiopian writers', <u>JSS</u> 25
(1980), pp.85-93.

Silbermann, A.M. (ed.), <u>Pentateuch with Rashi's commentary</u>,
London, 1946.

(Singer, S.), <u>The Authorised Daily Prayer Book</u>, many edd.

de Slane, Baron, <u>Catalogue des manuscrits arabes de la Biblio-</u>
<u>thèque nationale</u>, Paris, 1883-95.

Smalley, B., <u>The Study of the Bible in the Middle Ages</u>, 3rd. ed.,
Oxford, 1983.

Smoroński, K., 'Et Spiritus Dei ferebatur super aquas', <u>Biblica</u>
6 (1925), pp.140-56, 275-93, 361-95.

Snaith, J.G., 'Aphrahat and the Jews', in Emerton, J.A. and
Reif, S.C. (edd.), <u>Interpreting the Hebrew Bible: essays</u>
<u>in honour of E.I.J. Rosenthal</u>, Cambridge, 1982.

Soden, H. von, <u>Die Schriften des Neuen Testaments in ihrer</u>
<u>ältesten erreichbaren Textgestalt hergestellt auf Grund</u>
<u>ihrer Textgeschichte</u>, 2nd. ed., Göttingen, 1911, 1913.

Sofer, Simḥa Bunem David, <u>Sefer kəritot</u> (of Samson ben Yəṣḥaq),
Jerusalem, 1965.

Spanneut, M., 'Eustathe d'Antioche exégète', <u>TU</u> 92 (1966) (=
<u>Studia Patristica</u> 7), pp.549-559.

Sperling, H. and Simon, M., <u>The Zohar</u>, London and New York, 2nd.
ed. 1984.

Spicq, C., <u>L'Epître aux Hébreux</u>, Paris, 1952-3.

Sprenger, H.N., <u>Theodori Mopsuesteni Commentarius in XII Prophetas.</u>
<u>Einleitung und Ausgabe</u>, (<u>GOF</u>, Reihe Biblica et Patristica 1),
Wiesbaden, 1977.

Sprengling, M. and Graham, W.C., Barhebraeus' Scholia on the
 Old Testament, part I, Genesis - II Samuel, Chicago, 1931.

Staab, K., Paulus kommentare aus der griechischen Kirche,
 (Neutestamentliche Abhandlungen, Band 15), Münster, 1933.

Staàl, H., Mt. Sinai Arabic Codex 151, I: Pauline Epistles,
 C.S.C.O. vols. 452-3 (= Ar. 40, 41), Louvain, 1983.
 (For Acts and Catholic epistles, see C.S.C.O. vols. 462-3).
Stern, S.M., 'Ibn al-Ṭayyib's Commentary on the Isagoge', BSOAS
 19 (1957), pp.419-425.
 Medieval Arabic and Hebrew Thought, London, 1983.

Stone, M.E., Armenian Apocrypha relating to the Patriarchs and
 Prophets, Jerusalem, 1982.

Strack, H.L. and Billerbeck, P., Kommentar zum Neuen Testament
 aus Talmud und Midrasch, Munich, 3rd. ed., 1961.

Strelcyn, S., 'Une tradition éthiopienne d'origine juive yéménite
 concernant l'écriture', Rocznik orientalistyczny 23.1
 (1959), pp.67-72.

Sullivan, F.A., The Christology of Theodore of Mopsuestia,
 (Analecta Gregoriana vol.82, series facultatis theologicae,
 sectio B, no.29), Rome, 1956.

Swiggers, P., 'The Word Sibbōlet in Jud. XII.6', JSS 26/2
 (1981), pp.205-7.

Taʾammərä iyyäsus, see Grébaut, S'.

Taddesse Tamrat, Church and State in Ethiopia 1270-1527, Oxford,
 1972.

Talmage, F.E., David Kimhi. The Man and the Commentaries,
 Cambridge, Mass. and London, 1975.

Talmud, see Epstein, I., Schwab, M.

Tanna děbe Eliyyahu, see Braude, W.G. and Kapstein, I.J.

Taramaj mäzgäbä qalat, A.A., 1968 E.C. (prepared by debating
 association of Ethiopian University teachers).

Ten Napel, E., 'Einige Bemerkungen zu den Memrê des Emmanuel bar
 Shahhare', ZDMG supplement 4 (1980), pp.167-9.

Tewoflos, Abba (ed.), Mäzmurä dawit, A.A., 1950 E.C. (AC on Psalms).

Theodore bar Koni, see Griffith, S.H., Brade, L., Hespel, R.
  and Draguet, R.

Theodore of Mopsuestia, see Devreesse, R., Greer, R.A., Jansma,
  T., Sachau, E., Sprenger, H.N., Sullivan, F.A., Tonneau,
  R.M., van Rompay, L., Vosté, I.M., Wickert, U.

Theophilus of Antioch, see Zeegers-Vander Vorst, N.

Thiselton, A.C., The Two Horizons, Exeter, 1980.

Thompson, S., Motif-Index of Folk Literature, Bloomington,
  Indiana, 1932-6 (Indiana University Studies nos. 96, 97,
  100, 101, 105, 106, 108-112).

Tonneau, R.M., 'Texte syriaque de la Genèse, l'Héxaéméron', Le
  Muséon 59 (1946), pp.333-44.
  'Théodore de Mopsueste, Interprétation (du livre) de la
  Genèse', Le Muséon 66 (1953), pp.45-64.
  Sancti Ephraem Syri in Genesim et in Exodum commentarii,
  C.S.C.O. vols. 152-3 (= Syr. 71-2), Louvain, 1955.

Towner, W.S., The Rabbinic "Enumeration of Scriptural Examples",
  (Studia Post-Biblica), Leiden, 1973.

Trumpp, E., Der Kampf Adams (gegen die Versuchungen des Satans),
  oder: Das christliche Adambuch des Morgenlandes. Aethiopischer Text, verglichen mit dem arabischen Original-
  text, AKAW 15.3, München, 1881.
  Das Hexaëmeron des Pseudo-Epiphanius. Aethiopischer Text,
  verglichen mit dem arabischen Originaltexte und deutscher
  Uebersetzung, AKAW 16.2, pp.169-254, München, 1882.

Ullendorff, E., Ethiopia and the Bible, London, 1968.
  'Hebrew, Aramaic and Greek; the versions underlying Ethiopic
  translations of Bible and intertestamental literature',
  in Rendsburg, G. et al. (edd.), The Bible World. Essays
  in Honour of Cyrus H. Gordon, New York, 1980, pp.249-257.

van den Eynde, C., Commentaire d'Išoʿdad de Merv sur l'Ancien
  Testament, C.S.C.O. vols. 176, 179 (= Syr. 81-2, Ex.-
  Deut.); vols. 229-30 (= Syr. 96-7, Beth Mawtbe); vols.
  303-4 (= Syr. 128-9, Isa. and minor prophets); vols.
  328-9 (= Syr. 146-7, Jer., Ezek., Dan.); vols. 433-4
  (= Syr. 185-6, Psalms). (For Gen., see Vosté, I.M.).

van Rompay, L., 'A hitherto unknown Nestorian commentary on Genesis and Exodus 1-9.32 in the Syriac ms (olim) Diarbekr 22', OLP 5 (1974), pp.53-78.

'Išoʿ bar Nun and Išoʿdad of Merv: new data for the study of the interdependence of their exegetical works', OLP 8 (1977), pp.229-49.

'Le commentaire sur Gen.-Ex.9.32 du manuscrit (olim) Diyarbakir 22 et l'exégèse syrienne orientale du huitième au dixième siècle', OCA 205 (1978), pp.113-23.

Théodore de Mopsueste. Fragments syriaques du Commentaire des Psaumes, C.S.C.O. vols. 435-6 (= Syr. 188-9), Louvain, 1982.

van Winden, J.C.M., 'In the Beginning. Some observations on the Patristic Interpretation of Genesis 1:1', Vig.Chr. 17 (1963), pp.105-121.

Vaschalde, A., Iacobi Edesseni Hexaemeron seu in opus creationis libri septem, C.S.C.O. vol.97 (= Syr. II, 56 = Syr. 48, translation only; for text, see Chabot, I.-B.).

Dionysii bar Salibi commentarii in evangelia, C.S.C.O. vols. 113-4 (= Syr. II, 99 = Syr. 60-1).

Vasiliev, A., Kitab al-ʿUnvan, Histoire universelle écrite par Agapius, PO 5.4, 7.4, 8.3.

Vermes, G., The Dead Sea Scrolls in English, Harmondsworth, 1968.

Scripture and Tradition in Judaism, (Studia Post-Biblica), 2nd. ed., London, 1973.

Vööbus, A., History of the School of Nisibis, C.S.C.O. vol.266 (= Subs. 26), Louvain, 1965.

Voste, I-M., Theodori Mopsuesteni commentarius in evangelium Iohannis Apostoli, C.S.C.O. vols. 115-6 (= Syr. IV, 3 = Syr. 62-3), Louvain, 1940.

'La table ethnographique de Gen.X d'après Mar Išoʿdad de Merw', Le Muséon 59 (1946), pp.319-332.

and van den Eynde, C., Commentaire d'Išoʿdad de Merv sur l'Ancien Testament. I. Genèse, C.S.C.O. vols. 126 and 156 (= Syr. 67 and 75), Louvain, 1950, 1955.

Wace, H. and Schaff, P. (edd.), <u>A Select Library of the Nicene and Post-Nicene Fathers of the Christian Church</u>, A new series ..., New York, 1890 - (vol.7 includes Basil of Caesarea, <u>In Hexaemeron</u>).

Wacholder, B.Z., 'Biblical Chronology in the Hellenistic World Chronicles', <u>HTR</u> 61 (1968), pp.451-81.

Wäldä mika'el Bərhanä mäsqäl (ed.), <u>Gəbrä həmamat</u>, A.A., 1942 E.C.

Wäldä rufa'el, Mämhər and Gäbrä mädhən, Aläqa (edd.), <u>Wängel qəddus</u>, A.A., 1916 E.C. and reprints (AC to <u>MW</u> and gospels).

Wallace-Hadrill, D.S., <u>Christian Antioch. A study of early Christian thought in the East</u>, Cambridge, 1982.

Walton, B., <u>Biblia Sacra Polyglotta</u>, 1653-7.

<u>Wängel qəddus zä'əgzi'ənä wä'amlakənä wämädhaninä iyyäsus krəstos gəbrä hawaryat wämäl'əktatihomu lähawaryatihu qəddusan</u>, (Geez N.T.), Asmara (Mahbärä hawaryat Press), 1953 E.C.

<u>Wängel qəddus zä'əgzi'ənä wämädhaninä iyyäsus krəstos wämäsahəftihomu lähawaryat qəddusan</u>, (Geez N.T.), Bible Society of Ethiopia, 1979 A.D.

Weil, G.E., <u>Massorah gedolah, iuxta codicem leningradensem B 19a</u>, Rome/Stuttgart, 1971.

Weischer, B.M., 'Die äthiopischen Psalmen- und Qērlosfragmente in Erevan, Armenia', <u>OC</u> 53 (1969), pp.113-158.
<u>Qērellos I: Der Prosphonetikos, Über den rechten Glauben</u>' <u>des Kyrillos von Alexandrien an Theodosius II, Afrikanistische Forschungen</u> VII, Glückstadt, 1973.
<u>Qērellos III: Der Dialog, Dass Christus einer ist</u>'<u>des Kyrillos von Alexandrien</u>, <u>AF</u> 2, Wiesbaden, 1977.
<u>Qērellos IV 1: Homilien und Briefe zum Konzil von Ephesos</u>, <u>AF</u> 6, Wiesbaden, 1979.
<u>Qērellos IV 2: Traktate des Epiphanios von Zypern und des Proklos von Kyzikos</u>, <u>AF</u> 6, Wiesbaden, 1979.

<u>Qērellos IV 3: Traktate des Severianos von Gabala, Gregorios Thaumaturgos und Kyrillos von Alexandrien</u>, <u>AF</u> 7, Wiesbaden, 1980.
'Das christologische Florilegium in Qērellos II', <u>OC</u> 64 (1980).

Wensinck, A.J., <u>Mystic treatises by Isaac of Nineveh translated from Bedjan's Syriac text with an introduction and registers</u>, (Verhandelingen der Koninklijke Akademie van Wetenschappen: afdeeling letterkunde nieuwe reeks deel XXIII), Amsterdam, 1923.

Wickert, U., <u>Studien zu den Pauluskommentaren Theodors von Mopsuestia als Beitrag zum Verständnis der antiochenischen Theologie</u>, <u>BZNW</u> 27, Berlin, 1962.

Wilson, R. McL., 'The Early History of the Exegesis of Gen.1.26', <u>TU</u> 63 (= <u>Studia Patristica</u> 1), pp.420-437.

Wordsworth, J. and White, H.J. (edd.), <u>Nouum Testamentum domini nostri Jesu Christi latine secundum editionem S. Hieronymi ad codicum manuscriptorem fidem</u>, Oxford, 1889-1954.

Wright, W., <u>Catalogue of the Syriac Manuscripts in the British Museum, acquired since the year 1838</u>, London 1870-2.

<u>Yähaymanotənna yäsälot mäshaf</u>, A.A. (Tənsa'e zäguba'e P.P.), 1955 E.C.

Yahyā ibn 'Adī, see Endress G., Platti, E.

Yahyā ibn Sa'īd, see Kratchkovsky, I. and Vasiliev, A.

<u>Yalqut me'am lo'ez</u>, see Culi.

Young, F.M., 'Christological Ideas in the Greek Commentaries on the Epistle to the Hebrews', <u>JTS</u> XX.1 (1969), pp.150-63.

Zeegers-Vander Vorst, N., 'La création de l'homme (Gn.1.26) chez Théophile d'Antioche', <u>Vig.Chr.</u> 30 (1976), pp.258-267.

<u>Zohar</u>, see Sperling, H. and Simon, M., Matt, D.C.

Zotenberg, H., <u>Chronique de Jean, évêque de Nikiou</u>, Paris, 1883.

7.2   <u>BIBLIOGRAPHY OF ETHIOPIAN MANUSCRIPT CATALOGUES</u>.

The following is a list of the Ethiopian MS catalogues
consulted for this study (especially for the compilation of the
lists in 7.3 and 7.4 below). It is intended to be a complete list
of catalogues, omitting only some superseded shelf-lists, descriptions of single MSS, and catalogues of little or no relevance to
commentary studies (such as catalogues of magical scrolls). A
few catalogues that proved unavailable are listed separately at
the end of the bibliography.

d'Abbadie, A., <u>Catalogue raisonné de manuscrits éthiopiens</u>, Paris,
        1859.

Abbott, T.K., <u>Catalogue of the manuscripts in the Library of Trinity
        College Dublin</u>, Dublin, 1900, (p.402 only).

Aescoly, A., 'La colonie éthiopienne à Jérusalem. II Inventaire
        des manuscrits éthiopiens de cette colonie', <u>Æthiopica</u>
        1934, pp.44-9, 88-95.

Andrzejewski, T., Jakobielski, S., and Strelcyn, S., <u>Katalog
        Rekopisów Egipskich, Koptyjskich i Etiopskich</u>, Warszawa,
        1960, (pp.43-65 only).

Assemanus, S.E., <u>Bibliothecae Mediceae Laurentianae et Palatinae
        codicum mms. orientalium catalogus</u>, Florence, 1742-3, (pp.
        58-9, 92, 96-7, 431 only).

Bible Society, see Falivene.

Blanchart, J., 'Note sur les manuscrits rapportés d'Abyssinie par
        la mission Duchesne-Fournet' in Duchesne-Fournet, J.,
        <u>Mission en Éthiopie (1901-1903)</u>, Paris, 1909, (tome I, pp.
        289-440 and plates only).

Brockelmann, C., <u>Katalog der Handschriften der Stadtbibliothek zu
        Hamburg. Band III. Orientalische Handschriften: Katalog
        der Orientalischen Handschriften. Teil 1, Die arabischen,
        persischen, türkischen, malaiischen, koptischen, syrischen,
        äthiopischen Handschriften</u>, Hamburg, 1908, (pp.178-85 only).

Cerulli, E., 'I manoscritti etiopici della Biblioteca Nazionale di
        Atene', <u>RSE</u> 2 (1942), pp.181-90.

Cerulli, E., 'I manoscritti etiopici della Bibliothèque Royale di Bruxelles', RRAL fasc. 11–12, serie VIII, vol.IX, 1954 (Roma, 1955), pp.516–21.

Cerulli, E., 'I manoscritti etiopici della Chester Beatty Library in Dublino', MRAL serie VIII, vol.XI (1962), fasc. 6, pp.277–324.

Chaîne, M., 'Inventaire sommaire des manuscrits éthiopiens de Berlin acquis depuis 1878', ROC, 2e ser., tom.17 (1912), pp.45–68.

Chaîne, M., Catalogue des manuscrits éthiopiens de la Collection A. d'Abbadie, Paris, 1912.

Chaîne, M., Catalogue des manuscrits éthiopiens de la Collection Mondon-Vidailhet, Paris, 1913.

Chaîne, M., 'Catalogue des manuscrits éthiopiens des bibliothèques et musées de Paris, des départements et de collections privées, ROC 2e ser., tom. 9 (1914), pp.3–16, 247–65.

Chaîne, M., 'Les manuscrits éthiopiens de la bibliothèque des RR. PP. Capucins à Toulouse', Æthiops 1936, pp.8–16, 23–29.

Cohen, M., 'Rapport sur une mission linguistique en Abyssinie (1910–1911)', Nouvelles Archives des Missions Scientifiques, nouv. série, fasc.6 (1912), Paris.

Conti Rossini, C., 'Manoscritti ed opere abissine in Europa', RRAL, 5e sér, tom.VIII (1899), pp.606–637.

Conti Rossini, C., 'I manoscritti etiopici della Missione Cattolica di Cheren', RRAL, 5e sér., tom.XIII (1904), pp.233–55, 261–86.

Conti Rossini, C., 'Notice sur les manuscrits éthiopiens de la collection d'Abbadie', JA, 10th. series, t.XIX (1912), pp. 551–578; t.XX (1912), pp.5–72; 449–494; 11th. series, t.II (1913) pp.5–63; t.VI (1915), pp.189–238, 445–493.

Conti Rossini, C., 'Pergamene di Debra Dammò', RSO 19 (1940), pp.45–57.

Cowley, R., 'The Study of Geez Manuscripts in Tegré Province', JES vol.IX.1 (Jan.1971), pp.21–5 (and see also BSOAS XXXVII (1974) pt. 3, p.597, note 1).

Cunha Rivara, J., Catalogo dos manuscriptos da Bibliotheca Publica Eborense, tomo I, Lisboa, 1850, (p.249 only).

Dillmann, A., Catalogus codicum manuscriptorum orientalium, qui in Museo Brittanico asservantur. Pars III: Codices aethiopicos amplectens, London, 1847.

Dillmann, A., Catalogus codicum manuscriptorum Bibliothecae Bodleianae Oxoniensis. Pars VII: Codices aethiopici, Oxford, 1848.

Dillmann, A., Codices orientales Bibliothecae Regiae Hafniensis, Hafniae, 1857, (pars tertia, pp.78-9 only).

Dillmann, A., Die Handschriften-Verzeichnisse der königlichen Bibliothek zu Berlin. Band III:Verzeichniss der abessinischen Handschriften, Berlin, 1878.

Dorn, B., 'Ueber die aethiopischen Handschriften der öffentlichen Kaiserlichen Bibliothek zu St. Pétersburg', Académie Impériale des sciences de Saint-Pétersbourg. Bulletin scientifique, tom.3, no.10, col. 145-51 (St. Petersburg, 1838).

Dorn, B., 'Ueber einige dem Asiatische Institute des Ministeriums der Auswärtigen Angelegenheiten zugehörige Äthiopische Handschriften', Académie Impériale des sciences de Saint-Pétersbourg. Bulletin scientifique, tom. 2, no. 19, col. 302-4.

Dorn, B., Catalogue des manuscrits et xylographes orientaux de la Bibliothèque imperiale publique de St.-Pétersbourg, Imprimerie de l'Académie Impériale des Sciences. St. Péters-bourg, 1852, (pp.549-558 only).

Duchesne-Fournet, J., see Blanchart, J.

Ephraim Isaac, 'Catalogue of the Ethiopic (Géez) MSS in the Manuscript Library of the Armenian Patriarchate of Jerusalem', Le Muséon, tom.89 (1976), pp.179-194 .

Ephraim Isaac, 'Shelf list of Ethiopian manuscripts in the monasteries of the Ethiopian Patriarchate of Jerusalem', <u>RSE</u> XXX, pp.53-80.

Euringer, S., 'Verzeichnis der abessinischen Handschriften des Völkermuseums in Stuttgart', <u>Orientalia</u>, new series vol.IV, fasc. 3/4 (Rome, 1935), pp.465-483.

Ewald, H., 'Ueber die aethiopischen Handschriften zu Tübingen', <u>ZKM</u> 5 (1844), pp.164-201.

Ewald, H., 'Ueber eine zweite Sammlung aethiopischer Handschriften in Tübingen', <u>ZDMG</u> 1 (1847), pp.1-43.

Falivene, M.R. (compiler) and Jesson, A.F. (ed.), <u>Historical Catalogue of the Manuscripts of Bible House Library</u>, London, 1982.

Fleischer, H.O., <u>Catalogus codicum manuscriptorum orientalium Bibliothecae Regiae Dresdensis</u>, Lipsiae, 1831.

Flemming, J., 'Die neue Sammlung abessinischer Handschriften auf der Königlichen Bibliothek zu Berlin', <u>Zentralblatt für Bibliothekswesen</u>, XXIII.1 (1906), pp.7-21.

Galbiati, E., 'I manoscritti etiopici dell' Ambrosiana (Breve inventario)', <u>Studi in onore di Mons. Carlo Castiglioni</u> (<u>Fontes Ambrosiani 32</u>), Milano, 1957, pp.337-53.

Galbiati, E., 'I fonti orientali minori (siriaco, etiopico, armeno) dell' Ambrosiana', <u>Atti del congresso di studi sulla Lombardia e l'Oriente</u>, Milan, 1963, pp.190-6.

Getatchew Haile, see Macomber, W.F.

Gildemeister, J., <u>Catalogus librorum manu scriptorum orientalium qui in Bibliotheca Academica Bonnensi servantur</u>, Bonn Universitäts Bibliothek, 1864-76, (see pp.98-100).

de Goeje, M.J., <u>Catalogus codicum Orientalium Bibliothecae Academiae Lugduno-Batavae</u>, vol.V, Lugduni Batavorum, 1873, (see p.64).

Goldschmidt, L., Die abessinischen Handschriften der Stadtbibliothek zu Frankfurt a/M (Rüppell'sche Sammlung), Berlin, 1897.

Goodspeed, E.J., 'An Ethiopic Manuscript of John's Gospel', AJSL vol.XX (1903-4), pp.182-5.

Goodspeed, E.J., 'Ethiopic manuscripts from the Collection of Wilberforce Eames', AJSL vol.XX (1903-4), pp.235-44.

Grébaut, S., 'Les manuscrits éthiopiens de M.É. Delorme', ROC 1912, pp.113-32; 1914, pp.17-23, 174-82, 347-57; 1915-17, pp. 82-91, 408-15; 1918-19, pp.137-47.

Grébaut, S., 'Manuscrits éthiopiens appartenant à M.N. Bergey', ROC 1920-21, pp.426-42; 1925-6, pp.196-219.

Grébaut, S., 'Les mss. ethiopiens de M.N. Bergey', Æthiops I (1922), pp.12-14.

Grébaut, S., 'Catalogue des manuscrits éthiopiens de la Bibliotheque Ambrosienne', ROC 1934, pp.3-32.

Grébaut, S., 'Inventaire sommaire des manuscrits éthiopiens (géez) de la Mission Griaule', Aethiopica 1933, pp.23-35; 1934, pp. 16-22, 50-4, 65-9, 110-4; 1935, pp.27-32, 82-4, 154-61.

Grébaut, S., 'Les manuscrits éthiopiens de la Comtesse de Fels, princesse de Heffingen', Aethiopica 1935, pp.97-101; and Æthiops 1936, pp.3-8, 17-22; 1938, pp.2-6.

Grébaut, S., Catalogue des manuscrits éthiopiens de la Collection Griaule, Paris, vol.I,1938; vol.II, 1941; vol.III, 1944 (for vol.IV see Strelcyn).

Grébaut, S. and Tisserant, E., Codices aethiopici Vaticani et Borgiani, Barberinianus Orientalis 2, Rossianus 865, Vatican, 1935-6.

Guidi, I., Catalogo dei codici siriaci, arabi, etiopici, turchi e copti della Biblioteca Angelica, Florence, 1878, (pp.73-4 only).

Hagen, H., Catalogus codicum Bernensium (Bibliotheca Bongarsiana), Bernae, 1875, (p.74 only).

Haile, Getatchew, see Macomber, W.F.

Halén, H., Handbook of Oriental Collections in Finland (Scandinavian Institute of Asian Studies Monograph Series no.31), London and Malmö, 1978, (pp.104–8 only).

Hammerschmidt, E. and Jäger, O.A., Illuminierte äthiopische Handschriften, VOHD XV, Wiesbaden, 1968.

Hammerschmidt, E., Äthiopische Handschriften vom Tānāsee 1: Reisebericht und Beschreibung der Handschriften in dem Kloster des heiligen Gabriel auf der Insel Kebrān, VOHD XX.1, Wiesbaden, 1973.

Hammerschmidt, E., Äthiopische Handschriften vom Tānāsee 2: Die Handschriften von Dabra Māryām und von Rēmā, VOHD XX.2, Wiesbaden, 1977.

Hammerschmidt, E., Illuminierte Handschriften der Staatsbibliothek Preussischer Kulturbesitz und Handschriften vom Tānāsee (Codices Aethiopici Band 1), Graz, 1977.

Hammerschmidt, E. and Six, V., Äthiopische Handschriften 1: Die Handschriften der Staatsbibliothek Preussischer Kulturbesitz, VOHD XX.4, Wiesbaden, 1983.

Həruy Wäldä səllase, Baʾityopya yämmigäññu bägäʾəzənna bamarinna qwanqwa yätäsafu yämäsahəft katalog, A.A., 1928.

Imperial Ethiopian Government Antiquities Administration, Catalogue of the Ethiopian Manuscripts in the National Library of Ethiopia, A.A., 1962 (A.D., in Amharic).

Irmischer, J.C., Handschriften-Katalog der Königlichen Universitäts Bibliothek zu Erlangen, Frankfurt a.M., 1852, (pp.5–6 only).

Juel-Jensen, B. and Rowell, G. (edd.), Rock-Hewn Churches of Eastern Tigray. An Account of the Oxford University Expedition to Ethiopia 1974, Oxford, 1975, (pp.47–83, some plates, and errata; photographs of MSS are in the Bodleian Library).

Kamil, M., 'Les manuscrits éthiopiens du Sinaï', Annales
    d'Éthiopie 2(1957), pp.83–90.

Keller, A., 'Aethiopische Handschriften in Tübingen', Serapeum
    (Leipzig) 10 (1849), p.379.

Isaac E., see Ephraim Isaac.

Kokovtzov, P., 'Zametka ob efiopskich rukopisyach Imperatorskoi S.-
    Peterburgskoi Publitchnoi Biblioteki', ZVO 4 (1889), pp.106–11.

Kolmodin, J., 'Abessinische Bücherverzeichnisse', Le Monde Oriental
    10 (1916), pp.241–55.

Krackovskiy, I., 'O sobranim efiopskich rukopisey B.A. Turaeva',
    IRAN, 6 series, vol.XV (1921), pp.175–6.

Krackovskiy, I., 'Abissinskiy magiceskiy svitok iz sobraniya F.I.
    Uspenskogo', DAN 1928, pp.163–7.

Littmann, E., 'Die äthiopischen Handschriften im griechischen
    Klöster zu Jerusalem', ZA 15 (1901), pp.133–61.

Littmann, E., 'Aus dem abessinischen Klöster zu Jerusalem', ZA 16
    (1902), pp.102–24, 363–88.

Littmann, E., 'Preliminary report of the Princeton University
    Expedition to Abyssinia', ZA 20 (1907), pp.151–82.

Löfgren, O., 'Die abessinischen Handschriften der Evangeliska
    Fosterlands – Stiftelsen, Stockholm', Le Monde Oriental 23
    (1929), pp.1–22.

Löfgren, O., Katalog über die äthiopischen Handschriften in der
    Universitätsbibliothek Uppsala, Uppsala, 1974.

Lund, J.L.M., 'An Ethiopian Manuscript in the Astor Library',
    American Church Review XXXVI (1881), pp.189–221.

Macomber, W.F., 'Catalogue of Oriental Manuscripts in the
    Library of Seabury-Western Theological Seminary, Evanston,
    Illinois,' Le Muséon 92 (1979), pp.369–386.

Macomber, W.F. and Getatchew Haile, A Catalogue of Ethiopian Manu-
    scripts Microfilmed for the Ethiopian Manuscript Microfilm
    Library, Addis Ababa, and for the Hill Monastic Manuscript
    Library, Collegeville, Ann Arbor, Mich., University Micro-
    films International: vol.I (nos.1–300, by WFM, 1975); vol.
    II (nos.301–700, by WFM, 1976); vol.III (nos.701–1100, by
    WFM, 1978); vol.IV (nos.1101–1500, by GH, 1979); vol.V
    (nos.1501–1200, by GH and WFM, 1981); vol.VI (nos.2001–
    2500, by GH and WFM, 1982); vol.VII (nos.2501–3000, by
    GH and WFM, 1983); vol.VIII (nos.3001–3500, by GH, 1985).

Mai, A., Scriptorum veterum nova collectio e Vaticanis codicibus
    edita, Rome, 1831, (vol.V pp.94–100 in repaginated section
    towards end of volume).

Marrassini, P., 'I manoscritti etiopici del Museo Nazionale di
    Antropologia e Etnologia dell'Università di Firenze,
    Archivio per l'antropologia e la etnologia 114 (1984),
    pp.205–232.

Marrassini, P., 'I manoscritti etiopici della Biblioteca Medicea
    Laurenziana di Firenze', RSE XXX, pp.81–116.

Mazzatinti, G. and Pintor, F., Inventari dei manoscritti delle
    Biblioteche d'Italia, R. Biblioteca Nazionale Centrale,
    Forlì, 1902–3 (vol.XII, pp.104–5 only).

Mercer, S.A.B., 'An expedition to Abyssinia', JSOR Jan–Apr. 1931,
    pp.1–6.

Meyer, W., Die Handschriften in Göttingen (Verzeichniss der Hand-
    schriften im Preussischen Staate I), Berlin, vol.2, 1893;
    vol.3, 1894, (vol.2, p.538, and vol.3, pp.198–201, 308–14
    only).

Ministry of Education and Fine Arts, Department of Fine Arts and Culture (A.A.), Catalogue of Manuscripts Microfilmed by the Unesco Mobile Microfilm Unit in Addis Ababa and Gojjam Province, A.A., 1970 (A.D.).

Mordini, A., 'Il convento di Gunde Gundie', RSE 12, pp.29-70.

Müller, Fr., 'Die äthiopischen Handschriften der Kaiserlich-Königliche Hof-Bibliothek in Wien', ZDMG XVI (1862), pp.553-7.

Murad Kamil, Die abessinischen Handschriften der Sammlung Littmann zu Tübingen (ABKM XXI, 8), Leipzig, 1936.

Nau, F., 'Notices des manuscrits syriaques, éthiopiens et mandéens entrés à la Bibliothèque Nationale de Paris depuis l'édition des catalogues', ROC 1911, pp.271-323 (especially pp.311-3).

Perini, D.A., 'Catalogo dei Codici manoscritti ed oggetti portati dall' Oriente nel 1879 dal P. Agostino Ciasca Agostiniano', Bessarione 1903, pp.402-12; 1904, pp.58-71, 258-81.

Pertsch, L.C.W., Die orientalischen Handschriften der Herzoglichen Bibliothek zu Gotha, Gotha, 1893, (pp.1-6).

Pertsch, L.C.W. (ed.), Verzeichniss der Handschriften im Preussischen Staate I. Hannover. Die Handschriften in Göttingen. 3. Universitäts-Bibliothek, Berlin, 1894, (see pp.308-14).

Platt, T.P., A catalogue of the Ethiopic Biblical manuscripts in the Royal Library of Paris, and in the Library of the British and Foreign Bible Society ..., London, 1823.

Raineri, O., 'I mss. etiopici del Museo Diocesano di Bergamo', RRAL ser.VIII, vol.XXXVII (1983), pp.263-298.

Raineri, O., 'Libri di uso prevalentemente liturgico tra i mss « Cerulli Etiopici » della Vaticana', Ephemerides Liturgicae 1986, pp.171-185.

Raineri, O., 'I Mss etiopici della Biblioteca delle « Ephemerides Liturgicae » in Roma', Ephemerides Liturgicae 100.3 (1986), pp.334-9.

Rhodokanakis, N., 'Die äthiopischen Handschriften der K.K. Hofbibliothek zu Wien', SKAW 151 (1906), pp.1-93.

Riedel, W., Katalog över Kungl. Bibliotekets orientaliska handskrifter, Stockholm, 1923 (pp.20, 61 only).

Rodiger, E., Trumpp, E. and Krapf, J., Catalogus codicum manu scriptorum Bibliothecae regiae Monacensis, tom. 1, pars 4, München, 1875.

Ross, E.D., 'The Manuscripts collected by W. Marsden', BSOAS II (1921-3), pp.513-538.

Schodde, G.H., 'Beschreibung einer äthiopischen Handschrift der Königlichen Bibliothek zu Dresden', ZDMG 30 (1876), pp.297-301.

Simon, J., 'Répertoire des Bibliothèques publiques et privées contenant des manuscrits éthiopiens', ROC 1931-2, pp.178-96.

Simsar, M.A., Oriental Manuscripts of the John Frederick Lewis Collection, Philadelphia, 1937 (pp.202-7 only).

Strelcyn, S., Catalogue des manuscrits éthiopiens (Collection Griaule), tom.IV, Paris, 1954, (for vols. I-III, see Grébaut).

Strelcyn, S., 'Les manuscrits éthiopiens de quelques bibliothèques européennes décrits récemment', IV Congresso Internazionale di Studi Etiopici, Roma, 10-15 aprile 1972, Rome 1974, vol. II, pp.7-61.

Strelcyn, S., 'Catalogue of Ethiopian manuscripts of the Wellcome Institute of the History of Medicine in London', BSOAS 35.1 (1972), pp.27-55.

Strelcyn, S., 'Les nouveaux manuscrits éthiopiens de la Bibliothèque Royale de Bruxelles', JES XI.2 (1973), pp.169-88.

Strelcyn, S., Catalogue of Ethiopic Manuscripts in the John Rylands University Library of Manchester, Manchester, 1974.

Strelcyn, S., Catalogue des manuscrits éthiopiens de l'Accademia
    Nazionale dei Lincei, Fonds Conti Rossini et Fonds Caetani
    209, 375, 376, 377, 378, Roma, Accademia Nazionale dei
    Lincei, 1976.

Strelcyn, S., Catalogue of Ethiopian Manuscripts in the British
    Library acquired since the year 1877, London, 1978.

von Tischendorf, L.F.K., 'Die manuscripta Tischendorfiana in der
    Universitätsbibliothek zu Leipzig', Serapeum 8 (1847), pp.
    49-80, (see pp.73-4).

Tisserant, E., Catalogo della nostra di manoscritti e documenti
    orientali tenuta dalla Biblioteca apostolica vaticana e
    dall'archivio segreto ..., Vatican, 1935.

Tornberg, C.J., Codices Orientales bibliothecae regiae Universitatis
    Lundensis, Lundae, 1850, and Supplementa, Lundae, 1853.

Turaev, B. (see also Turaiev), 'Efiopskija rukopisi Muzeja Cerkovno-
    archeologičeskago Obščestva pri Kievskoj Duchovnoj Akademii',
    ZVO 12 (1899), pp.061-067.

Turaev, B., 'Efiopskija rukopisi Gatčinskago Dvorca', ZVO 1900,
    pp.01-07.

Turaev, B., 'Novyja sobranija efiopskich rukopisei v Peterburgě',
    ŽMNP čast' 358, 1905 no.4, Sovremennaja Lětopis, pp.15-27.

Turaev, B., 'Efiopskija rukopisi v S.-Peterburgě', ZVO 17 (1906),
    pp.115-248.

Turaev, B., 'Zamětki iz Efiopskich rukopisei Vaticana', VV 15
    (1908), pp.180-8.

Turaev, B., 'Iz armjano – abissinkich snošenij II: Efiopskie
    fragmenty Ečmiadzinskoj biblioteki', ZVO 21 (1911-12),
    pp.07-010.

Turaiev, B., 'Testi etiopici in manoscritti di Leningrado', RSE
    VII.1, 1948.

Ullendorff, E., Catalogue of the Ethiopian Manuscripts in the
    Bodleian Library, vol.II (Catalogi codd. mss. Bibliothecae
    Bodleianae, pars. VII), Oxford, 1951.

Ullendorff, E., 'The Ethiopic manuscripts in the Royal Library, Windsor Castle', <u>RSE</u> XII (1953), pp.71-9.

Ullendorff, E. and Wright, S.G., <u>Catalogue of Ethiopian Manuscripts in the Cambridge University Library</u>, Cambridge, 1961.

van Lantschoot, A., 'Inventaire sommaire des mss. Vaticans 261-99', <u>Collectanea Vaticana in honorem Anselmi M. Card. Albareda</u> (<u>Studi e testi</u> 219), Vatican, 1962, vol.I, pp.453-512.

Vollers, K., <u>Katalog der islamischen, christlich-orientalischen, jüdischen und samaritanischen Handschriften der Universitäts-Bibliothek zu Leipzig</u>, Leipzig, 1906 (pp.430-1 only).

Wickersheimer, C.A.E. (ed.), <u>Catalogue général des manuscrits des bibliothèques publiques de France</u>. Départements, tom.XLVII, Paris, 1923, (pp.771-3 only) .

Winckler, J.D., Κειμήλια <u>Bibliothecae Regiae Berolinensis Aethiopica descripta</u>, Erlangae, 1752.

Worrell, W.H., 'Studien zum abessinischen Zauberwesen', <u>ZA</u> 23 (1909), pp.149-83; 24 (1910), pp.59-96; 29 (1914-15), pp.85-141.

Wright, S.G., see Ullendorff, E.

Wright, W., 'List of the Magdala Collection of Ethiopic Manuscripts in the British Museum', <u>ZDMG</u> 1870, pp.599-616.

Wright, W., <u>Catalogue of the Ethiopic Manuscripts in the British Museum acquired since the year 1847</u>, London, 1877.

Wurmbrand, M., <u>Draft catalogue of the Ethiopian MSS in the Faitlovitch Collection</u> (now in the Tel Aviv University Library) (unpublished).

Uri, J., <u>Bibliothecae Bodleianae codicum manuscriptorum orientalium</u>, pars prima, Oxonii, 1787, (p.28 of pagination commencing with Syriac MSS).

Zanutto, S., <u>Bibliografia Etiopica: Manoscritti Etiopici</u>, Rome, 1932.

Zettersteen, K.W., 'Die abessinischen Handschriften der Königlichen Universitäts-bibliothek zu Upsala', <u>ZDMG</u> 53 (1899), pp.508-20.

Zotenberg, H., <u>Catalogue des manuscrits éthiopiens (gheez et amharique) de la Bibliothèque Nationale</u>, Paris, 1877.

Works not consulted because of unavailability:

Arnold, A. and Müller, A., <u>Verzeichnis der orientalischen Handschriften der Bibliothek des Halle'schen Waisenhauses</u>, Halle, 1876.

Bolotov, V., 'Description de deux manuscrits éthiopiens ...' (in Russian), in ? <u>Kharkovskaya obshchestvennaya biblioteka imeni V.G. Korolenko</u>, 1887.

Mauro da Leonessa, <u>Santo Stefano Maggiore degli Abissini</u>, Vatican, 1929.

Rogers, R.W., 'A Catalogue of manuscripts ... in the Library of Haverford College', <u>Haverford College Studies</u>, n.4, 1892, pp.28-50.

Turaev, B., catalogue articles reprinted in his <u>Pamiatniki ethiopskoi pismennosti</u>.

7.3   <u>GEEZ COMMENTARY MANUSCRIPTS</u>.

The following is a provisional listing of Geez commentary
MS materials, with incipits cited from the sources specified pre-
ceding the incipits. The list is supplementary to <u>TIA</u> pp.35-40,
4.1 and 5.1 above, and the information in the relevant MS catalogues.

For compiling the list, the catalogues listed in 7.2 above
have all been consulted, and it is hoped that the listing of whole
commentaries represents the current state of study fairly completely.
The listing of fragments, marginalia, and miscellanea, however, is
very incomplete, and is given only as a sample. I have personally
used the MSS in the collections at the B.L., Bodleian Library,
Cambridge, A.A. Nat. Lib., A.A. Holy Trinity Cathedral, and
Jerusalem, and in my own collection. For most other MSS, the list
may reproduce errors or confusions in the relevant MS catalogues.

Cataloguers' names are given in brackets, and refer to the
catalogues listed in 7.2. For EMML MSS, see W. Macomber and
Getatchew Haile. MSS numbered JE are in the Ethiopian archbishop's
residence in Jerusalem. For A.A. Nat. Lib. MSS see 'Imperial
Ethiopian Government'; for A.A. Unesco MSS see 'Ministry of Education'. For MSS numbered 'Cowley', see 7.5 below.

As a number of important commentaries are only known to be
extant in one or two MS copies, it is probable that investigations
will bring further materials to light.

Old Testament. <u>Haṭata orit,</u> translated from IAṬ's Questions, EMML
        1839 f.1a-48b, described in 4.1.3 above, incipit in catalogue
        notes on EMML 1839.

Octateuch. (i) <u>Mamhərä orit</u>, described in 4.1.2 (iii) above,
        incipits given below.
        (ii) Fragments in B.L. Or. 743.
        (iii) ? <u>TO</u> in A.A. Unesco 8/4, and ? Gundagundi (Mordini) 27.
        (iv) Theodoret on the 'Torah' in <u>Mashafä hawi</u> (e.g. B.L. Or.
        776 f.115b, 167a, 221a, 260a).

Pentateuch. (i) <u>Tərgwame orit</u>, translated from IAṬ, B.N. dᵗAbbadie 28, described in 4.1.2 (i) above, incipits given below.

(ii) <u>TO</u>, based on IAṬ, written by Məhərka dəngəl, EMML 2101, described in 4.1.2(ii) above, incipit in catalogue notes on EMML 2101.

Genesis. (i) <u>MO</u> (dᵗAbb.156 f.4a):

በአሰ ፡ እግዚአብሔር ፡ ሰብሐ ፡ ወመስተሣህል ፡ እወጋን ፡ ድሐፈ ፡
ወድሐፈ ፡ ዘይሰወድ ፡ መያሁር ። ዘእስተጋበእዎ ፡ ባግአምርነ ፡
መጸሕፍት ። ወረገሑስ ፡ አዘወድሐፈ ፡ ይዐጸሁር ፡ ወይተሬጐይም ፡
ቃላተ ፡ ወነገራተ ፡ ዘኡሬት ፡ እንተ ፡ የዓዕብ ፡ ወይስእን ። ዘይተሀባእ ፡
ወይደሓወር ፡ ለዘ ፡ ኢየአምር ፡ ብእሴ ፡ ---
ኡሬት ፡ ዘልሏት ። ኡሬት ፡ ብሄብ ፡ ሕግ ፡ ዘልሏት ፡ ብሄብ ፡
ዘፋንሬት ።

(ii) <u>TO</u> (dᵗAbb. 28 f.2a):

በአሰ ፡ __ ንወጋን ፡ ድሐፈ ፡ ተርንሜ ፡ ኡሬት ፡ ዘጸሐፈ ፡ ዮሐንስ ፡
እሬ ፡ ወርቅ ፡ __ ወድሐፈ ፡ ብሌት ፡ ዥሐንታሁ በጸዋዌ ፡ ጠፋእት ፡
በገቢኮናዌ ፡ ወእሰ ፡ ተሰዴጠ ፡ ዓዐጠ ፡ ዕዝሬ ፡ ንሁን ፡ ---
ወድሐፈ ፡ ቃዳማዌ ፡ ወሙእቹ ፡ ወድሐሬ ፡ ፋንሬት ፡ ኧፋል ፡
ቃዳማዌ ፡ ወዘይሬ ፡ በቃዳሪ ፡ ገብሬ ፡ እግሬ ፡ ሰማየ ፡ ወምድሬ ።
ወይመርእ ፡ ቦተ ፡ ኑበ ፡ ተሬክቦቱ ፡ ወቀፉመቹ ፡ ወጋንተኒ ፡ ---

(iii) EMML 2101.

(iv) Comment on Gen.1–11 in B.L. Or. 503 f.1a–4b; excerpts from similar text in JE 754E and EMML 3111.

(v) Fragment of introduction to Gen. in B.L. Or. 484 f.188b.

(vi) Fragment on Gen.7 in EMML 1929 f.171b, 171a.

(vii) Comment on Gen.48–9 in B.N. Zotenberg 64.

(viii) Legendary account of creation in <u>mäshaf zäċaräqa</u>, EMML 219 f.138b–139a.

(ix) The (? Felasha) work <u>bäqädami gäbrä əġziᵓabəher</u> in Tel Aviv Faitlovitch 3125.

(x) Fragments of ᵗJohn Chrysostomᵗ on the Hexaemeron in <u>Mäshafä hawi</u> (e.g. B.L. Or. 776 f.192a, 253a).

(xi) ? <u>Fəträtä adam</u> in Gundagundi (Mordini) 187.

Exodus. (i) <u>MO</u> (d'Abb.156 f.9a):

በዝልኋ ፡ ዓሞት ፡ እምእሰ ፡ ወፅኡ ፡ እስራኤል ፡ ተድሕፈ ፡ እሬት ፡
ዘፀት ፡ ዝውኁቲ ፡ ትርጒሜ ፡ ቃሉ ፡ ናሁኁ ። በሰ ፡ እዐዓዳቲሮሙ ፡ --

(ii) <u>TO</u> (d'Abb.28 f.38a):

ፋነሬ ፡ መጽሐፈ ፡ ዓገዶ ፡ ወውኁቲ ፡ ፀእት ፡ እዖግብዯ ፡ ጻፍል ፡
ቀዳጣዩ ፡ ዘተሰምዖሰ ፡ መጽሐፈ ፡ ፀእት ፡ እክሰበ ፡ ሁክቴ ፡
ዜና ፡ ፀእት ፡ ዓቂቀ ፡ ፭ ኤል ፡ እዖግብዯ ፡ --

(iii) EMML 2101.

(iv) Excerpts on Song of Moses and Miriam in <u>Mäshafä sawiros</u>.

(v) Commentary fragment in EMML 2055.

Leviticus. (i) <u>MO</u> (d'Abb.156 f.12b):

በ<u>ሁ</u>ወ<u> z</u> ፡ ዓሞት ፡ እዖዘ ፡ ወፅኡ ፡ እስራኤል ፡ እዖግብዯ ፡
ተድሕፈት ፡ እሬት ፡ ዘኔዋውይን ። ዝውኁቲ ፡ ፋነሬ ፡ ቃሉ ፡
ክሁፍ ። መባእ ፡ ዘያበውኁ ፡ ---

(ii) <u>TO</u> (d'Abb.28 f.54a):

መጽሐፈ ፡ ሣልሱ ፡ ወውኁቲ ፡ መጽሐፈ ፡ ካህናት ፡ ጻፍል ፡ ቀዳጣዩ ፡
እግዚእብሔር ፡ ይክበይ ፡ ክሰ ፡ ኢእዘዘሙ ፡ ሰሕዝብ ፡ ወዊዳ ፡
መሰዋዕት ፡ እንበይና ፡ ረገሕ ፡ --

(iii) EMML 2101.

Numbers. (i) <u>MO</u> (d'Abb. 156 f.13b):

በ<u>ሁ</u>ወ<u>I</u> ፡ ዓሞት ፡ እዖዘ ፡ ወፀኡ ፡ እስራኤል ፡ ተድሕፈ ፡ እሬት ፡
ዘኁልቁ ። ኁልቁ ፡ ዘተኅህለ ፡ እክሰ ፡ ይናገር ፡ ኄልቆሙ ፡
ሰእስራኤል ።

(ii) <u>TO</u> (d'Abb.28 f.64b):

መጽሐፈ ፡ ራብዕ ፡ ወውኁቲ ፡ መጽሐፈ ፡ ኄልቄ ፡ ጻፍል ፡ ቀዳጣዩ ፡
ወመፍቅዱስ ፡ ሰዝንቱ ፡ መጽሐፈ ፡ እዘክዎተ ፡ ኵሉ ፡ ስርዓታት ፡
እንተ ፡ ሠርዓ ፡ እግ ፡ ሰዲቀቀ ፡ ፭ ኤል ፡ ውስተ ፡ ገዳም ፡ መራር ፡ --

(iii) EMML 2101.

Deuteronomy. (i) <u>MO</u> (d'Abb.156 f.15a):

በ<u>ሃ</u> ፡ ዓሞት ፡ እዖእሰ ፡ ወፅኡ ፡ እስራኤል ፡ ተድሕፈ ፡ እሬት ፡ ዘዳግም ፡
ዝውኁቲ ፡ ትርጒሜ ፡ ቃሉ ፡ ሕተዖ ። ዓረቢሁ ፡ ዘ ፡ ሰዳ ፡ --

(ii) <u>TO</u> (d'Abb. 28 f.75a):

መጽሐፈ ፡ ሐምስ ፡ ወውኁቲ ፡ መጽሐፈ ፡ ወዳግም ፡ ሕግ ፡ ጻፍል ፡
ዳግማይ ፡ ወሰገሐሱ ፡ ሰሙሤ ፡ በዲዘሞ ፡ ሕግ ፡ ካሰ ፡ ይክዓዕ ፡
ሕዝብ ፡ ዳግማዩ ፡ ---

(iii) EMML 2101.

(iv) Comment on Dt. 33 in B.N. Zotenberg 64.

Joshua. (i) <u>MO</u> (d'Abb.157 f.45b):

እሬት ፡ ዘየሴበ ፡ ተጽሕፈ ፡ በልሳነ ፡ እሜሌቀ ፡ ወደተኔሰቀ ፡ ምስለ ፡
መጽሐፈ ፡ ነገሥት ፡ ዝውኁቱ ፡ ትርጓሜ ፡ ቃሉ ፡ እኩቱ ፡ ኢየሱስ ፡
ኳሬል ፡ መፉፃን ፡ __

(ii) <u>TO</u> (d'Abb.28 f.84a; Josh. continues to f.86b and
concludes incomplete):

ንወጥን ፡ በስመ ፡ እግዚእብሔር ፡ ሕያው ፡ ወወሀቤ ፡ ሕይወት ፡
ፋገሬ ፡ መጻሕፈ ፡ ኢየሱ ፡ ወልዱ ፡ ነዌ ፡ ክፋል ፡ ቃዳ ፡
ወይኌንንያቶስ ፡ በኁንት ፡ ዘኴሮሙ ፡ እግዚ ፡ __

Judges. <u>MO</u> (d'Abb.157 f.47a):

እሬት ፡ ዘመሳፋንት ፡ ተጽሕ ፈ ፡ በልሳነ ፡ እናሬዎን ፡ ዝውኁቱ ፡
ፋገሬ ፡ ቃለቱሉ ፡ ኁኁን ፡ ዝሬ ፡ ደተኔሰቀ ፡ ምስለ ፡ መጽሐፈ ፡
ነገሥት ፡ እዷሬ ፡ ዘ ፡ ኁግዚኁ ፡ __

Ruth. <u>MO</u> (d'Abb.157 f.50b):

እሬት ፡ ዘሩት ፡ ተጽሕፈ ፡ በልሳነ ፡ ሞእስ ፡ ፉኗወ3 ፡ ዘ ፡
ተፋሰሕት ፡ __

Samuel and Kings. Fragments in B.L. Or.743.

1 Samuel. (? <u>MO</u>) in B.N. d'Abbadie 39 f.156a-161a:

በስመ ፡ __ ትርጓሜ ፡ ነገሥት ፡ ወሀሎ ፡ ፩ ፡ ብእሲ ፡ እምነ ፡
እርማቴም ፡ ዘ ፡ ፋብር ፡ እምነ ፡ ፋብሬ ፡ ኤፍሬም ፡ ዘተውህበ ፡ ለነሀናት ፡ ፡
      also in d'Abb.157 f.51a-57a.

2 Samuel. (? <u>MO</u>) in d'Abb.39 f.161a-164b:

መጽሐፈ ፡ ነገሥት ፡ ካልእ ፡ ዘተጽሕፈ ፡ በልሳነ ፡ ዝርይ ፡ ወእሙ ፡
ሣልስት ፡ ዕለት ፡ ዘ ፡ ኁምእወ ፡ ገለኁ ፡ ዳዊት ፡ ኁምኡበ ፡ ሉ ፡
      also in d'Abb.157 f.57b-61b.

1 Kings. (? <u>MO</u>) in d'Abb. 39 f.164b-172b:

መጽሐፈ ፡ ነገሥት ፡ ሣልስ ፡ ተጽሕፈ ፡ በልሳነ ፡ ቃብጢ ፡ ትርጓሜ ፡
ቃሉ ፡ ዘይናጤ ፡ ወኁለፈ ፡ መዎዕሊሁ ፡ ዘ ፡ __
      also in d'Abb. 157 f.61b-67a.

2 Kings. (? <u>MO</u>) in d'Abb. 39 f.172b-174b:

 መድኅሬ ፡ ነገሠት ፡ ራብዕ ፡ ተድኅሬ ፡ በልሰነ ፡ ቅጶጦ ፡ ወበንዳሪቢ ፡
ወበሰ[ብ]ራይስጦ ። ዘሎሙ ፡ ብሕሩ ፡ ሳበዝ ፡ መዓዝ ፡ ወኡያሞፈ ሳሬ ፡
ሞተ ፡ እነአኩ ፡ እድረሬ ፡ ሞኁብ ፡ ዘ ፡ ኁያሞቢ ፡ እሉ ፡

    also in d'Abb. 157 f.67a-69b.

1 and 2 Chronicles. d'Abbadie 39 f.192b-195a and 195a-197b:

ትርንዐዬ ፡ ሳበ93 ። ሳበ93 ፡ ብ ፡ ክነገሠት ፡ የቀሬ ፡ ወጎንግ ፡ ዘ ፡
እሉፆሁ ፡ ለሰብኁ ፡ ዘደዘክኈዑሁ ፡ ሕዝቀኈል ፡ እሉቀለዶሊስ ፡

Jubilees. Fragments, notes and explanations of difficult words in
        B.L. Or. 743, B.N. Zotenberg 50 f.77b, Zotenberg 160,
        d'Abbadie 39 f.197b-198a, EMML 1945 f.133a-135a and 1b-2a.

Enoch. Fragments in B.L. Or. 743 and B.N. Zotenberg 160,
        ? Gundagundi (Mordini) 172.

Ezra. Fragments in B.L. Or. 743 and B.N. d'Abbadie 39 f.201b-202a.

Job. Fragments in <u>GH</u> (pr.ed. pp.103-5, 207-10, 293-5), Cambridge
        (Ullendorff and Wright) Add. 1570 f.173b, d'Abbadie 39 f.
        198a-b. ? Gundagundi (Mordini) 141.

Psalms. Fragments in Mashafa hawi (attributed to Basil of Caesarea,
        B.L. Or. 776 f.131b; attributed to Theodoret, Or. 776 f.78b,
        143a; attributed to John Chrysostom, Or. 776 f.54b, ? 121b,
        138a, 179a), in <u>HA</u> (attributed to John Chrysostom), and in
        Mashafa sawiros sect. 11 (on Ps.135 and 150); see also the
        dərsana mazmur (e.g. Wien Aeth. 16 (Rhodokanakis 1)) and the
        mazmura krəstos (e.g. B.L. Or. 534). Gundagundi (Mordini) 132.

Proverbs. Fragments in <u>GH</u> (pr.ed. pp.151-2, 121-2), in <u>HA</u> (attrib-
        uted to Basil of Caesarea), in Mashafa hawi (attributed to
        Basil of Caesarea, B.L. Or. 776 f.82a), and in B.N. d'Abbadie
        39 f.184b-185b.

Wisdom. Fragment in <u>GH</u> (pr.ed. pp.275-7).

Song of Solomon. (i) Geez version of Philo of Carpasia on Song 1.2–
14a in MS JE 300 E (MS 119 at Ethiopian archbishop's residence in Jerusalem), f.3a–20a.

(ii) Fragments in B.L. Or. 743, EMML 2481.

(iii) Commentary in B.N. d'Abbadie 39 f.178b–184b.

(iv) Gregory of Nyssa on Song 3.7 in Kəbrä nägäst ch.66.

(v) Gregory of Nyssa on Song in HA.

(vi) Tərgwame mahalləy in the Ethiopian monastery in
Jerusalem (Littmann's catalogue – possibly same as (i) above).

Ecclesiasticus. Fragments in B.N. d'Abbadie 39 f.185b–188a.

Isaiah. (i) Commentary in MS B.N. d'Abbadie 157 f.193a–227a:

በስመ ፡ እግዚእብሔር ፡ ወሐረ ፡ ወወስተሣሣህል ፡ ንወኝን ፡ ትርጓዜ ፡
ወድሐሪ ፡ ኢሳይያስ ፡ ሰዑል ፡ ቃል ፡ ስረኣት ፡ ዒቤሣ ፡ ትደልል ፡፡
እምሣጎፊ ፡ እምዖን ፡ ሙኝቹ ፡፡ ሎኣዲ ፡ ሀርኝየ ፡ በኝተ ፡ ይሉዲ ፡
ወበኝንተ ፡ ኢዮራስሌም ፡ ዘ ፡ ሀደሣውን ፡ ዓዌዌ ፡ ሰዐልዖን ·
ኢሳይስ ፡ ብሌል ፡ ቆሡዕ ፡ እምቀብሣ ፡ ትንቢት ፡ __

(ii) Fragments in GH (pr.ed. see 2.5 above), in Mashafa
hawi (attributed to Theodoret, B.L. Or. 776 f.72b; attributed to Basil of Caesarea, Or. 776 f.34a, 143b, 148a), and
in d'Abb. 39 f.198b–199b.

Jeremiah. Fragment in GH (pr.ed. pp.272–5).

Ezekiel. Fragments in B.L. Orient (Wright) 482 f.122a, Or. (Wright)
506 f.149a–159a, Or. (Strelcyn 68) 5085 f.186r–192r; B.N.
d'Abbadie 39 f.199b–201b, 140, 190.

Daniel. (i) Commentary in Wien Cod. Aeth. 16 (Rhodokanakis 1),
ff.17a–62b, see O. Löfgren, Die äthiopische Übersetzung des
Propheten Daniel:

በስመ ፡ እግዚእብሔር ፡ __ በድሐሪ ፡ ትርጓዜ ፡ ዳንኤል ፡

ነቢይ ፣ ___ እመ ፣ ሠላስ ፣ ዓሦተ ፣ ወእንግሊቱ ፣ ለኢዮአቄም ፣
___ ወኢዮአቄምስ ፣ ንጉሠ ፣ እምፉጎሩ ፣ እግዝ ፣ እኑ ፣ ሎ ፣
ውእቱ ፣ ወዶነ ፣ ዓዲ ፣ ደሠመደ ፣ ሳሎሞ ፣ ___

(ii) Commentary in B.N. d'Abbadie 157 f.76b–102b:

ትርንጌ ፣ ዓንኔል ፣ ወገብት ፣ ደተበሁሉ ፣ በእንተ ፣ ሠላስቱ ፣ እሑዱ ፣
ወሃይ ፣ ምናን ፣ ክልኤቱ ፣ ምእሰናን ፣ __

(iii) Fragments in GH (pr.ed. pp.124–5) and B.N. d'Abbadie
39 f.201b–202a.

(iv) ? A.A. Unesco 10/47.

Minor prophets. (i) Berlin (Hammerschmidt and Six 106) Ms. orient.
quart. 986 f.140a–199b; B.N. d'Abbadie 156 f.108a–130b; B.N.
d'Abbadie 157 f.103a–192a (see JRAS 1984 pp.268–9).

(ii) Commentaries different from the set in (i) above, in
Wien Cod. Aeth. 16 (Rhodokanakis 1).

Hosea. (i) d'Abb. 157, f.103a–124a:

ቃለ ፣ እግዚእብሔር ፣ ዘኮነ ፣ እስከ ፣ ዓበ ፣ ደብል ፣ ንጉሠ ፣ እስራኤል ።
ዓግሬ ። ነገሥተ ፣ ደሩዳ ፣ እለ ፣ ዘነርዑ ፣ ነቢደ ፣ ኢነገሡ ፣ ለ፮ ዘ፲፮ ፣
እንዝ ፣ ሰኮ ፣ ኢዮርብኣም ፣ ዓግሳዌ ፣ ዘውእቱ ፣ ወተልዋው ፣ ለ፲ ፣
ነገሥተ ፣ ሰማርደ ፣

also in d'Abb. 156; Berlin or.qu. 986; EMML 7410 f.30a–38a
(= A.A. Nat. Lib. 438/111); published in H.F. Fuhs, Die
äthiopischen Übersetzung des Propheten Hosea, pp.78–102.

(ii) Wien Cod. Aeth. 16, ff.62b–66b, published in H.F. Fuhs,
op.cit., pp.71–8:

በስመ ፣ ___ ቃል ፣ ዘእም ሆሴዕ ፣ ነቢይ ፣ ወደቤሎ ፣
እግዚእብሔር ፣ ለሆሴዕ ፣ ሑር ፣ እውስብ ፣ ___ ብእሲተ ፣
ዘማዌት ፣ እስተማስለ ፣ ባቲ ፣ ፲ ፣ ነገፉ ፣ እለ ፣ እምለኑ ፣
ክልኤቱ ፣ እልህምተ ፣ ዘወርቅ ፣ እለ ፣ እቀመ ፣ ኮሙ ፣
ኢዮርብኣም ፣ ንጉሠ ፣ በሰማርደ ፣ ገበፉ ፣ __

(iii) Fragment in C̣H (pr.ed. pp.152-4), and in M̈ashafä̈ hawi
(attributed to Theodoret).

Amos. (i) d'Abb. 157 f.124a-138b:

ቃለ ፡ እሞጽ ፡ ነቢይ ፡፡ ቃለ ፡ አሞጽ ፡ ዘኮነ ፡ እስ ፡ ኅ ፡ ይ ፡
ወትስልዕ ፡ እስነ ፡ ሞሠሬታቴሃ ፡ ፌ ፡ ቃለ ፡ አሞጽ ፡ ዘኮነ ፡
በኣቃሪም ፡ ዘፉቁሄ ፡ ዘ ፡ ትንቢት ፡ እሞጽ ፡ ተነግሪ ፡ በእቃሪም ፡
ዘፉቀሄ ፡ --

> also in d'Abb. 156; Berlin or.qu. 986; incomplete in
> EMML 7410 f.38b-42b.

(ii) Wien Cod. Aeth. 16 ff.66b-68b:

ቃል ፡ ዘአሞጽ ፡ ነቢይ ፡ ወደቤ ፡ ኃግዚእብሔር ፡ እሞጽዮን ፡
ነበበ ፡ --- ይቤ ፡ ዘንት ፡ እስወ ፡ ተነብዖ ፡ በእንተ ፡ ቤት ፡
ኃግዚእብሔር ፡ እሞልኡ ፡ ጣይት ፡ እሞቤተ ፡ ወቃሉስ ፡
ይስተርኢ ፡ ሐጕል ፡ --

Micah. (i) d'Abb. 157 f.138b-146a:

ቃለ ፡ እጒሪ ፡ ዘኮነ ፡ ኅበ ፡ ሚኪያስ ፡ ኮነ ፡ ሞንፈሰ ፡ ትንቢት ፡ በእፊ ፡
ሚኪያስ ፡ ዘርኅይ ፡ በእንተ ፡ ሰሞርያ ፡ ወበእንተ ፡ ኢዮርሳሌም ፡ ዘ ፡
ተነበዖ ፡ ለበተ ፡ ይሬዲ ፡ ወለ I ፡ ነገሩ ፡ ወደዮሩንፃወሙ ፡ እጒሪ ፡
ሰሞዕታ እነሙ ፡ --

> also in d'Abb.156; Berlin or.qu. 986.

(ii) Wien Cod. Aeth. 16 ff.68b-70b:

ቃል ፡ ዘሚኪያስ ፡ ነቢይ ፡ ፉሞዐ ፡ ሰረጋላት ፡ ላዕለ ፡ ኅንተ ፡
ትነብር ፡ --- ትርንፃ ፡ ይኤሞር ፡ በስሞ ፡ እሐቲ ፡ ሀገር ፡
ላዕለ ፡ ኙሉ ፡ --

Joel. (i) d'Abb. 157 f.146a-148b:

ቃለ ፡ ኃግዚእብሔር ፡ ዘኮነ ፡ ኅበ ፡ ኢዮኤል ፡ ዘ ፡ ኮነ ፡ ሞንፈሰ ፡
ተነብዖ ፡ ስሞዑ ፡ ዘንተ ፡ ኙልክነሙ ፡ ሊቃውንት ፡ ወእጹሞው ፡
ኙልክነሙ ፡ እለ ፡ ትነብሪ ፡ ዲበ ፡ ምፉር ፡ ዘ ፡ ስሞዓ ፡ ተነብዖ ፡
ወቃለ ፡ ተግሣጽ ፡ --

> also in d'Abb. 156; Berlin or.qu. 986.

(ii) Wien Cod. Aeth. 16 ff.70b–71b:

ቃል ፡ ዘኢየዔል ፡ ነቢይ ፡ ዘእትሬፈ ፡ ዕዩ ፡ በልጓ ፡ --- ትርጓሜ ፡ ይብል ፡ እስሞ ፡ ፋቄቀ ፡ ይሩዳ ፡ ወብንደም ፡ እለ ፡ ተርፉ ፡ እምዬዎ ፡ ሰናክሬም ፡ ንጉሠ ፡ ፋርስ ፡ --

Obadiah. (i) d'Abb. 157 f.148b–150a:

ዘርእዮ ፡ እብፉይ ፡ ዘ ፡ ተነበዮ ፡ ወርእዮ ፡ ብዙኀ ፡ ምንዳቤ ፡ ወቀትሎ ፡ ዘ ፡ ነሞ ፡ ይነሮሙን ፡ ሰብእ ፡ ኤፌምያስ ፡ ለፋቄቀ ፡ እ ፯ ኤል ፡ --

        also in d'Abb.156; Berlin or.qu. 986.

        (ii) Wien Cod. Aeth. 16 ff.71b–72b:

ቃል ፡ ዘእብፉይ ፡ ወይክሙን ፡ ወፋኃኔት ፡ --- ትርጓሜ ፡ ይብል ፡ በእንተ ፡ ግብረ ፡ ስርስቶስ ፡ ወፋሩን ፡ ወእስተርእዮቱ ፡--

Jonah. (i) d'Abb. 157 f.150a–151b:

ወሂነ ፡ ቃል ፡ እግዚእብሔር ፡ ኀበ ፡ ዮናስ ፡ ወልደ ፡ እማቴ ፡ ዘ ፡ ተንሂት ፡ ወትእዛዝ ፡ ለሰብእ ፡ ነነዌ ፡ ነነዬስ ፡ እሞወ ፡ ይእቲ ፡ ለእነተሩ ፡ ፋርስ ፡ --

        also in d'Abb.156; Berlin or. qu. 986.

        (ii) Wien Cod. Aeth. 16 f.72b:

ቃል ፡ ዘዮናስ ፡ ነቢይ ፡ ወተሬ ፡ ዮናስ ፡ ወተሐንኣ ፡ --- ትርጓሜ ፡ ኢዮና ፡ ነቢይ ፡ እብፉ ፡ ነሞ ፡ ይቱዪይ ፡ እምእግዚእብሔር ፡ ወወኀቲ ፡ የእምር ፡ ኅሒሎቱ ፡ --

Nahum. (i) d'Abb. 157 f.151b–156b:

ተሬፉ ፡ ነነዬ ፡ ወድሐሬ ፡ ራእይ ፡ አናዖይም ፡ ወብዱ ፡ ነበቀስይ ፡ ዘይቤ ፡ ብዙኀ ፡ ተንቤት ፡ ወፋፉፉ ፡ ራእይ ፡ ዘነነ ፡ እምኔሁ ፡ ሰበለ ፡ ሀገሬ ፡ ነነዬ ፡፡ ወበ ፡ ዘይቤ ፡ ተሬ ፡ ተንቤት ፡ ወተግሣፅ ፡ እምዮናስ ፡ ተፈጸወ ፡ በናዖይም ፡፡
        also in d'Abb.156; Berlin or.qu. 986.

(ii) Wien Cod. Aeth. 16 ff.72b-74a:

ቃል ፡ ዘናቦዓም ፡ ነቢይ ፡ ወሰኑ ፡ ይትቃወላጣ ፡
ለመቅሠፍት ፡ ሰባቱ ፡ --- ትርጓሜ ፡ ናናዔ ፡ ኣናተ ፡
እምእህጉሪ ፡ ፈርስ ፡ ይኤምር ፡ --

Habakkuk. (i) d'Abb. 157 f.156b-165a:

ዐንቀቅዓም ፡ ዘሣእምር ፡ እምሌዊ ፡ ተፈፈ ፡ ዘርእየ ፡ ዐንቀቅዓም ፡
ብዘን ፡ ተነበየ ፡ ወብዙን ፡ ርእየ ፡ እስከ ፡ ዓእዜኑ ፡ እነፅናሁ ፡ ---
እስ ፡ ካወ ፡ ዘይፈፅምም ፡ እምተዐገሥቴ ፡ --

             also in d'Abb.156; Berlin or.qu. 986.
          (ii) Wien Cod. Aeth. 16 ff.74a-75b:

ቃል ፡ ዘእንባቅዓም ፡ ነቢይ ፡ ወሙእቱስ ፡ ይናግሥ ፡ ለሰዉ ፡
ወይፈርግዐ ፡ --- ትርጓሜ ፡ ዘንተ ፡ ተናበየ ፡ እንባቅዓም ፡
እምፈሳሪ ፡ ይወዋሙ ፡ ስናንም ፡ (!) ንቱሠ ፡ ፈርስ ፡
ለ፲ ፡ ናገፈ ፡ ወእምፈሳሪ ፡ ወረሪ ፡ ወልእስ ፡ እግዜእ-ለሐር ፡ --

Zephaniah. (i) d'Abb. 157 f.165a-167b:

ቃለ ፡ እግዚ ፡ ዘኮነ ፡ ኀበ ፡ ሐፎንያስ ፡ ወልደ ፡ ኁስ ፡ ዘኮነ ፡
ወንፉስ ፡ እግዚ ፡ ውስተ ፡ እፉሉ ፡ ካመ ፡ ይትናበይ ፡ ቦቱ ፡
ወይገሣዱ ፡ ለካወ ፡ ይቤ ፡ ኦርምያስ ፡ --
             also in d'Abb. 156; Berlin or.qu. 986.

          (ii) Wien Cod. Aeth. 16   ff.75b-76b:

ቃል ፡ ዘሶፎንያስ ፡ ነቢይ ፡ ሐሊቅ ፡ የሐልቁ ፡ እምገደ ፡
ምፉር ፡ --- ትርጓሜ ፡ ዘሙእቲ ፡ እሌስኩወሙ ፡ ስእፉ ፡
ስብእ ፡ ገቢሎን ፡ ለስብእ ፡ ምፉሪ ፡ ርስት ፡ --

Haggai. (i) d'Abb. 157 f.168a-170a:

እስክ ፡ ኀበ ፡ ይብል ፡ እግዚ ፡ ቃል ፡ ሐጌ ፡ ፋናሪ ። ለካልእ ፡
እስክ ፡ ኀበ ፡ ይ ፡ ሐጌ ፡ ዘ ፡ ወልእን ፡ ወተነበየቴ ፡ ካና ፡ በ፪
ዓመተ ፡ መንግሥቴ ፡ ለዳርዮስ ፡ ንጉ[ሠ] ፡ ሜፋን ፡ ዘሙእቲ ፡
ሐወሑ ፡ ለፈሮስ ፡ --
             also in d'Abb. 156; Berlin or.qu. 986.

(ii) Wien Cod. Aeth. 16, ff.76b–77a:

ቃል ፡ ዘሕንፄ ፡ ናሁዴ ፡ በእንተ ፡ ዝንቱ ፡ ተቃውሞ ፡ ሰባዴ ᛫
ዝናሞ ፡ እያሌዕሉ ፡ --- ትርጓ[ሜ] ፡ ተሃነዮ ፡ ሐፄ ፡
በዝንቱ ፡ ፉሳፈ ፡ ተወዴጠ ፡ እያገቢሎን ᛬ ወሀለዎ ፡
ዘፈግቤሳ ፡ ወልፉ ፡ ሰላትያስ ፡ ወስፍሞሙ ፡ ወንጉሃሙ ᛫ --

Zechariah. (i) d'Abb. 157 f.170a–189a:

ዘሃርያስ ፡ ዘ ፡ ዝጓሬ ፡ እግዚአብሔር ፡ እያሌዋ ፡ ዘሃርያስ ፡ ናሁዴ ᛫
በሃልእ ፡ ፉሙት ፡ ወንግሡቸ ፡ --- ሃሳ ፡ ወንፈሳ ፡ ትዝቤት ፡ ናበ ፡
ዘሃርያስ ፡ በወዋዕሳ ፡ ትዝቤፉሙ ፡ ሉሐፄ ፡ ወለፉንኜሳ ᛫ --

                also in d'Abb. 156; Berlin or.qu. 986.

(ii) Wien Cod. Aeth. 16 ff.77a–83b:

ቃል ፡ ዘዘሃርያስ ፡ ናሁዴ ፡ ርእዩ ፡ በሊሊት ፡ ብእሴ ᛫
ዴጿሃን ፡ --- ትርጓዐ ፡ ፈረስ ፡ ቀይሕ ፡ ትእምርት ፡
በእንተ ፡ ሃዕወት ፡ ፉወ ፡ እሕዘብ ፡ እለ ፡ እሕሰሙ ᛫
ሳዕለ ፡ እዴሁፉ ᛫ --

                (iii) Fragment in G̲H̲ (pr. ed. pp.355–8).

Malachi. (i) d'Abb. 157 f.189a–192a:

ዘዌልእንያስ ፡ ናሁዴ ፡ ወዌልእንያስ ፡ ዌል ፡ ሐዋርዶ ፡ ተሀሀለ ᛫
እስወ ፡ ሙእቸ ፡ እዞርዶ ፡ ፩ እዓም ፯ ፉቀቅ ፡ ዘወፉዮሙ ᛫
ናዑክፈሃዶር ፡ ወሁስት ፡ እፉሃ ፡ እሳት ᛫ --

                also in d'Abb. 156; Berlin or.qu. 986.

(ii) Wien Cod. Aeth. 16 ff.83b–84a:

ቃል ፡ ዘዌልእንያስ ፡ ናሁዴ ፡ ተሬፈ ፡ ቃለ ፡ እግዚአብሔር ᛫
ሳዕለ ፡ እስኰኜሳ ፡ --- ትርጓዐ ፡ ወተበሀለ ፡ ሃወ ᛫
ሙእቸ ፡ እዞዴ ፡ ፩ ፡ እዓም ፯ ፉቀቅ ፡ እለ ፡ ወሬዎሙ ᛫
ናዑክፈሃ ፡ ጸር ፡ ሙስተ ፡ እፉን ᛫ --

New Testament.

M̈aqdəm̈a ẅangel. MSS are very numerous – e.g. B.L. Or. 508, 13264,
Add.16190; Bodleian (Dillmann) 12; Cambridge Add. 1165;
B.N. Zotenberg 33; Berlin (Dillmann 20) Peterm.II Nachtr.
43; EMML 2965, 3450.

Four gospels. (i) 'Coptic-Arabic gospel catena', complete in
Ṭanasee (Hammerschmidt) 30, Matthew only in MSS listed below.

(ii) Geez version of IAṬ's gospel commentary, incipits from
B.L. Or. 731 given below.

(iii) Comment in G̲H̲ headed dəhr̈a ẅangel (see 4.1.9 (i) above).

(iv) Ṭərgwame ẅangel z̈ak̈ambat, see Ṭanasee (Hammerschmidt) 91 ,
possibly the same as (i) or (ii) above.

(v) Fragments in EMML 1056.

Matthew. (i) 'Coptic-Arabic catena', incipit given fully in cata-
logue notes on B.N. Zotenberg 65, also contained in B.L.
(Dillmann) Add 16,220; Berlin (Dillmann 26) Peterm.II
Nachtr.52; Berlin (Hammerschmidt and Six 166.1) Hs.or.2283;
Ṭanasee (Hammerschmidt) 30; EMML 2068, 2088, 2797.

(ii) Geez version of IAṬ, B.L. Or. 731 f.12a:

በስመ ፡ -- ወዳሕፈ ፡ ሕፋት ፡ ለኢየሱስ ፡ ክርስቶስ ፡ ይቤ ፡
መተርጉም ፡ እስመ ፡ ይታጓ ሠሠ ፡ መተርጉሳን ፡ በእንተ ፡ ዝንቱ ፡
ክፋል ፡ ሐተተ ፡ ባዘዛ ፡ --

also in B.L. Or. 732, 734–6; B.L. Add. 16248 (Dillmann 12);
B.N. d'Abbadie 24, 191; Uppsala O Etiop.41 (L̈ofgren 37);
? Aksum (Kolmodin); A.A. Holy Trinity Cathedral 41; A.A.
Holy Trinity Theological College; A.A. Unesco 5/2, 10/50,
? 10/72, 12/4; EMML 368, 630, 1114;? Cerulli (Raineri) 2, 252,
(? also Gundagundi (Mordini) 48, 69, 175).

(iii) Anonymous commentary in B.L. Or. 731 f.142b–208b:

ይቤ ፡ ባዕዋስ ፡፡ ወሰበ ፡ ቆፋሐረት ፡ እሙ ፡ ለዮሴፍ ፡ --
ይቤ ፡ መተርጉም ፡ ባይፈሬ ፡ ዘይቤ ፡ ሐቀርያተ ፡ ያሳቱ ፡
ፋሓረተ ፡ ወኢይቤ ፡ ተወሰበተ ፡ --

(iv) Fragment in M̈ashafä̈ tä̈lmid attributed to Basil of Caesarea.

(v) Fragment in <u>HA</u> attributed to John Chrysostom.

(vi) Many extensive extracts from John Chrysostom in M̈ashafä̈ hawi, <u>passim</u>.

(vii) Fragment on Mt. 2.1–23 in Ṭanasee (Hammerschmidt) 91.

(viii) <u>Mä̈qdəmä̈ tərgwame wä̈ngelä̈ mattewos</u> in B.L. Or. 515 f.14a ff.

Mark. (i) 'Coptic–Arabic catena', MS Ṭanasee (Hammerschmidt) 30 f. 74a–94b:

በሰመ ፡ __ ትርጓሜ ፡ ወንጌል ፡ ዘብፁዕ ፡ ወቅዱስ ፡ ማርቆስ ፡ __

(ii) Geez version of IAṬ, B.L. Or. 731 f.209a:

በሰመ ፡ __ ይቤ ፡ ማርቆስ ፡ ቀዳሚሁ ፡ __ ይቤ ፡ መተርጒ ሞ ፡ ወብሂሎቱስ ፡ ቀዳሚሁ ፡ ለብስራተ ፡ ኢየሱስ ፡ ክርስቶስ ፡ ወኢይቤ ፡ ኆንተ ፡ መጽሐፈ ፡ ኢየሱስ ፡ ክርስቶስ ፡ __

also in B.L. Or. 732; B.N. d'Abbadie 24, 191; ? Aksum (Kolmodin); A.A. Unesco 10/50, 12/4; EMML 368.

(iii) Fragment in EMML 1054 f.1b.

Luke. (i) 'Coptic Arabic catena', Ṭanasee 30 f.95a–141a:

ወንጌል ፡ ዘሉቃስ ። በሰመ ፡ __ ንቀድም ፡ በረድኤተ ፡ እግዚእብሔር ፡ ትርጓሜ ፡ ወንጌል ፡ ዘሉቃስ ፡ እስመ ፡ ብዘነ ፡ እለ ፡ እለ ዙ ፡ ይሥዑሩ ፡ ነገረ ፡ በኆንተ ፡ ግብር ፡ ዘእምሬ ፡ በሎሌነ ፡ በካመ ፡ ወበጻሩነ ፡ እለ ፡ ቀዳሙነ ፡ ርኢዮቶ ፡ ወተልእኽነዎ ፡ በቃሉ ፡ ፈትፃሬ ፡ እትልዎ ፡ እምንንተ ፡ ወእመይቅ ፡ ለኵሉ ፡ በበመትሉ ሙ ። እጽሕፈ ፡ ለከ ፡ __

(ii) Geez version of IAṬ, B.L. Or. 731 f.223a:

በሰመ ፡ __ ይቤ ፡ ሉቃስ ፡ ሐዋርያ ፡ ኖሉር ፡ እስመ ፡ ብዘነ ፡ __ ይቤ ፡ ወተርጒሞ ፡ ወብሂሎቱስ ፡ ብዘነ ፡ ተገፉፈት ፡ እግሜረቱ ፡ ሐልዮ ፡ ካመ ፡ ሙኆተ ፡ ኢይብል ፡ በኆንተ ፡ ማቴዎስ ፡ ወማርቆስ ፡ __

also in B.L. Or. 732; B.N. d'Abbadie 24, 191; ? Aksum (Kolmodin); ? A.A. Unesco 10/72, 12/4; EMML 368, 2158.

John. (i) 'Coptic–Arabic catena', Ṭanasee 30 f.141b–

፮ በኆንተ ፡ ቃል ፡ ቀዳጣዊ ። ቀዳሚሁ ፡ ቃል ፡ ሙኆተ ፡ ወሙኆተ ፡ ቃል ፡ ኅበ ፡ እግዚእብሔር ፡ ሙኆተ ፡ __

(ii) Geez version of IAT, B.L. Or. 731 f.261a:

 በአሙ ፦ ደቤ ፦ ዮሐንስ ፦ በቀዳሚ ፦ ሃላ ፦ ቃል ፦ ሀላዉ ።
ደቤ ፦ መተርጉም ፦ እስሙ ፦ ይትጓሠሡ ፦ መተርጉማን ፦ በዝንቱ ፦
ን ፦ ተጓሠሃተ ፦ ብዙን ፦ --

    also in B.L. Or. 732; B.N. d'Abbadie 24, 191; Uppsala O
    Etiop.41 (Löfgren 37); ? Aksum (Kolmodin); A.A. Holy
    Trinity Cathedral 41; A.A. Unesco 5/2, ? 10/72, ? 12/4;
    EMML 368, 1114, 2158; ? Cerulli (Raineri) 302.

    (iii) Fragments attributed to John Chrysostom in HA,
    Mashafä tälmid, and Mashafä hawi (B.L. Or. 776 f.35a, 50b,
    62b, 88b, 103a, 105a, 139b, 140b, 189a, 205b, 219b).

Acts. (i) Fragments in Mashafä hawi attributed to Didymus (B.L. Or.
    776 f.162b) and to John Chrysostom (B.L. Or. 776 f.50b, 55b,
    156b, 161b, 191b).

    (ii) Fragment in Rylands (Strelcyn) 19 f.2a-4a and EMML 7410
    f.93a-94b.

Pauline corpus. (i) Tərgwame pawlos, described in 5.1.2 (ii) above,
    contained in MS B.L. Or. 13830 (and Cowley 33-4, and ? Aksum
    (Kolmodin) and ? Gundagundi (Mordini) 97); incipits are given
    below.
    (ii) Tərgwame felon felgos, described in 5.1.2 (iii) above,
    contained in MS B.L. Or. 13964 (and Cowley 35); incipits
    are given below.

Romans. (i) TP, MS Cowley 33 p.1:

ትርጓሜ ፦ መልእክታት ፦ ቀዳማዊ ፦ እንተ ፦ ፀሐፋ ፦ ጳስ ፦ ርዕጌ ፦ እዝ ፦
ሀሎ ፦ በቆሮንቶስ ፦ -- ምዕራፉ ፦ ቀዳማዊ ፦ እምይደውኮስ ፦ ገብረ ፦
ኢየሱስ ፦ ንርስቶስ ፦ --- ደቤ ፦ መተርጉም ፦ ወዘዝንራስ ፦ ብን[ንት] ፦
ዝንቱ ፦ መልእክታት ፦ ጳስ ፦ እሉ ፦ ሕዝብ ፦ ርሑቃን ፦ --

    (ii) TFF, MS B.L. Or. 13964 f.1a-25a (but the commentary on
    Romans is defective at its beginning and end).

    (iii) Fragments in Mashafä hawi attributed to John Chrysostom
    (B.L. Or. 776 f.142b, 260b).

1 Corinthians. (i) TP MS Cowley 33 p.78:

ዘቆሮንቶስ ፦ ቀዳማዊ ። ወዘሬ ፦ ዘነገርኩንሙ ፦ እስሙ ፦ እሳ ፦
ዘንዕፉኩንሙ ፦ -- ትርጓሜ ፦ ቀዳሜ ፦ ኑሉ ፦ ትትገአዘ ፦ በቤተ ፦
ንርስቲያን ፦ ወትትለአዎ ፦ ለማዕቡ ፦ ወሶ ፦ ዘእጎንፃ ፦ --

(ii) <u>TFF</u>, MS B.L. Or. 13964 f.27a–58a (but the commentary on 1 Cor. is defective at its beginning).

(iii) Fragments – see under 2 Cor.

2 Corinthians. (i) <u>TP</u>, MS Cowley 33 p.96:

ምዕራፍ ፡ ቀዳማዊ ፡ ‥ እምጾሙ ፡ ሐዋርያ ፡ ‥ ይቤ ፡
መተርጕም ፡፡ ወዘእስተላጸቅስ ፡ ሶሙ ፡ ጢሞቴዎስ ፡ ምስለ ፡
ሶሙ ፡ ወእስተቤተፎ ፡ በመጽሐፉ ፡ እስሙ ፡ ጾሙሎስ ፡
ቀዳሚ ፡ ለጢሞቴዎስ ፡ ፈነዋ ፡ ኀበ ፡ ሰሙ ፡ ‥

(ii) <u>TFF</u>, MS B.L. Or. 13964 f.58a–90b:

ለሰባእ ፡ ቆሮንቶስ ፡ ወተጹሕፈ ፡ እንዘ ፡ ሀሎ ፡ ብሔር ፡
ሌልጶስቦስ ፡ ‥ ፈኮን ፡ ተርጕመ ፡ ወይቤ ፡ ጾሙሎስ ፡ ሐዋርያ ፡
ለኀግዚአነ ፡ ኢየሱስ ፡ ክርስቶስ ፡ ልኢጎ ፡ ሙስተ ፡ እሕዛብ ፡
ቁሉ ፡ ለመፍሃኔ ፡ ሕዝብ ፡ ‥

(iii) Fragments (on 1 and 2 Cor.):

(a) in <u>HA</u> attributed to Cyril of Alexandria,

(b) in <u>HA</u> attributed to John Chrysostom,

(c) in <u>Mashafä hawi</u> attributed to John Chrysostom (B.L. Or. 776 f.50b, 58b, 67b, 84b, 96a, 106a, 114b, 141a, 166b, 173a, 220b, 223a, 260a),

(d) in B.L. Or. 527 f.137b–138.

Galatians. (i) <u>TP</u>, MS Cowley 33 pp.117–8:

መልእክት ፡ ኀበ ፡ ሰብእ ፡ ገላትያ ፡ ወምክንያት ፡ ጹሬጾቹስ ፡ ኪያሃ ፡
ኮነ ፡ ኀበ ፡ እሕዛብ ፡ እለ ፡ እምኑ ፡ በክርስቶስ ፡ ወምስለ ፡ ዕሥነቶሙ ፡
ኀበ ፡ ክርስቶስ ፡ ‥ ምዕራፍ ፡ ቀዳማዊ ፡ ‥ እምጾሙሎስ ፡ ሐዋርያ ፡ ‥
ቸርንዒ ፡ እስሙ ፡ ብሂሎቱስ ፡ በመልእክቱ ፡ ዘኢኮነ ፡ በእንተ ፡
ሰብእ ፡ ወኢኮነ ፡ እምሰብእ ፡ ‥

(ii) <u>TFF</u>, MS B.L. Or.13964 f.90b–103b:

በስሙ ፡ ‥ ለሰብእ ፡ ገላትያ ፡ ‥ ፈኮን ፡ ተርጕመ ፡ ወይቤ ፡ ናእምን ፡
ወኀነ ፡ ጾሙሎስ ፡ ተፈጥነ ፡ ሐዋርያ ፡ ለሰብእ ፡ ገላትያ ፡ ወኢኮነ ፡
በእንተ ፡ ሰብእ ፡ እለ ፡ በእንተ ፡ እግዚእብሔር ፡ ‥

(iii) Fragments in <u>Mashafä hawi</u> attributed to John Chrysostom (B.L. Or. 776 f.58b, 153a).

Ephesians. (i) T̲P̲, MS Cowley 33 p.132:

መልእክት ፡ ኀበ ፡ ሰብእ ፡ ኤፌሶን ፡ ወይእዜንtት ፡ ጽሒ ፎቴስ ፡ ኪያሃ ፡
ለሐዋርያ ፡ ብፁዓዊ ፡ ጳውሎስ ፡ ጸሐፈ ፡ ዘንተ ፡ መልእክተ ፡ ኀበ ፡ እሉ ፡
ሕዝብ ፡ እስመ ፡ ኢተራከዮሙ ፡ ገጸ ፡ በገጽ ፡ --- ምዕራፍ ፡ n̄ወ b̄ ፡
ዘኤፌሶን ፡ ኅምጸ ዉ ሎስ ፡ -- ትርጓሜ ፡ ወብሂሎቴስ ፡ ይትገሪ እን ፡
እግዚእ ብሔር ፡ እሉሉ ፡ --

(ii) T̲F̲F̲, MS B.L. Or. 13964 f.103b–116b:

ለሰብእ ፡ ኤፌሶን ፡ ወተጽሐፈ ፡ እንዘ ፡ ሀሎ ፡ በብሔረ ፡ ሮሜ ፡ --
ይትገሪእን ፡ እግዚ እብሔር ፡ -- ፌሎን ፡ ተርጎሙ ፡ ወይ ፡
ለቀዱሳን ፡ እሉ ፡ ኤፌሶን ፡ እሉ ፡ ነኑ ፡ ቀዱሳን ፡ ክርስቲያን ፡ --

(iii) Fragments attributed to John Chrysostom in H̲A̲, and in
Mäshafä hawi (B.L. Or. 776 f.50a, 57a, 85a, 88b, 261a).

Philippians. (i) T̲P̲, MS Cowley 34 p.1:

መልእክት ፡ ኀበ ፡ ሰብእ ፡ ፌልጴስዩስ ፡ ወይእዜንያt ፡ ጽሒፎቴስ ፡
ኪያሃ ፡ እስመ ፡ እሙንቱ ፡ ሕዝብ ፡ ነኑ ፡ ሠናይ ፡ ለሥርዓቶሙ ፡
ወርቱዓን ፡ በሃይማኖት ፡ -- ምዕራፍ ፡ n̄ወ z̄ ፡ እኅምጸ ዉ ሎስ ፡
ትርጓሜ ፡ ወዘ ይብ ፡ ኀበ ፡ ነኵሎሙ ፡ ቀዱሳን ፡ ወንዱሐን ፡
በኢየሱስ ፡ ክርስቶስ ፡ --

(ii) T̲F̲F̲, MS B.L. Or. 13964 f.116b–125a:

ተፈነወt ፡ መልእክት ፡ ለሰብእ ፡ ፌልጴስዩስ ፡ -- ነገረ ፡ ጳውሎስ ፡
ለነኵሎሙ ፡ ቀዱሳን ፡ -- ፌሎን ፡ ተርጎሙ ፡ ወይብ ፡ ጳውሎስ ፡
ወጢሞቴዎስ ፡ እግብርቲሁ ፡ ለኢየሱስ ፡ ክርስቶስ ፡ ለመፋነ ፡
ዓለም ፡ --

(iii) Fragments in H̲A̲ attributed to Gregory of Nyssa.

(iv) Fragments in Mäshafä hawi attributed to John Chrysostom
(B.L. Or. 776 f.140a, 153b, 163a, 192a, 219b).

Colossians. (i) T̲P̲, MS Cowley 34 p.9:

በስመ ፡ -- መልእክተ ፡ ጳውሎስ ፡ ኀበ ፡ ሰብእ ፡ ቆሎስይስ ፡ --
እኅምጸ ዉ ሎስ ፡ -- ፍገሬ ፡ ጸሐፈ ፡ ብፁዓዊ ፡ ጳውሎስ ፡
ለቆላሲ ይ ባዊያን ፡ እንዘ ፡ ኢያሬኅዮሙ ፡ ወዘይምህር ክ ፡ ለበላ ፡
ዘንተ ፡ በሂሎቴ ፡ ዘይብ ፡ ንሕነ ፡ ሰማዕና ፡ ሃይማኖተ ክሙ ፡ --

(ii) T̲F̲F̲, MS B.L. Or. 13964 f.125a–135a:

ጳውሎስ ፡ -- እሉ ፡ ውስተ ፡ ቆላስይስ ፡ -- ፌሎን ፡ ተርጎሙ ፡ ወይብ ፡
ለሰብእ ፡ ቆላስይስ ፡ ዘተፈነወ ፡ መልእክት ፡ እንዘ ፡ ሀለወ ፡ በሔረ ፡
ሮሜ ፡ ጳውሎስ ፡ ልኡ እን ፡ ለመፋኔ ፡ ሕዝብ ፡ --

(iii) Fragments in M̈ashafä̈ hawi attributed to John
Chrysostom (B.L. Or. 776 f.33b, 35a, 114b, 201a).

1 Thessalonians. (i) <u>TP</u>, MS Cowley 34 p.18:

ምዕራፉ ፡ ፲፬ እግዚአብሔሕ ፡ _ _ ትርጓሜ ፡ ዘዘክሮስ ፡ አስልዋኖስ ፡
በሠልእንቴ ፡ ደቤ ፡ ሐኖን ፡ ከመ ፡ ኢይፍኑ ፡ ኑፋቄ ፡ ሳዕለ ፡ እሎ ፡
ሕዝብ ፡ በእንቲእሉ ፡ በከመ ፡ ኑሳ ፡ በእንተ ፡ ኤሳፍሎ ፡ _ _

(ii) <u>TFF</u>, MS B.L. Or. 13964 f.135a-146b:

አሰብእ ፡ ተሰኮንቄ ፡ ወተድሕሬ ፡ እንዘ ፡ ሀሎ ፡ ብሔሬ ፡ እቲና ፡ _ _
ዘንተ ፡ ዘይቤከመሙ ፡ አእርቄዕት ፡ ከመ ፡ ይንብያው ፡ ውስተ ፡ ስብከተ ፡
ወንጌል ፡ ወተሰኮንቄ ፡ ወበኑሉ ፡ እቄያዊሪ ፡ እስዝ ፡ ኢይሬኑ ፡ _ _

(iii) Fragments – see under 2 Thess.

2 Thessalonians. (i) <u>TP</u>, MS Cowley 34 p.24:

ምዕራፉ ፡ ፲፬ወ፪ እግዚአብሔሕ ፡ _ _ ፉግሬ ፡ ደጋ ፡ ወ ሰኳ ፡
ምስሌናመው ፡ ዘደቤ ፡ እስመ ፡ ደጋ ፡ ዘሐፁር ፡ ሳዕለ ፡ ስብእ ፡
ኑሳ ፡ ፉስቤ ፡ እምደሉተ ፡ ወእማደ ፡ ውሉፁ ፡ ወድሕቀ ፡ _ _

(ii) <u>TFF</u>, MS B.L. Or. 13964 f.146b-152b:

አሰብእ ፡ ተሰኮንቄ ፡ ወተድሕሬ ፡ እንዘ ፡ ሀሎ ፡ ብሔሬ ፡ ሮጣይ ፡ _ _
ፉከሮን ፡ ትርጐመ ፡ ወደቤ ፡ አሰብእ ፡ ተሰኮንቄ ፡ ወተድሕሬ ፡ እንዘ ፡
ሀሎ ፡ ብሔሬ ፡ ሮጣይ ፡ _ _ _ ከመ ፡ ትእየሙ ፡ እንተመው ፡ ዘተፈነው ፡
እምኑብ ፡ አሉሩ ፡ _ _

(iii) Fragments (on 1 and 2 Thess.) in M̈ashafä̈ hawi
attributed to John Chrysostom (B.L. Or. 776 f.50a-b, 138b).

1 Timothy. (i) <u>TP</u>, MS Cowley 34 p.27:

ወልእንቴ ፡ ቀዳጣዪ ፡ ኑብ ፡ ጢሞቴዎስ ፡ ምዕራፉ ፡ ፲፬ወ፲
እግዚአብሔሕ ፡ _ _ ፉግሬ ፡ ወበሔከተሪ ፡ በኇንተ ፡ ወልእንቴ ፡
በቲኇዛዘ ፡ እንዚአስሔር ፡ ወበፈቃዲ ፡ እስመ ፡ ውኇቲ ፡ ይከእብ ፡
ሳዕለ ፡ ዝንቲ ፡ ግብር ፡ _ _

(ii) <u>TFF</u>, MS B.L. Or. 13964 f.152b-165b:

_ _ ፄውኮስ ፡ ገብሬ ፡ አኢየሉስ ፡ _ _ ፈፁተስ ፡ ትርጐመ ፡ ወደቤ ፡
ፄውኮስ ፡ ላእኑ ፡ ለወፁኑኔ ፡ ሕዝብ ፡ ቅሩዕ ፡ በተኇዛዘ ፡
እግዚ እስሔር ፡ _ _

(iii) Fragments – see under 2 Tim.

2 Timothy. (i) <u>TP</u>, MS Cowley 34 p.41-2:

በአሰወ ፡ -- መልእክት ፡ ቃዊግሞ ፡ ኅበ ፡ ጢሞቴዎስ ፡ --ምዕራፉ ፡
ሃ፬ወ፮ እጎም ፈጡሉስ ፡ -- ፍጎሬ ፡ ወበዚከሉቴሬ ፡ ሐዋርያ ፡
ኢየሱስ ፡ ክርስቶስ ፡ በፈቃዱ ፡ እግዚእብሔር ፡ ወበተስፋ ፡
ዘለእጎደወት ፡ ዘለሰይ ፡ ለሳ ፡ መጎፈልተ ፡ ጎገ ፡፡ ዘወኅቴ ፡
ኅበወ ፡ ለሊሁ ፡ ጎሳ ፡ ሐዋርያ ፡ --

     (ii) <u>TFF</u>, MS B.L. Or. 13964 f.165b-173a:

ለጢሞቴዎስ ፡ -- ፈለኮን ፡ ተርጕወ ፡ ወደበ ፡ ፈጡሉስ ፡
ሐዋርያሁ ፡ ለኢየሱስ ፡ መፈኅኔ ፡ ሕዝብ ፡ ወለክርስቶስ ፡
መፈኅኔ ፡ ሕዝብ ፡ መዚእ ፡ በፈቃዱ ፡ እግዚእብሔር ፡ --

     (iii) Fragments (on 1 and 2 Tim.) in M̈ashafä hawi, attributed
to John Chrysostom (B.L. Or. 776 f.50a-b, 57a, 116b, 119a,
140b, 152b, 153b, 172a, 202a).

Titus. (i) <u>TP</u>, MS Cowley 34 p.49:

በአሰወ ፡ -- መልእክት ፡ ኅበ ፡ ቲቶ ፡ ኅንተ ፡ ዳሐፈ ፡ እጎሜቃጡሉስ ፡ --
ምዕራፉ ፡ ሃ፬ወ፮ ፡ እጎ ፈጡሉስ ፡ -- ፍጎሬ ፡ ወዳኣሳ ፡ ዝንቴ ፡
ቲቶ ፡ ብእሴ ፡ ፪ሬ ፡ ፭ሉተ ፡ ኅሬሞ ፡ ፈጡሉስ ፡ --

     (ii) <u>TFF</u>, MS B.L. Or. 13964 f.173a-178b:

ፈጡሉስ ፡ ገብሬ ፡ እግዚእብሔር ፡ -- ፈለኮን ፡ ተርጕወ ፡ ወደበ ፡
ፈጡሉስ ፡ ገብሬ ፡ እግዚእብሔር ፡ ወልእኩ ፡ ለኢየሱስ ፡
ክርስቶስ ፡ ቆሉኅ ፡ መፈኅኔ ፡ ሕዝብ ፡ ኅወ ፡ እስብኅ ፡ --

Philemon. (i) <u>TP</u>, MS Cowley 34 p.53:

በአሰወ ፡ -- መልእክት ፡ ኅበ ፡ ሌልሞን ፡ ወምጎንደያተ ፡ ዳሐፈትስ ፡
ዲያዋ ፡ እጎሰወ ፡ ጎሳ ፡ ለሌልሞን ፡ ገብር ፡ ዘአሰወ ፡ እናሒሞስ ፡ --
ምዕራፉ ፡ ሃ፬ወ፰ እጎ ፈጡሉስ ፡ -- ፍጎሬ ፡ ወበዚከሉቴሬ ፡
እጎ ፈጡሉስ ፡ መቁኅ ፡ ለኢየሱስ ፡ ክርስቶስ ፈቃዱ ፡ ተመጎነዬ ፡
በዝንቴ ፡ --

     (ii) <u>TFF</u>, MS B.L. Or. 13964 f.178b-181a:

ፈጡሉስ ፡ መቁኅ ፡ ለኢየሱስ ፡ -- ፈለኮን ፡ ተርጕወ ፡ ወደበ ፡
ፈጡሉስ ፡ መቁኅ ፡ ለኢየሱስ ፡ ክርስቶስ ፡ ሶበ ፡ ይብጎ ፡
ዘናሠኅኔ ፡ በፈቃዱ ፡ ኅበ ፡ ኢፈቃፉኅ ፡ ለተምህርት ፡ ዘእሉ ፡ --

     (iii) Fragments in M̈ashafä hawi attributed to John
Chrysostom (B.L. Or. 776 f.41b, 139a).

Hebrews. (i) TP, MS Cowley 34 p.55:

በእሎሙ ፦ መፊእንተ ፡ ኀበ ፡ ዕብራዉያን ፡ ም[ዕ]ራፍ ፡ ፶ በበዘሩ ፡ ጸፉ ፡ ወበብዘሩ ፡ እምሳዕ ፦ ፍኀሬ ፡ ወበዜሎቱሬ ፡ በኀቡ ፡ ንጉሬ ፡ ወበኀሎ ፡ ነገር ፡ ፦ ፈቃፈ ፡ ነሙ ፡ ይመዴቀ ፡ በዝኅተ ፡ ፈልሙነ ፡ ዘሎሎ ፡ ማዕኅለ ፡ ነዲያተ ፡ ወማዕዕኅለ ፡ እግዜእ ፡ ክርስቶስ ፡ ፦

    (ii) TFF, MS B.L. Or. 13964 f.181a–216b:

በእሎሙ ፡ ፦ ንዱሐፈ ፡ ቅርጋዉ፤ ፡ ፈሙኮለ ፡ ለሰብእ ፡ ዕብራዉያን ፡ በብዘሩ ፡ ነገር ፡ ወበብዘሩ ፡ መፅኀፈሰተ ፡ ፦ ፈ ኮን ፡ ተርጎመ ፡ ወይበ ፡ በብዘሩ ፡ ነገር ፡ ፦ ወዝንተ ፡ ሶበ ፡ ይብል ፡ በብዘሩ ፡ ነገር ፡ ተኀበፈ ፡ ነዲያተ ፡ ነሙ ፡ ይመዴእ ፡ ክርስቶስ ፡ ለመፉኀረተ ፡ ውሉዱ ፡ ሰብኀ ፡፡

(iii) Geez version of John Chrysostom's Homilies on Hebrews,
and excerpts from them, described in 5.1.2 (i) above. The
fullest catalogue description is on EMML 2116, and the
work is also found in B.L. Add. 16197 (Dillmann 10), Or.
(Wright) 737–741, Or. (Strelcyn 59) 12513; B.N. d'Abbadie
20, 166, Zotenberg 66; Berlin (Dillmann 25) Peterm.II
Nachtr. 58; Tübingen (Ewald) 6; Uppsala O Etiop.21
(Löfgren 38); Jerusalem (Littmann, Greek monastery II),
Jerusalem (Littmann, Eth. monastery 252), Jerusalem (Aešcoly),
JE 343 E; Ṭanasee (Hammerschmidt) 37; Aksum etc. (Kolmodin);
Keren (Conti Rossini) 20, 21; A.A. Nat. Lib. 242, 243, 245;
EMML 46, 345, 513, 687, 948, (1200), 1764, 2377, 3002, 3406;

? Gundagundi (Mordini) 70, 98, ? 87.

Catholic epistles. See TIA p.40 and fragments in Berlin Ms.or.qu.986.

Revelation. (i) Tərgwame q̱ala̱msis, description, text, and trans-
lation in TIA, contained in MSS B.L. Or. 13830 part II,
EMML 2082 f.81a–106a, Cowley 34, Berlin (Dillmann 63) Peterm.
II Nachtrag 24, and   Cerulli Vatican 80 f.5a–43b; incipit

1. MS Vat. Cer. Eth. 80 contains a well-written twentieth century
copy of TQ, of the text-type referred to as A–B in TIA pp.65–70.

in Cowley 34 p.95:

 በአሙ ፡ -- ንወንን ፡ በድሉ ፡ ፋኅሬ ፡ ሊኁP ፡ P ሐንስ ፡ --
ምቀ ፁም ፡ ዘ P ሐንስ ፡ ኤ ደ ስ ቆ ደ ስ ፡ -- ፭ ፋ ኅ ሬ ፡ ወ ስ ሄ ኮ ተ ስ ፡
ዘ P ሐ ን ስ ፡ ኤ ደ ስ ፡ ቆ ደ ስ ፡ ዘ ቀ ስ ኝ ን ኝ ን ያ ፡ ስ ኻ ን ተ ፡
P ሐ ን ስ ፡ ኻ ሬ ፡ ወ ር ቀ ፡ --

(ii) Fragments in B.L. Or. 743; Uppsala O Etiop.52 (Löfgren
13); B.N. d'Abbadie 119 f.150; EMML 1056.

(iii) Geez poem on Rev. in B.L. Or. 574 f.1–8.

(iv) ? A.A. Unesco 8/3.

<u>Sinodos</u>. Fragments in B.L. Or. 743, and in <u>Mäshafä hawi</u> (e.g. B.L.
Or. 776 f.66a).

<u>Didəsqəlya</u>. Fragment in B.N. d'Abbadie 39 f.188a–190a.

<u>Qäleməntos</u>. Explanations of words and fragments in B.L. Or. 743;
B.N. d'Abbadie 97 f.96a; Accademia dei Lincei, Conti
Rossini (Strelcyn) 27 pp.180–1.

Books of the monks –

<u>Filkəsyus</u>. Fragment in ? EMML 418,
<u>Arägawi mänfäsawi</u>. Notes in EMML 2118, 2183.

Miscellanea related to Geez commentaries.

(i) Geez commentary on the ten commandments, attributed to
John Chrysostom and contained in <u>Sinodos</u>, see e.g. B.L. Or.
794, 481; B.N. Zotenberg 121 and (possibly a different text)
157 f.31b–; B.N. Griaule (Strelcyn Eth. 395) 91; Uppsala
O Etiop.39 (Löfgren 35); St. Petersburg (Turaev) VI;
EMML 362, 1189, 7410 f.125a–128b.

(ii) Commentary on the Lord's Prayer attributed to Gregory
of Nyssa and contained in <u>Mäshafä hawi</u> (e.g. B.L. Or. 776
f.167a).

(iii) Commentary on the Nicene Creed, by <u>Abunä</u> Bärtälomewos
in BFBS MS 176 (Cowley III) f.142b–144b, and credal expansions in this MS and BFBS 173 and 177.

(iv) Introductions and hypotheses to N.T. books – these are
analysed in my review of EMML <u>Catalogue</u> vol.VII in <u>JSS</u>, and

the following is a selection of additional MSS in which introductions are found:

(a) Gospels. Bodleian (Dillmann) X, XI, XII; B.N. Zotenberg 33; Berlin Ms.or.qu. 986; Wien Aeth. XX (Muller VI); St. Petersburg (Turaev) I, 4 and IV, 14(9); EMML 135–6, 154, 170, 174, 244, 287, 292, 330, 364, 388, 407, 416, 444, 468, 469, 565, 662, 686, 755, 767, 812, 858, 881, 1038, 1056, 1116, 1185, 1216, 2187, 2402, 2965, 3053, 3127, 3297, 3300, 3304, 3312, 3390, 3393, 3399, 3401, 3405, 3415, 3450.

(b) Acts. B.L. Or. 529 f.76a–, EMML 1982, 2210, 2372.

(c) Pauline corpus. B.L. Or. 528, 530; Add. 16248 (Dillmann 12); Bodleian (Dillmann) XV; B.N. d'Abbadie 130; Berlin Ms.or.qu. 846, 986, 989, 991; A.A. Nat. Lib. 36; EMML 128, 175, 656, 716, 1116, 1119, 1403, 1902, 1944, 1955, 1982, 2067, 2088, 2103, 2153, 2159, 2160, 2191, 2352, 2372, 2412, 2700, 2708, 2833, 2927, 3254.

(d) Catholic epistles. B.L. Or. 529, Add. 16248; Berlin Ms.or.qu. 846, 986; A.A. Nat. Lib. 36; EMML 585, 1119, 1403, 1944, 1948, 1955, 2067, 2103, 2155, 2159, 2209, 2372.

(e) Revelation. See TIA p.174 and B.L. Or. 526, 529, Add. 16248; Berlin Ms.or.qu. 846, 986; EMML 2160, 2191, 2210; introduction and history of John in EMML 585.

(v) Fäharäst (introduction to HA). Tanasee (Hammerschmidt) 50 f.2a–32a; EMML 154, 508, 1187, 1393, 2051.

(vi) Bios of (a) Cyril of Alexandria in e.g. B.L. Or. 744; EMML 639, 1993, 2108, 2385, 2847, (b) John Chrysostom in e.g. EMML 1200, 2116, 2377.

(vii) Collections of lexical and sawasəw material, e.g. in Dublin (Cerulli) 927; B.N. d'Abbadie 39, Zotenberg 150; Capucins (Chaîne) VI; St. Petersburg (Kokovcov) XX; St. Petersburg (Turaev) 19; EMML 2817, 2849.

(viii) Collections of historical and explanatory material, e.g. in B.L. (Wright) Or. 816, Add. 24990, 24991; B.L. (Dillmann 72) Add.16211; B.N. d'Abbadie 96, 157; Zotenberg

50, 64, 149; Mondon-Vidailhet (Chaîne) 19 (205); Griaule
(Strelcyn Eth. 386) 82; Duchesne-Fournet (Blanchart) 7;
Berlin (Dillmann 85) Ms.or.oct. 190; Pistoia ms.1 (Zanutto
item 158); Lincei, Conti Rossini (Strelcyn) 125; St. Petersburg (Turaev) III Nauk 56–8; EMML 259, 650, 954, 1370, 1543,
2092, 2342, 2440, 2855.

(ix) Computus, see O. Neugebauer, Ethiopic Astronomy, and
e.g. B.N. Zotenberg 160; EMML 941, 1056.

(x) Tənta haymanot. MSS are listed in 4.1.4 above.

(xi) The Aksimaros published by E. Trumpp, mentioned in
4.1.4 above. (In the MSS catalogues there may be some
confusion between this and similar works). See B.N. Zotenberg 175; Delorme (Grébaut) 3; Wien (Rhodokanakis 24)Aeth.19;
Jerusalem (Littmann, Eth. monastery) 265; ? A.A. Unesco 6/18,
7/6; Tigre (Cowley); ? Cerulli (Raineri) 165.

(xii) SFG (see 4.1.4 above). B.L. Or. 482 f.121b; Bod-
leian (Ullendorff 84, 85) Aeth. g.9 and Ind. Inst. Misc. 3;
B.N. d'Abbadie 156 f.3a–4a; Berlin Ms.or.qu. 994;
Jerusalem (Littmann, Eth. monastery) 266–8; ? JE 203E;
JE 702–8 E; A.A. Unesco 2/102, 6/27, 10/76; EMML 1054,
2114, 2302, 2135, 3111, ? 3412; Cerulli (Raineri) 272.

(xiii) Geez AAM and related texts. B.L. (Dillmann 15)
Add. 16199; Bodleian (Ullendorff 82, 85) Aeth. f.9 and
Ind. Inst. Misc. 3; B.N. d'Abbadie 151, 151 bis; Tübingen
(Ewald 4) Ms. aeth. 23; ? Jerusalem (Littmann, Eth.
monastery) 269–76; Hazzega and Sāʿdā Embā (Kolmodin);
Tigre (Cowley).

7.4   ANDƏMTA COMMENTARY MANUSCRIPTS.

The following is a provisional listing of AC MSS and their commonest incipits (cited from the sources first specified). It is supplementary to the information on the texts and printed editions contained in TIA pp.6–14.

For compiling the list, the catalogues listed in 7.2 above have all been consulted, but I have only personally used the MSS in the collections at the B.L., Bodleian Library, Cambridge, A.A. Nat. Lib., A.A. Holy Trinity Cathedral, and Jerusalem, and in my own collection; it should not be assumed, therefore, that all listed MSS are necessarily substantially similar to each other.

Cataloguers', names are given in brackets, and refer to the catalogues listed in 7.2. For EMML MSS, see W. Macomber and Getatchew Haile. MSS numbered JE are in the Ethiopian archbishop's residence in Jerusalem, except for ones noted as DG, which are at the Ethiopian Church Däbrä gännät. For A.A. Nat. Lib. MSS see 'Imperial Ethiopian Government'; for A.A. Unesco MSS see 'Ministry of Education'. For MSS numbered 'Cowley', see 7.5 below.

Many further AC MSS are to be found in Gondar and other centres of AC instruction.

AC Genesis. MS Cowley 1, pp.1-262:
ኦሪት ፡ ዘልደት ፡ ኦሪት ፡ ማለት ፡ ሕግ ፡ ማለት ፡ ነው ። የጥመስን ፡
የሐሳዌ ፡ መሲሕን ፡ የምጽአትን ፡ የመንግሥት ፡ ሰማያትን ፡ ነገር ፡
ትናገራለችና ።

Cowley 31, pp.1-64; B.L.Or. 13683D; Bodl. Aeth.d.15; EMML 1274, ? 1382, 1694, 2012; fragments in B.N. d'Abbadie 233, EMML 510, 1206, 175.

AC Exodus. MS Cowley 1, pp.263-380 and 2, pp.381-458:
ኦሪት ፡ ዘጸአት ፡ ሕግ ፡ ዘጸዓት ፡ ሲል ፡ ነው ። ያዕቆብ ፡ ወደ ፡
ግብፅ ፡ ፸ ፡ ሆኖ ፡ ወረዱ ፡ ብዙ ፡ ነበርና ፡ ከዚያ ፡ አያያዝ ፡
ኦሪት ፡ ዘጸዓት ፡ አለ ፡

Cowley 31, pp.64-111; B.L.Or. 13683D; Bodl. Aeth.d.15; EMML 1274, 1694.

AC Leviticus. MS Cowley 2,pp.553-691:
ኦሪት ፡ ዘሌዋውያን ፡ ... ሕግ ፡ ዘሌዋውያን ፡ ሲል ፡ ነው ።
በሌዊ ፡ ሌዋውያን ፡ ተብለዋል ፡ የሌዋውያንን ፡ ነገር ፡ የሚናገር ፡
መጽሐፍ ፡ ይህ ፡ ነው ።

Cowley 31, pp.112-130; B.L.Or. 13683D; Bodl. Aeth. d.15; EMML 1274, 1694; fragment in EMML 510.

AC Numbers. MS Cowley 2, pp.693-768 and 3, pp.769-857:
ኦሪት ፡ ዘኍልቍ ፡ ሕግ ፡ ዘኍልቍ ፡ ሲል ፡ ነው ፡ የሠሎቹን ፡
የቍጥሮቻቸውን ፡ ነገር ፡ የሚናገር ፡ መጽሐፍ ፡ ይህ ፡ ነው ።
ኦሪት ፡ ዘፀዓት ፡ የአበውን ፡ ነገር ፡ ይናገራል ፡ ኦሪት ፡ ዘኍልቍ ፡
የሠሎቹን ፡ ነገር ፡ ይናገራል ።

Cowley 31, pp.131-156; B.L.Or. 13683D; Bodl. Aeth. d.15; EMML 1274, 1694.

AC Deuteronomy. MS Cowley 3, pp.857-1080:
ኦሪት ፡ ዘዳግም ፡ + ዲዘትስ ፡ እንደመጣ ፡ ኦሪት ፡ ዘኃምስ ፡ ሲል ፡
በቀና ፡ ነበር ፡ ዘዳግም ፡ ያለበት ፡ ምስጢሩ ፡ አልታወቀም ፡
እንዲያም ፡ ታጠቃል ፡ ለኦሪት ፡ ዘኍልቍ ፡ ዳግም ፡ ብሎታል ።

Cowley 31, pp.157-175; B.L.Or. 13683D; Bodl. Aeth. d.15; EMML 1274, 1694.

AC Joshua. MS Cowley 2, pp.459-552:
ኦሪት ፡ ዘኢያሱ ፡ ሕግ ፡ ዘኢያሱ ፡ ሲል ፡ ነው ፡ ኢያሱ ፡ ማለት ፡
መድኃኒት ፡ ማለት ፡ ነው ፡ ኢሳይያስ ፡ ኢየሱስ ፡ ማለት ፡
መድኃኒት ፡ ማለት ፡ እንደሆነ ።

Cowley 31, pp.176–186;   B.L.Or. 13683E;   Bodl. Aeth. d.15;   EMML
1274, 1694.

AC Judges.   MS Cowley 4, pp.1071 (1081) – 1197:

እሪት ፡ ዘመሳፍንት ፡ --- ዜና ፡ ዘመሣፍንት ፡ ሔል ፡ ነው ፡
የመሣፍንትን ፡ ነገር ፡ የሚናገር ፡ መጽሐፍ ፡ ይህ ፡ ነው ።

Cowley 31, pp.187–205;   B.L.Or. 13683 E;   Bodl. Aeth. d.15;   EMML
1274, 1694;   fragment in EMML 510.

AC Ruth.   MS Cowley 4, pp.1199–1213:

እሪት ፡ ዘሩት ፡ --- ዜና ፡ ዘሩት ፡ ሔል ፡ ነው ፡ የሩትን ፡ ዜና ፡
የሚናገር ፡ መጽሐፍ ፡ ይህ ፡ ነው ፡

Cowley 31, pp.206–8;   B.L.Or. 13683 E;   Bodl. Aeth. d.15;   EMML
1274, 1694.

AC 1 Samuel.   MS Cowley 5, pp.1–240:

ነገሥት ፡ ቀዳማዊ ።   ቀዳማዊ ፡ ጎለ ፡ ንጉሥ ፤ ነገሥትያም ፡
ጎለ ፡ ቀዳማጉ ያን ፡ ጎለ ፡ በቃና ፡ ነገር ፡ ልማዱ ፡ መጽሐፍ ፡
ነው ።

Cowley 31;   B.L.Or. 13683 M;   Bodl. Aeth. c.11;   EMML 1281, 1693;
fragments in EMML 1206;   notes in EMML 3018.

AC 2 Samuel.   MS Cowley 5, pp.241–390 and 6, pp.391–426:

መጽሐፈ ፡ ነገሥት ፡ ዳግማዊ ፤ የነገሥታቸን ፡ ነገር ፡ የሚናገር ፡
ኻኛው ፡ መጽሐፍ ፡ ይህ ፡ ነው ።

Cowley 31;   B.L.Or. 13683 M;   Bodl. Aeth. c.11;   EMML 1281, 1693.

AC 1 Kings.   MS Cowley 6, pp.427–652:

ነገሥት ፡ ሣልስ ፡ ምዕራፍ ፡ ፩ ፡ ወዳዌትስ ፡ -- በተወለዱ ፡
በ፳ ፡ ዘመን ፡ በነገሠ ፡ በ፵ ፡ ዘመን ፡ ዓዌት ፡ እረፈ ፡
ስለ ም ን ፡ ፈንዮ ፡ እረፈ ፡ ሔሉ ፡ --

Cowley 31;   B.L.Or. 13683 M;   Bodl. Aeth. c.11;   EMML 1281, 1693.

AC 2 Kings.   MS Cowley 6, pp.653–792 and 7, pp.793–879:

ነገሥት ፡ ራብዕ ፡ --- ወኢምጽሐሬ ፡ -- እጸእብ ፡ ክሞት ፡ በኔለ ፡
የሟዓብ ፡ ስዎች ፡ ካዱ ።   እርኢስት ፡ ነው ።

Cowley 31;   B.L.Or. 13683 M;   Bodl. Aeth. c.11;   EMML 1281, 1693.

AC 1 Chronicles.   MS Cowley 8, pp.1–211:

ሐፃዓን ፡ ዘነገሥተ ፡ እስራኤል ፤ ሐፃዓን ፡ መሳት ፡ ዜና ፡
ዘነገሥተ ፡ እስራኤል ፡ ማሳት ፡ ነው ፡ በእስራኤል ፡ የነገሡ ፡
የእስራኤል ፡ ነገሥታት ፡ ወግ ፡ ታሪን ፡ ይህ ፡ ነው ።

Cowley 31;   Bodl. Aeth. c.11;   EMML 1199, 1281, 1693;   fragment in
EMML 1202.

AC 2 Chronicles. MS Cowley 9, pp.213–484:

ካልዕ ፡ ሐዋግዝ ፡ እምነገሥት ፡ ይሉዳ ፡ በይሉዳ ፡ ከነገሠ ፡
ነገሠታት ፡ የተገና ፡ ወግ ፡ ታሪኽን ፡ የሚናገር ፡ ሉለተኛ ፡
ክፍል ፡ ይህ ፡ ነው ።

Cowley 31; Bodl. Aeth. c.11; EMML 1199, 1281, 1693; fragment in
EMML 1202.

AC Jubilees. MS Cowley 22:

ነገረ ፡ ኩፋሌ ÷ ኩፋሌ ፡ ማለት ፡ ዘተክፋለ ፡ እምእሪት ፡ ማለት ፡
ነው ፡ ፆ ፡ የዘወኩን ፡ ክፍል ፡ የሚናገር ፡ ማለት ፡ ነው ፡

B.L. Or. 13683 E; Bodl. Aeth. d.15; B.N. d'Abbadie 154; EMML
1276, 1281, 1694; portions and fragments in EMML 101, 1693, 1847.

AC Enoch. MS Cowley 23:

ዘሄኖክ ፡ ነቢይ ÷ ሄኖክ ፡ ማለት ፡ ተሐፃሰ ፡ ማለት ፡ ነው ።
እግም ፡ በምግብ ፡ ምፃንይት ፡ ብሊት ፡ እንዳወመጠ ፡ ሄኖክም ፡
ከምግብ ፡ ተክልክሎ ፡ ተሐፃሶን ፡ እምንቱልና ።

B.L.Or. 13683 F; B.N. d'Abb. 161; EMML 1200, 1276, 1694; fragments
in EMML 1202, 1206; ? Cerulli (Raineri) 110.

AC Ezra. MS Cowley 10, pp.105–170:

እመ ፡ ቀዳሚ ፡ ዓመተ ፡ መንግሥቱ ፡ ለቂሮስ ፡ --- የፈርስ ፡
ንጉሠ ፡ ቂሮስ ፡ በነገሠ ፡ በመፂመራየው ፡ ዘመን ፡ ኤርምያስ ፡
ወኢሉቆ ፡ ፸ ፡ ዓመት ፡ --- ብሎ ፡ የተናገረው ፡ ቃለ ፡
እግዚ ፡ ከተፈፀመ ፡ ስኂለ ፡

Cowley 11, f.111a–119b.

AC Nehemiah. MS Cowley 10, pp.171–261:

ቃለ ፡ ሴንደ ፡ ወልዳ ፡ ዬልያ ÷ የኢልያ ፡ ልፁ ፡ ሴንደ ፡ የተናገረው ፡
ቃል ፡ ይህ ፡ ነው ። ታሪኽን ፡ ሴንደ ፡ ያስቀው ፡ ነሐምያ ፡ ነው ።

Cowley 11, f.120a–127a; Cowley 31.

AC Ezra Apocalypse (4 Ezra, <u>ᵻzra sutuʾel</u>). MS Cowley 11, f.1–88:

ዘዕዝራ ፡ ነቢይ ። ዕዝራ ፡ ማለት ፡ ረፃኄት ፡ ማለት ፡ ነው ፡ እሔርይ ፡
እልባዛር ፡ ሄልዛር ፡ ማለት ፡ ረፃኄት ፡ ማለት ፡ --- እንዳሆነ ፡ ይህስ ፡
እንዳ ፡ ነው ፡ ሊኑ ፡ ሁለቾ ፡ ነገፁ ፡ በተማረኩ ፡ በ፶ ፡
ዘመን ፡ ነው ፡

A.A. Nat. Lib. 16; EMML 1202, 1276.

AC 1 Esdras. MS Cowley 10, pp.1–105:

እዝራ ፡ ነቢይ ፡ ይህን ፡ እዝራን ፡ ስምይን ፡ ዘየወ ፡ ለእግዚእን ፡ ይለዋል ፡
ስምይን ፡ እረጋዊ ፡ ነው ፡ እንዳም ፡ ኢይቱ ፡ ሊልኽን ፡ ነው ።

Cowley 11 and 31; Bodl. Aeth. c.11; EMML 1276, 1281, 1693.

AC Tobit. MS Cowley 12, pp.1-57:

መጽሐፈ ፡ ጦቢት ÷ ጦቢት ፡ ማለት ፡ ሠናይ ፡ ማለት ፡ ነው ፡ ወርኽP ፡
ኽግዚእብሔC ፡ ክሙ ፡ ሠናይ ፡ ባለው ፡ ነሙ ፡ ጦብ ፡ ብኦ ፡ ኽንፉ 7ኛ ፡

A.A. Nat. Lib. 16;   EMML 1276.

AC Judith. MS Cowley 12, pp.59-139:

መጽሐፈ ፡ ዮዲት ÷ ዮዲት ፡ ማለት ፡ Pወገናዊት ፡ ማለት ፡ ነው ፡፡ ፉሕዮስ ፡
ቄሮስ ፡ ይ°ንፉዮስ ፡ ቄሮስ ፡ Pሚ ጋል ፡ PፈCስ ‹ንጉሥ ‹ ሳበC ፡፡

A.A. Nat. Lib. 16;   introduction only in EMML 1276.

AC Esther. MS Cowley 12, pp.141-198:

ዘእስቴC ÷ እስቴC ፡ ማለት ፡ ፀሐይ ፡ ማለት ፡ ነው ፡ ኽንፉ ይ° ፡
ሠሬገከ ፡ ፀሐይ ፡ ማለት ፡ ነው ፡ ይህስ ፡ ኽንፉ ዪ°ነ ው ፡ ቢ ሎ ፡
ኽCጠ ንስስ ፡ Pሚ ጋል ፡ PፈCስ ፡ ንጉሥ ፡ ሳበፈ ፡፡

A.A. Nat. Lib. 16;   EMML 1276.

AC Eth. 1 Maccabees. MS Cowley 13:

ዘመቃብ ያን ÷ መቃብ ያን ፡ ማለት ፡ ፀፈ ጓን ፡ በሃይ ዳ ዋ ዮ ት ፡ ፅ ታ ዛ ፫ ‹
በስ ዲ ት ፡ ማለት ፡ ነው ፡ ኽን ፉ ዪ° ፡ በእባ ታ ቸ ው ፡ በመ ቃ ብ ዮ ስ ፡
መ ቃ ብ ያ ን ፡ ተ ብ ለ ዋ ል ፡፡

B.L. Or. 13683 B;   A.A. Nat. Lib. 16;   A.A. Holy Trinity Cathedral
29;   EMML 1199, 1281, 1693.

AC Eth. 2 Maccabees. MS Cowley 13:

በ ኽ ን ት ፡ ዘ ሌ ክ በ ሙ ፡ _ _ _ PበC ይ ፡ ኽፉ ል ፡ በ ይ° ቶ ፡ ይ ፫ ን ፡
በ መ ስ ፄ ጠ ም ይ ፡ መ ቃ ቢ ስ ፡ ኽ ይ ሉ ፉ ዪ ፫ ፡ ኽ ን ዳ ጠ ፉ ቸ ው ፡ ይ ጠ ፉ በ ተ ፫ ፡
ሳ በ C ፡ Pሚ ና ገ C ፡ መ ጽ ሐ ፉ ፡ ይ ይ ህ ፡ ነ ው ፡፡

B.L. Or. 13683 C;   A.A. Nat. Lib. 16;   A.A. Holy Trinity Cathedral
29;   EMML 1199, 1281, 1693;   portion in Cowley 11.

AC Eth. 3 Maccabees. MS Cowley 38:

ወ ይ ተ ፈ ሡ ሐ ፡ ፉ ስ ያ ተ ፡ ግ ብ ጽ ፡ _ _ ሎ ለ ተ ፫ ፡ ኽ ፉ ል ፡ ፴ ፫ C ሶ ፡
፫ ኛ ው ን ፡ ኽ መ ጠ ፡ ፉ ስ ያ ተ ፡ ግ ብ ጽ ፡ P ተ ገ ሎ ፡ ይ° ፅ መ ና ን ፡
ና ቸ ው ፡

Cowley 11;   B.L. Or. 13683 C;   A.A. Nat. Lib. 16;   A.A. Holy Trinity
Cathedral 29;   EMML 1199, 1281, 1693.

AC Job. MS Cowley 24:

ዘ ኢ ዮ ብ ፡ ጻ ፉ ቅ ፡ ኢ ዮ ብ ፡ ማለት ፡ እ በ ገ ፡ ፴ ኔ ሬ ቃ ፡ ማለት ፡ ነው ፡
እ ሕ ዛ ብ ፡ ለ ል ፇ ች ቸ ው ፡ ስ ይ° ፡ ሊ ይ መ ሙ ፡ በ እ ማ ሬ ፡ በ እ ማ ሬ ፡
ና ገ C ፡ ነ ሙ ና ፡

B.L. Or. 13683 H;   Bodl. Aeth. e.27;   A.A. Nat. Lib. 16;   EMML 1280;
fragments in Bodl. Aeth. d.6 (= Ullendorff 101, containing intro-

duction to AC Job on f.4b, 3b, 2b, 4a) and EMML 1210;Cerulli (Raineri) 110.

AC Psalms. Pr. ed.:

ዳዊት ፡ ማለት ፡ ልብ ፡ እምላጎን ፡ ማለት ፡ ነው ፡ ወኢሠዪም ፡ ሶሎት ፡
ዘነበወ ፡ ልብየ ፡ ወየኀሥሥ ፡ ሶሎት ፡ ዘነበወ ፡ ልቡ ፡ እንጺል ።

EMML 678, 1070, 1202, 1230, 1238, 1278, 1426, 1851; fragment in
EMML 2468.

AC Məssale ('Proverbs'). Pr. ed.:

ሰሎሞን ፡ ማለት ፡ መሠተሳልያም ፡ ማለት ፡ ነው ። ዘሰኔ ፡ ዘሰነ ፡
ሰላም ፡ ስለበነ ፤ ዳዊት ፡ ኢኀግዚእስሐር ፤ እግዚእስሐር ፡ ነዳዊት ፡
በተራረቃስት ፡ ወለት ፡ ስለተወሰፈ ፡ መስተሳልያም ፡ ተብኪል ።
A.A. Nat. Lib. 16.

AC Tägsas. Pr. ed.:

ተገሣጸ ፡ ሰሎሞን ፡ -- ያለ ፡ ንርንር ፡ ወዳፉቾ ፡ የሚ ሆኑ ፡ ነገያት ፡
ጎህናት ፡ አይሁዳ ፡ ንጉሠ ፡ ለእዝቀያስ ፡ የጸፈለት ፡ ሰሎሞን ፡ የተናገረው ፡
ምኽንር ፡ እዝናት ፡ ይህ ፡ ነው ።
A.A. Nat. Lib. 16.

AC Wisdom. Pr. ed.:

ንበበ ፡ ሰሎሞን ፡ --- ዘነገሠን ፡ ለዳዊት ፡ ለሰሎሞንያም ፡ ቢቀፉሉ ፡
የተመቾ ፤ በኢየሩሳሌያም ፡ የነገሠ ፡ የዳዊት ፡ ልጅ ፡ የሰሎሞን ፡
ንበቡ ፤ ይህ ፡ ነው ።
A.A. Nat. Lib. 16.

AC Ecclesiastes. Pr. ed.:

ቃለ ፡ መጽብብ ፡ --- በኢየሩሳሌያም ፡ ለእስራኤል ፡ የነገሠ ፡ የዳዊት ፡
ልጅ ፡ መጽብብ ፡ ሰሎሞን ፡ የተናገረው ፡ ነገር ፡ ይህ ፡ ነው ።
ንጉሠን ፡ ለዳዊትያም ፡ ለሰሎሞንያም ፡ ቢቀፉሉ ፡ የተመቾ ።

A.A. Nat. Lib. 16; EMML 1276.

AC Song of Solomon. Pr. ed.:

መኃልየ ፡ መኃልዪ ፡ --- ስገእያት ፡ ስገሐ ፡ ማለት ፡ ነው ። ስሳው ፡
ኊልፉ ፡ እጋር ፡ ንቤብሉን ፡ ካመሰገኑ ፡ በኂስ ።
EMML 678, 1070, 1230, 1238, 1278, ? 1426, 1850; fragment in EMML
2468.

AC Ecclesiasticus. Pr. ed.:

ዘኢያት ፡ ኂራን ። ኂራን ፡ የገሀር ፡ ስም ፡ ነው ። ኢያሱ ፡
ማለት ፡ መፉኃፈት ፡ ማለት ፡ ነው ፤ ሎሬዕ ፡ ኂሳይያስ ፡ ኢየሉስ ፡
ማለት ፡ መፉኃፈት ፡ ማለት ፡ እንጀሮነ ።

EMML 1693.

AC Isaiah. MS Cowley 14, pp.1-204 and 15,pp.205-228:
ኢሳይያስ ፡ ማለት ፡ ቅቡዕ ፡ እምቅብዓ ፡ ትንቢት ፡ ማለት ፡ ነው ፡
እንድም ፡ መድኃኒት ፡ ማለት ፡ ነው ፤ ሆሴዕ ፡ ኢያሱ ፡ ኢየሱስ ፡
ማለት ፡ መድኃኒት ፡ ማለት ፡ እንደሆነ ፡
B.L. Or. 13683 K; Bodl. Aeth. c.12; EMML 1278, 1694; incomplete in EMML 1847; fragment in EMML 1202.

AC Jeremiah (Hebrew Jeremiah 1-52). MS Cowley 30 (introduction):
ኤርምያስ ፡ ማለት ፡ ብርሃን ፡ ማለት ፡ ነው ፡ ኤሎኤል ፡ ማለት ፡
ብርሃን ፡ ማለት ፡ እንደሆነ ፡ ቦ ፡ ቃል ፡ ማለት ፡ ነው ። ወወረዱ ፡ ኤር ፡
ቅዱስ ፡ ያለውን ፡ ቃል ፡ ቅዱስ ፡ መልእክት ፡ ቅዱስ ፡ ብለው ፡
እንዲተረጉሙት ።
Cowley 16, f.1-158 and 17, f.159-229; B.L. Or. 13683 I; A.A. Nat. Lib. 16; EMML 1280; notes in EMML 1698; fragments in EMML 1202, 2080.

AC Baruch. MS Cowley 29:
ባሮክ ፡ ዘ ፡ ነገረ ፡ መጽሐፍ ፡ ሲል ፡ ባሮክ ፡ የጻፈው ፡ መጽሐፍ ፡
ይህ ፡ ነው ፡ በኃምስ ፡ ዓመት ፡ ሲ ፡ ሴዴቅያስ ፡ በነገሠ ፡ በ፲፫ው ፡
ዘመን ፡ ቦ ፡ ወተቀንየ ፡ ኤልያቄም ፡ ሠለስተ ፡ ዓመተ ፡ ይላል ፡
ከሴዴቅያስ ፡ ሁለት ፡ አምስት ፡ ያለው ፡ ይህ ፡ ነው ።

EMML 1280.

AC Lamentations (Hebrew Lam.1-5). MS Cowley 17 f.229b-250b:
ሰቆቃው ፡ ኤርምያስ ፡ ነጊደ ፡ ነጊዶ ፡ ኤርምያስ ፡ የኢየሩሳሌምን ፡
ጥፋት ፡ የእኅሎቶቹ ፡ እስራኤልን ፡ ደስታቸውን ፡ አይቶ ፡
አዝኖ ፡ ተክዞ ፡ አልቅሶ ፡ የተናገረው ፡ ነገር ፡ ይህ ፡ ነው ።

B.L. Or. 13683 I; EMML 1280.

AC Epistle of Jeremiah (Lam.6). MS Cowley 30:
አርእያ ፡ መጽሐፍ ፡ ዘኤርምያስ ፡ ... የባቢሎን ፡ ንጉሠ ፡
ማርኮ ፡ በባቢሎን ፡ ወዲ ፡ እምለቸው ፡ የላከው ፡ ኤርምያስ ፡
የተናገረው ፡ ነገር ፡ ይህ ፡ ነው ።

AC Prophecy against Pashhur (Lam.7.1-5). MS Cowley 30:
ወይቤሎ ፡ ኤርምያስ ፡ ለጳስኮር ፡ ... ጽድቅን ፡ ሃይማኖትን ፡
ትቃወሟታላቹሁ ፡ እንዲ አባቶቻቹሁ ፡ ወዲቀቅኖሙ ፡ ሲ ፡
ልጆቻቹሁም ፡ ይቃወሟታል ፡

AC 4 Baruch (<u>Täräfä barok</u>, Lam.7.6–11.63).   MS Cowley 30:

ተራፋ ፡ ባሩ ፡ ዘባሮነ ፡ ሊ ፡ ለባሮነ ፡ ያተገለጸለት ፡ ከኤርምያስ ፡
የቀረው ፡ ያልተገለጸለት ፡ ይህ ፡ ነው ፡፡ ከኤርምያስ ፡ ያልተገለጸለት ፡
ለባሮነ ፡ እልተገለጸትም ፡ ብሎ ፡ ኤርምያስ ፡ ሊድፋ ፡ ከባሮነ ፡
የቀረው ፡ ይህ ፡ ነው ፡፡

notes in EMML 2080;   fragment in EMML 1202.

AC Ezekiel.   Pr. ed.:

ሕዝቅኤል ፡ ማለት ፡ ድኔ ሬ ፡ ድጎ ፡ እምላነን ፡ ማለት ፡ ነው ፡
ሕዝቅያስ ፡ ማለት ፡ ድኔ ሬ ፡ ድጎ ፡ ኧግዚእብሔር ፡ ማለት ፡
ኧንጻ በነ ፡፡ ነገፈ ፡ ከሎዊ ፡ ተውልጸ ፡ ከእ ሮነ ፡ ነው ፡ --

B.N. d'Abb. 190;   incomplete in EMML 1278.

AC Daniel.   MS Cowley 27:

ዘዳንኤል ፡ ነሊ ደ ✝ ዳንኤል ፡ ማለት ፡ ዳኛ ፡ ኧግዚእብሔር ፡
ፍታል ፡ ኧግዚእብሔር ፡ ማለት ፡ ነው ፡፡ የዳንኤል ፡ እናት ፡ ፲ ቱ ፡ ፊቀቅ ፡
ኢሳንደያ ፡ የኤስያቂያም ፡ ልፉች ፡ ናፐው ፡፡

B.L. Or. 13683 G;   A.A. Nat. Lib. 16;   EMML 1278, 1847;   fragment
in EMML 1202.

AC Hosea.   MS Cowley 18, pp.1–48:

ኢየሴ ፡ ማለት ፡ መዉኗሬት ፡ ማለት ፡ ነው ፡ ኢ ያ ሁ ፡ ኢ ሳ ይ ያ ስ ፡
ኢ የሱ ስ ፡ ማለት ፡ መዉኗሬት ፡ ማለት ፡ ኧንጻ በነ ፡

B.L. Or. 13683 A;   A.A. Nat. Lib. 16;   EMML 1280.

AC Amos.   MS Cowley 18, pp.48–79:

እምፀ ፡ ማለት ፡ ድኔ ሬ ፡ በኧግዚእብሔር ፡፡ ኧንጻም ፡ ድኔ ሬ ፡
ኧግዚእብሔር ፡ ኧንጻም ፡ ድጎ ፡ ኧግዚእብሔር ፡ ማለት ፡ ነው ፡፡

B.L. Or. 13683 A;   A.A. Nat. Lib. 16;   EMML 1280.

AC Micah.   MS Cowley 18, pp.79–106:

ሚ ኗ ያ ስ ፡ ማለት ፡ መኑ ፡ ከማነን ፡ መመኑ ፡ ከነመ ፡ ኧግዚእብሔር ፡
ማለት ፡ ነው ፡

B.L. Or. 13683 A;   A.A. Nat. Lib. 16;   EMML 1280.

AC Joel.   MS Cowley 18, pp.1–7–124:

ኢ ይ ኤ ል ፡ ማለት ፡ ፋ ሬ ደ ፡ ኧግዚ እ ብ ሔ ር ፡ ኧንጻ ም ፡ ፋ ሪ የ ፡
ኧግዚእብሔር ፡ ማለት ፡ ነው ፡፡

B.L. Or. 13683 A;   A.A. Nat. Lib. 16;   EMML 1280.

AC Obadiah.   MS Cowley 18, pp.124–131:

እብ ፉ ደ ፡ ማለት ፡ ገብረ ፡ ኧግዚእብሔር ፡ ማለት ፡ ነው ፡ ነገፈ ፡
ከነገፈ ፡ ኤፋ ሎ ም ፡ ነው ፡

B.L. Or. 13683 A;   A.A. Nat. Lib. 16;   EMML 1280.

AC Jonah. MS Cowley 18, pp.131–143:

ዮናስ ፡ ባለት ፡ ርግብ ፡ ባለት ፡ ነው ፡ ቴታ ፡ ተሳሥተህ ፡ ወዳ ፡
ሳሳዊ ፡ ሒፋ ፡ እለው ፡፡

B.L. Or. 13683 A;   A.A. Nat. Lib. 16;   EMML 1280.

AC Nahum. MS Cowley 18, pp.143–154:

ናየም ፡ ባለት ፡ ፈውስ ፡ እግዚአብሔር ፡ ፈዋሌ ፡ እግዚአብሔር ፡
ባለት ፡ ነው ፡ ታውልዱ ፡ እነገሩ ፡ ዘብኮን ፡ ነው ፡፡

B.L. Or. 13683 A;   A.A. Nat. Lib. 16;   EMML 1280.

AC Habakkuk. MS Cowley 18, pp.154–175:

ዕንባቆም ፡ ባለት ፡ ባኳያ፟ምር ፡ አገዊ ፡ ነገሪ ፡ ባለት ፡ ነው ፡
ይህም ፡ እንባቆም ፡ እዘወራሉን ፡ ለሚያናጽፁ ፡ ምስ ፡
ይዘ ፡ ሊሃፋ ፟ ። ።

B.L. Or. 13683 A;   A.A. Nat. Lib. 16;   EMML 1280.

AC Zephaniah. MS Cowley 18, pp.175–187:

ሶፎንያስ ፡ ባለት ፡ ስፋሬ ፡ ከራን ፡ ባለት ፡ ነው ፡ እንዳም ፡
ቀዲሲ ፡ ስሉን ፡ ባለት ፡ ነው ፡

B.L. Or. 13683 A;   A.A. Nat. Lib. 16;   EMML 1280.

AC Haggai. MS Cowley 18, pp.188–198:

ሐጌ ፡ ባለት ፡ መልእክ ፡ እግዚአብሔር ፡ እንዳም ፡ በዓል ፡
ባለት ፡ ነው ፡ ነገዱ ፡ እነገሩ ፡ ጋፋ ፡ ነው ፡፡

B.L. Or. 13683 A;   A.A. Nat. Lib. 16;   EMML 1280.

AC Zechariah. MS Cowley 18, pp. 198–254:

ዘካርያስ ፡ ባለት ፡ ዝኩር ፡ ዝክሪ ፡ እግዚአብሔር ፡ ባለት ፡
ነው ፡ ነገዱ ፡ እነገሩ ፡ ኮዋ ፡ ነው ፡፡

B.L. Or. 13683 A;   A.A. Nat. Lib. 16;   EMML 1280.

AC Malachi. MS Cowley 18, pp.255–271:

ሚልእንያስ ፡ ባለት ፡ መልእኳ ፡ እንዳም ፡ ሐዋርያ ፡ ባለት ፡ ነው ፡
ነገዱ ፡ እነገሩ ፡ ይሳዮር ፡ እባቴ ፡ ፋዱል ፡ እናቸ ፡ ጽግሌ ፡
ይገለሉ ፡፡

B.L. Or. 13683 A;   A.A. Nat. Lib. 16;   EMML 1280.

AC <u>Mäqdämä wängel</u>. Pr. ed.:

ይህን ፡ መጽሐፉ ፡ እምንዮስ ፡ እውሳብዮስ ፡ ተናገረውታል ፡፡
እናዚህስ ፡ ወሳሳ ታቸው ፡ ከሠለስቱ ፡ ምኳት ፡ በሬት ፡ ነውን ፡
ወይስ ፡ በኌላ ፡ ሊሉ ፡ በሬት ፡ ነው ፡፡

EMML 832, 1229, 1282, ? 2852;   fragment in EMML 1268 and 1270.

AC Matthew. Pr. ed.:

ብኩራተ ፡ ማቴዎስ ፡ --- ይህ ፡ ቃል ፡ የወለስቻ ፡ ምዕት ፡ ቃል ፡
ነው ፡ ንንተ ፡ ፈጋሬ ፡ እንዳማነው ፡ ቢሉ ፡ እንዚእነሱር ፡
እምቀዱሞ ፡ ዓለም ፡ ክልብ ፡ የሶነረውን ፡ በነቢያት ፡ ይናገረውን ፡
ለመፈጸም ፡ ሥጋ ፡ ሆነ ፡

Cowley 19;   B.N. Griaule (Strelcyn 638) 330;   JE 302 E (= DG 328);
JE 303 E (= DG 109);   A.A. Nat. Lib. 32, 35;   A.A. Unesco ? 1/12,
? 1/21, 2/32, 2/35;   EMML 277, 405, 832, 899, 1064, 1092, 1201, 1207,
1227, 1229, 1237, 1251, 1268, 1282;   fragments in EMML 630, 679, 1669;
Cerulli (Raineri) 142.

AC Mark. Pr. ed.:

ማርቆስ ፡ ማለት ፡ ንሁብ ፡ ማለት ፡ ነው ። ንሁብ ፡ ክለሉ ፡
እንዳቀነያም ፡ እስቀዱሞ ፡ ክክርስቶስ ፡ ኂላ ፡ ክለዋርያት ፡ ተምሪልና ።

B.L. Or. 13683 L;   B.N. Griaule (Strelcyn 638) 330;   A.A. Nat. Lib.
32, 35;   A.A. Unesco (as for Mt. above);   EMML 405, 832, 899, 1064,
1092, 1201, 1207, 1227, 1229, 1237, 1251, 1268, 1282;   fragments in
EMML 277, 679; Cerulli (Raineri) 142.

AC Luke. Pr. ed.:

ሉቃስ ፡ ማለት ፡ ዓቃቤ ፡ ሥርዐ ፡ ማለት ፡ ነው ። ቀዱሞ ፡ ዓቃቤ ፡
ሥርዐ ፡ ዘሥጋ ፡ ነበር ። ኂላ ፡ 7ን ፡ ዓቃቤ ፡ ሥርዐ ፡ ዘነፍስ ፡
ሆኑዋልና ።

B.N. Griaule (Strelcyn 638) 330;   A.A. Nat. Lib. 33, 35;   A.A.
Unesco (? 2/33 and as for Mt. above);   EMML 674, 832, 899, 1064,
1093, 1201, 1207, 1227, 1229, 1237, 1251, 1268, 1282;   part in A.A.
Nat. Lib. 32, EMML 277;   fragment in EMML 679 ; Cerulli (Raineri) 169.

AC John. Pr. ed.:

ብሥራተ ፡ __ ዮሐንስ ፡ __ ይህ ፡ ቃል ፡ የሠለስቻ ፡ ምኝት ፡ ነው ፡ --
እንዲ ፡ ማቴዎስ ፡ ተርኳ ፡ ዮሐንስ ፡ እንዲነቦቾ ፡ እንዲ ፡ ነቢያት ፡
እንዲ ፡ ወንዱ ምቾ ፡ እንዲ ፡ ሐዋርያት ፡ አይደፉም ፡

B.N. Griaule (Strelcyn 638) 330;   A.A. Nat. Lib. 33, 35;   A.A.
Unesco (as for Mt. above);   EMML 279, 674, 832, 899, 1064, 1093,
1201, 1207, 1227, 1229, 1237, 1251, 1268, 1282;   fragment in EMML
679; Cerulli (Raineri) 169.

AC Acts. Pr. ed.:

ወደሐፈ ፡ 7ነረ ፡ ሉኡ7ን ፡ __ ይህ ፡ ቃል ፡ የወለስቻ ፡
ምዕት ፡ ነው ፡   (continues as for Matthew).

JE 304 E;   EMML 832, 1063, 1201, 1226, 1228, 1270, 1277, 1669;
fragments in EMML 679, 1119.

AC Romans. Pr. ed.:

ሮም፡ ካሰጵ፡ እደሩ፡ እስቀፋጵም፡ ኾርስጠጣሊ ፡ትገሳ ፡ሳበር Ⅰ
ካሰጵ፡ እደሳጵም ፡ስጌስ ፡ሙሉፉ ፡ካጶተጵም ፡ሰፉሪሙገት ፡ ⸻

Cowley 20; JE 303 E (= DG 109); A.A. Nat. Lib. 34; A.A. Unesco
? 2/34; EMML 9, 20, 1063, 1091, 1226, 1228, 1269, 1277, 1669;
introduction only in EMML 679, 1200.

AC 1 Corinthians. Pr. ed.:

ሙሳ ኺንት ፡ ቀጰጣ፬ ፡ ⸻ ጙሌተኛ ፡ ዖሀጌ ጽፉ ፡ ሳሙ፭ ፡ቀጰጣ፬ ፡
እለ ፡ ቆሮንዱስ ፡ ስእካዶያ ፡ ዖሰ፮ ፡ ሙጌና ፡ ናት ።

Cowley 20; A.A. Nat. Lib. 34; A.A. Unesco ? 2/34; EMML 9, 20,
1063, 1091, 1226, 1228, 1269, 1277, 1669.

AC 2 Corinthians. Pr. ed.:

ሙሳ ኺንት ፡ ንሳኺት ፡ ⸻ ቀጰጣ፬ ፡ ስሆ ፡ ሳበር፭ ፡ንሳኺት ፡ እለ ፡
ተሪኺ ፡ ቀጰስ ፡ ጸሙሶስ ፡ ስሪሳኾስዖስ ፡ ጐ፫ ፡ ቲዱ፫ ፡
ሟዖቀ፬ፇሙ ፡ ፭ ፡ ስሆ ፡ ሰፉታል ።

Cowley 20; A.A. Nat. Lib. 34; A.A. Unesco ? 2/34; EMML 9, 20,
1063, 1091, 1226, 1228, 1269, 1277, 1669.

AC Galatians. Pr. ed.:

ንሳትዖ ፡ ዖዱሪ ፡ ፀርፀ ፡ ናት Ⅰ ቀꝗኄ ፡ ካስገፇ ፡ ዖ፭ናሙዖ፫ ፡
እዶሷስዖም ። ቀጰስ ፡ ጸሙሶስ ፡ ካዚሀ ፡ ንብፇ ፡ ⸻

Cowley 20; A.A. Nat. Lib. 34;   A.A. Unesco
? 2/34; EMML 9, 20, 1063, 1091, 1226, 1228, 1269, 1277, 1669;
fragment in EMML 1200.

AC Ephesians. Pr. ed.:

ኤፊስ፫ ፡ ዖዱሪ ፡ ፀርፀ ፡ ናት Ⅰ ቀꝗኄ ፡ ካስገፇ ፡ ዖ፭ናሙዖ፫ ፡
ሳሙ ፡ ቀጰስ ፡ ጸሙሶስ ፡ ንብፇ ፡ ⸻

Cowley 20; A.A. Nat. Lib. 34; A.A. Unesco ? 2/34; EMML 9, 20,
1063, 1091, 1226, 1228, 1269, 1277, 1669; fragment in EMML 1200.

AC Philippians. Pr. ed.:

ሪሳኾስዖስ ፡ ስሙቀጰ፫ ፪ ፡ ዖሰፇ ፡ ሙጌና ፡ ናት Ⅰ ስእካዶያ ፡
ቆሮ፫ዱስ ፡ ኺ፫ጰስፇ ፡ ⸻

MSS as for AC 2 Corinthians.

AC Colossians. Pr. ed.:

ቆለስዖስ ፡ ስሪሳኾስዖስ ፡ ኾሙገስ ፡ ዖሰፇ ፡ ሀገር ፡ ናት Ⅰ
ስ፯ኵዱC ፡ ኾሙገስ ፡ ኺንፉሪዝ ፡ ኺ፫ጰስ ።

MSS as for AC 2 Corinthians.

AC 1 Thessalonians. Pr. ed.:

__ ቀዳማዊ ፡ __ ዳግዒት ፡ የሢል ፡ ነውን ፡ ቀዳማዊ ፡ እለ ፡
ተሰኮንቄ ፡ በመቄፉንያ ፡ ራሲኩስቡስና ፡ በኢጎዩያ ፡ ቆሮንቶስ ፡
መሃክል ፡ ይአኝ ፡ እገር ፡ ናት ፡ በእሬንትና ፡ በዲባባ ፡ መሃክል ፡
ፉሬ ፡ ኺንዱለ ፡

MSS as for AC 2 Corinthians.

AC 2 Thessalonians. Pr. ed.:

ቀዳማዊ ፡ ብኩ ፡ ነበርና ፡ ሃልኸት ፡ እለ ፡ ንሕን ፡ ሕዬዋን ፡ __
ሲል ፡ ስምተው ፡ ምድኸት ፡ በኟውሎክ ፡ ረከ ፡ ይፉረጋሽ ፡
ህለዋል ፡

MSS as for AC 2 Corinthians.

AC 1 Timothy. Pr. ed.:

ጢሞቴዎስ ፡ የልስኖሬን ፡ ሰው ፡ ነው ፡ እገኝ ፡ እረጋዊ ፡
ነው ፡ ኺናኝ ፡ እዲሉፉዊት ፡ ናት ።

MSS as for AC 2 Corinthians.

AC 2 Timothy. Pr. ed.:

ቀዳማዊ ፡ ብኩ ፡ ነበርና ፡ ሃልኸት ፡ እለ ፡ ጢሞቴዎስ ፡ ኹለተኛ ፡
ሲ ይስተምር ፡ ሃሏ ዬን ፡ መከሬ ፡ እጽንተውበታል ፡

MSS as for AC 2 Corinthians.

AC Titus. Pr. ed.:

ቲቶ ፡ የቀርጤስ ፡ ሰው ፡ ነው ፲ ኺናቸም ፡ እገቸም ፡ እረጋውያን ፡
ናቸው ፲ በገ ፡ ህላቴናናቸን ፡ እዪት ፡ __

MSS as for AC Ephesians.

AC Philemon. Pr. ed.:

ራሲሞና ፡ የቀሳስይስ ፡ ሰው ፡ ነው ፡ በኟውሎክ ፡ ስብነት ፡
እምኑዋል ፡ ኺናሲሞስ ፡ የሢገል ፡ ገሬያ ፡ ነበረው ፡

MSS as for AC Ephesians.

AC Hebrews. Pr. ed.:

ዕብራውያን ፡ ማለት ፡ 0ዳውያ ፡ ራስግ ፡ ማለት ፡ ነው ፡
እገቶቻቸው ፡ ገብናን ፡ ፉርፉን ፡ ተሻግረው ፡ ወንተዋልና ።
እንኳም ፡ ፉለስያን ፡ ማለት ፡ ነው ።

Cowley 20; A.A. Nat. Lib. 34; A.A. Unesco ? 2/34; EMML 9, 20, 1063, 1091, 1226, 1228, 1269, 1270, 1277, 1669; fragments in EMML 1200.

AC 1 Peter. Pr. ed.:

ይህን ፡ መጽሐፉ ፡ ቅዱስ ፡ ጴንሮስ ፡ በስብካተ ፡ ቃሉ ፡ ሳመኑ ፡
በማተ ፡ ኺስሚፉሞስ ፡ ለተበተኑ ፡ ድዮ ለቻዋል ፡ የሃውሆናቸውስ ፡
የመበተና ቸውስ ፡ ምኸንንያት ፡ ኺናምን ፡ ነው ፡ ቢሉ ፡ __

Cowley 20; EMML 9, 832, 1063, 1207, 1210, 1226, 1228, 1270, 1277, 1669; brief commentary in EMML 2790.

AC 2 Peter. Pr. ed.:

ካዘዝህም ፡ ሠራኢ ፡ መንገሊ ፡ የአም ፡ ችንሣኽ ፡ ሙታን ፡ ፋሕፈት ፡ ሰማይ ፡
መምጽር ፡ የአም ፡ እንዳ ፡ ጊዜ ፡ ናውፁ ፡ ካተመመቁ ፡ ምን ፡ ምግገር ፡ ይኸል ፡
ብለዋል ፤ ለዚህ ፡ ሁሉ ፡ ይጽፈል ፡

MSS as for AC 1 Peter.

AC 1 John. Pr. ed.:

፩ኛ ፡ የሚድፈ ፡ ነውን ፡ ቀዳማዊ ፡ እለ ፡፡ ዮሐንስ ፡ መሢሕ ፡ እያ ፡
ሊያስተያምር ፡ ስምቶ ፡ ፈይምኝያስ ፡ አሥር ፡ እግዘታል ፡፡

Cowley 20; EMML 9, 1063, 1207, 1210, 1226, 1228, 1270, 1277, 1669.

AC 2 John. Pr. ed.:

ቀዳማዊ ፡ ስኮ ፡ ናበፈና ፡ ፈግዐዊት ፡ እለ ፡ ሁለተኛ ፡ ይጽፈል ፡
ምግዘት ፡ ሆና ፡ በፈቤት ፡ ልክስ ፡ ቀለብ ፡ እየተቀከለች ፡ የነገሥታቸን ፡
የመኳንንተን ፡ ልጆች ፡ የምታሳፍግ ፡ ሮምና ፡ የምትገል ፡ ሴት ፡
ናበፈች ፡፡

MSS as for AC 1 John.

AC 3 John. Pr. ed.:

ሣስተኛ ፡ ይጽፈል ፤ ጋዩስ ፡ የሚገል ፡ ፈግ ፡ ስው ፡ ናበፈ ፡
በቀለውፉዎስ ፡ ቄሣር ፡ ጊዜ ፡ --

MSS as for AC 1 John.

AC James. Pr. ed.:

ይዕቆብ ፡ ካገዉሉ ፡ ጽናት ፡ የተነሣ ፡ መንነ ፡ እግሬ ፡ ከሙ ፡ እግሬ ፡
ገሣል ፡ ይለዋል ፤ እግሬ ፡ እንፈ ፡ እግሬ ፡ ገሣል ፡ ሰያም ፡ ይምር ፡
ናበር ፡፡

MSS as for AC 1 John, plus fragment in EMML 832.

AC Jude. Pr. ed.:

ይሁዳ ፡ ይሁዳ ፡ ይሁዳ ፡ ታፈዎስ ፡ ይዕቆብም ፡ ይዕቆብ ፡ ፈቂቀ ፡
ዮሴፈ ፡ ናፈው ፡፡ እንፈም ፡ ይሁዳም ፡ ሌስ ፡ ይዕቆብም ፡ ሌስ ፡
ይለታወቀ ፡ ናፈው ፡

MSS as for AC 1 John.

AC Revelation. Pr. ed.:

ይህን ፡ መጽሐፈ ፡ ዮሐንስ ፡ ስለ ፡ ሣስት ፡ ናገር ፡ ተናግሮታል ፡
ፈቀ ፡ መፀመርቶ ፡ ይስተግለቸውን ፡ ገፈፈውስት ፡ ለመገሥፁ ፡
መጻገገ ፡ ካህናት ፡ ተስፖቶት ፡ --

Cowley 20; A.A. Holy Trinity Cathedral 29, 30; EMML 9, 832, 1063, 1199, 1200, 1207, 1226, 1228, 1270, 1277, 1669, 4986; introduction in EMML 1119; fragment in EMML 175.

AC Mar Yəshaq. Pr. ed.:
ይህን ፡ መጽሐፍ ፡ ማር ፡ ይስሐቅ ፡ ተናገሮታል ፡ የማር ፡ ይስሐቅ ፡
ብሔሩ ፡ ነገዱ ፡ ሀገሩ ፡ ሙላዱ ፡ ሶርያ ፡ ነው ። መጽሐፉ ፡ የተማረበት ፡
ምሥጢር ፡ ያገመረበት ፡ ቂሳርያ ፡ ነው ።

EMML 6; printed ed. in A.A. Unesco 1/30; marginal notes of commentary in B.L. Or. 760 and A.A. Nat. Lib.217.

AC Filkəsyus. Pr. ed.:
ሥርዓተ ፡ ብሕትውና ፡ በጳውሊ ፤ ሥርዓተ ፡ ምንኵስና ፡ በእንጦኒ ፡
ተዠምሯል ። የጳውሊ ፡ አባቱ ፡ ባለ ፡ ጸጋ ፡ ነበረ ።

JE 619 E; printed ed. in A.A. Unesco 1/30; fragments in EMML 2305; marginal notes of commentary in B.L. Or. 760 and A.A. Nat. Lib. 217.

AC Arägawi mänfäsawi. Pr. ed.:
ሥርዓተ ፡ ብሕትውና ፡ በጳውሎስ ፤ ሥርዓተ ፡ ምንኵስና ፡
በእንጦንስ ፡ ተዠምሯል ። እንጦንስ ፡ መቃርስን ፡ መቃርስ ፡
ጳኩሞንን ፡ ጳኩሞን ፡ ጳኵሚስን ፡ ...

incomplete in JE 628 E; pr. ed. in A.A. Unesco 1/30; fragments in EMML 734; marginal notes in B.L. Or. 760 and A.A. Nat. Lib. 217.

AC Qerəllos – History of Cyril (tarik zäqerəllos). MS Cowley 25:
ቄርሎስ ፡ ማለት ፡ ኃይል ፡ ሳሬዶ ፡ ማለት ፡ ነው ፡ ወይጼወው ፡ ቄሬ ፡
ሕዝቦሙ ፡ ለሶርያ ፡ እንዲል ፡ ኃይሉን ፡ ሕዝቦሙ ፡ ሳሬዱን ፡ ሕዝቦሙ ፡
ሲል ። ቦ ፡ አንበሳ ፡ ማለት ፡ ነው ፡

B.L. Or. 13683 J; A.A. Nat. Lib.

AC Qerəllos – Ǝstəgubu'. MS Cowley 25:
ነገር ፡ ዘጸሐፈ ፡ ቅዱስ ፡ ቄርሎስ ፡ ሊቀ ፡ ጳጳሳት ፡ ዘእስክንድርያ ፡
ለቴዎዶስዮስ ፡ ንጉሥ ፤ ነገር ፡ ዘተናገረ ፡ መጽሐፍ ፡ ዘጸሐፈ ፡ ሲል ፡
ነው ። የእስክንድርያው ፡ ሊቀ ፡ ጳጳስ ፡ ቄርሎስ ፡ ለንጉሡ ፡
ለቴዎዶስዮስ ፡ የጻፈው ፡ መጽሐፍ ፡ የተናገረው ፡ ነገር ፡ ይህ ፡ ነው ።

B.L. Or. 13683 J; Bodl. Aeth. c.13; A.A. Nat. Lib.

AC Qerəllos – Päladyos. MS Cowley 25:
ግጻዌ ፡ ድርሳን ፡ ዘቅዱስ ፡ ቄርሎስ ፡ ሊቀ ፡ ጳጳሳት ፡ ዘእስክንድርያ ፡
ዘሀሎ ፡ ፩ዱ ፡ ክርስቶስ ፡ ታሪኩ ፤ ይህን ፡ መጽሐፍ ፡ ቅዱስ ፡ ቄርሎስና ፡
ጳላድዮስ ፡ እየተከራከሩ ፡ ተናግረውታል ።

B.L. Or. 13683 J;   Bodl. Aeth. c.13;   A.A. Nat. Lib.

AC Qerəllos – Tärafä qerəllos. MS Cowley 26:

ዘኔዋፉጠስ ፡ ፈጸስ ፡ ዘኧንቅራ ፡ ዘገለተይ ። ይህን ፡ መጽሐፉ ፡
ለኧሙግዞተ ፡ ንጵጵሮስ ፡ የተሰበሰሙ ፡ ሰለተ ፡ ሞቄ ፡
ኤጺስቆፆሳት ፡ ተናግረሙታል ።

B.L. Or. 13683 J;   Bodl. Aeth. e.26;   A.A. Nat. Lib.;   EMML 1669.

AC Haymanotä abäw. MS Cowley 32:

ይህን ፡ መጽሐፉ ፡ በፒዜከሙ ፡ የተናሡ ፡ ሒቃሙንት ፡ ፉርሰሙታል ፡
ጽፈሙታል ፡ ተናግረሙታልም ፡ ይሳል ፡ ኧባ ፡ ሧኝኤስ ፡ ዘበገሪ ፡ እትራብ ፡
ወሠሊግ ፡ ኧባ ፡ ዮሐንስ ፡ ዘሣገሪ ፡ ሑርልስ ፡ ሰብስበሙታል ፡
መልሰሙታል ፡ ካፈለሙታልም ፡ ይሳል ፡ ኧባ ፡ ሧኝኤስ ፡ ገለሙ ፡ ኧባ ፡
እኝኤስ ፡ ይሳል ፡ የሀይ ፡ ቤተ ፡ እማርኛ ፡ ጏንተ ፡ ፈገሪስ ፡
ኧንፈይምፕሀሙ ፡ ቢሉ ፡---

B.L. Or. 13966;   ? Greek monastery, Jerusalem (Littmann) XIII;
A.A. Nat. Lib. 249;   EMML 1090, 1600;   introduction only in Cowley
36;   marginal commentary notes in EMML 1173, 3001.

AC Yohannəs afä wärq – Dərsan. Pr. ed.:

ይህን ፡ መጽሐፉ ፡ ብፀ፩ ፡ ፈሙኩስ ፡ ተናግሮታል Ṯ ዮሐንስ ፡ ኧፈ ፡
መርቅ ፡ ተርጓሞታል ። ዮሐንስ ፡ ኧፈ ፡ መርቅ ፡ ብሑሪ ፡ መሁለፉ ፡ .--
ኧንፈ፩ኪይ ፡ ፈሙ ።

? B.N. d'Abb. 145;   ? pr. ed. in Jerusalem (Aescoly).

AC Yohannəs afä wärq – Tägsas. Pr. ed.:

በኧንተ ፡ ፉሁፈፀ ። ብፀ፩ ፡ ፈሙኩስ ፡ ለ፩ብሪሙይን ፡ ጽሞ ፡ የሰፈፈሙን ፡
ጏታብ ፡ ዮሐንስ ፡ ኧፈ ፡ መርቅ ፡ ḡ̱ō ፡ ፉርሰን ፡ እፁርት ፡ ተርጓሞታ ።
ካዚሁም ፡ ካፉርሰኑ ፡ እነፈጽሮ Ṯ እይይዘ ፡ ḡ̱ō ተገሠ፩ ፡ ተናገፋል ።

as for Dərsan above.

AC Qəddase and associated prayers –

(i) AC Təmhərtä həbu'at. Pr. ed.:

በኧንተ ፡ ፉምሁርተ ፡ ፈቡፉተ ፡ .-- ፉፈፈን ፡ ጏተ ፡ በሕይወተ ፡ ሥጋ ፡
ሰለ ፡ ይስተጏረሙ ፡ መዝዝስ ፡ ይገለሳ ፡ ኝጭተ ፡ ተፈሡፆ ፡ ይስተጏረሙ ፡
ኪዱን ፡ ይገለሳ ፡

Cowley 21, 28;   B.L. Or. (Strelcyn 60) 11719;   A.A. Nat. Lib. 33;
EMML 1066, 1073, 1207, 1233, 1254, 1271, 1272, 1669;   fragment in
EMML 1119;   probably contained in MSS of AC Qəddase listed below.

(ii) AC <u>Kidan</u>. Pr. ed.:

ኪዳን ፡ ዘነገሁ ፡ ወለአኵንት ፡ ተናገራ‌ሙታል ፡ ቢሁ ፡ ለይፍን ፡
ክርሃን ፡ ገሌ ፡ ዚዜ ፡ ፍሙና ፡ ነገሁ ፡ የተ‌ሙ‌ቸ ፡ ዮ‌ሔፍና ፡ ፈ‌ቆ‌ዲ‌ሞ‌ስ ፡
ተናገራ‌ሙታል ፡ ቢሁ ፡ --

Cowley 21; B.L. Or. (Strelcyn 60) 11719; B.N. d'Abbadie 247
(Conti Rossini 243); ? JE 603 E, JE 604 E; EMML 1064, 1073, 1203,
1207, 1233, 1241, 1254, 1271, 1272, 1474, 1669; incomplete in EMML
2906.

(iii) AC <u>Mästäbqwə͗</u>. Pr. ed.:

ጸፍተ‌ሙ ፡ ዘ‌ሔ‌ሊት ። ባ‌ስ‌ል‌ዮ‌ስ ፡ ስ‌ር‌ዓ‌ት ፡ ቤት ፡ ክ‌ር‌ስ‌ቲ‌ያን ፡
ስ‌ር‌ዓ‌ት ፡ ቀ‌ዱ‌ሔ‌ን ፡ ስ‌ር‌ዓ‌ት ፡ ጸ‌ሎ‌ተ‌ን ፡ ተ‌ና‌ግ‌ኹ‌ል ። ዓ‌ሉ‌ሬ‌ን ፡
ሙ‌ስ‌ተ‌ብ‌ቁ‌ዕ ፡ ‌ክ‌ሊ‌ማ‌ቆ‌ስ ፡ ዘ‌ም‌ኹ‌ን ፡ ኪ‌ዳ‌ን ፡ ‌ክ‌ሙ‌ዕ‌ዱ‌ሔ‌ሬ ፡
ኪ‌ዳ‌ን ፡ እ‌ግ‌ን‌ጉ ፡ ተ‌ና‌ግ‌ሮ‌ታ‌ል ።

see MSS of AC <u>Qəddase</u> listed below.

(iv) AC <u>Liton</u>. Pr. ed.:

ሊ‌ጦ‌ን ፡ ዘ‌ነ‌ገ‌ሁ ፡ ዘ‌ሠ‌ሩ‌ይ ። ለ‌ባ‌ስ‌ል‌ዮ‌ስ ፡ ሊ‌ኖ‌ር‌ግ‌ይ ፡ የ‌ሚ‌ገ‌ሉ ፡
ሙ‌ጸ‌እ‌ፍ‌ት ፡ ‌ክ‌ሉ‌ት ፡ እ‌ስ‌ት‌ጉ‌ቡ‌ዕ ፡ ‌ማ‌ለ‌ት ፡ ‌ነ‌ሙ ።

see MSS of AC <u>Qəddase</u> listed below.

(v) AC <u>Qəddase</u>. Pr. ed.:

እ‌ግ‌ዚ‌እ‌ብ‌ሔ‌ር ፡ አ‌ዳ‌ም‌ን ፡ ‌ከ ፲ ፡ ባ‌ሕ‌ር‌ዩ‌ት ፡ ፈ‌ኖ‌ሮ ፡ በ‌ነ‌ፍ‌ስ ፡ እ‌ኗ‌ክ‌ሮ ፡
በ‌ገ‌ና‌ት ፡ እ‌ም‌ረ‌ሙ ። አ‌ዳ‌ም‌ም ፡ በ‌ገ‌ና‌ት ፡ ሊ‌ሞ‌ር ፡ ‌ሙ‌ኀ‌ነ ፡ ጸ‌ሎ‌ት ፡
ለ‌ይ‌ቶ ፡ ‌ይ‌ሞ‌ር ፡ ነ‌ብ‌ር ።

? JE 440 E; ? A.A. Unesco 6/29; EMML 1693; AC <u>sər͑atä qəddase</u>
only in EMML 455; fragments in EMML 517, 1056, 1157; pr. ed. in
Jerusalem (Aescoly) and EMML 898.

(vi) AC <u>Qəddase maryam</u>. Pr. ed.:

እ‌ስ‌ሙ‌ቴ‌ት ፡ ‌ቁ‌ር‌ግ‌ን ፡ ዘ‌ኌ‌ግ‌ዝ‌እ‌ት‌ነ ፡ ‌ማ‌ር‌ያ‌ም ፡ -- ሕ‌ር‌ይ‌ቆ‌ስ ፡ ‌ማ‌ለ‌ት ፡
ሓ‌ረ‌ይ ፡ ‌ማ‌ለ‌ት ፡ ‌ነ‌ሙ ። ለ‌ኹ‌ሙ‌ት ፡ ‌ሙ‌ር‌ጠ‌ሙ‌ታ‌ል‌ና ። እ‌ን‌ፉ‌ም ፡
ረ‌ቂ‌ቅ ፡ ‌ማ‌ለ‌ት ፡ ‌ነ‌ሙ ፡ --

JE 302 E (= DG 328); EMML 538, 1019, 1066, 1073, 1075, 1231, 1241,
1254, 1271, 1514, 1669, 1675; MSS of AC <u>Qəddase</u> listed above.

(vii) AC <u>Salotä haymanot</u> (Niceno–Constantinopolitan creed). Pr. ed.:

የ‌ቆ‌ስ‌ም‌ን‌ጢ‌ሞ‌ስ ፡ ብ‌ሔ‌ሬ ፡ ‌ሙ‌ላ‌ዱ ፡ ‌ኛ‌ን‌ት ፡ ነ‌ገ‌ሩ ፡ ‌ሙ‌ዱ‌ት ፡ ‌ነ‌ሙ ፡
ቢ‌ሁ ፡ እ‌ና‌ቸ ፡ ‌እ‌ይ‌ሁ‌ዳ‌ዊ‌ት ፡ የ‌ሮ‌ሔ ፡ ‌ስ‌ር‌ሙ ፡ እ‌ባ‌ት ፡ እ‌ረ‌ ‌ማ‌ዊ ፡
የ‌በ‌ሔ‌ን‌ጥ‌ይ ፡ ‌ስ‌ር‌ሙ ፡ ‌ና‌ፈ‌ሙ ።

(The incipit in MS Cowley 21 is as follows: የ‌ጸ‌ኹ‌ት ፡ ‌ህ‌ይ‌ማ‌ኖ‌ት ፡
ተ‌ራ‌ኹ‌ስ ፡ ‌ም‌ን ፡ ‌ም‌ን‌ን‌ት‌ያ‌ት ፡ እ‌ለ‌ሙ ፡ ቢ‌ሁ ፡ በ‌ሀ‌ገ‌ሩ ፡ ‌ይ‌ም‌ሥ‌ሊ‌ቅ ፡ ፮ ፡
ጎ‌ጉ‌ሠ ፡ ‌ነ‌በ‌ሩ ፡ ፫ ፡ ‌ል‌ፉ‌ኹ ፡ ‌ሙ‌ለ‌ፉ‌ና ፡ ‌ሞ‌ት ፡ በ‌ሙ‌ን‌ግ‌ሠ‌ት ፡ ቢ‌ማ‌ሁ ፡
ፊ‌ሊ‌ሳ‌ስ ፡ ---).

B.L. Or. 792, 9798 (Strelcyn 63); Cambridge Or. 1798; ? B.N. d'Abbadie 101, 212; JE 48 E; EMML 710, 1066, 1271, 1273, 1810, 2468, 2819.

(viii) AC Lord's Prayer. MS Cowley 21:

እንተሙስ ፡ ሶበ ፡ ተጼልይ ፡ --- እሉ ነ ፡ ዘበሰማያት ፡ እንዲ ለ ፡
 ጌታ ፡ በወንጌል ፡ ስለያጐን ፡ ዲርሱ ፡ እሉ ነ ፡ ዘበሰማያት ፡ እወ� ፡
ቢሉ ፡ ቀዱም ፡ ዮሐንስ ፡ ኧዜታ ፡ በሬት ፡ መንፈቅ ፡ እስተያም ፡
ነበር ፡ ይላሉ ᎓

B.L. Or. 792; B.N. Griaule (Strelcyn 621) 313; Ethiopian monastery Jerusalem (Littmann) 253; EMML 1254, 1310, 1547, 1810, 2819.

AC Wǝddase maryam. Pr. ed.:

ይኸነን ፡ መጽሐፉ ፡ ኧፍሬሳም ፡ ሶርያዊ ፡ ኧፍሬሳም ፡ ለብሐዊ ፡
ተነግሮታል ᎓ ሶርያዊ ፡ በ[ነጉ]ሩ Ⅰ ለብሐዊ ፡ በተግ[ነ]ሩ ፡ ይሰኛል " ይህም ፡
ቀዱስ ፡ ኧፍሬሳም ፡ የ[ያ]ዕ[ቆ]ብ ፡ ዘንድ[ለ]ን ፡ ዲቀ ፡ መ[ዘ]ሙር ፡ ነው ᎓

? B.N. d'Abbadie 101, 227; JE 555–558 E, JE 560–563 E, JE 559 E (= DG 164); Jerusalem (Aešcoly); A.A. Nat. Lib. 93; Aksum (Kolmodin); EMML 1019, 1066, 1073, 1075, 1233, 1241, 1254, 1271, 1514, 3412; incomplete in EMML 1669; fragment in B.N. Griaule (Strelcyn 591) 283.

AC Fǝtha nägäst – spiritual section. Pr. ed.:

ይኸነን ፡ መጽሐፉ ፡ ሠለስቱ ፡ ምዕነት ፡ ዲርሱ[ም]ታል ፡ ጽፉውታል "
እነርሳም ፡ ቀሲስ ፡ ኽዱርሰ ፡ መዳ ፡ ዓሪስ ፡ መልሶታል " ግንተ ፡
ነገራስ ፡ እንዲያም ፡ ነው ፡ ቢሉ ፡ ---

B.N. d'Abbadie 231; B.N. Mondon-Vidailhet (Chaîne) 49 (236); A.A. Nat. Lib. 233, ? 238; EMML 830, 1072, 1090, 1177, 1239, 1252, 1550–1; incomplete in EMML 1200–1; introd. in EMML 3003.

AC Fǝtha nägäst – corporal section. Pr. ed.:

እንቀጽ ፡ Ⅹ̄ወ፫ ᎓ በእንተ ፡ መብልዕ " እንቀጽ ፡ Ⅹ̄ወ፪ ፡ ብሎ ፡
ነበርና ፡ ኽዜያ ፡ እያዘ ፡ እንቀጽ ፡ Ⅹ̄ወ፫ ፡ እለ ፡ ህያ ፡ ሣስተኛው ፡
እንቀጽ ፡ የመብልን ፡ ነገር ፡ ይነግራል ፡ እንዲህ ፡ ይለውን ፡ ብሉ ᎓
እንዲህ ፡ ይለውን ᎓ እትብሉ ᎓ ብሎ ᎓ ----

B.N. Mondon-Vidailhet (Chaîne) 50 (237); A.A. Nat. Lib. 233, ? 238; EMML 830, 1072, 1090, 1177, 1239, 1252, 1483, 1550–1; incomplete in EMML 1200–1.

AC <u>Abušakər</u>. Marginal annotations in MS B.L. Or. 809:

እግዚአብሔር ፡ ፲፯ት ፡ እም ፡ --- ዝንት ፡ መጽሐፍ ፡ ዘፈሪሶ ፡
ተናግሮት ፡ እንየገር ፡ ብለን ፡ ተናገሩ ፡ ክተናገርሩ ፡ ሰኝስ ፡ የተናገርሳው ፡
ነገር ፡ ይሁ ፡ ነው ፡ ፡ ሶ ፡ ጽሮት ፡ እንደፈ ፡ ብለን ፡ ጽፈን ፡ ክነጽፍናው ፡
ሰኝስ ፡ የጸፍናው ፡ መጽሐፍ ፡ ይሁ ፡ ነው ፡ --- ቃል ፡ ዘተናገረ ፡
መጽሐፍ ፡ ዘጸሐፈ ፡ ፍርሳን ፡ ዘፈሪሶ ፡ ቢስ ፡ እንደ ፡ ነው ፡ ነገር ፡
ዘቅርኮስ ፡ ቃል ፡ ዘእጌፈሬስ ፡ ፍርሳን ፡ ዘፖሐንስ ፡ እፈ ፡ ወርቀ ፡
ቢስ ፡ እንደ ፡ እንዳየ ፡ --- እሉሻክር ፡ አስ ፡ ስብሐት ፡ ---
እሉሻክር ፡ የኝስ ፡ ስው ፡ ነው ፡ ይሳሉ ፡ አይፈሰም ፡ ፃንተ ፡ ስው ፡
ነው ፡ ፃንተ ፡ ስው ፡ የኝስ ፡ ግብራን ፡ ገሳጸስት ፡ ስዘይው ፡
ቀርትእስ ፡ ሻክር ፡ ማስት ፡ ስብሐት ፡ ማስት ፡ --

B.N. Griaule (Strelcyn 388) 84; ? A.A. Nat. Lib. 227, 229–231.

Miscellanea related to the AC tradition:
(i) translations without commentary (<u>nätala tərgwame</u>).
e.g. (a) of Pss., interlinear in B.N. d'Abbadie 41, ? A.A. Unesco
6/41; periphrastic in B.L. Or. 535, B.N. Zotenberg 21;
incomplete in Berlin (Dillmann 10) MS or.qu.412.

(b) 4 gospels, Geez and Amharic in EMML 1215; Amharic only in
EMML 1221.

(c) Acts, EMML 1108.

(d) Rev., EMML 1108.

(e) <u>Qəddase</u>, EMML 949, 1168, 1182.

(f) YAWT in B.L. Or. 742.

(ii) Marginalia and commentary notes, e.g. B.L. Add. 16253
(Dillmann 38); A.A. Nat. Lib. 5, 8, 234; EMML 679, 1187, 1200,
1201, 1206, 1234, 1337.

(iii) Unspecified O.T. commentary, A.A. Unesco 2/17 (? = A.A. Nat.
Lib. 16).

(iv) Amharic treatise on the Nicene Creed, EMML 1069, 1074.

(v) List of AC and other church teachers, B.N. Griaule (Strelcyn
580) 272.

(vi) Amharic computus, e.g. B.N. d'Abbadie 236, Mondon – Vidailhet
(Chaine) 28 (214); EMML 942, 989, 1064, 1073, 1075, 1094, 1104,
1149, 1187, 1202, 1210, 1227, 1231, 1233, 1234, 1243, 1251, 1271,
1274, 1276, 1419, 1468, 1676, 2114, 2402, 2588, 3247.

(vii) Amharic <u>AAM</u>, <u>qalä̈ haymanot</u>, and similar works, e.g. B.L. Add. 16206 (Dillmann 16), Add. 16221 (Dillmann 17); B.L. Add. 24183 (Wright 356); B.L. Or. 13267 (Strelcyn 51); Bodl. (Ullendorff) 82, 85; Cambridge Add. 1861, Or. 1880, Or. 1884; B.N. d'Abbadie 6, Zotenberg 100, Griaule (Strelcyn Eth. 617) 309, Griaule (Strelcyn Eth. 622) 314, Mondon-Vidailhet (Chaîne) 34 (220), 218, 219; Berlin (Dillmann 30) Peterm. II, Nachtr. 63; Berlin (Hammerschmidt and Six 67) or. oct. 1295; Littmann (Murad) 14; Vatican (Grébaut and Tisserant) 120; Hugo Odeberg, Uppsala (Löfgren 75); Stockholm (Löfgren) IX (499), XIV; St. Petersburg (Turaev) 17; Princeton (Littmann); Tel Aviv Faitlovitch (Wurmbrand 31, 32) 3131, 3132; A.A. Nat. Lib. 252, 258; EMML 23, 64, 305, 306, 379, 596, ? 632, 1131, 1288, 1423, 1425, 1447, 1458, 1468, 1495, 1648, 1708, 1810, 1815, 2121, 2138, 2187, 2840, 2852, 3247, 3408, 34-59; Bergamo (Raineri) 13, 15; Cerulli (Raineri) 143, 289; <u>haymanotä̈ abäw hawaryat</u> in EMML 1036; <u>qalä̈ haymanot</u> <u>wä̈mə̊ə̊dan</u> in Berlin (Hammerschmidt and Six) or.oct. 1289 and EMML 1310, 1315.

(viii) Amharic <u>sə̈nä̈ fə̊trät</u> texts, e.g. B.L. Add. 16246, Add. 16222 (Dillmann 18), Add. 24183 (Wright 356); Cambridge (Ullendorff and Wright) Or. 1740, Or. 1798, Or. 1876, Or. 1884; B.N. d'Abbadie 6, d'Abbadie (Conti Rossini 146), Griaule (Strelcyn) 617.2, Griaule (Strelcyn Eth. 623) 315, Griaule (Strelcyn Eth. 585) 277 , Griaule (Strelcyn Eth. 617) 309, Griaule (Strelcyn Eth. 622) 314; Berlin (Dillmann 37.1) Peterm.II, Nachtr. 59; Bonn (Gildemeister) 33; Vatican (Grébaut and Tisserant) 120, 123, 157; Pontificio Collegio Etiopico (Zanutto item 194 ms.2); JE 698 E, 700-2 E, 704 E, 709 E, DG 104; Tel Aviv Faitlovitch (Wurmbrand 31, 32) 3131, 3132; Ţanasee (Hammerschmidt) 53, 103; A.A. Nat. Lib. 266, 267; EMML 23, 306, 656, 716, 1036, 1203, 1205, 1210, 1288, 1315, 1392, 1495, 1708, 2154, 2169, 2852, 3247, 3408; Cerulli (Raineri) 121.

7.5.   Shelf-list of my personal collection of manuscripts and microfilm:

(a)   Manuscripts and photocopies of manuscripts:

The shelf-list following omits study notes and fragments. All
the MSS are written on paper, and are bound in ledgers or exercise
books unless they are noted as unbound. All were commissioned by
myself, and executed during the years 1967-1977 A.D., except nos. 19-21,
32, 37, 40-42 and 44. All are MSS, unless noted as photocopies.

All are basically of Gondarine provenance, except nos. 33-6 and
44. Nos. 1-10, 12-18, 25-6 and 32 were copied at Gəmja bet Maryam,
Gondar, from the MSS of Mämhər Wäldä sänbät Wäldä giyorgis, by permission
of Abba Kəflä maryam Yəmär; I am told that his MSS were dispersed
after the death of Abba Kəflä maryam. Nos. 22-3 and 31 were copied
or photocopied in Makalle, and no. 24 was photocopied in Addis Ababa.

Nos. 1-10, 12-18, 25-6 and 32 are the best MSS known to me of
these parts of the AC. Of these, nos. 1-10 and 12-18 contain the full
Geez texts commented on, in addition to the Amharic commentary; the
others are of varying degrees of completeness.

Cowley 1.
      (preface) copy of Amharic letter of Mämhər Wäldä sänbät; (pp.
1-262) AC Gen.; (pp.263-380) AC Ex.1.1-25.31. Copied by Mänbäru
Färrädä. 34 x 25 cm. Cited in this study as MS W.

2.   (pp.381-459, pages numbered consecutively with MS 1) AC Ex.
25.31 - end; (pp.459 (actually 461) - 552) AC Josh.; (pp.553-691)
AC Lev.; (pp.693-768) AC Num.1.1-16.8. Copied by Mänbäru Färrädä.
33 x 24 cm.

3.   (pp.769-857) AC Num.16.8 - end; (pp.857-1071 (actually 1081))
AC Deut. Copied by Mänbäru Färrädä. 33 x 24 cm.

4.   (pp.1071-1197) AC Judges; (pp.1199-1213) AC Rt.; (p.1214)
letter of Mämhər Wäldä sänbät Wäldä giyorgis. Copied by Mänbäru
Färrädä. 34 x 24 cm.

5.　　(pp.1–240) AC 1 Sam.; (pp.241–390) AC 2 Sam.1.1–20.18. Copied by Mänbäru Färrädä. 33 x 24 cm.

6.　　(pp.391–426) AC 2 Sam.20.18 – end; (pp.427–652) AC 1 Kgs.; (pp.653–792) AC 2 Kgs. 1.1–18.12. Copied by Mänbäru Färrädä. 33 x 24cm.

7.　　(pp.793–879) AC 2 Kgs. 18.12 – end. Copied by Mänbäru Färrädä. 32 x 19.5 cm.

8.　　(pp.1–211) AC 1 Chron. Copied by Mänbäru Färrädä. 32 x 22 cm.

9.　　(pp.213–484) AC 2 Chron. Copied by Mänbäru Färrädä. 32 x 22 cm.

10.　　(pp.1–105) AC 1 Esdras; (pp.105–170) AC Ezra; (pp.171–261) AC Nehemiah. Pp.1–170 are headed <u>qädamawi Əzra</u>, and pp.171–261 <u>kaləʿ Əzra</u>. Copied by Mänbäru Färrädä. 34 x 24 cm.

11.　　(ff.1a–88a) AC Ezra Apocalypse (i.e. 2 Esdras 3–14); (ff.88a–111a) AC 1 Esdras (briefer than in MS 10); (ff.111a–119b) AC Ezra; (ff.120a–127a) AC Nehemiah; (ff.128a–131a) AC Eth. 2 Macc. 18 – end; (ff.131a–145a) AC Eth. 3 Macc. Copied by Mogäs Getahun. 20 x 16 cm.

12.　　(pp.1–57) AC Tobit; (pp.59–139) AC Judith; (pp.141–198) AC Esther. Copied by Mänbäru Färrädä. 33 x 24 cm.

13.　　(ff.1a–107a) AC Eth. 1 Macc.; (ff.107a–162b) AC Eth. 2 Macc. A fuller commentary than in MS 11. Copied by Mogäs Getahun up to f.155a and completed by Mänbäru Färrädä. 32 x 20 cm.

14.　　(pp.1–204) AC Isa.1.1–61.1. 34 x 24 cm.

15.　　(pp.205–228, completion of no.14) AC Isa.61.1 – end. 34 x 24 cm.

16.　　(ff.1a–158b) AC Jer.1.1–34.5. From f.45b onwards copied by Mogäs Getahun. 32 x 20 cm.

17.　　(ff.159a–229b) AC Jer. 34.5 – end (continuation of no.16, the contents being AC Jer. 1–52); (ff.229b–250b) AC Lam.1–5. Copied up to f.248b by Mogäs Getahun. 32 x 20 cm.

18. (pp.1–48) AC Hos.; (pp.48–79) AC Amos; (pp.79–106) AC Micah; (pp.107–124) AC Joel; (pp.124–131) AC Obadiah; (pp.131–143) AC Jonah; (pp.143–154) AC Nahum; (pp.154–175) AC Hab.; (pp.175–187) AC Zeph.; (pp.188–198) AC Hag.; (pp.198–254) AC Zech.; (pp.255–271) AC Mal. Copied by Mogäs Getahun. 32 x 20 cm.

19. (ff.1a–287b) AC Matthew. Copied by several hands in 1960 E.C., purchased from Abba Gäbrä maryam Bihonänn in 1969 E.C. 20.5 x 16.5 cm.

20. (ff.3a–60a) AC Rom.; (ff.60a–102a) AC 1 Cor.; (ff.102a–123b) AC 2 Cor.; (ff.123b–135a) AC Gal.; (ff.135a–149a) AC Eph.; (ff.149a–156a) AC Phil.; (ff.156a–162a) AC Col.; (ff.162a–168a) AC 1 Thess.; (ff.168a–171a) AC 2 Thess.; (ff.171a–178a) AC 1 Tim.; (ff.178a–183a) AC 2 Tim.; (ff.183a–186b) AC Titus; (ff.186b–188b) AC Phm.; (ff.188b–228b) AC Heb.; (ff.228b–229a) notes of numbers of chapters, stichoi and citations in the Pauline epistles; (ff.229a–232a) prayers and other quotations from Mar Yəshaq; (ff.232b–245b) blank; (ff.246a–276b) AC 1 Pet.; (ff.276b–292a) AC 2 Pet.; (ff.292a–306b) AC 1 Jn.; (ff.306b–308b) AC 2 Jn.; (ff.308b–310b) AC 3 Jn.; (ff.310b–329b) AC James; (ff.329b–337b) AC Jude; (ff.337b–426a, of which ff.389b–394b are blank) AC Rev. Copied by many hands, early 20th. century, purchased from Abba Gäbrä maryam Bihonänn. 17 x 10.5 cm. Cited in this work and in TIA as MS R.

21. (ff.3a–32a) AC Kidan; (ff.32b–67a) AC Təmhərtä həbuʿat; (ff.67b–80b) AC on the Lord's Prayer; (ff.81a–101a) AC on the Niceno-Constantinopolitan Creed. Dated 1910 E.C., scribes named as Getahun and Mäkonnən, purchased in Addis Ababa market. 32 x 13 cm.

22. (pp.209–247, numbered continuously with no.31) AC Jubilees. Unbound, copied by Kalʾay Kiros from a copy belonging to Mälʾakä məhrät Yared Gərmay. 33 x 21.5 cm.

23. (pp.1–136) AC Enoch. Unbound, copied from a copy belonging to Mälʾakä məhrät Yared Gərmay. 33 x 21.5 cm.

24. (pp.1–109) AC Job. Photocopy, unbound, of copy belonging to Abba Şäggaye Bihonänn. 32 x 21.5 cm. (the original had 109 folios and a page size of about 21.5 x 16 cm.).

25.   (pp.1–10 in an exercise book) History of Cyril of Alexandria, in Amharic; (pp.1–44, 45–92, 93–140, 141–188, 189–232, 233–244, in 6 exercise books) AC P̈aladyos (Cyril's <u>Quod Christus sit unus</u>); (pp.1–76, 77–156, 157–236, 237–257 in 4 small ledgers) AC Ǝstǝgubuʼ (Cyril's <u>De recta fide</u> and book 1 of the <u>Prosphoneticus ad Reginas</u>). Copied by M̈anb̈aru F̈arr̈ad̈a. History, 20.5 x 16 cm. P̈aladyos, 20.5 x 17 cm. Ǝstǝgubuʼ, 31 x 20 cm.

26.   (pp.1–118) AC T̈ar̈af̈a Qerǝllos (i.e. the collection of homilies by Cyril of Alexandria and others). Unbound, copied by M̈anb̈aru F̈arr̈ad̈a. 33 x 22 cm.

27.   (ff.1–24, 25–49, 50–74, 75–89, 90–114, 115–117, in 6 exercise books) AC Daniel. Copied by myself, Qes F̈arr̈ad̈a Ayÿal̈a, and another copyist. 20 x 16 cm.

28.   (pp.1–14, 15–26, 27–38, 39–50, 51–61, 62–70, in 6 exercise books) AC Tǝmhǝrẗa hǝbuʻat. Copied by Qes F̈arr̈ad̈a Ayÿal̈a. 20 x 16 cm.

29.   (pp.1–3) AC Baruch; (p.1) list of chapter headings in Daniel. Unbound, copied by myself. 33 x 21.5 cm.

30.   (pp.1–4) AC introduction to Jeremiah (lacking in no.16–17); (pp.6–10 (there is no p.5)) AC Jer.36–44 (partially lacking in no.16–17); (pp.10–11) AC Epistle of Jeremiah (<u>Arʼaya m̈ashaf</u>); (p.11, but without clear incipit) AC Prophecy against Pashhur ; (pp.11–17) AC 4 Baruch (<u>T̈ar̈af̈a Barok</u>). Unbound, copied by Hayl̈a maryam Berhe. 33 x 22 cm.

31.   (pp.1–64) AC Gen., cited in this study as MS Y; (pp.64–111) AC Exodus; (pp.112–130) AC Lev.; (pp.131–156) AC Num.; (pp.157–175) AC Deut.; (pp.176–186) AC Josh.; (pp.187–205) AC Jdg.; (pp.206–208) AC Rt. MS no.22 is the continuation of this. Unbound, copied by Kalʼay Kiros from a copy belonging to M̈alʼak̈a mǝhr̈at Yared Gǝrmay. (pp.1–60) AC 1 Sam; (pp.60–105) AC 2 Sam; (pp.105–153) AC 1 Kgs.; (pp.153–194) AC 2 Kgs.; (pp.194–206) AC 1 Chron.; (pp.206–211) AC 2 Chron.; (pp.212–225) AC 1 Esdras; (pp.225–233) AC Nehemiah. Photocopy, unbound. Made from the copy belonging to M̈alʼak̈a mǝhr̈at Yared Gǝrmay. 33 x 21.5 cm.

32.   Photocopy of B.L. Orient 13966, AC <u>Haymanotä abäw</u>. The MS was purchased in Gondar from <u>Mämhər</u> Gäbrä əgziʾabəher Gäbrä həywät, and sold to the B.L. It has 999 foolscap folios. The photocopy is slightly reduced.

33.   <u>Tərgwame Pawlos</u>, a Geez commentary on the Pauline corpus (pp.1–78) Rom.; (pp.78–96) 1 Cor.; (pp.96–117) 2 Cor.; (pp.117–132) Gal.; (pp.132–142) Eph. Copied by Haylä maryam Bäläw. 31.5 x 20.5 cm.

34.   Continuation of no.33 (pp.1–9) Phil.; (pp.9–18) Col.; (pp.18–24) 1 Thess.; (pp.24–27) 2 Thess.; (pp.27–41) 1 Tim.; (pp.41–49) 2 Tim.; (pp.49–53) Tit.; (pp.53–55) Phm.; (pp.55–94) Heb.; (p.95) an excerpt from Cyril of Alexandria.
(pp.95–178) <u>Tərgwame Qälämsis</u>, a Geez commentary on Revelation. Copied by Fäntahun Däräs. 32 x 20 cm. Nos. 33 and 34 are a copy of a MS from Qälay Mädhane aläm, of which B.L. Orient 13830 parts 1 and 2 is also a copy.

35.   Photocopy of B.L. Orient 13964, <u>Tərgwame Felon Felgos</u>, a Geez commentary on the Pauline corpus, (f.1a–25a) Rom., defective at the beginning; (f.27a–58a) 1 Cor.; (f.58a–90b) 2 Cor.; (f.90b–103b) Gal.; (f.103b–116b) Eph.; (f.116b–125a) Phil.; (f.125a–135a) Col.; (f.135a–146b) 1 Thess.; (f.146b–152b) 2 Thess.; (f.152b–165b) 1 Tim.; (f.165b–173a) 2 Tim.; (f.173a–178b) Tit.; (f.178b–181a) Phm.; (f.181a–216b) Heb.
Copied by Haylä maryam Bäläw from a MS at Rima Mädhane aläm.

36.   (pp.1–20) introduction to AC <u>Haymanotä abäw</u>. Copied by <u>Mämhər</u> Gäbrä əgziʾabəher Gäbrä həywät from B.L. Orient 13966 when it was in his possession. 20.5 x 16.5 cm.

37.   (ff.1a–15a) <u>Nägärä haymanot</u>, in Amharic; (f.15b) a letter by the scribe, <u>Märi geta</u> Sämmann. 20.5 x 17 cm.

38.   (ff.1–27, 28–35, in two exercise books) AC Eth.3 Macc. Copied by <u>Mämhər</u> Gäbrä əgziʾabəher Gäbrä həywät. 21 x 16.5 cm.

39.   (ff.1a–17b) Eusebian canons. 20.5 x 16 cm.

40.   (ff.1a-45b) S̲ə̈nä fə̈trä̈t in Geez. Photocopy from MS in the possession of <u>Abba</u> La'ə̈kä̈ maryam Asrat. 21 x 16.5 cm.

41.   (ff.1a-13a) Yä̈tə̈qs mawča, a list of proof texts commonly quoted in the AC. Copied by <u>Mä̈mhə̈r</u> Gä̈brä̈ ə̈gzi'abə̈her Gä̈brä̈ hə̈ywä̈t. 20 x 15.5cm.

42.   (8 unbound photocopies) Yä̈tə̈qs mawča, different from no.41. Made from a MS in the possession of <u>Abba</u> La'ə̈kä̈ maryam Asrat. 30 x 21cm.

43.   (unnumbered title-page plus pp.1-247) Felasha prayers (<u>Yä̈kahə̈n mä̈shaf</u>). Photocopy of B.L. Or. 13965. Written by <u>Qes</u> Asrä̈s Yayyä̈h.

44.   Photocopy of BFBS (Falivene, Cowley XXVIII) MS 191, <u>Gä̈dlä̈ sadqan</u>.

(b)   <u>microfilm copies:</u>

EMML 1839, 2082, 2088, 2101, 7122, (7410).

Manchester Rylands (Strelcyn), parts of 15, 19 and 25.

B.N. d'Abbadie 39, 130, 156, 157, 195, 272.

B.N. Zotenberg 24 f.49-74.

B.N. Éth. 580 (Griaule 272).

Berlin, Petermann II, Nachtr. 24 (Dillmann 63) f.76-120.

Ṭǟnäsee (Hammerschmidt) 35.

Vatican Cerulli Ethiopic 80.

Wien Cod. Aeth. 16.

B.L. Orient 751 (part).

GENERAL INDEX

This is a brief index of chapters 1-6. Frequently occurring names are only indexed for their major appearances, and names which merely occur in lists are not indexed.

INDEX OF REFERENCES

This index lists references in chapters 1-6 to accounts of the Ethiopian interpretations of the specified parts of the Biblical and patristic texts. It does not include references to non-Ethiopian literatures, or to texts mentioned simply as corroborative examples.

UNIVERSITY OF CAMBRIDGE
ORIENTAL PUBLICATIONS PUBLISHED FOR THE
FACULTY OF ORIENTAL STUDIES

1   *Averroes' Commentary on Plato's Republic*, edited and translated by E. I. J. Rosenthal
2   *Fitzgerald's 'Salámán and Absál'*, edited by A. J. Arberry
3   *Ihara Saikaku: The Japanese Family Storehouse,* translated and edited by G. W. Sargent
4   *The Avestan Hymn to Mithra*, edited and and translated by Ilya Gershevitch
5   *The Fuṣūl al-Farabi. al-Farabi.* edited and translated by D. M. Dunlop (out of print
6   *Dun Karm, Poet of Malta*, texts chosen and translated by A. J. Arberry; introduction, notes and glossary by P. Grech
7   *The Political Writings of Ogyú Sorai*, by J. R. McEwan
8   *Financial Administration under the T'ang Dynasty,* by D. C. Twitchett
9   *Neolithic Cattle-Keepers of South India: A Study of the Deccan Ashmounds*, by F. R. Allchin
10 *The Japanese Enlightenment: A Study of the Writings of Fukuzawa Yukichi*, by Carmen Blacker
11 *Records of Han Administration*. Vol. I *Historical Assessment,* by M. Loewe
12 *Records of Han Administration*, Vol. II *Documents* by M. Loewe
13 *The Language of Indrafit of Orchā: A study of Early Braj Bhāṣā Bhasa Prose,* by R. S. McGregor
14 *Japan's First General Election, 1890*, by R. H. P. Mason
15 *A Collection of Tales from Uji: A Study and Translation of 'Uji Shui Monogtari'*, by D. E. Mills
16 *Studia Semitica*, Vol. I *Jewish Themes*, by E. I. J. Rosenthal
17 *Studia Semitica*, Vol. II *Islamic Themes*, by E. I. J. Rosenthal
18 A *Nestorian Collection of Christological Texts*, Vol. I *Syriac Text*, by Luise Abramowski and Alan E. Goodman
19 A *Nestorian Collection of Christological Texts*, Vol. II *Introduction, Translation, Indexes*, by Luise Abramowski and Alan E. Goodman
20 *The Syriac Version of the Pseudo-Nonnos Mythological Scholia*, by Sebastian Brock
21 *Water Rights and Irrigation Practices in Lahj*, by A. M. A. Maktari
22 *The Commentary of Rabbi David Kimhi on Psalms cxx-cl*, edited and translated by Joshua Baker and Ernest W. Nicholson
23 *Jalal āl-dīn al-Suyūṭī*, Vol. I *Biography and background*, by E. M. Sartain
24 *Jalal āl-dīn al-Suyūṭī*, Vol. II *"Al-Tahadduth biniumat allah"*, Arabic test by E. M. Sartain
25 *Origen and the Jews: Studies in Jewish–Christian Relations in Third Century Palestine*, by N. R. M. de Lange
26 *The 'Visaladevarāsa': A restoration of the text* , by John D. Smith
27 *Shabbetha Sofer and His Prayer-book*, by Stefan C. Reif
28 *Mori Ogai and the Modernization of Japanese Culture*, by Richard John Bowring
29 *The Rebel Lands: An investigation into origins of early Mesopotamian mythology*, by J. V. Kinnier Wilson
30 *Saladin: The politics of the Holy War*, by Malcolm Cameron Lyons and David Jackson
31 *Khotanese Buddhist Texts*, revised edition, edited by H. W. Bailey